Readings in Developmental Psychology

Readings in

Developmental Psychology

edited by

Mary Courage

broadview

Cataloguing in Publication Data

Main entry under title:

Readings in developmental psychology

ISBN 0-921149-19-0

1. Developmental psychology I. Courage, Mary Louise

BF713.5 1988   155   C88-093523-5

broadview press   in the U.S.: broadview press
P.O. Box 1243   421 Center St.
Peterborough, Canada, K9J 7H5   Lewiston, N.Y. 14092

Printed and bound in Canada by
Gagné Ltd.

Cover photo: Leah Balgaroo

Contents

Developments in Cognition and Language 153

Social Development: Interactions with Family and Friends ..269

Social Development: Aggression, Altruism, Moral Development, and Sex Differences 371

Preface

The study of developmental psychology has a long history. Philosophers and scientists have always looked to early development for clues to the nature of man, and generations of parents who have observed their children grow and change with age have informally been students of development. Only in the twentieth century however, has developmental psychology become a scientific discipline with emphasis on the systematic collection of the facts which describe developmental change, and the emergence of theories which attempt to explain why and how the observed changes occur.

The past generation has been a particularly active period of research, and one of the purposes of this collection of readings is to provide students with exposure to a representative sample of some of that research. In the ten years that I have been teaching developmental psychology, I have found that most textbooks survey a broad range of material fairly superficially. Although this material can be supplemented in lectures, I believe that students benefit from some first-hand exposure to original research reports. This exposure not only provides a little more depth than the usual textbook offers, but also develops an appreciation for the methodology that is the basis of research. The readings that I have selected were written by scientists who have been, or still are, active in their respective fields, and who have had their work published in professional journals and books. Since the book is intended primarily for undergraduate students, every attempt has been made to select papers that can be read and understood by students at that level of expertise.

The readings in this collection were selected with several additional considerations in mind. First, papers were chosen to reflect important research topics and issues normally covered in undergraduate textbooks in developmental psychology. These have been grouped under five general headings: (1) infant development, (2) early experience and behavior, (3) cognitive and language development, (4) social development: family and peer interactions and relationships, and (5) social development: sex differences, aggression, altruism, moral development. Within each of these general areas I have included a variety of papers that illustrate the specific interests that fall within that area. For example, the section on infancy includes papers on the development of visual perception, auditory perception, learning and memory, and infant attachment.

Secondly, while I wanted to include papers which represent current research and thought, I also felt it was important to include some classic papers by authors who have made a major contribution to developmental psychology and whose work has been instrumental in setting new directions for subsequent research. Papers by Jean Piaget, Albert Bandura, Robert Fantz, and Mary Ainsworth provide examples of such classic work.

Thirdly, I have included within each section some papers which are general discussion or review papers, and some which are specific research reports. For example, Martin Hoffman's paper on moral development is a good general paper which reviews important literature on the topic, and the papers by Sharon Nelson and by Terry Orlick are specific research reports of work on the development of moral judgements and cooperative behavior, respectively. Such combinations are intended to give readers an overview of the current state of knowledge in an area, and some understanding of the method by which such knowledge has been acquired through research.

Finally, I hope that this selection of readings enhances the student's interest in developmental psychology, fosters a healthy respect for the scientific approach to the study of development, and contributes to his/her understanding of the complex processes by which humans grow and change across the life span.

Section 1

Development in Infancy

Human infants are fascinating little people. Observing a newborn infant scanning his/her surroundings and orienting to the sound of a human voice, one cannot fail to wonder what this small, dependent creature can sense and how much he/she knows. William James, in 1890, believed that the newborn infant experiences only "a booming, buzzing, confusion", and John Locke wrote in 1693, that the infant was "tabula rasa", a blank slate waiting for the script of experience to give him or her individuality. Today, we know that these views underestimated the infant's competence. Although relatively immature at birth, the senses and nervous system of the infant are organized to begin processing information at once. Furthermore, babies assert their individuality from their earliest days. While much of the infant's early behavior is reflexive, each has his or her own biological and temperamental predispositions, and thus responds to the environment in his or her own characteristic way.

Although the infant is born with the potential for human skill and thought, these are not present at birth. Through the interactive effects of maturation and experience, and with an intrinsic curiosity to understand and master the environment, the infant undergoes a remarkable range of physiological, perceptual, cognitive, and social changes in the first year of life. He/she will acquire independent locomotion, learn and remember, begin to use spoken language to communicate, and develop at least a rudimentary sense of time, space and causality. The infant will also become a social being, adapting to a world of other humans. He/she will begin to develop a sense of self and will form a first emotional relationship, an attachment to the caretaker. These developmental changes do not occur in isolation, but are complexly interrelated.

Although scientific interest in infant development goes back about a hundred years, European thinkers such as Freud and Piaget long ago regarded infant experience as critically important for later development. Yet until the past twenty-five years, psychologists in North America focused their attention primarily on these later developmental periods, perhaps feeling that the inner world of the infant was not an appropriate subject for research in the Behaviorist tradition. The difficulties that they anticipated are quite real. The study of infant behavior presents many practical problems. Infants cannot talk to us, so we must rely on their nonverbal behavior to tell us what they know. Infants will respond to stimuli that are presented to them by scanning, orienting, smiling, and by showing surprise. Their nervous systems respond to stimuli and these reactions can be recorded electrophysiologically. They will also acquire new patterns of behavior through operant and classical conditioning. However, infant behavior can be difficult to interpret. If a baby responds differently to two stimuli we know that at some level he/she has discriminated between them. However, we cannot assume that the infant perceives or represents the difference between the stimuli in the same way that a mature adult would do. Furthermore, if the infant does not respond differently to the two stimuli we cannot conclude that he/she was unable to discriminate between them, as he/she may simply not be "telling" the observer that the discrimination has been made. Infants have little respect for science, and are often uncooperative, uninterested, and/or inattentive. Such problems present an enduring challenge to the patience and ingenuity of those who study infant development.

The papers selected for this chapter are intended to give the reader an exposure to a variety of research on infant development. The first paper is an early report by Robert Fantz, a pioneer in the field of infant perception. Fantz, noting that very young infants will visually explore their environments and prefer to look at certain stimuli over others, developed a Visual Preference technique for the assessment of infants' ability to discriminate form. Variations of this basic technique are still used in infant research today and have contributed enormously to our knowledge of perceptual development. The second paper, by Ian Bushnell, is a more recent example of the use of a version of the Fantz method to study infant perception of faces. Bushnell found that infants initially discriminate between faces on the basis of their external contours, but by about four or five months of age they use the internal features to discriminate between faces. Robert Fox and Cynthia McDaniel used the Fantz method to address a rather unusual aspect of infant perception, the identification of biological motion. It appears that four-month-old infants can identify the coordinated, rhythmic patterns that are characteristic of human movement, and seem to find them interesting. Although the significance of this early sensitivity to biological motion is not well understood, it is intriguing.

The paper by Peter Eimas describes his work on infants' perception of speech. Recent evidence also suggests that newborn infants may be especially sensitive to speech, and Eimas and his colleagues have found that infants at one month of age can discriminate between consonants such as "pa" and "ba". He also found that while infants' auditory discrimination of the sounds of their own language becomes more refined with experience, their discrimination of language sounds that are not part of refined with experience, their discrimination of language sounds that are not part of their native tongue becomes poorer.

Carolyn Rovee-Collier and her colleagues have used the infant's early learning ability to study the development of long-term memory. Their method is to teach infants an operant foot kick response that results in the reinforcing movement of an overhead mobile. Infants are removed from the situation and brought back to it at a later time. They found that three-month-old infants remembered and generalized the response eight days after the initial learning. In the research reported here, the authors found that two-month-old infants showed even better long-term memory performance following a technique called "reinstatement".

The final paper in this section, by Mary Ainsworth, is a review of some of her work on the development of an infant's attachment to his/her caretaker. She and her colleagues have found that the quality of this first emotional relationship is an extremely important predictor of later adaptation to a variety of cognitive and interpersonal situations. They have also found that certain maternal caretaking styles can affect the quality of the attachment that the infant develops.

Pattern Vision in Young Infants
Robert L. Fantz

William James described the infant's world as a "great blooming, buzzing confusion" (4). Two questions might be asked regarding this statement: first, what kinds of sensations are contained in the confusion, and second, is the confusion relieved by the beginnings of perceptual organization? Relative to the first question, considerable progress has been made in determining the elementary sensory dimensions to which the young infant is sensitive. For example, responsiveness to the intensive and spectral features of photic radiation and to movement is present at an early age (7). Regarding the second question, little information is available about supposedly complex functions such as form and spatial vision which involve configurations of stimuli. Since relevant data are lacking, there is a tendency to assume that visual organization and patterning are absent before considerable experience and learning has occurred. More definite information is desirable for several reasons. First, pattern and spatial vision is, in the adult, the most reliable and important source of information about the environment, so that the onset and development of this function is of great interest. Second, this topic has played a major role in theories of perception and neural functioning (2, 3, 5, 6).

The methods available for testing young infants are limited by the lack of verbal,

---

Originally published in *The Psychological Record*, 1958, 8, 43-47; reprinted with permission of the publisher.

manual, and locomotor response indicators. However, eye activity itself, which is a prominent part of the infant's behavior, can provide a clue to what is seen and how it is organized. When under controlled conditions an infant repeatedly looks more at one target than at another, and thus shows a visual preference for certain parts of the spectrum, it may be supposed that color is seen and discriminated. In the same way, consistent visual attention to stimuli differing only in pattern, regardless of position, is evidence for form or pattern vision.

In brief, the method used in this study was that of recording the relative lengths of visual fixation by an infant of simultaneously-presented patterns. The aim was to determine whether this technique offered a solution to the difficulties in studying early visual development. A similar method, used to test a chimpanzee infant, is described more fully elsewhere (1).

Subjects

The Ss were 30 infants selected from the waiting list of a university nursery school on the basis of age and availability for repeated testing. The age varied from one to fourteen weeks at the first test. Weekly test sessions were given when possible until ten records had been obtained.

Eight of the thirty Ss had to be dropped before this time due to persistent crying, fussing, or sleeping in the testing situation. Most of the results are based on the remaining 22 infants.

Procedure

The testing was carried out in the homes of the Ss in order to minimize disturbing factors. The infant was placed face up in a comfortable, form-fitting crib which prevented gross head and body movements. A uniform gray structure above the infant excluded vision of people or objects in the room and provided a background for two posterboard patterns. These patterns were located one ft. above the infant's head and were spaced one ft. apart. Illumination was provided from below the infant's field of view.

Four pairs of patterns were used during each test (Fig. 1). The identical triangles were included in control for the possibility of differential response to factors other than form or pattern differences. The cross and circle were equated in area. The bull's-eye and stripes patterns were equated in area of red and in outline form. The checkerboard was paired half of the time with the plain square of equal outline size and the remaining time with the smaller square equated in area of red. A duplicate set of patterns was used for part of the testing.

Fig 1. The stimulus patterns drawn to scale; the large squares measured five inches on a side. Shaded areas were bright red; blank areas were gray to match the background. Adjacent patterns were presented together; the checkerboard was paired with either large or small plain square on a given exposure.

Each pair was presented twice in succession, with reversed right and left positions for the second exposure. Thus eight test periods, each 30 sec. long, were given during a weekly test session. The order of presentation of the four pairs was random, and the initial positions within each pair also varied randomly.

Between exposures the patterns were hidden from view by a gray shield which contained a 4-inch hole directly overhead. A test exposure did not begin until the infant was looking at this central hole. Thus, there was an equal chance of eye movements toward the two patterns when they were suddenly exposed to view. The infant's eyes were observed through a 1/4 in. hole midway between the patterns. The total length of visual attention to each pattern was measured by pressing one of two telegraph keys while the corresponding pattern was fixated. Each key operated a timer. The time scores were then recorded at the end of the 30-sec. exposure.

It is difficult to be certain of the direction of gaze of an infant by unaided observation. This problem was solved by making use of the reflected images of the patterns. These images were clearly visible on the surface of the eyeball under proper lighting conditions. When a pattern was fixated, the image of that pattern coincided with the pupil of the eye. This provided a simple and reliable criterion of fixation.

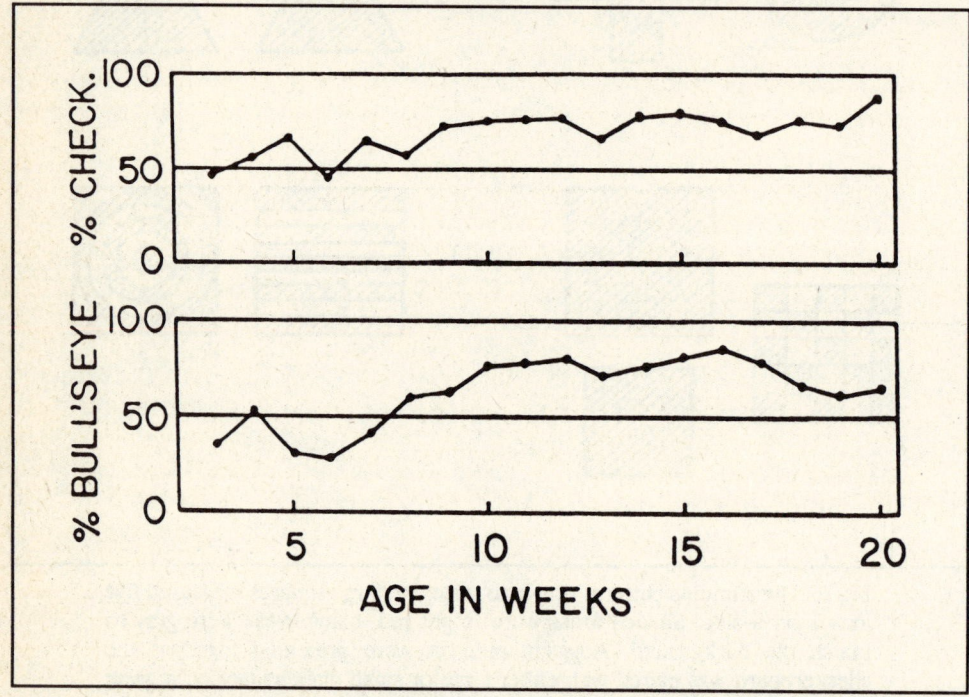

Fig 2.   Developmental preference curves for two pairs of patterns: checkerboard versus plain square and bull's-eye versus horizontal stripes. At each age is shown the relative amount of time for the two patterns out of the combined fixation time for both. Each point is the average for those Ss tested at that age; this number varies between 5 and 20 with the higher values at the middle ages.

The time scores for the two exposures of a pair of patterns were summated to balance out position preferences. Non-parametric tests of significance were used.

Results

Neither the control pair of triangles nor the cross and circle elicited consistent visual preferences. On the other hand, the two pairs presenting variations in type and degree of patterning gave results which were consistent both in successive tests and between Ss.

In total scores for all ten weekly sessions, 19 infants fixated the checkboard more than the square, compared to only 3 favoring the square. The results were similar for exposures using the large or small squares. Twenty Ss showed higher time scores for the bull's-eye, compared to two for the stripes. Both preferences are significant at the .001 level, indicating that the ability to discriminate patterns was present during the first six months of age.

Fig. 2 shows developmental curves for the two pairs of patterns which gave sig-

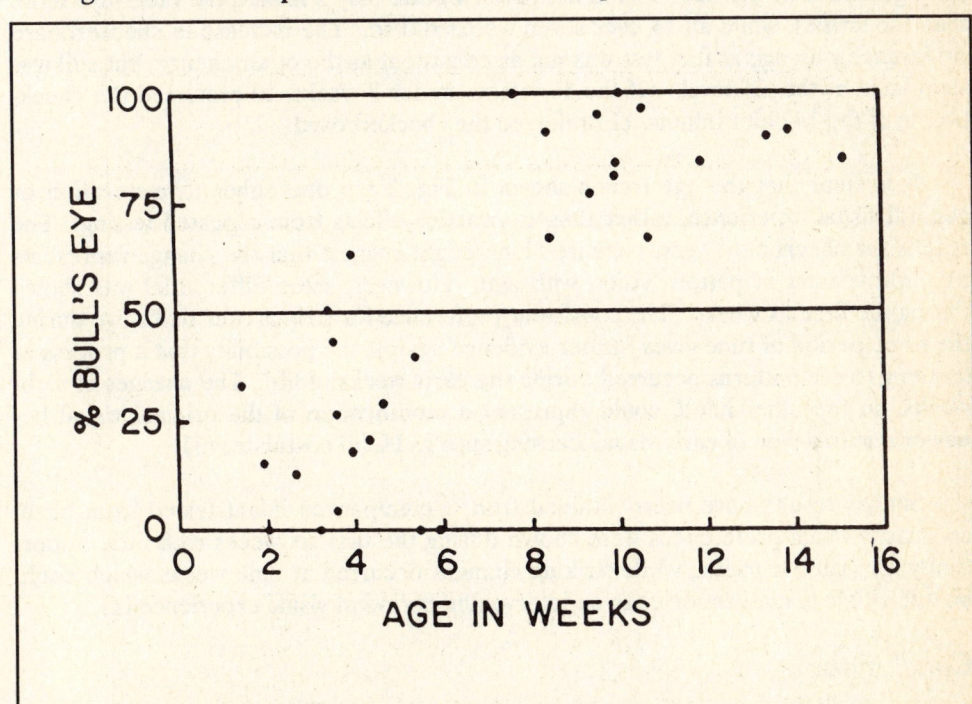

Fig 3. A scatterplot between age at first test and preference for the bull's-eye or stripes pattern. Each point is based on the combined fixation time for the two patterns during two 30-second exposures for a single S. The N is 30, including those infants dropped later in the experiment.

nificant overall results. An increase in the checkboard preference is evident around eight weeks. A reversal from a stripes to a bull's-eye preference was shown at eight weeks.

The latter change was an unexpected and unexplained finding, although it is one of the most consistent aspects of the results. Of the 12 infants who were first tested before eight weeks of age, 11 showed a clear reversal of preference from stripes to bull's eye. The 10 older infants all showed a consistent bull's-eye preference. The change of preference could not have been caused by an unknown change in testing procedure, experimental conditions, or stimulus patterns during the course of the experiment, since it occurred at widely varying dates for different Ss, and with duplicate sets of patterns.

The preference reversal was not related to amount of testing experience, as may be seen in Fig. 3. This is a scatterplot between age and preference score for the first testing of each S. Of the 16 Ss under seven weeks, only 2 fixated the bull's-eye more than the stripes, while all 14 over seven weeks did so. The increase in checkerboard preference with age at first test was not as consistent as the other change, but still was significant at the .05 level. Of the 16 infants under 7 weeks, 10 preferred the checkboard; of the 14 older infants, 11 preferred the checkerboard.

It is clear that the age trends shown in Fig. 2 are due either to maturation or general visual experience, rather than to practice effects from repeated testing. The results for checkboard versus square alone might suggest that the change represents an improvement in pattern vision with age. However, some differential was shown during the first six weeks. The consistent preference for stripes over bull's-eye during the same period of time gives further evidence against the possibility that a process of learning to see patterns occurred during the early weeks of life. The changes at eight weeks, on the other hand, could represent a modification of the original visual behavior due to a type of early visual learning such as Hebb postulates (3).

Similar results have been obtained from a chimpanzee infant tested from birth: consistent visual preferences were shown during the first six weeks with little opportunity for visual learning, while striking changes occurred at nine weeks which could be due either to maturation or to an intervening period of visual experience (1).

Conclusions

1. Visual patterns were discriminated by infants during the first six months, as evidenced by differential fixation times.

2. Changes in the strength or direction of the pattern preferences occurred around two months of age, independently of amount of testing.

3. Consistent visual preferences were present as early as the first two months, thus arguing against an extreme empiricistic view of the development of visual organization and pattern discrimination.

4. The determination of natural visual preferences among different stimuli is a powerful method of studying early visual development which can provide data of impor-

tance to theories of perception, learning, and neural functioning.

References

1. Fantz, R.L. Visual discrimination in a neonate chimpanzee. *Percept. mot. Skills.*, in press.

2. Gibson, J.J. *The perception of the visual world.* Boston: Houghton Mifflin, 1950.

3. Hebb, D.O. *The organization of behavior.* New York: Wiley, 1949.

4. James, W. *The principles of psychology.* New York: Holt, 1890.

5. Kohler, W. *Dynamics in psychology.* New York: Liveright, 1940.

6. Lashley, K.S. The problem of cerebral organization in vision. In H. Kluver (Ed.), *Visual mechanisms. Biol. Sympos.*, 1942, 7, 301-322.

7. Pratt, K.C. The neonate. In L. Carmichael (Ed.), *Manual of child psychology.* New York: Wiley, 1954. Pp. 215-291.

Discrimination of Faces by Young Infants

I.W.R. Bushnell

An experiment was conducted to obtain normative data concerning discrimination between human faces by infants under 6 months of age and to determine the information base required for this performance. Infants were habituated to a specific face and recovery of attention was monitored to a novel face, where one or more features was common to both faces. Results suggested that discrimination between photographs of adult, female faces is possible from 5 weeks of age, with critical information probably lying in the hair-face outline while internal features were relatively unimportant until the 19th week.

The human face is both salient and frequently encountered by the young infant and it may well provide significant information for differentiating people in the infants' environment. It appears that infants can discriminate between familiar and unfamiliar adults in terms of voice (Mills & Melhuish, 1974) and smell (Macfarlane, 1975) within the first weeks of life; it is less certain when visual discrimination of faces first occurs.

Existing studies on face discrimination may be divided into those which have adopted real faces and those using representations. Carpenter has conducted a series

Originally published in *Journal of Experimental Child Psychology*, 33, Copyright ©1982 Academic Press, Inc.; reprinted with permission of the publisher and author.

of studies using both real and representational faces in which infants were tested longitudinally through the first 2 months of life. In each study, from 2 weeks of age a significant difference in visual fixation was noted between the mother's face and a stranger's face or that of a mannequin (Carpenter, Tecce, Stechler, & Friedman, 1970; Carpenter, Note 4; Carpenter, 1974). It is difficult to draw conclusions about face discrimination from Carpenter's experiments because of problems evident in each of these studies. Olfactory and brightness cues were not properly controlled and the same stranger's face was apparently used in each study. However, other research using real faces has indicated that face discrimination is possible by 13 weeks of age (Caldwell, note 3) and 5 weeks of age (Maurer & Salapatek, 1976).

In studies analyzing differentiation of face photographs Fagan (1972) reported good discrimination at 22 weeks but none at 17 weeks. Cornell (1974) noted similar results where 19-week-olds failed to differentiate male and female faces in spontaneous visual preferences, while 23-week-olds succeeded. Fitzgerald (1968), using achromatic video stills, reported no discrimination between mother and female strangers at 5 and 9 weeks, but successful discrimination at 17 weeks. Finally, Cohen found in two studies that 18-week-olds could discriminate between two faces — male vs. female, female vs. female (Cohen, Note 5; Cohen, De Loache, & Pearl, 1977).

This considerable discrepancy in age at which face discrimination has been demonstrated for real and representational stimuli may result from a lack of control in the real face studies, particularly with regard to olfactory cues. Alternatively, the use of very short presentation and test times in representation studies (e.g., Fagan, 1972 and Cornell, 1974) may have reduced test sensitivity, as may the adoption of the dependent variable autonomic pupillary reflex in the case of Fitzgerald (1968).

Further research on this question may, therefore, be useful, particularly to determine what visual information is being used by the infant to discriminate between faces. Evidence regarding this is mostly indirect, coming from visual scanning studies and research into the necessary and sufficient stimuli for smiling. Evidence from scanning is fairly consistent, suggesting that in the first 2 months of life very few face features are fixated and most attention is paid to the hair-face outline. After the second month, however, more of the face is fixated and the eyes in particular receive a good deal of attention (Bergman, Haith, & Mann, Note 2; Donnee, Note 6; Maurer & Salapatek, 1976). The problem with fixation analysis, however, is that the relationship between direct line of regard and information pick-up cannot be assumed, but must be demonstrated.

A study of smiling behavior has presented a slightly different picture. Ahrens (1954) has stated that at 6 weeks eye dots elicit smiles and the face outline itself is unimportant, while by 13 weeks the full realistic face is required to elicit smiling.

Somewhat more direct evidence is available from fixation time experiments on the differentiation of faces varying in constituent features, although mainly with infants over 12 weeks of age. Fantz (1966), for example, showed infants a number of schematic faces and found a preference for faces with a normal eye arrangement over an off-center arrangement by 13 weeks, but not with younger infants. Similarly, Allyn (Note 1) reported that infants between 13 and 18 weeks spent more time looking at real faces or their filmed representations when these contained eyes than when they did not.

However one of the few systematic attempts to isolate the facial features salient to young infants is a study by Caron, Caron, Caldwell, & Weiss (1973) in which they used a habituation/dishabituation procedure. They familiarized 17- and 21-week-old infants to a distorted schematic face, monitored recovery to a regular face, and assumed the extent of this recovery would define the salience of the feature or arrangement of features affected. They looked at eyes, nose, mouth, hair, and face outlines, and varied the location of features relative to the standard face outline and found that at 17 weeks the nose-mouth distortions were far less likely to be detected than other distortions, especially of the eyes. This indicated that the nose-mouth was less salient than the eyes at this age. In addition, the proper location and symmetrical arrangement of the eyes was apparently available to infants. There was some suggestion that 17-week-olds were more sensitive to the hair-face outline than to the inner face configuration. The 21-week-olds, however, detected the nose-mouth distortions, and the inner face was as salient as the outer face and hairline.

The experiments described do not present an entirely cohesive picture although the general pattern emerges that infants respond at first to only a limited section of the face, either eyes or hairline, and gradually respond to more features and their interrelationships. In the light of previous research into the ontogeny of face perception, it was decided to look at the ability of young infants to discriminate between the face of their mother and that of a female stranger and to see how they were affected by the absence of specific feature information. The study was based on the principle that if only a single feature or a limited number of features are being used to discriminate between two faces, it should be possible to determine these by systematically equating features across a comparison pair of faces. Thus, if two faces have the same eyes and discrimination is based largely on eye information, there should be a failure to discriminate in this situation. A selection of features was, therefore, made and comparison faces equated on one or more of these features.

METHOD

The visual habituation-dishabituation paradigm was employed, with infants being repeatedly presented with a slide of their mother's face over a series of trials, each of 30-sec duration, until a criterion decrease in total fixation time per trial was registered.

The criterion set was that of two successive trials where the total fixation time was 25% less than that recorded on the previously most attended trial. The criteria used in some previous studies may appear to have been more strict. For example, Cohen, De Loache, and Pearl (1977) used a 50% decrement from the length of first fixation on the first trial to that on a subsequent trial. However, the criterion used here is less sensitive to chance variations in fixation time which can be encountered on a single trial. Once the criterion was reached, a novel slide of a stranger's face was presented for three successive trials.

Subjects

The subjects were found through a volunteer program at the Mill Road Maternity Hospital, Cambridge, England. Only infants with normal deliveries and no evidence of postnatal problems were tested. Three groups were obtained of 5-, 12-, and 19-week-olds with 10 infants in each group. One infant had to be replaced in the 12-week group due to persistent crying. Each infant made up to seven visits to the laboratory over a period extending to 3 weeks, with two test conditions normally being completed on each visit. The mean age at testing was 36.6 days (range 28-49), 81.6 days (range 70-91) and 131.2 days (range 119-140). Those sessions which were interrupted as a result of state variables were rerun on subsequent visits.

Stimuli

The faces (head and neck) of adult females were photographed on color slides when facing the camera. Each face was photographed five times, once in a normal state (N) and a further four times where one or more features were "standardized." This standardization of features across individuals was achieved by photographing the adult female while wearing:

(1) a small pair of dark-glass pince-nez to standardize the eye area (E),

(2) a closely fitting, light-colored, rubber bathing cap to standardize the hair (H),

(3) a flesh-colored rectangle of Elastoplast over the mouth (60 x 35 mm) to standardize the mouth (M),

(4) both pince-nez and wig together to standardize eyes and hair (EH).

These photographs were taken against a common background and with a standard light source. A photometer was used to select comparison pairs on the basis of luminance flux.

Equipment

Each infant was tested within an homogenous gray enclosure while sitting in an adjustable, padded infant chair reclined at 20 from the vertical. From the chair the infant viewed a rear-projection screen (60 x 60 cm) on which the face slides were displayed by means of a Leitz Pradovit projector. The faces measured approximately 25 x 20 cm and the screen-to-subject distance was 35 cm.

The observer viewed fixation behavior through an aperture within 15 cm of the face stimulus and recorded by button presses the length of each fixation to the face and the number of fixations within each 30-sec period. The criterion for fixation was the reflection of part of the face stimulus over the center of the pupil. Fixation data were recorded by means of Digital Equipment logic which also enabled automatic control of stimulus presentation, trial onset and duration. OMB 745 countertimers displayed data and a hard copy was produced on a Roxburgh Electronics Series RP19 Data Printer.

Stimulus presentation and trial onset were not simultaneous, the stimulus being presented first and the trial commencing with the first fixation.

Design

Each age group was tested under all six conditions. Each infant, therefore, was involved in the following six discriminations — between the faces of mother and female stranger — when (1) normal and expressionless (N), (2) the eye area was the same for both faces (E), (3) the mouth area was the same for both faces (M), (4) the hair was standardized across both faces (H), (5) the eyes and hair were standardized (EH). (6) the mother's face was shown throughout (as a control condition; c). A different stranger was used for each subject in each condition and the order in which conditions were given was randomized across subjects.

RESULTS

The data in the form of total fixation times within each 30-sec trial were analyzed by analysis of variance with separate analyses being undertaken for the Habituation and Test phases for each of the three age groups.

Habituation. The ANOVAs considered two within-subject variables, Conditions (6 levels) and Trials (4 levels). The Trials variable used the data from the last 2 min of habituation (i.e., 4 trials). At all ages the only factor to reach a significant F value was that of Trials (5 weeks, $F(3, 27) = 110.58$, $p < .001$; 12 weeks, $F(3, 27) = 210.03$, $p < .001$; 19 weeks, $F(3, 27) = 104.36$, $p < .001$). This effect was the result of the criterion decrement in fixation between the third and second to last trials of the habituation

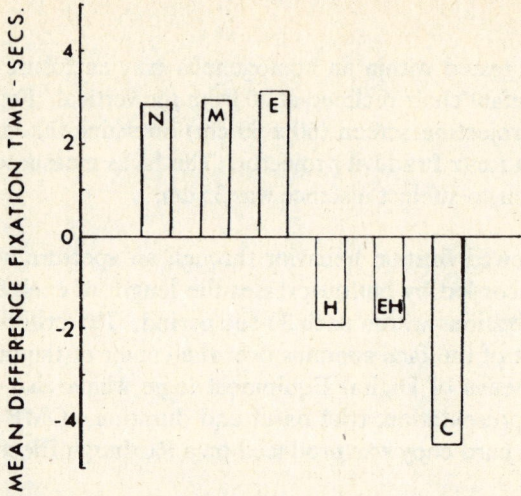

Fig 1. Mean difference fixation times across conditions for 5-week old subjects.

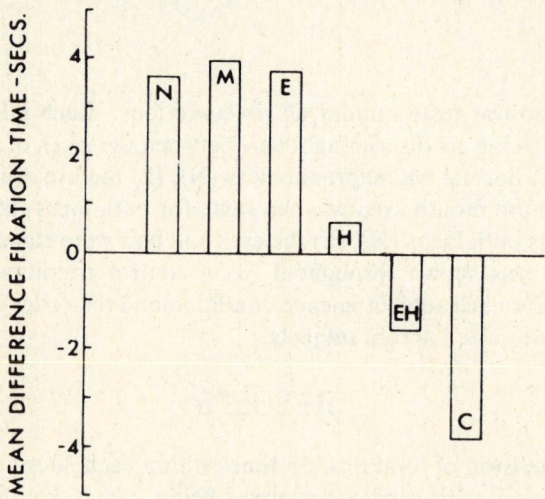

Fig 2. Mean difference fixation times across conditions for 12-week old subjects.

decrement in fixation between the third and second to last trials of the habituation phase.

Test. Separate ANOVAs for the Test trials data were carried out employing the variables Conditions (6 levels) and Trials (3 levels). The data for total fixation times per trial were adjusted for these analyses in order to achieve a sensitive measure of

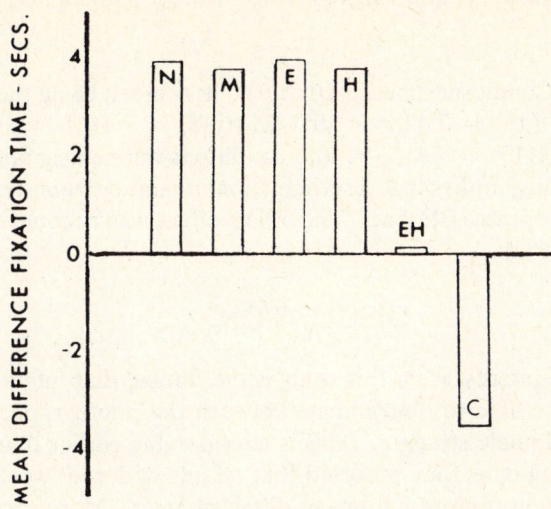

Fig. 3. Mean difference fixation times across conditions for 19-week old subjects.

response change during the Test phase compared with the Habituation phase. This was done for each subject by subtracting the arithmetic mean for the final two Habituation trials from the fixation time for each of the three Test trials. These mean difference fixation times can be seen in Figs. 1, 2, and 3.

At 5 weeks the ANOVA produced significant F values for both Conditions ($F(5, 45) = 6.94$, $p < .01$) and Trials ($F(2, 18) = 9.93$, $p < .01$), but not for the interaction. A Dunnett t test was used to compare each Condition's mean with the mean for the control (C) and this resulted in significant t values for Conditions N ($t(18) = 7.37$, $p < .05$), M ($t(10 = 8) = 7.51$, $p < .05$), and E($t(18) = 7.37$, $p < .05$). By this criterion, only in these Conditions was the mother discriminated from the stranger.

The Trials effect was accounted for by a reduction in fixation which occurred over the trials of this phase.

The ANOVA for the 12-week-old group produced a significant F value only for Conditions ($F(5, .45) = 8.53$, $p < .001$). A Dunnett t test indicated significant values for N ($t(18) = 7.49$, $p < .05$), M ($t(18) = 7.8$, $p < .05$), and E ($t(18) = 7.55$, $p < .05$), and thus discrimination of mother from stranger was only indicated in these cases.

Data from the 19-week group were analyzed by an ANOVA with both main effects reaching significance, Conditions (F(5, 45) = 5.81, p < .001) and Trials (F(2, 18) = 15.36, p < .001).

Comparing each Condition's mean with the control mean using the Dunnett t test indicated that the N (t(18) = 7.49, p < .05), M (t(18) = 7.41, p < .05), E (t(18) = 7.55, p < .05), and H(t(18) = 7.41, p < .05) conditions were all significantly different from the control C. This implies that discrimination of mother from stranger occurred in every condition except the EH one. The Trials effect was account for by a reduction in fixation across trials.

DISCUSSION

The first result of interest from this study is the finding that infants as young as 4 to 7 weeks of age were able to discriminate between the photographed face of their mother and that of a female stranger. This is considerably earlier than Fagan (1972) and Cornell (1974) found, as they reported that infants under 20 weeks of age could not discriminate between representations of different faces. More recently, however, Barrera and Maurer (in press) have described a study with 13-week-olds in which successful discrimination of female faces was found. What the present study and that of Barrera and Maurer have in common is the use of high quality color slides as stimuli and the adoption of a criterion habituation paradigm. This difference in technique combined with the careful testing of infants at their "best period" may be responsible for the present result. Certainly the evidence from discrimination of real faces would support the kind of time scale reported.

The question of what information is actually being processed can also be answered in part. The data do not support the view that the eyes may be of special importance for the young infant. It is probable that the basis for the observed discrimination between faces, at least by younger infants, was the outer contours of the face. This could have been the hair-face boundary, the hair itself, the outer hair-head boundary, or indeed a combination. Since all of these factors were affected by the hair standardization, the contribution of each cannot be assessed. The greater importance of the outer contours is attested to by the critical breakdown of face discrimination when the hair (but not the eyes or mouth) standardization was applied. A possible developmental change in this respect can be detected since the 5- and 12-week-olds failed to discriminate in the H condition while the 19-week-olds succeeded. However, the 19-week-olds failed on the EH condition, but not the E condition, confirming that hair information was still important.

The data from this study also allowed some test of the applicability of direct fixation analysis as an index of information pick-up. The scanning literature has demonstrated that infants under 8 weeks of age preferentially fixate outer face contours. It is, therefore, consistent with this that only outer face information had a direct effect on face discrimination at 5 weeks. However, both Bergman et al., (Note 2) and Maurer and Salapatek (1976) indicated that there should be equivalent fixation of inner and outer contour, or even preferential fixation of inner contour by the 8th week onward. If this were the case, the 12-week-olds in the present study should also not have appeared to use only the outer contours for discrimination. It may be that there are two aspects to be considered. One important factor is obviously the salience or attention worthiness of features and the scanning literature highlights this rather well. The outer face is particularly salient in the first 2 months of life, while the inner face becomes relatively more salient thereafter. However, salience can only be relevant to discrimination if the salient feature carries information that the infant can use. The 12-week-old infant may, therefore, attend to certain inner features, but may not be able to use the information from these features for effective discrimination because the differences between exemplars of these features may not be sufficiently great. This possibility is supported by the results of a study by Young-Browne, Rosenfeld, and Horowitz (1977) who reported significant discrimination in 12- to 14-week-olds between photographs of a male face differing only in the expression portrayed. Here the internal feature differences would have been enhanced by the adoption of different expressions. Thus, 12-week-olds may be able to detect and attend to inner features, but only discriminate when there are fairly large differences between exemplars, while 19-week-olds can respond to finer differences. The present data are largely consistent with face scanning research.

The performance of the 19-week-olds in this study accords quite well with the Caron, Caron, Caldwell, and Weiss (1973) finding that 17-week-olds respond more readily to alterations in the outer contours of a schematic face than those in the inner contours, while by 21 weeks an equivalent response is noted. Caron et al. did find that both eyes and mouth could be used to detect feature change by 21-week-olds, but the present study did not include a mouth/hair condition and thus it was not possible to compare results here.

In general, the young infants' limited capacity for processing visual input is confirmed, since removing only one face feature as a possible cue prevented discrimination at 5 and 12 weeks, while by 19 weeks a combination of two features prevent discrimination. The position appears to be that the 5-week-old infants are capable of differentiating represented faces by means of large contour differences in the outer part of the face, but inner features cannot be used for this purpose until perhaps 19 weeks of age. These are interesting results when Fagan and Singer's (1979) study is considered since they concluded that infants younger than 7 months are unlikely to make within-class (e.g., sex or age) face discriminations, but only across-class ones, and that simple features don't support such discriminations. However, successful within-class discrimination was also found by Young-Browne et al. (1977) and Barrera and Maurer (in press) with infants aged from 11 to 14 weeks and by Maurer and Salapatek (1976) with 5-week-olds.

It should of course be remembered that this study used static, face representations equated for brightness and coloring. The results may not, therefore, be easily generalized to real faces in the real world. For example, it is known that 5-week-olds will demonstrate a bonding-contour effect with static, geometric stimuli (Milewski, 1976), but where there is independent movement of a bounded element this effect disappears (Bushnell, 1979). Since the internal features of real faces are in frequent motion relative to the face outline, it would be expected that interval features will be fixated and information from them will be available even by 5 weeks.

REFERENCES

Ahrens, R. Beitrag zur entwicklung der physiognomie-und mimikerkennes. *Zeitschrift fur Experimentelle und Angewandte Psychologie*, 1954, 2, 412-454, 599-633.

Barrera, M.A., & Maurer, D. Recognition and discrimination of faces by the three-month-old infant. *Child Development*, in press.

Bushnell, I.W.R. Modification of the externality effect in young infants. *Journal of Experimental Child Psychology*, 1979, 28, 211-229.

Caron, A.J., Caron, R.F., Caldwell,R.C., & Weiss, S.J. Infant perception of the structural properties of the face. *Developmental Psychology*, 1973, 9, 385-399.

Carpenter, G.C. Visual regard of moving and stationary faces in early infancy. *Merrill-Palmer Quarterly*, 1974, 20, 181-194.

Carpenter, G.C., Tecce, J.J., Stechler, G., & Friedman, S. Differential visual behaviour to human and humanoid faces in early infancy. *Merrill-Palmer Quarterly*, 1970, 16, 91-108.

Cohen, L.B., De Loache, J.S., & Pearl, R.A. An examination of interference effects in infants' memory for faces. *Child Development*, 1977, 48, 88-96.

Cornell, E.H. Infants' discrimination of photographs of faces following redundant presentations. *Journal of Experimental Child Psychology*, 1974, 18, 98-106.

Fagan, J.F. Infants' recognition memory for faces. *Journal of Experimental Child Psychology*, 1972, 14, 453-476.

Fagan, J.F., & Singer, L.T. The role of simple feature differences in infants' recognition of faces. *Infant Behavior and Development*, 1979, 2, 39-45.

Fantz, R.L. Pattern discrimination and selective attention as determinants of perceptual development from birth. In A.H. Kidd & J.L. Rivoire (Eds.), *Perceptual development in children.* New York: International, 1966.

Fitzgerald, H.E. Autonomic pupillary reflex activity during early infancy and its relation to social and nonsocial visual stimuli. *Journal of Experimental Child Psychology,* 1968, 6, 470-482.

Maurer, D., & Salapatek, P. Developmental changes in the scanning of faces by young infants. *Child Development*, 1976, 47, 523-527.

Macfarlane, A. Olfaction in the development of social preferences in the human neonate. In *CIBA Foundation Symposium 33.* Elsevier/Excerpta Medica/North-Holland, 1975. Pp. 103-117.

Milewski, A. Infants' discrimination of internal and external pattern elements. *Journal of Experimental Child Psychology*, 1976, 22, 229-246.

Mills, M., & Melhuish, E. Recognition of mother's voice in early infancy. *Nature* (London), 1974, 252, 123-124.

Young-Browne, G., Rosenfeld, H.M., & Horowitz, F.D. Infant discrimination of facial expressions. *Child Development*, 1977, 48, 555-562.

REFERENCE NOTES

1. Allyn, G. *Infantile perception of the human face.* Unpublished Doctoral Dissertation, Bedford College, London, 1972.

2. Bergman, T., Haith, M.M., & Mann, L. *Development of eye contact and facial scanning in infants.* Paper presented at the meeting of the Society for Research in Child Development, Minneapolis, Minn., 1971.

3. Caldwell, B.M. *Visual and emotional reactions of an infant to his mother and other adult females.* Paper presented to the Tavistock Study Group on Mother-Infant Interaction, London, 1965.

4. Carpenter, G.C. *Mother-stranger discrimination in the early weeks of life.* Paper presented at the meeting of the Society for Research in Child Development, Philadelphia, 1973.

5. Cohen, L.B. *Concept acquisition in the human infant.* Paper presented at the meet-

ing of the Society for Research in Child Development, New Orleans, La., 1977.

6.   Donnee, L.H. *Infants' developmental scanning patterns to face and nonface stimuli under various auditory conditions.* Paper presented at the meeting of the Society for Research in Child Development, Philadelphia, 1973.

The Perception of Speech in Early Infancy
Peter D. Eimas

In perceiving speech human beings detect discrete phonemic categories and ignore much of the acoustic variation in the speech signal. Research with infants suggests the underlying perceptual mechanisms are innate.[1]

How is it that a child swiftly and seemingly without much effort learns to speak and understand? The process of language acquisition begins well before the first birthday, and most children use language with considerable skill by their third year. In contrast to the learning of reading or arithmetic, a child masters language without formal teaching; indeed, much of the learning takes place within a fairly limited linguistic environment, which does not specify the rules governing competent language use.

A possible explanation for the swift growth of a child's language skills is that language is not as complex as is generally thought, and consequently that such simple psychological principles as conditioning and generalization account for the speed with which it is learned. But research during the past several decades on the nature of language and the processes by which it is produced and understood has revealed not underlying simplicity but increasing complexity.

Experiments carried out by my colleagues and me at Brown University and by other investigators elsewhere have supported a different explanation, one derived from the view, of which the linguist Noam Chomsky is the most notable exponent, that inborn knowledge and capacities underlie the use of language. In studies of speech perception by infants we have found these young subjects are richly endowed with innate perceptual mechanisms, well adapted to the characteristics of human language, that prepare them for the linguistic world they will encounter.

The search for inborn mechanisms of speech perception developed from studies of the relation of the speech signal to phonemes, the perceptual units that correspond to the consonants and vowels of language. Phonemes are the smallest units of speech that affect meaning: only one phonemic difference sets apart the words late and rate, yet they are entirely distinct in meaning.

Workers at the Haskins Laboratories in New Haven, the Massachusetts Institute of Technology, Sweden's Royal Institute of Technology and elsewhere have shown that the speech signal is a complex of acoustic units: brief segments bounded by momentary pauses or peaks in intensity. The segments vary in duration and in the frequency, temporal relations and intensity of their constituent bands of concentrated acoustic energy, known as formants, and of noiselike acoustic components known as aspiration and frication. The variation in these acoustic parameters provides the information that is critical to the perception of phonemes.

.No direct, one-to-one correspondence holds, however, between individual acoustic segments and the phonemes we perceive. A single acoustic segment may encompass a consonant and a vowel; conversely, two distinct acoustic segments may contribute to a single consonantal sound. Furthermore, there is no direct relation between the segments' frequency and temporal characteristics and the phonemes we hear. A listener may recognize a range of stimuli, varying widely in a number of acoustic traits, as instances of the same phoneme. On the other hand, a small change in a single acoustic cue may in some situations change the phoneme that is perceived.

Consider the acoustic information that is sufficient to signal the distinction between the voiced stop consonant that begins the word bin and the voiceless stop consonant in pin. In both cases the speaker completely blocks the flow of air through the vocal tract just before the release of the utterance; in bin, however, the vocal cords begin to vibrate almost simultaneously with the release of air, whereas in pin vocal-cord vibration is delayed. The interval between the release of air and the onset of vocal-cord vibration, or voicing, is known as voice-onset time; it holds the crucial acoustic information that enables a hearer to distinguish bin from pin. No single value of voice-onset time defines each phoneme, however. Instead hearers typically perceive a range of values, reflecting different speakers, different instances of speech and differences in surrounding phonemic environment, as examples of the same phoneme.

The acoustic variables that define other phonemes are similarly fluid. For example, many phonemes are differentiated by place of articulation, the site of the constriction of the vocal tract that occurs as the sound is formed; the initial sounds of bin and din are examples. Among the acoustic cues that correspond to place of articula-

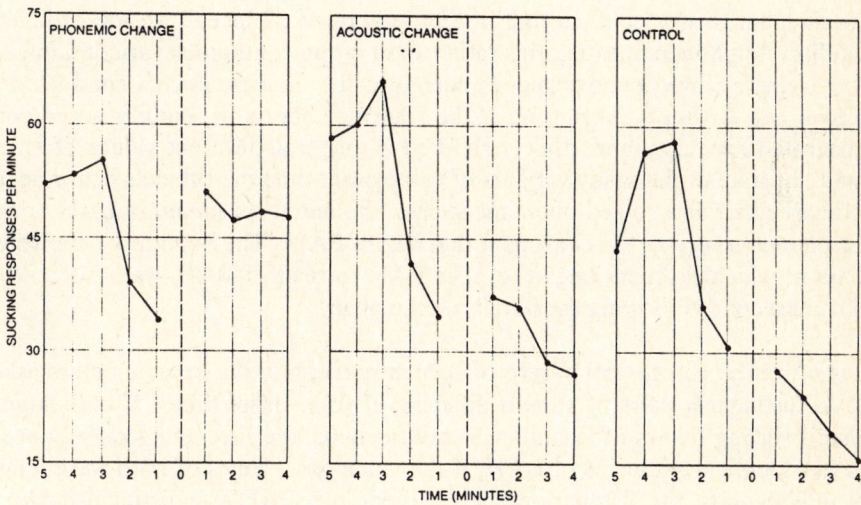

INFANTS' SUCKING RATE indicates their response to a series of speech sounds. In the author's experimental setup syllables of synthetic speech were played through the loudspeaker above the screen display of Raggedy Ann while a four-month old infant sucked on a pacifier connected to recording instruments. Graphs of mean sucking rate recorded under various experimental conditions with anumber of infants show that when a syllable beginning with a particular consonant was repeated sucking rate increased and then decreased as the stimulus became familiar. In some cases the sound changed at a time indicated by the broken line. In one group (left) the new sound represented a different consonant; sucking rate increased sharply, showing that the infants perceived a contrast. In a second group (middle) the stimulus differed acoustically from the preceding sound but corresponded to the same consonant, and there was little change in sucking rate. A control group of infants (right) experienced no change in stimulus.

tion and enable a hearer to distinguish such phonemes are the initial frequencies of the second and third formants: the formants that fall second and third from the bottom on a scale of frequency. Again no single value of these acoustic parameters characterizes each phoneme; a range of onset frequencies can signal the same place of articulation. Yet in spite of variation in the sounds corresponding to each phoneme we have little trouble deciding whether a speaker said din or bin. We are able in effect to listen through the variation in the signal and make categorical judgments of phonemic quality.

Experimental results confirm that in the perception of speech we are ordinarily aware of discrete phonemic categories rather than of the continuous variation in each acoustic parameter: we perceive speech categorically. In experiments conducted by Leigh Lisker and Arthur S. Abramson of the Haskins Laboratories adults heard computer-generated speech sounds that embodied a range of different values of voice-onset time. In spite of the many variants of voice-onset time the subjects heard nearly all the stimuli either as a voiced phoneme such as the initial consonant of BAH or as a voiceless phoneme such as the consonant that begins PAH. The boundary—the voice-onset time at which listeners began to hear PAH instead of BAH—was situated at about 30 milliseconds following the initial release of air.

To confirm the categorical nature of speech perception the experimenters asked subjects to distinguish pairs of stimuli differing in voice-onset time. If both sounds represented voicing delays of less than 30 milliseconds, the listeners generally heard them as two identical instances of BAH; if the voice-onset times of both were longer than 30 milliseconds, the listeners tended to hear two PAH's, indistinguishable although acoustically different. Only when the stimuli straddled the 30-millisecond boundary could subjects distinguish them consistently. Catherine G. Wolf, then at Brown University, obtained similar evidence of categorical perception in school-age children.

How much of this mechanism of categorical perception, which enables us to perceive speech reliably in spite of the lack of precision of the speech signal, is innate? The fact that speakers of different languages are attuned to somewhat different phonemic distinctions suggests that the influence of the linguistic environment on speech perception is powerful. Japanese speakers fail to perceive the contrast between the phonemes /r/ and /l/, a standard distinction in English; English speakers do not notice a fundamental contrast in voicing that distinguishes certain phonemes in Thai. Yet certain phonemic distinctions are present in languages throughout the world. It seemed possible to my colleagues and me that strong biological determinants, modified by later linguistic experience, might underlie the categorical perception of speech. To find out whether this is the case we did experiments with infants not yet able to speak, in whom one would expect the influence of their parents' language to be minimal.

In 1971 Einar R. Siqueland, Peter W. Jusczyk, James Vigorito and I examined the

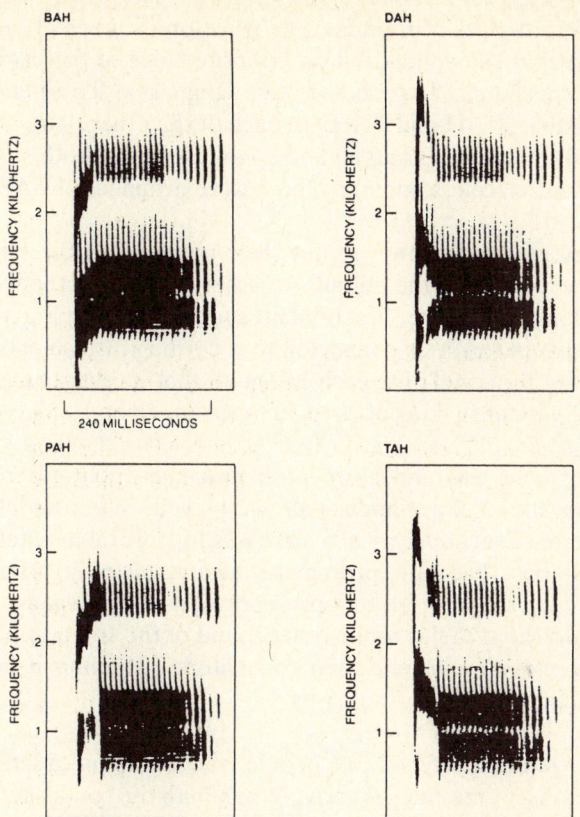

SPECTROGRAMS of syllables beginning with different stop consonants, so called because they require an interruption in the flow of air through the vocal tract, show the underlying differences in acoustic characteristics. The four acoustic signatures differ in the frequency and timing of their component bands of acoustic energy, known as formants.. The consonants paired horizontally are distinguished by the frequency at which the formants begin, a reflection of the point within the vocal tract at which constriction occurs, The frequency of the highest formant of the sound BAH, for example, begins at about two kilohertz and then rises, while that of the third formant of DAH begins at about three kilohertz and falls. Consonants paired vertically differ in voice-onset time, a measure of the delay between the release of air and the vibration of the vocal cords. In spectrograms for BAH and DAH a voice-onset time of zero is evident in the presence of periodicity, a series of spiky vertical striations that indicate vocal-cord vibration, at the beginning of all three formants. In spectrograms for PAH and TAH there is a gap before the lowest formant appears and periodicity begins in the two higher formants, reflecting a longer delay in onset of voicing.

perception of voice-onset time in one- and four-month-old infants. We exposed the infants to three different pairs of sounds. The voice-onset times of one pair were 20 and 40 milliseconds; thus the stimuli fell on opposite sides of the category boundary recognized by adult speakers of English and other languages. To adult ears the stimuli sounded like the syllables BAH and PAH. In each of the other pairs, with voice-onset times of zero and 20 milliseconds and 60 and 80 milliseconds, both stimuli fell on the same side of the voiced/voiceless boundary; both were instances of BAH or PAH.

Infants a few months old cannot report their perceptions directly. In order to gauge the infants' responses to the stimuli we resorted to a methodology called the high-amplitude sucking procedure. Each infant sucked on a pacifier wired to a pressure transducer, which in turn was connected to recording instruments. We adjusted the set-up's sensitivity separately for each infant so that in every case the apparatus recorded a base-line rate of sucking of 20 to 40 times a minute.

Once the experiment was underway, each time the apparatus recorded an instance of sucking one sound of a stimulus pair was played. When an infant encounters a new stimulus, its rate of sucking typically increases for several minutes, then gradually settles back to the base-line rate, presumably as a result of familiarization. When the sucking rates of our subjects fell to a preset level as they grew accustomed to the first sound, we shifted the stimulus to the other sound of the stimulus pair. If an infant grows familiar with one stimulus and then encounters a stimulus it perceives as different, its rate of sucking ordinarily increases.

The results showed that infants, like people who command a language, perceive differences in voice-onset time categorically. When both the sounds to which an infant subject was exposed lay on the same side of the 30-millisecond boundary, the shift from one sound to another evoked no increase in sucking rate. The infants appeared not to notice the change in voice-onset time. On the other hand, when the stimuli fell on opposite sides of the boundary, a sharp increase in sucking rate occurred at the shift, indicating that the infants perceived a change.

Other investigators and I have discovered further perceptual boundaries in infants' responses to the acoustic information in speech. Like adults, they respond categorically to changes in the onset frequency of the second and third formants, an acoustic cue that indicates differences in the place of articulation of a consonant. The same pattern holds in their responses to the acoustic cues that signal the distinctions between nasal and stop consonants, exemplified by the initial sounds of MAH and BAH, and between stop consonants and semivowels such as the initial sound of WAH.

It is difficult to see how learning could account for the mode of perception we have demonstrated in infants. What events during the first few weeks of life would train an infant to respond categorically to gradations of acoustic properties? A simpler view is that categorization occurs because a child is born with perceptual mechanisms that are tuned to the properties of speech. These mechanisms yield the forerunners of the phonemic categories that later will enable the child unthinkingly to convert the variable signal of speech into a series of phonemes and thence into words

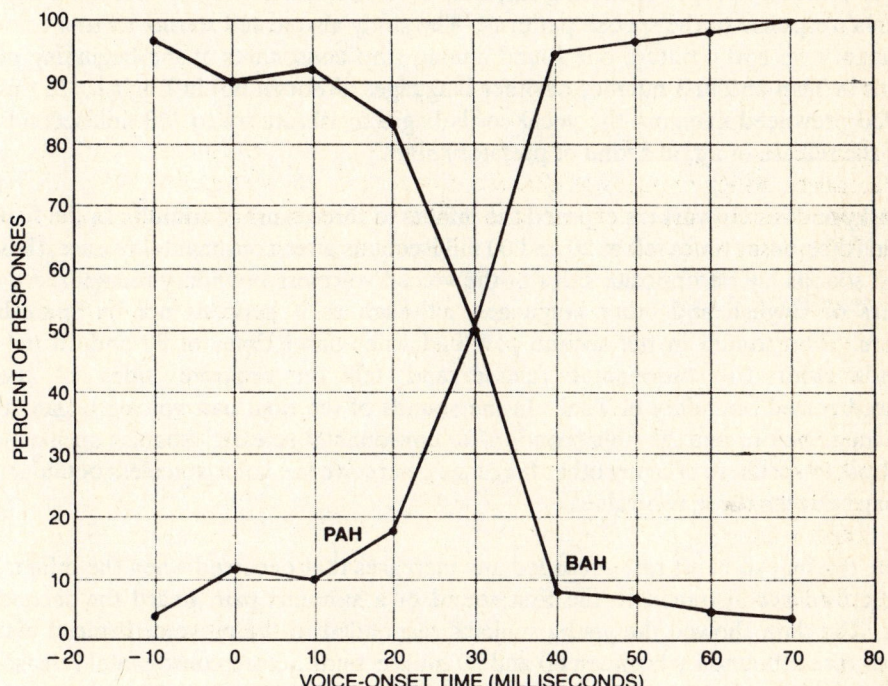

CATEGORICAL PERCEPTION is reflected in curves showing the relative proportions of responses when children were asked to identify a synthetic speech sound with a particular voice-onset time as an instance of a voiced (BAH) or a voiceless (PAH) consonantal sound. Instead of a linear change in the percentages the curves show that at voice-onset times of less than 30 milliseconds the children almost always identified the stimulus as BAH; when voice-onset time exceeded 30 milliseconds, they tended to hear the sound as PAH. The perpetual tendency shifted abruptly at 30 milliseconds. The study, done by Catherine G. Wolf at Brown University, suggests that perceptual categories, rather than continuous gradations in the acoustic properties of the speech signal, shape the perception of speech.

and meanings.

If these perceptual mechanisms do represent a biological endowment, they should be universal. The same perceptual patterns should occur in the infants of every linguistic background. In research reported in 1975 Robert E. Lasky, Ann Syrdal-Lasky and Robert E. Klein, then at the Institute of Nutrition in Panama, investigated the perception of voice-onset time by Guatemalan infants, born into a Spanish-speaking environment. The group's experimental methods differed from those used in our 1971 study: in place of changes in sucking rate they used changes in heart rate as the gauge of infants' response to the speech patterns. The study also tested sensitivity to a voicing category we had omitted, one found among stop consonants at the beginning of syllables in Thai and in a number of other languages although not in English. In this so-called prevoiced category the vocal cords begin to vibrate up to 100 milliseconds before the release of air, in a kind of prefatory hum.

Lasky and his co-workers exposed the infants to three pairs of stimuli. In the first pair the voice-onset times fell at 20 and 60 milliseconds after consonantal release; thus the two sounds lay on opposite sides of the voiced/voiceless boundary recognized by speakers of English and other languages, although as it happens not by Spanish speakers. The stimuli in the second pair had voice-onset times of 60 and 20 milliseconds prior to consonantal release and fell on opposite sides of the prevoiced/voiced boundary of Thai. In the sounds of the final pair voicing began 20 milliseconds before and 20 milliseconds after consonantal release. Spanish speakers, in contrast to speakers of many other languages, perceive the voice/voiceless boundary as falling between those two values.

The tracings of heart rate recorded any increases that occurred when the infants, having grown accoustomed to the first sound of a stimulus pair, heard the second sound. The data showed the young subjects responded to the prevoiced/voiced distinction, with a boundary between 60 and 20 milliseconds before consonantal release, and also to the voice/voiceless distinction with a boundary between 20 and 60 milliseconds following release. The voicing distinction peculiar to Spanish evoked no change in heart rate.

In 1976 Lynn A. Streeter, then at the Bell Laboratories, published evidence that infants born into a Kikuyu-speaking culture in Kenya display much the same perceptual pattern as the Guatemalan babies. Richard N. Aslin, David B. Pisoni, Beth L. Hennessy and Alan J. Perey of Indiana University recently completed the study of voice-onset-time sensitivity among infants in English-speaking communities by showing that they respond to the prevoiced/voiced contrast just as they do to the voiced/voiceless distinction. It appears that infants the world over are equipped with an inborn sensitivity to these three categories of voicing, whether or not the distinctions are important in their parent language.

The perception of speech is a complex and subtle process, which the studies of categorical perception described so far probe only in the simplest terms. The acoustic

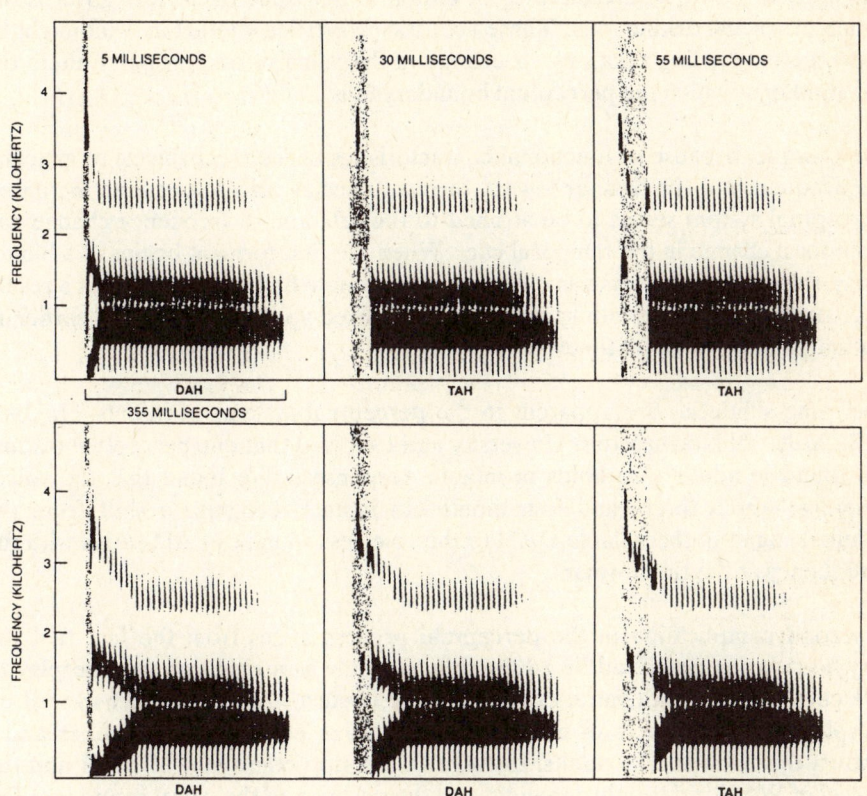

SHIFT IN A PERCEPTUAL BOUNDARY can occur when two acoustic cues are altered independently. The consonants beginning the six syllables shown in spectrographic form vary in voice-onset time and in the onset frequency of the lowest formant; to adult ears the sounds are the syllables DAH and TAH. At a high onset frequency (*top row, visible in the second and third spectrograms*) infants detected the DAH/TAH contrast between sounds having voice-onset times of five and 30 milliseconds. When the onset frequency was low (second and third spectrograms in the bottom row), voice-onset time had to increase to between 30 and 55 milliseconds before the infants reacted to the phonemic contrast. Such interactions between two acoustic variables are known as perceptual trading relations.

information that enables a listener to perceive distinctions in voicing illustrates the point. So far we have treated the essential information as a single continuum of time measuring the interval between consonantal release and the beginning of voicing. In ordinary speech, however, an interplay of temporal and spectral factors governs the perception of voicing distinctions. These acoustic properties interact in what might be called perceptual trading relations: a change in the value of one property alters the value of another at which the perceptual boundary falls.

For example, because of functional characteristics of the mechanisms of articulation, the frequency of the first, or lowest, formant rises as voice-onset time increases. Our perceptual system seems to be attuned to the relation: a frequency change can substitute for a change in the temporal cue. When the first formant begins at a higher frequency, the effect is the same as if the voice-onset time had lengthened. As a result, at higher onset frequencies adults perceive the voiced/voiceless boundary earlier in the continuum of voice-onset times.

The same subtleties are apparent in the perceptual systems of infants. In 1983 Joanne L. Miller of Northeastern University and I showed that one perceptual trading relation found in adults also holds in infants' responses. We found that the voice-onset time at which three- and four-month-old infants recognize a shift from the voiced initial sound of the syllable DAH to the voiceless sound of PAH varies with the onset frequency of the first formant.

A second complication in the perceptual process arises from the fact that the category boundaries perceived by adults shift not only as a result of the interplay of multiple cues but also with variations in acoustic context. In this respect as well infants display the forerunners of more mature patterns of perception. Miller and I have shown that infants, like adults, distinguish the stop consonant of BAH and the semi-vowel of WAH differently depending on the duration of the vowel sound that follows. The acoustic basis of the distinction is the length of the formant transitions: the periods needed for the central frequencies of the formants to reach the values appropriate for the vowel that follows. In the case of BAH the formant transitions are swift; with WAH they are slower. The longer the vowel duration is, however, the slower the formant transitions must be before infants recognize a change in stimulus from BAH to WAH.

Other quite complex effects of context on the categorization of speech by infants have been demonstrated. Jusczyk and his associates at the University of Oregon found a shift in the formant-onset frequencies at which infants detect a distinction between phonemes differing in place of articulation. The boundary value varied depending on whether an additional band of noiselike acoustic energy was present, signaling a fricative rather than a stop consonant.

The complex mechanism of categorical perception enables an individual to recognize phonemes consistently in spite of great variation in crucial acoustic parameters. Other kinds of variability blur the definition of the speech signal even further. The length of syllables, along with other temporal characteristics of speech, changes with rate of speech and patterns of emphasis; wide variations in the fundamental frequency of voicing and in the spacing of resonant frequencies occur as a result of the speaker's sex, age and emotional state. Some mechanism must enable us to listen through the variation to hear the same phoneme each time it is spoken. This phenomenon of perceptual constancy cannot be investigated directly in infants. But studies of infants' ability to form equivalence classes—groups of stimuli that evoke the same response in spite of obvious differences—suggest infants possess at least the forerunners of perceptual constancy.

Patricia K. Kuhl and her colleagues at the University of Washington have investigated the formation of equivalence classes for the sounds of speech in six-month-old infants. In the first stage of each experiment the Kuhl group trained infants to turn their head 90 degrees toward a loudspeaker whenever a series of contrasting stimuli interrupted a background sound; the sight of a colorful, moving toy that appeared above the loudspeaker as the contrasting sequence was played rewarded successful responses. In one experiment identical instances of the vowel sound /a/, as in POP, served as the background stimulus; identical versions of /i/, as in PEEP, provided the contrast. Once the training was complete the stimuli varied: the vowels, /a/ and /i/, remained the same but the infants now heard both vowels in a variety of voices and intonations. Sequences without contrasting stimuli, in which every sound was a variant of /a/, served as controls.

The infants' success in singling out contrasting stimuli and ignoring within-category acoustic variations during the control trials was impressive. When both inappropriate head-turnings and missed contrasts were counted, they averaged about 80 percent correct; in seven out of eight cases the infants scored better than if their responses had reflected chance. When Kuhl and her colleagues repeated the experiment with the acoustically less distinctive vowels /a/ and /o/ (as in PAW), the infants still could detect equivalent sounds, although less reliably; the proportion of correct responses fell to 67 percent and only four out of eight infants bettered the expected score for random responses.

When both the background and the contrasting sequences included arbitrarily chosen variants of both /a/ and /i/, however, the infants could not learn to differentiate members of the two sequences, in spite of the reward elicited by a correct response. They could not be trained to recognize an arbitrary grouping of sounds that had no linguistic property in common. They could respond correctly, indicating they had organized diverse stimuli into equivalence classes, only when the background and contrasting sequences represented different categories of speech. The finding is further evidence that long before infants can speak and understand they are particularly sensitive to the acoustic distinctions crucial to the comprehension of speech. It adds weight to the case for a set of inborn mechanisms that are specialized for speech perception.

The diversity among the sound systems of human languages makes it clear that environmental factors affect the perceptual dispositions with which an infant is born. What happens as the linguistic environment created by a child's parents and companions interacts with inborn perceptual mechanisms? It appears that perceptual horizons narrow as a child learns his or her native language. The child retains and probably sharpens those perceptual capacities that correspond to phonemic distinctions in the parental language but loses the ability to detect distinctions that do not occur in the native language.

Studies of voice-onset-time perception testify to the decline in some discriminative powers as the infant develops. While infants from diverse linguistic backgrounds respond to contrasts in prevoiced, voiced and voiceless initial consonants, adult speakers of some languages, including English, recognize only the distinction between the voiced and the voiceless categories. Although native adult Japanese speakers are virtually unable to perceive the distinction between the sounds of /r/ and /l/ without special training, I have found that the distinction is among those to which American infants—and presumably Japanese infants—have an inate sensitivity. Similarly, research by Janet F. Werker of Dalhousie University in Nova Scotia and Richard C. Tees of the University of British Columbia showed that six- to eight-month-old infants from an English-speaking background readily distinguish phonemic contrasts in Hindi and Salish, a North American Indian language. When they were tested again at the age of 12 months, the same infants, like English-speaking adults, did not detect the contrasts to which they had earlier been sensitive.

The decline in perceptual abilities through exposure to a restricted environment is familiar. When kittens are raised wearing goggles that limit the visual input of one eye to a series of horizontal stripes and that of the other eye to vertical stripes, corresponding areas of the visual cortex lose their sensitivity to stripes running in other directions. Such losses seem to be irreversible, no matter how varied the animal's later surroundings. In contrast, we can recover at least some of our initial capacities to detect the acoustic information underlying phonemic contrasts. For instance, when the acoustic information critical to phonemic distinctions in Hindi and Salish is embodied in sounds that usually are not heard as speech, English speakers can detect differences to which they are ordinarily insensitive.

Apparently the restricted linguistic environment of one's native language does not inactivate unused perceptual mechanisms completely. We learn to listen primarily for the acoustic distinctions that correspond to phonemic contrasts in our own language. Given the right task or instructions, however, we can detect unfamiliar acoustic distinctions even though we do not perceive them as marking phonemic contrasts. Furthermore, with enough experience the perception of non-native distinctions begins to operate at the phonemic level: after considerable experience with spoken English, native speakers of Japanese can distinguish the phonemes /r/ and /l/ categorically and almost as accurately as native English speakers. The fact that perceptual mechanisms available to us as infants can still operate in adulthood, after long disuse, confounds hypotheses that early experience with language immutably alters some of the mechanisms of speech perception.

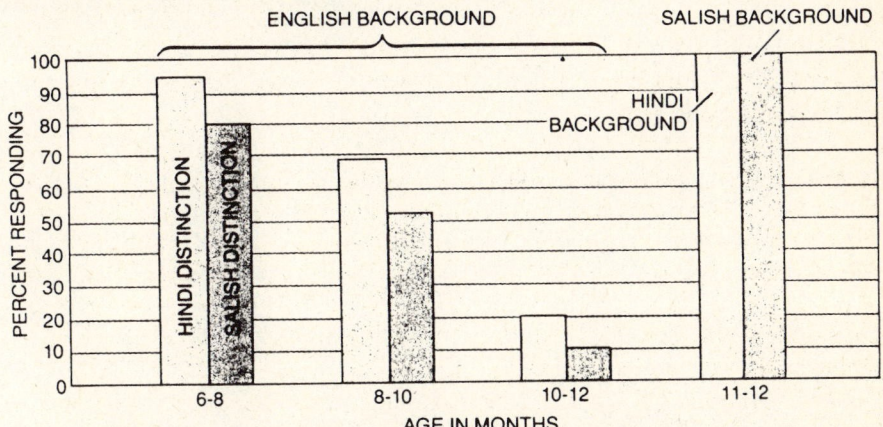

WANING OF UNUSED PERCEPTUAL POWERS is evident in the responses of infants from an English-speaking background to linguistic contrasts that are foreign to English. When Janet F. Werker of Dalhousie University in Nova Scotia and Richard C. Tees of the University of British Columbia simultaneously tested infants in different age groups, the proportion responding to consonantal contrasts from Hindi and Salish, a North American Indian language, fell rapidly with age. One-year-old Hindi and Salish infants, in contrast, retain the capacity to perceive the linguistic contrasts native to their respective languages.

The most dramatic demonstration of the innate mechanisms of perception other workers and I have studied, however, takes place in infancy, as a child begins to learn its parents' language. It is now clear that an infant is born with many of the underpinnings of later speech perception and comprehension. It may be that like the specialized anatomy of the vocal tract and the speech centers in the brain these innate perceptual capacities evolved specifically for the perception and comprehension of speech. They are an evolutionary answer to the need for each infant to acquire its parents' language and culture as early in life as possible. The effectiveness of these mechanisms is reflected in the swiftness with which a child joins the community of language.

Reactivation of Infant Memory

Carolyn K. Rovee-Collier,
Margaret W. Sullivan, Mary Enright,
Deborah Lucas and Jeffrey W. Fagen

The pervasive influences of early experiences on later behavior have been extensively documented, as have early memory deficits or "infantile amnesia" (1). Considered jointly, these phenomena pose a major paradox for students of development: How can the effects of early experiences persist into adolescence and adulthood if they are forgotten during infancy and early childhood? Campbell and Jaynes (2) proposed a resolution to this paradox in terms of reinstatement, a mechanism that maintains a memory which would otherwise be forgotten through occasional reencounters with the original training conditions over the period of development. Any given reencounter, however, would be insufficient to promote new learning in organisms lacking the early experience. Spear (3) attributed the efficacy of reinstatement procedures to improved retrieval produced by the reactivation of a sufficient number (or kind) of existing but otherwise inaccessible attributes of the target memory. He hypothesized that reexposure to stimuli from the original training context, which had been stored as attributes of the memory, could prime or arouse other attributes that represented the original experience, increasing their accessibility and, thus, the probability of their retrieval.

Originally published in *Science*, Vol. *208*, 1980. Copyright ©1980 by the American Association for the Advancement of Science. Reprinted with permission of the publisher and author.

"Reinstatement" or "reactivation" has been demonstrated in young and adult rats (2, 4, 5) and in grade-school children (6). We now report that a reactivation treatment can alleviate forgetting in 3-month-old infants after a retention interval as long as 4 weeks and that the forgetting function after a reactivation treatment is similar to the function after original training.

Our procedures were modeled after those of animal memory studies in which the experimenter trains a specific response in a distinctive context and later returns the subject to that context to see if the response is still produced. Because the retrieval cues are contextual and response production is assessed before reinforcement is reintroduced, the procedure is analogous to a test of cued recall (3).

In our studies, footkicks of 3-month-olds were reinforced by movement of an overhead crib mobile. The infant controlled both the intensity and frequency of the mobile movement by means of a ribbon connecting the ankle with the hook from which the mobile hung. This procedure, "mobile conjugate reinforcement," produces rapid acquisition and high, stable response rates attributable to the contingency and not to behavioral arousal (7). During nonreinforcement phases (baseline, retention tests, extinction), the mobile remained in view but was hung from a second mobile stand with no ribbon attachment and could not be activated by kicks.

Infants received three procedurally identical sessions in their home cribs. The first two were training sessions, spaced by 24 hours; the third followed a lengthy retention interval. Each session consisted of a 9-minute reinforcement phase preceded and followed by a 3-minute nonreinforcement period. In session 1, the initial 3-minute perod defined the baseline; in sessions 2 and 3, it was a long-term retention test of the effects of prior training. Total footkicks during this test (B) were expressed as a fraction of the infant's total kicks during the 3-minute nonreinforcement phase at the conclusion of the preceding session (A), which was an immediate retention test. The ratio B/A indexed the extent of an infant's forgetting from one session to the next. Ratios of > 1.00 indicated no forgetting, and < .00 indicated fractional loss (8).

A reactivation treatment was administered 24 hours before session 3. It consisted of a 3-minute exposure to the reinforcer (mobile movement) in a context identical to that of session 2 except that (i) the ribbon was not connected to the ankle but was draped over the side of the cirb, where it was drawn and released by the experimenter at a rate corresponding to each infant's mean response rate during the final 3 minutes of acquisition in session 2; and (ii) the infant was in a reclining seat, which minimized footkicks and altered the topography of those which did occur (9). These changes, as well as the brevity of the reminder, precluded the opportunity for new learning or practice during a reactivation treatment. Footkicks were recorded by the experimenter and, independently, by a second observer present for at least a third of the sessions and naive with respect to group assignment and session number. Pearson product-moment reliability coefficients were > .95 for all studies reported here.

In study 1, retention of conditioned footkicks was assessed 2 weeks after training. Infants [mean x age = 88.4 days, standard error(S.E.) = 3.3] were tested in three groups of six each: (i) a reactivation group received a 3-minute reminder 13 days after session 2 (24 hours before session 3); (ii) a no-reactivation group received training but

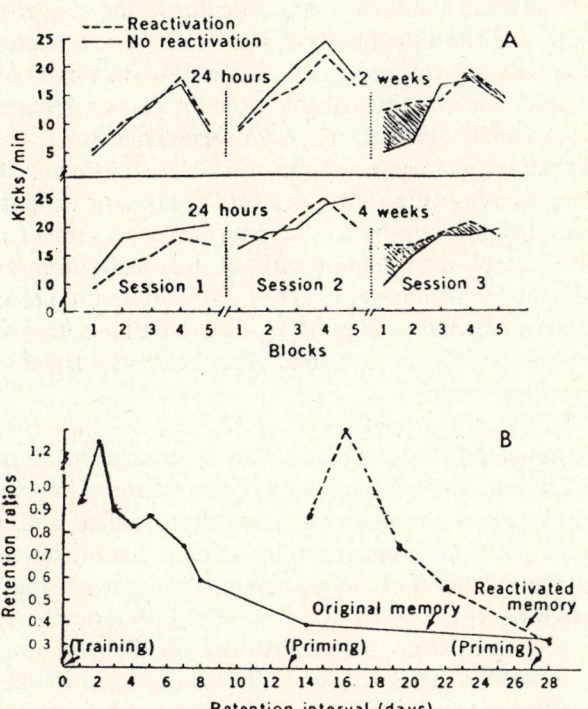

Fig 1. (A) Mean kicks per minute during training (sessions 1 and 2) and an identical session (session 3) occuring either 2 or 4 weeks after the completion of session 2. Blocks 1 and 5 are nonreinforcement phases; performance during long-term retention tests (block 1, session 2 or 3) is expressed as a fraction of the infant's performance during immediate retention tests (block 5, session 1 or 2, respectively). The reactivation group received a reminder 24 hours before the 2- or 4-week session; the facilitating or priming effect of the reactivation treatment is indicated by the hatched area, session 3.. (B) Retention ratios after 2 days of training (solid line) or two days of training plus a reactivation treatment (broken line); priming occurred 13 days after training for the single data point at the 28-day retention interval. Each data point represents at least five infants.

no reactivation treatment prior to session 3; and (iii) a familiarization/ reactivation control group received a procedure identical to that of the reactivation group except that infants in this group were removed from their cribs during the reinforcement phases of sessions 1 and 2 and thus had no training before session 3. The rates at which their reminders occurred were matched to those of the reactivation group.

Infants in this control group showed no change in response rate either within or across session (all t's < 1). Thus, infants of this age do not simply become more active over the 2-week interval, and their footkicking during the session-3 cued recall test is not a result of either elicited familiarity reactions or the reactivation treatment per se. The acquisition curve of this group in session 3, when reinforcement was introduced for the first time, was indistinguishable from the session-1 learning curves of the other two groups. An analysis of variance with repeated measures over sessions and blocks confirmed that response rates of the reactivation and no-reactivation groups did not differ during training (Fig. 1A). A 2 by 2 analysis of variance over retention rations yielded a significant group-by-session interaction: Although 24 hour retention ratios did not differ, the 14-day retention ratio of the reactivation group significantly exceeded that of the no-reactivation group (P < .01), whose ratio reflected a return to baseline performance of session 1 (Fig. 1B). The retention ratio of the reactivation group was as high as in the 24-hour measure. Thus, both prior training and a reminder are prerequisite for reactivation.

In study 2, we repeated the procedure with 18 infants (mean age = 76.9 days, standard error = 2.0) but doubled the length of the retention interval. The reactivation group (N = 9) received a reminder 27 days after training, and retention was assessed the next day. A significant group-by-sessions interaction (P < .03) again confirmed the superior retention of the reactivation group in session 3 relative to that of the no-reactivation group (N = 9), which received no reminder during the retention interval (Fig. 1B). As before, the groups had not differed during training (Fig. 1A) or in 24-hour retention performance. The 28-day ratio of the no-reactivation group reflected performance equivalent to their session-1 baseline level. The retention ratio (.96) of the reactivation group is remarkable in view of the relatively young age of the infants during training and the relatively large portion of their lives that 4 weeks constitutes.

In study 3, we determined the course of forgetting following a reactivation treatment. Twenty infants (mean age = 90.0 days, standard error = 1.3) received a reactivation treatment 13 days after training as described for study 1; however, session 3 now occurred 3, 6, 9, or 15 days (N = 5 per interval) after the reminder. This corresponded to 16, 19, 22, or 28 days, respectively, after the completion of training. The session-3 retention ratios, along with thsoe of the six infants tested 1 day after a reactivation treatment in study 1, were compared with retention ratios describing the original forgetting function. [We had previously obtained this function from 69 infants in a number of different experiments (10) carried out according to the same procedure as that used with the no-reactivation groups of this report.] At least five infants per retention interval contributed data 1, 2, 3, 4, 5, 7, 8, or 14 days after training (Fig. 1B). The no-reactivation group of study 2, tested after a 28-day retention interval, was also a control group for the reactivation group tested 15 days after the reminder (28 days after training).

Figure 1B is a composite of retention ratios of all groups tested after 2 days of training only ("original memory" function) or after 2 days of training plus a reactivation treatment ("priming") given either 13 (studies 1 and 3) or 27 (study 2) days after training ("reactivated memory" function). A one-way analysis of variance over all data points except that of the study-2 reactivation group indicated that ratios differed reliably as a function of retention interval (P < .025) and provided the error term for individual comparisons between means (Duncan's multiple range test). The latter indicated that the apparent increase above 1.00 in retention ratios in each function (Fig. 1B) was reliable; also, ratios of groups tested 8 (original memory function) and 19 (reactivated memory function) days after training did not differ from ratios of no-reactivation groups tested after retention intervals of 14 and 28 days, respectively. Regression analyses indicated that retention was a linear decreasing function of time since either training (P < .005) or priming (P < .005). Although the linear model provided a relatively poor fit in each instance, the intercepts and slopes of the two functions did not differ (t's < 1). Thus, forgetting of a reactivated memory followed the same temporal course as forgetting of the original experience.

Our findings confirm Campbell and Jaynes' (2) proposition that reinstatement is a potent mechanism through which experiences of early infancy can continue to influence behavior. An infant's reencounters with contextual aspects of prior training or an earlier experience can prime or recycle the remaining memory attributes and enhance access to them, alleviating forgetting which otherwise appeared complete weeks earlier. Moreover, a reencounter with the original context can maintain access to the target memory with the same efficacy as original training. Our findings also implicate reinstatement as the mechanism which, during infancy, facilitates the acquisition of the vast amount of learning characteristic of that period of development.

More generally, our findings support a distinction between availability and accessibility of information in memory and imply that failures to observe retention in infants should be discussed in terms of retrieval failures rather than memory deficits (3, 4). We think that procedures that improve accessibility to important retrieval cues will radically alter current views of infant memory (11) and that conditioning procedures, which permit a direct assessment of retention in infants, offer a promising means by which to bridge the gap between human and animal memory research.

References and Notes

1. F.A. Beach and J. Jaynes, *Psychol. Bull.* 51, 239 (1954); E.G. Schachtel, *Psychiatry* 10, 1 (1947).

2. B.A. Campbell and J. Jaynes, *Psychol. Rev.* 73, 478 (1966).

3. N.E. Spear, *ibid.* 80, 163(1973).

4. – – – – – and P.J. Parsons, in *Processes of Animal Memory*, D.L. Medin, W.A. Roberts, R.T. Davis, Eds. (Erlbaum, Hillsdale, N.J., 1976), p. 135.

5. C.F. Mactutus, D.C. Riccio, J.M. Ferek, *Science* 204, 1319 (1979).

6. K.K. Hoving, L. Coates, M. Bertucci, D.C. Riccio, *Dev. Psychol.* 6, 426 (1972).

7. C.K. Rovee-Collier and M.J. Gekoski, *Adv. Child Dev. Behav.* 13, 195 (1979).

8. Because operant levels are typically doubled or tripled during acquisition, retention ratios of .30 to .40 usually indicate performance at operant level. A 3-minute period of nonreinforcement at the conclusion of initial training sessions does not typically extinguish responding in infants 11 to 13 weeks of age.

9. During the reactivation treatment, infants produced responses at a rate of 0 to 2 kicks per minute; operant levels are typically 8 to 11 kicks per minute. In the infant seat, infants rarely exhibit the vertical leg thrusts, characteristic of conditioned responding: rather, their movements seem to be postural adjustments or horizontal squirming.

10. C.K. Rovee and J.W. Fagen, *J. Exp. Child Psychol.* 21, 1 (1976); M.W. Sullivan, C.K. Rovee-Collier, D.M. Tynes, *Child Dev.* 50, 152 91979); M.J. Gekoski, paper presented at the meeting of the Eastern Psychological Association, Hartford, Conn., 9 to 12 April 1980.

11. L.B. Cohen and E.R. Gelber, in *Infant Perception: From Sensation to Cognition*, L.B. Cohen and P. Salapatek, Eds. (Academic Press, New York, 1975), vol. 1, p. 347: J. Kagan *The Sciences* 19, 6 (1979); D.S. Ramsay and J.J. Campos, *Dev. Psychol.* 14, 79 (1978).

12. Study 1 of this research formed a portion of a dissertation submitted by M.W.S. to Rutgers University in partial fulfillment of the requirements for the Ph.D. J.Davis and L. O'Brien assisted in the data collection. Supported by NIMH grant 32307 to C.K.R.-C.

The Perception of Biological Motion by Human Infants

Robert Fox
Cynthia McDaniel

When a small number of luminous dots are attached to the torso and limbs of a moving human, and only the dots are visible, the pattern correctly conveys the human's activity. Walking, running, dancing, and even gender can be quickly perceived (1). The perceptions induced by these patterns of motion, dubbed "biological motion" by Johansson, have been taken as evidence that the visual system is sensitive to invariant higher-order stimulus information imbedded in the pattern. Further, this sensitivity has been hypothesized to be an innate capacity of the visual system rather than one acquired through experience (2).

As a test of this hypothesis, we investigated sensitivity to biological motion in human infants and found that a visual preference for such motion becomes manifest at 4 to 6 months of age. To gauge this sensitivity we used a forced-choice preferential looking technique, which provides an objective index of an infant's preference for visual stimulation (3). In our version of the technique, a pair of stimuli were presented side by side over a series of trials. One member of the pair, the target, consisted of a biological motion pattern, while the other member, the foil, consisted of moving dots that did not meet the criteria for biological motion. The left-right positions of target and foil were interchanged randomly and presented to an infant seated midway between them. An observer who could view the infant, but not the stimuli, was required to make forced-choice judgments about target location based on information obtained from observing the infant (3).

In our experiments, target and foil were made from videotapes displayed on a pair of monochrome video monitors placed side by side. Infants seated in the lap of a parent viewed the display from 30 cm; parents were blindfolded to prevent inadvertent cuing. One experimenter observed the infant through a peep-hole in an opaque screen surrounding the monitors, which concealed the observer from view. In a second experiment, we interchanged spatial positions of target and foil, by an electronic switch, in accord with a predetermined random schedule and gave feedback to the observer about the correctness of his or her responses. The number of trials obtained from each infant varied as a function of alertness and tractability; a minimum of ten trials were required for the retention of an infant in the experiment and no more than 30 trials were obtained from any given infant (4). Trials took about 15 seconds to complete and were initiated only when the infant appeared to be in position to view both displays.

In experiment 1, three groups of infants were tested at 2, 4, and 6 months (5). The target was a biological motion pattern depicting the profile of a human form running in place. The pattern was composed of ten dots located on the joints of the arms and legs and on the hip. The foil consisted of the same number of dots, each moving in an independent, randomly determined direction. For both patterns, the dots appeared as white disks against a darker background. The patterns were produced by video-recording the appropriate motions; adjustments of contrast and brightness during playback permitted only the dots to be seen (6).

The results of experiment 1 are given in Fig. 1A. Performance for the 2-month-old infants did not differ from chance [$t(9) = 0.61$]. Performance for the 4- and 6-month groups was significantly above chance [$t(9) = 9$; $t(9) = 5.25$, $P \leq .001$]. Since the dot size was considerably greater than the visual acuity threshold for 2-month-olds, their performance cannot be attributed to an inability to resolve the dot patterns (7). Nor did they appear less attentive than the other groups.

These results suggest that preference for biological motion appears by 4 months of age. Yet that conclusion must be qualified since there were differences between target and foil not confined strictly to the dimension of biological motion. The foil dots varied somewhat from the target dots in the rate and magnitude of their movement, and unlike the target dots, they were not periodically occluded by the limbs crossing the axis of the torso.

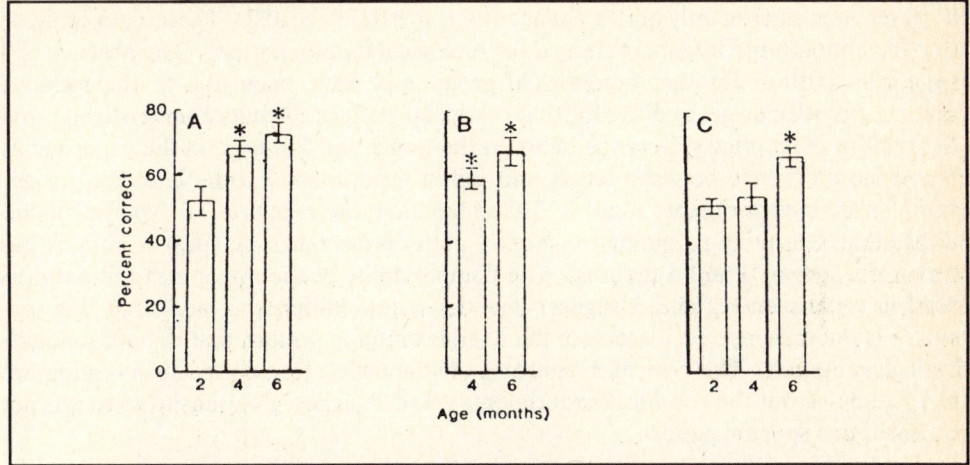

Fig 1. (A) The results of experiment 1. Means +/- standard errors for each age group. The asterisk indicates a significant departure from the chance level of 50 percent. (B) The results of experiment 2. (C) The results of experiment 3.

Experiment 2 was performed to determine if preference for biological motion was present when target and foil were more comparable. In this experiment the target was a human running in place (as in experiment 1), while the foil was the same form inverted 180°. For adult observers, such inversion severely impairs veridical perception of the human form. These stimuli were presented to two groups of infants (ten in each group) at 4 and 6 months of age (5) according to the same procedures used in experiment 1. Performance of both groups was significantly above chance [for the 4-month-old group, $t(9) = 4.64$, $P \leq .001$; for the 6-month-old group, $t(9) = 4.59$, $P \leq .001$]. These data indicate that the infants preferred the target even when the physical conditions of stimulation were identical for target and foil.

It is possible, however, that this preference is based on some unique attribute of the target. To test that possibility, a new biological motion pattern was constructed and used in experiment 3. This pattern was a pair of hands that appeared to come together to clasp an invisible glass and then withdraw. To produce this target pattern 15 dots were placed on the joints of the fingers and wrists of an actor and the hands video-taped as in the preceding experiments. For the foil stimulus, the same number of dots was placed on the hands at off-joint positions, a procedure known to impair the veridical perception of a biological motion pattern (6). These patterns were shown as in experiments 1 and 2 to three groups of infants 2, 4, and 6 months of age. Performance of the 2-month-olds [t(9) = 0.952, P > .05] and 4-month-olds [t(9) = 0.5, P > .05] did not differ from chance. The performance of the 6-month-olds, however, was significantly above chance [t(7) = 3.02, P = .02]. These data indicate that the 6-month-old infants preferred the biological motion pattern. The absence of a significant pattern for the 4-month-old group may have been due to the reduced salience between target and foil for that particular pattern. Adult observers who rated the relative perceptual difference between the target and foil used in the experiments found the difference between target and foil in experiment 3 to be less than for the stimuli used in experiments 1 and 2. Taken together, the results of all experiments indicate that sensitivity to biological motion patterns becomes manifest in infants between the ages of 4 and 6 months. The comparability of the target and foil patterns used in experiments 2 and 3 suggest that the critical difference mediating this sensitivity is the presence or absence of the complex motion pattern that defines uniquely biological motion. The critical dimensions of stimulation that define such motion are not yet known, yet the results of experiments 2 and 3 suggest that sensitivity to it is not confined to a specific pattern.

These data force us to conclude that young infants are sensitive to biological motion. This supports the hypothesis that the mechanism responsible for such sensitivity is largely intrinsic rather than acquired slowly through experience. Yet it is not obvious why the youngest infants did not exhibit this sensitivity. Perhaps a postnatal period of growth is required before such a mechanism becomes functional. A similar growth period has been proposed as a requisite for the emergence of stereoscopic depth termination (9).

References and Notes

1. J.E. Cutting, *Perception* 7, 393 (1978); _____, D.R. Proffitt, L.J. Kozolowski, *J. Exp. Psychol: Human Percept. Perform.* 4, 357 (1978); G. Johansson, *Percept. Psychophys.* 14, 201 (1973).

2. G. Johansson, *Handbook of Sensory Physiology*, vol. 8, *Perception*, M. Jacobson, Ed. (Springer-Verlag, Berlin, 1978), pp. 675-711; *Sci. Am.* 232, 76 (June 1975); in *Stability and Constancy in Visual Perception*, W. Epstein, Ed. (Wiley, New York, 1977); _____, G. von Hofsten, G. Jansson, *Annu. Rev. Psychol.* 31, 27(1980).

3. D.Y. Teller, *Infant Behav. Dev.* 2, 135 (1979). The forced-choice preferential looking method incorporates the same logic and methodology as the two-alternative forced-choice method used in contemporary psychophysical research. A statistically significant departure from chance (50 percent) implies both discrimination between the stimulus pair and a preference for one stimulus over its partner.

4. The number of infants with fewer than ten trials because of sleepiness, fussiness, or equipment failure were: experiment 1, one from each age group; experiment 2, one from each age group; experiment 3, one 2 month-old and two 6-month olds.

5. Experiment 1: 2 months, N = 10, range 68 to 79 days; 4 months, N = 10, range 111 to 130 days; 6 months, N = 10, range 164 to 190 days. Experiment 2: 4 months, N = 10, range 125 to 136 days; 6 months, N = 10, range 187 to 192 days. Experiment 3: 2 months, N = 10, range 63 to 70 days; 4 months, N = 10, range 122 to 132 days; 6 months, N = 8, range 190 to 210 days.

6. The target pattern was produced by video-recording a darkly garbed human running in place. Dots made of highly reflective tape were attached to limbs and torso. The foil pattern was produced by video-recording the motions of dots clustered in approximately the same area encompassed by the human runner. To facilitate clustering, each dot was attached to the end of a long wand; to provide motion the wands were moved manually by assistants, in apparently random directions. The background luminance of both video monitors was 25 cd/m^2; dot luminance was 51.3 cd/m^2; contrast (maximum - minimum/maximum + minimum) was 36 percent. Dot size in experiments 1 and 2 was 3.82° visual angle; in experiment 3 it was 1.15° visual angle.

7. V. Dobson and D.Y. Teller, *Vision Res*. 18, 1469 (1978).

8. J.E. Cutting, *J. Exp. Psychol: Human Percept. Perform*. 7.71 (1981)

9. R. Fox, R.N. Aslin, S.L. Shea, S.T. Dumais, *Science* 207, 323 (1980). For a review of investigations of stereopsis in infants see R. Rox [in *The Development of Perception: Psychobiological Perspectives*, R.N. Aslin, J.R. Albert, M.R. Petersen, Eds. (Academic Press, New York, 1981), vol. 2, pp. 335-381].

10. We thank J. Lappin and M. Powers for their comments on our manuscript and E. Francis, K. Kymbal, A. Menendez, and R. Patterson for assistance in testing infants. Supported by National Institutes of Health grant EY00590 to R.F.

Infant-Mother Attachment

Mary D. Salter Ainsworth

Bowlby's (1969) ethological-evolutionary attachment theory implies that it is an essential part of the ground plan of the human species--as well as that of many other species--for an infant to become attached to a mother figure. This figure need not be the natural mother but can be anyone who plays the role of principal caregiver. This ground plan is fulfilled, except under extraordinary circumstances when the baby experiences too little interaction with any one caregiver to support the formation of an attachment. The literature on maternal deprivation describes some of these circumstances, but it cannot be reviewed here, except to note that research has not yet specified an acceptable minimum amount of interaction required for attachment formation.

However, there have been substantial recent advances in the areas of individual differences in the way attachment behavior becomes organized, differential experiences associated with the various attachment patterns, and the value of such patterns in forecasting subsequent development. These advances have been much aided by a standardized laboratory situation that was devised to supplement a naturalistic, longitudinal investigation of the development of infant-mother attachment in the first year of life. This *strange situation*, as we entitled it, has proved to be an excellent basis for the assessment of such attachment in 1-year-olds (Ainsworth, Blehar, Waters, & Wall, 1978).

The assessment procedure consists of classification according to the pattern of behavior shown in the strange situation, particularly in the episodes of reunion after separation. Eight patterns were identified, but I shall deal here only with the three main groups into which they fell--Groups A, B, and C. To summarize, Group B babies use their mothers as a secure base from which to explore in the preseparation episodes; their attachment behavior is greatly intensified by the separation episodes so that exploration diminishes and distress is likely; and in the reunion episodes they seek contact with, proximity to, or at least interaction with their mothers. Group C babies tend to show some signs of anxiety even in the preseparation episodes; they are intensely distressed by separation; and in the reunion episodes they are ambivalent with the mother, seeking close contact with her and yet resisting contact or interaction. Group A babies, in sharp contrast, rarely cry in the separation episodes and, in the reunion episodes, avoid the mother, either mingling proximity-seeking and avoidant behaviors or ignoring her altogether.

COMPARISON OF STRANGE-SITUATION BEHAVIOR AND BEHAVIOR ELSEWHERE

Groups A, B, and C in our longitudinal sample were compared in regard to their behavior at home during the first year. Stayton and Ainsworth (1973) had identified a security-anxiety dimension in a factor analysis of fourth-quarter infant behavior. Group B infants were identified as securely attached because they significantly more often displayed behaviors characteristic of the secure pole of this dimension, whereas both of the other groups were identified as anxious because their behaviors were characteristic of the anxious pole. A second dimension was clearly related to close bodily contact, and this was important in distinguishing Group A babies from those in the other two groups, in that Group A babies behaved less positively to being held and yet more negatively to being put down. The groups were also distinguished by two behaviors not included in the factor analysis--cooperativeness and anger. Group B babies were more cooperative and less angry than either A or C babies; Group A babies were even more angry than those in Group C. Clearly, something went awry in the physical-contact interaction Group A babies had with their mothers, and as I explain below, I believe it is this that makes them especially prone to anger.

Ainsworth et al. (1978) reviewed findings of other investigators who had compared A-B-C groups of 1-year-olds in terms of their behavior elsewhere. Their findings regarding socioemotional behavior support the summary just cited, and in addition three investigations using cognitive measures found an advantage in favor of the securely attached.

COMPARISON OF INFANT STRANGE-SITUATION
BEHAVIOR WITH MATERNAL HOME BEHAVIOR

Mothers of the securely attached (Group B) babies were, throughout the first year, more sensitively responsive to infant signals than were the mothers of the two anxiously attached groups, in terms of a variety of measures spanning all of the most common contexts for mother-infant interaction (Ainsworth et al., 1978). Such responsiveness, I suggest, enables an infant to form expectations, primitive at first, that moderate his or her responses to events, both internal and environmental. Gradually, such an infant constructs an inner representation--or "working model" (Bowlby, 1969)--of his or her mother as generally accessible and responsive to him or her. Therein lies his or her security. In contrast, babies whose mothers have disregarded their signals, or have responded to them belatedly or in a grossly inappropriate fashion, have no basis for believing the mother to be accessible and responsive; consequently they are anxious, not knowing what to expect of her.

In regard to interaction in close bodily contact, the most striking finding is that the mothers of avoidant (Group A) babies all evinced a deep-seated aversion to it, whereas none of the other mothers did. In addition they were more rejecting, more often angry, and yet more restricted in the expression of affect than were Group B or C mothers. Main (e.g., in press) and Ainsworth et al. (1978) have presented a theoretical account of the dynamics of interaction of avoidant babies and their rejecting mothers. This emphasizes the acute approach-avoidance conflict experienced by these infants when their attachment behavior is activated at high intensity--a conflict stemming from painful rebuff consequent upon seeking close bodily contact. Avoidance is viewed as a defensive maneuver, lessening the anxiety and anger experienced in the conflict situation and enabling the baby nevertheless to remain within a tolerable range of proximity to the mother.

Findings and interpretations such as these raise the issue of direction of effects. To what extent is the pattern of attachment of a baby attributable to the mother's behavior throughout the first year, and to what extent is it attributable to built-in differences in potential and temperament? I have considered this problem elsewhere (Ainsworth, 1979) and have concluded that in our sample of normal babies there is a strong case to be made for differences in attachment quality being attributable to maternal behavior. Two studies, however (Connell, 1976; Waters, Vaughn, & Egeland, in press), have suggested that Group C babies may as newborns be constitutionally "difficult." Particularly if the mother's personality or life situation makes it hard for her to be sensitively responsive to infant cues, such a baby seems indeed likely to form an attachment relationship of anxious quality.

Contexts of Mother-Infant Interaction

Of the various contexts in which mother-infant interaction commonly takes place, the face-to-face situation has been the focus of most recent research. By many (e.g. Walters & Parke, 1965), interaction mediated by distance receptors and behaviors has been judged especially important in the establishment of human relationships. Microanalytic studies, based on frame-by-frame analysis of film records, show clearly that maternal sensitivity to infant behavioral cues is essential for successful pacing of face-to-face interaction (e.g., Brazelton, Koslowski, & Main, 1974; Stern, 1974). Telling evidence of the role of vision, both in the infant's development of attachment to the mother and in the mother's responsiveness to the infant, comes from Fraiberg's (1977) longitudinal study of blind infants.

So persuasive have been the studies of interaction involving distance receptors that interaction involving close bodily contact has been largely ignored. The evolutionary perspective of attachment theory attributes focal importance to bodily contact. Other primate species rely on the maintenance of close mother-infant contact as crucial for infant survival. Societies of hunter-gatherers, living much as the earliest humans did, are conspicuous for very much more mother-infant contact than are western societies (e.g., Konner, 1976). Blurton Jones (1972) presented evidence suggesting that humans evolved as a species in which infants are carried by the mother and are fed at frequent intervals, rather than as a species in which infants are left for long periods, are cached in a safe place, and are fed but infrequently. Bowlby (1969) pointed out that when attachment behavior is intensely activated it is close bodily contact that is specifically required. Indeed, Bell and Ainsworth (1972) found that even with the white, middle-class mothers of their sample, the most frequent and the most effective response to an infant's crying throughout the first year was to pick up the baby. A recent analysis of our longitudinal findings (Blehar, Ainsworth, & Main, Note 1) suggests that mother-infant interaction relevant to close bodily contact is at least as important a context of interaction as face-to-face is, perhaps especially in the first few months of life. Within the limits represented by our sample, however, we found that it was how the mother holds her baby rather than how much she holds him or her that affects the way in which attachment develops.

In recent years the feeding situation has been neglected as a context for mother-infant interaction, except insofar as it is viewed as a setting for purely social, face-to-face interaction. Earlier, mother's gratification or frustration of infant interest to both psychoanalytically oriented and social-learning research, on the assumption that a mother's gratification or frustration of infant instinctual drives, or her role as a secondary reinforcer, determined the nature of the baby's tie to her. Such research yielded no evidence that methods of feeding significantly affected the course of infant development, although these negative findings seem almost certainly to reflect methodological deficiencies (Caldwell, 1964). In contrast, we have found that sensitive maternal responsiveness to infant signals relevant to feeding is closely related to the security or anxiety of attachment that eventually develops (Ainsworth & Bell, 1969). Indeed, this analysis seemed to redefine the meaning of "demand" feeding--letting infant behavioral cues determine not only when feeding is begun but also when it is terminated, how the pacing of feeding proceeds, and how new foods are introduced.

Our findings do not permit us to attribute over-riding importance to any one context of mother-infant interaction. Whether the context is feeding, close bodily contact, face-to-face interaction, or indeed the situation defined by the infant's crying, mother-infant interaction provides the baby with opportunity to build up expectations of the mother and, eventually, a working model of her as more or less accessible and responsive. Indeed, our findings suggest that a mother who is sensitively responsive to signals in one context tends also to be responsive to signals in other contexts.

Practical Implications for Intervention

What I have so far summarized about research findings pertaining both to contexts of interaction and to qualitative differences in infant-mother attachment has implications for parenting education, for intervention by professionals to help a mother to achieve better interaction with her baby, and for the practices of substitute caregivers. I cannot go into detail here--and indeed such detail would need to be based on much fuller reports of the relevant research than I am able to include here. Among the intervention programs with which I am familiar, some parent-child development centers have reported success in the application of our research findings in improving and sustaining the rate of development of very young children through improving the quality of mother-infant interaction (e.g., Andrews, Blumenthal, Bache, & Wiener, Note 2). Furthermore, the expert clinical interventions of Fraiberg and her associates with families at risk have focused on increasing maternal responsiveness to infant behavioral cues (e.g., Shapiro, Fraiberg, & Adelson, 1976). It may be that such intervention, although obviously expensive, provides the most effective mode of helping dyads in which the difficulty stems from deep-seated difficulties in the mother's personality, such as the aversion to bodily contact characteristic of our Group A mothers.

Using The Mother as a Secure Base From Which to Explore

Attachment theory conceives of the behavioral system serving attachment as only one of several important systems, each with its own activators, terminators, predictable outcomes, and functions. During the prolonged period of human infancy, when the protective function of attachment is especially important, its interplay with exploratory behavior is noteworthy. The function of exploration is learning about the environment--which is particularly important in a species possessing much potential for adaptation to a wide range of environments. Attachment and exploration support each other. When attachment behavior is intensely activated, a baby tends to seek proximity contact rather than exploring; when attachment behavior is at low intensity a baby is free to respond to the pull of novelty. The presence of an attachment figure, particularly one who is believed to be accessible and responsive, leaves the baby open to stimulation that may activate exploration.

Nevertheless, it is often believed that somehow attachment may interfere with the development of independence. Our studies provide no support for such a belief. For example, Blehar et al. (Note 1) found that babies who respond positively to close bodily contact with their mothers also tend to respond positively to being put down again and to move off into independent exploratory play. Fostering the growth of secure attachment facilitates rather than hampers the growth of healthy self-reliance (Bowlby, 1973).

Response to Separation From Attachment Figures

Schaffer (1971) suggested that the crucial criterion for whether a baby has become attached to a specific figure is that he or she does not consider this figure interchangeable with any other figure. Thus, for an infant to protest the mother's departure or continued absence is a dependable criterion for attachment (Schaffer & Callender, 1959). This does not imply that protest is an invariable response to separation from an attachment figure under all circumstances; the context of the separation influences the likelihood and intensity of protest. Thus there is ample evidence, which cannot be cited here, that protest is unlikely to occur, at least initially, in the case of voluntary separations, when the infant willingly leaves the mother in order to explore elsewhere. Protest is less likely to occur if the baby is left with another attachment figure than if he or she is left with an unfamiliar person or alone. Being left in an unfamiliar environment is more distressing than comparable separations in the familiar environment of the home--in which many infants are able to build up expectations that reassure them of mother's accessibility and responsiveness even though she may be absent. Changes attributable to developmental processes affect separation protest in complex ways. Further research will undoubtedly be able to account for these shifts in terms of progressive cognitive achievements.

Major separations of days, months, or even years must be distinguished from the very brief separations, lasting only minutes, that have been studied most intensively both in the laboratory and at home. Securely attached infants may be able to tolerate very brief separations with equanimity, yet they are likely to be distressed in major separations, especially when cared for by unfamiliar persons in unfamiliar environments. Even so, Robertson and Robertson (1971) showed that sensitive substitute parenting can do much to mute separation distress and avert the more serious consequences of major separations.

Despite a steady increase in our understanding of the complexities of response to and effects of separation from attachment figures in infancy and early childhood, it is difficult to suggest clear-cut guidelines for parents and others responsible for infant and child care. So much depends on the circumstances under which separation takes place, on the degree to which the separation environment can substitute satisfactorily for home and parents, on the child's stage of development and previous experience, and on the nature of his or her relationship with attachment figures. No wonder that the issue of the separations implicit in day care is controversial. Further research is clearly needed. Meanwhile, it would seem wise for parents--if they have a choice--to move cautiously rather than plunging into substitute-care arrangments with a blithe assumption that all is bound to go well.

Other Attachment Figures

Many have interpreted Bowlby's attachment theory as claiming that an infant can become attached to only one person--the mother. This is a mistaken interpretation. There are, however, three implications of attachment theory relevant to the issue of "multiple" attachments. First, as reported by Ainsworth (1967) and Schaffer and Emerson (1964), infants are highly selective in their choices of attachment figures from among the various persons familiar to them. No infant has been observed to have many attachment figures. Second, not all social relationships may be identified as attachments. Harlow (1971) distinguished between the infant-mother and peer-peer affectional systems, although under certain circumstances peers may become attachment figures in the absence of anyone more appropriate (see, e.g., Freud & Dann, 1951; Harlow, 1963). Third, the fact that a baby may have several attachment figures does not imply that they are all equally important. Bowlby (1969) suggested that they are not--that there is a principal attachment figure, usually the principal caregiver, and one or more secondary figures. Thus a hierarchy is implied. A baby may both enjoy and derive security from all of his or her attachment figures but, under certain circumstances (e.g., illness, fatigue, stress), is likely to show a clear preference among them.

In recent years there has been a surge of interest in the father as an attachment figure, as reported elsewhere in this issue. Relatively lacking is research into attachments to caregivers other than parents. Do babies become attached to their regular baby-sitters or to caregivers in day-care centers? Studies by Fleener (1973), Farran and Ramey (1977), and Ricciuti (1974) have suggested that they may but that the preference is nevertheless for the mother figure. Fox (1977) compared the mother and the metapelet as providers of security to kibbutz-reared infants in a strange situation, but surely much more research is needed into the behavior of infants and young children toward caregivers as attachment figures in the substitute-care environment.

Consequences of Attachment

A number of investigators, including Main (1973, Note 3), Matas, Arend, and Sroufe (1978), and Waters, Wittman, and Sroufe (in press), having assessed the quality of 1-year-old's attachment, have followed the children through to ascertain whether this assessment bears a significant relationship to later behavioral measures in the second, third, or even sixth year of life. We (Ainsworth et al., 1978) have reviewed these investigations in some detail; only a brief summary can be given here.

In comparison with anxiously attached infants, those who are securely attached as 1-year-olds are later more cooperative with and affectively more positive as well as less aggressive and/or avoidant toward their mothers and other less familiar adults. Later on, they emerge as more competent and more sympathetic in interaction with peers. In free-play situations they have longer bouts of exploration and display more intense exploratory interest, and in problem-solving situations they are more enthusiastic, more persistent, and better able to elicit and accept their mothers' help. They are more curious, more self-directed, more ego-resilient--and they usually tend to achieve better scores on both developmental tests and measures of language development. Some studies also reported differences between the two groups of anxiously attached infants, with the avoidant ones (Group A) continuing to be more aggressive, noncompliant, and avoidant, and the ambivalent ones (Group C) emerging as more easily frustrated, less persistent, and generally less competent.

Conclusion

It is clear that the nature of an infant's attachment to his or her mother as a 1-year-old is related both to earlier interaction with the mother and to various aspects of later development. The implication is that the way in which the infant organizes his or her behavior toward the mother affects the way in which he or she organizes behavior toward other aspects of the environment, both animate and inanimate. This organization provides a core of continuity in development despite changes that come with developmental acquisitions, both cognitive and socioemotional.

This is not to insist that the organization of attachment is fixed in the first year of life and is insensitive to marked changes in maternal behavior or to relevant life events occurring later on. Nor is it implied that attachments to figures other than the mother are unimportant as supplementing or compensating for anxieties in infant-mother attachment--although too little is yet known about how various attachments relate together to influence the way in which infants organize their perception of and approach to the world. Despite the need for further research, however, the yield of findings to date provides relevant leads for policies, education in parenting, and intervention procedures intended to further the welfare of infants and young children.

REFERENCE NOTES

1. Blehar, M.C., Ainsworth, M.D.S., & Main, M. *Mother-infant interaction relevant to close bodily contact.* Monograph in preparation, 1979.

2. Andrews, S.R., Blumenthal, J.B., Bache, W.L., III, & Wiener, G. *Fourth year report: New Orleans Parent-Child Development Center.* Unpublished document, March 1975. (Available from Susan R. Andrews, 6917 Glenn Street, Metairie, Louisiana 70003.)

3. Main, M., & Londerville, S.B. *Compliance and aggression in toddlerhood: Precursors and correlates.* Paper in preparation, 1979.

REFERENCES

Ainsworth, M.D.S. *Infancy in Uganda: Infant care and the growth of love.* Baltimore, Md.: Johns Hopkins Press, 1967.

Ainsworth, M.D.S. Attachment as related to mother-infant interaction. In J.S. Rosenblatt, R.A. Hinde, C. Beer, & M. Busnel (Eds.), *Advances in the study of behavior* (Vol. 9). New York: Academic Press, 1979.

Ainsworth, M.D.S., & Bell, S.M. Some contemporary patterns of mother-infant interaction in the feeding situation. In A. Ambrose (Ed.), *Stimulation in early infancy.* London: Academic Press, 1969.

Ainsworth, M.D.S., Blehar, M.C., Waters, E., & Wall, S. *Patterns of attachment: A psychological study of the strange situation.* Hillsdale, N.J.: Erlbaum, 1978.

Bell, S.M., & Ainsworth, M.D.S. Infant crying and maternal responsiveness. *Child Development,* 1972, 43, 1171-1190.

Blurton Jones, N.G. Comparative aspects of mother-child contact. In N.G. Blurton Jones (Ed.), *Ethological studies of child behaviour.* London: Cambridge University Press, 1972.

Bowlby, J. *Attachment and loss: Vol. 1. Attachment.* New York: Basic Books, 1969.

Bowlby, J. *Attachment and loss: Vol. 2. Separation: Anxiety and anger.* New York: Basic Books, 1973.

Brazelton, T.B., Koslowski, B., & Main, M. The origins of reciprocity: The early mother-infant interaction. In M. Lewis & L.A. Rosenblum (Eds.), *The effect of the infant on its caregiver.* New York: Wiley, 1974.

Caldwell, B.M. The effects of infant care. In M.L. Hoffman & L.W. Hoffman (Eds.), *Review of child development research* (Vol. 1). New York: Russell Sage Foundation, 1964.

Connell, D.B. *Individual differences in attachment: An investigation into stability, implications, and relationships to the structure of early language development.* Unpublished doctoral dissertation, Syracuse University, 1976.

Farran, D.C., & Ramey, C.T. Infant day care and attachment behavior toward mother and teachers. *Child Development*, 1977, 48, 1112-1116.

Fleener, D.E. Experimental production of infant-maternal attachment behaviors. *Proceedings of the 81st Annual Convention of the American Psychological Association*, 1973, 8, 57-58. (Summary).

Fox, N. Attachment of kibbutz infants to mother. *Child Development*, 1977, 48, 1228-1239.

Fraiberg, S. *Insights from the blind.* New York: Basic Books, 1977.

Freud, A., & Dann, S. An experiment in group upbringing. *Psychoanalytic Study of the Child*, 1951, 6, 127-168.

Harlow, H.F. The maternal affectional system. In B.M. Foss (Ed.), *Determinants of infant behaviour* (Vol. 2). New York: Wiley, 1963.

Harlow, H.F. *Learning to love.* San Francisco: Albion, 1971.

Konner, M.J. Maternal care, infant behavior, and development among the Kung. In R.B. Lee & I. DeVore (Eds.), *Kalahari hunter-gatherers.* Cambridge, Mass.: Harvard University Press, 1976.

Main, M. *Exploration, play, and level of cognitive functioning as related to child-mother attachment.* Unpublished doctoral dissertation, Johns Hopkins University, 1973.

Main, M. Avoidance in the service of proximity. In K. Immelmann, G. Barlow, M. Main, & L. Petrinovich (Eds.), *Behavioral development: The Bielefeld Interdisciplinary Project.* New York: Cambridge University Press, in press.

Matas, L., Arend, R.A., & Sroufe, L.A. Continuity of adaptation in the second year: The relationship between quality of attachment and later competence. *Child Development*, 1978, 49, 547-556.

Ricciuti, H.N. Fear and the development of social attachments in the first year of life. In M. Lewis & L.A. Rosenblum (Eds.), *The origins of fear*. New York: Wiley, 1974.

Robertson, J., & Robertson, J. Young children in brief separation: A fresh look. *Psychoanalytic Study of the Child*, 1971, 26, 264-315.

Schaffer, H.R. *The growth of sociability*. London: Penguin Books, 1971.

Schaffer, H.R., & Callender, W.M. Psychological effects of hospitalization in infancy. *Pediatrics*, 1959, 25, 528-539.

Schaffer, H.R., & Emerson, P.E. The development of social attachments in infancy. *Monographs of the Society for Research in Child Development*, 1964, 3 (Serial No. 94).

Shapiro, V., Fraiberg, S., & Adelson, E. Infant-parent psychotherapy on behalf of a child in a critical nutritional state. *Psychoanalytic Study of the Child*, 1976, 31, 461-491.

Stayton, D.J., & Ainsworth, M.D.S. Individual differences in infant responses to brief, everyday separations as related to other infant and maternal behaviors. *Developmental Psychology*, 1973, 9, 226-235.

Stern, D.N. Mother and infant at play: The dyadic interaction involving facial, vocal, and gaze behaviors. In M. Lewis & L.A. Rosenblum (Eds.), *The effect of the infant on its caregiver*. New York: Wiley, 1974.

Walters, R.H. & Parke, R.D. The role of the distance receptors in the development of social responsiveness. In L.P. Lipsitt & C.C. Spiker (Eds.), *Advances in child development and behavior*. New York: Academic Press, 1965.

Waters, E., Vaughn, B.E., & Egeland, B.R. Individual differences in infant-mother attachment relationship at age one: Antecedents in neonatal behavior in an urban economically disadvantaged sample. *Child Development,* in press.

Waters, E., Wittman, J., & Sroufe, L.A. Attachment, positive affect, and competence in the peer group: Two studies in construct validation. *Child Development,* in press.

Section 2

Early Experience

D.O.. Hebb, in his *Textbook of Psychology*, defined experience as "sensory stimulation". As such, experience begins before birth, and may be either endogenous (from within the organism) or exogenous (from outside the organism). Broadly defined in this way, most of the papers in this collection of readings on child development are about the effects of early experience. Traditionally however, researchers in "early experience" have addressed three general questions. First, they have attempted to specify the type or quality of the experiences that are necessary for normal development to occur. Second, they have attempted to establish the amount or quantity of stimulation that an organism requires. Third, researchers have addressed the question of the timing of early experiences. Specifically, are there "critical" periods in development during which the organism is maximally sensitive to the effects of experience, but outside of which the organism is less sensitive, or insensitive to the effects of stimulation or deprivation? These three questions have been asked, and in some cases answered, with reference to physiological, social, perceptual, and cognitive development.

Early experience questions have typically been addressed in "intervention" studies in which subjects receive either enrichment or deprivation of a particular experience. In the enrichment study extra stimulation is provided to a group of subjects whose development is then compared in some way to that of a group who did not have the extra stimulation. The deprivation study involves the removal of some aspect of normal experience for one group of subjects, whose development is then compared to that of normally reared, nondeprived subjects. Much of this experimental work, especially that involving deprivation, is conducted on non-human species such as monkeys, rodents, dogs and cats. However, in some cases the experimental work was subsequent to some naturally occurring deprivation in which human subjects, who experienced a particular loss of stimulation, showed some deficiency in development. Thus, the early experience literature consists of both case studies and naturalistic observations of the effects of deprivation or enrichment, and more carefully controlled experimental work which has enabled scientists to specify how the quality, quantity, and timing of experience affects development in non-human species.

The knowledge obtained from such research has also provided some clarification of the "heredity (nature) versus environment (nurture)" question, which has been one of the oldest and most important theoretical issues in developmental psychology. While we no longer try to separate the influences of these factors, the study of early development has enabled scientists to describe the abilities that are present at birth, those which mature in the early months, and the manner in which early experiences facilitate or inhibit normal development. This research has made it clear that all development occurs through a complex interaction between hereditary predispositions and environmental stimulation, both before and after birth. Answers to the questions about the "how" and "why" of development will not only enrich our understanding of developmental processes, but will also find practical application. Parents, always eager to do what is "best" for their children, will become more aware of the capacities, needs and limitations of their babies. In addition, when scientists are able to describe the full range of capabilities that young infants possess and the way in which they develop, it will be possible to detect delays and deficiencies in development. Early detection of developmental problems may lead to earlier interventions and better long-term outcomes.

The diversity of the topics that are included in this section reflects the breadth of the early-experience literatures: only a sample of the research in this area has been included. The paper by Wayne Dennis is an early report on the effects of institutionalization on child development. It is representative of a number of studies which followed the publication of John Bowlby's report to the World Health Organization in 1951, documenting the devastating effects of early "maternal deprivation" on later development. Dennis examined the development of walking in children living in three orphanages that varied in the amount of practice that the children were permitted. He found that the development of this skill depended not only on maturation but also on experience. Experimental research on the effects of early maternal and social deprivation was conducted by Harry Harlow and his colleagues. The results of their carefully controlled experiments with subhuman primates were consistent with the naturalistic observation data on the effects of deprivation on human infants. The study included in this section describes their successful attempt to rehabilitate the behavior of monkeys that had been deprived of varying amounts of social contact with parents and/or peers.

The paper by Audrey Clark and Jeanette Hanisee is a more recent study which reports on the social and intellectual development of a group of Asian refugee children, who were at risk for developmental delay following such early experiences as traumatic separation from their parents and chronic undernutrition. These children were adopted into American families as infants and raised with all of the social advantages of the middle class environment. The level of performance shown by these children on tests of social and cognitive development when they were toddlers attests to the remarkable potential for recovery that is possible following entry into a favorable environment. In a similar vein, the paper by Philip Zeskind and Craig Ramey is the report of an intervention study in which newborn infants who had experienced prenatal malnutrition were provided with medical and nutritional attention, as well as an early curriculum for cognitive and social development. These children performed normally on developmental tests at 18 and 24 months of age, which indicated that the detrimental effects of early nutritional deprivation can be reversed.

Early experience begins before birth, and the paper by P. A. Fried and C. M. O'Connell is a recent study of the impact on development of prenatal exposure to certain chemicals commonly used by pregnant women. They report on the effects that alcohol, tobacco, cannabis, and caffeine use during pregnancy have on the subsequent growth of the child in the first two years after birth.

The paper by Terri Lewis and her colleagues describes the effects of the naturally occurring visual deprivation that was experienced by children who had cataracts on their eyes. Following removal of the cataracts, the development of the children's visual acuity, optokinetic nystagmus, and peripheral vision was assessed. The authors discuss their results in terms of the time in development at which the cataract formed, the length of time it was present, and how consistently the post-operative treatment of patching the good eye occurred. They compare the results of this visual deprivation in human subjects with that of carefully controlled, comparable studies of visual deprivation in cats.

Causes of Retardation among Institutional Children: Iran

Wayne Dennis

For some time it has been widely accepted that the early development of motor functions unfolds primarily on a maturational time schedule. This and other recent studies by Dennis provide a challenge to this view. They point to more important roles for early stimulation and opportunity for exercise of those functions.

A. Introduction

Considerable interest has recently been shown in the fact that in some institutions for children there occurs a decided retardation in behavioral development. The observations of Spitz (8, 9, 10) in particular have received much notice, chiefly because of the interpretations which Spitz has placed upon his data. In our opinion, the primary importance of these observations lies in their challenge to the theory that infant development consists largely of the maturation of a motor sequence which is little affected by learning.

Originally published in *The Journal of Genetic Psychology,* 1960, *96,* 47-59. Reprinted with permission of the Helen Dwight Reid Educational Foundation. Published by Heldref Publications, 4000 Albemarle St., N.W., Washington, D.C. 20016.

Aside from the investigations of Spitz, studies of behavioral retardation among institutional children have been few in number. The scarcity of such studies is due in large part to the fact that institutions in which conditions comparable to those described by Spitz can be found are not numerous. In many countries institutional care has been replaced by other methods of caring for dependent children. However, institutions in which behavioral development is retarded can still be found in countries which are "underdeveloped" not only in regard to modern technology but also in respect to newer methods for the care of foundlings and other homeless infants.

The present paper reports studies of development in three institutions in Tehran, the capital of Iran. In two of these institutions, children are exceedingly retarded in their motor development. In the third little retardation is present. It is believed that comparisons of child care in these institutions, and of behavioral development in them, will throw considerable light upon the nature of the environmental factors which influence motor development. This paper supplements a recent report on behavioral retardation in a Lebanese institution by Dennis and Najarian (4). In the earlier report attention was directed primarily to motor development in the first year of life, whereas in the present instance the period from one year to four years of age is the one with which we are mainly concerned. Preliminary observations indicated that development during the first year in the two Iranian institutions in which retardation occurs is essentially the same as in the Lebanese institution described in the previous paper. For this reason in the present study attention is given chiefly to the age period to which little attention was directed in the earlier report.

B. Description of the Institutions

The two institutions in which marked retardation occurs, which will be called institutions I and II, are supported chiefly by public funds; the third institution, to be labeled III, is supported by private funds. Several other children's institutions, both public and private, exist in Tehran. The present report should not be taken to imply that retardation prevails in the majority of Iranian institutions.

It is worthy of note that the number of children to be found in institutions in Tehran is quite large. This number is explained by several factors. For one thing, Tehran is a large city having approximately two million inhabitants. The recent growth of Tehran has taken place in the main through migration from villages. This has led to a considerable amount of social disorganization which has increased the number of illegitimate children, foundlings, abandoned children, orphans and half-orphans. Furthermore in Tehran at the present time, provisions for the care of dependent children, other than by institutionalization, are quite inadequate. Consequently, almost all children not living with parents or relatives are to be found in institutions.

1. Institution I. Institution I feels obligated to accept all foundlings and all aban-

doned children under three years of age who are brought to it. The population of the institution varies from day to day because of departures and admissions. During the time of the present study (September, 1958) the average daily population was about 600; of these about 275 were between birth and one year of age, 135 were between one and two years of age, and about 110 were between two and three years of age. While children above three years are generally transferred to other institutions, a few remain in Institution I beyond this age.

The excess of younger children over older children in Institution I may be due to several causes, including an increased intake rate in recent years, a higher death rate during the first year than in later years, return of older children to relatives, and transfer of older children to other institutions. The data at our disposal do not permit an assignment of relative weights to these factors.

More than nine-tenths of the children in Institution I are recorded as having been under one month of age at the time of their admission. When the actual date of birth is not known, an estimate of age at admission, based on weight, size, and appearance is made and placed in the child's record. The mother never accompanies the child to Institution I nor sees him after admission.

In general children are placed in individual cribs, although at times, because of over-crowding, two infants temporarily occupy the same crib. In such instances, the heads of the two babies are placed at opposite ends of the bed.

A child is bathed on alternate days. Except when being bathed, the younger children spend practically their entire time in their cribs. They are given milk and other liquids while lying in bed, the bottle being supported by a small pillow. When semi-solid foods are introduced, infants are sometimes held by an attendant and sometimes fed in bed. The children are placed in bed in the supine position. They are never placed prone and seldom get themselves into this position.

The paucity of handling is due primarily to the attendant-child ratio. On the average there were eight children per attendant. In addition to feeding the children, bathing them, and changing clothing and diapers, the attendants are also responsible for changing the bed-linen and cleaning the rooms, and have some responsibilities for preparing food. Each attendant is on duty 12 hours per day. In general there are 32 children and four attendants to a room, although this varies somewhat according to the size of the room. There is no assignment of attendants to particular children. The attendants have no special training for their work and are poorly paid. The emphasis on the part of the supervisors seems to be on neatness in the appearance of the rooms, with little attention to behavioral development.

In his crib the child is not propped up, and is given no toys. The child who can pull himself to sitting, and hence is in some danger of falling from his shallow crib, is placed, when awake, on a piece of linoleum on the composition stone floor of the room. Until he himself achieves the sitting position he remains in bed. In two rooms some of the children who can sit are seated in a row on a bench which has a bar across the front to prevent falling. Aside from these two benches and the frames for the cribs, the rooms have no children's furniture and no play equipment of any kind.

2. Institution II. This institution accepts children over three years of age. The children in this institution come mainly from Institution I. Child care practices in II are a continuation of the practices existing in I, but sanitation and cleanliness are poorer and the appearance of the children suggests that nutrition and health are poorer. However, in neither I nor II are there any records of growth in height or weight, and it was not possible for us to obtain any objective assessment of nutritional status.

3. Institution III. Institution III was established only one year prior to the present study. It was started primarily to demonstrate improved methods of institutional care. The children in III come from Institution I but are selected for transfer in the early months of life. It seems likely that those sent to Institution III are chosen from among the more retarded children. They remain in III until three years of age unless adopted before that date. The number of children per attendant is 3-4. Children are held in arms while being fed, are regularly placed prone during part of the time they are in their cribs, are propped up in a sitting position in their cribs at times and are placed in play pens on the floor daily when above four months of age. Numerous toys are provided. Attendants are coached in methods of child care, and supervisors emphasize behavioral development as well as nutrition and health.

Individual growth charts are available for each child in Institution III and show without exception that these children are much below prevailing weight norms on arrival but attain normal weight within a few months.

C. Types of Behavioral Data

Quantitative observations on the behavioral status of the groups described above were made only with regard to motor coordinations. Some general observations on social and emotional behaviour will be presented after motor behaviour has been discussed.

In respect to motor development, each child who was a subject of this study was classified with regard to his ability to meet each of the following behavioral criteria:

1. *Sit alone*. The child was placed in a sitting position on the floor. He was scored as sitting alone if he maintained this position for one minute. However, if a

child could maintain this position at all he ordinarily could maintain it indefinitely.

2. *Creep or Scoot.* The child was placed sitting on the floor and was encouraged to locomote by having the attendant hold a cookie, or extend her arms, toward the child at a distance of about six feet. He was scored as passing the test if he covered the distance in any manner. If he locomoted, his mode of progression was recorded. The modes of locomotion will be discussed at a later point.

3. *Stand by holding.* The child was held under the arms and placed adjacent to the horizontal bars of a child's bed. It was observed whether or not he grasped the bars and maintained a standing position.

4. *Walking by holding.* The child who could stand by holding was observed for some minutes to determine whether he took steps while holding. He was urged to walk by the attendant.

5. *Walk alone.* The child who could walk by holding objects was placed standing without support and was encouraged to walk to the outstretched arms of the attendant. The child was scored as walking alone if he took at least two steps without support.

In the above tests one of the attendants with whom the child was familiar was coached to make the tests while the experimenter remained at a distance of six feet or more from the child and somewhat behind him. This procedure was followed because it was found that the child's unfamiliarity with the experimenter often inhibited the child's behaviour if he was tested by the examiner himself. Communication between the attendant and the examiner was conducted via an Iranian interpreter. Tests were conducted among the children of a given room only after the experimenter and the interpreter had made several visits to the room and somewhat decreased the children's shyness. If a child failed a test the attendant was asked whether or not he could usually perform the required response. If the answer was positive, renewed efforts were made to elicit a successful performance. The experimenter is convinced that subjects who were scored as failing a test were actually unable to perform the required task.

The number of children tested at each age level in each institution are shown in Table I. In Institutions I and II the total number of children tested was 123. In selecting children to provide this sample, the children of appropriate ages were selected at random from each of several rooms, the rooms so far as we could determine not being unusual in any respect. However, we excluded from testing any child who had sensory or motor defects, who was ill or who had recently been ill. In Institution III all children between age one and three were tested. They totaled 51.

TABLE I

PER CENT OF EACH GROUP PASSING EACH TEST

Institutions	I	I	II	III	III
N	50	40	33	20	31
Ages	1.0–1.9	2.0–2.9	3.0–3.9	1.0–1.9	2.0–2.9
Sit alone	42	95	97	90	100
Creep or Scoot	14	75	97	75	100
Stand holding	4	45	90	70	100
Walk holding	2	40	63	60	100
Walk alone	0	8	15	15	94

D. Results of Tests

Table I shows the percent of each group which passed each test. The reader is asked to direct his attention first to the retardation which is evident in Institutions I and II. Among those children in Institution I who were between 1.0-1.9 years of age, fewer than half could sit alone and none could walk alone. In normative studies, of home-reared children, such as those conducted by Jones (6), Gesell (5), Dennis and Dennis (2) and others, it has been found that by nine months of age all normal non-institutional American children can sit alone. By two years of age nearly all can walk alone. A majority of the children of Institution I cannot perform these responses at ages at which almost all home-reared children can perform them. It will be noted that even between 2.0-2.9 years of age only 8 per cent of the children in Institution I are able to walk alone and only 15 per cent of those children in Institution II who are 3.0-3.9 years for age are able to walk alone. We are not aware that any groups so retarded as Groups I and II have previously been reported.

In Institution III the picture is different. Of those children between 2.0-2.9 years of age nearly every child is able to walk unaided. While these children do not equal the performance of home-reared children, their motor behaviour is much superior to that of children in Institutions I and II. In other words it is not institutionalization per se which handicaps Groups I and II since Group III children who are also institutionalized are but slightly retarded in motor development. The records of Group III also show that motor retardation is not a general characteristic of Tehran children.

Of special note is the difference in types of pre-walking locomotion between Institutions I and II on the one hand and Institution III on the other.

Of the 67 children in Institutions I and II who engaged in creeping or scooting, only 10 did so by creeping, i.e., going on hands and knees or on hands and feet. All others progressed by "scooting," i.e., their locomotion took place in the sitting position, the body being propelled forwarded by pushing with the arms aided by propulsion from the legs. Many children who could not walk were quite adept at scooting.

Since tests for creeping or scooting were made when the child was in a sitting position, it might seem that the frequency of scooting was due to the nature of the starting position. To test the effect of starting position, many subjects who were "scooters" were placed prone and offered a cookie at some distance, a powerful incentive for locomotion in these children. In each case the child first pushed himself to a sitting position and then scooted. Scooting was definitely the preferred mode of locomotion even when the child was placed prone. So far as we could determine, the majority of the scooters were completely unfamiliar with creeping.

In Institution III, the reverse situation prevailed. Of 15 children who were observed to creep or scoot, all progressed by creeping. No scooting whatsoever was seen in this institution, yet tests were made from the sitting position as with Groups I and II. When placed sitting and encouraged to locomote, the children leaned forward, got themselves on hands and knees, and crept.

E. Interpretative Comments on Motor Development

Let us examine now the probable reasons why the children in Institutions I and II were so severely retarded relative to home-reared children and why they were so much more retarded than children in Institution III. Several different possibilities need to be considered.

Attention should first be directed to malnutrition as a possible cause of retarded motor development. As noted earlier there can be no doubt that many of the children in Group I were much smaller and lighter than non-institutional children and children of the same age in Group III. There can be no doubt, too, that malnutrition can be so severe as to interfere with motor performance and motor progress. But the question at stake is not whether malnutrition can affect motor functions but whether malnutrition was in fact a major cause of the retardation of Groups I and II.

We are inclined to think that undernourishment was not the major factor. The following considerations have led us to this interpretation: In the first place, Groups I and II were not entirely listless and inactive. In this connection we need to bring out a fact that we have not noted in earlier sections, namely that these children engage to a considerable extent in automatisms such as head shaking and rocking back and forth. In many cases, these actions were quite vigorous. These activities tend to indicate that these children were not slow in motor development simply because of motor weakness.

The second consideration is somewhat similar to the first, namely, that the locomotor activities in which the children in Groups I and II engaged seem to require as much as or more energy than the locomotor activities which are usual at their respective ages, but in which they did not engage. For example, while few two-year-olds in Group I walked, three-fourths of them locomoted, chiefly by scooting. No physiological data are available, but it seems likely that the metabolic cost of covering a certain distance by scooting is as great as, or even greater than, the effort required to go the same distance by walking. Certainly this would be true for an adult, but of course one cannot argue from the adult to the child. At any rate the possibility exists that the reason that these children scooted was because this was the only form of locomotor skill which they had learned, not that they were too weak to walk.

This interpretation seems to be borne out by the fact that the pre-walking methods of locomotion were different in different groups. The retarded groups scooted. It is difficult to believe that malnutrition can lead to scooting rather than creeping. It is far from obvious that scooting is "easier" than creeping. If it is, why should not all children choose the easier method? In other words, the differences between groups seem to us to be due to the outcome of different learning situations rather than to differences in nutritional status.

What were the differences in the situations faced by Groups I and II and Group III which may account for the development of two different types of locomotion and different degrees of retardation? We suggest the following:

In Group III and in many homes infants are propped up in a sitting position, or held in a sitting position. In this position the child can raise his head and can partially raise his shoulders for short periods and can relax these efforts without falling. He can thus practice some elements of sitting. On the other hand, the child who remains on his back has no such opportunities to learn to sit. In some respects it is surprising that children who are never propped up or held on the lap are able to learn to sit at all. But it will be remembered that in Groups I and II some children could not sit until they were more than two years of age. Until they could sit alone, all forms of locomotion were impossible for them, because they were not placed in a position in which creeping was possible.

This is not true in Group III. In this group and in many homes, the child is frequently placed prone in bed or on the floor. In this position he can raise his head from the surface, push with his arms, raise his chest, pull his arms and legs beneath his body--in other words, he can practice acts which are employed in creeping. The child who lies on his back nearly every moment of the day is denied such practice. Thus one specific item of child care, i.e., occasionally placing the child face downward, may well contribute to the development of creeping in most children and its absence may account for the lack of creeping in Groups I and II.

The question may be raised as to why children in Institutions I and II did not get themselves into the prone position in their cribs. Repeated observations of these infants in their cribs showed that few ever attained the prone position. The probable reasons are the small size of the cribs and the softness of the beds, both of which made turning over very difficult.

It is likely that this item, i.e., absence of placement in the prone position, may lead to a delayed development not only in regard to creeping but also in respect to walking. The child who can creep can go to a piece of furniture, grasp it and pull to his knees. This may lead to walking on his knees while holding furniture. Many children go from knee walking to walking by holding to furniture and thence to walking alone. In contrast to the child who creeps, the child who scoots to a piece of furniture is sitting when he arrives at his goal and can attain a higher position only by lifting his entire weight by his arms. In our opinion, the lack of creeping accounts in large measure for the retardation in walking of Groups I and II.

We are well-aware that some persons have interpreted the behavioral retardation of institutional infants to emotional factors rather than to a paucity of learning opportunities. Some have even suggested that under certain conditions institutional infants simply "waste away" from psychological, not from medical causes, a process called marasmus.

If marasmus actually exists, it has somehow been escaped by several hundred children in Iranian institutions living under conditions which are supposed to foster it. Although the prevailing emotional tone of children in Institutions I and II is dysphoric, it is difficult to conceive of mechanisms whereby their unhappiness retards their motor development and causes them to scoot rather than to creep.

There remains the necessity of relating the results of the present study to certain findings reported earlier by the present author. We refer to a study which found no apparent effect of cradling upon the motor development of Hopi children (3) and a study which indicated that infant development can proceed normally under conditions described as "minimal social stimulation" (1). On the surface these results seem contradictory to those here reported, because the former studies found that environmental deprivations had but little effect whereas the present study reports that major consequences can ensure from them. In fact, however, the studies are not contradictory but complementary. To bring the results of these studies into harmony, one needs only to examine the kinds of deprivation which were involved and their severity. Certain differences among these studies seem to us to be crucial. The Hopi children were limited in regard to learning opportunities only while on the cradleboard. As we pointed out in our original report, they were on the cradleboard chiefly during these sleeping hours, when in any case little learning is expected to occur. When awake they were handled, held upright against the mother, placed sitting on her lap, and placed prone. Their deprivation of learning opportunities was much less than that encountered by the children in Institution I who 24 hours per day for many months remained in a supine position.

A similar contrast exists between Rey and Del, the subjects of an experiment in environmental deprivation, and children in Institution I and II. Rey and Del were not deprived to the same degree nor in the same manner as the institutional children described above. As the original report shows (1), Del and Rey, beginning at nine months, were regularly placed in a prone position on a pad on the floor. After it was found that they could not sit alone they were given special practice in sitting. Del and Rey were given special training in supporting their weight when held upright. Such training was not given in Institutions I and II.

These experiences with special training given to Del and Rey suggest that the retardation of the institutional children could be fairly rapidly remedied if intensive specialized practice were given them. Unfortunately it was not possible for us to undertake such experiments while we were in Tehran. The speed with which delayed skills can be developed remains an important problem for future researches with institutional children.

So far as the permanency of motor deficiencies is concerned it should be noted that Institution II had many children between ages 6 and 15 years who presumably were as retarded at ages two and three as were the children whose behaviour was described above. Yet these children were attending school, playing games, doing chores, and being trained in difficult skills, such as the weaving of Persian rugs. There was nothing in their general behaviour to suggest that any permanent consequences issued from the extreme retardation in motor development during the early years. To be sure, we have no direct evidence that these children were retarded at two and three years of age, but so far as we could ascertain there has been no change in the child care offered by Institutions I and II and no reason to suppose that their early development was different from that of their counterparts in the present study.

Finally let us note that the results of the present study challenge the widely-held view that motor development consists in the emergence of a behavioral sequence based primarily upon maturation. Shirley's chart of the motor sequence is a textbook favorite. It shows sitting alone at seven months, creeping at 10 months, and walking alone at 15 months. The present study shows that these norms are met only under favorable environmental conditions. Among the children of Institution I not only was sitting alone greatly retarded but in many cases creeping did not occur. Instead, an alternate form of locomotion was employed. These facts seem to indicate clearly that experience affects not only the ages at which motor items appear but also their very form. No doubt the maturation of certain structures, which as yet cannot be identified, is necessary before certain responses can be learned, but learning also is necessary. Maturation alone is insufficient to bring about most post-natal developments in behaviour. This is also the conclusion which we reached in the Del-Rey experiment, but the present study supports this position more dramatically because the limitations of learning in Institutions I and II are more drastic and more long-continued than were those in the Del-Rey study.

F. Social and Emotional Behaviour

Only incidental observations were made relative to social and emotional behaviour. Several of these had to do with the infants' reactions to visitors.

In the weeks preceding our test it appears that Institution I seldom had visitors. The children of Institution II formerly had few visitors but several weeks before our arrival a volunteer social service group, aware of the isolation of these children, began to make periodic visits to them, taking them from their beds, holding them, and carrying them about. Institution III also had several visitors, partly because of the demonstration nature of this orphanage.

Children in Institution I, probably because of their unfamiliarity with visitors, were somewhat afraid of us during our first visit. They did not smile with us and, in most cases, would cry if we picked them up. On repeated visits, however, they became more friendly, smiled at us, and before our work was completed some of them would hold out their arms to be carried.

Most of the children in Institution II were positive to visitors at the beginning of our work. Several employed attention-seeking devices before visitors and cried if other children were selected for attention. In contrast in Group III, probably because of the greater time spent with attendants and because of their familiarity with visitors, there was little fear of strangers and only limited attention seeking.

Eagerness for food appeared to be greatest in Institution II. In this institution there was much crying before meal time. Children of this group handled cups and spoons quite well. In general there was very little wasting of food on the part of these children. Cups of milk were reached for eagerly, handled carefully, and drunk rapidly. There were attempts, sometimes successful, on the part of those who had finished eating to obtain the food of others, and hitting, pinching, and biting were sometimes the outcomes of such clashes. Children who could not walk could nevertheless manage to attack others and to defend themselves with considerable skill. After feeding they became much more jovial and nearly every child could be made to smile or laugh by an adult who shook him lightly or tickled him.

G. Summary

This paper has presented data concerning behavioral development among 174 children, aged one year to four years, in three Iranian institutions. In Institutions I and II infant development was greatly retarded. The behavioral progress of children in the third institution was much less retarded. The interpretations offered for these differences in behaviour among the children of different institutions are as follows: the extreme retardation in Institutions I and II was probably due to the paucity of handling, including the failure of attendants to place the children in the sitting position and the prone position. The absence of experience in these positions is believed to have retarded the children in regard to sitting alone and also in regard to the onset of locomotion. The lack of experience in the prone position seems in most cases to have prevented children from learning to creep; instead of creeping, the majority of the children in Institutions I and II, prior to walking, locomoted by scooting. In Institution III, in which children were frequently handled, propped in the sitting position, and placed prone, motor development resembled that of most home-reared children. The retardation of subjects in Institutions I and II is believed to be due to the restriction of specific kinds of learning opportunities. This interpretation was found to be congruent with the results of other studies in environmental deprivation. In the light of these findings, the explanation of retardation as being due primarily to emotional factors is believed to be untenable. The data here reported also show that behavioral development cannot be fully accounted for in terms of the maturation hypothesis. The important contributions of experience to the development of infant behaviour must be acknowledged.

REFERENCES

1. Dennis, W. Infant development under conditions of restricted practice and of minimum social stimulation. *Genet. Psychol. Monog.*, 1941, 23:143-189.

2. Dennis, W., and Dennis, M.G. Behavioral development in the first year as shown by forty biographies. *Psychol. Rec.*, 1937, 1:349-361.

3. ------------. The effect of cradling practices upon the onset of walking in Hopi children. *J. Genet. Psychol.*, 1940, 56:77-86.

4. Dennis, W., and Najarian, P. Infant development under environmental handicap. *Psychol. Monog.*, 1957, 71:1-13.

5. Gesell, A. Infancy and Human Growth. New York: Macmillan, 1928.

6. Jones, M.C. The development of early behavior patterns in young children. *Ped. Sem.*, 1926, 33-537-585.

7. Shirley, M.M. The First Two Years: Vol. 1. Postural and Locomotor Development. *Inst. Child Welfare Monog. Series,* No. 6. Minneapolis: Univ. Minn. Press, 1933.

8. Spitz, R.A. Hospitalism, an inquiry into the genesis of psychiatric conditions in early childhood. *Psychoanal. Stud. Child.* 1945, 1:53-74.

9. Spitz, R.A. Hospitalism: A follow-up report. *Psychoanal. Stud. Child,* 1946, 2:113-117.

10. Spitz, R.A. Anaclitic depression. *Psychoanal. Stud. Child*, 1946, 2:313-342.

Social Rehabilitation of Isolate-Reared Monkeys

Stephen J. Suomi and Harry F. Harlow

Numerous researches have indicated that 6 or more months of total social isolation initiated at birth produces profound and apparently permanent social deficits in rhesus monkey subjects. Monkeys so reared fail to develop appropriate play, aggressive, sexual, and maternal behaviors but instead exhibit self-directed abnormalities such as self-clasping, huddling, and stereotypic rocking behaviors. Previous experimentation designed to rehabilitate isolate-reared subjects has not been successful. The present experiment successfully rehabilitated monkeys that spent the first 6 months of life in total social isolation. Following removal from isolation subjects were permitted to interact with socially normal monkeys 3 months chronologically younger than themselves. Within a few weeks isolate disturbance behaviors decreased substantially and were replaced by elementary socially directed activity. After 6 months of such exposure, the isolate subjects were virtually indistinguishable from their younger controls both in terms of absence of disturbance behaviors

---

Originally published in *Developmental Psychology*, 1972, 6, 487-496. Copyright ©1972 by the American Psychological Associaiton. Reprinted by permission of the publisher and author.

and sophistication of social behaviors. The process of the observed recovery and its implications for theoretical interpretations of the effects of isolation rearing are discussed.

The devastating effect of total social isolation upon monkey behavior is an exceptionally well-documented finding in primate behavioral research. Although 3 months of total social isolation from birth has yielded only transient and reversible behavioral effects (Boelkins, 1963; Griffin & Harlow, 1966), isolation for the first 6 months of life or more has consistently resulted in profound and permanent psychopathology (Harlow, Dodsworth, & Harlow, 1965; Harlow & Harlow, 1962; Harlow, Harlow, Dodsworth, & Arling, 1966; Mason, 1963; Rowland, 1964; Sackett, 1968a; Senko, 1966). Upon emergence from total social isolation, monkeys fail to exhibit age-appropriate social and exploratory behavior. Instead, their behavioral repertoire is dominated by self-directed activities, including self-clasping, self-mouthing, huddling, and stereotypic rocking. Such abnormalities persist as the subjects mature. Appropriate sexual responses are virtually absent among adult isolate-reared monkeys, and those females artificially inseminated typically display inadequate maternal behavior toward their initial offspring. Aggressive behavior of isolate-reared monkeys is commonly self directed or, when it occurs in social situations, inappropriately directed.

In contrast, isolation rearing apparently has little effect upon monkey learning capability. Although isolates are slower to adapt to most learning test situations (Harlow, Schiltz, & Harlow, 1969) and to extinguish certain nonreinforced behaviors previously operantly conditioned (Gluck, 1970), these deficits may be attributed to performance rather than intellectual variables. Once properly adapted to a Wisconsin General Test Apparatus, isolate-reared subjects solve complex learning problems as readily as do feral-born monkeys (Singh, 1969).

Two theoretical explanations for the socially destructive effects of isolation for monkeys have dominated the literature, although neither has had its origin in primate research. The "critical period" approach (Scott, 1962), initially an embryological concept and more recently applied by ethologists to avian attachment behavior (e.g., Lorenz, 1965), postulates that subjects progress through critical periods of social development. According to a strict interpretation of the theory, a subject denied appropriate social stimulation during a critical period will be rendered incapable of subsequent normal social development. A second theoretical position, stemming from research using canine subjects (Fuller & Clark, 1966), maintains that the bizarre behavior patterns exhibited by monkeys removed from isolation is the result of "emergence trauma," that is, a shock precipitated by an abrupt shift from an unstimulating environment to one of relatively high complexity.

In view of the apparent discrepancy between intellectual and social effects of isolation rearing and of the alternative theoretical explanation posited, numerous attempts to rehabilitate isolate-reared monkeys have been initiated. Virtually all of these efforts have been summarily unsuccessful, a result consistent with critical period theory. For example, researches designed to shape appropriate social behavior in isolate-reared monkeys via aversive conditioning procedures produced only limited behavioral changes which failed to generalize beyond the experimental situation (Sackett, 1968b). Efforts to alleviate postulated emergence trauma via gradual introduction to environments of increasing complexity did not achieve significant rehabilitation of isolate social behaviors (Clark, 1968; Pratt, 1969). Repeated exposure to socially competent age-mates also had little apparent therapeutic success (Harlow, Dodsworth, & Harlow, 1965). In fact, such exposure may have actually exaggerated isolate disturbance behavior. By 6 months of age, well-socialized monkeys have developed complex patterns of social interaction, including vigorous play and socially directed aggression. They will typically attack any stranger monkey introduced to their social group, and only if the stranger reciprocates the attack will it be "accepted" and mutual play follow. The monkey that does not fight back continues to be the victim of aggression. In retrospect, it is not surprising that isolate-reared subjects were consistently attacked when exposed to well-socialized peers nor is it surprising that these isolates failed to exhibit significant social recovery.

However, there exist data suggesting that isolate-reared subjects may be responsive to certain social agents and that exposure to such agents may have positive therapeutic value. Isolate-reared mothers who eventually submitted to their infants' efforts to maintain ventral contact usually exhibited adequate maternal behavior toward subsequent offspring (Harlow & Harlow, 1968). Also, monkeys exposed to heated surrogates upon emergence from isolation showed significant decreases in disturbance behavior after contacting the surrogates. In neither case was social rehabilitation complete. The isolate mothers continued to exhibit incompetent sexual behavior, and the isolates exposed to surrogates failed to develop a sophisticated social repertoire.

It seems obvious that any experimental effort designed to rehabilitate isolates via social exposure requires effective social agents or "therapists." What types of monkeys could be appropriate therapists? In view of the above data, one might select animals who would predictably initiate social contact with an isolate without displaying social aggression, and who themselves would exhibit simple social responses which gradually would become more sophisticated. Such requirements are fulfilled by socially experienced monkeys only 3 or 4 months old, for at this age clinging responses still form an integral part of their social repertoire, play is the primary stage of development, and aggressive behavior has not yet matured. In accord with these fundamental social considerations, the following rehabilitation study was initiated.

METHOD

Subjects

Isolates. Isolate subjects were four male rhesus monkeys (Macaca mulatta) born within a 2-week period. They were separated from their mothers at birth and maintained in the laboratory nursery (see Blomquist & Harlow, 1961) until their mean age was 10 days, when they were placed in individual isolation chambers (see Rowland, 1964) which effectively denied them physical and visual access to all social agents. The isolate subjects remained in the chambers until their mean age was 6 months.

Therapists. Therapist subjects were four female rhesus monkeys, also born within a 2-week period, but 3 months subsequent to the isolates. They were separated from their mothers at birth and maintained in the laboratory nursery for the first 30 days. They were then placed in individual quadrants of a quad cage, described by Suomi and Harlow (1969), and each monkey was provided with a heated simplified surrogate (see Harlow & Suomi, 1970). In addition, the therapists were permitted 2 hours of mutual social interaction 5 days per week. During three sessions per week they interacted as pairs within the quad cage; during the remaining 2-hour sessions per week they interacted as a group of four in a social playroom, described by Rosenblum (1961).

Procedure

Postisolation base-line period. When the mean ages of the isolates and therapists were 6 and 3 months, respectively, the isolates were removed from their chambers. All subjects were then placed in individual quadrants of two quad cages, with two isolates and two therapists in each cage. The therapists retained their surrogates and continued to receive 2 hours of social interaction 5 days per week as described above, while the isolates were not permitted to interact socially with other monkeys or with surrogates. The postisolation base-line period lasted 2 weeks.

Postisolation therapy period. Immediately after the base-line period, the following therapy procedure was initiated: (a) In therapy weeks 1-4, each isolate was allowed to interact with the therapist monkey adjacent to its quadrant for 2 hours per day, 3 days per week. (b) In therapy weeks 5-6, pair interaction (one isolate-one therapist) continued as described in a. In addition, the isolates were placed in the playroom with the therapists 1 hours per day, 2 days per week, in groups of four (two isolates, two therapists). (c) In therapy weeks 7-11, pair interaction (one isolate-one therapist) was reduced to two 2-hour sessions per week. The playroom sessions were expanded to three 1-hour sessions per week. (d) In therapy weeks 12-26, pair interaction was discontinued and replaced by two 2-hour session per week during which time all four members of each quad cage (two isolates, two therapists) were permitted free interaction within the quad cage. Playroom interaction continued as in c.

To summarize, following removal from isolation, the isolates were housed individually for a period of 2 weeks in order to assess postisolation behavioral levels. Twenty-six weeks of therapy followed. The first 4 weeks of therapy consisted of isolate-therapist interaction within the quad cage. Beginning at the fifth week, the isolates were also permitted social interaction with therapist and with each other in the playroom.

Data Collection

Beginning at 30 days of age, every subject was observed for two 5-minute periods, 5 days per week. Subject behaviors falling into each of 14 categories were measured for presence or absence during each of the twenty 15-second intervals which comprised the 5-minute session. The following behavioral categories were employed: self-groom (discrete, self-directed picking and/or spreading of the fur), self-mouth (oral contact, exclusive of biting, with any part of own body), self-bite (specific, vigorous, self-directed biting), self-clasp (clasping of any part of own body with hand(s) and/or foot (feet)), huddle (self-enclosed, fetallike position, incorporating any or all patterns of self-clasp, self-embrace, or lowered head), rock (repetitive, nonlocomotive forward and backward movement), spasm (single or repetitive convulsive jerk involving a major part of the body), stereotypy (identical body movements maintained in a rhythmic and repetitive fashion for at least three cycles), locomotion (ambulation of one or more full steps), environmental exploration (tactual and/or oral manipulation by subject or inanimate objects), vocalization (any sound emitted by subject), ventral cling (contact of own ventral body surface with another subject and/or surrogate), social contact (tactual and/or oral contact with another subject and/or surrogate, exclusive of ventral cling or play), and play (any socially directed play activity, including rough and tumble, approach-withdraw, and non-contact play). For each observation session, data consisted of 14 modified frequency scores, one for every behavioral category, each representing the total number of 15-second intervals during which behavior encompassed by the category was observed.

The observations were made between 9:00 a.m. and 5:00 p.m. by one of four testers, each of whom had been trained to a rigorous laboratory reliability criterion prior to the beginning of the experiment. Each subject's two daily observations were distributed as follows:

For isolate subjects (a) at 1-6 months there were two observations of each subject in the isolation chamber; (b) at 6-6 1/2 months (postisolation base line) there were two observations of the subject in the individual quadrant of the quad cage; (c) at 6 1/2-12 1/2 months (therapy period) there was one observation of each subject in the individual quadrant of the quad cage and one observation of each subject in the social situation (either the quad cage or playroom) to which it had been assigned that day.

For therapist subjects at 1-9 1/2 months there was one observation of each subject in the individual quadrant of the quad cage, the other of the subject in the social situation (either the quad cage or playroom) to which it had been assigned that day.

Data Analysis

Inspection of the data indicated that behaviors encompassed by four categories--self-groom, self-bite, spasm, and vocalization--were infrequently exhibited by any subjects, and therefore these categories were not analyzed statistically. Subject scores of the remaining 10 categories--self-mouth, self-clasp, huddle, rock, stereotype, locomotion, environmental exploration, and the social categories of ventral cling, social contact, and play--were analyzed in three stages.

First, behaviors of all subjects were traced from the end of the first to the sixth months of life in order to assess isolation effects during the period of confinement. For each of the above seven non-social categories, individual subject scores were summed over three 7-week periods, representing behaviors observed from 30 to 80 days, from 80 to 130 days, and from 130 to 180 days of age. Category means for each subject were calculated for each time period, representing the average number of 15-second intervals per observation session during the time block that behaviors encompassed by the category were observed. For each category the above means were subjected to a two-way repeated-measures analysis of variance, with group (isolate versus therapist) as the independent variable and time block as the repeated measure. The means were then compared by use of Duncan's new multiple-range test (Duncan, 1955), employing the Time Block × Subjects Within Groups mean square from the analysis of variance as the test denominator variance term. For the sake of parsimony, only the results of the Duncan tests are presented in this article.

Second, behavioral levels exhibited by the isolate subjects during the 2-week postisolation base line were directly compared to those observed during the final 50 days of isolation in order to determine possible "emergence trauma" effects. Two-tailed t tests were employed, one for each of the above nonsocial categories, to test for differences between category means calculated for the two time periods.

Finally, behavioral changes transpiring during the therapy period were examined. Home-cage behaviors of each isolate and control subject were summed for every category over each of the three 60-day projects which comprised the therapy period. Category means were calculated for each subject as above, and the means were subject to two-way repeated-measures analyses of variance, with groups as the independent variable and time block as the repeated measure, then compared by use of Duncan tests. Behaviors recorded during the quad cage interaction periods and during the playroom interaction sessions were separately analyzed in a similar fashion.

Again, only the results of the Duncan tests are presented, although the complete analyses may be obtained from the authors upon request.

Results

Three unequivocal findings emerged from the data analysis. First, isolate subjects developed significant behavioral abnormalities during the period of social isolation. Second, the isolate subjects exhibited virtually no trace of "emergence trauma" upon removal from isolation. Third and most important, the isolates showed significant recovery, in terms of both nonsocial and social behaviors, in all testing situations during the course of the therapy period.

Isolation Period Behaviors

As shown by Table 1, which presents the group means obtained from isolation period observations and the results of the Duncan tests, during the first 2 months of life isolate and therapist monkeys failed to differ significantly on any measure except locomotion, with the isolates locomoting less than the controls ($p < .05$). During the third and fourth months, the only significant group difference was in self-mouthing, with the therapists exhibiting higher levels ($p < .05$). However, during the final 2 months of the isolation period marked behavioral differences between isolates and therapists became evident. The isolates exhibited significantly higher levels of self-clasping ($p < .01$), rocking ($p < .05$), and stereotypy ($p < .01$) than the therapists, changes which reflected increases over previous levels by the isolates rather than decreases by the therapists. These behaviors have consistently been found in the past to differentiate isolate-reared monkeys from more adequately socialized controls. During this time period the isolates also exhibited lower levels of exploration than the therapists ($p < .05$). Thus, although the analysis disclosed few differences between isolate and therapist levels of behavior early in life, by 6 months of age the isolates were clearly exhibiting gross behavioral abnormalities in comparison with their therapist controls.

Postisolation Base-Line Behaviors

Comparison of the isolates' postisolation behavioral levels with their counterparts during the immediately preceding isolation period gave little indication of significant change following removal from isolation. No significant differences for any category were disclosed by the t tests. Thus, the data failed to substantiate the occurrence of measurable emergence trauma among the isolate subjects in this experiment. Rather, the isolates' abnormal behaviors, having developed during the period of isolation, remained at existing levels when the monkeys were removed from isolation.

TABLE 1

DUNCAN TEST ANALYSIS FOR ISOLATION PERIOD

Category	I	T
Self-mouth		
Period 1	9.5	7.7
Period 2	7.4	10.7
Period 3	10.2	9.0
Self-clasp		
Period 1	.8	.1
Period 2	3.1	.5
Period 3	5.8	.7
Huddle		
Period 1	1.1	.6
Period 2	4.2	.7
Period 3	4.9	1.9
Rock		
Period 1	.1	.6
Period 2	.3	.6
Period 3	2.2	.4
Stereotypy		
Period 1	.2	.1
Period 2	1.2	.1
Period 3	2.6	.0
Locomotion		
Period 1	10.2	13.3
Period 2	11.4	13.4
Period 3	11.4	13.3
Environmental exploration		
Period 1	7.4	8.9
Period 2	8.6	10.9
Period 3	8.1	11.5

Note.—I = isolate subjects, T = therapist subjects; Period 1 = 30–80 days, Period 2 = 81–130 days, Period 3 = 131–180 days of age. Significant differences: Self-mouth—$T - 2 > T - 1, I - 2$, $p < .05$. Self-clasp—$I - 3 > I - 1, T - 1, T - 2, T - 3, p < .01$; $I - 3 > I - 2, p < .05$. Huddle—$I - 3 > I - 1, p < .05$. Rock—$I - 3 > I - 1, I - 2, T - 1, T - 2, T - 3, p < .05$. Stereotypy—$I - 3 > I - 1, T - 1, T - 2, T - 3, p < .01$; $I - 3 > I - 2, p < .05$; $I - 2 > T - 3, p < .05$. Locomotion—$I - 1 < T - 1, T - 2, T - 3, p < .05$. Environmental exploration—$T - 3 > T - 1, I - 1, I - 2, I - 3, p < .05$; $T - 2 > I - 1, p < .05$.

Therapy Period Behaviors

The data from all three testing situations offered convincing evidence that significant gains were achieved by the isolate subjects during the therapy period. When first removed from their isolation chambers they exhibited high levels of disturbance behaviors and low levels of social behaviors, typical for monkeys socially isolated for the first 6 months of life. By the end of the therapy period, however, their behavioral levels were virtually indistinguishable from those of the socially competent therapist monkeys.

Behavior during quad cage therapy. That the isolates exhibited significant recovery in the quad cage interaction situation during the therapy period was evident from the results of the appropriate Duncan tests, listed in Table 2. During the first 60 days of the therapy period, isolate subjects exhibited significantly higher levels of self-mouthing ($p < .05$), self-clasping ($p < .01$), huddling ($p < .05$), and rocking ($p < .05$) behaviors and lower levels of locomotion ($p < .05$), clinging ($p < .05$), social contact (p .01), and play (p .05) than the therapist monkeys. These differences disappeared as the therapy period progressed, largely resulting from changes in isolate rather than therapist levels of behavior. From the sixty-first to the one hundred and twentieth day of therapy the two groups of monkeys differed significantly only with respect to locomotion, with the isolates exhibiting lower levels ($p < .05$). During the final 60 days of the therapy period there were no significant group differences on any of the category measures in the quad cage interaction situation.

Behavior during playroom therapy. As in the quad cage interaction sessions, the isolate subjects exhibited significant behavioral recovery during the playroom therapy sessions. Initially in the playroom they showed significantly higher levels of self-mouth, self-clasp huddle, and rock and significantly lower levels of locomotion, exploration, clinging, social contact, and play than the therapist monkeys (all $ps < .01$). During the fifty-first to the one hundredth day of the therapy period detectable group differences vanished except for the categories of self-clasp, for which the isolates showed higher levels than the therapist ($p < .01$) and locomotion, clinging, and play, for which the therapists exhibited higher levels ($p < .05$, $p < .05$, and $p < .01$, respectively). During the final 50 days of playroom therapy the only category to yield significant group differences was self-clasp, with isolates showing higher levels ($p < .05$). These findings are summarized in Table 2, which indicates that the convergence of isolate-therapist behavioral levels over time resulted primarily from changes in isolate rather than therapist levels. Thus, although 9 behavior categories differentiated isolates from therapists during the first days of playroom therapy, the groups were behaviorally equivalent by the end of the therapy period save for the isolates' elevated levels of self-clasping, and for this behavior the isolates showed a significant decline during the therapy period (0-50 days of therapy > 51-100 days of therapy > 101-150 days of therapy, $ps < .01$).

Behavior in home quadrants. Except for the specific interaction sessions, all subjects were individually housed in quadrants of the quad cages during the 6 months of the therapy period. Analysis of home quadrant behavioral levels during this period indicated that the isolates' recovery in the presence of the therapist monkeys generalized to home-cage behaviors in the absence of physical contact with the therapists.

TABLE 2
Duncan Test Analyses for Quad Cage Therapy, Playroom Therapy, and Home Quadrant

Category	Quad cage therapy[a]		Playroom therapy[b]		Home quadrant behavior[c]	
	I	T	I	T	I	T
Self-mouth						
Period 1	7.8	6.1	5.9	2.6	12.2	10.3
Period 2	3.6	4.0	2.7	2.0	11.6	9.3
Period 3	3.1	4.0	2.2	1.3	9.7	8.8
Self-clasp						
Period 1	7.3	.2	15.9	.4	6.1	.7
Period 2	3.3	1.7	6.6	1.3	4.4	1.1
Period 3	2.6	.8	3.6	.4	3.3	2.3
Huddle						
Period 1	4.4	.1	4.7	.0	5.2	.3
Period 2	2.0	.0	2.1	.0	2.6	1.1
Period 3	.1	.0	.5	.0	.8	.9
Rock						
Period 1	2.7	.8	5.6	.2	2.7	.6
Period 2	.7	.3	2.7	.2	.8	.3
Period 3	.4	.2	1.2	.0	.3	.4
Stereotypy						
Period 1	.1	.0	.4	.0	1.8	.0
Period 2	.6	.0	.0	.0	.5	.0
Period 3	.4	.4	.0	.0	.2	.1
Locomotion						
Period 1	13.2	16.1	9.4	19.0	10.3	12.8
Period 2	15.4	19.2	15.1	18.9	12.6	13.0
Period 3	17.6	18.3	17.3	18.4	13.6	14.2
Environmental exploration						
Period 1	11.0	12.0	6.7	10.5	7.8	10.8
Period 2	9.7	9.1	9.2	11.3	9.8	10.3
Period 3	10.3	9.7	10.3	12.0	10.3	9.9
Ventral cling						
Period 1	.3	1.0	.3	2.0		
Period 2	.1	.6	.0	.8	—	—
Period 3	.0	.3	.0	.3		
Social contact						
Period 1	4.7	7.5	1.2	4.5		
Period 2	4.9	5.9	2.5	4.1	—	—
Period 3	6.0	5.4	2.8	2.8		
Play						
Period 1	3.6	6.6	1.1	3.6		
Period 2	6.1	7.0	3.9	5.3	—	—
Period 3	6.8	7.2	2.0	2.8		

[a] Period 1 = 1–60 days, Period 2 = 61–120 days, Period 3 = 121–180 days of therapy. Significant differences: Self-mouth—I − 1 > I − 2, I − 3, T − 2, T − 3, p < .01; I − 1 > T − 1, p < .05; T − 1 > I − 2, I − 3, T − 2, T − 3, p < .05. Self-clasp—I − 1 > I − 2, I − 3, T − 1, T − 2, T − 3, p < .01; I − 1 > T − 1, p < .05. Huddle—I − 1 > I − 3, T − 1, T − 2, T − 3, p < .05. Rock—I − 1 > I − 2, I − 3, T − 1, T − 2, T − 3, p < .05. Stereotypy—no significant differences. Locomotion—I − 1 < I − 3, T − 2, T − 3, p < .01; I − 1 < T − 1, p < .05; I − 2, T − 3, p < .05. Environmental exploration—no significant differences. Ventral cling—T − 1 > I − 1, I − 2, I − 3, p < .05. Social contact—I − 1 < T − 1, p < .01; I − 2 < T − 1, T − 2, p < .05; Play—I − 1 < I − 2, I − 3, T − 1, T − 2, T − 3, p < .01.

[b] Period 1 = 1–50 days, Period 2 = 51–100 days, Period 3 = 101–150 days of therapy. Significant differences: Self-mouth—I − 1 > I − 2, I − 3, T − 1, T − 2, T − 3, p < .01; T − 3 < T − 1, I − 2, p < .05. Self-clasp—I − 1 > I − 2, I − 3, T − 1, T − 2, T − 3, p < .01; I − 2 > T − 1, T − 2, T − 3, p < .05; I − 2 > I − 3, p < .05. Huddle—I − 1 > I − 3, T − 1, T − 2, T − 3, p < .01; I − 1 > I − 2, p < .05. Rock—I − 1 > I − 3, T − 1, T − 2, T − 3, p < .01; I − 1 > I − 2, p < .05. Stereotypy—no significant differences. Locomotion—I − 1 < I − 2, I − 3, T − 1, T − 2, T − 3, p < .01; T − 1, T − 2, p < .05. Environmental exploration—I − 1 < I − 3, T − 1, T − 2, T − 3, p < .01; I − 1 < I − 2, p < .05; T − 2 < T − 1, p < .05. Ventral cling—T − 1 > T − 2, T − 3, I − 1, I − 2, I − 3, p < .01; T − 2 > I − 2, I − 3, p < .05. Social contact—T − 1 > I − 1, p < .01; T − 1 > I − 3, T − 2, T − 3, p < .05; I − 1 < T − 2, T − 3, p < .05. Play—I − 1 < I − 2, T − 1, T − 2, p < .01; I − 1 < T − 3, p < .05; T − 2 > T − 1, T − 3, I − 1, I − 2, I − 3, p < .01.

[c] Period 1 = 1–60 days, Period 3 = 61–120 days, Period 3 = 121–180 days of therapy. Significant differences: Self-mouth—I − 1 > I − 3, T − 1, T − 2, T − 3, p < .05; I − 2 > I − 3, T − 2, T − 3, p < .05. Self-clasp—I − 1 > I − 2, I − 3, T − 1, T − 2, T − 3, p < .01; I − 3 > T − 1, T − 2, T − 3, p < .01; I − 3 > I − 1, I − 2, T − 1, T − 2, T − 3, p < .01; I − 1 > I − 2, p < .05. Huddle—I − 1 > I − 3, T − 1, T − 2, T − 3, p < .01; I − 1 > I − 2, p < .05. Rock—I − 1 > I − 2, I − 3, T − 1, T − 2, T − 3, p < .01. Stereotypy—I − 1 > I − 2, I − 3, T − 1, T − 2, T − 3, p < .01. Locomotion—I − 1 < T − 3, p < .01; I − 1 < I − 3, T − 1, T − 2, p < .05. Environmental exploration—I − 1 < I − 2, I − 3, T − 1, T − 2, T − 3, p < .01.

The analysis is summarized in Table 2.

During the first 60 days of the therapy period isolates displayed significantly higher levels of self-mouth ($p < .05$), self clasp ($p < .01$), huddle ($p < .01$), rock ($p < .01$), and stereotypy ($p < .01$) and significantly lower levels of locomotion ($p < .05$) and exploration ($p < .01$) than the therapist monkeys. During the middle 60 days of the therapy period, group differences were evident only for the behaviors of self-mouth ($p < .05$) and self-clasp ($p < .01$), with isolates exhibiting higher levels of both behaviors. During the final 60 days of the therapy period, no significant group differences for any category were disclosed by the analysis.

Discussion

The primary finding of this experiment was that monkeys reared in total social isolation for the first 6 months of life exhibited significant recovery of virtually all behavioral deficits across all testing situations after appropriate therapeutic treatment. Reversal of the isolation syndrome to an equivalent degree over such a range of situations had not been previously achieved or approached via any experimental procedures.

Some previous rehabilitative attempts used social agents but failed to reverse the isolation syndrome. We feel that the crucial factor for successful rehabilitation in the present study was intrinsic to the nature of the social agents employed. As well as the fact that they were members of the same species as the isolates, these agents were chosen specifically in terms of behaviors they could be predicted to exhibit consistently and spontaneously at appropriate stages of the therapy program. Behavioral predictions were based upon years of research examining the normal social development of the rhesus monkey.

A sequential, subjective account of the actual rehabilitative process early in the therapy period illustrates the appropriateness of the therapist choice. The isolate subjects did not exhibit spontaneous recovery during initial exposures to the younger, socially normal monkeys, a fact that is not surprising since no isolate monkey had shown spontaneous recovery in previous experimental situations. Rather, the therapist monkeys actively initiated the first social interactions, and only then did the isolates gradually exhibit improvement. Specifically, the therapist monkeys' initial responses to the isolates were to approach and cling, while the isolates were typically immobile and withdrawn. Only after clinging had been initiated did the isolates reciprocate, and only when the therapists had directed play responses toward the isolates did isolate play behavior emerge. Once these interaction patterns were established, the isolates themselves initiated play bouts with progressively increasing frequency.

Although the process of rehabilitation was essentially continuous, it is possible to delineate two stages of isolate recovery. The first stage involved breaking down previously established patterns of abnormal, self-directed behaviors such as self-huddling and stereotypic rocking. This was achieved primarily through the clinging efforts of the therapist monkeys. An isolate receiving intimate social contact cannot effectively continue to rock and self-huddle. The breaking down of entrenched self-directed activity permitted the isolate subjects to engage in alternative behaviors, which took the form of elementary social contact, exploration, and locomotion.

The second stage involved developing the simple behaviors described above into a more complex socially appropriate behavioral repertoire. Again, the therapists apparently provided the crucial stimulation as they themselves developed a complex social repertoire in the course of normal maturation. With respect to these behavior patterns, isolate recovery was substantial.

Previous rehabilitative attempts which initially exposed isolate subjects to complex social stimulation failed to break down self-directed activity exhibited by the isolates, and recovery did not follow. Also, exposure to a surrogate was demonstrated to reduce isolate disturbance behavior, but because a surrogate cannot provide complex social stimulation those isolate subjects never developed complex social behaviors in the presence of a surrogate. In contrast, the present study provided the isolate subjects with a set of social stimuli designed to reduce self-directed activity, followed by a set of stimuli gradually increasing in social sophistication. In this case, the same group of therapist monkeys provided both types of stimulation and provided them in the appropriate temporal sequence during the course of their own normal social maturation.

These results suggest that a reexamination of traditional theoretical interpretations of isolation-rearing effects is required. The data from the present study are inconsistent with a strict interpretation of the critical period position, which implies that once a so-called critical period has transpired without social stimulation, normal social behaviors can never develop. The present results yield empirical testimony that relatively normal social development can occur following 6 months of total social isolation from birth provided that the isolates are exposed to appropriately selected social stimulation. One can conclude that either the first 6 months of life do not constitute a critical period for socialization of the rhesus monkey or that strict critical periods do not exist for this species. We prefer the latter interpretation. While it is obvious from numerous researches that the first 6 months of life are indeed critical for socialization under usual circumstances, a more apt terminology for this chronological span might be "sensitive period" or "sensitive phase" (Hinde, 1966).

Also, the postisolation base-line data do not specifically support an emergence trauma interpretation of isolation-rearing effects. Rather, the monkeys socially isolated in this study had developed obvious behavioral anomalies prior to emergence, but the data analysis disclosed no significant increments in these abnormalities following emergence. We do not claim that emergence from isolation has no behavioral consequences. The actual analysis compared preemergence behavioral levels with those encompassing a 2-week period following removal from isolation and may well have masked actual effects exhibited during the initial postisolation hours. However, acknowledgement of behavioral changes resulting from shifts in the environment is a far cry from attribution of persisting behavioral deficiencies to the process of environmental change.

It is appropriate at this point to express a certain degree of caution regarding the findings of this study, particularly in light of the absence of a group of control isolate-reared monkeys not exposed to therapists, although, in a sense, a decade of isolation research using monkeys provides an impressive body of control data. The above procedures resulted in a reversal of the isolation syndrome during the course of the experiment. However, since the isolate subjects have not yet reached physical maturity, assessment of their adult social capability is not possible at the present time. Further, the exact procedure described above may not be appropriate for monkeys subjected to longer periods of social isolation, nor will the procedure necessarily be effective if not instituted soon after the period of isolation.

Nevertheless, the fact that the isolates in this study did show marked social gains suggests that the *potential* for adequate social development is not necessarily destroyed by the isolation experience. Rather, the actual relationship between isolation rearing and social behavior may, in fact, be similar to the relationship between isolation rearing and learning capability. Previous researches have demonstrated that while isolation produces performance deficits in learning situations, intellectual capability remains relatively intact in monkey subjects. Apparently, adequate adaptation is required for adequate performance. With respect to social behavior, it may well be that previous studies have reported performance deficits only, that social capability remains viable despite the isolation experience, and that the requirement for rehabilitation is merely appropriate social stimulation. If this finding generalizes not only to other forms of early experience but also to other species, then the implications of the present experimentation for reversal of psychopathological behavior attributed to inadequate early experience become enormous.

REFERENCES

Blomquist, A.J., & Harlow, H.F. The infant rhesus monkey program at the University of Wisconsin Primate Laboratory. *Proceedings of the Animal Care Panel*, 1962, 11, 57-64.

Boelkins, R.C. The development of social behavior in the infant rhesus monkey following a period of social isolation. Unpublished master's thesis, University of Wisconsin, 1963.

Clark, D.L. Immediate and delayed effects of early, intermediate, and late social isolation in the rhesus monkey. Unpublished doctoral dissertation, University of Wisconsin, 1968.

Duncan, D.B. Multiple range and multiple F tests. *Biometrics,* 1955, 11, 1-42.

Fuller, J.L., & Clark, L.D. Genetic and treatment factors modifying the postisolation syndrome in dogs. *Journal of Comparative and Psychological Psychology,* 1966, 61, 251-257.

Gluck, J.P. Successive acquisitions and extinctions of bar pressing: The effects of differential rearing in rhesus monkeys. Unpublished master's thesis, University of Wisconsin, 1970.

Griffin, G.A., & Harlow, H.F. Effects of three months of total social deprivation on social adjustment and learning in the rhesus monkey. *Child Development,* 1966, 37, 533-547.

Harlow, H.F., Dodsworth, R.O., & Harlow, M.K. Total social isolation in monkeys. *Proceedings of the National Academy of Sciences*, 1965, 54, 90-96.

Harlow, H.F., & Harlow, M.K. The effect of rearing conditions on behavior. *Bulletin of the Menninger Clinic,* 1962, 26, 213-224.

Harlow, H.F., & Harlow, M.K. Effects of various mother-infant relationships on rhesus monkey behaviors. In B.M. Foss (Ed.), *Determinants of infant behavior.* Vol. 4. London: Methuen, 1968.

Harlow, H.F., Harlow, M.K., Dodsworth, R.O., & Arling, G.L. Maternal behavior of rhesus monkeys deprived of mothering and peer associations in infancy. *Proceedings of the American Philosophical Society*, 1966, 110, 58-66.

Harlow, H.F., Schiltz, K.A., & Harlow, M.K. Effects of social isolation on the learning performance of rhesus monkeys. In C.R. Carpenter (ed.), *Proceedings of the Second International Congress of Primatology.* Vol. 1. New York: Karger, 1969.

Harlow, H.F., & Suomi, S.J. The nature of love--simplified. *American Psychologist,* 1970, 25, 161-168.

Hinde, R.A. *Animal behavior.* New York: McGraw Hill, 1966.

Lorenz, K. *Evolution and modification of behavior*. Chicago: University of Chicago Press, 1965.

Mason, W.A. Social development of rhesus monkeys with restricted social experience. *Perceptual and Motor Skills,* 1963, 16, 263-270.

Pratt, C.L. The developmental consequences of variations in early social stimulation. Unpublished doctoral dissertation, University of Wisconsin, 1969.

Rosenblum, L.A. The development of social behavior in the rhesus monkey. Unpublished doctoral dissertation. University of Wisconsin, 1961.

Rowland, G.L. The effects of total isolation upon learning and social behavior of rhesus monkeys. Unpublished doctoral dissertation, University of Wisconsin, 1964.

Sackett, G.P. Abnormal behavior in laboratory reared rhesus monkeys. In M.W. Fox (ed.), *Abnormal behavior in animals*. Philadelphia: Saunders, 1968. (a)

Sackett, G.P. The persistence of abnormal behavior in monkeys following isolation rearing. In R. Porter (Ed.), *The role of learning in psychotherpay*. London: Churchill, 1968. (b)

Scott, J.P. Critical periods in behavior development. *Science*, 1962, 138, 949-958.

Senko, M.G. The effects of early, intermediate, and late experiences upon adult macaque sexual behavior. Unpublished master's thesis, University of Wisconsin, 1966.

Singh, S.D. Urban monkeys. *Scientific American*, 1969, 221, 108-115.

Suomi, S.J., & Harlow, H.F. Apparatus conceptualization for psychopathological research in monkeys. *Behavioral Research Methods and Instrumentation,* 1969, 1, 247-250.

Intellectual and Adaptive Performance of Asian Children in Adoptive American Settings

E. Audrey Clark and Jeanette Hanisee

This study sought to determine the presence of developmental delay in adopted Asian children who had suffered disruptive early childhood experiences. The 25 pre-school-age subjects in the sample had been adopted from Southeast Asia. All were found to have experienced one or more forms of preadoptive deprivation. The Peabody Picture Vocabulary Test (PPVT) and the Vineland Social Maturity Scale (VSMS) were used to measure the children's levels of intellectual and social competence, respectively. The results indicate that the adopted Asian children exceed the performance levels established by the original standardization groups for the PPVT and VSMS at a highly significant level.

The United States is having a major influx of Asian refugees, including a number of children who have been adopted by American families. Most of these children have experienced separation, institutionalization, deprivation, or malnutrition, factors that have been associated with developmental delay. For this reason, some professionals and prospective parents fear that the adopted Asian child will not measure up to American peers.

Originally published in *Developmental Psychology*, 1982, 18, 595-599. Copyright ©1982 by the American Psychological Association. Reprinted by permission of the publisher and author.

It is not difficult to find support for this concern. The classic studies of Spitz (1945; Spitz & Wolf, 1946) supported the notion that institutionalization of infants and young children is likely to cause irreversible mental and emotional damage. Douglas (1975) found that prolonged or repeated hospital admission in early childhood was associated with later behavior disturbances. Bowlby's (1970) work suggested that maternal deprivation is profoundly detrimental to early development. In addition, malnutrition has been implicated in affecting early brain growth (Dobbing, 1970; Dobbing & Sands, 1973; Winick & Rosso, 1969). Clarke and Clarke (1976) wrote that the view that the early years of infant development are critical has become so widely accepted as to be implicit in the decision making of research workers and practioners alike.

Despite this barrage of pessimistic findings regarding the prognosis for children experiencing early social disruption, other evidence suggests that children can endure significant deprivation without permanent injury. Kagan and Klein (1973) indicated that even though children were stimulus deprived during their first years of life, they were able to perform competently by age 11. Skodak and Skeels (1949) found that white infants from low socioeconomic backgrounds showed substantial gains when placed in adoptive homes with upper income, educated parents. In their new environment, adoptees showed mental functioning that greatly surpassed that of their biological mothers.

Some of these more optimistic research findings have included Asian children. Scarr and Weinberg's (1976) research on the placement of black and interracial children (including eight Asian adoptees) in upper-middle-class, educated, white families supported the Skodak & Skeels (1949) study. The mental test scores of the adoptees were significantly higher (1 SD) than those of their nonadopted peers living with biological families in the same locale. Rathbun (1964/1976) investigated 33 foreign children adopted in the United States. This group of Greek, Korean, Japanese, Italian, Armenian, Austrian, and mixed-parentage children were found to be adequate or notably superior on measures of IQ and general competence 6 years after placement.

Furthermore, Winick, Meyer, and Harris (1975) found that a group of severely malnourished Korean children later placed in United States adoptive homes exceeded mean values of United States children on group intelligence tests. The severely malnourished group had a mean IQ score of 102. This is in contrast to a mean IQ of 58 found in a study of similarly malnourished children who were returned to their original home environments after hospitalization for malnutrition (Hertzig, Birch, Richardson, & Tizard, 1972). Clarke and Clarke (1976) concluded that most studies of children who have spent early lives in chaotic conditions indicate that these children turn out to be more "normal" or less "maladapted" than expected, if placed in better environments.

Few studies have dealt exclusively with Asian adoptees and have also included both measures of intelligence and adaptive behavior. This research sought to fill that gap by investigating the levels of intellectual and adaptive development of Asian children who had been placed in adoptive homes in the United States. It was reasoned that average or better performance in both areas would be substantial evidence that the children were not developmentally delayed. The research compared subjects' mean scores on the Peabody Picture Vocabulary Test (PPVT; Dunn, 1965) and the Vineland Social Maturity Scale (VSMS; Doll, 1965) with standardization data. Scores were also examined for differences associated with sex, age at time of placement and testing, presence of siblings in the home at time of placement, health history, number of foster placements, and length of stay in the adoptive home.

METHOD

Subjects

The sample of Asian adoptees was obtained by telephone through the membership lists of organizations for families with cross-racial adoptees. Part of the sample was referred by members of these organizations or by other contacts. Of the first 29 families contacted that seemed to fit the established criteria, 21 were members, 7 were referred by members, and 1 was referred by a personal contact of the researcher. One of the families later declined to participate for job-related reasons. Three other participants in the study were also eliminated due to inappropriate age, race, or length of placement. The final sample of 25 consisted of 11 boys and 14 girls (age range, 31-71 months; mean age, 44 months). There were 12 from Vietnam, 8 from Korea, 3 from Cambodia, and 2 from Thailand. All subjects had been placed in the adoptive home prior to 36 months of age and had been in the adoptive home a minimum of 23 months. (The range of time spent in the home was 23-57 months, with a mean of 33 months.) All subjects were in good health at the time of the study. All families were English-speaking United States citizens.

Test Instruments

The PPVT is a standardized picture-vocabulary intelligence measure that has been shown to correlate moderately well with measures such as the Stanford-Binet Intelligence Scale (Dunn, 1965). Hughes (1965) showed a positive correlation of the PPVT and the Wechsler Intelligence Scale for Children (WISC) among black and white rural children. Corwin (1965) found strong correlations between the PPVT and WISC with children of Mexican-American descent. She noted that children limited in Anglo cultural and language experience scored lower than nonlimited peers. Shotwell, O'Connor, Gabet, & Dingman (1969) recommended the PPVT for assessing mental ability while recognizing, however, its limitations for individual IQ prediction.

The PPVT was used because it is especially appropriate for the preschool child, requiring only the ability of the subject to see pictures, hear the examiner's request, interpret the meaning of the stimulus word, and point to the picture of choice. The examiner was experienced in administering the test to preschool children.

The VSMS is a measure of social competence obtained by interviewing the parent about the child's performance on a series of age-graded skills representative of activities of daily life. The expectation was that the inclusion of an adaptive measure would reduce penalties caused by sole reliance on a verbal measure of intelligence.

Procedure

Data were obtained from the administration of the PPVT (Dunn, 1965) and the VSMS (Doll, 1965), both of which are standardized measures. Twenty percent of the subjects from the original sample were randomly selected to be retested by a second interviewer after an interval of 6 months to establish reliability. In addition to the standardized instruments, two questionnaires were administered to parents of the subjects to gain information on background variables.

Two questionnaires were sent to the subjects' parents and were reviewed with the examiner on the examination dates. Questionnaire 1 provided information on the parents' age, income, education, language, and citizenship, as well as age and number of children in the home. Questionnaire II established the subjects' age, country of origin, health, length of placement, and background variables that might have affected development (health, hospitalization, institutionalization, foster care).

Means and standard deviations for these children were compared with those of the original standardization groups on the PPVT and VSMS. A matrix of correlations was prepared including age at adoption, age at testing, sex, preadoption health status, number of foster placements, number of months in the adoptive home, and PPVT and VSMS scores.

Assessments took place in the subject's home. The parent was interviewed with the VSMS, and the completed questionnaires were reviwed for accuracy and expansion. The PPVT (Form B) was then administered to the subject. Verification of the original results was attempted by randomly selecting 20% of the subjects from the original sample for retesting 6 months later by a second examiner. The PPVT alternate form (Form A) was administered at the retest, and the VSMS was readministered to the parents.

Results and Discussion

The histories of the subjects obtained from the adoptive parents included several factors that might have been predictive of delayed development. In terms of health, the prognosis for high scores was pessimistic. Sixteen of the subjects were reported to have been malnourished at some time during infancy. Fourteen of these were in sufficiently poor condition to have required hospitalization prior to or on arrival in the United States. The diagnosis included malnutrition, dehydration, muscle weakness, and in some cases pneumonia.

All of the subjects had experienced infant separation from their mothers and biological families. All had at one time lived in orphanages, foster homes, hospitals, or a combination of these. Most of the Vietnamese subjects were evacuated from Vietnam during the last stages of United States military involvement in 1975. There was little or no screening of adoptable versus unadoptable children at that time. The sample, therefore, may have included children with emotional and developmental disabilities.

The mean performance of the children on the PPVT was in the superior range (M = 120; SD = 16) when compared to Dunn's (1965) normative group (see Table 1).

Table 1

Performance of Asian Adoptees Compared to Standardization Groups on PPVT and VSMS

Subjects	*M* scores	*SD*	*t*(24)
PVVT			
Asian adoptees	120	16	6.11*
Standardization group	100	15	
VSMS			
Asian adoptees	137	20	9.06*
Standardization group	100	10	

Note. PVVT = Peabody Picture Vocabulary Test; VSMS = Vineland Social Maturity Scale. *N* (Asian adoptees) = 25.
* *p* < .001.

Individual scores ranged from 89 to 143. A t test comparing the subjects to the normative group was significant (p < .001). These scores on an English-language-based measure are remarkable in view of the background of the children, which included a late start in English language development.

The above-average scores obtained by the sample on the PPVT may be the result of the adoptive home environment. The adoptive families were highly educated and were higher than average in income and occupational status. Only 1 child was adopted into a family with an annual income of less than $15,000, whereas 11 were placed in families earning more than $25,000 per year (1978 figures). Both parents typically had college degrees. When employed, mothers of the subjects held jobs such as teachers, advanced clerical workers, and social workers. Fathers of adoptees were characteristically employed as engineers, ministers, and teachers.

The subjects' average score was in the superior range of the VSMS also (M = 137; SD = 20) (see Table 1). The range of scores was from 86 to 186. A t test for the mean difference groups was significant (p < .001). Performance on the VSMS was, in fact, relatively higher than performance on the PPVT. The first inclination was to attribute this to the one exceptionally high score. Even if this score were excluded, however, the mean would be 134.

The higher VSMS performance may be related to the many items at the pre-school-age level that are motor dependent. That is, social skill at this age is more closely related to both gross and fine motor development and coordination than it is at later age levels. Examples are skills such as buttoning, handling table utensils, and going up and down stairs. The examiner observed that the adopted Asian children seemed to be accelerated in motor development as compared with Anglo children of the same age. Parents reported that some of the subjects who as babies in institutions were too weak to sit had developed the capacity to pick up objects with their toes and transfer them to their hands. This would seem to constitute unusual motor skill, especially in view of the infants' already weakened condition.

The generally high scores of the group raised the question of whether or not the chaos surrounding the early lives of the children could have yielded underestimates of chronological age, which would have, in turn, been responsible for overestimation of competence. Examination of the data revealed that of 13 children whose birth dates were known, 10 were relinquished at birth to adoption agencies. Children with less-certain birth dates were those found abandoned during somewhat later infancy (3 to 12 months). Since most of the children were placed with social agencies early in life, there appears to have been relatively little opportunity for gross errors in age estimation.

Another explanation of the unusually high scores of the VSMS might be some sort of systematic bias by the sole interviewer. But retests of a small sample of the group 6 months later verified that these children were operating far above age expectations. The scores recorded by the second researcher were consistently higher than those obtained by the original investigator.

Another explanation of superior performance might be that the children were off-spring of better-than-average biogenetic stock. No known selection process was involved to lend substance to such a suspicion, but it cannot be ruled out. Perhaps less-strong babies perished before adoption was possible, given the grave environmental circumstances that prevailed. Likewise, even if superior biogenetics were implicated, they could not be attributed to any single racial or ethnic group. More likely, the infants represented a racial melange, with Asian origin their only real common bond.

Table 2

Pearson Correlation Coefficients Between Eight Variables Associated With Asian-Born Adoptees

Variable	1	2	3	4	5[a]	6[b]	7	8
1. Age at placement	—	.18	−.09	.16	.26	−.47*	−.11	−.12
2. Age at testing			.55	.05	.22	−.49*	−.18	−.01
3. Months since placement				−.05	−.06	−.27	−.05	−.05
4. Foster placements					−.04	.67*	.10	−.12
5. Sex						−.14	−.05	.55*
6. Health status							.27	.67*
7. PVVT								.20
8. VSMS								—

Note. PVVT = Peabody Picture Vocabulary Test; VSMS = Vineland Social Maturity Scale. $N = 25$.
[a] Males = 1; Females = 2.
[b] Well = 1; hospitalized = 2.
* $p < .05$.

No significant correlation was found between the subjects' scores on the PPVT and the VSMS (see Table 2), perhaps because the scores of the sample were concentrated in the upper end of the range.

Correlations revealed that children who had been hospitalized prior to adoption achieved higher scores on the VSMS than their counterparts ($r = .67$, $p < .01$) and that girls scored somewhat higher than boys ($r = .55$, $p < .01$). A history of hospitalization or sex was not significantly correlated with PPVT scores. Also, hospitalized children were both younger at time of placement and at time of testing than the group in its entirety.

Presence of older siblings in the home might have been expected to affect language acquisition. No support was found for this expectation. The chi-square test between scores obtained on the PPVT and VSMS and presence of siblings in the home at the time of placement indicated no significant differences.

When verification of results was attempted by reexamining a randomly selected portion of the original subjects, the Pearson product-moment correlation between the two examiners on the PPVT was .78. This corresponds closely to the correlation of .77 reported by Dunn (1965) for the two test forms. The test-retest correlation for the VSMS by the two examiners was .65. Test-retest correlations over a 6-month period for the VSMS standardization group are unavailable, but the 2-year test-retest correlation in the standardization is .57 (Doll, 1953).

Although the group that was reexamined was admittedly small, the data collected provided some assurance that the original results were not grossly in error. Examiners agreed that the group of Asian adoptees performed better than had the original normative groups.

It can be said of all scores and statistical data resulting from this study that no indication was present of a disabling developmental delay in the sample group of adopted Asian children. Performance on the PPVT and VSMS by the 25 Asian children adopted by American parents gives reason to believe that participation of subjects in normal family and school activities in this country should be successful. It can also be said that there was sufficient evidence present in the personal backgrounds of the subjects to justify developmental delay had it occurred. The results tend to substantiate the observations of Clarke and Clarke (1976) and others, who have noted the resiliency of children who have suffered seemingly great environmental damage.

REFERENCES

Bowlby, J. Disruption of affectional bonds and its effects on behavior. *Journal of Contemporary Psychotherapy,* 1970, 2(2), 75-86.

Clarke, A.M., & Clarke, A.D.B. *Early experience: Myth and evidence.* New York: Free Press, 1976.

Corwin, B.J. The influence of cultural and language on performance of individual ability tests. *Journal of School Psychology,* 1965, 3(3), 41-47.

Dobbing, J. Undernutrition and the developing brain. *American Journal of Diseases of Children*, 1970, 120, 411-415.

Dobbing, J., & Sands, J. Quantitative growth and development of the human brain. *Archives of Disease in Childhood*, 1973, 48, 757-767.

Doll, E.A. *The measurement of social competence.* Minneapolis: Educational Publishers, 1953.

Doll, E.A. *Vineland Social Maturity Scale.* Circle Pines, Minn.: American Guidance Service, 1965.

Douglas, J.W.B. Early hospital admissions and later disturbances of behavior and learning. *Developmental Medicine and Child Neurology,* 1975, 17, 456-480.

Dunn, L.M. *Peabody Picture Vocabulary Test.* Circle Pines, Minn.: American Guidance Service, 1965.

Hertzig, M.E., Birch, H.G., Richardson, S.A., & Tizard J. Intellectual levels of school children severely malnourished during the first two years of life. *Pediatrics,* 1972, 49, 814-824.

Hughes, R.B. A comparison of WISC and Peabody scores of Negro and white rural school children. *American Journal of Mental Deficiency,* 1965, 69, 877-880.

Kagan, J., & Klein, R.E. Cross-cultural perspectives on early development. *American Psychologist,* 1973, 28, 947-961.

Rathburn, C. Untitled study, 1964. In A.M. Clarke & A.D.B. Clarke (Eds.), *Early experience: Myth and evidence.* New York: Free Press, 1976.

Runyon, R., & Haber, A. *Fundamentals of behavioral statistics* (2nd ed.). Reading, Mass.: Addison-Wesley, 1971.

Scarr, S., & Weinberg, R.A. IQ test performance of black children adopted by white families. *American Psychologist,* 1976, 10, 726-739.

Shotwell, A.M., O'Connor, G., Gabet, Y., & Dingman, H.F. Relation of the Peabody Picture Vocabulary Test IQ to the Stanford-Binet IQ. *American Journal of Mental Deficiency,* 1969, 74, 39-42.

Skodak, M., & Skeels, H.M. A final follow-up study of one hundred adopted children. *Journal of Genetic Psychology,* 1949, 75, 85-125.

Spitz, R.A. Hospitalism: An inquiry into the genesis of psychiatric conditions in early childhood. *The Psychoanalytic Study of the Child,* 1945, 1, 53-74.

Spitz, R.A., & Wolf, K.M. Anaclitic depression: vol. 2. An inquiry into the genesis of psychiatric conditions in early childhood. *The Psychoanalytic Study of the Child,* 1946, 2, 313-342.

Winick, M., Meyer, K.K., & Harris, R.C. Malnutrition and environmental enrichment by early adoption. *Science*, 1975, 190, 1173-1175.

Winick, M., & Rosso, P. The effect of severe early malnutrition on cellular growth of human brain. *Pediatric Research*, 1969, 3(2), 181-184.

Fetal Malnutrition:
An Experimental Study of Its Consequences on Infant Development in Two Caregiving Environments

Philip Sanford Zeskind and Craig T. Ramey

The consequences of early malnutrition on human behavior have been the concern of those interested in shaping social policy and of those interested in understanding fundamental processes of development. Although a substantial amount of research has been directed toward the effects of infantile malnutrition on subsequent intellectual and social development (for reviews, see Birch 1972; Kaplan 1972; Lester 1977), a general paucity of experimental-manipulative study characterizes the work on the consequences of fetal malnourishment.

An infant may be born already malnourished if it receives insufficient supplies of essential nutrients in utero because of inadequate maternal diet. This malnourishment may also occur if placental transport is impaired or if the fetus incorrectly metabolizes

Originally published in *Child Development*, 1978, 49, 1155-1162. Copyright ©1978 by the Society for Research in Child Development, Inc.; reprinted with permission of the publisher and author.

available nutrients (Birch 1971). Traditionally, the nutritional status of the newborn has been determined by comparing the birthweight of the baby with norms established for similar babies of the same gestational age (Lubchenco, Hansman, Dressler, & Boyd 1963). The term "small-for-date" has been used to describe the infant whose birth weight is below the tenth percentile for its gestational age and who is considered fetally malnourished (Birch 1971). Another measure of fetal growth and nutrition is Rohrer's ponderal index, or PI (in Brazelton, Parker, & Zuckerman 1976), a ratio of birth weight (in grams) $\times 100$/the cube of crown-heel birth length (in centimeters). A weight-length ratio of less than 2.17 for the 37-week gestation baby and 2.20 for the baby of 38 weeks' gestation or greater usually signifies a late gestational nutritional deficiency (Brazelton et al. 1976) and has been used in the diagnosis of fetal malnutrition to identify those full-term infants who are at or below the the third percentile of weight-length norms (Miller & Hassanenin 1971, 1973). Unlike the weight-for-age norms, this index of fetal malnutrition is relatively independent of the sex, race, and parity of the baby and the physical size of the mother.

Both the weight-height and weight-for-age norms have been predictive of specific behavioral characteristics that may differentiate the fetally malnourished from well-nourished newborn. For example, fetally malnourished newborns show deficits in a number of basic reflexes by small-for-date (Michaelis, Shulte, & Nolte 1970) and low PI (Als, Tronick, Adamson, & Brazelton 1976) criteria. When evaluated on the Brazelton Neonatal Behavioral Assessment Scale (Brazelton 1973) both small-for-date (Lester & Zeskind, in press) and low-PI newborns (Als et al. 1976; Lester & Zeskind, in press; Lestern, Note 1) make poor use of available stimulation and have deficient social interactive behaviors. Further, the spectrum analyses of the cry sounds of both small-for-date (Lester & Zewskind, in prss; Zeskind & Stern, Note 2) and low-PI (Lester & Zeskind, in press; Lester, Note 1) newborns show a number of acoustic and temporal deviations (including an unusual, high pitch) when compared with control infants. These behavioral characteristics have led to the description of the fetally malnourished infant as generally apathetic, unresponsive to environmental stimuli, and irritable when aroused (Als et al. 1976; Birch 1971).

Studies of the more long-term consequences of being small-for-date have shown standardized intelligence-score deficits (Weiner 1970), special educational needs (Rubin, Rosenblatt & Balow 1973), and poor intellectual performances (Fitzhardinge & Steven 1972; Stimmler 1970) of the target infants at school age. However, the severity of the deficit has been shown to be a function of the level of the infant's socioeconomic status (Birch 1971; Drillien 1970) since severely economically impoverished home environments are generally nonsupportive of optimal intellectual development (Heber, Dever, & Conry 1968).

These differential outcomes associated with socioeconomic status levels underscore the need for more than a linear model of development that emphasizes the one-to-one relation between anthropometric signs of fetal malnourishment and poor developmental outcome. According to a transactional model of development (e.g., Sameroff & Chandler 1975), the detrimental effects of prenatal nutrition may be maintained or exacerbated in a "nonsupportive" caregiving environment, yet may be ameliorated in a caregiving environment that is "supportive" of optimal development. Essential features of this organismic view of development are the bidirectional nature of the forces regulating development and the dynamic quality of both the infant and environment. Specifically, environmental forces act upon the infant to change its behavioral propensities during development. The resulting developmental changes in behavioral repertoire act to alter the environment that is encountered during the next infant-environment interaction. Thus, one must examine not only the caregiver's contribution to the quality of the caregiver-child interaction but also the status of the infant as a demand characteristic to which the caregiver responds (Bell 1968, 1971). To the extent that fetal malnourishment is associated with differing demand characteristics, one would expect that fetally malnourished babies would be treated differently by their primary caregivers than babies who are not fetally malnourished. Further, fetally malnourished babies reared in a caregiving environment that does not attenuate deletious demand characteristics should have less supportive mother-infant interaction patterns over time than infants reared in an environment designed to successfully alter those deleterious demand characteristics independently of the mother.

Although Lester (Note 1) has described this synergistic relation between the fetally malnourished infant and its caregiving environment, the influence of the postnatal caregiving environment on the infant's development and how the infant's changing status affects the nature of that caregiving environment have yet to be experimentally demonstrated. For example, the differential outcomes of fetally malnourished infants from different socioeconomic status levels may be more than the products of the supportive or nonsupportive postnatal caregiving environments in which the infants develop. Other pediatric risk factors that may prenatally influence developmental outcome, such as a lack of prenatal care or a poor obstetric history, are more highly related to lower socioeconomic status levels than higher ones (Birch & Gussow 1970). Further, in assessing the impact of the developing infant on the caregiving environment, unless fetally malnourished infants have been randomly assigned to two environments--one in which recovery is expected and another in which the detrimental effects of fetal malnourishment are expected to be maintained--a change in the nature of the caregiver's behavior in one group could be interpreted as the cause, rather than the result, of the infant's changing demand characteristics. Of course, ethical considerations preclude placing infants in an environment that is known to be nonsupportive of optimal development.

One way to demonstrate the usefulness of a transactional model would be to select infants from a low socioeconomic status background, a background in which the detrimental effects of fetal malnourishment are expected to be maintained, and to place some of these infants in an experimental treatment program designed to be supportive of optimal intellectual development. Although the program to be described below was not constituted primarily to test the interaction between prenatal and postnatal risk factors, the random assignment of infants from a very low socioeconomic status background to an instructional day-care program or to a nonintervention home-control group (enrichment vs. nonenrichment) fulfilled the criteria for a natural experiment. The purpose of this longitudinal study was to examine the predictive utility of anthropometric characteristics at birth for an infant's intellectual development in what may be considered supportive and nonsupportive postnatal caregiving environments. The early detrimental effects of fetal malnourishment were expected to be ameliorated in the day-care environment yet maintained in the high-risk home environment. Further, we believed that the lasting detrimental effects of fetal malnutrition would feed back and affect the nature of the caregiving environment.

Method

Subjects. Subjects were chosen from participants involved in a longitudinal educational program designed to prevent socioculturally caused mental retardation. Program participants were chosen for their high risk status as defined by a number of criteria indicating very low socioeconomic status (Ramey & Smith 1977). After infants were born, families qualified to join the program were first pair matched as closely as possible on a number of variables and then assigned randomly to either an educational day-care program or a nonintervention control group. The variables used for the matching procedure were the total score of socioeconomic risk indicators from a high-risk index[1], *maternal IQ, number of siblings, and sex of the infant. All infants in the program were black.*

The intent of the day-care program was to provide conditions that would be supportive of optimal intellectual and social development. Intervention began before the age of 3 months and included social work, medical and nutritional services, and an educational curriculum. Children attended the program approximately 8 hours per day, 5 days per week, 50 weeks per year. At the day-care center the educational curriculum stressed the development of basic language and cognitive skills and social cooperation. The control infants received similar social work and medical and nutri-

---

1   The high-risk index described by Ramey and Smith (1977) contains
    sociodemographic factors which have been assigned weights arbitrarily. Scores
    on this index can range from 0 to 50

tional services but did not attend the day-care center's educational program. For a more complete description of the day-care center, a number of publications detail the operations and educational curricula of the program (Ramey, Collier, Sparling, Loda, Campbell, Ingram, & Finkelstein 1976; Ramey, Holmberg, Sparling, & Collier 1977) and the nature of the program's social environment (Finkelstein, Dent, Gallacher, & Ramey 1978).

Criteria for inclusion in this study were based on the absence of several pediatric risk indicators. We selected only those infants who were full term and full birth weight, had both 1- and 5-min Apgar scores of 7 or greater, and had no serious prenatal and perinatal complications. The anthropometric characteristics available on the birth records were used to calculate the ponderal indices for each of these babies. We excluded infants who had ponderal indices above the ninety-seventh percentile (3.0) since this high ponderal index may be related to other pediatric risk conditions. After this selection process was completed the day-care-center and home control groups were still very comparable on the total score of high-risk index (experimental: mean X = 18.7, SD = 4.3; control: mean X = 22.5, SD = 6.6Z), maternal IQ (experimental: mean X = 87.5, SD = 9.4; control: mean X = 82.6, SD = 13.1), number of siblings (experimental: mean X = .43, SD = .92; control: mean X = .60, SD = 1.2), and sex

TABLE 1

MEANS AND SDs OF GESTATION AGES AND ANTHROPOMETRIC BIRTH CHARACTERISTICS

	GESTATIONAL AGE (Weeks)		BIRTH WEIGHT (g)		BIRTH LENGTH (cm)		PONDERAL INDEX	
GROUP	$\bar{X}$	SD	$\bar{X}$	SD	$\bar{X}$	SD	$\bar{X}$	SD
Center:								
Low PI........	39	1.4	2,908	379	51.8	1.6	2.08	.10
Normal PI.....	39.9	1.4	3,295	502	50.5	2.2	2.54	.20
Control:								
Low PI........	40.4	.89	2,834	163	51.1	1.1	2.12	.03
Normal PI.......	40.3	1.20	3,394	381	50.6	1.9	2.63	.17

of the infant (experimental percentage female = 51.3; control percentage female = 52.5). Five infants were identified in both the center and home groups as having ponderal indices at or below the third percentile. Four groups were thus determined: (1) 17 well-nourished and (2) 5 fetally malnourished infants involved in the early intervention program, and (3) 15 well-nourished and (4) 5 fetally malnourished infants in the home control group. Table 1 contains the means and standard deviations of the gestational ages and anthropometric characteristics of these four groups.

Procedure.

Infants were tested in a standardized laboratory setting on the Bayley Scales of Infant Development at 3 and 18 months of age and on the Stanford-Binet intelligence test at 24 months of age. For this study the Mental Development Index (MDI) subscale of the Bayley test was analyzed. These standardized indices of intellectual performance offered scores that could be compared with other studies of the consequences of fetal malnourishment.

Because we were interested in the effects of fetal malnutrition on the caregiver's

TABLE 2
MEANS AND SDs OF STANDARDIZED TEST SCORES

Group	BAYLEY MDI 3 MONTHS		BAYLEY MDI 18 MONTHS		STANFORD-BINET 24 MONTHS	
	$\bar{X}$	SD	$\bar{X}$	SD	$\bar{X}$	SD
Center:						
Low PI..........	92.5	2.5	104.4	9.0	95.8	9.6
Normal PI........	100.9	11.7	105.5	13.9	94.8	10.7
Control:						
Low PI..........	91.2	3.5	86.8	3.8	77.8	2.3
Normal PI.......	96.9	9.7	93.3	13.1	83.9	8.1

[2] Calculations of degrees of freedom in t tests with separate variance estimates often result in different degrees of freedom in each of the tests (Hays 1973).

behavioral interaction with the infant, assessments of maternal involvement with the subjects were made with the aid of the Maternal Involvement subscale of the Home Observation for Measurement of the Environment (HOME) developed by Caldwell, Heider, and Kaplan (Note 3). Observations were made in the home when infants were 6 and 18 months of age. All intelligence and maternal involvement assessments were made by examiners who were unaware of the infant's prenatal nourishment condition.

Results and Discussion

Intelligence. Table 2 contains the means and standard deviations of the Bayley

MDI scores at 3 and 18 months of age and the Stanford-Binet scores at 24 months of age for low-and normal-PI infants under two different environmental conditions. One-tailed t tests were performed on the standardized test scores for each of the four groups at each assessment occasion. Separate variance estimates were used to calculate the t's if tests of homogeneity of variance showed that the group variances differed significantly.[2]

At 3 months of age, the low-PI infants showed lower MDI scores than the normal-PI infants in both the control group, $t(18) = 1.93$, $p < .04$, and the center group, $t(18) = 2.63$, $p < .01$. At this assessment occasion no differences were evidenced between the control and center groups for either the low- or normal-PI groups. Based on these data we suggest that the control and center groups were similar on MDI measures within the low-PI and normal-PI groups, and that infants with low ponderal indices had significantly lower Bayley MDI scores than infants with normal ponderal indices as early as 3 months of age.

The difference in MDI scores between low- and normal-PI infants in the home control group continued to exist at the 18-month assessment, $t(18) = 1.71$, $p < .05$. However, after the day-care infants had participated in the center program for more than 15 months, the difference between the low- and normal-PI infants disappeared, $t(20) = .16$, $p < .45$. Whereas the two low-PI groups (center and control) did not differ at 3 months of age, at 18 months the low-PI infants in the center environment showed higher MDI scores than their counterparts in the control environment, $t(8) = 4.01$, $p < .002$. Similarly, the normal-PI infants in the day-care environment had higher MDI scores than normal-PI infants in the control group at 18 months of age, $t(30) = 2.55$, $p < .008$. Based on the finding that the normal-PI infants in day care showed higher test scores than normal-PI infants in the control group, we suggest that the influences of the day-care environment were supportive of intellectual development relative to the influences of the low socioeconomic status home environments. In other words, the differences that characterized the fetally malnourished infants at 3 months of age were ameliorated in the supportive environment of an enriched day-care program yet were maintained in the nonsupportive high-risk home environment.

The 18-month assessment findings were replicated at 24 months with measures on the Stanford-Binet scale. One-tailed t tests showed that although the low- and nor-

---

2   Calculations of degrees of freedom in t tests with separate variances estimates often result in different degrees of freedom in each of the tests (Hays 1973)

TABLE 3

MEASURES OF MATERNAL INVOLVEMENT
AT 6 AND 18 MONTHS OF AGE

	6 MONTHS		18 MONTHS	
GROUP	$\bar{X}$	SD	$\bar{X}$	SD
Center:				
Low PI.........	4.2	1.8	3.0	1.6
Normal PI.......	3.5	1.3	3.1	1.3
Control:				
Low PI.........	3.0	1.2	1.6	.5
Normal PI......	3.6	1.7	2.7	1.5

mal-PI groups could not be differentiated in the day-care sample, t(20) = .18, p < .43, fetally malnourished infants showed lower Stanford-Binet scores than the normal-PI infants within the control group sample, t(18) = 2.63, p < .008. The day-care infants had higher scores than control infants in both the low-PI, t(4) = 4.08, p < .008, and normal-PI groups, t(30) = 3.21, p < .001.

Maternal involvement.. Table 3 contains the means and standard deviations of the Maternal Involvement subscale of the HOME Inventory for the low-and normal-PI infants in the center and control groups at 6 and 18 months. One-tailed t tests showed no differences in the amount of maternal involvement with the infants between any of the groups at 6 months of age. At the 18-month assessment occasion mothers of the low-PI infants in the non-intervention group showed significantly less maternal involvement with their children than mothers of the normal-PI infants in the non-intervention group, t(18) = 2.43, p < .01, and mothers of the low-PI infants in the center group t(8) = 1.87, p < .05. No other differences between groups were found at the 18-month assessment. Thus, although the mothers in the four groups showed similar amounts of involvement with their infants at 6 months of age, the mothers of those fetally malnourished babies who still showed the effects of the fetal malnourishment at 18 months of age showed less involvement with their babies than the mothers in the other groups. To the extent that the random assignment of babies to the two caregiving environments resulted in comparable group qualities of maternal style, it is reasonable to suggest that the persevering detrimental effects of fetal malnourishment, reflected in lower MDI scores, affected the quality of care the baby received.

Previous studies on the interaction of newborn characteristics and environmental influences have tended to use differing socioeconomic status levels to represent environments varying in supportiveness (e.g., in Sameroff & Chandler 1975). The present study was concerned with the experimental manipulation of postnatal environmental factors on the development of fetally malnourished infants, all of whom were of very low socioeconomic status. These findings indicate that the detrimental effects of fetal malnourishment on intellectual performance may be found as early as 3 months of age, may be ameliorated in a supportive environment by 18 months of age, and may be maintained in a nonsupportive environment until at least 2 years of age.

How can we best explain these differential outcomes of the day-care and control low-PI infants? One suggestion is that by modifying growth and chemical maturation of the brain during the rapid brain growth of the last trimester of pregnancy (Dobbing 1970) fetal malnourishment directly affects intellectual competency. However, the nature of the direct relation between structural insult to the central nervous system due to inadequate nutrition and subsequent intellectual capacity remains to be adequately delineated. In addition, according to the logic of this direct causation model, the differential outcome of the two fetally malnourished infant groups would be the result of a persevering condition of postnatal malnourishment in the low-PI infants of the control group relative to the experimental group. However, when the babies were 18 months of age, a comparison of the norms of the weight-height percentiles established by the National Center for Health Statistics (1976) showed that the low-PI infants in the control group (mean $X = 61$, SD $= 42.6$) actually had higher rankings than the low-PI infants in the experimental group (mean $X = 40$, SD $= 22.4$), $t(8) = 5.6$, $p < .001$.

Birch (1971) proposed an alternative model which emphasizes a more indirect, functional relation between fetal malnutrition and an infant's intellectual development. According to his model, a lower IQ score is only one measure of the fetally malnourished infant's impoverished functional relation with its environment. Projected into a more general model of the development of the infant born at risk, these functional relations may be manifested in the transactions between the infant and its caregiving environment (Sameroff & Chandler 1975). The developmental outcome of an infant is not implicit in the infant or the environment exclusively; rather, it is a result of how the characteristics of the infant and environment continually alter one another throughout the process of development. These transactions begin prenatally and include the complex relations among the developing organism and both the intrauterine and extrauterine environments (Gottlieb 1976). Postnatally, the transactions continue as the effects of the baby's behaviors on the caregiving environment operate as a function of that envoronment's supportive or nonsupportive characteristics. The response of the environment to the baby affects the process of the baby's recovery and thus its subsequent behavior (Sameroff & Chandler 1975).

Although the transactional nature of the relationship between infant and environment is implicit in an organismic approach to development, there is little available experimental evidence for these processes in human infancy. At this time we can only speculate about how some of the behaviors characteristic of the fetally malnourished infant may transact with the caregiving environment. For example, the full-term yet fetally malnourished baby shows poor use of stimulation and has deficient social interaction processes as measured by the Brazelton Scale (Als et al. 1976; Lester & Zeskind, in press; Lester, Note 1). Poorly responsive infants, as determined by this scale, may have caregivers who are less responsive and sensitive to the baby's actions (Field 1977; Osofsky 1976). Pollitt (1973) has suggested that in an economically stressed home mothers may respond to a lethargic, malnourished infant by showing withdrawal and neglect. Further, the high-pitched cry characteristic of the low-PI baby (Lester & Zeskind, in press, Lester, Note 1) may be more distressing, grating, and aversive to listeners when compared with normal cry sounds but may also be perceived as a signal that the infant is "sick" (Zeskind & Lester 1978). These perceptions may provide a basis for differential responses to fetally malnourished infants, depending on the supportive or nonsupportive nature of the caregiving environment (Zeskind, Note 4). Ultimately, the nature of the caregiver's responsiveness to the baby's social behaviors may be related to the infant's Bayley mental scores (e.g., Clarke-Stewart 1973).

The findings of this longitudinal study may be explained by this infant-environment transactional model. For this investigation we chose only those babies who were full term and full birth weight and who showed no major abnormal clincial signs at birth other than the ponderal indices we calculated. However, the expectations of the caregivers for a healthy baby may have been violated. In an economically stressed home, an environment which was nonsupportive of optimal intellectual growth even with well-nourished babies, the mothers of socially unresponsive infants who have aversive, grating, and distressing cry sounds may have become less involved with their infants than mothers of normal-PI infants. Without supportive care, the low-PI baby may have continued to be unresponsive to the social environment and to have a grating cry sound. Over a time of continued unresponsivity the caregiver may have withdrawn, and a cycle of unresponsive infant-environment transactions may have developed.

In the day-care center's environment the cycle may never have been established. The day-care center's program is designed to provide an environment which is responsive to the baby's needs. The environmental responsivity ranges from proper nutritional and health care to a professional concern for affection and education. In this supportive environment, a poorly responsive infant with a "sick"-sounding cry may have elicited special care and attention. As the initially stressed infant recovered its behavioral organization may have improved, resulting in improved social interaction process (Als, Tronick, Lester, & Brazelton 1977) and an amelioration of the distressing qualities of the baby's cry sound (Lester & Zeskind 1979; Zeskind, Note 4). Without the baby's continued unresponsivity and aversive cry the caregiver, at home, may continue to be as involved with her infant as other caregivers of the same socioeconomic status.

In summary, we have presented some experimental longitudinal evidence of the transactional nature of the development of the infant born at risk. Specifically, the outcome of the infant who shows anthropometric signs of fetal malnourishment is a function of the supportive qualities of the infant's caregiving environment, an environment to which the infant itself contributes. Future study of the functional consequences of the infant's behaviors in caregiving environments varying in supportiveness may lead to understanding the basic processes involved in the nonoptimal development of some infants who are born at risk.

Reference Notes

1. Lester, B.M. Maternal nutrition and fetal outcome. In F. Rebelsky (Chair), The pollution of the fetus. Symposium presented at the meeting of the American Psychological Association, San Francisco, August 1977.

2. Zeksind, P.S., & Stern, K. Acoustic analysis of the cry response. In B.M. Lester (Chair), Influences on the behavior of the newborn. Symposium presented at the meeting of the Southeastern Psychological Association, Atlanta, March 1975.

3. Caldwell, B.; Heider, J.; & Kaplan, B. The inventory of home stimulation. Paper presented at the meeting of the American Psychological Association, New York, 1966.

4. Zeskind, P.S. Beyond a sign of pathology: a functional perspective of the cry sound of the risk infant. Paper presented at the meeting of the Southeastern Conference on Human Development: A Regional Convention of the Society for Research in Child Development, Atlanta, April 1978.

References

Als, H.; Tronick, E.; Adamson, L; & Brazelton, T.B. The behavior of the full-term yet underweight newborn infant. *Developmental Medicine and Child Neurology*, 1976, 18, 590-602.

Als, H.; Tronick, E.; Lester, B.M.; & Brazelton, T.B. The Brazelton Neonatal Behavioral Assessment Scale (BNBAS). *Journal of Abnormal Child Psychology*, 1977, 5, 215-231.

Bell, R.Q. A reinterpretation of the direction of effects in studies of socialization. *Psychological Review*, 1968, 75, 81-95.

Bell, R.Q. Stimulus control of caretaker behavior by offspring. *Developmental Psychology* 1971, 4, 63-72.

Birch, H.G. Functional effects of fetal malnutrition. *Hospital Practice*, 1971, March, 134-148.

Birch, H.G. Malnutrition, learning, and intelligence. *American Journal of Public Health*, 1972, 62, 773-784.

Birch, H.G., & Gussow, J.D. *Disadvantaged children: health, nutrition, and school failure.* New York: Harcourt, Brace, & World; Grune & Stratton, 1970.

Brazelton, T.B. *Neonatal Behavioral Assessment Scale.* Philadelphia: Lippincott, 1973.

Brazelton, T.B.; Parker, W.B.; & Zuckerman, B. Importance of behavioral assessment of the neonate. In L. Gluck (Ed.), *Current problems in pediatrics.* Chicago: Year Book Medical Publishers, 1976.

Clarke-Stewart, K.A. Interactions between mothers and their children: characteristics and consequences. *Monographs of the Society for Research in Child Development,* 1973, 38(6-7, Serial No. 153).

Dobbing, J. Undernutrition and the developing brain. In W. Himwich (Ed.), *Developmental neurology.* Springfield, Ill.: Thomas, 1970.

Drillien, C.M. Intellectual sequelae of fetal malnutrition. In H.A. Waisman & G.R. Kerr (Eds.), *Fetal growth and development.* New York: McGraw-Hill, 1970.

Field, T.M. The effects of early separation, interactive deficits, and experimental manipulations of infant-mother face-to-face interaction. *Child Development,* 1977, 48, 763-771.

Finkelstein, N.W.; Dent, C.; Gallacher, K.; & Ramey, C.T. Social behaviors of infants and toddlers in a day-care environment. *Developmental Psychology,* 1978, 14(3), 257-262.

Fitzhardinge, P.M., & Steven, E.M. The small-for-date infant, II: Neurological and intellectual sequelae. *Pediatrics,* 1972, 50, 50-57.

Gottlieb, G. Conceptions of prenatal development: behavioral embryology. *Psychological Review,* 1976, 83(3), 215-234.

Hays, W.L. *Statistics for the social sciences* (2d ed.), New York: Holt, Rinehart & Winston, 1973.

Heber, R.F.; Dever, R.B.; & Conry, J. The influence of development. In H.J. Prehm, L.A. Hamerlynck, & J.E. Crossen (Eds.), *Behavioral research in mental retardation.* Eugene: University of Oregon Press, 1968.

Kaplan, B.J. Malnutrition and mental deficiency. *Psychological Bulletin,* 1972, 78(5), 321-334.

Lester, B.M. The consequences of infantile malnutrition. In H.E. Fitzgerald and J.P. McKinney (Eds.), *Developmental psychology: studies in human development.* Homewood, Ill.: Dorsey, 1977.

Lester, B.M., Zeskind, P.S. The organization of crying in the infant at risk. In T.M. Field, A.M. Sostek, S. Goldberg, & H.H. Shuman (Eds.), *Infants born at risk.* New York: Spectrum, 1979.

Lester, B.M., & Zeskind, P.S. Brazelton scale and physical size correlates of neonatal cry features. *Infant Behavior and Development*, in press.

Lubchenco, L.D.; Hansman, C.; Dressler, M.; & Boyd, E. Intrauterine growth as estimated from live-born birth-weight data at 24 to 42 weeks of gestation. *Pediatrics*, 1963, 32, 793-800.

Michaelis, R.; Shulte, F.J.; & Nolte, R. Motor behavior of small-for-gestational age newborn infants. *Journal of Pediatrics,* 1970, 76, 208-213.

Miller, H.C., & Hassanein, K. Diagnosis of impaired fetal growth in newborn infants. *Pediatrics,* 1971, 48, 511-522.

Miller, H.C., & Hassanein, K. Fetal malnutrition in white newborn infants: maternal factors. *Pediatrics*, 1973, 52, 504-522.

National Center for Health Statistics. NCHS growth charts, 1976. *Monthly Vital Statistics Report,* 1976, 25(3, suppl.). Rockville, Md.: Health Resources Administration.

Osofsky, J. Neonatal characteristics and mother-infant interaction in two observational situations. *Child Development,* 1976, 47, 1138-1147.

Pollitt, E. Behavior of infant in causation of nutritional marasmus. *American Journal of Clinical Nutrition,* 1973, 26, 264-270.

Ramey, C.T.; Collier, A.; Sparling, J.J.; Loda, F.A.; Campbell, F.A.; Ingram, D.L.; & Finkelstein, N.W. The Carolina Abecedarian Project: a longitudinal and multi-disciplinary approach to the prevention of mental retardation. In T.D. Tjossem (Ed.), Intervention strategies for high risk infants and young children. Baltimore: University Park Press, 1976.

Ramey, C.T.; Holmberg, M.; Sparling, J.H.; & Collier, A.M. An introduction to the Carolina Abecedarian Project. In B.M. Caldwell & D. J. Stedman (Eds.), *Infant education: a guide for helping handicapped children in the first three years*. New York: Walker, 1977.

Ramey, C.T., & Smith, B.J. Assessing intellectual consequences of early intervention with high-risk infants. *American Journal of Mental Deficiency,* 1977 81(4), 318-324.

Rubin, R.; Rosenblatt, C.; & Balow, B. Psychological and educational sequelae of prematurity. *Pediatrics,* 1973, 52, 352-363.

Sameroff, A., & Chandler, M.J. Reproductive risk and the continuum of caretaking casualty. In F.D. Horowitz (Ed.), *Review of child development research*. Vol. 4. Chicago: Unviersity of Chicago Press, 1975.

Stimmler, L. Infants who are small-for-gestational age. *Proceedings of the Royal Society of Medicine*, 1970, 63, 500-501.

Weiner, G. The relationship of birth weight and length of gestation to intellectual development at ages 8 to 10 years. *Journal of Pediatrics,* 1970, 76, 694-699.

Zeskind, P.S., & Lester, B.M. Acoustic features and auditory perceptions of the cries of newborns with prenatal and perinatal complications. *Child Development,* 1978, 49(3), 580-589.

Effects on Perceptual Development of Visual Deprivation during Infancy

Terri L. Lewis, Daphne Maurer, and Henry P. Brent

SUMMARY   We measured three aspects of vision in children treated for unilateral congenital cataract: visual resolution, the symmetry of optokinetic nystagmus (OKN), and peripheral vision. Good visual resolution was achieved by children who had had the earliest treatment and who had had the normal eye patched close to 50% of the waking time throughout early childhood. All children treated for unilateral congenital cataract showed a marked asymmetry of OKN regardless of the age of treatment. One child with early treatment who could be tested with the Goldmann perimeter also showed especially poor sensitivity in the nasal visual field in her aphakic eye. We found no such deficits in the vision of children who had had normal visual experience during early infancy and then later developed cataracts in one or both eyes. The limitations observed in children treated for congenital cataract are similar to those reported in nor-

Originally published in *British Journal of Ophthalmology*, 1986, 70, 214-220. Copyright ©1987 by the British Medical Association; reprinted with permission of the publisher and author.

mal human infants, in normal kittens, and in cats which were visually deprived early in life.

Much of what we know about the effects of visual deprivation comes from studies of cats which had one eye sutured shut during a critical period shortly after birth. Such cats later show limitations in many aspects of vision, including visual resolution[1], peripheral vision (reviewed by Maurer and Lewis[2]), and the symmetry of optokinetic nystagmus[3][4]. These three aspects of vision are also poorly developed in normal kittens[5-8] and in normal human infants[9-11].

We were interested in determining whether monocular deprivation during early infancy affects the development of these abilities in humans as it does in cats. To do so we turned to a population of children who had been born with a dense, central cataract in one eye. (This condition is similar to lid suture in cats because only diffuse light passes through the cataract.) The cataract had been treated surgically by removing the natural lens of the eye, rendering the eye aphakic. The aphakic eye was fitted with a contact lens which restored nearly normal visual input. Parents were then instructed to patch the normal eye 50% of the waking time. We measured three aspects of vision in these children: visual resolution, the symmetry of optokinetic nystagmus (OKN), and peripheral vision.

Experiment I. Visual Resolution

Visual resolution has been tested both in normal kittens and in normal human infants by showing subjects black-and-white stripes of varying width paired with a grey stimulus of the same mean luminance. The width of the smallest stripes chosen over grey provides a measure of visual resolution. Numerous studies have shown that visual resolution is poorly developed at birth both in cats and in humans[10].

Adult cats which had been monocularly deprived for a period after birth also show poor visual resolution in the previously deprived eye. The best visual resolution achieved depends on the *duration* of deprivation such that, the longer the deprivation, the poorer the visual resolution[1]. However, the visual resolution of the formerly deprived eye can be improved if the normal eye is sewn shut when the deprived eye is opened[1], a procedure called reverse-suturing. The visual resolution of visually deprived cats also depends on the *timing* of deprivation. Giffin and Mitchell[5] demonstrated this in cats which were monocularly deprived for 23 days beginning at 42, 64, or 87 days of age. Only the cats which had been monocularly deprived from 42 days of age failed to recover normal visual resolution in the deprived eye. Thus in cats the effect of deprivation on the development of visual resolution depends on when the deprivation begins, how long it lasts, and whether or not reverse-suturing occurs. The purpose of the first experiment was to determine whether similar principles apply to humans who had been monocularly deprived.

MATERIALS AND METHODS

We measured the Snellen acuity of 13 children who had been deprived from birth for varying periods of time because of a dense and central congenital cataract in one eye (congenital group). For comparison we measured the Snellen acuity of 30 children who had had normal visual experience until an injury caused a dense central cataract to develop in one eye sometime after the age of 3 years (traumatic group). During the Snellen test the aphakic eyes were corrected optically to focus at infinity.

RESULTS AND DISCUSSION

Fig. 1 shows the Snellen acuity of the deprived eye for the congenital group plotted as a function of duration of deprivation, that is, the time from birth until the cataract was removed surgically and the aphakic eye fitted with an appropriate contact lens. The two children who had had the shortest periods of deprivation and who had had the normal eye patched close to 50% of the waking time throughout early childhood had the best Snellen acuities (6/12 and 6/15). The remaining 11 children

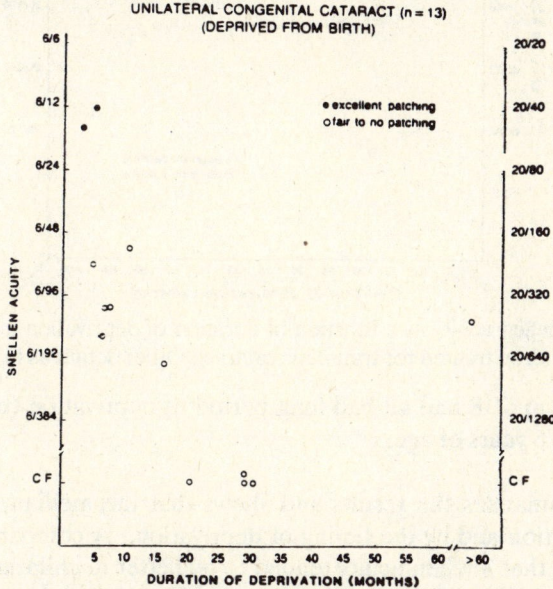

Fig 1. Snellen acuity as a function of duration of deprivation in the aphakic eye of children treated for unilateral congenital cataract. Snellen acuities are shown in metres on the left axis and in feet on the right axis. Filled circles represent the results from children who had the normal eye patch close to 50% of the waking time throughout early childhood. Open circles represent results from children who did not.

who had poorer Snellen acuities had had longer periods of deprivation and/or little or no patching of the normal eye.

Fig. 2 shows the Snellen acuity of the deprived eye for the traumatic group plotted as a function of duration of deprivation, that is, the time from when the cataract was first diagnosed as dense and central until the cataract was removed surgically and the aphakic eye fitted with an appropriate contact lens. All but five children had Snellen acuities of at least 6/18, regardless of the duration of deprivation and regardless of whether or not they had patched the normal eye. The five children with Snellen

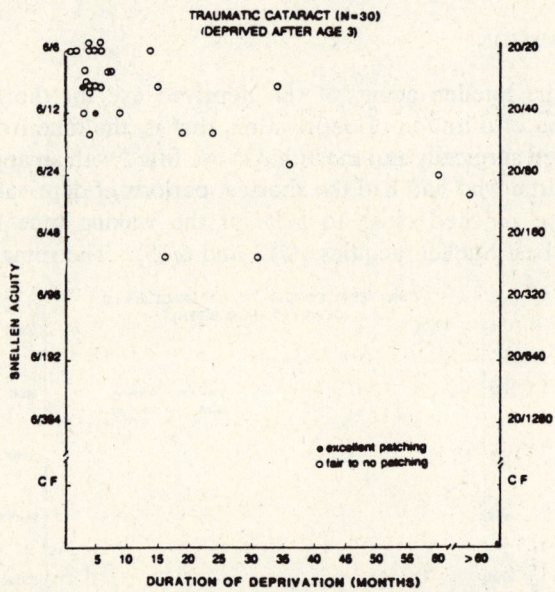

Fig 2. Snellen acuity as a function of duration of deprivation in the aphakic eye of children treated for traumatic cataract. Other details as in Fig. 1.

acuities worse than 6/18 had all had long period of deprivation (more than one year) beginning before 6 years of age.

Table 1 summarises the results and shows that the median acuity is influenced both by the duration and by the timing of deprivation. A comparison of the columns in Table 1 shows that Snellen acuity tended to be better in children who had had relatively short periods of deprivation (less than six months) than in children who had had longer periods of deprivation. A comparison of the rows in Table 1 shows that Snellen acuity tended to be better in children deprived after 3 years of age than in those deprived from birth. Moreover, there appears to be an interaction between duration and timing of deprivation such that the worst acuities were shown by children who had had long periods of deprivation beginning at birth. What is not illustrated in Table 1 is that

	Duration of deprivation	
	<6 months	*≥6 months*
Deprivation beginning from birth (congenital cataract)	6/15	6/190
Deprivation later (traumatic cataract)		
Beginning age 3 to 6	6/10·5	6/24
Beginning after age 6	6/7·5	6/8

Table 1. Median acuity as a function of duration and timing of deprivation.

the potentially poor outcome of early deprivation can be tempered by regular patching of the normal eye.

In summary, our results from tests of Snellen acuity show that visual deprivation during infancy does not prevent the development of good visual resolution, provided the deprivation is short and provided that, following the deprivation, the normal eye is patched regularly. Deprivation at a later age does not lead to the same deficiencies. These results are similar to those from monocularly deprived cats.

Experiment II. Symmetry of optokinetic nystagmus

A second aspect of vision measured in monocularly deprived children was the symmetry of optokinetic nystagmus. OKN is a series of jerky eye movements elicited by a repetitive pattern moving across the visual field. Thus the eyes follow a part of the pattern (slow phase) and then saccade back to pick up another part (fast phase). In normal adult humans and cats OKN can be elicited easily both when stripes move from the temporal visual field toward the nasal field (for example, from right to left for the right eye) and when they move from the nasal visual field towards the temporal visual field (for example, from left to right for the right eye)[12 13]. Thus their OKN is 'symmetrical'. In contrast, young human infants and kittens show consistent OKN when stripes move temporally to nasally but little or no OKN when stripes move in the opposite direction.[6 8 9 14-16] We refer to this difference in the ease of eliciting OKN in the two directions as 'asymmetrical OKN'.

Like human newborn babies and kittens, cats which were monocularly deprived shortly after birth also show asymmetrical OKN[3 4 17]. Moreover, this asymmetry is present both in the previously deprived eye and in the non-deprived eye[3 4 17] (but see Malach et al.[6]). To determine whether deprivation affects similarly the symmetry of OKN in humans monocularly deprived from birth, we tested children treated for a dense unilateral congenital cataract (congenital group). For comparison, we also tested normal subjects and children who had had normal visual experience until they incurred a traumatic cataract sometime after 3 years of age (traumatic group).

MATERIALS AND METHODS

The congenital group consisted of 17 children who had had a dense central cataract diagnosed in one eye at a median age of 2 months (range birth to 6 months). The cataract had been removed surgically at a median age of 5.5 months (range 2 to 28 months) and the aphakic eye fitted with an appropriate contact lens at a median age of 9 months (range 3 to 29 months). At the time of the asymmetry test the children ranged in age from 1 to 13 years (median = 5 years). Refractive errors ranged from +2.0 D to +24.75 D (median = +16.5) in the aphakic eyes and from plano to +3.0 D (median = plano) in the normal eyes. For the eight children old enough to read an eye chart Snellen acuities ranged from 6/12 to merely light perception (median = 6/60) in the aphakic eyes and from 6/6 to 6/7.5 (median = 6/6) in the normal eyes. We tested the normal eye of all 17 children but were able to test only six aphakic eyes primarily because of latent nystagmus in many cases.

The traumatic group consisted of 13 children who had incurred a dense cataract at a median age of 8.5 years (range 3 to 13 years). The cataracts had been removed surgically at a median age of 9 years (range 3 to 13 years), and the aphakic eyes had been fitted with an appropriate contact lens at a median age of 9 years (range 3 to 14 years). The median duration of deprivation was five months (range 1 to 34 months). At the time of the asymmetry test the median age of this group was 12 years (range 3 to 17 years). Their refractive errors ranged from +10.5 D to +17.5 D (median = +14.0 D) in the aphakic eye and from plano to -1.0 D (median = plano) in the normal eye. The 12 children old enough to read an eye chart had Snellen acuities ranging from 6/6 to 6/30 (median = 6/12) in the aphakic eye and from 6/6 to 6/9 (median = 6/6) in the normal eye. We tested the aphakic eye of all 13 children and the normal eye of eight.

The normal subjects (n = 26) ranged in age from 1 year to adulthood (median age = 4 years). We tested the right eye of half the subjects and the left eye of the other half.

For the OKN test each subject had one eye occluded and sat 50 cm from a 90° x 90° rear projection screen surrounded by black plywood. Black-and-white vertical stripes (0.6 cycles/deg) were swept across the screen at a velocity of 13 deg/s by a 35 mm slide projector projecting through a rotating mirror. Shielded peepholes on either side of the screen permitted a clear view of the subject's unoccluded eye, but not of the stimuli. The test included 39 randomly ordered 7 s trials: 15 trials with stripes moving temporally to nasally, 15 trials with stripes moving nasally to temporally, and 9 control trials with a moving blank field. An observer decided during each trial whether OKN definitely occurred, possibly occurred, or definitely did not occur.

RESULTS AND DISCUSSION

The observer never reported definite OKN when the field was blank except during one trial for one subject.

For each eye, we used a two-tailed χ^2 test to compare the frequency of trials on which OKN definitely occurred when stripes moved temporally to nasally versus the frequency when stripes moved nasally to temporally. Fig. 3 shows the difference between these two frequencies for each eye tested. A positive difference score means that definite OKN was observed on a greater proportion of trials when stripes moved temporally to nasally than when they moved nasally to temporally. Conversely, a negative difference score means that OKN was observed on a greater proportion of trials when stripes moved nasally to temporally than when they moved temporally to nasally. An asterisk indicates that a difference was significant by the χ^2 test (that is, asym-

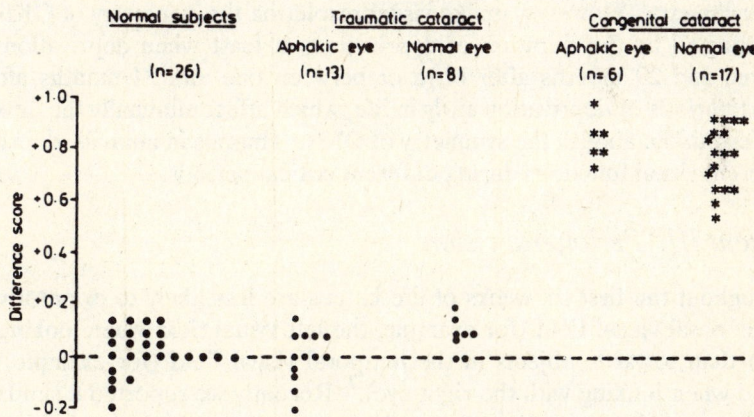

Fig. 3. Asymmetry of OKN in three groups of subjects. See text for details.

metrical OKN) and a dot indicates that a difference was not significant (that is, symmetrical OKN).

In normal subjects and in both eyes of children treated for traumatic cataract definite OKN was observed on virtually every experimental trial. Thus their difference scores tended to cluster around zero, and in no case was there a significant asymmetry by the χ^2 test (see Fig. 3). In contrast for the congenital group definite OKN was observed on most trials when stripes moved temporally to nasally but on few trials when stripes moved nasally to temporally. Thus in this group all the difference scores were positive and the asymmetry was significant by the χ^2 test in every aphakic and normal eye tested. The magnitude of the asymmetry was not related to the duration of deprivation nor the patching regimen. Children who had had early treatment and aggressive patching of the normal eye had asymmetries just as large as those who had had later treatment with little or no patching of the normal eye.

Factors other than early pattern deprivation per se might have contributed to the observed asymmetries. For example, asymmetrical OKN has been reported in subjects with amblyopia,[13 14] with estropia,[13 14 16] or with reduced stereopsis for whatever reason.[13] However, none of these factors was more common in children in the congenital group, all of whom showed asymmetrical OKN, than in children in the traumatic group, none of whom showed asymmetrical OKN.

Like our findings for visual resolution the timing of deprivation appears to affect the development of symmetrical OKN. Children deprived from birth showed a marked asymmetry of OKN, but those deprived after 3 years of age showed no such marked asymmetry. However, unlike visual resolution the symmetry of OKN appears to be unaffected by the duration of deprivation, at least when deprivation lasts between three and 29 months after birth or between one and 34 months after age 3. Even short periods of deprivation early in life, which affect minimally the development of visual resolution, abolish the symmetry of OKN. Thus, as in animals, deprivation affects different visual functions during different critical periods.

Experiment III. Peripheral vision

Throughout the first six weeks of life kittens are less likely to orient towards objects in the nasal visual field (for example, the left visual field when looking with the right eye) than towards objects in the temporal visual field (for example, the right visual field when looking with the right eye).[7] Recently we reported a similar pattern of results in young human infants shown lines of varying width located either at 30° in the temporal visual field or at 20° in the nasal visual field.[11] We assumed that, if infants could see a line, they would look towards it more often than they looked in the same direction on control trials when the field was blank. When lines were located at 30 in the temporal visual field 1-month-old infants detected the narrowest line we presented, a line only 1.5° wide. In contrast, when lines were located at 20° in the nasal visual field, they detected a 'line' 25.6° wide but showed no evidence of detecting a line even 12.8° wide. Thus 1-month-olds show at least an eightfold difference in the size of line they can detect at those locations. Normal adults on the other hand are *better* at detecting objects located at 20° in the nasal visual field than objects located at 30° in the temporal visual field.[18]

Cats which were monocularly deprived during a critical period shortly after birth, like young human infants and kittens, are especially poor at detecting stimuli in the nasal visual field of the deprived eye[7] reviewed by Maurer and Lewis.[2] To determine whether monocular deprivation has similar effects in humans we used the Goldmann perimeter to measure sensitivity along the horizontal meridian in one child treated for a unilateral congenital cataract. For comparison we also tested a child with no known eye disorders and children who had normal visual experience until they developed cataracts in one or both eyes.

MATERIALS AND METHOD

Two subjects, A and B, were tested extensively. Patient A was a 12-year-old child who had had a dense central cataract diagnosed in her left eye by 3 months of age. The cataract was removed at 4 1/2 months and the aphakic eye fitted with a contact lens at 5 months. Subsequently her normal eye had been patched at least 50% of the waking time throughout early childhood, and at the time of the perimetry test she had 6/12 acuity in her aphakic eye and 6/6 acuity in her normal eye. Patient B was a 13-year-old child with 6/6 vision in each eye and no known eye problems. Five additional eyes from four children were tested less extensively by perimetry. All of these children had had normal visual experience and then developed dense, central cataracts in one eye or both eyes. Three of these patients had had developmental cataracts and one a traumatic cataract. Other details are listed in Table 3.

We used the Goldmann perimeter to test each eye of patient A with a 6.25 min spot of light (object I) and with a 13 min spot of light (object II) every 10° along the horizontal meridian from 30 to 60° in the temporal visual field, and from 10 to 60° in the nasal visual field. For comparison we tested one eye of patient B with a 6.25 min spot of light at the same locations. The remaining subjects were tested only at 30° in the temporal visual field and at 20° in the nasal visual field. In each case the subject's task was to identify the one of two 2 s intervals during which a spot of light had appeared. At each location we used a staircase to determine the intensity at which the subject could identify the correct interval 75% of the time (PEST with W = 1, initial step size = 1 log ml; final step size = 0.05 log ml).[19]

RESULTS AND DISCUSSION

The results for patients A and B are shown in Figs. 4 (6.25 min spot) and 5 (13 min spot). At every location A required more intensity to detect light with her aphakic eye than with her normal eye, which gave results similar to those from the normal control subject, B. Table 2 summarises the threshold intensities for patients A and B at 20° in the nasal visual field and at 30° in the temporal visual field, the locations we had tested in normal 1-month-olds.[11] Like patient B and like normal adults,[18] A's normal eye had lower thresholds at 20° in the nasal visual field than at 30°

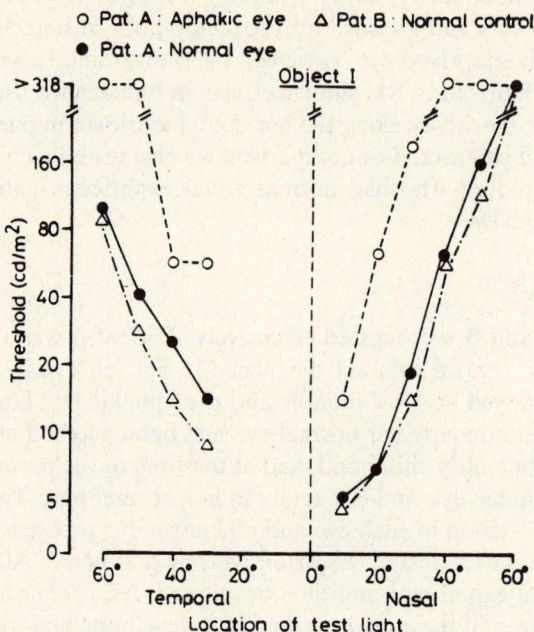

Fig. 4. The threshold luminance for detecting a 6.25 min spot of light (object 1) at various locations along the horizontal meridian for the aphakic and normal eyes of patient A, who was treated for a unilateral congenital cataract, and for one eye of patient B, who had no eye disorders. We did not test 20° in the temporal visual field because the blind spot interferes with the detection of small targets at that location.

Subject	Condition	Object size	Threshold (cd/m²)	
			20° Nasal	30° Temporal
A	Aphakic eye	I	63·5	56·6
		II	22·5	8·5
A	Normal eye	I	7·1	14·2
		II	<4·0	4·8
B	Normal	I	7·1	9·0

Table 2. Threshold intensities for patient A (treated for unilateral congenital cataract) and B (normal control subject) at 20° in the nasal visual field and at 30° in the temporal visual field.

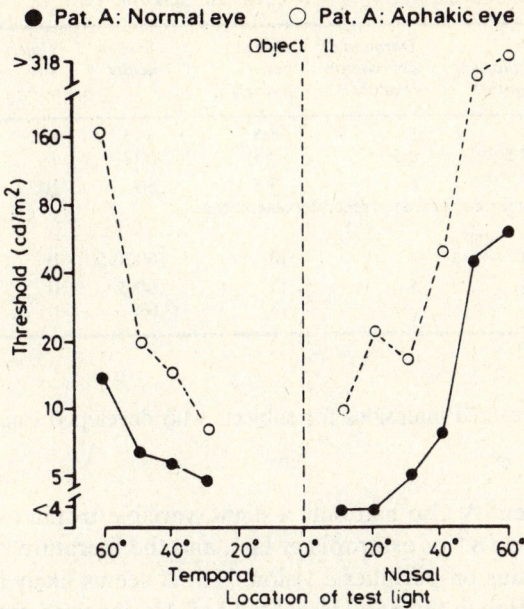

Fig. 5. The threshold luminance for detecting a 13 min spot of light (object II) at various locations along the horizontal meridian for the aphakic and normal eyes of patient A. Other details in Fig. 4.

in the temporal visual field. In contrast, unlike normal adults but like normal 1-month-olds, A's aphakic eye had *higher* thresholds at 20° in the nasal visual field than at 30° in the temporal visual field.

Table 3 lists thresholds for lights at those locations in the children who had had normal visual experience until they later developed cataracts. In every case threshold intensity at 20° in the nasal field was equal to, or lower than, threshold intensity at 30° in the temporal field. This pattern is like that of normal adults and very different from the pattern we observed in the aphakic eye of patient A, the child treated for a unilateral congenital cataract. It is evident that aphakia per se does not account for greater threshold elevation (that is, lower sensitivity) in the nasal as compared with the temporal field.

It is also unlikely that associated problems such as amblyopia or strabismus accounted for the results. Patient A had achieved 6/12 vision in her aphakic eye and showed especially poor detection in the nasal visual field, while one child in the control group (patient E) who had only 6/120 vision in her aphakic eye showed no such

Table 3   *Threshold intensities for subjects who developed cataracts after birth*

Subject	Condition	Age of diagnosis (months)	Duration of deprivation (months)	Age at test (years)	Snellen acuity	Object size	Threshold (cd/m²)	
							20° Nasal	30° Temporal
C	Dev OD[1]	12	5	8·5	6/15	I	28·4	56·6
	Dev OS	7·5	6·5	8·5	6/12	I	14·2	112·9
D	Dev OD	17	6	7·5	6/9	III	4·5	89·7
	Dev OS	Not tested because of secondary membrane						
E	Normal OD	Not tested						
	Dev OS	20	4	10	6/120	II	28·4	35·7
F	Traum OD[2]	145	5	13	6/7·5	II	5·7	5·7
	Normal OS	—	—	13	6/6	II	<4·0	4·5

[1]Developmental cataract.
[2]Traumatic cataract.

Table 3.   Threshold intensities for subjects who developed cataracts after birth.

nasal field loss. Patient A also had only a slight, variable tropia (4^Δ esotropia to 6^Δ exotropia at near; 6^Δ to 8^Δ of exotropia at far), and the literature suggests no consistent effect of strabismus on peripheral vision.[20-22] It seems likely that our finding of especially poor detection in the nasal visual field of A's deprived eye is related at least in part to the visual deprivation caused by a congenital cataract. If that is the case, then early visual deprivation affects the development of humans' visual fields in much the same way it affects the development of kittens' visual fields. In both cats and humans deprivation depresses sensitivity in the nasal visual field, so that, like the young human infant or the young kitten, the deprived eye is less sensitive to stimuli in the nasal field than at corresponding locations in the temporal field.

Conclusions

We have discussed three aspects of vision which are incompletely developed at birth in cats and in humans: visual resolution, the symmetry of OKN, and peripheral vision. In cats these abilities are adversely affected by monocular deprivation early in life. Thus after such deprivation visual resolution is reduced, OKN is asymmetrical, and cats fail to orient toward objects in the nasal visual field. After short periods of deprivation, some of these effects are reversible, especially if the normal eye is then sutured shut. Deprivation at a later age does not lead to the same deficiencies. Our results so far suggest that these same principles apply in humans who have been visually deprived in one eye during early infancy by the presence of a dense central cataract.

References

1. Mitchell DE. Sensitive periods in visual development. In: Aslin RN, Alberts JR, Petersen MR eds. *Development of perception: 2: The visual system.* New York: Academic Press, 1981:3-39.

2. Maurer D, Lewis TL. A physiological explanation of infants' early visual development. *Can J Psychol* 1979; 33:232-52.

3. Van Hof-van Duin J. Early and permanent effects of monocular deprivation on pattern discrimination and visuomotor behaviour in cats. *Brain Res* 1976; 111:261-76.

4. Van Hof-van Duin J. Development of visuomotor behavior in normal and light-deprived cats. In: Smith V, Keen J, eds. *Clinics in developmental medicine.* London: Spastics International Medical Publications, 1979; 73:112-23.

5. Giffin F, Mitchell DE. The rate of recovery of vision after early monocular deprivation in kittens. *J Physiol (Lond)* 1978; 274:511-37.

6. Malach R, Strong M, Van Sluyters RC. Analysis of monocular optokinetic nystagmus in normal and visually deprived kittens. *Brain Res* 1981; 210:367-72.

7. Sireteanu R, Maurer D. The development of the kitten's visual field. *Vision Res* 1982; 22:1105-11.

8. Van Hof-van Duin J. Direction preference of optokinetic responses in monocularly tested normal kittens and light deprived cats. *Arch Ital Biol* 1978; 116:471-7.

9. Atkinson J. Development of optokinetic nystagmus in the human infant and monkey infant: an analogue to development in kittens. In: Freeman RD, ed. *Developmental neurobiology of vision.* New York: Plenum, 1979:277-87.

10. Fantz R, Ordy J, Udelf M. Maturation of pattern vision in infants during the first six months. *J Comp Physiol Psychol* 1962; 55:907-17.

11. Lewis TL, Maurer D, Blackburn K. The development of young infants' ability to detect stimuli in the nasal visual field. *Vision Res* 1985; 25:943-50.

12. Braun JJ, Gault FP. Monocular and binocular control of horizontal optokinetic nystagmus in cats and rabbits. *J Comp Physiol Psychol* 1969; 69:12-6.

13. Schor CM, Levi DM. Disturbances of small-field horizontal and vertical optokinetic nystagmus in amblyopia. *Invest Ophthal Vis Sci* 1980; 19:668-83.

14. Atkinson J, Braddick O. Development of optokinetic nystagmus in infants: an indicator of cortical bionocularity? In: Fisher DF, Monty RA, Senders JW, eds. *Eye movements: cognition and visual peception.* Hillsdale, New Jersey: Erlbaum, 1981:53-64.

15. Naegele J, Held R. The postnatal development of monocular optokinetic nystagmus in infants. *Vision Res* 1982; 22341-6.

16. Naegel JR, Held R. Development of optokinetic nystagmus and effects of abnormal visual experience during infancy. In: Jeannerod M, Hein A, eds. *Spatially oriented behavior,* New York: Springer, 1983:155-74.

17. Hoffmann KP. Control of the optokinetic reflex by the nucleus of the optic tract in the cart. In: Hein A. Jeannerod M, eds. *Spatially oriented behavior.* New York: Springer, 1983:135-53.

18 Frisén L, Glansholm A. Optical and neural resolution in peripheral vision. *Invest Ophthal Vis Sci* 1975; 14:528-36.

19 Taylor M, Creelman C. PEST: efficient estimates on probability functions. *J Acoust Soc Am* 1967; 41:782-7.

20. Duke-Elder S, Wybar K, *System of Ophthalmology.* Vol. 6. London: H Kimpton, 1973; 6:313-4.

21. Feldman J, Taylor A. Obstacle to squint training—amblyopia. *Arch Ophthalmol* 1942; 27:851-68.

22. Schmidt D, Reuscher A, Kommerell G. Uber das nasale Gieschtsfeld bei Strabismus fixus divergens. *Grafes Arch Klin Exp Ophthalmol* 1971; 183:97-104.

A Comparison of the Effects of Prenatal Exposure to Tobacco, Alcohol, Cannabis and Caffeine on Birth Size and Subsequent Growth

P.A. Fried and C.M. O'Connell

Maternal use of cigarettes, alcohol, cannabis, and caffeine was established for four time periods: prepregnancy, first trimester, third trimester and average use over pregnancy. The relationship between such usage and growth parameters of offspring followed up from birth to 12 and 24 months of age were examined. Of the soft drugs used, nicotine had the most pronounced effect. After adjustment for other relevant variables, nicotine use prior to and during pregnancy was negatively related to weight and head circumference at birth. Furthermore, third trimester nicotine use was a stronger predictor of decreased weight and head circumference at birth than was first trimester use. The results obtained are consistent with ponderal index (PI) literature suggesting a recovery of growth retardation in infants with a lowered PI. Average consumption of greater than one

Originally published in *Neurotoxicology and Teratology,* 1987, 9, 79-85.

ounce of absolute alcohol per day was negatively related to birth weight and length. Neither cannabis nor caffeine use had a significant negative effect on any growth parameter.

The interest in birth weight as a measure of assessing the success of pregnancy derives from the well documented association between small-for-date babies and morbidity at birth or in the neonatal period (e.g., [32]). Over the years a large number of exogenous, controllable factors have been associated with intrauterine growth retardation. One of the best documented of such agents is maternal smoking [1,14]. It has been consistently reported, in many countries and among many social strata, that infants born to mothers who smoked during pregnancy tend to be lighter in weight than infants born to non-smokers. The effect is dose dependent and is not due to a shortened gestation period. Although the mechanisms by which smoking induces the slowed fetal growth have not been definitively determined, it does not appear that undernutrition is the causative factor [3,20].

The longer term effects of maternal smoking are less definitive. A number of workers have reported slight (but statistically significant) growth retardation in offspring up to 11 years of age [7,9,30] while others have found the growth retardation seen at birth does not persist [4,19]. It is noteworthy that only in the work of Barr et al. [4] was the potential confound of alcohol included in the statistical model used to examine the longer term effects on growth of intrauterine exposure to maternal smoking.

Although there is a general consensus that the offspring of alcoholics are at risk for intrauterine growth retardation that persists into childhood [41] the effects on fetal growth of drinking at non-alcoholic levels during pregnancy are not as clear [4,22-24,39,42].

An association between the lifestyle habits of cigarette smoking and alcohol consumption has been repeatedly noted [2,37,39] and several workers have found that effects of alcohol and smoking on birth weight potentiate each other [27,37]. No follow-up of these samples have been reported.

Approximately ninety percent of women report an intake of some caffeine from various sources during pregnancy [23,44]. When using an algorithm based on analyzed coffee and tea samples, volume consumed and other predictor variables, only daily caffeine levels of greater than 300 mg were found to be associated with infants having lowered birth weights and smaller head circumferences [44]. This is consistent with the findings of Kuzma and Sokol [25]. In a study examining growth in infants at eight months of age no effect of in utero caffeine exposure was noted [4].

Marihuana, used by an estimated 12 percent of pregnant women [10,13,17,18] has usually [11,16] but not always [22] been found to be associated with reduced birth weight when confounding factors are controlled [16,26].

The present work is a prospective investigation of growth parameters of children assessed at birth, 12 and 24 months of age. The subjects of this report are part of the Ottawa Prenatal Prospective Study [15] and as such a considerable body of information with respect to drug use and potentially confounding factors have been collected and can be statistically controlled for in this work.

METHOD

The Ottawa Prenatal Prospective Study is an ongoing longitudinal investigation examining the effects of a number of socially used drugs during pregnancy. Cannabis, alcohol and cigarettes are the primary independent variables and a wide variety of pregnancy and neonatal outcome variables have been and are currently being assessed [11].

To date approximately 700 women have been interviewed several times during their pregnancies regarding their use of drugs prior to pregnancy and during each trimester of pregnancy. Of these women, a follow-up cohort was selected whose offspring were assessed beyond birth. These included all those who used cannabis (either marihuana or hashish) regularly during pregnancy, those who were the heavier social alcohol drinkers and those who were the heavier cigarette smokers. In addition, approximately 50 women who were non-cannabis users and who abstained or drank little alcohol and who were non- or very light cigarette smokers were randomly selected and were also followed.

The average age of women in the present study was 28.9 years; slightly above the mean age of all women who gave birth in the participating hospitals during 1981 (i.e., 27 years). The mean family income of $31,675.42 is nonsignificantly lower than the average family income of $36,247.22 for the Ottawa metropolitan area in 1981, as reported by Statistics Canada. As might be expected in a volunteer sample, the average level of education was somewhat higher than that in the general population. In a population-based hospital survey of women giving birth in the Ottawa region, it was reported that 49.03% of the women had greater than a high school education [40]; in the present study the proportion is 65.68%.

Mothers-to-be were informed of the study by their obstetrician or notices in waiting rooms of pre-natal clinics in three of the largest hospitals in the city of Ottawa. Upon volunteering to participate, each subject was given a structured interview once during each of the trimesters remaining in her pregnancy. During each of the interviews, typically conducted in the home of the mother-to-be by a trained female interviewer, information was collected on socio-economic status, mother's health (both presently and prior to pregnancy), obstetrical history of previous pregnancies, father's medical history, a 24-hour dietary recall (including caffeine estimates) and past and present drug use with particular emphasis upon alcohol, cigarette and cannabis usage. Repeat interviews included questions asked in previous interviews and allowed the investigators to estimate consistency of self-report. When an inconsistency was reported (e.g., if estimates of prepregnancy use differed between second and third trimester interviews), the higher figure was utilized for analysis. The procedures for the deter-

TABLE 1

COMPARISON OF ORIGINAL SAMPLE AND FOLLOW-UP SAMPLES ON VARIABLES OF INTEREST

Variables (mean values)	Original Sample n = 667	12 and 24 Month Follow-Up n = 123
Birth Weight (g)	3485.90 ($\pm$533.91)	3540.65 ($\pm$466.56)
Birth Length (cm)	51.39 ($\pm$2.84)	51.36 ($\pm$2.38)
Head Circumference (cm)	34.54 ($\pm$1.83)	34.75 ($\pm$1.50)
Gestation Length (weeks)	39.63 ($\pm$1.76)	39.77 ($\pm$1.36)
Pregnancy Number	2.24 ($\pm$1.37)	2.51 ($\pm$1.27)
Mother's Weight Prepregnancy (kg)	58.32 ($\pm$9.72)	57.98 ($\pm$8.84)
Mother's Total Weight Gain (kg)	14.65 ($\pm$5.06)	14.80 ($\pm$4.96)
Mother's Height (cm)	162.18 ($\pm$6.60)	161.89 ($\pm$5.73)
Family Income ($)	31,675.42 ($\pm$15,793.29)	30,164.01 ($\pm$14,838.25)

mination of the soft drug use have been described in detail elsewhere [15].

Briefly, alcohol consumption was broken down into beer, wine and liquor and both quantity and pattern of consumption being noted and then converted to average ounces of absolute alcohol (AA) per day. For cigarette use a nicotine score was developed by multiplying the number of cigarettes smoked by the nicotine content of the brand specified. Cannabis use was described in terms of the number of joints used per week.

Average daily caffeine use was calculated according to the number and size of servings of coffee, tea, cola beverages, and other dietary sources of caffeine consumed during pregnancy. As the measure of caffeine use was extracted from a 24-hour dietary recall recorded at each prenatal interview and as not all subjects had been interviewed for all three trimesters, a weighted mean based on the maximum amount of caffeine information on each subject was calculated. This calculated amount was taken as a conservative estimate of caffeine consumption in each of the maternal time periods of soft drug use examined in this study. Nicotine, alcohol, cannabis and caffeine scores were transformed to a logarithmic scale to reduce skewness and minimize the effect of extreme outliers.

For the present report, the sample assessed at birth consisted of 667 newborns (male and female) and their mothers. All infants were the result of singleton births and were without any major congenital malformations. At 12 and 24 months of age, growth parameters were available from 123 of the follow-up cohort. This number represents those subjects who fit the criteria of drug use mentioned above and whose children reached two years of age at the time the present study was undertaken. The growth data subsequent to the birth of the infants was obtained at the time of behavioural testing and was collected by assessors who were unaware of the drug histories of the mothers.

The statistical analysis utilized was multiple linear regression. All predictor variables were entered in all regressions. The unique contribution of each predictor was determined by the size of the change in R^2 after all other, potentially confounding, variables were entered [38]. Four time periods of maternal soft drug use were of interest; prepregnancy (i.e., during the year prior to recognition of pregnancy), first trimester, third trimester, and drug use averaged over pregnancy. Separate regressions were computed for each of three outcome variables; weight, length/height, and head circumference--at each of three ages of the offspring--birth, 12 months and 24 months--using drug consumption information from each of the four maternal time periods. In all, 36 of these regression equations were computed. Pairwise deletion of missing data was employed, resulting in the sample sizes ranging from 641 to 667 in the regressions on outcomes at birth, and from 117 to 123 in the regressions involving outcomes at 12 and 24 months.

The predictor variables were: consumption of nicotine, alcohol, cannabis and caffeine; mother's weight prior to pregnancy; mother's total weight gain during pregnancy; mother's height; pregnancy number; length of gestation; sex of child; and family income. Mother's education had been considered for inclusion as a predictor variable but was found to be highly correlated with nicotine consumption ($r = -.336$, $p = 0.001$) and was excluded because of possible multicollinearity.

To assess the representativeness of the 12 and 24 month subsamples, compared to the total sample of infants examined at birth, the following procedure was employed. Regression analysis on outcomes at birth using only those subjects for whom 12 and 24 month data was available were computed. The relationships among the predictor and birth outcome variables on these smaller subsamples were compared to those seen in regressions employing the whole of the original sample.

RESULTS

Comparison of Samples

The subjects which constituted the 12 and 24 month follow-up subsamples were highly similar to the original birth sample considered. This includes the mean values of non-drug predictor variables (e.g., maternal weight) and the mean birth measures, regardless of whether the samples were based on maternal information from prepregnancy, first trimester, third trimester or average over pregnancy time periods. The mean values for these variables, from the sub-samples based on the "average over pregnancy" time period, are presented in Table 1. The mean values for weight, length, and head circumferences at birth for the original and follow-up subsamples fell between the 50th and 75th percentiles for infants born at 39-39.9 weeks gestation [5].

Regression analysis on outcomes at birth using only those subjects for whom 12 and 24 month data were available revealed that the same relationships between the predictor variables and the outcome variables at birth were present in the large original sample as well as in the smaller subsamples of subjects who were followed to 12 and 24 months.

When comparing the 12 and 24 month follow-up subsamples to the original sample on the basis of maternal drug use, differences with regard to the proportion of drug users within each subsample were noted. The percentage of users of each drug (nicotine, alcohol, cannabis and caffeine) increased across the birth, 12 month, and 24 month subsamples (Table 2). This reflects the focus of the follow-up portion of the Ottawa Prenatal Prospective Study, as the offspring of regular and/or heavy users are most likely to be followed. The 12 and 24 month follow-up subsamples remained similar to the original sample with regard to a pattern of declining drug consumption over the course of pregnancy. Fewer women were users of the drugs of interest during the third trimester as compared to the first trimester. This was true for both the original and follow-up samples. The drop in percentage of users was 5% for nicotine, approximately 7% for alcohol and approximately 8% for cannabis.

Non-Drug Predictor Variables

Mother's weight gain during pregnancy was significantly positively related to all birth measurements as was pregnancy number and length of gestation. Prepregnancy weight was associated only with birth weight and maternal height was associated only with birth length. Sex was significantly related to all outcome measures at birth and 12 months of age such that males were significantly larger on all measures than were females. The same was true for the measures of weight and head circumference at 24 months of age. Head circumference at 24 months was also positively linked with

TABLE 2
COMPARISON OF SAMPLES ON DRUG USE AVERAGED OVER PREGNANCY

Soft Drug	Original Sample (n = 667)	12 and 24 Month Follow-Up (n = 123)
Cigarettes		
Percentage who used	28.49 (190)	54.47 (67)
Mean amount consumed (mg/day)	10.05 (±11.37)	11.93 (±12.58)
Range	0.03–60.0	0.03–60.0
Alcohol		
Percentage who used	85.91 (573)	94.31 (116)
Mean amount consumed (oz AA/day)	0.21 (±0.404)	0.31 (±0.687)
Range	0.003–6.74	0.003–6.74
Cannabis		
Percentage who used	15.14 (101)	33.33 (41)
Mean amount consumed (joints/week)	6.64 (±19.19)	9.09 (±18.10)
Range	0.33–151.7	0.33–105
Caffeine		
Percentage who used	82.61 (551)	84.55 (104)
Mean amount consumed (mg/day)	107.08 (±131.10)	147.63 (±212.75)
Range	2.96–1852.96	5.92–1852.96

mother's weight gain over pregnancy and with length of gestation.

Family income did not contribute significantly to the variance in any of the outcome measures.

The non-drug variables as a group accounted for significant proportions of explained variance in the outcome variables in 27 of the 36 regressions computed. The equations where these variables did not account for a significant proportion of the explained variance in outcome were those involving height and weight at 24 months of age (i.e., 4 time periods x 2 dependent variables = 8 regressions) and one regression involving weight at 12 months using third trimester drug information. In this last equation the contribution of the non-drug predictors approached significance ($p = 0.06$).

All of the predictor variables (including drug variables) together accounted for significant proportions of the explained variance in 29 of the 36 regression equations. Three of the four regressions on head circumference at 12 months and all of the regressions involving height at 24 months were not significant. All equations involving outcome at birth were significant, accounting for 30 to 40% of the explained variance. At the 12 month follow-up from 14% (n.s.) to 23% (p < .01) of variance was accounted for; at 24 months the range was from 13% (n.s.) to 30% (p < .001).

Drug Predictor Variables

Of the drug variables studied, nicotine had the most consistent effect across maternal drug use time periods. The effects of nicotine on birth weight was significant and negative (p < .05) in every regression.

Analyses involving the sample at birth (n = 667) revealed that consumption of 16 mg of nicotine per day (approximately 1 pack) during the year preceding pregnancy was associated with a decrease in birth weight of 99.0 g (p = 0.02). During the first trimester consumption of a pack of cigarettes per day was associated with a decrease in birth weight of 134.39 g (p = 0.004). The same amount consumed in late pregnancy was associated with a greater decrease of 181.01 g (p.001) and, if averaged over pregnancy a pack per day was linked with an intermediate decrease of 154.84 g in birth weight (p = 0.002).

Nicotine consumption either before or during pregnancy did not significantly influence birth length. However the contribution of the third trimester nicotine measure approached significance (p = 0.07).

Nicotine consumption was linked with decreased head circumference at birth in the prepregnancy regression equation. A pack of cigarettes per day during the year preceding pregnancy was associated with a decrease of 0.32 cm in head circumference at birth (p = 0.04).

An analysis of the ponderal index (PI = weight $\times 100/\text{length}^3$) indicated no differences between the babies of the heavy cigarette smokers (> 16 mg nicotine/day) and the rest of the sample when the analysis was based on prepregnancy or first trimester data. However, children born to women who smoked heavily during the third trimester had (non-significantly) lower PI's when compared to the rest of the sample, t(56) = 1.52, p = 0.07, one-tailed. A significant reduction in PI was noted among the newborns of heavy smokers when the smoking habits were based upon use averaged over pregnancy, t(53) = 2.48, p = 0.009, one-tailed.

Nicotine was not significantly related to any of the outcomes at 12 or 24 months of age.

In none of the regression analyses was alcohol consumption found to contribute in a negative fashion to any of the growth parameters. However, when the alcohol variable was analyzed by dividing the women into groups of those who consumed more than one ounce of absolute alcohol per day (n = 21) and the remainder of the sample based on averaged over pregnancy alcohol consumption, a significant difference was noted. Both birth weight and birth length in the offspring of the heavier social drinkers was significantly reduced, $t(627) = 1.86$, $p = 0.03$, one-tailed; $t(613) = 2.00$, $p = 0.025$, one-tailed, respectively. No effects were noted at 12 or 24 months.

Cannabis consumption figured prominently in six regression equations, all involving outcomes at 24 months of age. The consumption of five joints per week (i.e., "heavy" use [15]) in the year preceding pregnancy was associated with an increase of 530.17 g in weight ($p < .01$). Consumption of five joints per week during the first trimester was linked with a weight increase of 539.16 g ($p = 0.02$); third trimester use with a 623.16 g increase ($p = 0.02$); and five joints per week averaged over pregnancy was associated with a 596.69 g ($p = 0.01$) increase in weight at 24 months. Heavy cannabis consumption prepregnancy was also linked with a 0.98 cm increase in height ($p = 0.03$) while heavy use averaged over pregnancy was associated with an increase of 1.10 cm in height ($p = 0.05$) at 24 months of age.

The variable of caffeine consumption did not significantly contribute to a slowed growth at any of the time periods assessed. When the caffeine variable was analyzed by dividing the women into groups of those who consumed more than 300 mg per day (n = 22) and the rest of the sample a non-significant decrease in birth weight of 173.9 g was associated with heavier caffeine use, $t(21.8) = 1.0$, $p = 0.14$, one-tailed.

As neither alcohol or caffeine showed a relationship to any of the outcome measures and because the number of regular cannabis users (i.e., > 1 joint/week) was relatively small, an interactive component was not entered in any of the regression equations. However inspection of mean birth weight for each level of nicotine consumption by each level of cannabis consumption suggested an "offsetting" rather than a potentiating of cannabis on birth weight when used in conjunction with nicotine. The mean birth weight of babies born to women who were "heavy" consumers of both drugs during pregnancy was 3556.75 g whereas babies born to heavy smokers who did not use cannabis had a mean birth weight of 3278.41 g. For babies born to abstainers from both substances, the average birth weight was 3530.89 g.

Only 11 women reported using any other drugs of abuse (which by and large included cocaine and amphetamines with only one reported intake of LSD) and this use was limited to one or two intakes early in pregnancy. There was no reported use of these drugs during the third trimester. Three of these 11 women continued to participate in the study until their children were two years of age. Use of minor tranquilizers was reported by seven women early in pregnancy. This number dropped to four by the third trimester. Only two of the seven who used tranquilizers in the first trimester and only one of the four who reported use in the third trimester remained in the follow-up (12 and 24 month) sample. A comparison of babies born to women who had not used these drugs revealed no significant difference in birth weight.

DISCUSSION

A new finding in this study was the interaction between the timing of cigarette use during pregnancy and its relative differential effects on growth parameters at birth. Although both first and third trimester maternal use of cigarettes significantly influenced birth weight, the effect of third trimester use was more marked with a decrease of 181.01 g (associated with the daily use of 16 mg of nicotine per day) versus a decrease of 134.39 g with a similar use in the first trimester.

These observations are consistent with seemingly divergent findings in the literature. For example Butler and Goldstein [7] reported that birth weight was affected more by the smoking later in pregnancy (the third trimester effect noted in the present work) but Herriott et al. [21] noted that even when mothers stopped smoking early in pregnancy, their babies at term were lighter than those of non-smoking mothers (influence of the first trimester noted in the present work).

Further, in the two reports in which maternal smoking was not significantly related to infant size beyond the neonatal period it appears, although not directly stated, that the smoking behaviour was based on habits after the first trimester of pregnancy [4,19]. A poorer prognosis for intrauterine growth retardation associated with early gestational factors has been noted elsewhere [29,33].

Villar et al. [43] discuss the ponderal index (PI) as a means of detecting those infants who are underweight for their length as a result of third trimester growth reduction. Because of the disproportionate retardation of weight compared to length such infants have a low PI. In the present work heavy smoking averaged over pregnancy or heavy smoking during the third trimester was associated with a lower PI whereas first trimester smoking was not. Villar et al. [43] observed that infants who are small and who have low PI catch up within a year to normal weight and length. This finding is consistent with the present observation of the children "catching-up" by twelve months of age.

The catch-up growth and the lowered PI noted in the babies born to mothers whose smoking habits are based on third trimester and averaged over pregnancy usage suggest that the etiology of the reduced birth weight has a fetal malnourishment basis [43] which could, in turn, be due to a restriction of maternal weight gain. The importance of maternal weight gain during prgnancy in determining birth weight has been reported (with particular reference to a poor, black, urban population; [34]). It was likewise found to be an important contributor to the variance in growth parameters at birth in the present study. However, consistent with other reports [8], controlling for the influence of maternal weight gain still leaves a significant proportion of the variance in birth weight which is explained by maternal smoking. In the present study, maternal nourishment was no different among heavy smokers as contrasted to the rest of the sample. The lowered birth weight, which is reversible, is therefore suggestive of a possible impairment in the fetal ability to utilize nourishment *in utero*.

It is important to recognize that although the Ottawa study used nicotine values as the basis for evaluating the extent of smoking behaviour of the women, it cannot be assumed that nicotine is the constituent that is associated with the reported observations. Nearly 2000 compounds have been identified in cigarette smoke [28] and, in addition to nicotine, carbon monoxide and cyanide, have been implicated in observed fetal effects [1].

In this work, as in reports outlined previously, cannabis was not found to be associated with reduced growth. In fact, at 24 months of age a positive association between marihuana use and weight and height was noted. However, as described elsewhere [31], the heavy cannabis users tended to consume more calories and protein than control subjects and thus the increased growth in the offpsring may reflect this aspect of their life-style. It is also noteworthy that the report of lowered birth weight associated with cannabis usage [22] was observed in a sample that had poor nutrition (see [12]).

Alcohol consumption in the present work was associated with a reduction in birth weight and length only in the offspring of women who consumed more than one ounce of absolute alcohol per day throughout pregnancy. At this level some, but not all, workers have reported a significant reduction in birth weight [22-24,39,42], while only at quantities averaging more than 12 times those seen in the present work has long term growth retardation between noted [4].

The trend toward a negative effect of heavy caffeine on birth weight and the subsequent lack of effect at 12 and 24 months is consistent with most reports in the literature [4,23,25,26,44]. The lack of statistical significance at birth is most likely a reflection of the small number of heavy consumers of caffeine.

Finally, although a significant amount of variance in many of the growth parameters was accounted for by maternal smoking, the proportion of explained variance was small. It is worthwhile noting that even the non-drug predictor variables (e.g., weight prepregnancy, weight gain, pregnancy number, gestation length), which were highly significant predictors of birth measurements were no longer significant predictors at 12 and 24 months. Therefore it is not surprising that the drug variables, which although significant at birth did not explain as much variance as the non-drug variables, were no longer significant at 12 and 24 months. It is quite apparent that the developmental consequnce of prenatal exposure to drugs is a complex interaction that must take into account both *in utero* and postnatal factors [35].

ACKNOWLEDGEMENTS

The authors wish to thank Ken Innes for his assistance in the preparation of this manuscript. The research was supported by Health and Welfare, Canada and the March of Dimes Foundation, U.S.

REFERENCES

1. Abel, E.L. Smoking during pregnancy: A review of effects on growth and development of offspring. *Hum Biol* 52:593-626, 1980.

2. Alpert, J.J., N. Day, E. Dooling, R. Hingson, E. Oppenheimer, H.L. Rosett, L. Weiner and B. Zuckerman. Maternal alcohol consumption and newborn assessment: Methodology of the Boston City Hospital Prospective Study. *Neurobehav Toxicol Teratol* 3:195-201, 1981.

3. Anderson, G.D., E.N. Blidner, S. McClemont and J.C. Sinclair. Determinants of size at birth in a Canadian population. *Am J Obstet Gynecol* 150:236-244, 1984.

4. Barr, H.M., A.P. Streissguth, D.C. Martin and C.S. Herman. Infant size at 8 months of age: Relationship to maternal use of alcohol, nicotine, and caffeine during pregnancy. *Pediatrics* 74:336-341, 1984.

5. Blidner, I.N., S. McClemont, G.D. Anderson and J.C. Sinclair. Size-at-birth standards for an urban Canadian population. *Can Med Assoc J* 130:133-140, 1984.

6. Brandt, I. Growth dynamics of low birth weight infants with emphasis on the perinatal perod. In: *Human Growth*, edited by J.M. Tanner. New York: Plenum Publishing Company, 1978, pp. 557-617.

7. Butler, N.R. and H. Goldstein. Smoking in pregnancy and subsequent child development. *Br Med J* 4:573-575, 1973.

8. Davies, D.P., O.P. Gray, P.C. Ellwood and M. Abernethy. Cigarette smoking in pregnancy: Associations with maternal weight gain and fetal growth. *Lancet* i:385-387, 1976.

9. Dunn, H.G., A.K. McBurney, S. Ingram and C.M. Hunter. Maternal cigarette smok-

ing during pregnancy and the child's subsequent development: I. Physical growth to the age of 6 1/2 years. *Can J Public Health* 67:499-505, 1976.

10. Fried, P.A. Marihuana use by pregnant women: Neurobehavioral effects in neonates. *Drug Alcohol Depend* 6:415-424, 1980.

11. Fried, P.A. Marihuana use during pregnancy: Pre- and post-natal consequences. In: *Neurobehavioral Teratology,* edited by J. Yanai. Amsterdam: Elsevier Biomedical Press, 1984, pp. 275-285.

12. Fried, P.A. Postnatal consequences of maternal marihuana use. In: *Current Research on the Consequences of Maternal Drug Abuse,* edited by I.M. Rinkert. NIDA Research Monograph 59. Rockville, MD: NIDA, 1985.

13. Fried, P.A., K.S. Innes and M.V. Barnes. Soft drug use prior to and during pregnancy: A comparison of samples over a four year period. *Drug Alcohol Depend* 13:161-171, 1984.

14. Fried, P.A. and H. Oxorn. *Smoking for Two: Cigarettes and Pregnancy.* New York: Free Press/MacMillan & Sons, 1980.

15. Fried, P.A., B. Watkinson, A. Grant and R.M. Knights. Changing patterns of soft drug use prior to and during pregnancy: A prospective study. *Drug Alcohol Depend* 6:323-343, 1980.

16. Fried, P.A., B. Watkinson and A. Willan. Marihuana use during pregnancy and decreased length of gestation. *Am J Obstet gynecol* 150:23-27, 1984.

17. Gibson, G.T., P.A. Baghurst and D.P. Colley. Maternal alcohol, tobacco and cannabis consumption and the outcome of pregnancy. *Aust NZ J Obstet Gynaecol* 23:15-19, 1983.

18. Greenland, S., K. Staisch, N. Brown and S. Gross. The effects of marihuana use during pregnancy. I. A preliminary epidemiologic study. *Am J Obstet Gynecol* 143:408-413, 1982.

19. Hardy, J.B. and E.D. Mellits. Does maternal smoking during pregnancy have a long term effect on the child? *Lancet* 2:1332-1336, 1972.

20. Haworth, J.C., J.J. Ellestad-Sayed, J. King and L.A. Dilling. Relation of maternal cigarette smoking, obesity and energy consumption to infant size. *Am J Obstet Gynecol* 138:1185-1189, 1980.

21. Herriott, A., W.Z. Billewica and F.E. Hytten. Cigarette smoking in pregnancy. *Lancet* 1:771-773, 1962.

22. Hingson, R., J.J. Alpert, N. Day, E. Dooling, H. Kayne, S. Morelock, E. Oppenheimer and B. Zuckerman. Effects of maternal drinking and marihuana use of fetal growth and development. *Pediatrics* 70:539-546, 1982.

23. Jacobson, S.W., G.G. Fein, J.L. Jacobson, P.M. Schwarts and J.K. Dowler. Neonatal correlates of prenatal exposure to smoking, caffeine, and alcohol. *Infant Behav Dev* 7:253-265, 1984.

24. Kaminski, M., M. Franc, M. Lebouvier, C. Du Mazaubrun and C. Rumeau-Rouquette. Moderate alcohol use and pregnancy outcome. *Neurobehav toxicol Teratol* 3:173-181, 1981.

25. Kuzma, J.W. and R.J. Sokol. Maternal drinking behavior and decreased intrauterine growth. *Alcoholism* 6:396-402, 1982.

26. Linn, S., S.C. Schoenbaum, R.R. Monson, B. Rosner, P.G. Stubblefield and K.J. Ryan. No association between coffee consumption and adverse outcomes of pregnancy. *N Engl J Med* 306:141-145, 1982.

27. Little, R.E. Moderate alcohol use during pregnancy and decreased infant birth weight. *Am J Public Health* 67:1154-1156, 1977.

28. Longo, L.D. Some health consequences of maternal smoking. Issues without answers. In: *Birth Defects: Original Article Series*, vol 18. White Plains, NY: March of Dimes Birth Defects Foundation, 1982, pp. 13-31.

29. Mille, H.C. and A.T. Merritt. *Fetal Growth in Humans.* Chicago: Year Book Medical Publishers, 1979.

30. Naeye, R.L. and E.C. Peters. Mental development of children whose mothers smoked during pregnancy. *Obstet Gynecol* 64:601-607, 1984.

31. O'Connell, C.M. and P.A. Fried. An investigation of prenatal cannabis exposure and minor physical anomalies in a low risk population. *Neurobehav Toxicol Teratol* 6:345-350, 1984.

32. Ounsted, M., V. Moar and W.A. Scott. Perinatal morbidity and mortality in small-for-dates babies: The relative importance of some maternal factors. *Early Hum Dev* 5:367-375, 1981.

33. Redmond, G. Effect of drugs on intrauterine growth. *Clin Perinatol* 6:5-19, 1979.

34. Rush, D. Cigarette smoking during pregnancy: The relationship with depressed weight gain and birthweight. An updated report. In: *Birth Defects Risks and Consequences,* edited by S. Kelly, E.B. Hook, D.T. Janerick and I.H. Porter. New York: Academic Press, 1976, pp. 161-172.

35. Sameroff, A.J. and M.J. Chandler. Reproductive risk and continuum of caretaking casualty. In: *Review of Child Development Research*, Vol 4, edited by F.D. Horowitz, E.M. Hetherington, S. Scarr-Salapatek and G. Siegel. Chicago: University of Chicago Press, 1975.

36. Sokol, R.J., S.I. Miller and G. Reed. Alcohol abuse during pregnancy. An epidemiologic study. *Alcoholism* 4:135-145, 1980.

37. Sokol, R.J., S.J. Miller, S. Debanne, N. Golden, G. Collins, J. Kaplan and S. Martier. The Cleveland NIAAA prospective alcohol-in-pregnancy study: The first year. *Neurobehav Toxicol Teratol* 3:203-209, 1981.

38. SPSS Inc. *SPSS-X.* New York: McGraw-Hill, 1983.

39. Staisey, N.L. and P.A. Fried. Relationship between moderate maternal alcohol consumption during pregnancy and infant neurological development. *J Stud Alcohol* 44:262-270, 1983.

40. Stewart, P.J. and G.C. Dunkley. Smoking and health care patterns among pregnant women. *Can Med Assoc J* 133:989-994, 1985.

41. Streissguth, A.P., C.S. Herman and D.W. Smith. Stability of intelligence in the fetal alcohol syndrome. *Alcoholism* 2:165-170, 1978.

42. Streissguth, A.P., D.C. Martin, J.C. Martin and H.M. Barr. The Seattle longitudinal prospective study on alcohol and pregnancy. *Neurobehav Toxicol Teratol* 3:223-233, 1981.

43. Villar, J., J.M. Belizan, J. Spalding and R.E. Klein. Postnatal growth of intrauterine growth retarded infants. *Early Hum Dev* 6:265-271, 1982.

44. Watkinson, B. and P.A. Fried. Maternal caffeine use before, during and after pregnancy and effects upon offspring. *Neurobehav Toxicol Teratol* 7:9-17, 1985.

Section 3
Developments in Cognition and Language

The word *cognition* comes from the Latin verb which means "to know", and in psychology the term refers to the study of the mental processes through which knowledge is acquired. Thus, perception, attention, memory, problem solving, and thinking are aspects of the study of cognition. As all our waking hours involve some of the mental activities that we call cognitive, the impact of these processes on our daily lives is enormous. Cognitive development refers to the changes that occur in these abilities as children accumulate age and experience. At the turn of the century G. Stanley Hall, widely viewed as the founder of developmental psychology in America, recognized the importance of discovering the contents of children's minds. Hall devised the questionnaire as a tool for the study of the children's minds, and his work was followed by decades of research into the nature and assessment of intelligence. Thus, the earliest work in cognition was in the psychometric tradition.

A new direction in the study of children's minds was initiated by the Swiss scientist, philosopher, and educator, Jean Piaget. Piaget viewed intelligence, not as a group of intellectual traits to be quantified, but as a process whereby the child actively constructs or understands his/her environment. Piaget formulated a theory which described how this understanding matured and became more sophisticated across four age-related stages of development. Children's thinking at each stage was qualitatively different from previous and subsequent stages. Intellectual growth was more than the acquisition of facts. Thus, the range of logical problems and relationships that the child could be expected to understand depended on the mental operations that he/she possessed at a particular stage of development. Passage through the stages is the result of the biological pressure to adapt to and understand the environment, and the active will to organize and reorganize their knowledge. Piaget's theory was both intriguing and controversial. The mental activities that he addressed were unique. While psychometricians were quantifying and assessing intelligence, Piaget was writing about such characteristics of thought as object permanence, egocentrism, animism, irreversibility, and the ways in which children learn to solve logical problems such as class inclusion, transitivity, and conservation. The first paper in this section is by Piaget and is an introduction to his stage theory of cognitive development. Piaget's work was criticized in America because his methodology was informal and subjective, and many of his terms were difficult to operationalize. However, his impact on the field of cognitive development was enormous, and his work set the direction for research for decades to come.

One of the aspects of Piaget's theory that has been most frequently criticized is his treatment of the preschool, or preoperational, child. Children in this stage of thought were seen primarily in terms of their limitations, of the things that they could not do and the logical problems that they were apparently unable to solve. This view was influential in directing others to view preschoolers' abilities negatively. The paper by Rochel Gelman presents persuasive evidence that Piaget underestimated the ability of the preoperational child to solve problems, in part because his tasks were misleading or overly complex. She shows that if the task demands of logical problems are minimized, preschoolers demonstrate a range of competence that Piaget would not have expected.

In the past twenty years the information processing approach to cognition has become firmly established in the field of cognitive development and has continued to grow in importance. Information processing is not a single theory, but rather a framework in which a variety of research can be considered. These theorists view cognitive processes as the flow of information through the senses and the brain. The flow begins with sensory input, continues inside the brain where it is represented, transformed, and stored in memory, and ends with output, or retrieval of the information on demand. Thinking involves manipulation of data which comes in from the environment or which is already in the system. Cognitive development is marked by the increase in efficiency that occurs as children become more knowledgeable and more strategic information processors.

Three of the papers in this section represent the information processing approach to cognitive development. Judy DeLoache and Ann Brown report a study of young children's memory using a paradigm in which they hide an object and observe whether the child searches for it, and whether or not the search is successful. They found that two-year-olds are not only able to retrieve hidden objects, but are systematic and organized in the way they search. William Fabricius and Henry Wellman have studied retrieval processes in older children. Specifically, they looked at children's knowledge of the circumstances under which external cues will effectively aid recall, and found age differences in 7-, 9-, and 11-year-olds' understanding of cue use. Finally, the paper by Katherine McCartney and Katherine Nelson is an investigation of the way in which children represent knowledge. They found that children represent many of their everyday experiences as "scripts" - prototypes or rough outlines of these experiences that have been encoded and that help them to organize their worlds.

The development of language is an important aspect of cognitive development. Historically, there have been arguments over whether language determined cognition, or whether cognition determined language. While there have been no clear answers to this question, we do know that the two are integrally related. Consequently, papers on the development of language and communication have been included in this section.

Two of these papers demonstrate humans' strong predisposition to acquire language. Susan Goldin-Meadow and Carolyn Mylander report that a group of deaf children, who could not use spoken language, and whose parents did not expose them to manual language, developed among themselves a system of gestural communication which had many of the characteristics of natural language. The paper by Janet Werker and Richard Tees is a follow up to a study they did on phonemic discrimination in infancy. In that paper they found that infants were able to discriminate among phonemes that were not a part of their native language, whereas adult subjects could not do this very well. The paper reported here traces the decline in this ability to make phonemic discriminations that are not a part of our language environment.

In the two final papers, the relationship between cognition and language as communication is considered. Henry Wellman and Jacques Lempers report that the conversations of two-year-olds in natural settings show a remarkable sensitivity to some of the rules of communication interactions. The paper by Amye Warren-Leubecker and John Bohannon is an experimental study of preschoolers' ability to communicate, and the way in which they modify their conversations according to the feedback they receive from their partners during a communication.

Development and Learning

Jean Piaget

In his opening remarks Piaget makes a distinction between development and learning—development being a spontaneous process tied to embryogenesis, learning being provoked by external situations. He proceeds to discuss the concept of an operation as an interiorized action linked to other operations in a structure. Four stages of development are enumerated—sensori-motor, pre-operational, concrete operations, and formal operations. Factors explaining the development of one structure of operations from another are discussed—maturation, experience, social transmission, and equilibration. Equilibration is defended as the most fundamental factor. Commenting on the inadequacy of the stimulus-response approach to understanding learning, Piaget presents evidence negating the effectiveness of external reinforcement in hastening the development of operational structures. These operational structures can be learned only if one bases the learning on simpler, more elementary structures— only if there is a natural relationship and development of structures. The learning of these structures is held to follow the same basic laws as does their natural development, i.e., learning is

Originally published in *Piaget Rediscovered. A Report of the Conference on Cognitive Studies and Curriculum Development,* edited by R. Ripple and V. Rockcastle, Cornell University, 1964. Reprinted with permission.

> subordinated to development. Piaget concludes that the fundamental relation involved in development and learning is assimilation, not association.

My dear colleagues, I am very concerned about what to say to you, because I don't know if I shall accomplish the end that has been assigned to me. But I've been told that the important thing is not what you say, but the discussion which follows, and the answers to questions you are asked. So this morning I shall simply give a general introduction of a few ideas which seem to me to be important for the subject of this conference.

First I would like to make clear the difference between two problems: the problem of *development* in general, and the problem of *learning*. I think these problems are very different, although some people do not make this distinction.

The development of knowledge is a spontaneous process, tied to the whole process of embryogenesis. Embryogenesis concerns the development of the body, but it concerns as well the development of the nervous system, and the development of mental functions. In the case of the development of knowledge in children, embryogenesis ends only in adulthood. It is a total developmental process which we must re-situate in its general biological and psychological context. In other words, development is a process which concerns the totality of the structures of knowledge.

Learning presents the opposite case. In general, learning is provoked by situations—provoked by a psychological experimenter; or by a teacher, with respect to some didactic point; or by an external situation. It is provoked, in general, as opposed to spontaneous. In addition, it is a limited process—limited to a single problem, or to a single structure.

So I think that development explains learning, and this opinion is contrary to the widely held opinion that development is a sum of discrete learning experiences. For some psychologists development is reduced to a series of specific learned items, and development is thus the sum, the cumulation of this series of specific items. I think this is an atomistic view which deforms the real state of things. In reality, development is the essential process and each element of learning occurs as a function of total development, rather than being an element which explains development. I shall begin, then, with a first part dealing with development, and I shall talk about learning in the second part.

To understand the development of knowledge, we must start with an idea which seems central to me—the idea of an *operation*. Knowledge is not a copy of reality. To know an object, to know an event, is not simply to look at it and make a mental copy, or image, of it. To know an object is to act on it. To know is to modify, to transform the object, and to understand the process of this transformation, and as a consequence to understand the way the object is constructed. An operation is thus the essence of knowledge; it is an interiorised action which modifies the object of knowledge. For instance, an operation would consist of joining objects in a class, to construct a classification. Or an operation would consist of ordering, or putting things in a series. Or an operation would consist of counting, or of measuring. In other words, it is a set of actions modifying the object, and enabling the knower to get at the structures of the transformation.

An operation is an interiorised action. But in addition, it is a reversible action; that is, it can take place in both directions, for instance, adding or subtracting, joining or separating. So it is a particular type of action which makes up logical structures.

Above all, an operation is never isolated. It is always linked to other operations, and as a result it is always a part of a total structure. For instance, a logical class does not exist in isolation; what exists is the total structure of classification. An asymmetrical relation does not exist in isolation. Seriation is the natural, basic operational structure. A number does not exist in isolation. What exists is the series of numbers, which constitute a structure, an exceedingly rich structure whose various properties have been revealed by mathematicians.

These operational structures are what seem to me to constitute the basis of knowledge, the natural psychological reality, in terms of which we must understand the development of knowledge. And the central problem of development is to understand the formation, elaboration, organization, and functioning of these structures.

I should like to review the stages of development of these structures, not in any detail, but simply as a reminder. I shall distinguish four main stages. The first is a sensory-motor, pre-verbal stage, lasting approximately the first 18 months of life. During this stage is developed the practical knowledge which constitutes the substructure of later representational knowledge. An example is the construction of the schema of the permanent object. For an infant, during the first months, an object has no permanence. When it disappears from the perceptual field it no longer exists. No attempt is made to find it again. Later, the infant will try to find it, and he will find it by localizing it spatially. Consequently, along with the construction of the permanent object there comes the construction of practical, or sensory-motor, space. There is similarly the construction of temporal succession, and of elementary sensory-motor causality. In other words, there is a series of structures which are indispensable for the structures of later representational thought.

In a second stage, we have pre-operational representation — the beginnings of language, of the symbolic function, and therefore of thought, or representation. But at the level of representational thought, there must now be a reconstruction of all that was developed on the sensory-motor level. That is, the sensory-motor actions are not immediately translated into operations. In fact, during all this second period of pre-operational representations, there are as yet no operations as I defined this term a moment ago. Specifically, there is as yet no conservation which is the psychological criterion of the presence of reversible operations. For example, if we pour liquid from one glass to another of a different shape, the pre-operational child will think there is more in one than in the other. In the absence of operational reversibility, there is no conservation of quantity.

In a third stage the first operations appear, but I call these concrete operations because they operate on objects, and not yet on verbally expressed hypotheses. For example, there are the operations of classification, ordering, the construction of the idea of number, spatial and temporal operations, and all the fundamental operations of elementary logic of classes and relations, of elementary mathematics, of elementary geometry and even of elementary physics.

Finally, in the fourth stage, these operations are surpassed as the child reaches the level of what I call formal or hypothetic-deductive operations; that is, he can now reason on hypotheses, and not only on objects. He constructs new operations, operations of propositional logic, and not simply the operations of classes, relations and numbers. He attains new structures which are on the one hand combinatorial, corresponding to what mathematicians call lattices; on the other hand, more complicated group structures. At the level of concrete operations, the operations apply within an immediate neighborhood: for instance, classification by successive inclusions. At the level of the combinatorial, however, the groups are much more mobile. These, then, are the four stages which we identify, whose formation we shall now attempt to explain.

What factors can be called upon to explain the development from one set of structures to another? It seems to me that there are four main factors: first of all, *maturation*, in the sense of Gesell, since this development is a continuation of the embryogenesis; second, the role of *experience* of the effects of the physical environment on the structures of intelligence; third, *social transmission* in the broad sense (linguistic transmission, education, etc.); and fourth, a factor which is too often neglected but one which seems to me fundamental and even the principal factor. I shall call this the factor of *equilibration* or if you prefer it, of self-regulation.

Let us start with the first factor, maturation. One might think that these stages are simply a reflection of an interior maturation of the nervous system, following the hypotheses of Gesell, for example. Well, maturation certainly does play an indispensable role and must not be ignored. It certainly takes part in every transformation that takes place during a child's development. However, this first factor is insufficient in itself. First of all, we know practically nothing about the maturation of the nervous system beyond the first months of the child's existence. We know a little bit about it during the first two years but we know very little following this time. But above all, maturation doesn't explain everything, because the average ages at which these stages appear (the average chronological ages) vary a great deal from one society to another. The ordering of these stages is constant and has been found in all the societies studied. It has been found in various countries where psychologists in universities have redone the experiments but it has also been found in African peoples for example, in the children of the Bushmen, and in Iran, both in the villages and in the cities. However, although the order of succession is constant, the chronological ages of these stages varies a great deal. For instance, the ages which we have found in Geneva are not necessarily the ages which you would find in the United States. In Iran, furthermore, in the city of Teheran, they found approximately the same ages as we found in Geneva, but there is a systematic delay of two years in the children in the country. Canadian psychologists who redid our experiments, Monique Laurendeau and Father Adrien

Pinard, found once again about the same ages in Montreal. But when they redid the experiments in Martinique, they found a delay of four years in all the experiments and this in spite of the fact that the children in Martinique go to a school set up according to the French system and the French curriculum and attain at the end of this elementary school a certificate of higher primary education. There is then a delay of four years, that is, there are the same stages, but systematically delayed. So you see that these age variations show that maturation does not explain everything.

I shall go on now to the role played by experience. Experience of objects, of physical reality, is obviously a basic factor in the development of cognitive structures. But once again this factor does not explain everything. I can give two reasons for this. The first reason is that some of the concepts which appear at the beginning of the stage of concrete operations are such that I cannot see how they could be drawn from experience. As an example, let us take the conservation of the substance in the case of changing the shape of a ball of plasticene. We give this ball of plasticene to a child who changes its shape into a sausage form and we ask him if there is the same amount of matter, that is, the same amount of substance as there was before. We also ask him if it now has the same weight and thirdly if it now has the same volume. The volume is measured by the displacement of water when we put the ball or the sausage into a glass of water. The findings, which have been the same every time this experiment has been done, show us that first of all there is conservation of the amount of substance. At about eight years old a child will say, "There is the same amount of plasticene." Only later does the child assert that the weight is conserved and still later that the volume is conserved. So I would ask you where the idea of the conservation of substance can come from. What is a constant and invariant substance when it doesn't yet have a constant weight or a constant volume? Through perception you can get at the weight of the ball or the volume of the ball but perception cannot give you an idea of the amount of substance. No experiment, no experience, can show the child that there is the same amount of substance. He can weigh the ball and that would lead to the conservation of weight. He can immerse it in water and that would lead to the conservation of volume. But the notion of substance is attained before either weight or volume. This conservation of substance is simply a logical necessity. The child now understands that when there is a transformation something must be conserved because by reversing the transformation you can come back to the point of departure and once again have the ball. He knows that something is conserved but he doesn't know what. It is not yet the weight, it is not yet the volume; it is simply a logical form — a logical necessity. There, it seems to me, is an example of a progress in knowledge, a logical necessity for something to be conserved even though no experience can have lead to this notion.

My second objection to the sufficiency of experience as an explanatory factor is that this notion of experience is a very equivocal one. There are, in fact, two kinds of experience which are psychologically very different and this difference is very important from the pedagogical point of view. It is because of the pedagogical importance that I emphasize this distinction. First of all, there is what I shall call physical experience, and secondly, what I shall call logical-mathematical experience.

Physical experience consists of acting upon object and drawing some knowledge about the objects by abstraction from the objects. For example, to discover that this pipe is heavier than this watch, the child will weigh them both and find the difference in the objects themselves. This is experience in the usual sense of the term—in the sense used by empiricists. But there is a second type of experience which I shall call logical-mathematical experience where the knowledge is not drawn from the objects. This is not the same thing. When one acts upon objects, the objects are indeed there, but there is also the set of actions which modify the objects.

I shall give you an example of this type of experience. It is a nice example because we have verified it many times in small children under seven years of age, but it is also an example which one of my mathematician friends has related to me about his own childhood, and he dates his mathematical career from this experience. When he was four or five years old—I don't know exactly how old, but a small child --he was seated on the ground in his garden and he was counting pebbles. Now to count these pebbles he put them in a row and he counted them one, two, three, up to ten. Then he finished counting them and started to count them in the other direction. He began by the end and once again he found ten. He found this marvelous that there were ten in one direction and ten in the other direction. So he put them in a circle and counted them that way and found ten once again. Then he counted them in the other direction and found ten once more. So he put them in some other direction and found ten once more. So he put them in some other arrangement and kept counting them and kept finding ten. There was the discovery that he made.

Now what indeed did he discover? He did not discover a property of pebbles; he discovered a property of the action of ordering. The pebbles had no order. It was his action which introduced a linear order or a cyclical order, or any kind of an order. He discovered that the sum was independent of the order. The order was the action which he introduced among the pebbles. For the sum the same principle applied. The pebbles had no sum; they were simply in a pile. To make a sum, action was necessary—the operation of putting together and counting. He found that the sum was independent of the order, in other words, that the action of putting together is independent of the action of ordering. He discovered a property of actions and not a property of pebbles. You may say that it is in the nature of pebbles to let this be done to them and this is true. But it could have been drops of water, and drops of water would not have let this be done to them because two drops of water and two drops of water do not make four drops of water as you know very well. Drops of water then would not let this be done to them, we agree to that.

So it is not the physical property of pebbles which the experience uncovered. It is the properties of the actions carried out on the pebbles and this is quite another form of experience. It is the point of departure of mathematical deduction. The subsequent deduction will consist of interiorizing these actions and then of combining them without needing any pebbles. The mathematician no longer needs his pebbles. He can combine his operations simply with symbols and the point of departure of this mathematical deduction is logical-mathematical experience and this is not at all experience in the sense of the empiricists. It is the beginning of the coordination of actions, but this coordination of actions before the stage of operations needs to be supported by concrete material. Later, this coordination of actions leads to the logical-mathematical structures. I believe that logic is not a derivative of language. The source of logic is much more profound. It is the total coordination of actions, actions of joining things together, or ordering things, etc. This is what logical-mathematical experience is. It is an experience of the actions of the subject, and not an experience of objects themselves. It is an experience which is necessary before there can be operations. Once the operations have been attained this experience is no longer needed and the coordinations of actions can take place by themselves in the form of deduction and construction for abstract structures.

The third factor is social transmission — linguistic transmission or educational transmission. This factor, once again, is fundamental. I do not deny the role of any one of these factors; they all play a part. But this factor is insufficient because the child can receive valuable information via language or via education directed by an adult only if he is in a stage where he can understand this information. That is, to receive the information he must have a structure which enables him to assimilate this information. This is why you cannot teach higher mathematics to a five-year old. He does not yet have structures which enable him to understand.

I shall take a much simpler example, an example of linguistic transmission. As my very first work in the realm of child psychology, I spent a long time studying the relation between a part and a whole in concrete experience and in language. For example, I used Burt's test employing the sentence, "Some of my flowers are buttercups." The child knows that all buttercups are yellow, so there are three possible conclusions: the whole bouquet is yellow, or part of the bouquet is yellow, or none of the flowers in the bouquet is yellow. I found that up until nine years of age (and this was in Paris, so the children certainly did understand the French language) they replied, "The whole bouquet is yellow or some of my flowers are yellow." Both of those mean the same thing. They did not understand the expression, "some _of_ my flowers." They did not understand this _of_ as a partitive genitive, as the inclusion of some flowers in my flowers. They understood some of my flowers to be my several flowers as if the several flowers and the flowers were confused as one of the same class. So there you have children who until nine years of age heard every day a linguistic structure which implied the inclusion of a sub-class in a class and yet did not understand this structure. It is only when they themselves are in firm possession of this logical structure, when they have constructed it for themselves according to the developmental laws which we shall discuss, that they succeed in understanding correctly the linguistic expression.

I come now to the fourth factor which is added to the three preceding ones but which seems to me to be the fundamental one. This is what I call the factor of equilibration. Since there are already three factors, they must somehow be equilibrated among themselves. That is one reason for bringing in the factor of equilibration. There is a second reason, however, which seems to me to be fundamental. It is that in the act of knowing, the subject is active, and consequently, faced with an external disturbance, he will react in order to compensate and consequently he will tend towards equilibrium. Equilibrium, defined by active compensation, leads to reversibility. Operational reversibility is a model of an equilibrated system where a transformation in one direction is compensated by a transformation in the other direction. Equilibration, as I understand it, is thus an active process. It's a process of self-regulation. I think that this self-regulation is a fundamental factor in development. I use this term in the sense in which it is used in cybernetics, that is, in the sense of processes with feedback and with feedforward, of processes which regulate themselves by a progressive compensation of systems. This process of equilibration takes the form of a succession of levels of equilibrium, of levels which have a certain probability which I shall call a sequential probability, that is, the probabilities are not established a priori. There is a sequence of levels. It is not possible to reach the second level unless equilibrium has been reached at the first level, and the equilibrium of the third level only becomes possible when the equilibrium of the second level has been reached, and so forth. That is, each level is determined as the most probable given that the preceding level has been reached. It is not the most probable at the beginning, but it is the most probable once the preceding level has been reached.

As an example, let us take the development of the idea of conservation in the transformation of the ball of plasticene into the sausage shape. Here you can discern four levels. The most probable at the beginning is for the child to think of only one dimension. The most probable at the beginning is for the child to think of only one focus on the length, and that the width has a probability of 0.2. This would mean that of ten children, eight will focus on the length alone wihout paying any attention to the width, and two will focus on the width without paying any attention to the length. They will focus only on one dimension or the other. Since the two dimensions are independent at this stage, focusing on both at once would have a probability of only 0.16. That is less than either one of the two. In other words, the most probable in the beginning is to focus only on one dimension and in fact the child will say, "It's longer, so there's more in the sausage." Once he has reached this first level, if you continue to elongate the sausage, there comes a moment when he will say, "No, now it's too thin, so there's less." Now he is thinking about the width, but he forgets the length, so you have come to a second level which becomes the most probable after the first level, but which is not the most probable at the point of departure. Once he has focused on the width, he will come back sooner or later to focus on the length. Here you will have a third level where he will oscillate between width and length and where he will discover that the two are related. When you elongate you make it more thin, and when you make it shorter, you make it thicker. He discovers that the two are solidly related and in discovering this relationship, he will start to think in terms of the transformation and not only in terms of the final configuration. Now he will say that when it gets longer it gets thinner, so it's the same thing. There is more of it in length but less of it in width. When you make it shorter it gets thicker; there's less in length and more in width, so there is compensation—compensation which defines equilibrium in the sense in which

I defined it a moment ago. Consequently, you have operations and conservation. In other words, in the course of these developments you will always find a process of self-regulation which I call equilibration and which seems to me the fundamental factor in the acquisition of logical-mathematical knowledge.

I shall go on now to the second part of my lecture, that is, to deal with the topic of learning. Classically, learning is based on the stimulus-response schema. I think the sitmulus-response schema, while I won't say it is false, is in any case entirely incapable of explaining cognitive learning. Why? Because when you think of a stimulus-response schema, you think usually that first of all there is a stimulus and then a response is set off by this stimulus. For my part, I am convinced that the response was there first, if I can express myself in this way. A stimulus is a stimulus only to the extent that it is significant and it becomes significant only to the extent that there is a structure which permits its assimilation, a structure which can integrate this stimulus but which at the same time sets off the response. In other words, I would propose that the stimulus-response schema be written in the circular form — in the form of a schema or of a structure which is not simply one way. I would propose that above all, between the stimulus and the response there is the organism, the organism and its structures. The stimulus is really a stimulus only when it is assimilated into a structure and it is this structure which sets off the response. Consequently, it is not an exaggeration to say that the response is there first, or if you wish at the beginning there is the structure. Of course we would want to understand how this structure comes to be. I tried to do this earlier by presenting a model of equilibration or self-regulation. Once there is a structure, the stimulus will set off a response, but only by the intermediary of this structure.

I should like to present some facts. We have facts in great number. I shall choose only one or two and I shall choose some facts which our colleague, Smedslund, has gathered. (Smedslund is currently at the Harvard Center for Cognitive Studies.) Smedslund arrived in Geneva a few years ago convinced (he had published this in one of his papers) that the development of the ideas of conservation could be indefinitely accelerated through learning of a stimulus-response type. I invited Smedslund to come to spend a year in Geneva to show us this, to show us that he could accelerate the development of operational conservation. I shall relate only one of his experiments.

During the year that he spent in Geneva he chose to work on the conservation of weight. The conservation of weight is, in fact, easy to study since there is a possible external reinforcement, that is, simply weighing the ball and the sausage on a balance. Then you can study the child's reactions to these external results. Smedslund studied the conservation of weight on the one hand, and on the other hand, he studied the transitivity of weights, that is, the transitivity of equalities if $A = B$ and $B = C$, then $A = C$, or the transitivity of the qualities if A is less than B, and B is less than C, then A is less than C.

As far as conservation is concerned, Smedslund succeeded very easily with five- and six-year-old children in getting them to generalize that weight is conserved when the ball is transformed into a different shape. The child sees the ball transformed into a sausage or into little pieces or into a pancake or into any other form, he weighs it, and he sees that it is always the same thing. He will affirm it will be the same thing, no matter what you do to it; it will come out to be the same weight. Thus Smedslund very easily achieved the conservation of weight by this sort of external reinforcement.

In contrast to this, however, the same method did not succeed in teaching transitivity. The children resisted the notion of transitivity. A child would predict correctly in certain cases but he would make his prediction as a possibility or a probability and not as a certainty. There was never this generalized certainty in the case of transitivity.

So there is the first example, which seems to me very instructive, because in this problem in the conservation of weight there are two aspects. There is the physical aspects and there is the logical-mathematical aspect. Note that Smedslund started his study by establishing that there was a correlation between conservation and transitivity. He began by making a statistical study on the relationships between the spontaneous responses to the questions about conservation and the spontaneous responses to the questions about transitivity, and he found a very significant correlation. But in the learning experiment, he obtained a learning of conservation and not of transitivity. Consequently, he was successful in obtaining learning of what I called earlier physical experience (This is not surprising; it is simply a question of noting facts about objects.) but he was not successful in obtaining a learning in the construction of the logical structure. This doesn't surprise me either, since the logical structure is not the result of physical experience. It cannot be obtained by external reinforcement. The logical structure is reached only through internal equilibration, by self-regulation, and the external reinforcement of seeing the balance did not suffice to establish this logical structure of transitivity.

I could give many other comparable examples, but it seems to me useless to insist upon these negative examples. Now I should like to show that learning is possible in the case of these logical-mathematical structures, but on one condition—that is, that the structure which you want to teach to the subjects can be supported by simpler, more elementary, logical-mathematical structures. I shall give you an example. It is the example of the conservation of number in the case of one-to-one correspondence. If you give a child seven blue tokens and ask him to put down as many red tokens, there is a preoperational stage where he will put one red opposite each blue one. But when you spread out the red ones, making them into a longer row, he will say to you, "Now, there are more red ones than there are blue ones."

Now how can we accelerate, if you want to accelerate, the acquisition of this conservation of number? Well, you can imagine an analogous structure but in a simpler, more elementary, situation. For example, with Mlle. Inhelder, we have been studying recently the notion of one-to-one correspondence by giving the child two glasses of the same shape and a big pile of beads. The child puts a bead into one glass with one hand and at the same time a bead into the other glass with the other hand. Time after time he repeats this action, a bead into one glass with one hand and at the same time a bead into the other glass with the other hand and he sees that there is always the same amount on each side. Then you hide one of the glasses. You cover it up. He no longer sees this glass but he continues to put one bead into it while putting at the same time one bead into the other glass which he can see. Then you ask him whether the equality has been conserved, whether there is still the same amount in one glass as in the other. Now you will find that very small children, about four years old, don't want to make a prediction. They will say, "So far, it has been the same amount, but now I don't know. I can't see anymore, so I don't know." They do not want to generalize. But the generalization is made from the age of about five and one-half years.

This is in contrast to the case of the red and blue tokens with one row spread out, where it isn't until seven or eight years of age that children will say there are the same number in the two rows. As one example of this generalization, I recall a little boy of five years and nine months who had been adding the beads to the glasses for a little while. Then we asked him whether, if he continued to do this all day and all night and all the next day, there would always be the same amount in the two glasses. The little boy gave this admirable reply, "Once you know, you know for always." In other words, this was recursive reasoning. So here the child does acquire the structure in this specific case. The number is a synthesis of class inclusion and ordering. This synthesis is being favored by the child's own actions. You have set up a situation where there is an iteration of one same action which continues and which is therefore ordered while at the same time being inclusive. You have, so to speak, a localized synthesis of inclusion and ordering which facilitates the construction of the idea of number in this specific case, and there you can find, in effect, an influence of this experience on the other experience. However, this influence is not immediate. We study the generalization from this recursive situation to the other situation where the tokens are laid on the table in rows, and it is not an immediate generalization but it is made possible through intermediaries. In other words, you can find some learning of this structure if you base the learning on simpler structures.

In this same area of the development of numerical structures, the psychologist Joachim Wohlwill, who spent a year at our Institute at Geneva, has also shown that this acquisition can be accelerated through introducing additive operations, which is what we introduced also in the experiment which I just described. Wohlwill introduced them in a different way but he too was able to obtain a certain learning effect. In other words, learning is possible if you base the more complex structure on simpler structures, that is, when there is a natural relationship and development of structures and not simply an external reinforcement.

Now I would like to take a few minutes to conclude what I was saying. My first conclusion is that learning of structures seems to obey the same laws as the natural development of these structures. In other words, learning is subordinated to development and not vice-versa as I said in the introduction. No doubt you will object that some investigators have succeeded in teaching operational structures. But, when I am faced with these facts, I always have three questions which I want to have answered before I am convinced.

The first question is, "Is this learning lasting? What remains two weeks or a month later?" If a structure develops spontaneously, once it has reached a state of equilibrium, it is lasting, it will continue throughout the child's entire life. When you achieve the learning by external reinforcement, is the result lasting or not and what are the conditions necessary for it to be lasting?

The second question is, "How much generalization is possible?" What makes learning interesting is the possibility of transfer of a generalization. When you have brought about some learning, you can always ask whether this is an isolated piece in the midst of the child's mental life, or if it is really a dynamic structure which can lead to generalizations.

Then there is the third question, "In the case of each learning experience what was the operational level of the subject before the experience and what more complex structures has this learning succeeded in achieving?" In other words, we must look at each specific learning experience from the point of view of the spontaneous operations which were present at the outset and the operational level which has been achieved after the learning experience.

My second conclusion is that the fundamental relation involved in all development and all learning is not the relation of association. In the stimulus-response schema, the relation between the response and the stimulus is understood to be one of association. In contrast to this, I think that the fundamental relation is one of assimilation. Assimilation is not the same as association. I shall define assimilation as the integration of any sort of reality into a structure, and it is this assimilation which seems to me fundamental in learning, and which seems to me the fundamental relation from the point of view of pedagogical or didactic applications. All of my remarks today represent the child and the learning subject as active. An operation is an activity. Learning is possible only when there is active assimilation. It is this activity on the part of the subject which seems to me underplayed in the stimulus-response schema. The presentation which I propose puts the emphasis on the idea of self regulation, on assimilation. All the emphasis is placed on the activity of the subject himself, and I think that without this activity there is no possible didactic or pedagogy which significantly transforms the subject.

Finally, and this will be my last concluding remark, I would like to comment on an excellent publication by the psychologist Berlyne. Berlyne spent a year with us in Geneva during which he intended to translate our results on the development of operations into stimulus-response language, specifically into Hull's learning theory. Berlyne published in our series of studies of genetic epistemology a very good article on this comparison between the results of Geneva and Hull's theory. In the same volume, I published a commentary on Berlyne's results. Now the essence of Berlyne's results is this: our findings can very well be translated into Hullian language, but only on condition that two modifications are introduced. Berlyne himself found these modifications quite considerable, but they seemed to him to concern more the conceptualization than the Hullian theory itself. I'm not so sure about that. The two modifications are these. First of all, Berlyne wants to distinguish two sorts of responses in the S-R schema. First, responses in the ordinary, classical sense, which I shall call "copy responses", and secondly, what Berlyne called "transformation responses." Transformation responses consist of transforming one response of the first type into another response of the first type. These transformation responses are what I called operations, and you can see right away that this is a rather serious modification of Hull's conceptualization because here you are introducing an element of transformation and thus of assimilation and no longer the simple association of stimulus-response theory.

The second modification which Berlyne introduces into the stimulus-response language is the introduction of what he calls internal reinforcements. What are these internal reinforcements? They are what I call equilibration or self-regulation. The internal reinforcements are what enable the subject to eliminate contradictions, incompatibilities, and conflicts. All development is composed of momentary conflicts and incompatibilities which must be overcome to reach a higher level of equilibrium. Berlyne calls this elimination of incompatibilities internal reinforcements.

So you see that it is indeed a stimulus-response theory, if you will, but first you add operations and then you add equilibration. That's all we want!

Editor's note: A brief question and answer period followed Professor Piaget's presentation. The first question related to the fact that the eight-year-old child acquires conservation of substance prior to conservation of weight and volume. The question asked if this didn't contradict the order of emergence of the pre-operational and operational stages. Piaget's response follows:

The conservation of weight and the conservation of volume are not due only to experience. There is also involved a logical framework which is characterized by reversibility and the system of compensations. I am only saying that in the case of weight and volume, weight corresponds to a perception. There is an empirical contact. The same is true of volume. But in the case of substance, I don't see how there can be any perception of substance independent of weight or volume. The strange thing is that this notion of substance comes before the two other notions. Note that in the history of thought, we have the same thing. The first Greek physicists, the pre-socratic philosophers, discovered conservation of substance independently of any experience. I do not believe this is contradictory with the theory of operations. This conservation of substance is simply the affirmation that something must be conserved. The children don't know specifically what is conserved. They know that since the sausage can become a ball again there must be something which is conserved, and saying "substance" is simply a way of translating this logical necessity for conservation. But this logical necessity results directly from the discovery of operations. I do not think that this is contradictory with the theory of development.

Editor's note: The second question was whether or not the development of stages in children's thinking could be accelerated by practice, training, and exercise in perception and memory. Piaget's response follows:

I am not very sure that exercise of perception and memory would be sufficient. I think that we must distinguish within the cognitive function two very different aspects which I shall call the figurative aspect and the operative aspect. The figurative aspect deals with static configurations. In physical reality there are states, and in addition to these there are transformations which lead from one state to another. In cognitive functioning one has the figurative aspects --for example, perception, imitation, mental imagery, etc.

Secondly, there is the operative aspect, including operations and the actions which lead from one state to another. In children of the higher stages and in adults, the figurative aspect are subordinated to the operative aspects. Any given state is understood to be the result of some transformation and the point of departure for another transformation. But the pre-operational child does not understand transformations. He does not have the operations necessary to understand them so he puts all the emphasis on the static quality of the states. It is because of this, for example, that in the conservation experiments he simply compares the initial state and the final state without being concerned with the transformation.

In exercising perception and memory, I feel that you will reinforce the figurative aspects without touching the operative aspect. Consequently, I'm not sure that this will accelerate the development of cognitive structures. What needs to be reinforced is the operative aspect—not the analysis of states, but the understanding of transformations.

Preschool Thought
Rochel Gelman

I find it noteworthy that this special issue has provided for a separate essay on preschool thought. Until very recently, almost all researchers of cognitive development have made a habit of contrasting the preschooler with the older child. Preschoolers have been characterized as lacking the classification abilities, communication skills, number concepts, order concepts, memorial skills, and a framework for reasoning about causal relationships between events that older children are granted. Indeed, had one written an essay on preschool thought five years ago, the conclusion might have been that preschoolers are remarkably ignorant. In this essay I review some of the evidence that has begun to pile up against the view that preschoolers are cognitively inept. I then consider why we failed to see what it is that preschoolers can do and possible misinterpretations of the recent findings.

It is commonplace to read about the egocentrism of preschool children. The idea is that the young child either is unable to take the perspective of another child or adult or, worse yet, believes his or her own perspective is the same as that of others. Such general statements derive support from a variety of studies. When asked to describe an abstract shape for another child, a preschooler will sometimes use private labels, for example, "mommy's hat" (Glucksberg, Krauss, & Weisberg, 1966). The child's talk in the presence of others often goes on without any attempt to coordinate this talk with that of other speakers; the child seems not to care who else is speaking, what they say,

---

or whether he or she is being listened to. "He feels no desire to influence his listener nor to tell him anything; not unlike a certain type of drawing room conversation where everyone talks about himself and no one listens" (Piaget, 1955, p. 32). When asked to choose a picture that represents the view of a mountain seen by someone opposite the child, the child selects the representation that matches what the child sees (Piaget & Inhelder, 1956)!

In 1973, Marilyn Shatz and I reported on our studies of the speech used by 4-year-olds when they talked to 2-year-olds, peers, or adults. We found that our subjects generally used short and simple utterances when they described the workings of a toy to their 2-year-old listeners. In contrast, these same 4-year-old children used longer and more complex utterances when describing the same toy to their peers or adults (Shatz & Gelman, 1973). Was it possible that these children, who were presumed to be egocentric speakers by the research community at large, were adjusting their speech in accordance with their perception or conception of their listeners' different abilities and needs? As it turns out, yes. We (Gelman & Shatz, 1977) found that 4-year-olds' speech to a 2-year-old serves different functions and contains somewhat different messages than does their speech to adults. Speech to 2-year-olds serves to show and tell, to focus, direct, and monitor attention; speech to adults includes talk about the child's own thoughts and seeks information, support, or clarification from adults. Adult-directed speech also contains hedges about statements of fact, indicating that the child recognizes that he or she may be wrong and that the adult could challenge his or her statements. The children in our experiments were clearly taking the different needs and capacities of their listeners into account when talking to them. They hardly seem egocentric!

What about the claim that preschoolers think their visual perspective is the same as that of another person? Here again the presumed is contradicted. In an elegant series of experiments with 1-3-year-old children, Lempers, Flavell, and Flavell (1977) demonstrated over and over again that it is simply wrong to deny preschoolers an ability to distinguish their perspective from that of others. In the "show-toy task," 1-3-year-old children showed toys to adults so that the front side was visible to the adult. This means they turned away from themselves the front of the toy and thereby deprived themselves of their original perspective. When asked to show pictures, almost all the 2- and 3-year-olds turned the front side to the adult and thereby ended up seeing the blank back of the picture. Still younger children showed the picture horizontally rather than egocentrically, that is, they did not simply hold the picture upright and thus show the back to their adult cohort in the task.

More recently, Flavell, Shipstead, and Croft (Note 1) dispelled the rumor that preschoolers believe that the closing of their own eyes deprives others of visual information about them. In fact, there is so much evidence now coming in about the perspective-taking abilities of preschoolers (for reviews, see Gelman, 1978; Shatz,

1978) that I find it hard to understand how I or anyone else ever held the belief that preschoolers are egocentric.

In retrospect one might argue that the perspective-taking abilities of preschoolers make sense. Young children do interact with others and they do talk. If they did not have any perspective-taking abilities, how could they ever communicate (cf. Fodor, 1972)? The argument might continue that we may have been wrong on the perspective-taking front, but surely we were correct in our characterization of other cognitive abilities. After all, number concepts seem much removed from the daily interactions of a preschooler. Besides, they constitute abstract ideas--the kind of ideas that everyone knows are very late in cognitive development. All of this may well be true; nevertheless, preschoolers know a great deal about the nature of number. I and my collaborators have shown that children as young as 2 years honor the principles of counting and are able to use a counting algorithm to reason numerically, for example, to determine that an unexpected change in the numerical value of a set occurred because of surreptitiously performed addition or subtraction. (See Gelman & Gallistel, 1978, for a review of the arithmetic reasoning abilities of preschoolers.)

Successful counting involves the coordinated application of five principles (Gelman & Gallistel, 1978). These are as follows: (1) The one-one principle--each item in an array must be tagged with one and only one unique tag. (2) The stable-order principle--the tags assigned must be drawn from a stably ordered list. (3) The cardinal principle--the last tag used for a particular count serves to designate the cardinal number represented by the array. (4) The abstraction principle--any set of items may be collected together for a count. It does not matter whether they are identical, three-dimensional, imagined, or real, for in principle, any discrete set of materials can be represented as the contents of a set. (5) The order-irrelevance principle--the order in which a given object is tagged as one, two, three, and so on, is irrelevant as long as it is tagged but once and as long as the stable-order and cardinal principles are honored. Number words are arbitrary tags. The evidence clearly supports the conclusion that preschoolers honor these principles. They may not apply them perfectly, the set sizes to which they are applied may be limited, and their count lists may differ from the conventional list, but nevertheless the principles are used. Thus, a 2-year-old may say "two, six" when counting a two-item array and "two, six, ten" when counting a three-item array (the one-one principle). The same child will use his or her own list over and over again (the stable-order principle) and, when asked how many items are present, will repeat the last tag in the list. In this example, the child said "ten" when asked about the number represented by a three-item array (the cardinal principle).

The fact that young children invent their own lists suggests that the counting principles are guiding the search for appropriate tags. Such "errors" in counting are like the errors made by young language learners (e.g., "I runned"). In the latter case, such errors are taken to mean that the child's use of language is rule governed and that these rules come from the child; we are not likely to hear speakers of English using such words as *runned, footses, mouses, unthirsty,* and *two-six-ten.* We use similar logic to account for the presence of idiosyncratic count lists.

Further facts about the nature of counting in young children support the idea that some basic principles guide their acquisition of skill at counting. Children spontaneously self-correct their count errors, and perhaps more important, they are inclined to count without any request to do so. If we accept the idea that the counting principles are available to the child, the fact that young children count spontaneously without external motivation fits well. What's more, the self-generated practice trials make it possible for a child to develop skill at counting.

Still other cognitive domains exist for which it has been possible to reveal considerable capacity on the part of the young child. There are conditions under which preschoolers classify according to taxonomic categories (Rosch, Mervis, Gray, Johnson, & Boyes-Braem, 1976), classify animate and inanimate objects separately (Keil, 1977; Carey, Note 2), and use hierarchical classifications (Keil, 1977; Mansfield, 1977; Markman & Siebert, 1976). They can be taught to use a rule of transitive inference (Trabasso, 1975). They can be shown to be sensitive to temporal order (Brown, 1976). They believe, as do adults, that causes precede their effects (Bullock & Gelman, 1979; Kun, 1978). They use rules to solve problems (Siegler, 1978), and so on. In short, they have considerable cognitive abilities. Why, then, has it taken us so long to see them? I think there are two related reasons.

First, we simply did not look. Indeed, we seemed to choose to ignore facts that were staring us in the face. Consider the case of counting prowess in the young child. It is now clear that preschoolers can and do count. But many of us, myself included, who researched number concepts in children started out with the view that preschoolers were restricted to the use of a perceptual mechanism for number abstraction. The idea was that their representation of number was governed by the same pattern-recognition abilities that are used to distinguish one object from another. Just as they distinguish "cowness" and "treeness," they presumably distinguished "twoness" and "threeness." I don't remember how many times I saw preschoolers counting in my various experiments before I finally recognized they were indeed able to count, no matter what our theories led us to believe. I do remember one 3-year-old telling me that he much preferred one task over another, that being the one in which it was possible to count! And it took us a while to recognize the ubiquitous tendency for 4-year-olds to talk down to 2-year-olds.

The failure to recognize facts that contradict existing theories is not unique to those who study cognitive development. Time and time again we read in the history of science of similar cases. It seems as if we have a general tendency to resist new facts if their recognition means giving up a theory without being able to come up with another that will account for the new as well as the old facts. I believe that we now know enough about the nature of the development of number concepts to be able to deal with the apparent contradictions between the new and old research findings. The young child seems unable to reason about number without reference to representations of specific numerosities, representations obtained by counting. With development, the child's reasoning moves from a dependence on specific representations to an algebraic stage in which specific representations of numerosity are no longer required. In the conservation task, the child has to make inferences about equivalence and nonequivalence on the basis of one-to-one correspondence. It matters not what the particular numbers of items in the two displays are. If they can be placed in one-to-one correspondence, then they are equal by definition. If we are correct, then the abilities we have uncovered can be seen as the beginning understanding of number. In this light their existence need not be seen as contradictory findings. Indeed, once one begins to talk about precursors of later cognitive abilities it is no longer unreasonable to start the search for those concepts and capacities the preschooler must have if he or she is to acquire complex cognitive abilities. We should expect to find domains in which they are quite competent--if only we look.

Recent work on the learning and memorial abilities of young children endorses my belief that there are many cases in which it will suffice to decide to look for competence in order for us to take note of it. As Carey (1978) pointed out, young children perform an incredible task by learning the lexicon of their native language. She estimated that 6-year-old children have mastered to some degree about 14,000 words. To do this, the children need to learn about nine new words a day from the time they start speaking until the time they reach their sixth birthday. This is truly a remarkable accomplishment. So what if the preschooler fails on a task that requires him or her to sort consistently by taxonomic category? The same child has to have some classification abilities in order to learn the lexicon so rapidly. To be sure, the child probably does not learn the full meaning of every new word the first time that word is heard. But as Carey showed, "One or a very few experiences with a new word can suffice for the child to enter it into his or her mental lexicon and to represent some of its syntactic and semantic features." Given this and the continued exposure to that word, it is then possible for a child to learn more about it and to reorganize his or her lexicon and the conceptual framework involved therein.

Nelson (1978) made it clear that young children readily learn the scripts that describe the class of events they encounter. Others (e.g., Mandler, in press) have shown young children to have excellent memories for stories--a fact that really should not surprise us, given the young child's interest in hearing stories.

Although some abilities are so pervasive that simply deciding to attend to them will make them evident, this is not true for a wide variety of cognitive skills, for example, reading and metacognitive skills. This brings me to the second reason for our failure, until recently, to acknowledge the cognitive capacities of preschoolers.

Many of the young child's cognitive abilities are well concealed and require the modification of old tasks or the development of new tasks for their revelation. I return to the question of early number concepts. Young children systematically fail Piaget's number conservation task. With this task, they behave as if they believe that the number of objects in a row changes when items are pushed together or spread apart. They thus begin by agreeing that two rows placed in one-to-one correspondence represent equal amounts; when they see one row lengthened, however, they deny the continued equivalence.

In an effort to control for a variety of variables that might have interfered with the child's possible belief in the invariance of the numerical value of a set despite the application of a lengthening transformation, my colleagues and I developed what we call "the magic task" (Gelman, 1972). The task involves two phases. The first establishes an expectancy for the continued presence of two sets of two given values, say, 3 and 2, despite the repeated covering and uncovering of those sets. To avoid reference to number or the use of ambiguous terms such as *more* or *less*, one of these displays is designated "the winner," and the other "the loser." These are covered and children have to find the winner and tell us why they have or have not done so once they uncover a display. As luck would have it, preschoolers decide on their own that numerical value is the determinant for winning and losing status. They thus establish an expectancy for two particular numerical values. Then, unbeknownst to the child, the second phase of the experiment begins when the experimenter surreptitiously alters one of the expected displays. Across different conditions and experiments, the changes involve addition, subtraction, displacement, change in color of the original objects, and even a change in identity of the original objects. Children who encounter a change in number produced by subtraction or addition say that the expected number has been violated, typically identify the number of elements present and the number that should be present, and make explicit reference to the transformation that must have been performed--even if they did not see it. In contrast, children who encounter the effects of irrelevant transformations say the number of elements is as expected despite the change in length of a display, or in the color, or in the identity of an element in that display.

According to the results of the magic task, preschoolers know full well that lengthening or shortening an array does not alter the numerical value of a display. Still, these same children fail the conservation task. But note how different these tasks are. In the conservation task the child has to judge equivalence on the basis of one-to-one correspondence, correctly interpret questions that are ambiguous, watch the transformation being performed, and then ignore the effect of that transformation. In the magic task the child need not make judgments of equivalence based on one-to-one correspondence, he or she need not (indeed cannot) see the transformation being performed, and there are no ambiguous terms to misinterpret. In other words, the magic task is a very stripped down version of the conservation task. Likewise, many other tasks that show preschoolers in a positive light have downgraded the complexity of the tasks that they fail, altered the instructions, changed the stimuli used, embedded the question of interest in games preschoolers play, provided extensive pretraining before testing on the target task--In short, in many cases it has been necessary to develop tasks and experimental settings to suit the preschool child (Gelman, 1978). This is easier said than done. Consider the magic game which *was* designed to meet our best guesses as to how to elicit the number-invariance rules honored by the young child.

Bullock and Gelman (1977) modified the magic task in order to determine whether preschoolers could compare two number pairs. In particular, the question was whether they would recognize that the number pair 1 and 2 was like 3 and 4 insofar as 1 and 3 were both "less" and 2 and 4 were both "more." Children between the ages of 2 1/2 and 4 were first shown one-item and two-item displays, and they established expectancies for a set of one and a set of two items. Half the children were told that the one-item array was the winner; half were told that the two-item array was the winner. From the experimenter's point of view this was also a more-less comparison task. To determine whether the 21/2-4-year-old children in the experiment knew this, we surreptitiously replaced the original displays with three-item and four-item displays and asked which of these was the winner. Many of the older children were confused by this question and said that neither was the winner--an observation which in point of fact was correct. When asked to make the best possible choice, the children then went on to choose the display that honored the relation they were reinforced for during the expectancy training. Apparently the children did not immediately realize that it was all right to make a judgment of similarity, given the fact that neither of the new displays was identical to either of the original displays. Our variation in question format served to tell them that the transfer task called for a similarity judgment. My point here is that we started out with a task that was designed for young children and still we found that the task presented problems.

This example of the subtle ways in which a task can confound the assessment of those early cognitive abilities that are generally buried is not an isolated one. I have discussed others elsewhere (Gelman, 1978), and for me they are very sobering. They make it clear that in many cases, it takes more than a decision to look for early cognitive abilities. It is often exceedingly difficult to know how to design tasks so that they will be suitable for use with young children. I believe this derives in part from the fact that many of the preschoolers' cognitive abilities are fragile and as such are only evident under restricted conditions--at least compared with the conditions under which older children can apply their knowledge. This brings me to my next point.

Some might take the recent demonstrations of early cognitive abilities to mean that preschoolers are miniature adults as far as their cognitions are concerned. This is not what I want people to conclude, and should they so conclude it would not be in the best interests of either those who study cognitive development or the child. The fact remains that despite the recent demonstration of some complex cognitive abilities, young children fail a wide range of tasks that seem so simple for older children. I believe that many of the best insights into the nature of development will come from understanding exactly what conditions interfere with the use and accessibility of those capacities the young child does possess. These insights may also be of the greatest educational relevance. However, these insights can only come after we have uncovered the basic capacities that make cognitive growth a possibility.

What I do want people to realize is that we have been much too inclined to reach conclusions about what preschoolers cannot do, compared with what their older cohorts can do on a variety of tasks. We must cease to approach young children with only those tasks that are designed for older children. The time has come for us to turn our attention to what young children can do as well as to what they cannot do. Without a good description of what young children do know, it's going to be exceedingly difficult, if not impossible, to chart their course as they travel the path of cognitive development. What's worse, we run the serious risk of making unwarranted statements about the nature of preschool curricula. I have had people tell me that there is no point in teaching young children about numbers, since preschoolers cannot conserve numbers. This, I submit, is a non sequitur. The conservation task is but one index of numerical knowledge, and it is beginning to look like it is an index of a rather sophisticated knowledge.

My message is quite straightforward. We should study preschoolers in their own right and give up treating them as foils against which to describe the accomplishments of middle childhood. We have made some progress in recent years, but there is still plenty of room for those who are willing to take on the mind of the young child.

REFERENCE NOTES

1. Flavell, J.H., Shipstead, S.G., & Croft, K. *What young children think you see when their eyes are closed.* Unpublished manuscript, Stanford University, 1978.

2. Carey, S. *The child's concept of animal.* Paper presented at the meeting of the Psychonomic Society, San Antonio, Texas, November 1978.

REFERENCES

Brown, A.L. The construction of temporal succession by preoperational children. In A.D. Pick (Ed.), *Minnesota symposium on child psychology* (Vol. 10). Minneapolis: University of Minnesota Press, 1976.

Bullock, M., & Gelman, R. Numerical reasoning in young children: The ordering principle. *Child Development*, 1977, 48, 427-434.

Bullock, M., & Gelman, R. Preschool children's assumptions about cause and effect: Temporal ordering. *Child Development*, 1979, 50, 89-96.

Carey, S. The child as word learner. In M. Halle, J. Bresnan, & G.A. Miller (Eds.), *Linguistic theory and psychological reality*. Cambridge, Mass.: Massachusetts Institute of Technology Press, 1978.

Fodor, J.A. Some reflections on L.S. Vygotsky's Thought and language. *Cognition*, 1972, 1, 83-95.

Gelman, R. Logical capacity of very young children: Number invariance rules. *Child Development*, 1972, 43, 75-90.

Gelman R. Cognitive development. In L.W. Porter & M.R. Rosenzweig (Eds.), *Annual review of psychology* (Vol. 29). Palo Alto, Calif.: Annual Reviews, 1978.

Gelman, R., & Gallistel, C.R. The child's understanding of number. Cambridge, Mass.: Harvard University Press, 1978.

Gelman, R., & Shatz, M. Appropriate speech adjustments: The operation of conversational constraints on talk to two-year-olds. In M. Lewis & L.A. Rosenblum (Eds.), *Interaction, conversation, and the development of language*. New York: Wiley, 1977.

Glucksberg, S., Krauss, R.M., & Weisberg, R. Referential communication in nursery school children: Method and some preliminary findings. *Journal of Experimental Child Psychology*, 1966, 3, 333-342.

Keil, F. *The role of ontological categories in a theory of semantic and conceptual development*. Unpublished doctoral dissertation, University of Pennsylvania, 1977.

Kun, A. Evidence for preschoolers' understanding of causal direction in extended causal sequences. *Child Development*, 1978, 49, 218-222.

Lempers, J.D., Flavell, E.R., & Flavell, J.H. The development in very young children of tacit knowledge concerning visual perception. *Genetic Psychology Monographs*, 1977, 95, 3-53.

Mandler, J.M. Categorical and schematic organization. In C.R. Puff (Ed.), *Memory, organization, and structure.* New York: Academic Press, in press.

Mansfield, A.F. Semantic organization in the young child: Evidence for the development of semantic feature systems. *Journal of Experimental Child Psychology,* 1977, 23, 57-77.

Markman, E.M. & Siebert, J. Classes and collections: Internal organization and resulting holistic properties. *Cognitive Psychology*, 1976, 8, 561-577.

Nelson, K. How young children represent knowledge of their world in and out of language: A preliminary report. In R. Siegler (Ed.), *Children's thinking: What develops?* Hillsdale, N.J.: Erlbaum, 1978.

Piaget, J. *The language and thought of the child.* London: Routledge & Kegan Paul, 1955.

Piaget, J., & Inhelder, B. *The child's conception of space.* London: Routledge & Kegan Paul, 1956.

Rosch, E., Mervis, C.B., Gray, W.D., Johnson, D.M. & Boyes-Braem, P. Basic objects in natural categories. *Cognitive Psychology*, 1976, 8, 382-439.

Shatz, M. The relationship between cognitive processes and the development of communication skills. In C.B. Keasey (Ed.), *Nebraska symposium on motivation* (Vol. 26). Lincoln: University of Nebraska Press, 1978.

Shatz, M., & Gelman, R. The development of communication skills: Modifications in the speech of young children as a function of listener. *Monographs of the Society for Research in Child Development*, 1973, 38(2, Serial No. 152).

Siegler, R.S. The origins of scientific reasoning. In R.S. Siegler (Ed.), *Children's thinking: What develops?* Hillsdale, N.J.: Erlbaum, 1978.

Trabasso, T.R. Representation, memory and reasoning: How do we make transitive inferences. In A.D. Pick (Ed.), *Minnesota symposium on child psychology* (Vol. 9). Minneapolis: University of Minnesota Press, 1975.

Where Do I Go Next? Intelligent Searching by Very Young Children

Judy S. DeLoache and Ann L. Brown

A memory-based search task was used to investigate the organization of searching by very young children. The task required the child to remember in what natural location in his or her own home a toy had been hidden. Both an older (27 months) and a younger (21 months) group of subjects achieved a high level of errorless retrievals. To examine the children's ability to search differentially as a function of their own level of certainty that they remembered the location of the toy, two surprise trials were included on which the toy was hidden as usual but was then moved without the subject's knowledge. The children's search behavior on these surprise trials was compared to their error trials (occasions on which the child initially searched the wrong location). Both age groups showed greater persistence in their initial search on surprise than on error trials, indicating that their retrieval effort was based on their level of subjective certainty. The two age groups displayed different patterns in the subsequent searching that they did: The older, but not the younger, subjects searched differently on surprise and error trials. On surprise trials they searched selectively and intelligently, confining their search

Originally published in *Developmental Psychology*, 1984, 20, 37-44. Copyright ©1984 by the American Psychological Association. Reprinted with permission of the publisher and author.

primarily to locations that were nearby or in some way related to the place where the toy had actually been hidden. The related searching of the older children suggested that they had made intelligent guesses about plausible alternative locations for the missing toy.

Very young children generally perform quite well in tasks requiring them to remember the location of a hidden object (e.g., Horn & Myers, 1978; Perlmutter et al., 1981), especially if the object is hidden in a natural location in the large-scale environment (DeLoache, 1980; DeLoache & Brown, 1983; DeLoache, Cassidy, & Brown, 1983). Since young children willingly search the environment to retrieve an object before they reliably search internally to retrieve stored information, memory-based search tasks may represent an especially good domain for examining the emergence of simple forms of mnemonic organization.

In the present research we asked whether in a situation in which their basic memory performance is excellent, very young children would be capable of a very simple form of metamemory (Flavell, 1979; Wellman, 1983). In particular, can they accurately assess the current state of their own memory and then use that assessment to guide their subsequent behavior? We know that older subjects do so. In internal memry tasks, children as young as kindergarten age allocate retrieval effort based on subjective certainty or feeling of knowing judgments: The more certain they are that they know something not immediately retrievable, the more extensive and persistent are their efforts to retrieve it (Posnansky, 1978, Wellman, 1977).

We used a memory-based search task in which the child watches while a toy is hidden in a natural location in the home (e.g., behind a chair). After a delay interval, the child is allowed to retrieve the toy. One-and-a-half and 2-year-old children generally achieve a high level of performance in this task, with errorless retrievals averaging 75% or better across several studies (DeLoache & Brown, 1979, 1983; DeLoache, Cassidy, & Brown, 1983).

To see if subjective certainty influences young children's retrieval or search behavior, we employed a surprise procedure, a technique frequently used in object-permanence research to illuminate the infant's understanding and expectations about objects (e.g., Charlesworth, 1969; Gelman, 1972; LeCompte & Gratch, 1972; Ramsay & Campos, 1978). On two of the hide-and-seek-trials, the toy was hidden as usual but was surreptitiously moved without the child's knowing it. We expected that the persistence with which the 18- to 30-month-old subjects searched would provide an indirect assessment of their level of certainty: The more certain children are that they remember the correct location, the longer they should continue searching there after failing to find the toy immediately.

We therefore compared the persistence of the children's searching on surprise trials with any error trials that occurred, that is, all regular trials on which they mistakenly searched an incorrect place first. In both cases, the child's initial search had failed to retrieve the toy. On surprise trials they were in fact at the correct location and hence should have been confident of their choice. On error trials the children were wrong—they may have forgotten the correct location or become confused—so their level of certainty should have been considerably less. Thus, we expected to observe greater persistence in searching for the toy on surprise than on error trials.[1]

We were especially interested in whether any subsequent searching that the children did would also be influenced by their confidence in the correctness of their initial search. A reasonable and intelligent response to the surprising absence of an object at its remembered location is to search plausible alternative locations. Imagine a woman who fails to find her car keys on the coffee table where she remembers leaving them. She might consider the possibility that she has misremembered some detail with respect to the precise location and thus search all around the table surface or even check to see if the keys have been brushed off the table onto the floor. Or she might find out if someone else moved the keys. Thus, this hypothetical adult selects from all the potential locations in the room only those places that are near or in some way related to where she remembers the keys should be. In other words, she confines her searching to places that would be plausible locations of the keys if her memory for where she left them is essentially correct.

Where would a young child search next, after failing to find a toy where he or she expected it would be? We examined the types of locations searched to see if the subjects searched intelligently on surprise trials, that is, if they tended to restrict their searching to locations related or near to the actually correct location. Searching related locations should occur more frequently on surprise than on error trials, since certainty that the toy was hidden in a particular location specifies reasonable alternative locations to be searched.

---

1   We had planned to obtain a more direct assessment of surprise, independent from the search persistence measure, by videotaping and analyzing the children's facial expressions on discovering the absence of their toy (as Gelman (1972) and others have done to assess surprise). However, the usual reaction of the children on the surprise trials was to immediately turn to their mothers or the experimenter, and hence away from the camera, so these data were not obtained.

Method

Subjects

The subjects were 12 boys and 12 girls, equally divided into a younger group whose mean age was 21 months (18 to 23 months) and an older group with mean age 27 months (25 to 30 months). Data from one additional subject were eliminated, because her performance on the basic task was so poor it would have been difficult to interpret her behavior on surprise trials.

Procedure

To ensure that performance was high before the surprise trials were presented, we asked the parents to introduce the hide-and-seek game to their own children, using a stuffed toy approximately 9 in. (22.9 cm) high (Big Bird, Mickey Mouse) as the object to be hidden.

On each trial the child watched while the experimenter hid the toy[2] in a natural location in the home (under couch or chair cushions, under pillows, behind doors or pieces of furniture, and so forth). The child's attention was always called to the act of hiding, but the hiding places were never named. After the toy was hidden, a timer was set for a specified interval; the child was told that when the bell rang, he or she could get the toy. During the delay interval, the subject's activity was not controlled, with the exception that he or she was not allowed to retrieve the toy or hover near it.[3]

All trials were videotaped, and written records were also made. Two experimenters were present, one to operate the video camera and one to conduct the

---

2 Because of a provocative finding in an earlier study, the person who hid the toy was varied, with the experimenter hiding it on one half of the Day 1 trials and the subject hiding it on the other half. Since performance was identical regardless of who hid the toy, a subsequent experiment also failed to find a reliable effect for this variable, the manipulation and analysis are not discussed.

3 The delay interval was shortened on Day 2 so it would be possible to have more trials than were given on Day 1. In the several studies conducted with this task, the length of the delay interval appears to have little or no effect.

hide-and-seek game with the child. A trial was scored as correct (an errorless retrieval) only if the subject went to the correct location without first searching any other place. If a subject made an error, he or she was permitted to search other locations for approximately 1 min. Then, if necessary, hints were given to enable the child to find the toy.

All subjects participated in two days of testing. The first day included one practice (1-min interval) and four regular trials, two each with 3- and 5-min delay intervals, with order of interval length counterbalanced across subjects. During the delay interval for at least one of these trials, some pretext was presented for taking the child out of the room in which the game was played. This was done so that the subject would not notice something different about the surprise trials on Day 2, when it was essential that he or she be out of the room while the toy was moved from its hiding place. On Day 2, each subject received six trials. The first had a 1-min delay interval, and Trials 2 through 6 had 2-min intervals.

The surprise trials were the second and fifth trials on day 2.[4] The toy was hidden as usual but was moved by one experimenter while the child was out of the room. On the first surprise trial, the toy was always moved to one of two large shopping bags the experimenters brought. After the initial search of the correct location, approximately one minute was allowed during which the child was permitted or encouraged to continue searching. At the end of one minute the experimenter showed the subject where the toy was, saying, "Big Bird wanted to surprise you, so I helped him hide in my bag." This was done to make sure the children understood that nothing mysterious or magical had been responsible. It also enabled us to see if they would use that information to guide their searching on the second surprise trial, that is, to see if the next time they failed to find the toy where expected, they would draw the reasonable influence that someone had moved it again.

Results

The overall level of performance on Day 1, when no surprise trials were given, was 75% errorless retrievals for both the old and young groups, data that are quite comparable to those found in other research with the hide-and-seek task (DeLoache &

---

4   Only one subject failed to search the correct location on a surprise trial. On this occasion the experimenter managed to surreptitiously move the toy back to the original hiding place and then gave hints to help the subject find it. The next trial was made a surprise trial.

Brown, 1983; DeLoache, Cassidy, & Brown, 1983). An Age × Trial Blocks mixed analysis of variance (ANOVA) of the mean number of errorless retrievals produced no significant effects. Performance at the 3- and 5-min intervals was identical.

Comparison of Surprise and Error Trials

Persistence of initial searching. We expected that the subjects would be more surprised at the absence of the toy and hence more persistent in searching on surprise than on error trials. From the videotapes, the length of the initial search was timed in seconds. Strict criteria were adopted for scoring the occurrence of a search, in part to rule out instances in which a child simply scanned around the room without actively searching. The subject had to either move some obstacle out of the way (e.g., open a door, lift up a cushion) or reorient her body (e.g., get down to look under a couch), and she had to check a place that could in fact completely conceal the toy. Timing of the initial search began when the children first moved an obstacle or reoriented themselves and ended when they ceased actively searching that place.[5]

---

5   A second, naive observer independently timed the searching of eight subjects (4 young and 4 old, randomly selected from the 18 subjects who had made at least one error). The correlation between the two observers' recordings was .98.

Variable	Young (n = 10)[a]		Old (n = 8)[a]	
	Surprise	Error	Surprise	Error
No. of trials	20	25	16	15
Mean no. of searches per trial	0.90	0.63	1.38	0.90
Mean no. of related searches per trial	0.40	0.20	1.13	0.31[b]

[a] Four old and two young subjects had no errors, so their data are not included.
[b] $p < .05$.

Table 1. Additional Searching on Surprise and Error Trials

Variable	Young (n = 12)	Old (n = 12)
Mean no. of related searches per trial	0.33	1.04**
Proportion of all searches that were related	44%	76%*
Proportion of first searches that were related	55%	95%**
No. of trials with a related search	0.67	1.42**
Mean no. of searches per trial	0.88	1.38
Mean no. of trials with any searches	1.33	1.58

* p < 10 (one-tailed). **p < .05.

Table 2. Searching by Young and Old Subjects on Surprise Trials

The initial search times were compared for surprise and error trials, using data from the 18 subjects who made at least one error in the study (4 old and 2 young subjects had 100% errorless retrievals). The hypothesized difference was confirmed: Both the old and young children were more persistent, in fact spent almost twice as long, when searching the correct place (M = 6.42 s on surprise trials than when they were searching the incorrect location (M = 3.54 s for error trials). The main effect for surprise versus error trials, $F(1, 16)$ = 6.44, p < .05, was the only significant result in a 2 (age) ×2 (trials) mixed ANOVA of the initial search times. In addition, the children were somewhat more likely to return and research the initial location of surprise (42%) than on error trials (18%), although this difference was not significant.

Search data. After their initial unsuccessful search on surprise and error trials, the subjects usually (71% of the trials) went on to search one or more additional locations. The number of additional searches ranged from 0 to 6. All these additional searches were classified according to their relationship to the initial location searched (the correct location on surprise trials, the place the subject had mistakenly searched first on error trials) or to the first surprise trial location. A search was scored as "related" if it fell into one or more of the following three categories: (a) a nearby or adjacent location (e.g., after looking under one couch cushion, the child looked under the next cushion or behind the couch); (b) an analogous location (after looking under a pillow at one end of the couch, the subject looked under a different pillow at the other end of the couch); (c) the surprise Trial 1 location (subjects sometimes looked in the bag to which the experimenter had moved the toy on the first surprise trial). Any searches not falling in these categories were considered "unrelated" (after looking under a couch cushion, the subject searched inside a desk drawer).

We had expected that the subjects might search differently on surprise and error trials, and in particular, that related searching would be more common on surprise trials. As shown in Table 1, this was true for older subjects; their mean number of related searches was significantly greater on surprise than on error trials (Wilcoxon matched-pairs signed-ranks tests, p < .05; Wilcoxon, 1949). For the younger children, however, the mean number of related searches did not differ significantly for surprise or error trials. Thus, the older children, but not the younger ones, organized their retrieval efforts differently as a function of whether their initial search was correct.

The difference in the number of related searches found for the older subjects could be an artifact, if they simply searched more actively on surprise than on error trials. This was not the case, however. Considering the mean number of searches of any kind (related and/or unrelated combined), slightly more searches were conducted on surprise trials than on error trials (see Table 1), but for neither age group did the difference even approach significance (Wilcoxon tests). Also, no differences were found for the proportion of surprise and error trials on which subjects searched at least one additional place following their initial search.

Surprise Trials

To examine further the age difference in differential related searching, the data from the surprise trials only of all 24 subjects were analyzed. As shown in Table 2, several analyses indicated that the older subjects were more likely to search related locations than were the younger subjects. (a) A significant age difference was found for the *mean number* of related searches (the range of scores was 0 to 3.0 for the older and 0 to 1.0 for the younger subjects). Eleven of the 12 older subjects had one or more related searches per surprise trial, while only one young subject did (Fisher's exact probability test, p < .05). (b) The proportion of all searches that were related was significantly greater for the older than for the younger subjects (p < .05, one-tailed): Only one old subject had less than 50% related searches, whereas over half the young subjects did. (c) The older subjects more often searched a related location on the first search following the initial, unsuccessful one. In fact, all but one of the older subjects always went directly from the correct surprise trial location to a related one. A significant age difference was found in the number of subjects whose first searches were related 100% of the time versus those for whom 50% or less were related (p < .05). (d) Finally, a comparison of the number of surprise trials with related searches (one or more) revealed that the majority of the old subjects searched related locations on both of their surprise trials, but most of the young subjects did not (p < .05). Only one older subject had no related search trials, whereas only one subject had related searches on both trials.

Analyses of base rates of searching again suggested that the differential rates of related searching for the two age groups were not simply due to differences in overall level of searching. (a) There was no significant difference in the total number of searches of any kind (related plus unrelated) for the old and young subjects. (b) The old and young subjects did not differ in the number of surprise trials on which additional searching of any kind occurred.

Qualitative Aspects of Searching

Qualitative aspects of search data supplement the quantitative data reported above. On surprise trials, the old subjects frequently searched a new location (48% of their searches) — one that had never been used as a hiding place but that was usually (75% of the time) related to the correct location. The young subjects seldom (19%) searched a new location; they most frequently (62%) returned to a location that had served as the hiding place on a previous trial, especially the immediately preceding one. The two age groups searched the experimenter's bag equally often on the second surprise trial (18% and 19% of their searches for the old and young subjects, respectively).

On the error trials, nearly all of the initial search errors (93% for the old group and 77% for the young group) were due to a subject searching a hiding place from a previous trial, especially the immediately preceding one. The two age groups were equally likely to correct themselves, that is, to go from the initial, erroneous search directly to the correct location (33% and 38% of their trials for the old and young subjects, respectively). Considering all the additional searches that occurred on error trials, the old and young groups had equal proportions of related searches (21% and 22%, respectively).

In summary, the main results showed contrasting patterns of searching for the two age groups. The older subjects searched differently on surprise and error trials, with their modal response on surprise trials being to search one or more related locations. The younger subjects conducted fewer related searches. Their modal response on both surprise and error trials was to search a location that had served as a previous hiding place.

Discussion

The data provide evidence of very early manifestations of metamemory. The search-persistence data suggest that the 18- to 30-month old children based their retrieval effort on how certain they were of the correctness of their initial response. Both age groups searched significantly longer on surprise trials, when they were in fact correct, than on error trials, when they were mistaken. They also tended to re-search the correct location on surprise trials. A typical example of a persistent search is the surprise trial behavior of a 23-month-old boy: He looked under the couch cushion where his toy had been hidden, then pulled the cushion completely off the couch and examined the area, turned around to say "No!" to his mother, and then turned back and briefly checked the correct hiding place again.

These results are analogous to those obtained with adults and older children (Posnansky, 1978; Wellman, 1977) for internal retrieval of stored information, rather than retrieval of an object from the external environment (as in the present study). In both cases, children's retrieval effort is based on their assessment of their own memory state — of how much they think they know or how well they think they know it. That children are capable of this form of metamemory earlier in an external memory task such as the hide-and-seek game is consistent with other research showing that metamemory skills are generally exercised earlier with respect to external variables (Gordon & Flavell, 1977; Yussen & Levy, 1977).

The older children's memory assessment also guided their subsequent search behavior, so that they displayed qualitatively different patterns of searching on surprise and error trials. On surprise trials the old subjects almost always (95%) began their additional searching at locations that were in some way related either to the correct location or to their previous surprise trial experience, and three fourths of their total surprise trial searches were so related. In contrast, less than one fourth of their error trial searches were related.

The related surprise trial searching of the older children suggests that they (like the hypothetical adult with the lost car keys) may have generated plausible hypotheses to explain the toy's absence that then guided their subsequent search efforts. The fact that the older children often searched locations that were analogous to the correct location (48% of their related searches) suggests that they sometimes assumed that they had misremembered a detail about the toy's location, such as which specific one of a category of locations it was. Supporting examples include a child's going from the couch pillow under which the toy was hidden to a different pillow at the other end of the couch or to a pillow on a chair.

The older subjects occasionally (16% of their related searches) seemed to consider the possibility that some intervening event may have displaced the toy. A 30-month-old searched both under and beside the couch in which his toy had been hidden. Another subject explicitly verbalized his hypothesis: He looked in the desk drawer in which his toy had been hidden, said "Did Mickey Mouse fall out?" and then proceeded to search behind the desk.

Some children also realized that a social agent might be responsible for the toy's absence. On the second surprise trial, several subjects (five old and four young) inferred (correctly) that the experimenter had again moved their toy; they went immediately from their initial search to the experimenter's bag, the place to which the toy had been moved on the first surprise trial. A 29-month-old girl whirled around from her initial search of the correct location, yelling to the experimenter "In your bag!". She then ran immediately to look in the bag, saying "Jackie, *you* took him."

These children thus demonstrated understanding of the adult experimenter as an independent causal agent with respect to the location of their toy, an ability Fisher and Jennings (1981) have argued is a reflection of representational capacity. The conception of social agency revealed here is fairly complex: The child infers that his or her toy is missing for the same reason that it was missing earlier—because the experimenter moved it from its original location. Thus, the child uses his or her memory of the previous surprise trial to understand the current one, to infer not only that the experimenter moved the toy but also where she probably hid it. It is interesting that none of the children ever accused an adult of being responsible for the toy's absence on the first surprise trial. On her first surprise trial, the 29-month-old girl referred to above exclaimed, "Darn! Somebody taked him!" but she gave no evidence of suspecting that any of the adults present was the guilty party. Even a group of older pilot subjects (36 months old) never voiced any suspicions the first time their toy was unaccountably missing.

Evidence for the argument that the older children attempted to figure out plausible explanations for the toy's absence is the fact that one half of the surprise trial searches were of completely new locations (i.e., ones that had never been used as hiding places) but were usually related to the correct location. Thus, the older children selected places to search because they were plausible alternative locations for the toy and not because they had enjoyed any past association with it.

The search behavior of the subjects in this research can be examined in the light of the categorization of two types of selective search proposed by Wellman and Somerville (1983). The searching of the younger children clearly represents the less mature type, spatial associative searching, which involves searching a particular location because it is associated in the subject's mind with the object. When they failed to find their toy, whether on surprise or error trials, the younger children tended to search in places where it had been hidden before, reminiscent of the typical error in delayed-response tasks of searching for an object where one has previously found it (Daehler, Bukatko, Benson, & Myers, 1976; Loughlin & Daehler, 1973; Horn & Myers, 1978; Perlmutter et al., 1981; Webb, Massar, & Nadolny, 1972).

To a certain extent, the search behavior of the older subjects also fits the definition of spatial associative search, since the related locations were in some way associated with the initial location or with the toy. However, the related searching of the older children may also qualify as an example of the more mature form of searching defined by Wellman and Somerville: Deliberate or logical selective search "requires the ability to conceive of many possible locations, deliberately ruling out some and logically selecting others" (Wellman & Somerville, 1983). For example, Wellman and his colleagues (Haake, Somerville, & Wellman, 1980; Wellman, Somerville, & Haake, 1979) have reported that older preschool children are capable of deducing a critical search area for a lost object based on where they last saw the object and where they discovered it to be missing. In the present study, the older subjects used information about where they last saw a missing object to make an intelligent guess as to where it might now be. Their tendency to select new related locations on surprise trials indicates that the older children conceive of several possibile locations to search on the basis of their relation to the original hiding place. Their search behavior is thus more mature than the associative searching that characterizes the younger subjects, but it may still be less sophisticated than some of the forms of logical searching observed for older preschool children by Wellman and his colleagues.

References

Charlesworth, W.R. (1969). Surprise and cognitive development. In D. Elkind & J.H. Flavell (Eds.), *Studies in cognitive development: Essays in honor of Jean Piaget* (pp. 257-314). New York: Oxford University Press.

Daehler, M., Bukatko, D., Benson, K., & Meyers, N. (1976). The effects of size and color cues on the delayed response of very young children. *Bulletin of the Psychonomic Society*, 7, 65-68.

DeLoache, J.S. (1980). Naturalistic studies of memory for object location in very young children. *New Directions for Child Development*, 10, 17-32.

DeLoache, J.S., & Brown, A.L. (1979). Looking for Big Bird: Studies of memory in very young children. *The Quarterly Newsletter of the Laboratory of Comparative Human Cognition*, 1, 53-57.

DeLoache, J.S., & Brown, A.L. (1983). Very young children's memory for the location of objects in a large-scale environment. *Child Development*, 54, 888-897.

DeLoache, J.S., Cassidy, D.J., & Brown, A.L. (1983). *Precursors of mnemonic strategies in very young children's memory for the location of hidden objects*. Unpublished manuscript, University of Illinois.

Fischer, K.W., & Jennings, S. (1981). The emergence of representation in search: Understanding the hider as an independent agent. *Developmental Review*, 1, 18-30.

Flavell, J.H. (1979). Metacognition and cognitive monitoring: A new area of cognitive-developmental inquiry. *American Psychologist*, 34, 906-911.

Gelman, R. (1972). Logical capacity of very young children: Number invariance rules. *Child Development*, 43, 75-90.

Gordon, F.R., & Flavell, J.H. (1977). The development of intuitions about cognitive cueing. *Child Development*, 48, 1027-1033.

Haake, R., Somerville, S.C., & Wellman, H.M. (1980). Logical ability of young children in searching a large-scale environment. *Child Development*, 51, 1299-1302.

Horn, H., & Myers, N.A. (1978). Memory for location and picture cues at ages two and three. *Child Development*, 49, 845-856.

LeCompte, G.K., & Gratch, G. (1972). Violation of a rule as a method of diagnosing infants' levels of object concept. *Child Development*, 43, 385-396.

Loughlin, K.A., & Daehler, M.A. (1973). The effects of distraction and added perceptual cues on the delayed reaction of very young children. *Child Development*, 44, 384-388.

Perlmutter, M., Hazen, N., Mitchell, D.B., Grady, J.C., Cavanaugh, J.C., & Flook, J.P. (1981). Pictures cues and exhaustive search facilitate very young children's memory for location. *Developmental Psychology*, 17, 109-110.

Posnansky, C.J. (1978). Age- and task-related differences in the use of category size information for retrieval of categorized items. *Journal of Experimental Child Psychology*, 26, 373-382.

Ramsay, D.S., & Campos, J.J. (1978). The onset of representation and entry into Stage 6 of object permanence development. *Developmental Psychology*, 14, 79-86.

Webb, R.A., Massar, B., & Nadolny, T. (1972). Information and strategy in the young child's search for hidden objects. *Child Development*, 43, 91-104.

Wellman, H.M. (1977). Tip of the tongue and feeling of knowning experiences: A developmental study of memory monitoring. *Child Development*, 48, 13-21.

Wellman, H.M. (1983). Metamemory revisited. In M.T.H. Chi (Ed.), *Trends in memory development research*. New York: S. Karger. *Contributions to human development*.

Wellman, H.M., & Somerville, S.C. (1982). The development of human search ability. In M.E. Lamb & A.L. Brown (Eds.), *Advances in developmental psychology* (Vol. 2; pp. 41-84). Hillsdale, N.J.: Erlbaum.

Wellman, H.M., Somerville, S.C., & Haake, R.J. (1979). Development of search procedures in real-life spatial environments. *Developmental Psychology*, 15, 530-542.

Wilcoxon, F. (1949). *Some rapid approximate statistical procedures*. New York: American Cyanamid Company.

Yussen, S.R., & Levy, V.M. (1977). Developmental changes in knowledge about different retrieval problems. *Developmental Psychology*, 13, 114-120.

Children's Understanding of Retrieval Cue Utilization

William V. Fabricius and Henry M. Wellman

Children's knowledge of how to use external retrieval cues to aid memory was investigated in first, third, and fifth graders. To understand the logic of effective cue utilization one must know not only that cues are useful but that a specific cue is useful only if it is located where one will be when it is time to remember, and placed so one will encounter it automatically. Stories representing effective and ineffective cue locations were constructued. Many first graders believed that all cue locations were effective; the discrimination of ineffective locations showed a clear order of acquisition by age. Those first graders had little understanding of external retrieval cues as mnemonic means. As soon as children achieved this understanding, it was coordinated with temporal requirements for using cues effectively. However, full understanding of the temporal criteria required a series of developments. Children at first knew only that a cue encountered after the time to do the task would be ineffective. Next, children understood that a cue would be ineffective if it were encountered after the time one had to remember to do the task. Finally, most fifth graders knew that even a cue encountered before the task might be ineffective if the cue appeared greatly in advance of the time one had to remember. Results were discussed in terms of the importance of investigating children's integrated knowledge, or theories, about memory.

In children's effort to understand their world they encounter human cognition. They themselves and others possess internal mental states such as dreams, engage in symbolic processes such as language, and perform cognitive tasks such as remembering. Research on the development of metacognition—the development of knowledge of cognition—has probed the child's knowledge regarding language, attention, dreams, the brain, comprehension, and memory. By far the most research has focused on metamemory--the child's understanding of memory (Flavell & Wellman, 1977). It is surprising that metamemory research has focused almost solely on children's acquisition of certain memory "facts." There are numerous investigations of children's knowledge that some variable influences memory performance; for instance, that categorization aids recall (Moynahan, 1973), that recognition is easier than recall (Speer & Flavell, 1979), that study time limits memorization (Wellman, 1977). What this research fails to capture, however, are the child's further ideas about how memory variables work. After one knows that a particular factor influences memory there is much to learn about the limits of this influence, the conditions when it is optimal or attenuated, and the reasons and ways in which it operates. We know little of children's larger knowlege of memory, their theories that qualify and organize the effects of different influences on memory performance.

The specific memory theory of interest here is the child's qualified, organized knowledge of external retrieval cues. External retrieval cues (e.g., calendars, notes to oneself, and strings around the finger) provide a powerful strategy for solving everyday memory problems. The organization of a typcial kitchen presents one example. There may be canisters of different size and color to cue memory for the location of the flour, the sugar, and the coffee; arrangement of items in cupboards to cue memory for their locations; the trash periodically placed by the back door to facilitate remembering to put it out; and notes taped to the refrigerator as reminders of errands or desired behaviors (e.g., snacking less).

Adults report frequent strategic use of external retrieval cues (Herrman & Neisser, 1978). Kreutzer, Leonard, and Flavell (1975) found that kindergarteners (as well as older children) also showed a striking tendency to mention the usefulness of external memory cues. In that study there were no developmental differences in knowing that external retrieval cues could be useful but there were informal indications that older children's knowledge was possibly more complete, more qualified, and more integrated within a larger knowledge of other memory factors and processes.

Only informal indications were apparent because the evidence stemmed from a few subjects' spontaneous comments. More precise information would require that children make judgments about the usefulness of cues placed in a variety of different locations, carefully selected to provide full insight into the logic of their understanding.

Consider the sequence of events involved in instructing someone to do X tomorrow, followed by the person's use of some external cue to remember X. An effective cue should be obvious to the person so as to remind him or her wherever he or she is tomorrow when it is time to do X. Thus the cue should be at a particular place and time, but the whole scenario is filled with other places and times (e.g., the time and place the person is first instructed to remember, the place the task itself will take place, etc.). Many of these times and places are spatiotemporally connected with the person and the task but only some are truly good cue locations. By probing children's knowledge of the efficacy of different cue locations, the present study investigated the development of children's extended, organized knowledge of how external retrieval cues aid memory.

Method

Subjects

Sixteen first graders (M age = 7 years 1 month), 16 third graders (M = 9 years 0 months), and 16 fifth graders (M = 11 years 2 months) participated; there were equal numbers of boys and girls at each age. Children were from a school in a racially mixed, predominantly working-class school district in southeastern Michigan.

Materials

Two cutouts representing houses and one representing a school were shown on a horizontal 146 × 40 cm green board. The houses were in the lower left and right corners, and the school was centered along the upper edge. The school was divided into two classrooms. Each location (house or classroom) included two drawings of tables. One table in each pair included a drawer, which was an extra piece of paper attached so that it formed a hollow pocket. Pathways were drawn between the two houses and the school. In addition, there were color pictures of a boy and a girl, a small brown cardboard book, and a small white note with the word *book* printed on it. The boy or girl characters each had a shirt pocket and a bookbag that could hold the note (similar to the drawers on the desk). When in the drawer or bookbag, the note was not visible to the character; when it was attached to the table top or in the shirt pocket it appeared clearly visible.

Task

There were two story scenarios in which the character had to remember to take the book someplace and in which the note could be located in a number of different locations as a reminder. A note was used as the retrieval cue because a note was the modal strategy mentioned by all subjects in the Kreutzer et al. (1975) study. The following cue locations were used. The *instruction* location was where the story character was when he or she was told in the evening to remember to do the task the next day; thus, the cue at that location would be encountered before the time to remember the task. A second location was where the character would *be* when it was time to remember to do the task. The cue here would be encountered at the time to remember and before the time to do the task. The *task* location was where the character had to remember to go in order to do the task. Here the cue would be encountered after the time to remember, but at the time to do the task. The *destination* location was where the character's routine would end up, regardless of whether the task was remembered or not; thus, the cue would be encountered after the time to do the task. An *irrelevant* location was also included that was a place the character would not normally visit; the cue would not be encountered here at all. Finally, a movable cue location was possible, which was *with* the character (shirt pocket or bookbag). Among these locations the most effective cue locations were those with the character and where the character would be, because in both cases the cue could remind the character at the appropriate time and place. Ineffective locations were instruction, task, destination, and irrelevant locations.

The above task of retrieval cue knowledge concerns knowledge of cue location. A second aspect of cue effectiveness is that the cue should be placed so that it is likely to be encountered incidentally, without its having to be intentionally remembered or searched for. For the present task this dimension was represented as cue visibility; stories contrasted visible (table top or shirt pocket) and nonvisible (drawer or bookbag) cue placements in each cue location. Cue location and visibility interact: effective locations are good only if the cue is visible; ineffective locations are bad regardless of cue visibility.

In each scenario, the house and classroom on the left were the character's, those on the right were called the "friend's house" and the "other classroom":

Scenario 1. The character was located at home, and the book was at the friend's house. The character was instructed at night to remember to get the book from the friend's house on the way to school tomorrow and to take it to his or her classroom. The cue locations judged for this scenario were (a) be (at home); (b) irrelevant (the other classroom); and (c) with. In each location, the note could be placed visibly or nonvisibly.

Scenario 2. The character was at the friend's house, where he or she was spending the night, and the book was in the other classroom. At night the character was told to remember to get the book tomorrow after school, and to take it home. The character was to spend all the next day in his or her classroom. Cue locations tested were (a) instruction (friend's house); (b) be (his or her classroom); (c) task (other classroom); (d) destination (home); and (e) with. Visible and nonvisible placements of the cue were made.

Procedure

Each child received a judgment task followed by a choice task.

Judgment task. The child was asked whether each depicted cue placement was a good or bad place for the note to be to remind the character. Sixteen judgments, one each in the 8 x 2 (Location x Visibility) combinations, were obtained. The eight locations are the three in Scenario 1 plus the five in Scenario 2. Locations were blocked by scenario; thus, one scenario was described and all the locations relevant to it were judged one by one, before the next scenario was introduced. Scenario order was counterbalanced across subjects, and order of locations within scenarios was in one of two random orders. Visibility was blocked by location; at half the locations, the subject judged the visible placement first. Visibility order within locations was counterbalanced across subjects. The boy character was used in one scenario, the girl in the other; the first one used represented the sex of the subject.

The various home and school locations were first explained to the subject. It was emphasized that the note would be visible to the character if placed on a table top or in the shirt pocket but invisible in the drawer or bookbag. Further, it was stated that the drawer or bookbag were empty today, so that there would be no other reason to look in them. For Scenario 1, the character and book were placed appropriately, and the subject was told:

> The boy (girl) is home at night, and his mother tells him to remember
> to take his book to school tomorrow morning. But the book is at his
> friend's house. So tomorrow morning he has to remember to go to
> his friend's house and pick up his book and take it to school.

The experimenter then moved the character and book while reiterating the last sentence of the story. To ensure attention and comprehension, the subject was asked to move the character and book appropriately and to reiterate the last sentence. All children did this correctly. Then the experimenter asked, "What if the note were here (placing it in one of the locations)? Would that be a good place or a bad place for the note to be to remind him (her) to get this book?" Subjects were asked to explain why they thought it was a good or bad place. If any subject's explanation indicated a contradiction of the story constraints (e.g., "the boy would look in the bookbag for something else and see the note") the subject was corrected and a new judgment taken. The procedure for Scenario 2 was identical to that for Scenario 1.

Choice task. Here the subject was given the note, each scenario was described again, and the subject was asked to find the "very best" place for the note to be and to put it there. Before choosing, the subject was reminded of all the possible locations for the note to be.

The entire procedure took about 20 minutes. Subjects were seen in a second session, which was a replication but in reverse scenario order, 3-7 days after the first session. All subjects completed both sessions.

Results

Initial analysis of the data revealed no effects due to sex of subject; consequently sex was not a factor in any subsequent analyses.

Judgment Task

Understanding of cue location. Visible locations were examined first in order to determine whether children differentiated among effective (with, be) and ineffective (irrelevant, destination, task, instruction) locations. Children received a score of 0, 1 or 2 for correctly judging a cue location in neither, one, or both sessions, respectively. A 3 ×2 ×8 (Grade ×Scenario Order ×Cue Location mixed analysis of variance (ANOVA) on these scores revealed no effects involving order (Fs < 1.81). The effect of grade was significant, $F(2,42) = 18.73$, $p < .001$. Scheffe contrasts showed that first graders (M = 1.41) were significantly worse at judging cue location than were third graders (M = 1.75) or fifth graders (M = 1.87; ps < .05), who did not differ from each other. The effect of location was also significant, $F(7,294) = 56.46$, $p < .001$. The numbers of correct judgments for the four effective locations ranged from 1.96 to 2.0; numbers correct for irrelevant, destination, task, and instruction locations were 1.72, 1.66, 1.46, and .64, respectively. As a result of the ceiling effect for the effective locations, the Grade ×Location interaction also achieved significance, $F(14,294) = 7.93$, $p < .001$.

The order of difficulty for judging various cue locations was examined in a scalogram analysis (Green, 1956), depicted in Table 1. Children's judgments for each location were scored as correct (+) if they were consistently correct across sessions and as incorrect (-) if they were either inconsistent or consistently incorrect. First, third, and fifth graders were consistent 86%, 93%, and 91% of the time, respectively. Effective locations were treated as a single unit since performance on them was essentially perfect. Five patterns of responses across locations resulted from judging increasing numbers of locations correctly. The number of children at each grade level conforming to each of the five patterns is shown in Table 1. Only five children showed nonscalable patterns. The coefficient of reproductibility (Rep_a) is .98. The index of consistency (I) is .73 (greater than .50 is significant). Response patterns were significantly related to age; comparing Patterns 1-3 versus Patterns 4-5 at the three grades, $X^2(2) = 17.7$, p < .001.

Cue locations and grades	Pattern					
	1	2	3	4	5	Other
Criteria for assigning subject to a pattern						
Effective cue locations judged good (with and be)	+	+	+	+	+	
Ineffective cue locations judged bad						
Irrelevant	−	+	+	+	+	
Destination	−	−	+	+	+	
Task	−	−	−	+	+	
Instruction	−	−	−	−	+	
Number of subjects in each pattern						
First grade	7	1	3	4	0	1
Third grade	0	0	2	9	2	3
Fifth grade	0	0	1	6	8	1
All grades	7	1	6	19	10	5

Note: A + indicates that subjects judged these items correctly in each of the two sessions. A − indicates that subjects judged these items correctly in only one or neither of the two sessions.

Table 1. Response Patterns to Effective and Ineffective Cue Locations at the Three Grade Levels.

As is clear from Table 1, it is the discrimination among ineffective locations that accounts for the developmental change. Pattern 1 subjects, (seven first graders) made no distinctions among effective and ineffective locations; they did not consistently judge ineffective locations as bad. However, these subjects' responses were not a result of a simple response bias to say "good" to all cue locations. Only one of the seven showed that pattern, whereas the rest judged some locations to be bad on one session or the other.

Understanding of cue visibility. Understanding the role of cue visibility involves the understanding that any location judged good becomes bad if the cue is not immediately visible. Subjects who judged an ineffective location as bad when the cue was visible also judged the corresponding nonvisible cue placement at that location as bad. The rate was .94, 1.0, and .98 at first, third, and fifth grades, respectively. Thus a proportion score was calculated equaling the number of times a nonvisible location was judged bad when the corresponding visible location was judged good, divided by the subjects' total number of visible good judgments. This score ranges from 0 to 1.0 with increasing values indicating increasing knowledge that an effective cue location becomes ineffective if the cue is not visible. A 3×2 (Grade $\times$ Scenario Order) ANOVA revealed a significant effect due to grade, $F(2,42) = 8.36$, p.< 001. Scheffe contrasts showed that first graders $(M=.51)$ were significantly worse than third graders $(M=.81)$ and fifth graders $(M=90; ps < .001)$, who did not differ from each other. The effect of scenario order was also significant, $F(1,42) = 6.63$, p $< .05$ (M for Order 1-2 $= .84$; M for Order 2-1 $= .63$.

The pattern of the data is clearest if children's understanding of cue visibility is examined for subjects in each of the response patterns. Patterns 2 and 3 were collapsed and then subjects in the various patterns were compared in relation to the above score, $F(3,42)=10.94$, p $< .001$. This effect was due to Pattern 1 $(M=.20)$ differing from each of the other three patterns (Scheffe contrasts, ps $< .05$), which did not differ among themselves $(M=.65, .86,$ and $.84$, for Patterns 2/3, 4, and 5, respectively). The difference between Pattern 1 and the others did not result from the fact that Pattern 1 was comprised entirely of first graders; the eight first graders using the other response patterns $(M=.72)$ also performed significantly better on cue visibility than the first graders using Pattern 1 $(M=.20)$, $t(13) = 3.71$, p $< .01$.

Explanations of judgments. The explanations given for judgments were categorized into those that (a) described the story character as intentionally searching for the note (e.g., "If he doesn't see the note at home or in his class, he'll know it has to be in the other class so he'll just go and get it"; "She'll look for it cause she has to remember to find the note"), (b) referred to the spatial requirement that the note should be where it could be encountered ("She will see it there"; "He's not going there"), or (c) added a temporal requirement to Type b ("He can see it in the morning when he leaves"; "She will see it too late"; "She'll have it with her when she needs to remember"). Seventeen percent of the explanations were uncategorizable, and the largest group of those (9%) were explanations that did not allow a clear decision between Types a and b ("She wouldn't find the note"). Remaining explanations included "don't know" and "other" reasons. Intercoder reliability between two coders, calculated on 25% of the responses, was 93.7%.

Explanation type was related to response pattern. Explanations of Type a accounted for 65% of categorizable Pattern 1 explanations, but for only 23%, 5%, and 3% of categorizable explanations in Patterns 2/3, 4, and 5, respectively. All seven subjects in Pattern 1 gave at least one Type a explanation, versus only 53% of those in Patterns 2-5 (Fischer's exact p < .01). Explanations of Type b accounted for 32% in Pattern 1 and for the majority in Patterns 2/3, 4, and 5: 62%, 76%, and 66% respectively. Type c explanations, however, showed a steady increase across response patterns: 2%, 15%, 19%, and 31%, respectively. All Pattern 4 and 5 subjects gave at least one Type c explanation versus 50% of the Pattern 1 and 2/3 subjects (Fisher's exact p < .001).

Choice Task

It is possible that children would differ less given a different type of judgment to make. If asked to find the very best place for the cue, most children might agree that it should be in one of the effective locations. That is, they may have judged certain ineffective locations as good in some sense, but when asked about the best location they might then apply more adult-like criteria. It should be noted that the choice task does not involve simply remembering the responses given in the judgment task, but requires selecting one location as best. Since all subjects judged all effective locations as good, they had those locations in common to draw upon.

Each subject made four choices of the best location (one for each scenario in each session). Pattern 1 subjects chose the visible, effective locations as the best locations only 47% of the time, whereas the percentages for Patterns 2/3, 4, and 5 subjects were 75%, 89%, and 100%, respectively. Subjects were categorized as to whether or not they made any choice of an ineffective location (including any nonvisible cue placement and any visible placement in an ineffective location). Subjects in Patterns 1-3 were combined and were tested against Pattern 4 and 5, $x^2(2) = 17.49$, p < .001. Twelve out of 14 subjects in Patterns 1-3 made at least one choice of an ineffective location, whereas only 42% of Pattern 4 and none of Pattern 5 subjects did so.

Discussion

The results are best discussed in terms of the observed response patterns. Pattern 1 subjects did not distinguish effective from ineffective cue locations; they considered all cue locations as helpful. One possibility is that these subjects merely misunderstood the story sequences. However, all subjects could reiterate the stories correctly. Any misrepresentation of the story constraints obvious from the subject's explanations were corrected and new judgments were elicited. The stories involved familiar locales (home and school) and familiar sequences and constraints. The other more likely explanation is that many of the first graders understood that "cues help" yet did not understand the basic means-ends relation between the cue and remembering. Essentially, Pattern 1 subjects were insensitive to the spatial requirement that the cue and person should automatically come together at some point in the person's routine. This is shown both by their judgments that the irrelevant location would be effective and by their greater likelihood of identifying nonvisible locations as good. Instead,

Pattern 1 subjects indicated that the person remembered the cue before encountering it. This was seen in their high proportion of references to the story character's intentional search for the note. Indeed, we were struck by the number of first graders who clearly stated that the character would look in the drawer or bookbag in order to find the note. The logic that appears to be used by these subjects is one in which the retrieval cue and the memory target are separate or parallel memory goals, not coordinated into a means-ends relationship (Paris, 1978).

The present data further suggest that children's first understanding of retrieval cues as mnemonic means rather than memory goals themselves is embedded in some understanding of temporal requirements for their effective use. Since there was only one subject using Pattern 2, the data do not suggest that the children first understood the spatial requirement — that the character and note should automatically come together — without also having some idea about when this should occur. Rather, awareness of spatial and temporal requirements together appeared in Pattern 3. Pattern 3 subjects understood cue visibility and the ineffectiveness of the irrelevant location (both reflecting the spatial requirement). They also applied a temporal requirement in judging the destination location ineffective but the task location effective; namely, that the cue must be encountered at or before the time to do the task. Pattern 4 subjects knew the task location would be ineffective. Thus the temporal requirement employed by Pattern 4 subjects states that the cue must be encountered at or before the time to remember the task. Finally, Pattern 5 subjects realized that a cue encountered too long in advance of the time to remember would be ineffective. The developing sensitivity to temporal factors affecting cue utilization is reflected in subjects' increasing references with age to temporal factors in their explanations of their judgments.

These findings are important for two reasons: because of the memory domain investigated and because of the approach adopted. First, the present study adds to previous research on the child's knowledge and use of retrieval cues (Gordon & Flavell, 1977; Kobasigawa, 1974; Ritter, 1978). The present data make clear how children's early knowledge of retrieval cues becomes extensively qualified and organized during the school years. Most generally, the data described the child's growing knowledge of how to take advantage of his or her memory's automatic operation. Most studies of memory strategies focus on techniques for deliberately encoding or deliberately retrieving information. There has been little investigation of strategies used to obviate deliberate effortful remembering altogether. Yet this class may represent the most used, or certainly the most sought-after, solution to a variety of memory problems. The effective use of external memory devices or cues is probably the prototypic example of this sort of strategy (e.g., keeping addresses in an address book instead of memorizing them, putting your package by the door to ensure that you mail it). The present data show the development of an understanding of how retrieval cues should optimally be utilized to automatically obviate more deliberate memory efforts.

The importance of the present approach to investigating metamemory concerns the adequacy and comprehensiveness of our descriptions of children's knowledge of cognition. The results indicate that even children's early appreciation of some memory variable is likely to be part of a systematic approach to, or theory about, that variable's operation. A high level of consistency was found among subjects between the judgement and choice tasks, attesting to the robustness of these opinions. Our further understanding of metamemory development will require elaborating the theories children hold about memory. This approach to metamemory research yields important implications for the study of metamemory's role in memory performances. Several studies of the relationship of metamemory and memory performance have shown little correlation between the two (e.g., Cavanaugh & Borkowski, 1980; Salatas & Flavell, 1976). However, the metamemory tested in such studies has been children's knowledge that some variable or variables influence memory peformance. Yet knowledge that some variable exercises some influence does not represent knowledge of when and where it operates or how it competes with other factors. It is the child's development of more comprehensive theories of memory variables, as studied in the present research, that provides the appropriate framework in which to fully understand the development of metamemory and to search for its connections with memory behavior.

REFERENCES

Cavanaugh, J.C., & Borkowski, J.G. Searching for metamemory-memory connections: A developmental study. *Developmental Psychology,* 1980, 16, 441-435.

Flavell, J.H., & Wellman, H.M. Metamemory. In R.V. Kail & J.W. Hagen (Eds.), *Perspectives on the development of memory and cognition.* Hillsdale, N.J.: Erlbaum, 1977.

Gordon, F.R., & Flavell, J.H. The development of intuitions about cognitive cueing. *Child Development,* 1977, 48, 1027-1033.

Green, B.F. A method of scalogram analysis using summary statistics. *Psychometrika,* 1956, 21, 79-88.

Herrman, D.J., & Neisser, V. An inventory of everyday memory experiences. In M.M. Gruenberg, P.E.M. Orris, & R.N. Sykes (Eds.), *Practical aspects of memory.* New York: Academic Press, 1978.

Kobasigawa, A. Utilization of retrieval cues by children in recall. *Child Development,* 1974, 45, 127-134.

Kreutzer, M.A., Leonard, C., & Flavell, J.H. An interview study of children's knowledge about memory. *Monographs of the Society for Research in Child Development*, 1975, 40(1, Serial No. 159).

Moynahan, E.D. Development of knowledge concerning the effect of categorization on free recall. *Child Development*, 1973, 44, 238-246.

Paris, S.G. Coordination of means and goals in the development of mnemonic skills. In P.A. Ornstein (Ed.), *Memory development in children*. Hillsdale, N.J.: Erlbaum, 1978.

Ritter, K. The development of knowledge of an external retrieval cue strategy. *Child Development*, 1978, 49, 1227-1230.

Salatas, H., & Flavell, J.H. Behavioral and metamnemonic indicators of strategic behaviors under remember instructions in first grade. *Child Development*, 1976, 47, 81-89.

Speer, J.R., & Flavell, J.H. Young children's knowledge of the relative difficulty of recognition and recall memory tasks. *Developmental Psychology*, 1979, 15, 214-217.

Wellman, H.M. Preschoolers' understanding of memory-relevant variables. *Child Development*, 1977, 48, 1720-1723.

Children's Use of Scripts In Story Recall

Kathleen A. McCartney

Katherine Nelson

Recent work on children's comprehension of stories (Brown, 1975, 1976; Mandler & Johnson, 1977; Stein & Glenn, 1979) has called into question the claims made by Piaget (1926) and Fraisse (1963) that children's memories are "completely jumbled up" and are not sequential, causal, or deductive. The recent work, based on the notion of a story schema or story grammar, and using stories that are more relevant to children's own experience, has shown that children of 4 to 7 years are capable of sequential, logically connected recall of stories under favorable circumstances.

The notion of a story schema came originally from Bartlett (1932), who postulated that people use pre-existing schemata as guides to comprehension. One type of schema that has been related to story understanding by adults is a script as defined by Schank and Abelson (1977), that is, a mental representation of the sequence of actions called for in a familiar situation. Bower, Black & Turner (1979) report that, when given script-like stories for recall, adult subjects tended to confuse actions that were

---

Originally published in *Discourse Processes*, 1981, 4, 59-70. Reprinted with pemission of the publisher and author.

stated with actions not stated but strongly implied by the script.

Nelson (1979) has used the script construct to suggest one means children use to organize knowledge of their world. She described a script as a kind of model of repeated familiar experience which is called into play in the appropriate verbal or situational context. The model contains certain basic or obligatory events in sequence and predicts open slots for optional objects and events and what they may contain, and appropriate roles in the action and who can fill them. That is, there is a skeletal sequential structure that is called up in context and is filled in as needed with context-appropriate optional slot fillers and details (Nelson, 1979, p. 256).

In an investigation of preschoolers' knowledge about the routine events associated with having a meal in three different settings, Nelson (1979) found commonality among reports, reliable sequencing of actions, and a lack of personal, idiosyncratic, or egocentric detail, in contrast to the expectations of the Piagetian model. These findings have since been replicated with different children and different events, showing consistently that children's knowledge about mealtimes and about many other experiences appears to fit the script model (Nelson, in preparation).

.It is clear then that children can remember sequences of actions told as stories or experienced in real life; that they have scripts for familiar events; and that adults use scripts in comprehending stories. Can it be shown that children's scripts similarly guide their comprehension and memory for stories? If so, it might be suggested that script-type knowledge is an important foundation stone for the development of a story schema.

One step toward examining this question is to study children's recall for stories built around familiar scripts, in order to determine how such scripts are used. This was the aim of the present study. An analysis of the story recall in terms of a script model contrasted the frequency of recall of designated core events and other logically-consistent, supporting filler events. Kindergarteners and second graders were chosen as participants, to determine whether there were developmental changes in the ability to use script knowledge in story recall, and to evaluate the occurrence of egocentric interferences and difficulty in sequencing ability attributed to young children by Piaget and Fraisse.

The stories were composed of three sequences of activities within the theme of a typical evening in the life of a young child. The stories varied in sequence emphasis in order to see whether there were age differences in recall of components and sequences. It was hypothesized that subjects' changes would be logically consistent within the stories' theme, reflecting personal experience or familiarity with the specified routines.

METHOD

Subjects

Twenty-four kindergarteners and 24 second graders, from two neighboring elementary school districts, participated in the study; in each group, half the subjects were girls and half were boys. The kindergarteners ranged in age from 5;3.5 (years; months) to 6;4.5 (mean X = 5;9). The second graders ranged in age from 7:3.5 to 8:6.5 (mean X = 7;8). The children were white, from English-speaking families in a middle class suburban area.

Materials

Two stories were constructed about a typical evening in the life of a young child. Each story contained an introduction, a dinner script, full or abridged, a television event, and a bed script, full or abridged. Thus, the stories did not vary in topic, but rather in emphasis. In one story the dinner script was emphasized, and in the other the bed script was emphasized. Each full script consisted of 14 events, where event was defined as a character action (e.g., brushing one's teeth). The events chosen were extracted from verbal responses of preschoolers collected by Nelson (unpublished) and from informal verbal responses of adults collected by the experimenter to the questions, "What happens when you eat dinner?" and "What happens when you go to bed at night?" In the event selection an attempt was made to integrate the most frequently cited responses of both groups. Each abridged script consisted of 7 of the 14 events from the full script. These 7 events were judged as more salient than the remaining filler events by the two experimenters who collected the adult and child verbal protocols; the selection reflects their consensus. These salient or core events include the anchor events (i.e., the first and last events), and the main events (e.g., eating dinner and going to sleep), among others. The filler events provide logically-consistent information which serves to support the more salient events; these filler events represent routine actions as well, as opposed to more novel events.

Thus, the dinner-emphasis story consisted of the introduction, the full dinner script, the television event, and the abridged bed script, while the bed-emphasis story consisted of the same introduction, the abridged dinner script, the same television event, and the full bed script. The full and abridged scripts controlled for number of script events, number of sentences, and number of words. The full scripts consisted of 14 events, 11 sentences, and 101 words; the abridged scripts consisted of 7 script events, 6 sentences, and 50 words. Since the introduction and television event were common to both stories, the stories are equivalent along the above-specified dimensions. Note that the ratio of the full to the abridged script with respect to the words and events is 2:1.

A complete specification of the stories can be found in Table 1. Note that the introduction does not contain event knowledge but state knowledge (a distinction made by Mandler and Johnson, 1977), namely that the child character "enjoys spending night time" with his or her parents and that "tonight would be a lot like other nights."

Girls heard a story, dinner or bed, about a character named Rose, boys about a character named George. The stories were recorded on audio tape by an adult who was naive to the hypothesis of the study. Two copies of the four stories (Rose — dinner emphasis, Rose — bed emphasis, George — dinner emphasis, and George — bed emphasis) were recorded, in an effort to control for possible pragmatic effects (e.g., intonation). Story copy was counterbalanced within groups. The tapes were presented to the children on a Califone Cassette Recorder 3530. Children's story recalls were recorded on audio tape as well.

Procedure

Subjects were seen individually in an empty classroom. After introductions, children were invited to play some games with the experimenter.

When the child seemed to feel comfortable, and after at least 2 games of lotto, the game pieces were pushed to the opposite side of the table and the tape recorder was pulled forward. Subjects were told, "I'd like us to listen to a story someone made for me about a girl(boy) named Rose(George). After you hear the story, you can make your own tape of the same story. Then we can listen to your tape together. Are you ready to listen to the story?"

Following the story presentation, a 2-minute delay was filled by having the child put away the lotto game while the experimenter got the child's tape ready.

Next, subjects were asked to record their stories. Most children were eager to do so, though a few needed prompting (e.g., "What was the story about?"); only one kindergarten male had to be replaced as a subject for failure to record. Further prompting was given (e.g., "Go on.") when children paused. When the child appeared to have finished, he or she was asked the final probe, "Can you remember anything else that happened?"

After completing their story recalls, children were asked a series of questions regarding what parts of the story they liked, didn't like, and would change.

Scoring

The story reconstructions were scored for the presence or absence of each event by one judge. A second judge coded 8 reconstructions, 2 of which were randomly selected from each of the following 4 groups: kindergarten females, kindergarten males, second grade females, and second grade males. The judges agreed 94% of the time. In addition, the reconstructions were scored for number of event inventions (e.g., "After supper Rose did her homework."); number of event changes, where the child either made a significant phrase change which did not change the meaning of the event (e.g., "Rose said, 'May I be excused?'" for "Then Rose asked if she could leave the table.") or made a significant content change which still managed to carry the gist of the event's meaning (e.g., "And he said, 'No, it's too late.'" for "Her father said, 'sorry Rose, but you have school tomorrow.'"); and number of detail inventions or changes (e.g., "pink nightgown" for "green pajamas"). Agreement between the judges was perfect on the identification of these categories.

Total number of words used in the story reconstructions was also scored, as was total number of experimenter probes following the child's first utterance and preceding the child's last utterance.

RESULTS

A three-way (grade X gender X story) ANOVA was performed for number of words and number of events recalled. As expected, both show only grade effects ($F_{1,40} = 6.36$, $p < .02$ for words; $F_{1,40} = 10.10$, $p < .005$ for events), with second graders producing more words and more events than kindergarteners.

As a first step in an effort to investigate whether a skeletal, script-like event structure determined children's recall, a comparison was made between anchor/main events and the remaining shared events of the dinner-and bed-emphasis stories, excluding the two-sentence introduction (see Table 1 for a listing of the 17 shared events). Using a three-way (grade X gender X event, where event is a repeated factor) ANOVA, it was shown that anchor and main events were recalled better ($F_{1,704} = 13.89$, $p < .001$) than the remaining events. In fact, an examination of the rank ordering the shared events recalled across story emphasis showed that the kindergarteners' top five events include the three main events (events 11, 17, and 31-- see Table 1) and the two anchor events (events 3 and 31); the second graders' top five include two of the three main events and both anchors. Of interest is the fact that even the poorest recallers were sensitive to anchor and main events. The three poorest recallers, all kindergarteners, produced reconstructions consisting only of main events (e.g., "Bed. Watching television. Dinner.")

It was hypothesized that designated core events (the 7 events rated as most important) would be remembered better than filler events (the remaining 7 supporting events). As Figure 1 shows, this prediction seems to have held only for subjects in the dinner-emphasis condition. Separate event comparisons for dinner- and bed-emphasis groups, using a three-way (grade X gender X event) ANOVA, confirmed this

TABLE 1
Story Events

In dinner emphasis story	In bed emphasis story	Story event
I	I	(1) Rose enjoyed spending night-time with her parents
I	I	(2) Tonight would be a lot like other nights
C(A)	C(A)	(3) When Rose's mother yelled, "Dinner-time,"
C	C	(4) Rose was playing in her bedroom.
F		(5) Rose ran into the kitchen
F		(6) and asked, "What's for dinner?"
F		(7) Rose's father told her they were having her favorite, spaghetti.
C	C	(8) Then she washed her hands in the bathroom.
C	C	(9) Rose's Mother served them all a dish of spaghetti,
F		(10) and her father poured the milk.
C(M)	C(M)	(11) Then they all started eating their dinner.
F		(12) Rose's parents asked her what she had done at school that day.
F		(13) Then her parents talked about their day at work.
F		(14) Soon everyone finished eating.
C	C	(15) They had chocolate cake for dessert.
C(A)	C(A)	(16) Then Rose asked if she could leave the table.
C(M)	C(M)	(17) After dinner Rose and her parents watched some TV.
C(A)	C(A)	(18) After a while Rose's father said, "It's bedtime, Rose."
	F	(19) "Just a little longer?" she asked.
	F	(20) "Sorry Rose, but you have school tomorrow."
C	C	(21) Rose went to get ready for bed.
C	C	(22) She put on her favorite pair of green pajamas.
C	C	(23) In the bathroom she brushed her teeth
C	C	(24) and washed her face.
	F	(25) Then Rose's parents came to tuck her in.
	F	(26) Rose asked for a bedtime story,
	F	(27) so her mother told her one about life on a farm.
C	C	(28) After the story, Rose's mother and father kissed her good-night.
	F	(29) Her father shut off the light,
	F	(30) and whispered, "Sweet dreams."
C(M,A)	C(M,A)	(31) Soon Rose was fast asleep.

I stands for introduction
C stands for core event
M stands for main event, a type of core event
A stands for anchor event, also a type of core event
F stands for filler event

observation. Dinner-emphasis subjects recalled core events better ($F_{1,240} = 6.14$, p.02), while bed-emphasis subjects recalled core and filler events equally well ($F_{1,240}$). Though the failure of subjects to differentiate between core and filler events in the bed-emphasis story may reflect a problem with the initial adult rating, an alternate interpretation seems more likely. A rank ordering of events remembered by bed-emphasis subjects showed a three event sub-sequence (events 18, 19, and 20) to be highly salient; only the first event was rated a core event. Complementary evidence for event contiguity or cohesiveness is suggested by an examination of a less salient event sub-sequence. Only four dinner-emphasis subjects recalled event 12 (see Table 1), where Rose's parents ask her what she has done at school. Of those four, all recalled the following related event, where Rose's parents talk about their day at work. Thus, one can consider the dinner and bed scripts as higher-ordered sequences. The memory organizing properties of sub-sequences, of course, follows from this examination.

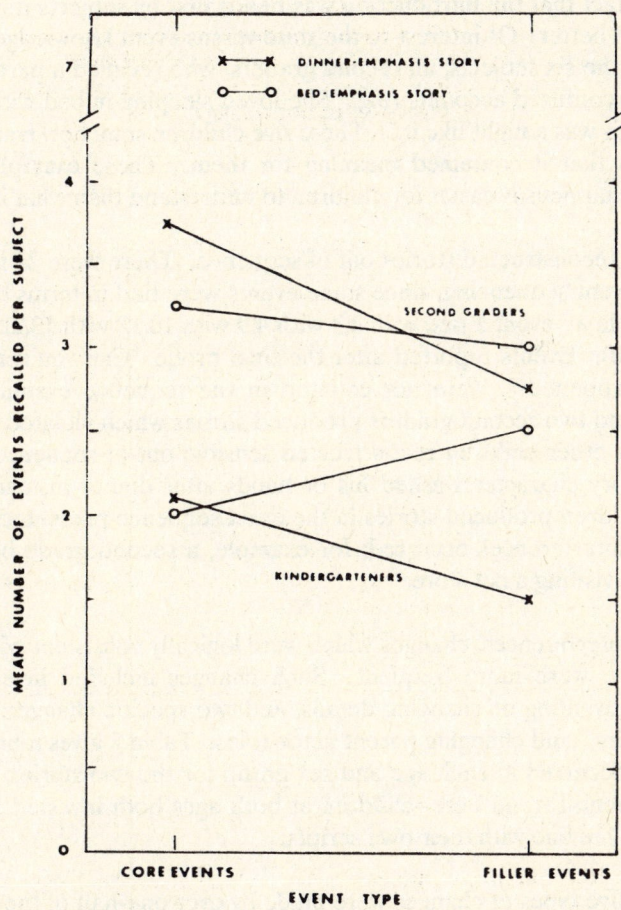

Fig. 1. Mean number of events recalled as a function of event type.

Having shown that anchor events are more easily recalled, one might be tempted to conclude that this is due to a serial position effect; however, this does not seem to be the case. A comparison of the first four shared events (events 1, 2, 3, and 4) and the last four shared events (23, 24, 28, and 31) with the nine remaining, middle shared events showed no recall difference ($F_{1,704} < 1$). Meyer and McConkie (1973) have found that structural importance rather than serial position determines what will be recalled, and indeed this seems to be the case. For example, the introduction was recalled less well than the remaining shared events ($F_{1,704} = 53.66$, $p < .001$) as predicted, possibly because it contains state (factual) rather than event (action) knowledge. The fact that the introduction was heard first by subjects did not seem to help them recall it better. Of interest to the state versus event knowledge comparison is the fact that of the six subjects, all second graders, who recalled a part of the introduction, five gave confused accounts (e.g., "She loved sleeping in bed with her mother and father, and this was a night like it.") These five children somehow transformed the introduction such that it contained meaning for them. These examples speak for themselves—what happens is easier for children to understand than what is.

Few children reconstructed stories out of sequence. There were 24 separate time units in need of event sequencing, since some events were tied in terms of time of occurrence (see Table 1: event 1 tied with 2,3 with 4,9 with 10,12 with 13,22 with 23 with 24, and 29 with 30). Events reported after the final probe, "Can you remember anything else that happened?" were not counted in the sequence examination. Five kindergarteners and two second graders produced stories which violated the sequencing pattern. Four other children reconstructed sensible out-of-sequence reconstructions (e.g., the story character washed his or hands after dinner instead of before). Thus, 37 of 48 children produced stories in the exact sequence presented. Only 3 obvious egocentric interferences occurred; for example, a second grade boy began his story with George visiting a pet store.

More subtle interferences, changes which were logically consistent within the typical evening theme, were more frequent. Such changes included inventing events, changing events, inventing or changing details, and two specific changes: mentioning "upstairs/downstairs," and changing parent actor roles. Table 2 gives a break-down of the changes that occurred in each age and sex group for the two stories. There is no obvious developmental trend here—children at both ages both invested and changed events, presumably in line with their own scripts.

Three of the five types of changes were made by over one-half of the subjects, the remaining two changes by over one-third. Also of interest is the fact that only four subjects produced stories containing none of the five changes examined, while 35 of the 48 subjects produced stories containing two or more types of changes.

In order to determine whether children were sensitive to the variation in emphasis between the event sequence, an analysis was performed on the ratio between the number of events recalled in the emphasized script (i.e., perfect recall would reflect a 14 to 7, or 2 to 1 ratio). A three-way (grade X gender X story) ANOVA using an arcsin transformation showed only grade to have had a significant effect ($F_{1,40} = 4.85$, p < .03; see Figure 2). The second graders gave 2.3 times as much information about the emphasized script, while kindergarteners gave only 1.3 times as much information. A particularly interesting developmental finding is the fact that kindergarteners and second-graders did not differ in the number of events reported for the unemphasized script (gender X grade X story, $F_{1,40} < 1$), while the groups did differ in the number of events reported for the emphasized script ($F_{1,40} = 14.55$, p < .001), with second graders reporting more events.

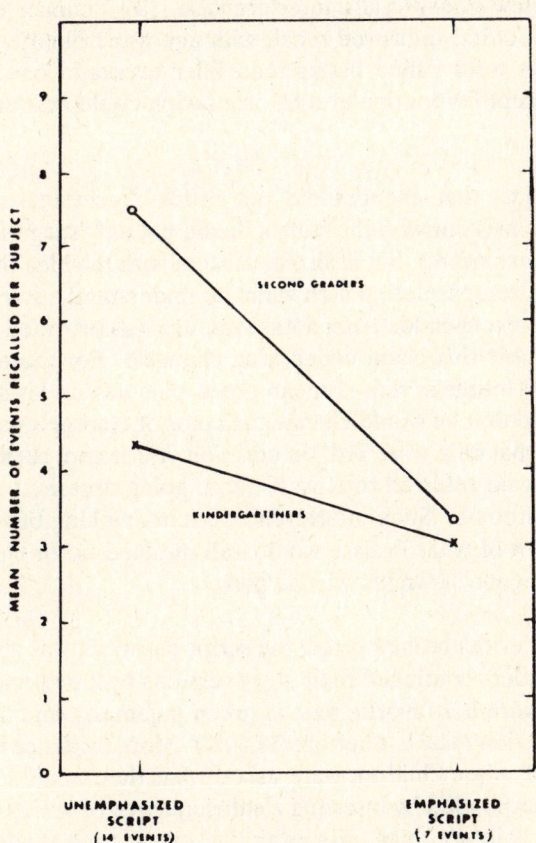

Fig. 2. Mean number of events recalled as a function of script emphasis.

During the questioning period following recall, 11 kindergarteners and 2 second graders referred to events not reported in their story reconstructions, implying that children knew more than the task elicited.

DISCUSSION

The purpose of the present study was to examine children's recall for script-based stories in an effort to determine whether the script model could account for the knowledge representations used by children. The major findings of the study are: (1) Structural importance and not serial position was shown to guide recall, as evidence by the fact that anchor and main events were recalled better than filler events. (2) Children were able to sequence properly (i.e., 37 of 48 subjects produced exactly correct sequences) with few idiosyncratic interferences. (3) Younger children recalled main events as well as older; improved recall with age was primarily for filler events. Moreover, core events were called better than filler events in one story. It seems reasonable that a concept for routine events, or a script, could account for these findings.

In addition, the fact that changes did not reflect "incidental associations" but rather were logically consistent with the story's theme not only suggests that memory is reconstructive of past experience but is also consistent with the idea that children have an ordered knowledge representation with which to understand a story about a typical evening in the life of a young child. Anecdotal evidence was provided during the questioning period to support this claim concerning changes. For example, one second grade boy referred to George's "red — I mean green pajamas" in his story reconstruction, and then later said that he would change the color of George's pajamas to red because his own favorite pajamas were red. In addition, it does not seem too speculative to infer that children who referred to Rose/George going upstairs to bed themselves have second floor bedrooms. Such interferences seem anything but incidental. The claim here is that much of what Fraisse would call jumbled up or egocentric reflects structure imposed from one's own knowledge base.

Further anecdotal evidence supporting the script construct was abundant. For example, two second graders continued their story versions past bedtime (e.g., "And she went to bed and she wore her favorite pair of green pajamas. And the next morning she got up from bed. Didn't she eat her breakfast?") More evidence was given during the questioning period, when children were asked what they would change about the story. Four children responded by inserting a sub-sequence of events which reportedly matched their own daily routines. For example, one second grade girl responded that she would change "the part where you had to go to bed. You could go outside for a little bit and then you could watch TV and then you have your snack and then go to bed." It seems clear that these children noticed violations between the story and their own representations for similar events. Also of interest is the fact that nearly every child, when asked, cited a change he or she would make in the story, and that for the most part children wanted to add mundane events which complemented the story's theme (e.g., "I would have Rose go outside after dinner.") As shown in Table 2, there was no apparent difference between children of different ages in either the number or type of changes imposed on the story. Although one might expect development of this kind (for example, that older children would make fewer changes, that is, assimilate less to their own script) none were apparent in this study.

TABLE 2
Subject frequencies for story reconstruction changes

Type of Change	Group				
	Dinner emphasis story				
	Kindergarteners		Second graders		
	Boys	Girls	Boys	Girls	Total
Invented event(s)	2	1	4	3	10
Changed event(s)	5	3	6	4	18
Changed/invented detail(s)	3	4	3	3	13
Mentioned up/downstairs	4	2	4	4	14
Changed parent actor role(s)	2	4	4	4	14
	16	14	21	18	69
	Bed emphasis story				
Invented event(s)	4	4	3	4	15
Changed event(s)	2	3	1	6	12
Changed/invented detail(s)	2	2	0	0	4
Mentioned up/downstairs	2	3	2	4	11
Changed parent actor role(s)	1	0	3	3	7
	11	12	9	17	49

Note. There are 6 subjects per group.

However, evidence for the orderly development of scripts was provided. The fact that kindergarteners and second graders did not differ in their memory for the unemphasized scripts (consisting of designated core events), while there was a grade difference in recall for the emphasized script events, supports the hypothesis that a basic structure develops early. Filler events are added later. Probably two variations of a script develop: a stereotypic one, and a personal one. This would explain why second graders refrained from reporting personal events in their recalls, and yet indicated a desire to include seemingly personal events during the question period.

In conclusion, it has been shown that children's stories are less egocentric than was once thought. Children's performance may be dependent upon the content of story material; they seem to do better with event as opposed to state knowledge. Because the script model is an event sequence model and because children appeared to use script knowledge to guide story output, as evidenced by their changes, it is proposed that the script model may serve as a valid model of one type of children's knowledge representation. Many questions regarding the development of script knowledge, stereotypic and personal, and the role of script knowledge in imposing structure remain. The answers to such questions could have far-reaching implications, particularly with regard to understanding cognitive operations in young children.

REFERENCES

Bartlett, F.C. *Remembering.* Cambridge, England: Cambridge Unviersity Press, 1932.

Bower, G. Experiments on story understanding and recall. *Quarterly Journal of Experimental Psychology,* 1976, 23, 511-524.

Bower, G.H., Black, J.B., & Turner, T.J. Scripts in memory for text comprehension. *Cognitive Psychology*, 1979, 11, 177-220.

Brown, A.L. The development of memory: Knowing, knowing about knowing, and knowing how to know. In H.W. Reese (Ed.), *Advances in child development and behavior*, (Vol. 10). New York: Academic Press, 1975. (a)

Brown, A.L. Recognition, reconstruction, and recall of narrative sequences by preoperational children. *Child Development*, 1975, 46, 156-166. (b)

Brown, A.L. The construction of temporal succession by preoperational children. In A.D. Pick (Ed.), *Minnesota symposium on child psychology,* (Vol. 10). Minneapolis: University of Minnesota, 1976. (a)

Brown, A.L. Semantic integration in children's reconstruction of narrative sequences. *Cognitive Psychology*, 1976, 8, 247-262. (b)

Fraisse, P. *The Psychology of time.* New York: Harper, 1963.

Mandler, J.M. & Johnson, N.S. Remembrance of things parsed: Story structure and recall. *Cognitive Psychology*, 1977, 9, 111-151.

Meyer, B.J.F. & McConkie, G.W. What is recalled after hearing a passage? *Journal of Educational Psychology,* 1973, 65, 109-117.

Nelson, K. Cognitive development and the acquisition of concepts. In R.C. Anderson, R.J. Spiro, & W.E. Montague (Eds.), *Schooling and the acquisition of knowledge*. Hillsdale, N.J.: Erlbaum, 1977.

Nelson, K. How children represent their world in and out of language. In R.S. Siegler, (Ed.), *Children's thinking: What develops?* Hillsdale, N.J.: Erlbaum, 1979.

Piaget, J. *The language and thought of the child*. New York: Harcourt Brace, 1926.

Piaget, J. *The child's concept of time*. London: Routledge and Kegan Paul, 1969.

Rumelhart, D.E. Notes on a schema for stories. In D.G. Bobrow and A. Collins (eds.), *Basic processes in reading: Perception and comprehension*. Hillsdale, N.J.: Erlbaum, 1976.

Schank, R.C. & Abelson, R.P. *Scripts, plans, goals, and understanding*. Hillsdale, N.J.: Erlbaum, 1977.

Stein, N.L. & Glenn, C.G. An analysis of story comprehension in elementary school children. In R. Freedle (Ed.), *New directions in discourse processing*. Norwood, N.J.: Ablex, 1979.

Gestural Communication in Deaf Children: Noneffect of Parental Input on Language Development

Susan Goldin-Meadow and Carolyn Mylander

The deaf children in our study had hearing parents who elected to educate them by the oral method (1). We reported earlier (2) that, although these children had not been exposed to conventional sign language, they were able to develop a gestural communication system with some of the observed properties of early child language: consistent ordering of elements (the placement of words, or gestures, for certain semantic elements in consistent orders within a sentence) (3); differential probabilities of production of elements (the explicit production of words, or gestures, for certain semantic elements in a sentence more often than for other semantic elements) (4); and recursion (the concatenation of more than one proposition within a sentence) (5)). Thus it appeared that they were able to develop a structured and productive communication system without a conventional linguistic model.

It was possible, however, that the children's hearing parents influenced the structure of this gesture system. We investigated two likely parental influences on the child's system: modeling, where the child learns the structure of his or her gestures,

---

either by imitation or induction, from the structure of the parents' gestures; and shaping, where the structure in the child's gestures is reinforced by differential parental responses.

To determine whether the deaf children in our study might merely be imitating an adult's gestures, we videotaped four of the children and their mothers during play sessions. We classified the children's gestures as (i) spontaneous, if they were not preceded by parental gesture or were different from the parent's immediately preceding gestures, or (ii) imitated, if they were exact or partial imitations of the parent's immediately preceding gestreus. Imitated gestures were found to be infrequent: 2 percent (1 of 58) of Karen's gestures, 5 percent (7 of 144) of Marvin's, 7 percent (7 of 93) of Abe's, and none (0 of 27) of Mildred's.

We next considered the possibility that the children induced a structure from their parents' gestures. We noted at the outset that gesture, not speech, was the children's primary means of communicating (only 1 to 4 percent of the children's communications contained meaningful speech); the mothers communicated by both gesture and speech (83 to 96 percent of the mothers' communications contained speech). Despite the fact that for a hearing person gesture and speech might form an integrated communication system, we chose to analyze mothers' communications from what we took to be their deaf children's point of view and therefore included only the mothers' gestures in our analyses (6). The gestures of six deaf children and their mothers were transcribed according to a system developed earlier (2, 7). Reliability--agreement between two coders in independently noting and segmenting individual gestures and assigning them to semantic categories--ranged from 83 to 100 percent. Two types of denotative signs were coded: deictic signs (pointing gestures which indicated objects) and characterizing signs (gestures whose forms were transparently related to the actions they represented--for example, a closed fist bobbed near the mouth to characterize the act of eating). Deictic and characterizing signs could be concatenated to form simple sign sentences that conveyed one proposition [for example, gestures for "jar twist," indicating that the jar (object acted upon, or "patient" in the linguist's terminology) had been twisted open (act)], or complex sign sentences that conveyed at least two propositions [for example, "jar twist blow," a request that the jar (patient) be twisted open (act_1) and bubbles be blown (act_2)] (8). We stress that we use linguistic terms such as sentence loosely and only to suggest that the deaf child's gesture strings share certain elemental properties with early sentences in child language.

We found that for five of the six children in our experiment the probability of producing in a two-sign sentence a sign for an intransitive actor ("boy" in the proposition "boy goes to mother") was comparable to the probability of producing a sign for a patient ("boy" in the proposition "mother hits boy"), and distinct from the probability of producing a sign of a transitive actor ("boy" in the proposition "boy hits mother") (Fig. 1). This same probability pattern was found in only two mothers, one of whom was the mother of Abe, the only child who did not convincingly show the pattern. Thus, the systems of mother and child differed in the probability of certain semantic

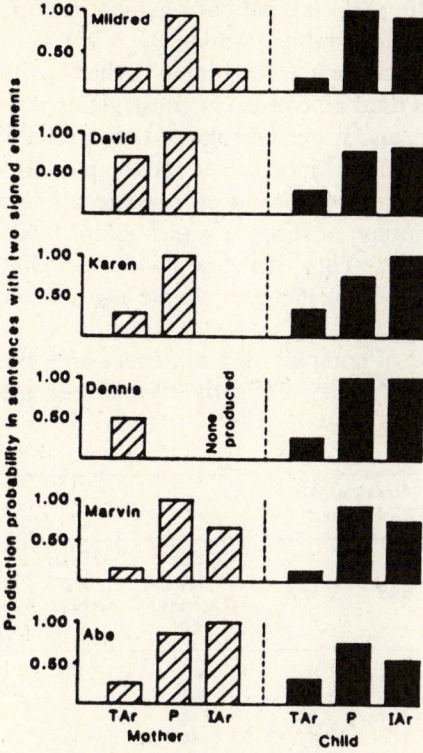

Fig. 1. Production-probability patterns in simple sign sentences of mother and child. Probabilities were calculated only from sign sentences with two explicit semantic elements: Mildred's mother used 14 transitive sentences (the data base for the transitive actor and patient probabilities) and 4 intransitive sentences (the data base for the intrasitive actor probability); her child used 22 and 2, respectively. David's mother used 10 transitive sentences and 1 intransitive sentence; her child used 54 and 16, respectively. Karen's mother used 7 transitive sentences and 1 intransitive sentence; her child used 23 and 4, respectively. Dennis's mother used 2 transitive sentences and no intransitive sentences; her child used 10 and 1, respectively. Marvin's mother used 6 transitive sentences and 8 intransitive sentences; her child used 30 and 4 respectively. Abe's mother used 8 transitive sentences and 2 intransitive sentences; her child used 29 and 19, respectively. *TAr*, transitive actor; *P*, patient; *IAr*, intransitive actor.

roles (intransitive actor, patient, or transitive actor) being signed explicitly in two-sign sentences.

Furthermore, each of the six children's simple two-sign sentences could be characterized by at least one reliable construction order: patient-act, such as "grape eat" [David (N = 38) and Dennis (N = 11), P < .01; Mildred (N = 27), P < .05; Karen (N = 25), P < .10; χ^2 tests]; patient recipient (recipient, the end point of a change of location), such as "cup table" [Marvin (N = 15), P < .01; David (N = 19), P < .001; χ^2 tests]; or actor-act, such as "dog jump" [Abe (N = 11), P = 0.002; χ^2 test]. In contrast, three mothers used no consistent construction orders, and the other three (mothers of Mildred, Abe, and Karen) displayed only a reliable patient-recipient construction order (N - 8, P = 0.07; binomial for each), an order not used by any of their children. Moreover, five children produced sentences following their own reliable construction orders an average of three sessions before their mothers produced any sign sentences in that order. Thus, the deaf children's reliable construction orders were not modeled by their hearing mothers' simple sign sentence.

We also analyzed use of complex sign sentences and found that all six children used complex sign sentences more frequently (9) and four used complex sign senten-

Child	Age (months)	Session first observed		Child		Mother	
		Child	Mother	Complex sign sentences (N)	Total sign sentences (%)	Complex sign sentences (N)	Total sign sentences (%)
David	34 to 44	1	1	88*	26	8	12
Marvin	35 to 50	1	6	38†	23	2	6
Karen	37 to 50	1	6	31‡	22	1	4
Dennis	26 to 30	1		4§	11	0	0
Abe	27 to 45	2	5	45‖	25	1	3
Mildred	16 to 44	5	4	11¶	12	2	2

*Chi-squares were performed by comparing each child's complex sign sentences to those of his mother. $\chi^2(1)$ = 5.62, P < 0.02.   †$\chi^2(1)$ = 3.79, P < 0.10.   ‡$\chi^2(1)$ = 2.87, P < 0.10.   §Dennis's mother produced nine sign sentences but none was complex.   ‖$\chi^2(1)$ = 8.06, P < 0.01.   ¶$\chi^2(1)$ = 5.12, P < 0.05.

Table 1. Complex sign sentences produced by six deaf children of hearing parents and their mothers.

ces earlier than did their mothers (Table 1). Taken together the data suggest that the structure of the deaf child's sign sentences was not induced from the mother's gestural model (10, 11).

We next considered the possibility that the structure of the deaf child's sign sentences was in some way shaped by differential parental responsiveness to those sentences. Following Brown and Hanlon (12), we categorized the responses of the mothers and the experimenter to the sign sentences of four deaf children subjects as either sequiturs (relevant and comprehending reactions to the child's sentence) or nonsequiturs (queries, irrelevant responses, misunderstandings, no responses, or responses of doubtful classification). We considered the child's sentence order to be preferred if it conformed to that child's reliable order and nonpreferred if it did not; for example, since Marvin reliably produced sentences with patient-recipient orders, sentences with this order were considered preferred for him, and recipient-patient sentences, nonpreferred. We found that the deaf child's sentences with preferred orders were no more likely to be followed by sequitur responses than were sentences with nonpreferred orders [49 percent (24 of 49) preferred and 47 percent (8 of 17) nonpreferred; P > 0.50, Fisher's exact test with children individually tested]. Thus the child's preference for particular sign orders does not appear to be a function of communication pressure from the adult.

To determine whether communication pressure was shaping the deaf child's production-probability pattern we looked at sequiturs that followed sentences with preferred production-probability patterns (two-sign sentences with either an explicit patient, an explicit intransitive actor, or an implicit transitive actor) and sentences with nonpreferred patterns (two-sign sentences with either an explicit transitive actor, an implicit patient, or an implicit intransitive actor). We found that sentences with preferred production-probability patterns were no more likley to receive sequitur responses from the mother or experimenter than were sentences with nonpreferred patterns [46 percent (32 of 69) preferred and 50 percent (9 of 18) nonpreferred; P > 0.67, Fisher's exact test with children indivdually tested].

Finally, to determine whether contingent approval might have shaped the structure of the deaf children's sign sentences, we coded (12) the mother's and the experimenter's responses as approvals if they contained smiles or nods or complied with the child's request or query, and as disapprovals if they contained headshakes or frowns or did not comply with the child's request or query (sentences not responded to were not counted). We found that sentences following preferred sign orders were no more likely to be approved by mother or experimenter than were sentences following nonpreferred orders [65 percent (22 of 34) preferred and 67 percent (8 of 12) nonpreferred; P > 0.42, Fisher's exact test with children individually tested]. Further, approval of sentences with preferred production-probability patterns was found to be similar to that for sentences with nonpreferred patterns [73 percent (29 of 40) preferred and 83 percent (10 of 12) nonpreferred; P > 0.25, Fisher's exact test with children individually tested]. In sum, it appears that neither communication pressure nor contingent approval shaped the deaf children's sign orders or probabilities of sign production.

Our observations indicate that a child in a markedly atypical language learning environment can apparently develop communication with language-like properties without a tutor modeling or shaping the structural aspects of communication. These results suggest that the child has a strong bias to communicate in language-like ways.

References and Notes

1. That is, rather than learn a sign language such as American Sign Language or Signed English, the children were taught to read lips and to produce spoken English through kinesthetic cues. At the time of our study, the children (all of whom had severe to profound hearing losses) were producing only a few single words and never combined words into sentences.

2. S. Goldin-Meadow and H. Feldman. Science 197, 401 (1977); H. Feldman, S. Goldin-Meadow, L.R. Gleitman, *Action, Gesture and Symbol*, A Lock, Ed. (Academic Press, New York, 1978), pp. 349-414; S. Goldin-Meadow, *Studies in Neurolinguistics*, H.Whitaker and H.A. Whitaker, Eds. (Academic Press, New York, 1979), vol. 4, pp. 125-209.

3. D.I. Slobin, in *Studies of Child Language Development*, C.A. Ferguson and D.I. Slobin, Eds. (Holt, Rinehart & Winston, New York, 1973), pp. 175-208.

4. L. Bloom, P. Miller, L. Hood, in *The 1974 Minnesota Symposium on Child Psychology*, A. Pick, Ed. (Univ. of Minnesota Press, Minneapolis, 1975), pp. 3-55.

5. R. Brown, *A First Language* (Harvard Univ. Press, Cambridge, Mass., 1973).

6. Although the children could in principle have been getting speech input through lip reading, in fact they seemed to understand little of the English spoken to them. Indeed, the structure of the children's gesture systems did not reflect the structure of English; in particular, the children's construction orders differed from those found in canonical English sentences, and the children's production-probability pattern was an analog of the structural case-marking pattern of ergative languages and therefore was distinct from the accusative case-marking pattern seen in English (S. Goldin-Meadow and C. Mylander, in preparation).

7. Criteria for sign sentences were the same for mother and child: if the hands did not relax between the production of two signs, these two signs were considered part of one sentence.

8. For examples of complex sentences, see S. Goldin-Meadow, *In Language Acquisition: The State of the Art*, L.R. Gleitman and E. Wanner, Eds. (Cambridge Univ. Press, New York 1982), pp. 51-77.

9. Quantitative differences such as these are inconclusive since they suggest only that certain structures are less frequent in mother's gestures than in the child's. However,

in order to argue that the child induces consistent structure from the infrequent instances of structure found in his mother's gestures, one must allow that the child is coming to the learning situation with a bias toward making those inductions.

10. Although the camera might have inhibited the mother's gesture production overall, it is unlikely that the camera affected the way in which the mother structured or failed to structure her gestures. The "camera-shy" hypothesis is further weakened by the fact that, for five mothers, the rate of single-sign production was higher for mother than for her child (although each mother's rate of production of the more compelx sign sentence form was half that of her child).

11. It is possible that individuals other than parents (such as siblings or the experimenters themselves) included the development of the gesture system, but three of the ten deaf children had no siblings, suggesting that interaction with a sibling was not necessary to develop a structured gesture system. Experimenters made every effort not to gesture to the deaf children, and few of children's gestures were imitations of the experimenter's gestures (2 percent, 1 of 58, overall); the experimenter produced so few gestures on videotape that anlaysis for structural properties was unnecessary.

12. R. Brown and C. Hanlon, *Cognition and the Development of Language,* J.R. Hayes, Ed. (Wiley, New York, 1970), pp. 11-54.

13. We thank L. Gleitman, J. Huttenlocher, M. McClintock, W. Meadow, E. Newport, M. Shatz, M. Silverstein, and T. Trabasso for comments and R. Church, E. Eichen, M. Morford, and D. Unora for videotape coding. Supported by NSF grant BNS 77-05990 and by grants from the Spencer Foundation.

Developmental Changes Across Childhood in the Perception of Non-native Speech Sounds

Janet F. Werker and Richard C. Tees

Abstract. In this research children at three different ages, 4, 8, and 12 years, were compared on their ability to discriminate two (non-English) Hindi speech contrasts. This work followed from earlier research (Werker, Gilbert, Humphrey, & Tees, 1981) showing a developmental decline between infancy and adulthood in cross-language speech perception abilities. The present research was designed to try to identify the time in development when the loss of the ability to discriminate the non-native (Hindi) speech contrasts would be present. Results show that the decline is evident by 4 years of age, suggesting that important reorganizations in linguistic perceptual abilities occur in early childhood.

Recent research on cross-language speech perception has yielded data pointing to a substantial difference in the ability of infants and adults to discriminate non-native speech contrasts. Although there is some suggestion that linguistic experience may act to alter the ease in which linguistic contrasts are differentiated (Eilers, Gavin, & Wil-

Originally published in *Canadian Journal of Psychology*, 1983, 37, 278-286. Copyright ©1983 Canadian Psychological Association. Reprinted with permission.

son, 1979), the evidence seems to indicate that regardless of specific linguistic experience, infants can discriminate nearly every contrast on which they have been adequately tested (Aslin, Pisoni, Hennessy, & Perey, 1981; Holmberg, Morgan, & Kuhl, 1977; Streeter, 1976; Eilers, Oller, & Gavin, Note 1). In contrast other investigations have revealed that adults may have difficulty differentiating non-native speech contrasts (Lisker & Abramson, 1970; MacKain, Best, & Strange, 1980; Miyawaki, Strange, Verbrugge, Liberman, Jenkins, & Fujimura, 1975). Two studies have addressed the question of the adult/infant differences by directly comparing their ability to differentiate non-native contrasts (Trehub, 1976; Werker, Gilbert, Humphrey, & Tees, 1981). In both cases, infants showed significantly superior performance to that of adults. In fact, Werker et al. showed adult English speakers to be unable to discriminate one of the non-English (Hindi) contrasts even after (albeit limited) training.

Although it is clear that there are differences in cross-language speech perception between infants and adults, very little work has examined the ontogeny of this decline. Zlatin and Koenigsknecht (1976) have shown that specific linguistic experience may act to solidify relevant linguistic boundaries in young children. The question of whether this solidification implies a concurrent weakening of non-relevant boundaries has not been addressed.

Most work investigating speech perception in the child has been designed to test native language perception rather than cross-language perception. Much of this research has been motivated by the work of Jakobson (1968). Jakobson advocates a theory of phonological development in which sounds that are common across natural languages are acquired earlier than sounds which have a more limited distribution. In support of this, speech perception work with young children has yielded data suggesting a developmental increase between the ages of 2 to 7 years in the accuracy of discrimination of native speech contrasts that have a restricted representation both within and across natural languages (Eilers & Oller, 1976; Garnica, 1973; Shvachkin, 1973). Barton (1980) has recently shown that children between the ages of 2 and 7 are able to discriminate any native-language phonemic contrast if they are tested in a low memory procedure using words with which they are familiar. Barton feels his findings do not negate the claim that accuracy of discrimination of phonetic contrasts (i.e., from nonsense words) improves with age (Gilbert, 1975), but that the findings do undermine a theory of gradual perceptual acquisition as proposed by Jakobson. The methodological sophistication of Barton's work makes it most comparable with infant data; indeed, his findings, in contrast to those of others, are consistent with infant work by showing that even very young children can perceive all the distinctions which are phonemic in their own language.

Further information relevant to developmental changes in speech perception is provided by research on second language acquisition. Much of this research has been designed to test Lenneberg's (1967) hypothesis that perceptual flexibility exists until accent-free, whereas those learning a new language afterwards will not. Considerable research has provided support for this hypothesis (Asher & Garcia, 1969; Cochrane & Sachs, 1979; Fatham, 1975; Seliger, Krashen, & Ladefoged, 1975). However, the hypothesis has recently been questioned by theorists who argue that older language learners may actually be more proficient given equal time and equal instruction than young children at learning all aspects (including phonology) of a new language (McLaughlin, 1977; Stern, 1976). In support of this, recent research looking at English speakers learning Dutch provides evidence that older children and adults may learn both proper pronunciation (Snow & Hoefnagel-Hohle, 1977) and discrimination (Snow & Hoefnagel-Hohle, 1978) of non-native sounds more easily than younger children.

The present research directly explores non-native speech perception across childhood to try to determine if the decline between infancy and adulthood in non-native perceptual abilities occurs around puberty (as suggested by Lenneberg), or if it occurs much earlier in childhood as implied by some of the other studies reviewed above. In addition, this research addresses the generality of such a decline by examining perception of two very different non-English speech contrasts, since it is conceivable that some cross-language boundaries may be perceptually weaker than others (i.e., it has been suggested that the prevoicing boundary is weaker than the voiced-voiceless boundary in voice onset time; cf. Eilers, Gavin, & Wilson, 1979). "Weaker" boundaries could disappear (leading to a braoder perceptual category) earlier in development without specific experience than more robust boundaries.

METHOD

Subjects

There were 12 English-speaking subjects tested at each of three ages (4, 8, and 12) on three different speech contrasts. An approximately equal number of boys and girls were tested at each age. The subjects were unilingual English speakers with, at most, limited second language training. None of the English subjects had any training in a language which differentiates the two speech contrasts under consideration. As a control procedure, two bilingual Hindi-English speaking children aged 4 and 5 were also tested.

Stimuli

The English contrast used was the voiced bilabial versus alveolar contrast, /ba/-/da/, where place of articulation is the critical distinction. The first (non-English) Hindi contrast was the unvoiced, unaspirated retroflex versus dental stop, /ta/-/ta/, where place of articulation is also the critical distinction. Although the acoustic characteristics of retroflexion are not that well understood, it appears that the burst and at least the first three formant transitions are necessary to achieve reliable identification among native speakers (see Stevens & Blumstein, 1975). Acoustic analysis of our natural tokens (See Fig. 1A) showed the main cues differentiating these sounds to be in the burst and in the third formant transition with only the slope of the second formant transition varying significantly.

The second Hindi contrast employed was the unvoiced, aspirated dental stop versus the breathy voiced dental stop, /t^h-/d^h/, in which a difference in voice onset time (VOT) was the critical distinction. The VOT for an average /t^h/ token was 131.3 msec compared with -121.5 msec for an average /d^h/ token in this study (see Werker et al., 1981). As evident in our spectrograms (see Fig. 1B), periodicity precedes the release burst at the level of Formant 1 for the breathy voicing sound.

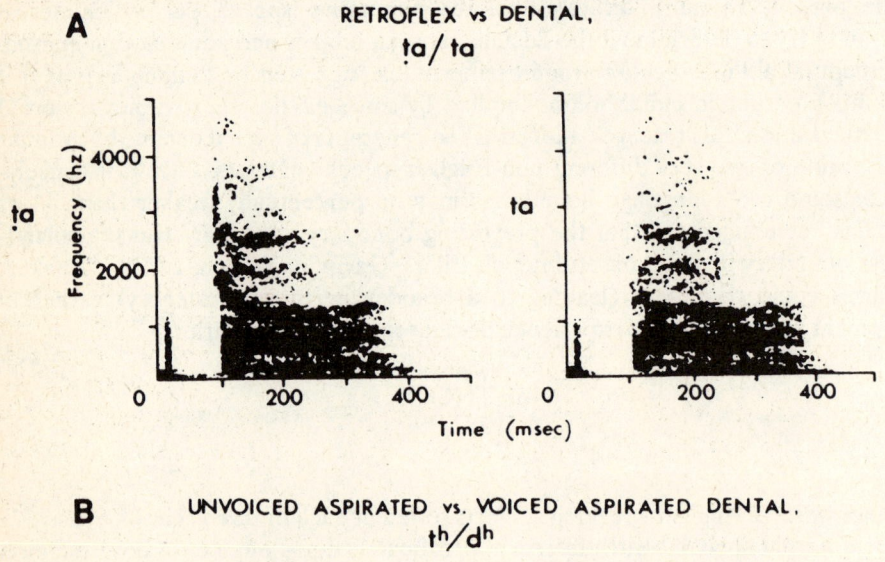

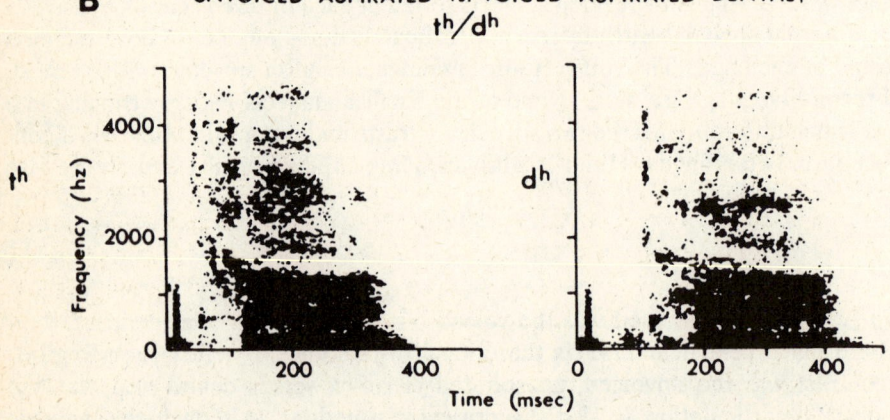

Fig. 1. Spectrograms for representative tokens of (A) /ṭa/ versus /ta/ and (B) /t^h/ versus /d^h/ Hindi stop consonant contrasts.

Four exemplars of each sound were used. The several exemplars were chosen so that the distribution of duration, fundamental frequency, and intonation contour overlapped in each of the contrasting pairs. Since multiple natural exemplars were used, subjects could not discriminate the sound pairs on the basis of irrelevant allophonic variation; rather, subjects had to ignore non-phonetic variation and respond only to the phonetic change. In some ways this is similar to the perceptual constancy paradigm as used by Kuhl (1980), since the subjects must discriminate varying multiple tokens according to phonetic category. In this experiment, however, the variability within each phonetic category was much more limited since sounds were recorded by a single speakers, and care was taken to ensure that the intonation contour in all stimulus exemplars was relatively flat. The average duration of a stimulus exemplar was 500 msec, with a 1500 msec intertrial interval. All stimuli were recorded from a native Hindi speaker in the phonetics laboratory at the University of British Columbia. Final tokens were digitized and aligned with the PDP-224 computer at Haskins Laboratories.

Procedure

All subjects were tested in a simple discrimination paradigm which had minimal memory requirements (cf. Carney, Widin, & Viemeister, 1977) and was similar to the infant Head Turn (HT) paradigm (Werker et al., 1981). In this paradigm, the subject was instructed to press a button when there was a change in the speech stimuli. Feedback was provided by reinforcing correct button presses with the illumination of lights inside a smoked plexiglas box. When the lights came on, a toy animal inside the box became apparent. Lights did not come on following an incorrect button press, providing feedback to indicate a false positive response.

To familiarize subjects with the paradigm, and to ensure that they could perform the required discrimination task, subjects in all age groups were first tested on their ability to discriminate multiple tokens of the English /ba/-/da/ contrast according to phonetic category. If they could not reach criterion on this second pair, they were excluded from the study for being unable to perform the required task. After testing subjects on both Hindi contrasts, all subjects in all age groups who had failed both contrasts were tested again on the /ba/-/da/ sound pair. Although this retesting was undertaken to ensure that each child had a positive experience in the laboratory setting, it also provided the necessary control to show that negative results were not simply an artifact of the inability to perform the required task. It was only necessary to exclude one child, a 4-year old, from the study.

In this study, the tapes were set up dichotically, and lined up for onset on each of the tracks. That is, stimuli from the one phoneme category /ba/ were on Track 1, and stimuli from the other category /da/ were on Track 2. Change trials were initiated by stimuli from the other category /da/ were on Track 2. Change trials were initiated by changing tracks. Modifications were made in the equipment to ensure that irrelevant clues such as clicks could not aid in the discrimination. All stimuli were played on a Revox A-77 tape recorder,, and projected over a single-driver speaker at approximately 65 dB SPL in a Tracoustics double-walled sound attenuated booth.

The timing for presentation of control (no change) and experimental (change) trials, and for activation of the lights was controlled by a logic system. Experimental trials occurred at irregular intervals (every 4 to 15 tokens). All responses were recorded on a Grason Stadler event recorder so that correct hits, false positives, and misses could be scored. An 8 out of 10 correct response to change trials with a maximum of either 2 misses or 2 false positives was considered criterion for evidence of discrimination abilities. Because of the number of false positive possibilities, the probability of achieving this criterion by chance alone is extremely low (p < .001). Criterion for deciding which subjects could not reach criterion was set at 30 change trials. That is, if a subject did not show evidence of approaching the pre-established criterion by 30 change trials, testing was stopped and it was assumed that the subject could not discriminate the contrast.

RESULTS

The number of subjects who reached and did not reach criterion on each of the two Hindi sound contrasts is reported in Table 1, along with relevant data from our previous research. An analysis of proportions based on the Scheffe theorem (Marascuilo, 1966) was applied to these new data, together with data from the three groups tested under identical conditions earlier (Werker et al., 1981). This analysis was designed to compare the proportion of individuals either reaching or not reaching

TABLE 1

Number of Subjects in Each Group Reaching or Not Reaching Criterion on the Two Hindi Speech Contrasts

Reached Criterion	(1)* English Infants	(2) English 4 years	(3) English 8 years	(4) English 12 years	(5)* English Adults	(6)* Hindi Adults	(7)* Trained Eng-Adults
The retroflex/dental contrast /ṭa-ta/							
YES	11	0	0	1	1	5	0
NO	1	12	12	11	9	0	10
The voicing contrast /t^h-d^h/							
YES	10	0	4	4	4	5	7
NO	2	12	8	8	6	0	3

* Data from Werker et al., 1981

In the case of the Hindi Retroflex/Dental contrast, the overall Chi-square obtained from the analysis of proportions had a probability of $p < .05$ ($\chi^2 = 42.693$), suggesting significant differences between the six groups of subjects tested. To determine which groups varied significantly, a series of pair-wise comparisons between two groups was performed, based on Marascuilo (1966).

Comparisons between Group 1 with Groups 2, 3, and 4, and between Group 6 with Groups 2, 3, and 4 were all significant, but none of the comparisons between Groups 2, 3, 4, and 5 or between Groups 1 and 6 were significant. In summary, the Hindi adults (Group 6) and English infants (Group 1) discriminated these contrasts significantly better than the other groups. Furthermore, there were no changes or differences across childhood (ages 4, 8, and 12) in the ability to discriminate this contrast according to phonemic category; that is, subjects at all three ages were poor and not significantly different from one another.

In the case of the Hindi unvoiced aspirated dental versus unvoiced unaspirated dental contrast, the overall Chi-square obtained was significant ($p < .05$; $\chi^2 = 24.617$). A series of multiple comparisons was again performed to determine which groups varied.

The following comparisons between two groups reached significance: these were Group 1 versus 2 and Group 6 versus 2, 3, 4, and 5. The English infants (Group 1) performed better than the 4-year olds (Group 2), and the Hindi adults performed better than all groups except the English infants. Although the decline in the ability to discriminate this contrast according to phonemic category is not as pronounced as it is for the first contrast (possibly because it is a perceptually easier difference), it can be seen that the decline is evident by age 4. To understand these data further, a series of individual Chi-squares was run comparing two groups. These analyses showed the comparisons between children aged 8 and 12 with the 4-year-old children to be significantly different ($p < .05$; $\chi^2 - 7.5$). This suggested that the 4-year olds performed more poorly on this contrast than the older children.

It is useful to note that no English-speaking 4-year old even approached the 8 out of 10 criterion on either Hindi contrast, although they could all discriminate the English /ba/-/da/. Two further children in both the 8- and 12-year old groups did reach a 7 out of 10 criterion on the voicing contrast /t^h/-/d^h/. It is interesting that although the error patterns for the 4-year olds were highly variable, these children showed more false positive responses overall in the case of the Hindi voicing contrast and more misses in the case of the Hindi place contrast.

As a final measure to control for the possibility that the lack of non-native discriminative abilities in the 4-year English group was a function of an inappropriate task procedure for children this age (cf. Tallal, Stark, Kallman, & Mellits, 1980), an attempt was made to test same-aged Hindi-speaking children. It is difficult to find children this age in the Vancouver area who are fluent in Hindi (most of the Indian population speaks Punjabi, with some Urdu and Tamil); however, we were able to test two children, aged 4 and 5, who were bilingual Hindi-English speakers. Both children reached criterion on both Hindi contrasts within fewer than 15 test trials, showing that young children can perform in this procedure.

Table 1 summarizes the results of the present study and compares them with earlier work with infants and adults. In summary, it is clear that the 7-month-old infants of English speaking parents could discriminate both Hindi contrasts, whereas English speaking adults could not discriminate either contrast without training. Data from Group 7 shows that training significantly improved performance for adults on the VOT contrast, $/t^h/-/d^h/$, but did not affect performance on the retroflex/dental contrast, $/ \underset{.}{t}a/-/ta/$. In the present study, the 8- and 12-year olds both performed at the level of the English adults (analysis showed no significant difference between these three groups). Although it is clear that the infants and Hindi adults were superior on both contrasts relative to the other groups, it is also apparent that the 4-year olds performed poorly relative to the other groups on the voicing contrasts.

DISCUSSION

These findings suggest that non-native speech discrimination does not decline in a gradual linear fashion across development. Most importantly, the effects of specific linguistic experience seem to be evident by age 4. Such a finding is not surprising given that 4-year-old children are already relatively accomplished speakers. However, this finding is inconsistent with the hypothesis suggested by Lenneberg (1967) that linguistic perceptual flexibility should be maintained until puberty. Rather, these results provide support for the alternative notion that second language learning may not necessarily be easier in early childhood. Furthermore, the relative recovery of discrimination by age 8 for the VOT contrast suggests that simple maturational explanations may not suffice, and that a more complex explanation may be required, taking both the acoustic parameters of the speech sounds and the level of cognitive development of the children into account. In the paradigm we used in which subjects were required to discriminate multiple natural tokens according to phonetic category, subjects may have been predisposed to adopt a native-language phonemic strategy. That is, by being first tested on /ba/ versus /da/, subjects could have adopted a perceptual strategy based on the phonemic categories of their native language to guide their performance. It may be that the 4-year olds are simply rigid rule followers (as has been shown in other cognitive tasks, cf. Kogan, 1974) and cannot easily drop that phonemic strategy to attend to the phonetic or acoustic features differentiating the sounds, whereas the 8- and 12-year olds are more capable of adopting such a task-specific perceptual strategy. We are currently investigating such an interpretation in our lab by varying perceptual set conditions (predispose subjects to an acoustic or a phonetic set) and by using different discrimination procedures (e.g., same/different).

REFERENCE NOTE

1. Eilers, R.E., Oller, D.K., & Gavin, W.J. *A cross-linguistic study of infant speech perception*. Paper presented at the Southeastern Conference on Human Development, Atlantta, Georgia, 1978.

REFERENCES

Asher, J.J., & Garcia, R. The optimal age to learn a foreign language. *Modern Language Journal,* 1969, 53, 334-341.

Aslin, R.N., Pisoni, D.B., Hennessy, B.L., & Perey, A.J. Discrimination of voice onset time by human infants: New findings and implications for the effect of early experience. *Child Development,* 1981, 52, 1135-1145.

Barton, D. Phonemic perception in children. In G.H. Yeni-Komshian, J.F. Kavanagh, and C.A. Ferguson (Eds.), *Child phonology: Volume 2, Perception.* New York: Academic Press, 1980.

Carney, A.E., Widin, G.P., & Viemeister, N.F. Noncategorical perception of stop consonants differing in VOT. *Journal of the Acoustical Society of America, 1977, 62, 961-970.*

Cochrane, P.M., & Sachs, J. Phonological learning by children and adults in a laboratory setting. *Language and Speech*, 1979, 22, 145-150.

Eilers, R.E., Gavin, W.J., & Wilson, W.R. Linguistic experience and phonemic perception in infancy: A cross-linguistic study. *Child Development,* 1979, 50, 14-18.

Eilers, R.E., & Oller, D.K. The role of speech discrimination in developmental sound substitutions. *Journal of Child Languag*e, 1976, 3, 319-329.

Fatham, A. The relationship between age and second language productive ability. *Language Learning,* 1975, 25, 245-253.

Garnica, O.K. The development of phonemic speech perception. In T.E. Moore (Ed), *Cognitive development and the acquisition of language*. New York: Academic Press, 1973.

Gilbert, J.H.V. Speech perception in children. In A. Cohen and S.E. Nootebom (Eds.), *Structure and process in speech perception*. Heidelburg: Springer-Verlag, 1975.

Holmberg, T.L., Morgan, K.V., & Kuhl, P.A. Speech perception in early infancy: Discrimination of fricative consonants. *Journal of the Acoustical Society of America*, 1977, 62, Supplement 1, 599.

Jakobson, R. *Child language, aphasia, and phonological universals*. The Hague: Morton, 1968.

Kogan, N. *Cognitive styles in infancy and early childhood*. Hillsdale, N.J.: Lawrence Erlbaum Associates, 1974.

Kuhl, P.K. Perceptual constancy for speech-sound categories in early infancy. In G.H. Yeni-Komshian, J.F. Kavanagh, and C.A. Ferguson (Eds.), *Child phonology: Volume 2, Perception*. New York: Academic Press, 1980.

Lenneberg, E.H. *Biological foundations of language*. New York: Wiley, 1967.

Lisker, L., & Abramson, A.S. The voicing dimensions: Some experiments in comparative phonetics. In *Proceedings of the Sixth International Congress of Phonetic Sciences*. Prague: Academia, 1970.

MacKain, K.S., Best, C.Y., & Strange, W. Native language effects on the perception of liquids. *Journal of the Acoustical Society of America*, 1980, 27, 527.

Marascuilo, L.A. Large scale multiple comparisons. *Psychological Bulletin*, 1966, 69, 280-290.

McLaughlin, B. Second-language learning in children. *Psychological Bulletin*, 1977, 84, 438-459.

Miyawaki, K., Strange, W., Verbrugge, R.R., Liberman, A.M., Jenkins, J.J., & Fujimura, O. An effect of linguistic experience: The discrimination of (r) and (l) by native speakers of Japanese and English. *Perception and Psychophysics*, 1975, 18, 331-340.

Seliger, H., Krashen, S., & Ladefoged, P. Maturational constraints in the acquisition of a native-like accent in second language-learning. *Language Sciences*, 1975, 20-22.

Shvachkin, N.K. The development of phonemic speech perception in early childhood. In C.A. Ferguson and D.I. Slobin (Eds.), *Studies of child language development*. New York: Holt, Rhinehart, and Winston, 1973.

Snow, C.E., & Hoefnagel-Hohle, M. Age differences in the pronunciation of foreign sounds. *Language & Speech,* 1977, 20, 357-365.

Snow, C.E., & Hoefnagel-Hohle, M. The critical period for language acquisition: Evidence from second language learning. *Child Development*, 1978, 49, 1114-1128.

Stern, H.H. Optimal age: Myth or reality? *The Canadian Modern Language Review,* 1976, 32, 283-294.

Stevens, K.N., & Blumstein, S.E. Quantal aspects of consonant production and perception: A study of retroflex stop consonants. *Journal of Phonetics*, 1975, 3, 215-233.

Streeter, L. Language perception of two-month-old infants shows effect of both innate mechanisms and experience. *Nature,* 1976, 259, 39-41.

Tallal, P., Stark, R., Kallman, C., & Mellits, D. Perceptual constancy for phonemic categories: A developmental study with normal and language-impaired children. *Applied Psycholinguistics*, 1980, 1, 49-64.

Trehub, S. The discrimination of foreign speech contrasts by infants and adults. *Child Development,* 1976, 47, 466-472.

Werker, J.F., Gilbert, J.H.V., Humphrey, K., & Tees, R.C. Developmental aspects of cross-language speech perception. *Child Development*, 1981, 52, 349-355.

Zlatin, M.A., & Koenigsknecht, R.A. Development of the voicing contrast: A comparison of voice onset time in stop perception and production. *Journal of Speech and Hearing Research*, 1976, 19, 93-111.

The Naturalistic Communicative Abilities of Two-Year-Olds

Henry M. Wellman

Jacques D. Lempers

A commonsense description of a socialized communicator would have to include the following:(1) he must engage other participants in interaction and sustain the interaction through a sequence of exchange (engagement); (2) he must take the role of the other by accommodating his messages to what the recipient needs to know (role taking); (3) he must also be attuned to the recipient's reaction and reformulate his message in response to cues from him (response to feedback). Piaget's (1955) concept of socialized communication seems to include these three features; his description of egocentric communication implies that these ingredients are missing in the communication of young children. While Piaget came to a pessimistic view of the preschool child's abilities in this area, recent investigations have led to a reappraisal of the communicative ability of young children. Concerning engagement, Mueller (1972) and Garvey and Hogan (1973) showed that 3-year-olds engaged other children in in-

---

teraction and sustained mutual interaction over a number of exchanges. Concerning role taking, Maratsos (1973) showed that children as young as 3 modified their communication if the listener's needs were made highly salient (if the listener was blindfolded). Lempers, Flavell, and Flavell (in press) observed role-taking behaviors in children aged 1-3. Children were directed to show objects to or point out referents for their mothers. Thus they were asked to send certain "look at this" communications to a receiver. In some cases, 18-month-olds varied their behaviors to effectively point out referents, and 2-year-olds varied their behaviors to effectively display referents. Concerning response to feedback, Peterson, Danner, and Flavell (1972) found that 4-year-olds would reformulate their messages if explicitly requested to by a listener ("Tell me something different') but not in response to an implicit request ("I don't understand").

A number of unanswered questions arise from this brief review. What is the nature of communication in children younger than 3 or 4? What abilities do young children evidence in communications initiated on the child's own accord (he is *not* directed what to communicate, as in Lempers et al., in press)and when the listeners' needs are not especially salient (as in Maratsos 1973)? Finally, with an eye to Lempers et al., what is the communicative ability of young children when the term "communication" is broadened to include messages that are non-verbal such as pointing and showing? The present study reports on the naturally occurring communications of 2-year-olds, including the child's competence in engaging others, adapting his communications to the requisites of listener and situation, and his responses to feedback. The focus is one form of referential communication—messages where the communicator's intent is to get his listener to look at a particular referent.

Method

Five boys and five girls, aged 2-2 to 3-0, participated. Two boys and two girls (mean age 2-5) were observed in a toddler play group which met once a week for 6 weeks. Six children (mean age 2-6) were part of a 13-child preschool class, meeting twice a week for an academic year. Both groups met in the same classroom.

Sony half-inch videotapes of the children's ongoing behaviors were recorded from an observation booth. One hour of tape was filmed per session, with one child the focus for 10 min and other children the foci in successive 10-min segments. Order of filming was randomly determined. In all, 10 1-hour videotapes were recorded, with each child the focus a total of 1 hour but also appearing on the tape when not the focus.

The tapes were scanned for instances of communication where the communicators' intent was to point out, show, or display a particular referent. Two scales were used to describe each interaction, one describing the communicative situation and the other describing the communicator's behavior. The following list shows these two scales.

Communicative Situation

Receiver-Communicator

1. Proximity
   - (+) Receiver 5 feet or less from communicator
   - (—) Receiver more than 5 feet away
2. Involvement
   - (+) Communicator and receiver interacting together or playing in same small group in last 90 sec.
   - (—) Communicator and receiver not interacting in last 90 sec.
3. Attention
   - (+) Receiver looking at communicator
   - (—) Receiver not looking at communicator
4. Obstacle
   - (+) Absence of visual obstacle between communicator and receiver
   - (—) Presence of obstacle
5. Availability
   - (+) Receiver not involved with any other person
   - (—) Receiver actively engaged with other person

Communicator-Referent

6. Proximity
   - (+) Communicator 5 feet or less from referent
   - (—) Communicator more than 5 feet from referent
7. Involvement
   - (+) communicator playing with or attending to referent in last 90 sec.
   - (—) Communicator has not interacted with referent in last 90 sec.
8. Attention
   - (+) Communicator looking at referent
   - (—) Communicator not looking at referent
9. Obstacle
   - (+) Absence of obstacle between communicator and referent
   - (—) Presence of obstacle

Receiver-Referent

10. Proximity
    - (+) Receiver 5 feet or less from referent
    - (—) Receiver more than 5 feet from referent
11. Involvement
    - (+) Receiver playing with or attending to referent in last 90 sec.
    - (—) Receiver has not interacted with referent in last 90 sec.
12. Attention
    - (+) Receiver looking at referent
    - (—) Receiver not looking at referent

13. Obstacle
  (+) Absence of obstacle between receiver and referent
  (—) Presence of obstacle

Communicator's Behavior
1. Verbal attention getters
   (+) Communicator says "Hey," other's name, "You," etc. preceding communication
   (—) Absence of the above
2. Nonverbal attention getter
   (+) Communicator waves at receiver, bangs referent, repeatedly stabs at referent, touches or grabs receiver preceding communication
   (—) Absence of above
3. Points
   (+) Communicator points to object to show it to receiver
   (—) Absence of pointing
4. Shows
   (+) Communicator picks on the displays referent to receiver or gives the referent to the receiver
   (—) Absence of above
5. Takes referent
   (+) Communicator carries referent to receiver
   (—) Absence of above
6. Takes receiver
   (+) Communicator takes or leads receiver to referent
   (—) Absence of above
7. Removes obstacle
   (+) Communicator removes obstacle between receiver and referent or between receiver and self
   (—) Absence of above
8. Verbal comment
   (+) Communicator makes verbal utterances about referent
   (—) Absence of above
9. Orients referent
   (+) When showing a referent with a definite proper orientation, communicator deliberately orients referent
   (—) Communicator does not deliberately orient referent
10. Attention
   (+) Communicator looks at receiver while communicating or immediately afterwards
   (—) Absence of above

The scale describing the situation was divided into three subparts, one describing the situation between the communicator and the receiver, one between the communicator and the referent, and one between the receiver and the referent. Each attribute of the situation was scored dichotomously in terms of whether it was assumed that the situation was relatively easier (+) or harder (—) to communicate in. Each attribute of the communicator's behavior was scored in terms of whether its presence (+) was assumed to make the communicator's intent easier to understand than its absence (—). Every communication was also rated in terms of the response it produced from the intended receiver, including: (a) no response—receiver does not look at referent or at communicator; (b) looks at communicator—receiver looks at communicator, not at the referent; (c) negative verbal feedback—receiver says "What," "I don't see it," or otherwise indicates a lack of understanding; and (d) adequate response—receiver attends to referent and/or verbally communicates that he has understood the message. Finally, any further communication by the communicator occurring within 5 sec. and about the same referent was analyzed by rating the subsequent behavior according to the categories of communicator's behavior.

Two independent observers (one blind to the purposes of the study) rated the tapes. Reliability on a random sample was .81 for selecting communicative instances and ranged from .89 to 1.00 (M = .96) for the individual categories.

Results

There were 300 communicative interactions, ranging from 17 to 58 instances per subject. Of these, 236 were directed to adults and 64 were directed to 2-year-old peers. An average of 80% of each subject's communications were directed to adults (ranged 53%-100%). Table 1 shows the percentage of times each of the attributes for both situations and behaviors were rated plus. In describing the situation the percentage of pluses is generally higher for messages directed to peers than to adults, t(11) = 3.76, p < .01. Each situation was given a score (0-13) by summing up the number of attributes rated "plus" (low scores indicating difficult situations); each instance of communicative behavior was given a score (1-10) summing up the pluses (low scores indicating use of few communicative behaviors). There were no differences in any of the following analyses due to the different classroom groups or due to sex.

Engagement. —As the bottom row of table 2 shows, 79% of the messages (range 60%-92%) met with an adequate response. Communicators were able to engage receivers even in more difficult situations and engagement did not depend on the sophistication of adult receivers, since there were no differences in adequate responses for adult versus peer receivers (79% vs. 78% success) or for situations receiving a high, medium, or low number of pluses (87%, 75%, and 78% success).

Role taking. —Situation scores were correlated with behavior scores. Over all instances r(298) = -.71, p < .001 (difficult situations were related to much communicative behavior, easy situations to less behavior). For messages directed to adults r(234) = -.72, p < .001; for messages directed to peers r(62) = .60, p < .001. For in-

TABLE 1

MEAN PERCENTAGE OF TIMES EACH
ATTRIBUTE WAS RATED PLUS

	Messages to Adults	Messages to Peers
Communicative situation:		
1. Rec-com proximity....	84	98
2. Rec-com involvement..	85	80
3. Rec-com attention....	38	45
4. Rec-com obstacle.....	95	98
5. Rec-com availability...	75	92
6. Com-ref proximity....	90	94
7. Com-ref involvement..	79	92
8. Com-ref attention.....	92	92
9. Com-ref obstacle......	97	98
10. Rec-ref proximity.....	78	91
11. Rec-ref involvement...	49	67
12. Rec-ref attention......	24	41
13. Rec-ref obstacle.......	87	89
	75	83
Communicator's behavior:		
1. Verbal attention getters	7	2
2. Nonverbal attention getters..............	4	2
3. Points..............	53	45
4. Shows.............	49	55
5. Takes referent........	20	6
6. Takes receiver.......	1	2
7. Removes obstacle.....	4	3
8. Verbal comment.......	82	64
9. Orients referent.......	4	3
10. Attention...........	69	72
	29	25

TABLE 2

RECEIVER'S RESPONSE TO COMMUNICATOR'S MESSAGE

Communicator's Response to Feedback	No Response	Negative Verbal Feedback	Looks at Communicator	Adequate Response	Total
Recommunicates using more communicative behaviors......................	8 (3)	2	1	0	11 (3)
Recommunicates using same no. of communicative behaviors..............	13 (3)	7	1 (1)	4	25 (4)
Recommunicates using fewer communicative behaviors...................	6	2	0	2	10
Does nothing......................	23 (7)	0	0	231 (50)	254 (57)
Total......................	50 (13)	11 (0)	2 (1)	237 (50)	300 (64)

NOTE.—Nos. shown in parentheses are just for those messages directed to peers; nos. shown outside of parentheses are for the total messages to adults and to peers.

dividuals, $r = -.50$ or better for nine of the 10 children.

The scheme for rating communicative situations was designed to include many attributes that may have been important for communicative behavior; which were the attributes important to 2-year-olds? Each attribute describing the situation was individually correlated with the total communicative behavior score across all 300 communicative interactions. All correlations were negative and significant ($p < .05$), though significances are inflated due to large sample size. For the five attributes defining the receiver-communicator situation, the mean $r = -.39$; for communicator-referent attributes the mean $r = -.21$; for receiver-referent attributes, mean $r = -.39$, $F(2,18) = 6.33$, $p < .01$. Subsequent Newman-Keuls tests at the .05 level showed that communicator-referent attributes were different from both other classes of attributes which did not differ from each other. For all three attributes referring to proximity, mean $r = -.38$; for involvement, mean $r = -.33$; for attention, mean $r = -.29$; for obstacles, mean $r = -.24$; and for the one attribute referring to communicator-receiver availability, $r = -.54$, $F(4,36) = 11.99$, $p < .01$. Subsequent tests at the $p < .05$ level showed that availability was different from all other classes of attributes and that proximity was different from obstacles.

Response to feedback. — Table 2 also shows how the communicator dealt with feedback in his further activity. The communicator may not have communicated about the same referent subsequently (did nothing), or he could have recommunicated by using more (higher number of pluses), the same, or less communicative behaviors than before. In 54% of the cases where the communicators received no response, they recommunicated their message in some form; in only 3% of the cases where they received an adequate response did they recommunicate. Many fewer messages received negative-verbal feedback or looks-at-communicator feedback, but in 100% of these cases (where there was some indication that the communicator made contact with the receiver and the receiver just did not understand) the message was recommunicated.

Discussion

In certain simple, naturally occurring referential communications 2-year-old children engaged other listeners about 80% of the time, adapted their messages to the demands of receiver and situation, and were differentially responsive to a range of feedback including (a) when the listener understood, (b) when he became engaged with the communicator but did not understand, and (c) when he paid no attention to the message at all. Communicators' messages were related mostly to information about the relation of receiver and referent and the relation of receiver and communicator. Information about the communicator's own position in relation to the referent was much less influential in message formulation. From an egocentric point of view, one would expect an opposite pattern, where the communicator's message was formulated on the basis of the communicator's position rather than the receiver's.

The present data indicate a lack of egocentric role taking in this respect. As could be reasonably expected, the single most important piece of information utilized was the receiver's availability — his present uninvolvement in some other pressing matter.

Children of this age made a sharp distinction between adults and peers as receivers. They chose to communicate to adults more often than peers and only communicated to peers when it was easier to do so. For every child observed, the correlation between situations and communicative behaviors was better for messages to adults than for messages to peers. Even the correlation for messages to peers was substantial, but the children more closely tailored their messages to the receiver's needs when the receiver was an adult than when he was another 2-year-old.

It was surprising that children this young evidenced the communicative skills that they did in the naturally occurring situations sampled in this study. Other studies have shown poor performances by older subjects (Flavell, Botkin, Fry, Wright, & Jarvis 1968; Glucksberg, Krauss, & Higgs 1975). However, the present study observed only a select sample of possible communications — those that dealt with the present spatial locations of single external referents. This study is not alone in suggesting that very young children are relatively knowledgeable about objects in the external environment and about others' perception of the presence or absence of objects (Lempers et al., in press; Masangkay, McClusky, McIntyre, Sims-Knight, Vaughn & Flavell 1974). The information content of such messages intuitively seems simpler than messages about absent referents (absent in time or absent in space), internal referents (one's own or other's feelings, motivations, thoughts, etc.), and relationships of one or more referents (relationships over space or over time, the functions of referents, etc.). Studies such as those using a Krauss and Glucksberg paradigm (see Glucksberg et al. 1975), for example, have involved messages to receivers who were spatially absent from the communicator and inferences about the internal associations of listeners. In this regard, note that in the present data information about proximity was much more related to communicative behavior than was information about visual obstacles. Essentially when visual obstacles were present either the referent or receiver or both were visually absent. Thus the data indicate some real differences in young children's abilities for communicating about present versus absent objects and to present versus absent receivers.

In sum, the present research demonstrates an intriguing amount of communicative competence in very young children. It also demonstrates the need for a clearer, rigorous theory of differing types of communicative tasks and messages.

REFERENCES

Flavell, J.H.; Botkin, P.T.; Fry, C.L.; Wright, J.W.; & Jarvis, P.E. *The development of role-taking and communication skills in children*. New York: Wiley, 1968.

Garvey, G., & Hogan, R. Social speech and social interaction: egocentrism revisited. *Child Development*, 1973, 44, 562-568.

Glucksberg, W.; Krauss, R.M.; & Higgins, E.T. The development of referential communication skills. In F.D. Horowitz (Ed.), Review of child development research. Vol. 4. Chicago: University of Chicago Press, 1975.

Lempers, J.D.; Flavell, E.R.; & Flavell, J.H. The development in very young children of tacit knowledge concerning visual perception. *Genetic Psychology Monograhs,* in press.

Maratsos, M. Nonegocentric communication abilities in preschool children. *Child Development,* 1973, 44, 697-700.

Masangkay, Z.S.; McCluskey, K.S.; McIntyre, C.W.; Sims-Knight, J.; Vaughn, B.E.; & Flavell, J.H. The early development of inferences about the visual percepts of others. *Child Development*, 1974, 45, 357-366.

Mueller, E. The maintenance of verbal exchanges between children. *Child Development*, 1972, 43, 930-938.

Peterson, C.L.; Danner, F.W.; & Flavell, J.H. Developmental changes in children's repsonses to three indications of communicative failure. *Child Development*, 1972, 43, 1463-1468.

Piaget, J. *The language and thought of the child.* New York: World, 1955.

The Effects of Verbal Feedback and Listener Type on the Speech of Preschool Children

Amye Warren-Leubecker and John Neil Bohannon III

The present study simultaneously assessed the relative contributions of feedback indicative of comprehension and the apparent age of the listener, either an adult or a doll which resembled a toddler, in a 2 (listeners) $\times 2$ (types of feedback, C = comprehension, NC = non-comprehension) design. Two groups of children a 3-year-old (N = 13, 7 boys, 6 girls) and a 5-year-old group (N = 12, 6 boys, 6 girls) were asked to tell stories to both the adult and doll in both C and NC conditions. The doll was constructed with an internal speaker such that it could actually carry on a conversation with the children. The coversations were taped, transcribed, and scored for mean length of utterance (MLU), transitional utterance length to each C and NC signal, and the proportion of child questions, exact self-repetitions, repetition and reductions, and rephrases/elaborations. The data analysis revealed that all children appropriately modified the length of their utterances (MLU) in the doll condition but not in the adult condition, indicating that they were sensitive to both the feedback and the nature of their listeners. Older children were more likely than younger children, and girls more likely than boys to adjust the length of their utterances appropriately to each type of feedback, slightly increasing the length of the subsequent utterance to a C signal and decreasing the length to an NC signal. The younger children were also more likely to respond with a simple repetition to NC cues from the adult.

Mature communicative competence requires the ability to use language appropriate in differing contexts. Piaget (1926) and others (Flavell, Botkin, Fry, Wright, & Jarvis, 1968) have maintained that preschool children are too "egocentric" to adapt their speech to the communicative needs of different listeners. Flavell et al. (1968) found that older children's messages to a blindfolded adult differ greatly from their messages to an adult who could observe the topic of conversation, whereas the younger children's messages do not differ as much. The same pattern was noted by Higgins (Note 1) in children's messages to a "stranger" vs. those addressed to a "neighbor" who had some information in common with the child speaker. In summary, older children are more likely than preschoolers to modify their messages to fit the perceived characteristics of their listeners (see Glucksberg, Krauss, & Higgs, 1975, for a review).

In contrast, several studies have shown that preschool children are capable of adapting their speech to different listener characteristics. Menig-Peterson (1975) and Maratsos (1973) found adjustments in the speech of preschool children when the listener had not observed, or was not capable of observing the target stimulus or event. Others (Shantz & Gelman, 1973; Sachs & Devin, 1976) have found that young children will reliably adjust to the length and complexity of their utterances when speaking to younger children or dolls.

Verbal feedback is also a salient cue provided by the listener. When an adult listener signals a comprehension failure, most adult speakers will respond with a longer, or elaborated message; whereas signals of comprehension result in shortening of subsequent messages (Maclay & Newman, 1960). In contrast, if the listener is a child or an adult "foreigner" who is not a native language speaker, then cues of noncomprehension yield shorter subsequent utterances (measured in mean length of utterance or MLU) than signals of successful comprehension (Bohannon & Marquis, 1977; Warren-Leubecker & Bohannon, 1982). Therefore, appropriate speech adjustments appear to depend upon both the verbal feedback and the perceived listener characteristics.

Whether preschool children respond to verbal feedback in a manner similar to adults has been questioned. According to Glucksberg & Krauss (1967), third and fifth grade children and adults lengthen and elaborate their initial statements when listeners supplied noncomprehension feedback (i.e., "I don't understand"). Kindergarten children, however, typically responded with silence or mere repetition of their initial utterance. Flavell et al. (1968) reported similar effects of noncomprehension feedback as a function of age. In contrast, Garvey (1979) argued that her 3-year-old subjects exhibited sensitivity to feedback when they repeated their prior utterance in response to a signal of comprehension difficulty.

Clearly, verbal feedback and perceived listener characteristics simultaneously influence the speaker's behavior in most communicative contexts. Unfortunately, none of the previous studies simultaneously assessed both factors. The present study attempted to examine the speech adjustments of preschool children to different listeners: an adult and a doll. At the same time, the verbal cues of comprehension and noncomprehension (identical to those manipulated by Bohannon & Marquis, 1977) were varied. If children rely on the obvious aspect of relative age, then the subjects should address longer utterances to the adult regardless of the verbal feedback. If children are sensitive to the verbal cues then adjustments should occur regardless of the perceived age of the listener. This design also assessed the extent to which the relative age of the listener (adult or doll) modified the child's response to the various forms of feedback. In addition, the developmental trend of simplified speech was assessed by comparing a group of 3-year-old speakers with a group of 5-year-old speakers.

METHOD

Subjects

The subjects for the present study were 25 preschool children in a private daycare center in northern Atlanta, Georgia. The children were divided into two groups, a 3-year-old group (mean age = 3 years, 6 months, SD = 5.05 months) and a five-year-old group (mean age = 5 years, 1 month, SD = 5.31 months). The younger group contained six males and seven females; the older group was composed of six males and six females. The males and females did not significantly differ as to their ages, and all the children were middle class.

Design

The design of the study was a 2 (types of listeners, adult and talking doll) $\times 2$ (type of feedback, comprehension and noncomprehension) $\times 2$ (ages of subjects, 3- vs. 5-year-olds) $\times$ 2 (genders of subjects, boys vs. girls). The first two variables were within subject manipulations, and age and gender were the grouping variables.

Equipment

This study utilized a talking doll which was constructed from a commercially available baby doll. The doll was approximately 70 cm in length and had the appearance of a 12- to 18-month-old child. The doll was made to talk by inserting a small speaker in the chest cavity. Holes were drilled in the chest to allow clear voice reproduction and the doll came with clothes that cover up the speaker holes yet did not interfere with the sound quality. The speaker wire was concealed in the doll's pants leg and no child mentioned or seemed to notice it during the test sessions. The children's conversations were recorded on a stereo cassette tape via a wireless microphone strategically placed near the doll. Picture story books were available to the children during all conversations.

Procedure

Initially, all the subjects played with the adult experimenters for an average of 1/2 hr prior to any testing to familiarize them with their future conversational partners. They were then invited to converse individually with either the adult or the doll (appropriately nicknamed Chatty Cathy). The order of interaction (adult or doll first) and condition (comprehension "C", or noncomprehension "NC") were randomized across children. Familiar picture story books were available to the children during all interactions to assist conversation.

In the C condition, the adult or doll signaled complete comprehension of everything the child uttered. The responses were: *sure, ok, I see, yeah,* and appropriate responses to the child's questions. In the NC condition the adult and doll responded with the following responses: *what, huh*, imitation of the child's previous utterance, or statements such as, "I don't understand." To minimize the obvious transitions between conditions, each condition was separated by a significant pause, either between days of testing or during a change of story books.

All children were tested individually. They sat across a small table from their conversational partner and were simply asked if they would like to tell a story to the partner, either an adult or the doll. The interactions were viewed from behind a one way mirror and allowed the experimenter who was the voice of Chatty to keep abreast of the context of the conversation. The voice of Chatty was a high-pitced male falsetto (the best attempt of the experimenters at the prosodic voice quality of a toddler). All conversations lasted 5-10 min. and were tape recorded.

Results

The tape conversations were transcribed and scored for mean length of utterance (MLU) using the Bohannon and Marquis (1977) techniuqe, which treats all independent clauses as separate utterances and trends to make the MLU measure more conservative. Transitional MLUs were also scored using the Bohannon and Marquis (1977) technique. This calculates the relative utterance length change, either longer or shorter, following a comprehension or noncomprehension cue from the listener. Transitional MLUs were calculated for both the adult and doll condition for each child.

The transcripts were also scored for the number of child questions that occurred in each condition, the number of exact repetitions, repetition/reductions, and elaborations/rephrases. Exact repetitions were defined as any exact reproduction of an utterance that occurred in the prior conversational turn. Repetitions/reductions were defined as any reproduction of one or more content words from an immediately preceding utterance (preserving the original word order) without adding any new information. Elaborations/rephrases were defined as any utterance that retained the content of the previous statement yet added new information or phrased it in an entirely new way. The number of the various types of repetitions, elaborations, and questions were divided by the total number of the child's utterances that occurred in that condition to obtain a percentage score for each type of utterance.

The MLU data were anayzed in a 2 (feedback) ×2 (listeners) ×2 (ages) ×2 (genders) split-plot, factorial analysis of variance. The analysis revealed an age main effect, $F(1,21) = 8.60$, p. < 01. This was not surprising in that the 5-year-olds used longer utterances (mean MLU = 6.32 morphemes) than the 3-year-old children (mean MLU = 5.37 morphemes). The significant main effect of feedback, $F(1,21) = 7.28$, $p < .02$, indicated that all the children used longer utterances (mean MLU = 6.05 morphemes) when their listeners signaled comprehension rather than noncomprehension (mean MLU = 5.61 morphemes). The significant listener by feedback interaction, $F(1,21) = 6.29$, $p < .03$, is shown in Table 1. A Fisher's LSD test for multiple comparisons among means revealed that all the children significantly (p < .01) modified their speech only when addressing the doll (mean MLUs = 6.30 vs. 5.51 morphemes). None of the other conditions significantly differed from each other (see Table 1). This suggests that the children shortened their utterances to signals of noncomprehension only when the signals originated from a childlike source. The single sex effect in the analysis was a three-way interaction with listener and age. The authors feel that this was an artifact that did not significantly alter the strong pattern of effects evidenced by the other variables in the analysis.

The transitional MLUs were analyzed in a manner identical to that described above. The main effect of the different types of feedback, $F(1,21) = 90.11$, $p < .001$, indicated that regardless of any other factor, the children tended to shorten (mean decrease = -1.37 morphemes) their utterances subsequent to a noncomprehension cue (NC) vs. an increase in utterance length (mean increase = +.12) subsequent to a comprehension signal (C). The significant age by feedback interaction, $F(1,21) =$

TABLE 1
MEAN LENGTH OF UTTERANCE BY LISTENER AND
FEEDBACK TYPE

Listener	Feedback type	
	Comprehension	Noncomprehension
Adult	5.80"	5.70
Doll	6.30	5.51

" Mean differences greater than .59 are significant
($p < .01$) according to a Fisher's least significant
difference test.

5.38, p < .03, revealed that the older children responded more appropriately (mean C change = +.14, mean NC change = -1.74) to the different types of feedback, than the younger children (mean C change = +.10, mean NC change = -1.04). The significant sex by feedback interaction, $F(1,21) = 5.73$, p < .03, indicated that the girls of both ages (mean C change = +.32, mean NC change = -1.57) were more sensitive to the feedback cues than the boys (mean C change = -.08, mean NC change = -1.20).

A similar analysis was performed on the percentage of elaborations in the conversations which revealed another main effect of feedback, $F(1,21) = 106.83$, p < .001. This was due to all the subjects elaborating their prior statements more to signals of noncomprehension (mean = 13.4%) in contrast to cues of comprehension (mean = 1.7%). The significant listener by feedback interaction, $F(1,21) = 4.29$, p < .05, indicated that all the children elaborated in the noncomprehension conditon more to the adult (mean = 15%) than to the doll (11.8%). The percentages of elaborations that occurred in the comprehension condition did not differ significantly (adult mean = 1.6% vs. 1.9% to the doll).

The percentage of exact repetitions and repetition/reductions could not be analyzed using the above method simply because few children used these types of utterances under the comprehension conditions. Chi square analyses indicated that significantly more exact repetitions, $\chi^2(1) = 7.06$, p < .01, occurred in the noncomprehension conditions (mean = 9.2%) than in the comprehension conditions (mean = .9%). A similar analysis $\chi^2(1) = 5.85$, p < .02) revealed more repetitions/reductions in the noncomprehension condition (mean = 9.4%) than in the comprehension condition (mean = 1.4%). Therefore, only the data from the noncomprehension conditions were analyzed using a 2 (listeners) ×2 (ages) ×2 (genders) split-plot, factorial analysis of variance for the percentages of both exact repetitions and repetitions/reductions.

The analysis of the exact repetition data from the noncomprehension conditions revealed a significant effect of age, $F(1,21) = 5.88$, $p < .03$, because the 3-year-old children repeated themselves (mean $= 12.2\%$) more often than the older children (mean $= 5.9\%$). There was also a main effect of listener, $F(1,21) = 4.75$, $p < .05$, indicating that all the children tended to exactly repeat themselves more with the adult as listener (mean $= 10.9\%$) than with the doll as listener (mean $= 7.5\%$).

Discussion

It is clear from the data that the children could respond to both the available feedback and the appearance of their listeners. The significant listener by feedback interaction in the MLU analysis was the result of all the children shortening their utterances when the doll signaled comprehension difficulty and lengthening their statements when the doll signaled comprehension success (see Table 1). No such adjustments occurred when the adult gave the same types of signals. This suggests that the preschool children in the Shatz and Gelman (1973) study used short utterances because of both the younger children's appearance and the younger child's language immaturity. On the other hand, the failure of young children to modify their speech in the Flavell et al. (1968) study may have been due to the fact that their subjects' listeners were adults. If the relative age (appearance) of the listener was the only cue used by children, then the doll's feedback indicating comprehension failure should have had no effect.

When adults are confronted with noncomprehending adults, for example when talking to retardates (Pratt, Bumstead, & Raines, 1976), or to foreigners (Warren-Leubecker & Bohannon, 1982), reductions in MLU occur. It is possible that young children cannot conceive of a native, adult speaker who would need simple speech. Thus, the most frequent response in the adult-NC condition was to simply repeat the prior utterance. This was especially true for the 3-year-old children in the adult-NC condition where almost 20% of all the utterances were self-repetitions of one form or another. It is possible that with more exposure to the slow-witted adult in the NC condition, even the youngest children would modify their speech as they would to a child.

Developmental trends were noted in the MLU transitions and exact repetitions analyses. The MLU transition analysis revealed that older children responded more appropriately to feedback, by increasing utterance length more in response to signals of comprehension and decreasing more to noncomprehension cues than the younger children. Interestingly, there was no listener by feedback interaction in the MLU transition analysis to mirror the same effect in the MLU data. It appears that the effects of listener characteristics are strongest for utterances not preceeded by a feedback cue. If the listener is an adult, then utterances that introduce new topics or information tend to be longer than if the listener is a doll. Once feedback indicating comprehension success or failure of that message has been provided, speakers appear to rely on the feedback more than any other cue when producing subsequent utterances on that same topic (Warren-Leubecker & Bohannon, 1982). Since the MLU transition anlaysis only examines the differing lengths of utterances separately by a feedback cue, and since topic introduction typically occurs without preceding feedback, the listener effect may be obscured in this analysis. On the other hand, the MLU transitions data clearly show the increasing sensitivity to feedback with age.

The analyses of repetitions also reflected the 5-year-olds' greater communicative abilities. The older children were less likely to exactly repeat themselves in response to noncomprehension signals than the younger children. This appeared to be especially true when their listeners provided several consecutive noncomprehension cues. Whereas the older children would repeat themselves once or twice, then modify their initial messages, the younger children tended to persevere in their repetitions, making few adjustments to their original utterances. In fact, the most frequent adjustment of the younger children was merely to increase the loudness of the subsequent repetition. Younger children also tended to use repetition/reductions more frequently with the adult listener than with the doll. This is contrary to the pattern exhibited by mature speakers, who typically repeat and reduce more to younger listeners than to peers (Bohannon & Marquis, 1977; Stine & Bohannon, in press; Warren-Leubecker & Bohannon, 1982). The older children showed some evidence of the more mature pattern.

In summary, the present study has shown that even 3-year-old children can and do modify their speech depending on both feedback and their listeners' characteristics. The discrepancies between the results of this study and others (Glucksberg & Krauss, 1967; Flavell et al., 1968) may be due less to the young children's communicative immaturity than the type of task and listeners used. The typical referential communication task is by nature very restricted, to allow precise control over the topics to be described. However, this tight control may also place restrictions on the type and amount of modifications possible. If the initial message in a referential communication task is inadequate, an exact repetition is insufficient to repair the communication

TABLE 2

PROPORTION OF UTTERANCE TYPE BY FEEDBACK CONDITION

Type of utterance	Feedback	
	Comprehension	Noncomprehension
Elaborations	1.7%	13.4%*
Questions	5.3%	5.6%
Exact repetitions	.4%	9.2%*
Repetition/reductions	.5%	9.4%*
Total	7.9%	37.6%

* Comprehension–noncomprehension difference significant, $p < .01$.

failure. The content of the message must be modified for successful communication. In a more natural conversation setting, such as used in the present study, a repetition, or repetition/reduction, or an utterance changed in grammatical form but not in content, may suffice.

The present study also reaffirmed the power of verbal feedback from an immature (appearing) listener to control the length and complexity of a speaker's utterances, even if the speakers are only 3 years old. In addition, the appearance of certain types of utterances such as elaborations, exact repetitions, and repetition/reductions, is determined by the feedback provided by the listener (see Table 2). Both 3- and 5-year-old children made fewer adjustments when speaking to a noncomprehending adult, which suggests an ability to estimate a listeners' language skill based upon their appearance. Analyses of MLU transitions and the proportion of questions, exact repetitions, and repetition/reductions revealed developmental trends. The data suggest that the older children repeated themselves less often, modified their speech more to differing feedback, and asked question more appropriately across the experimental conditions than the younger children.

REFERENCES

Bohannon, J.N., & Marquis, A. Children's control of adult speech. *Child Development,* 1977, 48, 1002-1008.

Bohannon, J.N., Stine, E.L., & Ritzenberg, D. Motherese: The effects of experience and feedback. *Bulletin of the Psychonomic Society*, 1982, 19, 201-204.

Flavell, J.H., Botkin, P.T., Fry, C.L., Wright, J.W., & Jarvis, P.E. *The development of role-taking and communication skills in children.* New York: Wiley, 1968.

Garvey, C. Contingent queries and their relations in discourse. In E. Ochs & B. Schieffelin (Eds.), *Developmental pragmatics.* New York: Academic Press, 1979.

Glucksberg, S., Krauss, R., & Higgins, T. The development of referential communication skills. In F.D. Horowitz (Ed.), *Review of child development research* (Vol. 4). Chicago: Univ. of Chicago Press, 1975.

Maclay, H., & Newman, S. Two variables affecting the message in communication. In D.K. Wilner (Ed.), *Decisions, values, and groups.* New York: Pergamon, 1960.

Maratsos, M. Nonegocentric communication abilities in preschool children. *Child Development*, 1973, 44, 697-700.

Menig-Peterson, C.L. The modification of communicative behavior in preschool aged children as a function of the listener's perspective. *Child Development*, 1975, 46, 1015-1018.

Piaget, J. *Language and thought of the child*. New York: Harcourt, Brace & World, 1926.

Pratt, M., Bumstead, D., & Raines, N. Attendant staff speech to the institutionalized retarded: Language use as a measure of the quality of care. *Journal of Child Psychology and Psychiatry*, 1976, 17, 133-144.

Sachs, J., & Devin, J. Young children's use of age appropriate speech styles in social interaction and role-playing. *Journal of Child Language*, 1976, 3, 81-98.

Shatz, M., & Gelman, R. The development of communication skills: Modifications in the speech of young children as a function of listener. *Monographs of the Society for Research in Child Development*, 1973, 38 (5, Serial No. 152).

Stine, E.L., & Bohannon, J.N. Imitation, interaction and acquisition. *Journal of Child Language*, in press.

Warren-Leubecker, A., & Bohannon, J.N. Expectation and feedback in speech to foreigners. *Journal of Psycholinguistic Research*, 1982, 11, 207-215.

REFERENCE NOTE

1. Higgins, E.T. *A social and developmental comparison of oral and written communication skills*. Unpublished doctoral dissertation, Columbia University, 1973.

Section 4
Social Development: Interactions with Family and Friends

Children are social creatures. From early infancy, they are especially responsive to the qualities of the human voice and to spoken language. They smile, show pleasure and are soothed by the presence of other humans, and they form strong emotional attachments to their caretakers. The attachment figure serves as a source of security for the child in times of illness, fatigue, or threat, and the presence of the caretaker enables the child to cautiously explore a novel environment. The paper by Mary Ainsworth in Section 1 of this book describes some important work on the development of infant attachment.

As early as six months of age, infants direct social behavior to one another, exchanging looks, smiles, vocalizations and later, toys. Toddlers and preschoolers derive much pleasure from peer interactions and it is widely believed that play fosters both cognitive and social development. The skills that children develop during peer interactions prepare them for more mature social interactions and form the basis for life-long friendships. The paper by Zick Rubin in this section describes some of the "skills of friendship" that children acquire, and some of the implications for social development that can follow from having, or not having these skills.

While children experience security, pleasure, and friendship in their associations with other humans, they are also shaped and molded by these others. Although they come into the world without culture, children learn in a few short years to acquire the attitudes, values, and traditions that characterize the culture into which they were born. Parents are the first and perhaps most influential socializers. As such, their direct instruction and their behavior provide children with powerful lessons in social development. In addition to transmitting general cultural values, parents have their own unique styles or "philosophies" of child rearing. Research shows that styles of parent behavior tend to vary along the dimensions of warmth-hostility, and permissive-ness-control. Although generations of parents and other experts in child development have debated over which combinations of warmth and control are "best", research has not yet provided definite answers. The paper by Diana Baumrind presents some of her work on three parenting styles that she identified as authoritative, permissive, and authoritarian, and the impact of these styles on certain personality characteristics of preschool children.

Since parent-child interactions are so important for early social development several other papers in this section are also devoted to this topic. Jay Belsky's paper on mother-father-infant interactions provides a description of the similarities and differences in the ways in which mothers and fathers relate to their 15-month-old infants in a naturalistic situation. Contrary to some existing research, Belsky found more similarities than differences between the behavior of parents as they looked after and played with their infants. Marilyn Svejda and her colleagues present a review and discussion of the literature on the significance of the parent-to-infant bond of attachment that begins to develop in the early postpartum period. It has been suggested that any separation of infant and mother during this "sensitive" period could inhibit or delay the formation of the attachment bond and lead to inadequate caretaking. They argue that while early contact is important for both mother and child, separation of the pair need not be harmful to their relationship. Susan Goldberg also discusses this issue in her paper on premature birth. She describes some of the characteristics of premature infants which make early parent-infant interactions with these children different from, and sometimes more difficult than relationships with full-term infants.

In the past two decades family structures and relationships have changed from the traditional nuclear pattern of a male parent who was employed outside the home and a female parent who stayed home to be a homemaker and caretaker of the children. The increasing rate of divorce in the past two decades has left many single parent families who must cope on their own with the complexities of family life. However, children must also make adjustments following a divorce between their parents, and some of these changes and adjustments are discussed in the paper by Mavis Hetherington.

Other significant social changes in family structure have occurred with the increasing number of mothers of young children who now work full time outside their homes. This phenomenon has resulted in much debate over the impact of "working mothers" on the development of children. Whether the consequent changes in both women's and men's roles will have positive or negative effects on child development in the long term is unclear. However, the changes are inevitable and remain only to be adapted to and evaluated. The paper by M. Ann Easterbrooks and Wendy Goldberg examines some of the effects of maternal employment on mother-toddler and father-toddler relationships.

A significant effect of the increase in the number of women working outside their homes is that more children are being raised in day care centers. This phenomenon has been quite controversial, with critics arguing that raising children in "institutions" will have detrimental effects on development, and proponents claiming that high quality day care is good for children and in no way compromises the parent-child relationship. Jay Belsky has written a review of the literature on the impact of the day care experience on children's cognitive, social, and emotional development.

Socialization and Instrumental Competence in Young Children

Diana Baumrind

For the past 10 years I have been studying parent-child relations, focusing upon the effect of parental authority on the behavior of preschool children. In three separate but related studies, data on children were obtained from three months of observation in the nursery school and in a special testing situation; data on parents were obtained during two home observations, followed by an interview with each parent.

In the first study, three groups of nursery school children were identified in order that the child-rearing practices of their parents could be contrasted. The findings of that study (Baumrind, 1967) can be summarized as follows:

1. Parents of the children who were the most self-reliant, self-controlled, explorative, and content were themselves controlling and demanding; but they were also warm, rational, and receptive to the child's communication. This unique combination of high control and positive encouragement of the child's autonomous and independent strivings can be called *authoritative* parental behavior.

---

2. Parents of children who, relative to the others, were discontent, withdrawn, and distrustful, were themselves detached and controlling, and somewhat less warm than other parents. These may be called *authoritarian* parents.

3. Parents of the least self-reliant, explorative, and self-controlled children were themselves noncontrolling, nondemanding, and relatively warm. These can be called *permissive* parents.

A second study of an additional 95 nursery school children and their parents, also supported the position that "authoritative control can achieve responsible conformity with group standards without loss of individual autonomy or self-assertiveness" (Baumrind, 1966, p. 905). In a third investigation (Baumrind, 1971), patterns of parental authority were defined so that they would differ from each other as did the authoritarian, authoritative, and permissive combinations which emerged from the first study.

PATTERNS OF PARENTAL AUTHORITY

Each of these three authority patterns is described in detail below, followed by the subpatterns that have emerged empirically from the most recent study. The capitalized items refer to specific clusters obtained in the analysis of the parent behavior ratings.

The *authoritarian* parent[2] attempts:

> to shape, control and evaluate the behavior and attitudes of the child in accordance with a set standard of conduct, usually an absolute standard, theologically motivated and formulated by a higher authority. She values obedience as a virtue and favors punitive, forceful measures to curb self-will at points where the child's actions or beliefs conflict with what she thinks is right conduct. She believes in inculcating such instrumental values as respect for authority, respect for work, and respect for the preservation of order and traditional structure. She does not encourage verbal give and take, believing that the child should accept her word for what is right (Baumrind, 1968, p. 261).

---

2 In order to avoid confusion, when I speak of the parent I will use the pronoun "she", and when I speak of the child, I will use the pronoun "he", although, unless otherwise specified, the statement applies to both sexes equally.

Two subpatterns in our newest study correspond to this description; they differ only in the degree of acceptance shown the child. One subpattern identifies families who were Authoritarian but Not Rejecting. They were high in Firm Enforcement, low in Encourages Independence and Individuality, low in Passive-Acceptance, and low in Promotes Nonconformity. The second subpattern contained families who met all the criteria for the first subpattern except that they scored high on the cluster called Rejecting.

The *authoritative* parent, by contrast with the above, attempts:

> to direct the child's activities but in a rational issue-oriented manner. She encourages verbal give and take, and shares with the child the reasoning behind her policy. She values both expressive and instrumental attributes, both autonomous self-will and disciplined conformity. Therefore, she exerts firm control at points of parent-child divergence, but does not hem the child in with restrictions. She recognizes her own special rights as an adult, but also the child's individual interests and special ways. The authoritative parent affirms the child's present qualities, but also sets standards for future conduct. She uses reason as well as power to achieve her objectives. She does not base her decisions on group consensus or the individual child's desires; but also, does not regard herself as infallible, or divinely inspired (Baumrind, 1968, p. 261).

Two subpatterns correspond to this description, differing only in the parents' attitudes towards normative values. One subpattern contained families who were Authoritative and Conforming. Like the Authoritarian parents described above, these parents had high scores in Passive-Acceptance. However, they also had high scores in Encourages Independence and Individuality. The second subpattern contained parents who met the criteria for the first subpattern, but who also scored high in Promotes Nonconformity.

The *permissive* parent attempts:

> to behave in a nonpunitive, acceptant and affirmative manner towards the child's impulses, desires, and actions. She consults with him about policy decisions and gives explanations for family rules. She makes few demands for household responsibility and orderly behavior. She presents herself to the child as a resource for him to use as he wishes, not as an active agent responsible for shaping or altering his ongoing or future behavior. She allows the child to regulate his own activities as much as possible, avoids the exercise of control,

and does not encourage him to obey externally-defined standards. She attempts to use reason but not overt power to accomplish her ends (Baumrind, 1968, p. 256).

We were able to locate three subpatterns reflecting different facets of this prototypic permissiveness. One subpattern, called Nonconforming, typified families who were nonconforming but who were not extremely lax in discipline and who did demand high performance in some areas. The second subpattern, called Permissive, contained families who were characterized by lax discipline and few demands, but who did not stress nonconformity. The third subpattern contained families who were both nonconforming and lax in their discipline and demands; hence, they are referred to as Permissive-Nonconforming.

INSTRUMENTAL COMPETENCE

Instrumental Competence refers to behavior which is socially responsible and independent. Behavior which is friendly rather than hostile to peers, cooperative rather than resistive with adults, achievement rather than nonachievement-oriented, dominant rather than submissive, and purposive rather than aimless, is here defined as instrumentally competent. Middle-class parents clearly value instrumentally competent behavior. When such parents were asked to rank those attributes that they valued and devalued in children, the most valued ones were assertiveness, friendliness, independence, and obedience, and those least valued were aggression, avoidance, and dependency (Emmerich & Smoller, 1964). Note that the positively valued attributes promote successful achievement in United States society and, in fact, probably have survival value for the individual in any subculture or society.

There are people who feel that, even in the United States, those qualities which define instrumental competence are losing their survival value in favor of qualities which may be called Expressive Competence. The author does not agree. Proponents of competence defined in terms of expressive, rather than instrumental, attributes, value feelings more than reason, good thoughts more than effective actions, "being" more than "doing" or "becoming," spontaneity more than planfulness, and relating intimately to others more than working effectively with others. At present, however, there is no evidence that emphasis on expressive competence, at the expense of instrumental competence, fits people to function effectively over the long run as members of any community. This is not to say that expressive competence is not essential for effective functioning in work as well as in love, and for both men and women. Man, like other animals, experiences and gains valid information about reality by means of both noncognitive and cognitive processes. Affectivity deepens man's knowledge of his environment; tenderness and receptivity enhance the character and effectiveness of any human being. But instrumental competence is and will continue to be an essential component of self-esteem and self-fulfillment.

One subdimension of instrumental competence, here designated *Responsible vs. Irresponsible*, pertains to the following three facets of behavior, each of which is related to the others:

(a) *Achievement-oriented vs. Nonachievement-oriented.* This attribute refers to the willingness to persevere when frustration is encountered, to set one's own goals high, and to meet the demands of others in a cognitive situation as opposed to withdrawal when faced with frustration and unwillingness to comply with the teaching or testing instructions of an examiner or teacher. Among older children, achievement-orientation becomes subject to autogenic motivation and is more closely related to measures of independence than to measures of social responsibility. But in the young child, measures of cognitive motivation are highly correlated with willingness to cooperate with adults, especially for boys. Thus, in my study, resistiveness towards adults was highly negatively correlated with achievement-oriented behavior for boys, but not for girls. Other investigators (Crandall, Orleans, Preston & Rabson, 1958; Haggard, 1969) have also found that compliance with adult values and demands characterizes young children who display high achievement efforts.

(b) *Friendly vs. Hostile Behavior Towards Peers.* This refers to nurturant, kind, altruistic behavior displayed toward agemates as opposed to bullying, insulting, selfish behavior.

(c) *Cooperative vs. Resistive Behavior Towards Adults.* This refers to trustworthy, responsible, facilitative behavior as opposed to devious, impetuous, obstructive actions.

A second dimension of child social behavior can be designated Independent vs. Suggestible. It pertains to the following three related facets of behavior:

(a) *Domineering vs. Tractable Behavior.* This attribute consists of bold, aggressive, demanding behavior as opposed to timid, nonintrusive, undemanding behavior.

(b) *Dominant vs. Submissive Behavior.* This category refers to individual initiative and leadership in contrast to suggestible, following behavior.

(c) *Purposive vs. Aimless Behavior.* This refers to confident, charismatic, self-propelled activity vs. disoriented, normative, goalless behavior.

The present review is limited to a discussion of instrumental competence and associated antecedent parental practices and is most applicable to the behavior of young children rather than adolescents.

SOCIALIZATION PRACTICES RELATED TO RESPONSIBLE VS. IRRESPONSIBLE BEHAVIOR

The reader will recall that I have defined Responsible vs. Irresponsible Behavior in terms of Friendliness vs. Hostility Towards Peers, Cooperation vs. Resistance Towards Adults, and High vs. Low Achievement Orientation. Socialization seems to have a clearer impact upon the development of social responsibility in boys than in girls, probably because girls vary less in this particular attribute. In my own work, parents who were authoritative and relatively conforming as compared with parents who were permissive or authoritarian, tended to have children who were more friendly, cooperative, and achievement-oriented. This was especially true for boys. Nonconformity in parents was not necessarily associated with resistant and hostile behavior in children. Neither did firm control and high maturity demands produce rebelliousness. In fact, it has generally been found that close supervision, high demands for obedience and personal neatness, and pressure upon the child to share in household responsibilities are associated with responsible behavior rather than with chronic rebelliousness. The condition most conducive to antisocial aggression, because it most effectively rewards such behavior, is probably one in which the parent is punitive and arbitrary in his demands, but inconsistent in responding to the child's disobedience.

Findings from several studies suggest that parental demands provoke rebelliousness only when the parent both restricts atuonomy of action and does not use rational methods of control. For example, Pikas (1961), in a survey of 656 Swedish adolescents, showed that differences in the child's acceptance of parental authority depended upon the reason for the parental directive. Authority based on rational concern for the child's welfare was accepted well by the child, but arbitrary, domineering, or exploitative authority was rejected. Pikas' results are supported by Middleton and Snell (1963) who found that discipline regarded by the child as either very strict or very permissive was associated with rebellion against the parents' political views. Finally, Elder (1963), working with adolescents' reports concerning their parents, found that conformity to parental rules typified subjects who saw their parents as having ultimate control (but who gave the child leeway in making decisions) and who also provided explanations for rules.

Several generalizations and hypotheses can be drawn from this literature and from the results of my own work concerning the relations of specific parental practices to the development of social responsibility in young children. The following list is based on the assumption that it is more meaningful to talk about the effects of patterns of parental authority than to talk about the effects of single parental variables.

1. *The modeling of socially responsible behavior facilitates the development of social responsibility in young children, and more so if the model is seen by the child as having control over desired resources and as being concerned with the child's welfare.*

The adult who subordinates his impulses enough to conform with social regulations and is himself charitable and generous will have his example followed by the child. The adult who is self-indulgent and lacking in charity will have his example followed even if he should preach generous, cooperative behavior. Studies by Mischel and Liebert (1966) and by Rosenhan, Frederick and Burrowes (1968) suggest that models who behave self-indulgently produce similar behavior in children and these effects are even more extensive than direct reward for self-indulgent behavior. Further, when the adult preaches what he does not practice, the child is more likely to do what the adult practices. This is true even when the model preaches unfriendly or uncooperative behavior but behaves toward the child in an opposite manner. To the extent that the model for socially responsible behavior is perceived as having high social status (Bandura, Ross & Ross, 1963), the model will be most effective in inducing responsible behavior.

In our studies, both authoritative and authoritarian parents demanded socially responsible behavior and also differentially rewarded it. As compared to authoritative parents, however, authoritarian parents permitted their own needs to take precedence over those of the child, became inaccessible when displeased, assumed a stance of personal infallibility, and in other ways showed themselves often to be more concerned with their own ideas than with the child's welfare. Thus, they did not exemplify prosocial behavior, although they did preach it. Authoritative parents, on the other hand, both preached and practiced prosocial behavior and their children were significantly more responsible than the children of authoritarian parents. In this regard, it is interesting that nonconforming parents who were highly individualistic and professed anticonforming ideas had children who were more socially responsible than otherwise. The boys were achievement-oriented and the girls were notably cooperative. These parents were themselves rather pacific, gentle people who were highly responsive to the child's needs even at the cost of their own; thus, they modeled but did not preach prosocial behavior.

2. *Firm enforcement policies, in which desired behavior is positively reinforced and deviant behavior is negatively reinforced, facilitate the development of socially responsible behavior, provided that the parent desires that the child behave in a responsible manner.*

The use of reinforcement techniques serves to establish the potency of the reinforcing agent and, in the mind of the young child, to legitimate his authority. The use of negative sanctions can be a clear statement to the child that rules are there to be followed and that to disobey is to break a known rule. Among other things, punishment provides the child with information. As Spence (1966) found, nonreaction by adults is sometimes interpreted by children as signifying a correct response. Siegel and Kohn (1959) found that nonreaction by an adult when the child was behaving aggressively resulted in an increased incidence of such acts. By virtue of his or her role as an authority, the sheer presence of parents when the child misbehaves cannot help but affect the future occurrence of such behavior. Disapproval should reduce such actions, while approval or nonreaction to such behavior should increase them.

In our studies, permissive parents avoided the use of negative sanctions, did not demand mannerly behavior or reward self-help, did not enforce their directives by exerting force or influence, avoided confrontation when the child disobeyed, and did not choose or did not know how to use reinforcement techniques. Their sons, by comparison with the sons of authoritative parents, were clearly lacking in prosocial and achievement-oriented behavior.

3. *Nonrejecting parents are more potent models and reinforcing agents than rejecting parents; thus, nonrejection should be associated with socially responsible behavior in children provided that the parents value and reinforce such behavior.*

It should be noted that this hypothesis refers to nonrejecting parents and is not stated in terms of passive-acceptance. Thus, it is expected that nonrejecting parental behavior, but not unconditionally acceptant behavior, is associated with socially responsible behavior in children. As Bronfenbrenner pointed out about adolescents, "It is the presence of rejection rather than the lack of a high degree of warmth which is inimical to the development of responsibility in both sexes" (1961, p. 254). As already indicated, in our study authoritarian parents were more rejecting and punitive, and less devoted to the child's welfare than were authoritative parents; their sons were also less socially responsible.

4. *Parents who are fair, and who use reason to legitimate their directives, are more potent models and reinforcing agents than parents who do not encourage independence or verbal exchange.*

Let us consider the interacting effects of punishment and the use of reasoning on the behavior of children. From research it appears that an accompanying verbal rationale nullifies the special effectiveness of immediate punishment, and also of relatively intense punishment (Parke, 1969). Thus, by symbolically reinstating the deviant act, explaining the reason for punishment, and telling the child exactly what he should do, the parent obviates the need for intense or instantaneous punishment. Immediate, intense punishment may have undesirable side effects, in that the child is conditioned through fear to avoid deviant behavior, and is not helped to control himself consciously and willfully. Also, instantaneous, intense punishment produces high anxiety which may interfere with performance, and in addition may increase the likelihood that the child will avoid the noxious agent. This reduces that agent's future effectiveness as a model or reinforcing agent. Finally, achieving behavioral conformity by conditioning fails to provide the child with information about cause and effect relations which he can then transfer to similar situations. This is not to say that use of reasoning alone, without negative sanctions, is as effective as the use of both. Negative sanctions give operational meaning to the consequences signified by reasons and to rules themselves.

Authoritarian parents, as compared to authoritative parents, are relatively unsuccessful in producing socially responsible behavior. According to this hypothesis, the reason is that authoritarian parents fail to encourage verbal exchange and infrequently accompany punishment with reasons rather than that they use negative sanctions and are firm disciplinarians.

SOCIALIZATION PRACTICES RELATED TO INDEPENDENT VS. SUGGESTIBLE BEHAVIOR

The reader will recall that Independent vs. Suggestible Behavior was defined with reference to: (a) Domineering vs. Tractable Behavior, (b) Dominance vs. Submission, (c) Purposive vs. Aimless Activity, and (d) Independence vs. Suggestibility. Parent behavior seems to have a clearer effect upon the development of independence in girls than in boys, probably because preschool boys vary less in independence.

In my own work, independence in girls was clearly associated with authoritative upbringing (whether conforming or nonconforming). For boys, nonconforming parent behavior and, to a lesser extent, authoritative upbringing were associated with independence. By independence we do not mean anticonformity. "Pure anticonformity, like pure conformity, is pure dependence behavior" (Willis, 1968, p. 263). Anticonforming behavior, like negativistic behavior, consists of doing anything but what is prescribed by social norms. Independence is the ability to disregard known standards of conduct or normative expectations in making decisions. Nonconformity in parents may not be associated in my study with independence in girls (although it was in boys) because females are especially susceptible to normative expectations. One can hypothesize that girls must be trained to act independently of these expectations, rather than to conform or to anticonform to them.

It was once assumed that firm control and high maturity demands lead to passivity and dependence in young children. The preponderance of evidence contradicts this. Rather, it would appear that many children react to parental power by resisting, rather than by being cowed. The same parent variables which increase the probability that the child will use the parent as a model should increase the likelihood that firm control will result in assertive behavior. For example, the controlling parent who is warm, understanding, and supportive of autonomy should generate less passivity (as well as less rebelliousness) than the controlling parent who is cold and restrictive. This should be the case because of the kinds of behavior reinforced, the traits modeled, and the relative effectiveness of the parent as a model.

Several generalizations and hypotheses can be offered concerning the relations between parental practices and the development of independence in young children:

1. *Early environmental stimulation facilitates the development of independence in young children.*

It took the knowledge gained from compensatory programs for culturally disadvantaged children to counteract the erroneous counsel from some experts to avoid too much cognitive stimulation of the young child. Those Head Start programs which succeed best (Hunt, 1968) are those characterized by stress on the development of cognitive skills, linguistic ability, motivational concern for achievement, and rudimentary numerical skills. There is reason to believe that middle-class children also profit from such early stimulation and enrichment of the environment. Fowler (1962) pointed out, even prior to the development of compensatory programs, that concern about the dangers of premature cognitive training and an overemphasis on personality development had delayed inordinately the recognition that the ability to talk, read, and compute increase the child's self-respect and independent functioning.

Avoidance of anxiety and self-assertion are reciprocally inhibiting responses to threat or frustration. Girls, in particular, are shielded from stress and overstimulation, which probably serves to increase preferences for avoidant rather than offensive responses to aggression or threat. By exposing a child to stress or to physical, social, and intellectual demands, he or she becomes more resistant to stress and learns that offensive reactions to aggression and frustration are frequently rewarding. In our studies, as the hypothesis would predict, parents who provided the most enriched environment, namely the nonconforming and the authoritative parents, had the most dominant and purposive children. These parents, by comparison with the others studied, set high standards of excellence, invoked cognitive insight, provided an intellectually stimulating atmosphere, where themselves rated as being differentiated and individualistic, and made high educational demands upon the child.

2. *Parental passive-acceptance and overprotection inhibits the development of independence.*

Passive-acceptant and overprotective parents shield children from stress and, for the reasons discussed above, inhibit the development of assertiveness and frustration tolerance. Also, parental anxiety about stress to which the child is exposed may serve to increase the child's anxiety. Further, willingness to rescue the child offers him an easy alternative to self-mastery. Demanding and nonprotective parents, by contrast, permit the child to extricate himself from stressful situations and place a high value on tolerance of frustration and courage.

According to many investigators (e.g., McClelland, Atkinson, Clark & Lowell, 1953), healthy infants are by inclination explorative, curious, and stress-seeking. Infantile feelings of pleasure, originally experienced after mild changes in sensory stimulation, become associated with these early efforts at independent mastery. The child anticipates pleasure upon achieving a higher level of skill, and the pleasure derived from successfully performing a somewhat risky task encourages him to seek out such tasks.

Rosen and D'Andrade (1959) found that high achievement motivation, a motivation akin to stress-seeking, was facilitated both by high maternal warmth when the child pleased the parent and high maternal hostility and rejection when the child was displeasing. Hoffman et al. (1960) found that mothers of achieving boys were more coercive than those who performed poorly, and it has also been found (Crandall, Dewey, Katkovsky & Preston, 1964) that mothers of achieving girls were relatively nonnurturant. Kagan and Moss (1962) reported that achieving adult women had mothers who in early childhood were unaffectionate, "pushy," and not protective. Also, Baumrind and Black (1967) found paternal punitiveness to be associated positively with independence in girls. Finally, in a recent study (Baumrind, 1971), there were indications for girls that parental nonacceptance was positively related to independence. That is, the most independent girls had parents who were either not passive-acceptant or were rejecting.

Authoritarian control and permissive noncontrol both may shield the child from the opportunity to engage in vigorous interaction with people. Demands which cannot be met, refusals to help, and unrealistically high standards may curb commerce with the environment. Placing few demands on the child, suppression of conflict, and low standards may understimulate him. In either case, he fails to achieve the knowledge and experience required to desensitize him to the anxiety associated with nonconformity.

3. *Self-assertiveness and self-confidence in the parent, expressed by an individual style and by the moderate use of power-oriented techniques of discipline, will be associated with independence in the young child.*

The self-assertive, self-confident parent provides a model of similar behavior for the child. Also, the parent who uses power-oriented rather than love-oriented techniques of discipline achieves compliance through means other than guilt. Power-oriented techniques can achieve behavioral conformity without premature internalization by the child of parental standards. It may be that the child is, in fact, more free to formulate his own standards of conduct if techniques of discipline are used which stimulate resistiveness or anger rather than fear or guilt. The use of techniques which do not stimulate conformity through guilt may be especially important for girls. The belief in one's own power and the assumption of responsibility for one's own intellectual successes and failures are important predictors of independent effort and intellectual achievement (Crandall, Katkovsky & Crandall, 1965). This sense of self-responsibility in children seems to be associated with power-oriented techniques of discipline and with critical attitudes on the part of the adult towards the child, provided that the parent is also concerned with developing the child's autonomy and encourages independent and individual behavior.

In my study, both the authoritative and the nonconforming parents were self-confident, clear as well as flexible in their child-rearing attitudes, and willing to express angry feelings openly. Together with relatively firm enforcement and nonrejection, these indices signified patterns of parental authority in which guilt-producing techniques of discipline were avoided. The sons of nonconforming parents and the daughters of authoritative parents were both extremely independent.

4. Firm control can be associated with independence in the child, provided that the control is not restrictive of the child's opportunities to experiment and to make decisions within the limits defined.

There is no logical reason why parents' enforcing directives and demands cannot be accompanied by regard for the child's opinions, willingness to gratify his wishes, and instruction in the effective use of power. A policy of firm enforcement may be used as a means by which the child can achieve a high level of instrumental competence and eventual independence. The controlling, demanding parent can train the child to tolerate increasingly intense and prolonged frustration; to broaden his base of adult support to include neighbors, teachers, and others; to assess critically his own successes and failures and to take responsibility for both; to develop standards of moral conduct; and to relinquish the special privileges of childhood in return for the rights of adolescence.

It is important to distinguish between the effects on the child of restrictive control and of firm control. Restrictive control refers to the use of extensive proscriptions and prescriptions, covering many areas of the child's life; they limit his autonomy to try out his skills in these areas. By firm control is meant firm enforcement of rules, effective resistance against the child's demands, and guidance of the child by regime and intervention. Firm control does not imply large numbers of rules or intrusive direction of the child's activities.

Becker (1964) has summarized the effects on child behavior of restrictiveness vs. permissiveness and warmth vs. hostility. He reported that warm-restrictive parents tended to have passive, well-socialized children. This author (Baumrind, 1967) found, however, that warm-controlling (by contrast with warm-restrictive) parents were not paired with passive children, but rather with responsible, assertive, self-reliant children. Parents of these children enforced directives and resisted the child's demands, but were not restrictive. Early control, unlike restrictiveness, apparently does not lead to "fearful, dependent and submissive behaviors, a dulling of intellectual striving, and inhibited hostility," as Becker indicated was true of restrictive parents (1964, p. 197).

5. *Substantial reliance upon reinforcement techniques to obtain behavioral conformity, unaccompanied by use of reason, should lead to dependent behavior.*

To the extent that the parent uses verbal cues judiciously, she increases the child's ability to discriminate, differentiate, and generalize. According to Luria (1960) and Vygotsky (1962), the child's ability to "order" his own behavior is based upon verbal instruction from the adult which, when heeded and obeyed, permits eventual cognitive control by the child of his own behavior. Thus, when the adult legitimizes power, labels actions clearly as praiseworthy, explains rules and encourages vigorous verbal give and take, obedience is not likely to be achieved at the cost of passive dependence. Otherwise, it may well be.

It is self-defeating to attempt to shape, by extrinsic reinforcement, behavior which by its nature is autogenic. As already mentioned, the healthy infant is explorative and curious, and seems to enjoy mild stress. Although independent mastery can be accelerated if the parent broadens the child's experiences and makes certain reasonable demands upon him, the parent must take care not to substitute extrinsic reward and social approval for the intrinsic pleasure associated with mastery of the environment. Perhaps the unwillingness of the authoritative parents in my study to rely solely upon reinforcement techniques contributed substantially to the relatively purposive, dominant behavior shown by their children, especially by their daughters.

6. *Parental values which stress individuality, self-expression, initiative, divergent thinking, and aggressiveness will facilitate the development of independence in the child, provided that these qualities in the parent are not accompanied by lax and inconsistent discipline and unwillingness to make demands upon the child.*

It is important that adults use their power in a functional rather than an interpersonal context. The emphasis should be on the task to be done and the rule to be followed rather than upon the special status of the powerful adult. By focusing upon the task to be accomplished, the adult's actions can serve as an example for the child rather than as a suppressor of his independence. Firm discipline for both boys and girls must be in the service of training for achievement and independence, if such discipline is not to facilitate the development of an overconforming, passive life style.

In our study, independence was clearly a function of nonconforming but nonindulgent parental attitudes and behaviors, for boys. For girls, however, nonconforming parental patterns were associated with independence only when the parents were also authoritative. The parents in these groups tended to encourage their children to ask for, even to demand, what they desired. They themselves acquiesced in the face of such demands provided that the demands were not at variance with parental policy. Thus, the children of these parents were positively reinforced for autonomous self-expression. In contrast to these results, the authoritarian parents did not value willfulness in the child, and the permissive parents were clearly ambivalent about rewarding such behavior. Further, the permissive parents did not differentiate between mature or praiseworthy demands by the child and regressive or deviant demands. These permissive parents instead would accede to the child's demands until patience was exhausted; punishment, sometimes very harsh, would then ensue.

CONCLUSIONS

Girls in Western society are in many ways systematically socialized for instrumental incompetence. The affiliative and cooperative orientation of girls increases their receptivity to the influence of socializing agents. This influence, in turn, is often used by socializing agents to inculcate passivity, dependence, conformity, and sociability in young females at the expense of independent pursuit of success and scholarship. In my studies, parents designated as authoritative had the most achievement-oriented and independent daughters. However, permissive parents whose control was lax, who did not inhibit tomboy behavior, and who did not seek to produce sex-role conformity in girls had daughters who were nearly as achievement-oriented and independent.

The following adult practices and attitudes seem to facilitate the development of socially responsible and independent behavior in both boys and girls:

1. Modeling by the adult of behavior which is both socially responsible and self-assertive, especially if the adult is seen as powerful by the child and as eager to use the material and interpersonal resources over which he has control on the child's behalf.

2. Firm enforcement policies in which the adult makes effective use of reinforcement principles in order to reward socially responsible behavior and to punish deviant behavior, but in which demands are accompanied by explanations, and sanctions are accompanied by reasons consistent with a set of principles followed in practice as well as preached by the parent.

3. Nonrejecting but not overprotective or passive-acceptant parental attitudes in which the parent's interest in the child is abiding and, in the preschool years, intense; and where approval is conditional upon the child's behavior.

4. High demands for achievement and for conformity with parental policy, accompanied by receptivity to the child's rational demands and willingness to offer the

child wide latitude for independent judgment.

5. Providing the child with a complex and stimulating environment offering challenge and excitement as well as security and rest, where divergent as well as covergent thinking is encouraged.

These practices and attitudes do not reflect a happy compromise between authoritarian and permissive practices. Rather, they reflect a synthesis and balancing of strongly opposing forces of tradition and innovation, divergence and convergence, accommodation and assimilation, cooperation and autonomous expression, tolerance and principled intractability.

REFERENCES

Aberle, D.F. & Naegele, K.D. Middle-class fathers' occupational role and attitudes toward children. *Am. J. Orthopsychiat.,* 1952, 22, 366-378.

Bandura, A., Ross, D. & Ross, S.A. A comparative test of the status envy, social power, and the secondary-reinforcement theories of identificatory learning. *J. abnorm. soc. Psychol.,* 1963, 67, 527-534.

Barry, H., Bacon, M.K. & Child, I.L. A cross-cultural survey of some sex differences in socialization. *J. abnorm. soc. Psychol.,* 1957, 55, 327-332.

Baumrind, D. Effects of authoritative parental control on child behavior. *Child Develpm.,* 1966, 37, 887-907.

-----. Child care practices anteceding three patterns of preschool beahvior. *Genet. Psychol. Monogr.,* 1967, 75, 43-88.

-----. Authoritarian vs. authoritative parental control. *Adolescence,* 1968, 3, 255-272.

-----. Current patterns of parental authority. *Develpm. Psychol. Monogr.,* 1971, 4(1), 1-102.

-----. From each woman in accord with her ability. *School Rev.,* Feb. 1972, in press. (a)

-----. An exploratory study of socialization effects on black children: Some black-white comparisons. *Child Develpm.,* 1972, in press. (b)

Baumrind, D. & Black, A.E. Socialization practices associated with dimensions of competence in preschool boys and girls *Child Develpm.,* 1967, 38, 291-327.

Becker, W.C. Consequences of different kinds of parental discipline. In M.L. Hoffman & L.W. Hoffman (eds.), *Review of Child Developmental Research,* Vol. 1. New York: Russell Sage Foundations 1964. Pp. 169-208.

Bronfenbrenner, U. Some familial antecedents of responsibility and leadership in adolescents. In L. Petrullo & B.M. Bass (eds.), *Leadership and Interpersonal Behavior.* New York: Holt, Rinehart and Winston, 1961. Pp. 239-271.

Brown, D. Sex role development in a changing culture. *Psychol. Bull.*, 1958, 55; 232-242.

Crandall, V., Dewey, R., Katkovsky, W. & Preston, A. Parents' attitudes and behaviors and grade school children's academic achievements. *J. genet. Psychol.,* 1964, 104, 53-66.

Crandall, V., Katkovsky, W. & Cradall, V.J. Children's beliefs in their own control of reinforcements in intellectual-academic achievement situations. *Child Develpm.*, 1965, 36, 91-109.

Crandall, V., Orleands, S., Preston, A. & Rabson, A. The development of social compliance in young children. *Child Develpm,* 1958, 29, 429-443.

Dinitz, S., Dynes, R.R. & Clarke, A.C. Preference for male or female children: Traditional or affectional. *Marriage and Family Living*, 1954, 16, 128-130.

Eiduson, B.T. *Scientists, Their Psychological World*, New York: Basic Books, 1962.

Elder, G.H. Parental power legitimation and its effects on the adolescent, *Sociometry*, 1963, 26, 50-65.

Emmerich, W. & Smoller, F. The role patterning of parental norms. *Sociometry*, 1964, 27, 382-390.

Fowler, W. Cognitive learning in infancy and early childhood. *Psychol. Bull,* 1962, 59, 116-152.

Haggard, E.A. Socialization, personality, and academic achievement in gifted children. In B.C. Rosen, H.J. Crockett & C.Z. Nunn (eds.), *Achievement in American society.* Cambridge, Mass.: Schenkman Publishing, 1969. Pp. 85-94.

Heilbrun, A.B. Sex differences in identification learning. *J. genet. Psychol.*, 1965, 106, 1885-193.

Hoffman, L., Rosen, S. & Lippitt, R. Parental coerciveness, child autonomy, and child's role at school. *Sociometry,* 1960, 23, 15-22.

Horner, M.S. Sex differences in achievement motivation and performance in competitive situations. Unpubl. doctoral dissertation, Univ. of Michigan, 1968.

Hunt, J. McV. Toward the prevention of incompetence. In J.W. Carter, Jr. (Ed.), *Research Contributions from Psychology to Community Mental Health.* New York: Behavioral Publications, 1968.

Kagan, J. & Moss, H.A. *Birth to Maturity: A Study in Psychological Development.* New York: John Wiley, 1962.

Keniston, E. & Keniston, K. An American anachronism: the image of women and work. *Am. Scholar,* 1964, 33, 355-375.

Luria, A.R. Experimental analysis of the development of voluntary action in children. In *The Central Nervous System and Behavior.* Bethesda, Md.: U.S. Dept. of Health, Education, & Welfare, National Institutes of Health, 1960. Pp. 529-535.

Maccoby, E.E. (Ed.), *The Development of sex differences..* Stanford, Calif.: Stanford Univ. Press, 1966.

McClelland, D., Atkinson, J., Clark, R. & Lowell, E. *The achievement Motive.* New York: Appleton-Century-Crofts, 1953.

McKee, J.P. & Sherrifs, A.C. The differential evaluation of males and females, J. Pers., 1957, 25, 356-371.

Middleton, R. & Snell, P. Political expression of adolescent rebellion. *Am. J. Sociol.,* 1963, 68, 527-535.

Mischel, W. & Liebert, R.M. Effects of discrepancies between observed and imposed reward criteria on their acquisition and transmission. *J. pers. soc. Psychol.,* 1966, 3, 45-53.

Parke, R.D. Some effects of punishment on children's behavior. *Young children,* 1969, 24, 225-240.

Pikas, A. Children's attitudes toward rational versus inhibiting parental authority. *J. abnorm. soc. Psychol.,* 1961, 62, 315-321.

Roe, A. *The Making of a Scientist.* New York: Dodd, Mead, 1952.

Rosen, B.C. & D'Andrade, R. The psychological origins of achievement motivation. *Sociometry,* 1959, 22, 185-218.

Rosenhan, D.L., Frederick, F. & Burrowes, A. Preaching and practicing: Effects of channel discrepancy on norm internalization. *Child Develpm.,* 1968, 39, 291-302.

Rossi, A. Women in science: why so few? In B.C. Rosen, H.J. Crockett, & C.Z. Nunn (Eds.), *Achievement in American Society.* Cambridge, Mass.: Schenkman Publishing, 1969. Pp. 470-486.

Siegel, A.E. & Kohn, L.G. Permissiveness, permission, and aggression: The effects of adult presence or absence on aggression in children's play. *Child Develpm.,* 1959, 36, 131-141.

Spence, J.T. Verbal-discrimination performance as a function of instruction and verbal reinforcement combination in normal and retarded children. *Child Develpm.,* 1966, 37, 269-281.

Terman, L.M. & Oden, H.H. *The Gifted Child Grows Up.* Stanford, Calif.: Stanford Univ. Press, 1947.

Vygotsky, L.S. *Thought and Language.* Cambridge, Mass.: M.I.T. Press, 1962.

Walberg, H.J. Physics, femininity, and creativity. *Develp. Psychol.,* 1969, 1, 47-54.

Willis, R.H. Conformity, independence, and anitconformity. In L.S. Wrightsman, Jr. (ed.). *Contemporary Issues in Social Psychology.* Belmont, Calif.: Brooks/Cole Publishing, 1968. Pp. 258-272.

Parent to Infant Attachment:
A Critique of the Early "Bonding" Model

Marilyn J. Svejda,

Betty Jean Pannabecker, and Robert N. Emde

Introduction

Most research exploring attachment has been concerned with the development of the infant's attachment to his or her parents, especially to the mother. Historically, much less attention has been devoted to the parental attachment systems–the parents' growth of love for the infant. A major step toward looking at the development of parental attachment came about through pioneering work of Klaus and Kennell and their associates (Klaus, Jerauld, Kreger, McAlpine, Steffa, & Kennell, 1972) who explored the manifestations of the mother's tie to her infant in the time shortly after the infant's birth. Subsequently, investigations have extended to the forgotten member of the triad–the father. Now, additional research has led to a need for reassessing the nature of the parent-infant attachment system.

The goals of this chapter are twofold: (1) to briefly review the research concern-

Originally published in *The Development of Attachment and Affiliative Systems,* edited by R. Emde and R. Harmon. New York: Plenum, 1982. Reprinted with permission of the publisher and author.

ing the importance of the time after birth for the development of maternal and paternal attachment systems, and (2) to suggest, on the basis of this, that the 'bonding' model of paternal attachment is misleading.

MOTHER-TO-INFANT ATTACHMENT

The original model for the importance of early contact for human mothers came from work with animals. In some animals, for example sheep and goats, separation of the young from the mother shortly after birth had a profound effect on subsequent maternal behavior. Ungulate mothers whose lambs or kids were removed soon after birth and returned one or more hours later butted their infants away when they approached, and withdrew from the young's attempts to nurse (Collias, 1956; Klopfer, Adams, & Klopfer, 1964). Those mothers that were not separated from their young, or separated following a 5-10 minute period of contact immediately after birth, did not engage in these aberrant behaviors (Hersher, Moore, & Richmond, 1958). Thus the evidence was strong for the importance of the interval immediately after birth for the formation of the social bond between ungulate mothers and infants.

A Review of Maternal Bonding Research

The prototype for the several studies exploring the importance of the immediate postpartum period for maternal attachment in human mothers came from the Cleveland study of Klaus and associates (Klaus et al., 1972). In that study two groups of primiparous mothers of healthy fullterm infants had different amounts of contact with their infants immediately after delivery and during the next three postpartum days. The mothers of this study were from an inner-city disadvantaged poor population (most were unmarried teenagers who had not completed high school). Routine care mothers had the usual hospital contact: a glimpse of the infant shortly after birth, a 6-12 hour separation, and 20-30 minutes of contact every 4 hours for feeding. Extended contact mothers had their nude infants 1 hour within the first 3 hours after birth and 5 hours additional each day for the next 3 hospital days. At one month, extended contact mothers showed more soothing behavior when their infants became upset, engaged in more *en face* and fondling behavior during the feeding, and reported greater reluctance to leave their infants in the care of another person than did routine care mothers.

Since the original Cleveland study, there has been increasing interest in the possible influence of biological factors in the development of maternal attachment. Attachment, defined as a unique emotional relationship between two people which is specific and endures through time, is thought to be indexed by various behaviors including fondling, prolonged gazing, and cuddling which serve to maintain proximity and express affection to the infant (Kennell, Trause, & Klaus, 1975). The biological basis of maternal attachment has been postulated as a result of findings from several studies which emphasize the importance of *contact* between mother and infant in the *time interval shortly after birth* — the maternal 'sensitive period.' Early contact is seen as the facilitator for a rapid process of mother to infant attachment more commonly known as bonding (Carlsson, Fagerberg, Horneman, Hwang, Larsson, Rodholm, Schaller, Danielsson, & Gundewell, 1978; de Chateau & Wiberg, 1977; Hales, Lozoff, Sosa, & Kennell, 1977; Klaus et al., 1972; Konton, 1978). In these studies evidence for maternal bonding has been found in increased frequencies of affectionate behaviors (e.g., looking *en face*, holding, fondling, and rocking the infant) by those mothers who are given early contact with their infants as compared with those mothers who are given their infants for the first time several hours following birth. The effects of early contact on maternal behavior have been seen as soon as 36 hours (de Chateau & Wiberg, 1977; Hales et al., 1977) and have been seen as late as two and five years (Klaus & Kennell, 1976).

The notion that early contact between mother and infant may have positive effects on their relationship has great theoretical and practical importance. Nonetheless, although most of the research on mother-infant contact shortly after birth tends to support the importance of early contact, careful review of these studies indicates that the generalizable effects of early contact have not been convincingly demonstrated.

First, different effects have been reported even when similar dependent measures and paradigms were used. For instance, in one study primiparous mothers given skin-to-skin contact with their infants shortly after birth engaged in significantly more affectionate behaviors at 36 hours (looking *en face*, fondling) than did control mothers (Hales et al., 1977). Yet in a similar study (de Chateau & Wiberg, 1977) no significant differences were found in affectionate behaviors at 36 hours between control mothers and mothers given skin-to-skin contact with their infants.

Second, the effects of early contact have been subtle. Differences between early contact and routine care (control) mothers often have been marginally significant (e.g., Klaus et al., 1972), and some behaviors, especially those involved in caretaking (e.g., burping, cleansing) do not seem to be affected by early contact (de Chateau & Wiberg, 1977; Klaus et al., 1972).

Third, some behaviors which differentiated early contact (sits up more) from routine care mothers (leans on elbow) (de Chateau & Wiberg, 1977) are not in accord with behaviors that more typically characterize maternal attachment.

Finally, important methodological features (e.g., random assignment to contact conditions, blind scoring, control for demand characteristics) were not always evident in earlier studies.

Early Contact Fails to Generalize

In view of the practical importance of maternal attachment, the unclear findings to date, and the absence of important methodological features in earlier work, we were encouraged to design a study that included several methodological and procedural controls which would allow us to test the notion that early enhanced contact facilitates maternal attachment behavior (Svejda, Campos, & Emde, 1980).

Thirty lower-middle-class, healthy, primiparous mothers were randomly assigned to an extra contact (15 minutes of skin-to-skin contact in the delivery room, 45 minutes of contact in the recovery room, and 1 1/2 hours at each feeding for the next 7 feedings) or routine care group (5 minutes of contact while mother and infant were wheeled from the delivery room, no contact in the recovery room, and 20-30 minutes at each feeding for the next 7 feedings). Mothers were not informed about differences in contact conditions or the study's purpose until the study was completed. To avoid comparison about different contact conditions only one study mother was on the unit at a time. Nonstudy roommate mothers of extra contact mothers also had extra contact in order to reduce feelings of specialness in study mothers. Manipulation checks revealed that nurses spent an equal amount of time with all mothers. Mothers and infants were videotaped at 36 hours postpartum during an unstructured interaction and a breast feeding.

Results indicated that mothers in the two groups were very similar in their responses toward their infants. No significant differences were obtained on 28 discrete response measures or on categories of pooled response measures (i.e., affectionate, caretaking, or proximity-maintaining behaviors) as a function of early contact. We did, however, find a few sex differences related to contact condition. Early contact mothers talked more to their female infants and were more affectionate toward them during the unstructured interaction while routine care mothers touched their female infants more and looked *en face* more often at their male infants.

In general, we found little support for effects of early contact on maternal behavior. Futher, the high frequency of attachment behaviors in routine care mothers suggested to us that these mothers were attached to their infants. While other studies did not state that mothers *not* having early contact were unattached, they do seem to imply that the quality of attachment was compromised in these mothers.

The results of our research are less surprising in view of other recent research reporting little support for meaningful effects of early contact on maternal behavior. One study (Leiderman & Seashore, 1975) compared mothers of fullterm infants and mothers of prematures who either had contact with their infants after delivery or who were separated from them. Differences observed in maternal behavior at one week and one month had largely disappeared at one year. Instead, parity, socioeconomic status, sex of infant, and play behavior of infant were significant predictors of maternal responsiveness (Leiderman & Seashore, 1975). At a two-year follow-up even these factors had disappeared as predictors of maternal behavior. In the words of Leiderman (1978), "it would appear that subsequent post-discharge events had major influence in reducing variations we found among groups in the first postpartum year" (p. 51). Interestingly, early separation may have had a more general effect on family stability since families in the separated group had a higher divorce rate (Leiderman, 1978).

Carlsson and associates obtained initial support for the effects of early contact on maternal behavior but effects did not persist on follow-up study. Primiparous mothers who were given early contact showed more affectionate behaviors (e.g., talks, smiles, touches, rocks) than did later contact mothers on the second and fourth day postpartum (Carlsson et al., 1978). However, a follow-up study at 6 weeks showed no statistically significant differences between groups of mothers on 18 discrete response measures or on pooled response categories (contact vs. noncontact behaviors) (Carlsson, Fagerberg, Horneman, Hwang, Larsson, Rodholm, Schaller, Danielsson, & Gundewall, 1979).

Finally, Taylor's research group (Taylor, Taylor, Campbell, Maloni, & Dickey, 1979) reported no differences between groups of mothers as a function of early contact on several measures: (a) time spent with their infants during the postpartum hospital stay, (b) responses to questions reflecting attachment, (c) responses on the Neonatal Perception Inventory at 2 days and at 1 month, and (d) the quality of the mother-infant interaction reflected during feeding at 2 days and 1 month. Some modest sex effects were obtained during feeding in favor of early contact mothers of males at the day 2 and at the 1 month observation.

What conclusions can be drawn about the effects of early contact on maternal attachment behavior?

Shortcomings of the Bonding Model

First, the general case for maternal bonding as currently conceptualized (i.e., as involving a sensitive period for infant contact immediately after birth) is weak. The diversity of findings in the several early contact studies suggests that the generality of the effect can be questioned.

Second, the evidence to date suggests a need to investigate other factors that may facilitate maternal responsiveness. One factor is the set of variables associated with a more economically advantaged population, for example, job, income, and education. A regular income provides the family with means to afford a private physician who can be consulted about matters related to pregnancy, delivery, and child care. Further, increased educational opportunities, including prenatal education, may enable the mother to identify many ways of relating to her infant and providing for his or her care. It is of interest that in studies reporting little or no effect of early contact, mothers were primarily middle-class, high school or college educated, married and living in stable families, and had husbands who were available during labor and/or delivery (Carlsson et al., 1979; Leiderman, 1978; Svejda et al., 1980; Taylor et al., 1979).

Another factor which may play a significant role in facilitating the mother's responsiveness to her infant is the existence of support systems--family members, friends, physicians, and nurses. Especially important may be the father's presence at delivery. Wilson (1977) found that a significant predictor for the mother's responsiveness in the delivery room (e.g., talking to and touching the infant) was the father's general responsiveness, and that maternal responsiveness in the delivery room significantly predicted the mother's general responsiveness during a hospital feeding. Thus it seems quite possible that maternal behavior could be affected by the support provided by the father at delivery.

The characteristics of the infant and his or her ability to engage in interaction may also have important affects on maternal behavior. In early contact studies little attention has been given to the role of the infant as a participant in the first encounter with his or her parents.

Third, the bonding model proposed by the early contact work does not take into account the dynamic nature of the relationship between mother and infant. Maternal attachment appears to be an ongoing process and is probably not consolidated by any one experience or event (Harmon & Emde, in press). That events take place during a specified time interval, for example, immediately after birth, does not necessarily mean that they have a lasting impact on the development of the mother-infant relationship. In fact, long-term follow-up on infants of early contact mothers shows, in general, that these infants do not differ in any important way from infants of control mothers (de Chateau, 1979; Leiderman, 1978; Kennell, Jerauld, Wolfe, Chesler, Kreger, McAlpine, Steffa, & Klaus, 1974). To advocate the primacy of time-locked events tends to diminish the importance of subsequent interactions and events in the ongoing relationship between mother and infant. Further, such a position carries the potential for limiting or denying conceptualizing motherhood as a developmental process in its own right.

FATHER-TO-INFANT ATTACHMENT

Caregiving of the Father

Whereas it is true that mother-to-infant attachment has been a topic of relatively recent concern, father-to-infant attachment has been limited to even more recent interest. It was not long ago that fathers were thought to be unimportant for infant development; instead of becoming involved with their infants, the standard wisdom was that fathers were to become involved with their offspring in childhood when they became important influences for sex role, moral, and cognitive development. As Lamb (1977) has noted, recent studies of the father-infant relationship, with infants aged six months to two years, have indicated that the infant is clearly attached to the father by the second half of the first year. Thus, since we now know that father-to-infant attachment exists, it becomes relevant to ask about its beginnings. Is early contact important to facilitate this process? Is there anything analogous to maternal bonding in the immediate postpartum period?

Although childbearing used to be considered "women's work" with traditional attitudes keeping fathers away, there has been a dramatic historical change brought about by the childbirth education movement. Fathers have now become involved in prenatal classes and they assist their wives during labor and delivery. Hospital rules have been altered to allow husbands to attend deliveries, and fathers have been able to hold their infants in the delivery room and to participate in infant care during the postpartum hospital stay. It is now common for fathers to express pleasure and some confidence in the caring of their newborn infants.

A number of studies of early father-infant interaction documented these changes. Greenberg and Morris (1974) interviewed fathers within 48 hours of the delivery of their infants and noted a strong desire in the fathers to touch and hold their infants. Greenberg and Morris labelled this phenomenon "engrossment." Parke and O'Leary (1973) observed mother-infant, father-infant, and mother-father-infant interaction during the first 48 hours and found that fathers were very active participants in interactions with their infants whether or not the mothers were present. Only a few differences were found between mothers' and fathers' behavior with their infants. Mothers and fathers were found to be equally competent to meet their infants' needs during feeding.

Parke and Sawin (1977) observed father-infant and mother-infant interaction in a feeding situation and in a play situation at three times: during the postpartum hospital stay, at three weeks of age, and at three months of age. They concluded that fathers, again, were active participants in interaction with infants and that mutual regulation and adaptation between infant and parent begins in the newborn period. Both parents are seen to be active and sensitive figures in the early social development of their infants.

A Test of Father Bonding

The original Cleveland study (Klaus et al., 1972) of early enhanced mother-infant contact served as a paradigm for our father-infant study. Experimental and hospital control groups were recruited prenatally (Pannabecker, Emde, & Austin, in press). Fathers in the experimental group were given extra contact with their infants during the postpartum hospitalization; however, the contact differed from the Klaus et al. (1972) study of mothers in several respects. Fathers had two periods of extra contact with their infants, one on each of the first two days postpartum. Although the amount of time added was only 50 minutes, this doubled the amount of infant contact fathers in the experimental group had compared to fathers in the control group. During extra contact, fathers were given information about selected physical and behavioral characteristics of their newborn infants. A hospital control group of fathers received the same information about physical and behavioral characteristics of newborn infants but without the contact with their own infant. (This group was introduced to control for the educational effect of learning about infants in general without added contact between fathers and their own particular infants.) An office control group was recruited on the last day of the postpartum hospital stay to control for effects which may have been due to expectations related to being in the study up until that time (demand characteristics). All three groups of parents attended their infant's one-month pediatric checkup and observations were made of fathers' interactions with their infants.

Our results were striking. No differences were found between groups of fathers on 103 measures of father-infant interaction, either during the infant's physical examination or while father was dressing the infant and performing other unstructured activities. Our measures included *en face* behavior, and father-to-infant affectionate behaviors, as well as behaviors of other kinds. Thus enhancing early father-to-infant contact, under the conditions of this study, did not result in differences similar to those reported after enhancing mother-to-infant contact. How do we understand this?

The fact that all three groups of fathers attended childbirth education classes and the birth of their infant may have wiped out any differences related to other amounts of early contact. Peterson, Mehl, and Leiderman (1979) found that the father's participation in the birth and his attitude toward it were the most significant variables in predicting father attachment from 1 to 3 months postpartum. Alternatively, our lack of differences among groups may have been due to the fact that families were from a middle-class, educated, and childbirth-prepared population where early contact would have less of an impact than would be the case with families from a disadvantaged population. But perhaps the outstanding finding of our study concerned the large amount of involvement and participation of fathers with their infants at both the newborn and one-month age period. Like the previous studies of Parke and his collaborators, fathers were actively interested and demonstrated affection toward their infants. Obviously, not having the added early contact did *not* result in their not becoming attached. Certainly the case for the bonding model has been made more strongly for mothers where there has been a biological overtone. Since there is little or no evidence for an early contact or sensitive period phenomenon in the development of paternal attachment, it seems fortunate that the concept of bonding has been less frequently applied to fathers.

CONCLUSION

Bonding Model No Longer Useful

The pioneering work of Klaus and Kennell and their associates has facilitated important theoretical advances in emphasizing the parental side of the developing affiliative relationship between parents and infants. It has also led to important humanistic advances by encouraging hospitals to provide options for parents to be with their infants in the immediate postpartum period.

Still, we conclude that the bonding model, which grew out of this work, is no longer useful. In our view, it is misleading in the following ways:

1. The model carries the implication that parents who lack early contact do not love their babies or somehow are compromised. There is little or no research support for this position, especially for middle-class or advantaged populations.
2. The model carries the implications of a biologically-based sensitive period for attachment. This may further imply to some that attachment is primarily for mothers and is time-limited.
3. The model emphasizes newborn contact for attachment in such a way that it could lead to a relative neglect of the importance of interaction in infancy and early childhood.
4. The model is oversimplified. It tends to encourage a unidirectional view of the development of the attachment-interactive process. Current models of development are interactional and transactional and are more appreciative of factors in the family network.
5. There is a problem of reification. This was illustrated by a recent hospital nursing note which read "do not remove the baby to the nursery until bonding has taken place." As a metaphor, bonding reminds us of "getting stuck." Thus it can detract from the *process* aspects of a developing dynamic relationship between parent and infant.
6. Clinically, many parents cannot be with their infants; others may not choose to. Yet, because of some ideas fostered by the bonding model, they may feel disappointed and/or guilty for not having the opportunity to become "bonded."

In summary, the early work on maternal bonding has focused increased interest on mother and infant togetherness at the time of birth and made us more aware of parents' eagerness to participate more actively in the birth process. We have witnessed the great joy parents experience from this contact. Thus it seems important that parents have the opportunity for contact with their infants after delivery. However, they should not be led to believe that early contact is the direct route to maternal attachment, or that its absence confers difficulty. We recommend that the bonding model be discontinued as a misleading metaphor.

REFERENCES

Carlsson, S.G., Fagerberg, H., Horneman, G., Hwang, C.-P., Larsson, K., Rodholm, M., Schaller, J., Danielsson, B., & Gundewall, C. Effects of amount of contact between mother and child on the mother's nursing behavior. *Developmental Psychobiology*, 1978, 11, 143-150.

Carlsson, S.G., Fagerberg, H., Horneman, G., Hwang, C.P., Larsson, K., Rodholm, M., Schaller, J., Danielsson, B., & Gundewall, C. Effects of various amounts of contact between mother and child on the mother's nursing behavior: A follow-up study. *Infant Behavior and Development*, 1979, 2, 209-214.

Collias, N.E. The analysis of socialization in sheep and goats. *Ecology*, 1956, 37, 228-239.

de Chateau, P. *Long-term effects of early post-partum contact.* Research display discussion session, Society for Research in Child Development, San Francisco, March 1979.

de Chateau, P., & Wiberg, B. Long-term effect on mother-infant behavior of extra contact during the first hour postpartum. I. First observation at 36 hours. *Acta Paediatrica Scandinavica*, 1977, 66, 137-143.

Greenberg, M., & Morris, N. Engrossment: The newborn's impact upon the father. *American Journal of Orthopsychiatry*, 1974, 44, 520-531.

Hales, D.J., Lozoff, B., Sosa, R., & Kennell, J.H. Defining the limits of the maternal sensitive period. *Developmental Medicine and Child Neurology*, 1977, 19, 454-461.

Harmon, R.J., & Emde, R.N. Beyond maternal bonding: Clinical and research perspectives. *Journal of Nervous and Mental Disease* (in press).

Hersher, L., Moore, A.U., & Richmond, J.B. Effects of post-partum separation of mother and kid on maternal care in the domestic goat. *Science*, 1958, 128, 1342-1343.

Kennell, J.H., Jerauld, R., Wolfe, H., Chesler, D., Kreger, N.C., McAlpine, W., Steffa, M., & Klaus, M.H. Maternal behavior one year after early and extended post-partum contact. *Developmental Medicine and Child Neurology*, 1974, 16, 172-179.

Kennell, J.H., Trause, M.A., & Klause, M.H. Evidence for a sensitive period in the human mother. In *Parent-infant interaction* (Ciba Foundation 33-new series). New York: Elsevier, 1975.

Klaus, M.H., Jerauld, R., Kreger, N.C., McAlpine, W., Steffa, M., & Kennell, J.H. Maternal attachment importance of the first post-partum days. *New England Journal of Medicine*, 1972, 286, 460-463.

Klaus, M.H., & Kennell, J.H. *Maternal-infant bonding.* St. Louis: Mosby, 1976.

Klopfer, P.H., Adams, D.K., & Klopfer, M.S. Maternal "imprinting" in goats. *Proceedings, National Academy of Science,* 1964, 52, 911-914.

Kontos, D. A Study of the effects of extended mother-infant contact on maternal beahvior at one and three months. *Birth and the Family Journal,* 1978, 5, 133-140.

Lamb, M.E. Father-infant and mother-infant interaction in the first year of life. *Child Development,* 1977, 48, 176-181.

Leiderman, P.H., & Seashore, M.J. Mother-infant neonatal separation: Some delayed consequences. In *Parent-infant interaction* (Ciba Foundation Symposium 33-new series). New York: Elsevier, 1975.

Leiderman, P.H. The critical period hypothesis revisited. Mother to infant social bonding in the neonatal period. In F.D. Horowitz (Ed.), *Early developmental hazards: Predictors and precautions.* American Academy for Advancement of Science, Selected Symposium 9, Boulder: Westview Press, 1978.

Pannabecker, B.J., Emde, R.N., & Austin, B.C. The effect of early extended contact on father-newborn interaction. *Journal of Genetic Psychology* (in press).

Parke, R.D., & O'Leary, S. *Family interaction in the newborn period: Some findings, some observations and some unresolved issues.* Paper presented at Biennial Meetings of the International Society for the Study of Behavior Development, Ann Arbor, August 1973.

Parke, R.D., & Sawin, D.B. *The family in early infancy: Social interactional and attitudinal analyses.* Paper presented at Society for Research in Child Development, New Orleans, March 1977.

Peterson, G.H., Mehl, L.E., Leiderman, P.H. The role of some birth-related variables in father attachment. *American Journal of Orthopsychiatry,* 1979, 49(2), 330-338.

Svejda, M.J., Campos, J.J., & Emde, R.N. Mother-infant "bonding": Failure to generalize. *Child Development,* 1980, 56, 775-779.

Taylor, P.M., Taylor, F.H., Campbell, S.B., Maloni, J., & Dickey, D. *Effects of extra contact on early maternal attitudes, perceptions and behaviors.* Paper read at the meetings of the Society for Research in Child Development, San Francisco, March 1979.

Wilson, L. *A predictive analysis of early parental attachment behavior.* Paper read at the meetings of the Society for Research in Child Development, New Orleans, March 1977.

Premature Birth: Consequences for the Parent-Infant Relationship

Susan Goldberg

The normal pattern of interaction in which both infant and parent initiate and respond to mutually complementary behavior is difficult to establish when the infant is premature.

Imagine, if you will, the sound of a young infant crying. For most adults it is a disturbing and compelling sound. If it is made by your own infant or one in your care, you are likely to feel impelled to do something about it. Most likely, when the crying has reached a particular intensity and has lasted for some (usually short) period of time, someone will pick the baby up for a bit of cuddling and walking. Usually, this terminates the crying and will bring the infant to a state of visual alertness. If the baby makes eye contact with the adult while in this alert state, the caregiver is likely to begin head-nodding and talking to the baby with the exaggerated expression and inflections that are used only for talking to babies. Babies are usually very attentive to this kind of display and will often smile and coo. Most adults find this rapt attention and smiling exceedingly attractive in young infants and will do quite ridiculous things for these seemingly small rewards.

I have used this example to illustrate that normal infant behaviors and the be-

Originally published in *American Scientist*, 1979, 67, 214-220. Reprinted with permission of the publisher and author.

haviors adults direct toward infants seem to be mutually complementary in a way that leads to repeated social interactions enjoyed by both infants and adults. Consider now the experiences of a baby whose cry is weak and fails to compel adult attention, or the baby (or adult) who is blind and cannot make the eye contacts that normally lead to social play. When the behavior of either the infant or the adult is not within the range of normal competence, the pair is likely to have difficulties establishing rewarding social interactions. Premature birth is one particular situation in which the interactive skills of both parents and infants are hampered.

Recent studies comparing interactions of preterm and full-term parent-infant pairs have found consistently different patterns of behavior in the two groups. Before we turn to these studies, it will be useful to introduce a conceptual framework for understanding parent-infant interaction and a model within which the findings can be interpreted.

A conceptual framework

In most mammalian species, the care of an adult is necessary for the survival, growth, and development of the young. One would therefore expect that such species have evolved an adaptive system of parent-infant interaction which guarantees that newborns will be capable of soliciting care from adults and that adults will respond appropriately to infant signals for care. Where immaturity is prolonged and the young require the care of parents even after they are capable of moving about and feeding without assistance, one would also expect the interactive system to be organized in a way that guarantees the occurrence of social (as opposed to caregiving) interactions that can form the basis for a prolonged parent-child relationship. It is not surprising to find that when these conditions are met, the parent-infant interaction system appears to be one of finely tuned reciprocal behaviors that are mutually complementary and that appear to be preadapted to facilitate social interaction. Furthermore, as the example given earlier illustrates, both parents and infants are initiators and responders in bouts of interaction.

This view is quite different from that taken by psychologists in most studies of child development. For most of the relatively short history of developmental psychology it was commonly assumed that the infant was a passive, helpless organism who was acted upon by parents (and others) in a process that resulted in the "socialization" of the child into mature forms of behavior. In popular psychology this emphasis appeared as the belief that parents (especially mothers) were responsible for their child's development. They were to take the credit for successes as well as the blame for failures.

In the last fifteen years, the study of infant development has shown that the young infant is by no means passive, inert, or helpless when we consider the environment for which he or she is adapted — that is, an environment which includes a responsive caregiver. Indeed, we have discovered that infants are far more skilled and competent than we originally thought. First, the sensory systems of human infants are well developed at birth, and their initial perceptual capacities are well matched to the kind of stimulation that adults normally present to them. Infants see and discriminate visual patterns from birth, although their visual acuity is not up to adult standards. Young infants are especially attentive to visual movement, to borders of high contrast, and to relatively complex stimuli. When face to face with infants, adults will normally present their faces at the distance where newborns are best able to focus (17-22 cm) and exaggerate their facial expressions and movements. The result is a visual display with constant movement of high contrast borders.

A similar phenomenon is observed in the auditory domain. Young infants are most sensitive to sound frequencies within the human vocal range, especially the higher pitches, and they can discriminate many initial consonants and vocal inflections. When adults talk to infants, they spontaneously raise the pitch of their vocies, slow their speech, repeat frequently, exaggerate articulation and inflection. Small wonder that young infants are fascinated by the games adults play with them!

In addition, researchers have found that when adults are engaged in this type of face-to-face play they pace their behavior according to the infant's pattern of waxing and waning attention. Thus the infant is able to "control" the display by the use of selective attention. At the same time, studies have found that babies are most likely to smile and coo first to events over which they have control. Thus, infants are highly likely to smile and gurgle during face-to-face play with adults, thus providing experiences which lead the adult to feel that he or she is "controlling" an interesting display. We will return to the notion of control and the sense of being effective as an important ingredient in parent-infant relationships.

A second respect in which infants are more skilled and competent than we might think is their ability to initiate and continue both caregiving and social interactions. Although the repertoire of the young infant is very limited, it includes behaviors such as crying, visual attention, and (after the first few weeks) smiling, which have compelling and powerful effects on adult behavior. Almost all parents will tell you that in the first weeks at home with a new baby they spent an inordinate amount of time trying to stop the baby's crying.

Crying is, at first, the most effective behavior in the infant's repertoire for getting adult attention. When social smiling and eye contact begin, they too become extremely effective in maintaining adult attention. In one study, by Moss and Robson (1968), about 80 percent of the parent-infant interactions in the early months were initiated by the infant. Thus, the normally competent infant plays a role in establishing the contacts with adults that provide the conditions necessary for growth and development.

Competence motivation: a model

The actual process by which this relationship develops is not clearly understood, but we can outline a plausible model that is consistent with most of the available data. A central concept in this model is that of competence motivation, as defined by White (1959). In a now-classic review of research on learning and motivation in many species, White concluded that behaviors that are selective, directed, and persistent occur with high frequency in the absence of extrinsic rewards. He therefore proposed an intrinsic motive, which he called competence motivation, arising from a need to cope effectively with the environment, to account for behavioral phenomena such as play, exploration, and curiosity. Behavior that enables the organism to control or influence the environment gives rise to feelings of efficacy that strengthen competence motivation. White pointed out that much of the behavior of young infants appears to be motivated in this manner. Why else, for example, would infants persist in learning to walk when they are repeatedly punished by falls and bruises?

At the other extreme, Seligman (1975) has demonstrated that animals, including humans, can quickly learn to be helpless when placed in an unpleasant situation over which they have no control. This learned helplessness prevents effective behavior in subsequent situations where control is possible. It has been suggested that an important part of typical parent-infant interaction in the early months is the prompt and appropriate responses of the parent to the infant's behavior, which enable the infant to feel effective. The retarded development often seen in institutionalized infants may arise from learned helplessness in a situation where, though apparent needs are met, this occurs on schedule rather than in response to the infant's expression of needs and signals for attention. There is a general consensus among researchers in infant development that the infant's early experiences of being effective support competence motivation, which in turn leads to the exploration, practice of skills, and "discovery" of new behaviors important for normal development.

I have suggested elsewhere (1977) that competence motivation is important to parents as well. Parents bring to their experiences with an infant some history that determines their level of competence motivation. However, their experiences with a particular infant will enhance, maintain, or depress feelings of competence in the parental role. Unlike infants, parents have some goals by which they evaluate their effectiveness. Parents monitor infant behavior, make decisions about caregiving or social interaction, and evaluate their own effectiveness in terms of the infant's subsequent behavior.

When parents are able to make decisions quickly and easily and when subsequent infant behavior is more enjoyable or less noxious than that which prompted them to act, they will consider themselves successful in that episode. When parents cannot make decisions quickly and easily and when subsequent infant behavior is more aver-

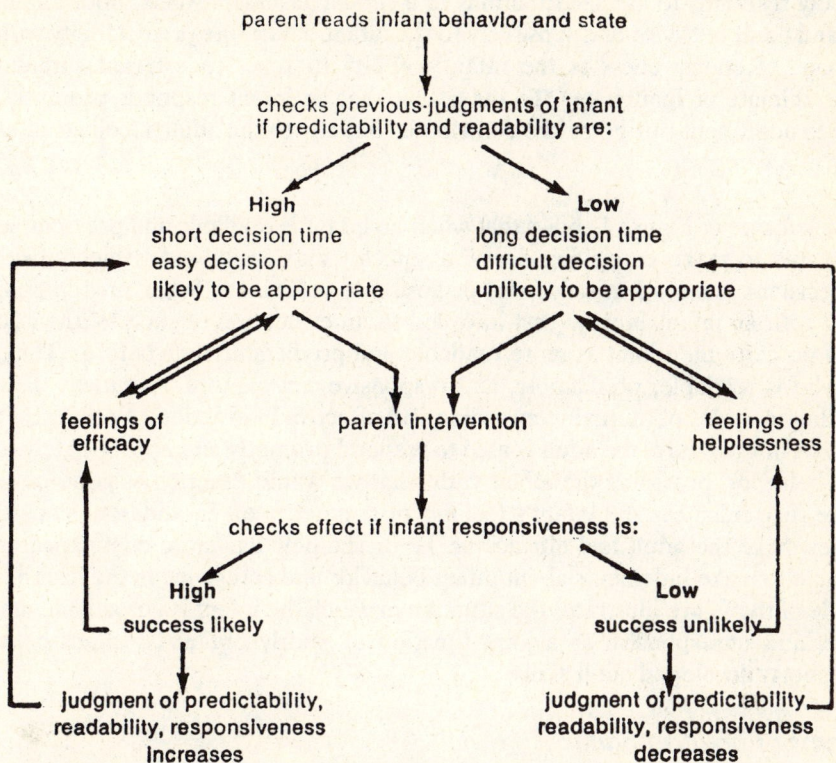

Fig. 1. An adult who has experienced a successful interaction with an infant (left) perceives the infant as "readable" and predictable and acquires a feeling of competence in further interactions. The good and sensitive care that results causes the infant to feel more competent in turn at eliciting the appropriate responses, and thus a cycle of successful interaction is established. The reverse of this pattern is illustrated in the right side of the figure.

sive or less enjoyable than that which led them to intervene, they will evaluate that episode as a failure. Figure 1 illustrates this process, and the following discussion is intended to clarify the model depicted.

The normally competent infant helps adults to be effective parents by being readable, predictable, and responsive. Readability refers to the clarity of the infant's signalling--that is, how easily the adult can observe the infant and conclude that he or she is tired, hungry, eager to play, etc. Although there may be some infants who are easier for everyone to read than others, readability within the parent-infant pair is a joint function of infant behavior and the adult's skill in recognizing behavior patterns.

Predictability refers to the regularity of the infant's behavior — whether sleeping, waking, feeding, and elimination follow a recognizable pattern and whether the infant repeatedly responds to similar situations in a similar fashion. Again, both infant behavior and adult behavior and sensitivity to the infant determine predictability within a given pair. Reponsiveness is the infant's ability to react to external stimulation, whether animate or inanimate. To the extent that an infant responds promptly and reliably to adult behavior he or she contributes directly to the adult's feelings of effectiveness as a caregiver.

The left side of Figure 1 shows that when an infant is readable and predictable the adult is able to make caregiving decisions quickly and easily and is highly likely to make decisions that lead to successful or desirable outcomes. When an adult has interacted with an infant in ways that have led to an evaluation of success, the adult is likely to perceive the infant as more readable and predictable than before. Thus, the infant who is readable, predictable, and responsive can capture an initially disinterested adult in cycles of mutually rewarding and effective interaction. Notice also that, in this part of the figure, the adult is able to respond promptly and appropriately to the infant's behavior, providing the infant with what we would describe as good or sensitive care that enhances the infant's feelings of competence. In addition, since these successes make the adult feel efficacious, he or she now has more confidence and is better able to make judgments about infant behavior and caregiving in the future. The right side of the figure illustrates the situation in which the infant is unreadable, unpredictable, and unresponsive as a joint function of poorly organized infant behavior and/or poorly developed adult skills.

Problems of preterm pairs

Under normal conditions, the natural reciprocity of adult and infant behavior guarantees that each member of the pair is provided with frequent opportunities to feel effective. A review of what is known about preterm infants and their parents will indicate that such pairs have a greater probability of falling into the patterns on the right side of the figure than do their full-term counterparts. Most preterm pairs eventually do develop successful relationships. However, the available data also indicate that they must make compensatory adjustments to enable them to overcome initial disadvantages.

Premature infants are those who are born after fewer than 37 weeks of gestation and weigh under 2,500 g. Infants who were born small for their age or with known congenital defects are not included in the samples of the studies I am describing. The most obvious fact of premature birth is that parents are confronted with an infant who is relatively immature and may not have developed the care-soliciting or social behaviors available to the full-term infant.

Several studies, including my own (Goldberg et al., in press), which have systematically evaluated the behavior of preterm infants (close to term or hospital discharge), have reported that they spent less time alert, were more difficult to keep in alert states, and were less responsive to sights and sounds (a ball, a rattle, a moving face, and a voice) than the full-term comparison group. Furthermore, preterm infants who had experienced respiratory problems following birth rarely cried during the newborn examinations, even though some of the procedures (e.g., undressing, testing reflexes) are mildly stressful and provoke crying from full-term infants. This suggests that these preterm infants are not likely to give adults clear distress signals.

The effectiveness of the preterm infant's cry in compelling adult attention has not been studied extensively. However, at the University of Wisconsin (Frodi et al. 1978), mothers and fathers were shown videotapes of full-term and preterm infants in crying and quiescent states. A dubbed sound track made it possible to pair the sound and the picture independently. Physiological recordings taken from the viewing parents indicated that the cry of the premature infant was physiologically more arousing than that of the full-term infant, and particularly so when paired with the picture of the preterm baby. Furthermore, ratings of the cries indicated that parents found that of the premature baby more aversive than that of the full-term infant. Thus, although the preterm infant may cry less often, this can be somewhat compensated for by the more urgent and aversive sound of these cries. If a parent is able to quiet these cries promptly, they clearly serve an adaptive function. If, however, the infant is difficult to pacify or frequently irritable, it is possible that the aversive experience will exceed the parent's level of tolerance or that he or she will experience repeated feelings of helplessness that can be damaging to the interactive relationship.

Thus far, we have assumed that the less competent behavior of the preterm infant is primarily attributable to immaturity. Often prematurity is associated with other medical problems that depress behavioral competence. In addition, the early extrauterine experiences of preterm infants in intensive-care nurseries probably do little to foster interactive competence and may, in fact, hinder its occurrence. Procedures such as tube feedings, repeated drawing of blood samples, temperature taking, and instrument monitoring often constitute a large proportion of the preterm infant's first encounters with adults. There are few data on the effects of specific medical procedures and since these procedures cannot ethically be withheld on a random schedule, this is a difficult area to study. However, numerous studies have attempted to foster early growth and development of preterm infants by adding specific kinds of experiences.

An example of a study from the first category is one in which 31 preterm infants were gently rocked for 30 minutes, three times each day, from their fifth postnatal day until they reached the age of 36 weeks postconception. They were compared to 31 unrocked preterm babies of similar gestational age, weight, and medical condition. The experimental infants were more responsive to visual and auditory stimulation and showed better motor skills as well.

Other studies have tried to treat preterm infants more like their full-term counterparts. In one study 30 preterm infants weighing 1,300-1,800 grams at birth were randomly assigned to experimental and control groups. The infants in the experimental group were given extra visual stimulation by placing mobiles over their cribs and were handled in the same manner as full-term infants for feeding, changing, and play. The control group received hospital care standard for the preterm nursery, which meant that handling was kept to a minimum. Although initial weights and behavioral assessments had favored the control group, at 4 weeks postnatal age, the experimental group had gained more weight and showed better performance on the behavioral assessment than the controls.

Like these two examples, all of the other studies which provided extra stimulation to preterm infants showed gains in growth and/or development for the babies in the experimental group beyond those of the control group. Thus, although we do not know whether routines of intensive care interfere with early development, we do know that the behavioral competence of preterm infants can be enhanced by appropriate supplemental experiences.

On the parents' side, premature birth means that parenthood is unexpectedly thrust upon individuals who may not yet be fully prepared for it. Beyond the facts of not having finished childbirth preparation classes or having bought the baby's crib, it may be that more fundamental biological and psychological processes are disrupted. A beautiful series of studies by Rosenblatt (1969) has explored the development of maternal behavior in rats. As in humans, both male and female adult rats are capable of responding appropriately to infants. However, the hormonal state of the adult determines how readily the presence of infants elicits such behaviors. Furthermore, hormonal changes during pregnancy serve to bring female rats to a state of peak responsiveness to infants close to the time of delivery. Other animal studies indicate that experiences immediately after delivery are important for the initiation of maternal behavior. In many mammalian species removal of the young during this period may lead to subsequent rejection by the mother.

We do not have comparable hormonal studies of human mothers, but it seems likely that hormonal changes during pregnancy may serve similar functions. There is some evidence that among full-term births, immediate postpartum experiences contribute to subsequent maternal behavior. A series of studies by Klaus and Kennell (1976) and their colleagues provided some mothers with extra contact with their infants soon after birth. In comparison with control groups, these mothers were observed to stay closer to their babies, to touch and cuddle them more, and to express more reluctance to letting others care for their babies after leaving the hospital. Klaus and Kennell have summarized these studies and interpreted them as indicating that there is an optimal or "sensitive" period for initiating maternal behavior in humans. As further evidence they cite studies in which preterm infants are found to be over-represented among reported cases of child abuse, neglect, and failure to thrive. These disturbing statistics, they suggest, reflect the effects of parent-infant separation during the sensitive period.

Even if one does not accept the idea of the sensitive period as described by Klaus and Kennell (and many developmental psychologists do not), it is clear that parents whose preterm infants must undergo prolonged hospitalization have few opportunities to interact with them. Even in the many hospitals that encourage parents to visit, handle, and care for their babies in intensive care, the experiences of parents with preterm infants are in no way comparable to those of parents with full-term infants.

If you have ever visited a friend under intensive care in the hospital, you will have some idea of the circumstances under which these parents must become acquainted with their infants. Neither parents nor infants in this situation have much opportunity to practice or develop interactive skills or to experience the feelings of competence that normally accompany them. Parents also have little opportunity to learn to read, predict, or recognize salient infant behaviors. In a study conducted at Stanford University, Seashore and her colleagues (1973) asked mothers to choose themselves or one of five other caregivers (e.g., nurse, grandmother) as best able to meet their infants' needs in numerous caregiving and social situations. Mothers who had not been able to handle their first-born preterm infants chose themseves less often than mothers in any other group sampled.

Thus, both infants and parents in preterm pairs are likely to be less skilled social partners than their full-term counterparts, because the development of interactive capacities has been disrupted and because they have had only limited opportunities to get acquainted and to practice. In addition, during the hospital stay, parents of preterm infants already have little self-confidence and lack the feeling of competence. Ordinarily, an interactive pair in which one member has limited competence can continue to function effectively if the partner is able to compensate for the inadequate or missing skills. In the case of parent-infant pairs, because the infant's repertoire and flexibility are limited, the burden of such compensatory adjustments necessarily falls upon the parent.

Observations of interactions

Six studies to date have compared parent-infant interaction in full-term and preterm pairs. They were carried out in different parts of the country with different populations and different research methodologies. Yet there seems to be some consistency in findings that is related to the age of the infant at the time of observation (which also reflects the duration of the parent-infant relationship). Each study involved repeated observation of the same parent-infant pairs, though the number of observations and the length of the studies vary.

Those studies which observed parents and infants in the newborn period typically report that parents of preterm infants are less actively involved with their babies than parents of full-term infants. Relative to full-term infants, preterm infants were held farther from the parent's body, touched less, talked to less, and placed in the face-to-face position less often. Subsequent observations of the same pairs usually indicated that the differences between preterm and full-term pairs diminished with time, as parents in the preterm group became more active. Thus, it appears that the initiation of interaction patterns considered "normal" for full-term pairs is delayed in preterm pairs. In my own study (DiVitto and Goldberg, in press) I found that for one kind of parental behavior- cuddling the baby- the preterm infants never received as much attention as the full-term infants in spite of increases over time. Over the first four months, parents cuddled preterm infants more at later feeding observations, but they were never cuddled as much as the full-term infants at the very first (hospital) observation. Thus, the development of some kinds of interactions in the preterm group can be both delayed and depressed.

In contrast with these observations of very young infants, studies of older infants reported a very different pattern. Regardless of the observation situation (feeding, social play, or object play), preterm infants were less actively engaged in the task than were full-term infants, and their parents were more active than those of full-term infants. In one study of this type, Field (1977) placed each mother face to face with her baby, who sat in an infant seat, and asked her to "talk to your baby the way you would at home." Infant attention and parent activity were coded. Infants in the preterm group squirmed, fussed, and turned away from their mothers more than those in the full-term group, and preterm mothers were more active than full-term mothers. Instructions that decreased maternal activity ("Try to imitate everything your baby does") increased infant attention in both groups, while those that increased maternal activity ("Try to get your infant to look at you as much as possible") decreased infant attention in both groups.

Field's interpretation of these findings assumed that infants used gaze aversion to maintain their exposure to stimulation within a range that would not overtax their capacities for processing information. Thus, when mothers' activity decreased, infants were able to process the information provided without the need to reduce stimulation. Field also suggested that since the *imitation* condition provided stimulation that was matched to the infant's behavior, it might be more familiar and thus easier for the infant to process. It is possible that the greater initial fussing and gaze aversion reflected information-processing skills that were less developed than those of full-term infants.

Brown and Bakeman (in press) observed feedings in the hospital, one month after discharge, and three months after discharge. Their findings are somewhat different from the overall trend because they were similar at all observations. Behavior segments were assigned to four categories: *mother acts alone, baby acts alone, both act,* and *neither acts.* In comparing preterm and full-term pairs, they reported that preterm infants acted alone less frequently than full-term infants, while mothers of preterm infants acted alone more often than those of full-term infants. Furthermore, in preterm pairs, the *neither acts* state was most likely to be followed by *mother acts alone* while in the full-term pairs, it was equally likely to be followed by activity by the baby or the mother.

In my own research (DiVitto and Goldberg, in press; Brachfeld and Goldberg 1978) there are two sets of data consistent with these findings. First, we found that parent behavior during feedings in the hospital, and at the 4-month home and laboratory visits, was related to infant behavior in the newborn period. Regardless of their condition at birth, infants who had been difficult to rouse as newborns received a high level of functional stimulation from parents (e.g., position changes, jiggling the nipple). Infants who had been unresponsive to auditory stimulation as newborns received high levels of vocal and tactile stimulation during feedings. Thus, the parents of infants who were unresponsive as newborns appeared to work harder during feedings in the first four months than did the parents whose newborns were more responsive.

We also observed the same pairs at 8 months of age in a free-play situation. Four toys were provided and parents were asked to "do what you usually do when [name] is playing." In this situation, both at home and in the laboratory, preterm infants (particularly those who had been very young and small at birth and had respiratory problems) played with toys less and fussed more than the full-term group. Parents in the preterm group stayed closer to their babies, touched them more, demonstrated and offered toys more, and smiled less than those in the full-term group.

Another study with somewhat younger infants also fits this pattern. Beckwith and Cohen (1978) observed one wake-sleep cycle at home one month after discharge. Since babies were born and discharged at different ages, the age of the infants varied: some were relatively young, while others were closer in age to the older groups in other studies. All were born prematurely. However, Beckwith and Cohen found that mothers whose babies had experienced many early complications devoted more time to caregiving than those who had babies with fewer problems.

All these studies concur in indicating that parents with preterm infants or preterm infants with more serious early problems devote more effort to interacting with their babies than do their full-term counterparts. In most of the studies this was coupled with a less responsive or less active baby in the preterm pairs. Thus, it appears that parents adapt to the less responsive preterm baby by investing more effort in the interaction themselves. As Brown and Bakeman put it, the mother of the preterm infant "carries more of the interactive burden" than her full-term counterpart. From our own laboratory, there is some evidence that other adults have a similar experience with preterm infants. At our regular developmetnal assessments at 4, 8, and 12 months, staff members rated the preterm group as being less attentive to the tasks, less persistent in solving them, and less interested in manipulating objects than the full-term group. In addition, staff members found it necessary to spend more time with the preterm group to complete the required tasks.

The consistency of these findings suggests that in pairs with a preterm infant, adults use a common strategy of investing extra time and effort to compensate for their less responsive social partner. It is important to note that while this seems to be a widely adopted strategy, it is not necessarily the most successful one. In Field's study (1977) a decrease in maternal activity evoked infant attention more effectively than an increase. In our own observations of 8-month-old infants, increased parent involvement did not reduce the unhappiness of the sick preterm group, and some play sessions had to be terminated to alleviate infant distress. Hence, while there seem to be some consistent strategies by which parents compensate for the limited skills of their preterm infants, these pairs may continue to experience interactive stress in spite of or even because of these efforts. Continuation of such unrewarding interactions, as Figure 1 indicates, is a threat to continued effective functioning of the interactive system.

The data reviewed above provide little evidence on the duration of interactive differences between full-term and preterm pairs. Among researchers in the field, there seems to be an informal consensus which holds that such differences gradually disappear, probably by the end of the first year. In my own research, a repetition of the play sessions at 12 months revealed no group differences. At 11-15 months, Leiderman and Seashore (1975) report only one difference: mothers of preterm babies smile less frequently than those of full-term babies. However, in Brown and Bakeman's study, group differences were observed as late as preschool age in rated competence in social interactions with adults (teachers) and peers. These data are too meager and scattered to support a firm conclusion on the duration of group differences.

This review has focused only upon the ways in which premature birth may stress the parent-infant interaction system. Preterm infants are generally considered to be at higher risk for subsequent developmental and medical problems than their full-term counterparts. In order to understand the reasons for less than optimal developmental outcomes, it is important to bear in mind that premature births occur with high frequency among population subgroups where family stress is already high (e.g., young, single, black, lower-class mothers). Most of the research designs which would allow us to disentangle the independent contributions of each medical and social variable to long-term development are unethical, impractical, or impossible to carry out with human subjects.

The early approach to studying the consequences of prematurity was to consider each of these medical and social variables as "causes" and the physical and intellectual development of the child as the "effect." The data reviewed here indicate that we cannot think in such simple terms. Prematurity (or any other event which stresses the infant) stresses the parent-infant interaction system and indeed the entire family. The way in which the family is able to cope with these stresses then has important consequences for the child's development. A major finding of the UCLA study was that for preterm infants, as full-term infants, a harmoniously functioning parent-infant relationship has beneficial effects on development in other areas, such as language, cognition, motor skills, and general health. Prematurity, like many other developmental phenomena, can best be understood as a complex biosocial event with multiple consequences for the child and the family.

Furthermore, in the absence of sophisticated medical technology, the vast majority of the births we have been discussing would not have produced live offspring. In evolutionary history, though it would have been adaptive for infants' initial social skills to be functional some time before birth was imminent, there was no reason for these preadapted social skills to be function at 6 or 7 months gestation. Premature births include only a small proportion of the population, but our ability to make such infants viable at younger and younger gestational ages by means of artificial support systems may be creating new pressures for differential selection. The fact that the majority of preterm pairs do make relatively successful adaptations indicates that the capacity to compensate for early interactive stress is one of the features of the parent-infant interaction system.

REFERENCES

Beckwith, L., and S.E. Cohen. 1978. Preterm birth: Hazardous obstetrical and postnatal events as related to caregiver-infant behavior. *Infant Behav. and Dev.* 1.

Brachfeld, S., and S. Goldberg. Parent-infant interaction: *Effects of newborn medical status on free play at 8 and 12 months.* Presented at Southeastern Conference on Human Development, Atlanta, GA, April 1978.

Brown, J.V., and R. Bakeman. In press. Relationships of human mothers with their infants during the first year of life. In *Maternal Influences and Early Behavior,* ed. R.W. Bell and W.P. Smotherman. Spectrum.

DiVitto, B., and S. Goldberg. In press. The development of early parent-infant interact as a function of newborn medical status. In *Infants Born at Risk,* ed. T.

Field, A. Sostek, S. Goldberg, and H.H. Shuman. Spectrum.

Field, T.M. 1977. Effects of early separation, interactive deficits, and experimental manipulations on mother-infant interaction. *Child Development* 48:763-71.

Frodi, A., M. Lamb, L. Leavitt, W.L. Donovan, C. Wolff, and C. Neff. 1978. Fathers' and mothers' responses to the faces and cries of normal and premature infants. *Devel. Psych.* 14.

Goldberg, S. 1977. Social competence in infancy: A model of parent-infant interaction. *Merrill-Palmer Quarterly* 23:163-77.

Goldberg, S., S. Brachfeld, and B. DiVitto. In press. Feeding, fussing and play: Parent-infant interaction in the first year as a function of newborn medical status. In *Interactions of High Risk Infants and Children*, ed. T. Field, S. Goldberg, D. Stern and A. Sostek, Academic Press.

Kennell, J.H., and M.H. Klaus. 1976. Caring for parents of a premature or sick infant. In *Maternal-Infant Bonding* ed. M.H. Klaus and J.H. Kennell. Mosby.

Klaus, M.H., and J.H. Kennell. 1976. *Maternal-Infant Bonding*. Mosby.

Leiderman, P.H., and M.J. Seashore. 1975. Mother-infant separation: Some delayed consequences. In *Parent-Infant Interaction*. CIBA Foundation Symp. 33. Elsevier.

Moss, H.A., and K.S. Robson. The role of protest behavior in the development of parent-infant attachment. Symposium on attachment behavior in humans and animals. *Am. Psych. Assoc.* Sept. 1968.

Rosenblatt, J.S. 1969. The Development of maternal responsiveness in the rat. *Am. J. Orthopsychiatry* 39:36-56.

Seashore, M.J., A.D. Leifer, C.R. Barnett, and P.H. Leiderman. 1973. The effects of denial of early mother-infant interaction on maternal self-confidence. *J. Pers. and Soc. Psych.* 26:369-78.

Seligman, M.R. 1975. *Helplessness: On Development, Depression and Death.* W.H. Freeman.

White, R. 1959. Motivation reconsidered: The concept of competence. *Psych. Review* 6:297-333.

Mother-Father-Infant Interaction: A Naturalistic Observational Study

Jay Belsky

To investigate infant preferences for interaction with mother versus father, similarities and differences in maternal and paternal behavior, and the influence of a second parent's presence on parent-infant interaction, 40 middle-class families with infants 15 months of age were observed in their own homes on 2 separate weekdays, for 2 hours each day. Analysis revealed more similarities than differences in maternal and paternal behavior, limited preferences for interaction with same-sex children, and more active parenting when alone with the child than when in the presence of the spouse. Infant behavior was similarly influenced by social situation, with more social behavior directed toward each parent when alone with them. Finally, covariance analysis revealed that displayed general preferences for interaction with father were primarily a function of parental behavior. These results are discussed in light of past research on the mother-father-infant system.

Originally published in *Developmental Psychology*, 1979, 15, 601-607. Copyright ©1979 by the American Psychological Association. Reprinted by permission of the publisher and author.

In his recent critique of developmental psychology, McCall (1977) noted that because of their reliance on manipulative, laboratory research methods, investigators have preferred to study what may influence development rather than determine what does influence development under "typical natural circumstances." Examination of recent attempts by developmental psychologists to redress their past neglect of the role of the father during infancy clearly validates this appraisal. (For a review, see Parke, 1978.) Clarke-Stewart (1978) has noted that the distinction between competence and performance limits the generalizability of results emerging from many of these studies.

These comments notwithstanding, the evidence accumulated to date regarding mother-infant and father-infant relationships leads to several interesting conclusions, though inconsistency is evident within the literature. Parke (1978) has recently observed in reviewing the research on attachment and parental preference that although both parents are consistently preferred to strangers as objects of attachment, "the question of whether there is a preference for mother versus father has yielded less consistent results" (p. 569).

There is greater consensus among researchers regarding similarities and differences in maternal and paternal behavior and the influence of a spouse's presence on parent-infant interaction (i.e., second-order effects). Fathers appear more likely than mothers to engage their infants in physical play and to hold them in the course of playing; maternal play is more likely to focus on objects and conventional social games (e.g., peek-a-boo), and holding tends to occur during the provision of basic physical care (Clarke-Stewart, 1978; Lamb, 1977b, 1977c; Parke & O'Leary, 1976). Observational data also consistently indicate that each parent's active involvement with the child is reduced, as is the quantity of behavior directed by the infant toward each parent, when the parent-infant dyad is transformed into the parent-parent-infant triad (Clarke-Stewart, 1978; Lamb, 1976a, 1977a, 1978a, 1978b; Parke & O'Leary, 1976).

Since many of these summarized data are based on studies carried out in laboratory or hospital settings (e.g., Lamb, 1976a, 1976b; Parke & O'Leary, 1976; Spelke, Zelazo, Kagan, & Kotelchuck, 1973; Weinraub & Frankel, 1977) or in homes under conditions that may not truly reflect infants' daily experiences with their parents (e.g., Lamb, 1977a, 1978b), the goal of this investigation was to address three questions raised in previous research by examining behavioral data gathered during fully naturalistic observations of family interaction: (a) Do fathers and mothers differ in their styles of playing with and their reasons for holding their infants when they are observed going about their daily household routines? (b) Does parental involvement decrease as a function of presence of spouse under such conditions? (c) Is infant behavior susceptible to similar second-order effects? And, finally, (d) do infants in their 2nd year of life prefer to interact with one parent over the other? With regard to this final question, emphasis in this investigation was placed on what Lamb (1976b) has labeled affiliative behavior (e.g., vocalize to, show/offer) rather than attachment behavior (e.g., fuss to, cling to), as no attempt was made to stress the child.

In light of our desire to study parent-infant interaction during naturally occurring family routines so that comparisons could be made with the results of more manipulative studies, a coding system was devised to distinguish between 15-sec time-sampling intervals in which (a) mother was with child and father was not present, (b) father was with child and mother was not present, and (c) both parents were together with child. It is important to note, with regard to second-order effects that will be reported, that no distinction was made between periods in which the parent was psychologically removed from the scene (not in same or adjacent room with parent and child) or physically unavailable (out of the house). Further, it must be recognized in considering the data to be reported that mothers and fathers were not observed under exactly the same circumstances, since we studied mother-infant, father-infant, and mother-father-infant interaction during periods of the day that parents considered representative of the time they regularly spent with their infants.

Method

Sample

Forty families with infants 15 months of age were recruited from the Ithaca and Cortland, New York, areas to participate in the research. An introductory letter and follow-up phone call were used. Names of prospective families were culled from birth announcements in local newspapers. To maintain sample homogeneity, study families were restricted to those that were traditional in their household division of labor (father working and mother serving as primary caregiver) and in which one or both parents had some college education. Rate of acceptance among such families was 58%.[2] In 24 households the infants were male (10 firstborn, 14 later born), and in 16 they were female (8 firstborn, 8 later born). The occupations of fathers participating in the study varied greatly and included salesman, small businessman, doctor, lawyer, elementary and high school teacher, and graduate student. Only a limited number of families (19%) participating were affiliated with a college or university.

---

2 Of 73 families called to participate in the investigation, only 4 in which mothers were working agreed to participate. Thus, the homogeneity of the sample was as much a function of self-selection as experimental design.

Design

Families were observed on 2 separate weekdays for 2 hours each day. Prior to home observations, mothers and fathers were visited by the observer (the author). The purposes of these initial visits were (a) to describe in more detail the nature of the study (to learn about the infant's world), (b) to establish rapport so as to decrease parental self-consciousness and the potential for displaying socially desirable behavior during formal data collection, and (c) to schedule the home observations.

The observations were scheduled to assure the sampling of segments of the day that could be considered representative of the infant's experience with each of his or her parents; to maximize the likelihood of observing father-infant interaction; and to sample the following three situations: mother with child and father not present, father with child and mother not present, and both parents together with child.

Eighty percent of the observations were scheduled in late afternoon, beginning 1 hour before the father's arrival at home from work and continuing for an additional hour following his arrival. The hour before the father's arrival was scheduled to insure sampling of the situation in which infants and mothers spent the majority of their time together. The hour following the father's arrival was scheduled to insure representative sampling of the time in which fathers were available to their infants. There were several adjustments to time to obtain the desired parent-child pairings in some families.

Behavior recording. The presence/absence of 15 parent and 8 infant behaviors listed on a precoded checklist was recorded during alternating 15-sec observe-record periods throughout each 2-hour observation. Parental behaviors selected for coding were culled from home-based research on mother-infant interaction highlighting developmentally facilitative parental styles (e.g., Beckwith, 1971; Clarke-Stewart, 1973) and from researches highlighting differences in mother-infant and father-infant interaction (e.g., Lamb, 1977c; Parke & O'Leary, 1976). The infant behaviors coded were play with toy, explore nontoy object[3] (e.g. pots and pans), express pleasure (e.g., smile, laugh), fret/cry, vocalize to parent, vocalize to no one, move toward parent, and

---

3   Play with toys and exploration of nontoy objects were distinguished in the coding to determine whether children's self-selected activities predicted their exploratory competence assessed in a semistructured play situation administered subsequent to the completion of the home observations. These data are discussed in another report (Belsky, 1979).

show/offer to parent. The parental behaviors coded were attend to child, speak to child, teach (e.g., label object), stimulate (i.e., focus attention on object or event), restrict (physical and verbal), and read to self/watch TV; five categories of physical contact including caretake (e.g., diapering, washing), positive affection (e.g., kiss/hug), soothe, play, and simple (i.e., all other holding); and three categories of play including social (e.g., peek-a-boo, patty-cake, chase), object mediated (usually with toy), and vigorous motion (e.g., tossing in the air, bouncing on knee). Additionally, a measure of verbal response rate was created by calculating the proportion of infant vocalizations to which parents verbally responded.

Reliability assessment was based on the rate of interobserver agreement in coding the presence of a behavior in the same 15-sec period. Tests of agreement were carried out prior to formal data collection and following 4 weeks of training. Across all tests of reliability, percentage of agreement (agreements/agreements plus disagreements) ranged from 72% (teach) to 100% (soothe), with a mean of 87%. The author conducted all observations once adequate levels of interobserver agreement were achieved.

In addition to recording parent and infant behavior, each 15-sec period was categorized in terms of one of the three situations noted earlier. Being with the child was operationally defined as being in the same room with or in the room adjacent to that containing the child. Thus, the first hour of observation before father came home was coded entirely as a period in which the mother was alone with the child.[4] Following father's arrival, the situation was free to vary according to naturally occurring family patterns. Since these patterns varied across families, resulting in unequal observation times in each situation, scores on all behaviors were prorated in terms of a standard 30-min period in each situation (comprised of 120 15-sec periods) to permit comparison between social situations and across families. Across the entire sample, mothers were observed alone with their infants for an average of 257 15-sec periods (range: 152-300), fathers for 85 periods (range: 10-214), and both parents together for 213 periods (range: 108-251).

---

4   Since parents clearly understood that the observer was not present to function as a baby sitter, it was an infrequent occurrence when the mother was not in the same or adjacent room with the child during the period prior to the father's arrival.

Results

The data sets from the 2 days were summed together and treated as one, since there were no significant differences across the two sets. Scores on any behavior could

Table 1

Adjusted Mean Frequencies of Parental Behaviors in One-Parent and Two-Parent Situations

| | Situation | | | | F ratios[a] | | |
| | One-parent | | Two-parent | | | | |
Behavior	Mother	Father	Mother	Father	Parent (A)	Situation (B)	A × B
Speak to	131	131	79	81		17.27	
Verbal response rate	43	52	30	26		51.86	
Attend to	201	194	164	158		16.53	
Stimulate[b]	46	35	21	19	4.80	29.18	
Teach	18	14	9	6		17.52	
Restrict	12	9	6	5		9.42	
Read/watch TV	16	30	15	37			
Play							
Social	9	15	7	7		7.06	
Object mediated	6	9	2	5		5.78	
Vigorous motion	2	7	1	1		11.54	
Physical Contact							
Simple	33	46	18	27		19.86	
Caretake	14	3	8	4	9.87		5.91
Positive affection[b]	6	2	2	3			4.13
Soothe	3	1	1	2			
Play	11	21	4	9		21.54	

Note. Length of observation time in each situation was controlled; number of 15-sec periods in each situation was employed as covariate.

[a] $F \geq 4.14$, $p < .05$. $F \geq 7.47$, $p < .01$. $df = 1, 33$.

[b] Significant Parent × Sex of Child interaction (see text).

range from 0 to 240, the latter figure representing the total number of 15-sec periods in an hour.

A correlational analysis was carried out to determine whether the prorated parent and infant scores were systematically affected by the differing amounts of time that families were actually observed in each of the three situations. This analysis revealed that parents observed for longer periods of time directed less behavior toward their infants. No systematic relation between observation time and behavior scores was discerned in the case of infants. Given these results, there was a need to control the effect of observation time in subsequent analyses of parental data, but not in analyses of infant data.

Parental Behavior

The 15 parental behaviors were subjected to 2 (parent: mother, father) x 2 (situation: one parent, two parent) x 2 (sex) x 3 (birth order)[5] repeated-measures analyses of covariance. The parent and situation factors were the repeated measures. The number of 15-sec periods that each family was actually observed in each situation was employed as the covariate to control for the above noted influence of observation time on parental scores. Results are discussed in three parts, representing the first three main effects of the analyses. All higher order interactions are discussed whenever pertinent within these three sections. The effects of birth order are not considered, since they did not in any way systematically influence the findings to be discussed. As in other studies (e.g., Jacobs & Moss, 1976), firstborns received consistently more attention from both mothers and fathers than did later borns.

Mother-father differences. When observation time was statistically controlled, maternal behavior and paternal behavior were more similar than different. Only 2 of the 15 coded behaviors significantly differentiated between parents (stimulate, caretaker), with mothers exceeding fathers, and both of these main effects were qualified by significant higher order interactions (see Table 1). In the case of stimulate, a Parent × Sex of Child interaction indicated that mothers and fathers alike preferred to interact with their same-sex children, $F(1,33) = 6.41$, $p < .05$. A significant Parent × Situation interaction on the variable caretaker revealed that although mothers exceeded fathers in care-taking in both one-parent and two-parent situations, the difference between parents was most marked in the former context.

Significant Sex of Parent × Sex of Child and Parent × Situation interactions also emerged for the variable position affection, indicating that parents were more likely to kiss/hug their same-sex children, $F(1,33) = 7.61$, $p < .01$, and that mothers exceeded fathers in this behavior in the one-parent situation, whereas fathers slightly exceeded mothers when both parents were together.

---

5   Three levels of birth order were included in the model (firstborn, later born of same gender as older sibling, and later born of gender different from all older siblings) in an attempt to determine whether differences between firstborn and later born were mediated by contrasts between the gender of later borns and their older siblings.

In general, these results are in agreement with previously reported comparisons of maternal and paternal behavior. Parental similarities far outweigh differences (e.g., Clarke-Stewart, 1978; Pedersen, Yarrow, Anderson, & Cain, 1978) though mothers spend more time providing basic physical care while in physical contact with their infants than do fathers (Lamb, 1977c). The absence of significant differences between parents in the area of play, which at first appears at odds with parental comparisons reported by Lamb (1977c) and Clarke-Stewart (1978) and reviewed by Parke (1978), is easily reconciled with them. Inspection of Table 1 reveals that fathers in the present study engaged in more vigorous-motion play than did mothers, but that this parental difference was not reliable. A similar nonsignificant parental difference on a variable labeled *physical* play was reported by Lamb (1977c) in his study of 7- to 8- and 12- to 13-month-olds. Since Clarke-Stewart (1978) found that fathers' role as playmate increased from 15 to 30 months, these trends could precede the subsequent differences Clarke-Stewart observed while studying older children.

Son-daughter differences. Other than the previously noted Sex of Parent × Sex of Child interactions, parents were observed to treat their sons and daughters similarly. No significant differences were discerned in parental behavior as a function of their children's gender.

One-parent/two-parent situation differences. As the data in Table 1 indicate, mothers and fathers alike were consistently more active in interacting with their infants when their spouses were not present than when they were present. For 11 of 15 behaviors coded, this differences between situations was statistically reliable.

This general reduction in parental behavior probably results from parents' tendencies to share their parenting responsibilities when afforded the opportunity in the two-parent situation. It may also be that this decrease is directly (and inversely) tied to the adult-adult communication made possible by the presence of the second parent (cf. Pedersen et al., 1978). Consideration of these second-order effects from the child's point of view suggests that parents may also have been responding to their toddlers' limited attentional and interactive competencies. The fact that children received generally the same amount of attention in the two-parent as in the one-parent situation provides some indirect support for this explanation. The present investigation provided no means for taking apart these competing explanations.

Infant Behavior

It was necessary to divide the eight infant behaviors into two sets of variables and to employ different statistical models in analyzing them, since there existed only a single score for each of the non-parent-directed behaviors (play, explore, cry, express

Table 2
Mean Frequency of Infant Behavior Directed Toward Each Parent in One-Parent and Two-Parent Situations

| | Situation | | | | F ratios[a] | |
| | One-parent | | Two-parent | | | |
Behavior	Mother	Father	Mother	Father	Parent	Situation
Move toward	18	19	10	12		35.68
Show	7	8	4	6		5.98
Vocalize to	21	28	11	13	4.67[b]	28.75

[a] $F \geq 4.14$, $p < .05$. $F \geq 7.47$, $p < .01$. $df = 1, 34$.
[b] Qualified by higher order Parent × Sex of Child interaction (see text).

pleasure, vocalize to no one) and two scores (one for each parent) for each of the parent-directed behaviors (vocalize to move toward, show/offer). The five non-parent-directed behaviors were subjected to 3 (situation) ×2 (sex) ×3 (birth order) repeated-measures analyses of variance; situation was the repeated measure. Results of these analyses indicated that the frequencies with which children played with toys, explored nontoy objects, expressed pleasure and distress, and vocalized to no one were not systematically influenced by any of these factors or their interactions.

Infant behavior directed at parents was systematically influenced by parent, situation, and sex. The 2 (parent) ×2 (situation) ×3 (sex) ×2 (birth order) repeated-measures analyses of variance indicated that toddlers were significantly more likely to move toward, show or offer things to, and vocalize to each parent while with only one parent than while in the presence of both simultaneously (see Table 2). Inspection of the relevant means displayed in Table 2 reveals, however, that the total amount of behavior toddlers directed toward their parents in the two-parent situation (mother plus father) was roughly equivalent to that directed at either parent when alone with them.

The data displayed in Table 2 also indicate that infants were significantly more likely to vocalize to (p < .05) and slightly more likely to move toward (*ns*) and show things to (*ns*) their fathers than to their mothers. Several significant Parent ×Sex of Child interactions revealed that these general trends were primarily a function of sons' preferences for interaction with their fathers; for move toward, F(1,34) = 7.12, p < .01, for vocalize to, F(1,34) = 6.08, p < .01.

Since previous research suggested that infants in their 2nd year of life have affiliative preferences for social interaction with their fathers (Lamb, 1976b, 1977c; Lamb, Note 1), it was of theoretical interest to determine whether the above noted interactive preferences were a function of some psychological disposition on the part of the child or, more simply, a behavioral response to differential parental behavior. The above analyses were repeated, statistically controlling for parental activity to address this issue. Following Lamb (1976a), frequency of parental vocalizations was employed as a covariate, since it was considered to be a general index of parental activity.

When parental activity was statistically controlled, the previously observed significant differences in favor of father on the vocalize-to-parent variable disappeared, as did the Sex of Parent × Sex of Child interactions discussed above. These results, which are in agreement with those reported by Lamb (1977c; Lamb, Note 2) and Clarke-Stewart (1978), clearly indicate that observed preferences for interaction with fathers are primarily a function of parental behavior.

Discussion

The results derived from this home-based observational investigation, in which family interaction was completely unstructured and parents were free to do as they pleased with no directives from the experimenter, are in general agreement with many of the findings emerging from more manipulative studies of mother-father-infant interaction. This suggests, contrary to my initial suspicions, that the results of these latter researches are robust and provide a generally accurate picture of the family system during infancy.

The results of this investigation may be limited in several ways—most importantly by the fact that mothers were observed after they had spent an entire day in the parenting role, whereas fathers were observed while still fresh in this role. In defense of this design, it should be noted that at least for those families studied, this observational strategy maintained the ecological integrity of parents' experiences. From parents' descriptions of their daily schedules, it was clear that mothers spent relatively extended periods in the parenting role while fathers spent relatively brief periods in this capacity and, as a consequence, that there was no such thing as psychologically equivalent periods of the day for mothers and fathers (cf. Pedersen et al., 1978).

Nevertheless, it could still be argued that had parents been observed at other times of the day, different findings might have emerged (e.g., more significant mother-father differences). The variation observed in both mothers' and fathers' behavior mitigates this argument somewhat. Indeed, it is reasoned that when parents are directed to go about their everyday household routines so that fully naturalistic observations can be made, the natural and thus representative variation that exists in parental behavior is displayed.

Reference Notes

1. Lamb, M. *Infants, fathers, and mothers: Interaction at 8-months-of-age in the home and in the laboratory.* Paper presented at the convention of the Eastern Psychological Association, New York, April 1976.

2. Lamb, M. *Development and function of parent-infant relationships in the first two years of life.* Paper presented at the biennial meeting of the Society for Research in Child Development, New Orleans, Louisiana, March 1977.

REFERENCES

Beckwith, L. Relationships between infants' vocalizations and their mothers' behavior. *Merrill-Palmer Quarterly*, 1971, 17, 211-216.

Belsky, J. A family analysis of parental influence on infant exploratory competence. In F. Pedersen (Ed.), *The father-infant relationships: Observational studies in a family context.* New York: Praeger Special Studies, 1979.

Clarke-Stewart, K.A. Interactions between mothers and their young children: Characteristics and consequences. *Monographs of the Society for Research in Child Development*, 1973, 38(6-7, Serial No. 153).

Jacobs, B., & Moss, H. Birth order and sex of sibling as determinant of mother-infant interaction. *Child Development*, 1976, 47, 315-322.

Lamb, M. Effects of stress and cohort on mother- and father-infant interaction. *Developmental Psychology*, 1976, 12, 435-443. (a)

Lamb, M. Twelve-month-olds and their parents: Interaction in a laboratory playroom. *Developmental Psychology*, 1976, 12, 237-244. (b)

Lamb, M. The development of mother-infant and father-infant attachments in the second year of life. *Developmental Psychology*, 1977, 13, 631-648. (a)

Lamb, M. The development of parental preferences in the first two years of life. *Sex Roles*, 1977, 3, 495-497. (b)

Lamb, M. Father-infant and mother-infant interaction in the first year of life. *Child Development,* 1977, 48, 167-181. (c)

Lamb, M. Infant social cognition and "second order" effects. *Infant Behavior and Development*, 1978, 1, 1-10. (a)

Lamb, M. The effects of social context on dyadic social interaction. In M. Lamb, S. Soumi, & G. Stephenson (Eds.), *Social interaction analysis: Methodological issues*. Madison: University of Wisconsin Press, 1978. (b)

McCall, R. Challenges to the science of developmental psychology. *Child Development*, 1977, 48, 333-344.

Parke, R. Perspectives on father-infant interaction. In J. Osofsky (Ed.), *Handbook of infancy*. New York: Wiley, 1978.

Parke, R., & O'Leary, S. Father-mother-infant interaction in the newborn period: Some findings, some observations, and some unresolved issues. In K. Riegel & J. Meucham (Eds.), *The developing individual in a changing world: social and environmental issues*. The Hague, Netherlands: Mouton, 1976.

Pedersen, F., Yarrow, L., Anderson, B., & Cain, R. Conceptualization of father influences in the infancy period. In M. Lewis & L. Rosenblum (Eds.), *The social network of the developing infant*. New York: Plenum Press, 1978.

Spelke, E., Zelazo, P., Kagan, J., & Kotelchuck, M. Father interaction and separation protest. *Developmental Psychology,* 1973, 9, 83-90.

Weinraub, M., & Frankel, J. Sex differences in parent-infant interaction during free play, departure, and separation. *Child Development,* 1977, 48, 1240-1249.

Effects of Early Maternal Employment on Toddlers, Mothers, and Fathers

M. Ann Easterbrooks

Wendy A. Goldberg

A family system orientation was adopted in studying the effects of early maternal employment on toddler development and mothers' and fathers' parenting styles. The 75 families with firstborn 20-month-olds varied in maternal employment status (nonemployed, part-time, and full-time). Observations were conducted of qualitative dimensions of parent-child relationships (toddler-mother and toddler-father attachment and child-parent problem-solving behavior), quantitative dimensions of family time allocation, and parental child-rearing attitudes. Maternal employment was not related to toddler outcomes (security of attachment or problem-solving behavior). It was related to the amount of time mothers spent with their children and to some child-rearing attitudes and behaviors of fathers and mothers. Results highlight the importance of examining direct (mother-child) and indirect (father-child) effects in the study of early maternal employment and the ability of families to adapt to a variety of life-styles.

The employment of mothers outside the home can no longer be considered a non-traditional life-style for families with young children. Over the past few decades, the number of employed mothers in two-parent families has risen steadily, with the rate of increase particularly high for families with infants and preschool-age children. In 1960, only 19% of mothers with children under 6 years were employed (Barnett & Baruch, 1978). Even by 1970, maternal employment was still a non-normative pattern in the United States: 34.5% of mothers with children under the age of 3 years were employed. In contrast, by March 1983, over half (56.1%) of mothers with children less than 3 years old were employed outside the home (Waldman, 1983).

The increasing proportion of employed mothers of infants and young children has been accompanied by concern about the potential effects of maternal employment on children's development. Historically, the roots of this concern lie in the linkage between early maternal deprivation and childhood developmental pathologies. The pioneering work of Spitz (1946) and Bowlby (1951) sensitized the public to the possible adverse effects of any lengthy or repeated separations of infant from mother. This research, which promoted the primacy of the bond between infant and mother, strengthened arguments for traditional family role organization.

The subsequent empirical literature documenting the direct effects of maternal employment on mothers and their young children (infancy to preschool age) is far from conclusive. Research has reported (a) few or no effects of maternal employment; (b) more intense, frequent, or positive interaction in employed mother-child dyads; or (c) diminished quantity or quality of interaction in these pairs (Hock, 1980; Schacter, 1981; Schubert, Bradley-Johnson, & Nuttal, 1980). Further inquiry reveals that differences related to poorer adaptation in babies of employed mothers many reflect variations in stability of life circumstances that are not related to maternal employment per se (Vaughn, Gove, & Egeland, 1980), or variations in employment characteristics such as number of hours per week mothers are employed and length of employment prior to participation in the research study. To evaluate the impact of maternal employment alone, there must be sufficient stability in the environment unrelated to maternal employment (i.e., ruling out poverty and instability of other family relationships) to allow attribution to findings to mother's employment status.

Recently, researchers have become concerned about the implications of maternal employment status for other family relationships, particularly that between father and child. The indirect effect of maternal employment on child-father relationships is also not conclusive, but several interesting suggestions have emerged. Namely, the impact of early maternal employment may be most salient for infant-father, not infant-mother, relationships and exert different effects for boys and girls in the first year of life. In one study (Pedersen, Cain, Zaslow, & Anderson, 1982), when infants were less than 6 months old, maternal employment diminished the amount of interaction between fathers and infants. Although subsequent observations when infants were 12 months failed to replicate these patterns (Zaslow, Pedersen, Suwalsky, & Rabinovich, 1983), trends in the data indicated that sons in employed-mother families experienced less cognitive stimulation from parents. A similar interaction between parent and child gender emerged for attachment relationships at 1 year of age in another investigation (Chase-Lansdale, 1981). Maternal employment was not associated with 1-year-olds' attachments to their mothers; however, there were more insecure boy-father attachments in employed-mother families than in nonemployed-mother families.

It is important to note that research suggesting adverse effects of maternal employment on infant boys' relationships with their fathers has studied infants only during the first year of life, primarily in families where mothers were employed full-time and returned to work early in the first year (in most cases within 3 months of the infant's birth). In fact, these findings may reflect relatively transitory adjustments of parents and infants to maternal employment. In the face of change related to resumption of employment, mothers and fathers may experience a period of fluctuation while they renegotiate family and work roles. Following early resumption of maternal employment, infant boys may suffer greater disruption in their interactions, especially with their fathers, but these effects may diminish as parents and children adapt to these family circumstances.

While the disruptive effects of maternal employment may disappear with time, there is another alternative: We may find "sleeper effects" of maternal employment during infancy that become evident only in the second or third years of life, or only after mothers have been employed for periods of a year or more. This possibility emphasizes the need for longitudinal research, as well as for studies investigating children of different ages. There may be differential effects of maternal employment that are related to children's age or developmental competencies and capacities for developing active coping strategies (e.g., the capacity for symbolic representation of mother in her absence or the ability to benefit from peer contact in day-care settings).

It is especially important to investigate father-child relationships during toddler-hood, when fathers traditionally become more involved with their children, particularly their sons (Clarke-Stewart, 1977; Lamb, 1977). It may be that increased father involvement at this time ameliorates the potential negative effects of early maternal employment on toddler-father relationships. Alternatively, adverse effects of maternal employment may be amplified if husbands of employed women are crowded out (Pedersen et al., 1982) from interaction at a time when fathers characteristically become more salient to their toddlers.

The diversity of research findings to date suggests that maternal employment is best viewed in a family context in order to examine the possibility of differential effects on various dimensions of family life. By investigating the impact of maternal employment on parents as well as children, we may be able to construct a process model (e.g., the direct and indirect effects) of the manner in which maternal employment is integrated into family relationships. For example, mother's employment may be related to quantitative (e.g., time allocation) as well as qualitative (e.g., attitudes) aspects of family relationships; interactional styles that typify employed-mother families and differentiate them from nonemployed-mother families may be evident only on weekdays and not weekends, when employment-related constraints are lessened. Moreover, the effects of maternal employment on children may be transactional (related to sex of child, for example) and may be either domain specific (i.e., limited to attachment, parent-child interaction, or cognitive competence) or more pervasive. An additional potentially critical, but largely overlooked, factor in the study of maternal employment is whether mothers are employed part-time or full-time. Although most studies do not consider the extent of maternal employment, it appears that it is full-time employment that is related to poorer outcomes for children, not employment per se (Alvarez, Bronfenbrenner, & Henderson, 1983; Schwartz, 1983).

The present study was designed to investigate the impact of maternal employment — direct (mother-child) and indirect (father-child) effects — in families with toddlers. Maternal employment effects on the father-child relationship are considered indirect or second-order because it is employment variations of the mother and not the father that are being examined. In this sample, maternal employment was a well-established aspect of family life, increasing our confidence that observed effects were not simply reflecting transitory adjustments. We highlight a family orientation to the study of maternal employment by examining multiple dimensions of family life: toddlers' attachment relationships with both of their parents and toddlers' behavior in a problem-solving task; the impact of maternal employment on parental perceptions, child-rearing attitudes, and sensitivity in interaction with their toddlers; and quantitative aspects of family time distribution. In addition, this study was designed to explore differences in family relationships according to whether mothers are employed part- or full-time. On the basis of previous research, we expected that if negative effects of maternal employment were found in our study, they would be more evident in the full-tme employed-mother families because of the increased demands and strain of integrating full-time employment and family roles.

Method

Subjects

Subjects were 73 families (72 fathers participated) with 20-month-old firstborn only children. The families were Caucasian and middle class; mean and mode on Hollingshead's (1978) four-factor index of social status was 2 (range = 1-4, with 1 representing the highest social status category). Mean age of mothers was 30 years, and of fathers 31 years. Families were recruited from county birth records, Lamaze classes, and notices in local pediatricians' offices.

All mothers had been employed outside of the home prior to the baby's birth. At the time of the study, 24 mothers had not been employed since the birth of their children; 23 mothers were employed part-time, range = 8-25 hours per week, mean = 18 hours per week; and 26 mothers were employed full-time, range = 32-50 hours per week, mean = 41 hours per week. Employed women held primarily professional (30%), teaching (22%), technical (33%), or clerical and sales positions (15%). Sixty-three percent (n = 29) of the employed mothers had resumed their employment by the time their babies were 6 months old; 85% (n = 42) had been continuously employed for at least 1 year prior to the time of study, and the nonemployed group showed a similar continuity. In nonemployed-mother families there were 10 girls and 14 boys, part-time employed-mother families had 10 girls and 13 boys, and the full-time employed-mother families had 14 girls and 12 boys. Analysis of variance tests were conducted on the overall Hollingshead index (mean for all groups was Class 2, range = 1-4 for nonemployed and 1-3 for part-time and full-time); maternal education (mean for all groups was college graduate, range = high school graduate-graduate degree); occupational level (prior to the baby's birth for nonemployed women; mean for all groups was technical, range = clerical/sales-professional); and family monetary level (mean for all groups was $20,000-$30,000, range = $7,500-$40,000 for nonemployed and $12,500- over $50,000 part-time and full-time). There were no significant differences among the employment groups for any of these four variables, all $Fs(2, 73) < 1.32, ns$). In the vast majority of employed-mother families, alternate care was provided by babysitters and spouses; day care was seldom used.

Procedures and Measures

Families were seen in a laboratory playroom on two occasions, separated by 3-4 weeks. One visit involved observation of the mother-child dyad; the other involved father and child. At each visit, toddlers and parents were observed in the Ainsworth and Wittig (1969) Strange Situation procedure for assessment of security of either toddler-mother or toddler-father attachment. Following the Strange Situation and a clean-up period, parent-child dyads were observed in a problem-solving task. All assessments were videotaped for later analysis. Finally, mothers and fathers completed questionnaires concerning child-rearing attitudes, maternal employment, and daily time allocation. Order of mother-child and father-child visits was counterbalanced; analyses revealed no order effects.

Quality of toddler-parent attachment relationships was assessed and rated in the standard procedure for the Strange Situation (see Ainsworth, Blehar, Waters, & Wall, 1978). Classificiation of security of attachment was made according to the three major categories — secure (Group B), insecure-avoidant (Group A), and insecure-resistant (Group C) — and the accompanying eight subgroups. Interrater reliability for this project, conducted on all 73 families, averaged 94%.

Following the Strange Situation, toddlers and their mothers and fathers were observed in a 5-min problem-solving task. The task, completing a jigsaw puzzle, was designed to be too difficult for toddlers to complete independently, allowing us to observe children's styles of approaching a difficult task and individual differences in parental assistance. Rating scales (5 points; 1 = low, 5 - high) were devised to measure quality of toddler affect and task orientation (degree of autonomous effort, off-task behavior, persistence) and parental behavioral sensitivity (encouragement, quality of technical assistance). Interrater reliability (calculated as agreements divided by agreements + disagreements), assessed on all videotapes, averaged .99 for each of the toddler ratings and .91 for parental sensitivity. Strange Situation and problem-solving behaviors were rated independently by different raters, as was rating of different family members on the problem-solving task. Raters were blind to the maternal employment status of the families.

Mothers and fathers completed questionnaires assessing (a) attitudes about maternal employment, (b) child-rearing attitudes, and (c) daily time allocation. The maternal employment questionnaire focused on perceptions of the impact of maternal employment on parent-child relationships. Perceptions were coded into categories of positive effects, negative effects, mixed positive and negative effects, and no effect of maternal employment on parent-child relationships. Interrater reliability for these categories, calculated on 50% of statements, was .96. Parents' attitudes about child rearing were indexed with the Parental Attitudes Toward Childrearing questionnaire (PACR). This instrument yields four subscales of parental warmth, strictness, encouragement of independence, and aggravation (extent to which parents are bothered and worried about the child). Questions are measured on 6-point Likert-type scales. Information was also obtained on mother's and father's daily time allocation; in this report we focus on parental reports of number of hours per day spent in various family units (playing with child, alone with child, with spouse and child together). Estimates were calculated separately for weekdays and weekends, and an average of mother and father estimates is reported. Details of the rating scales and questionnaires are reported elsewhere (Easterbrooks & Goldberg, 1984; Goldberg & Easterbrooks, 1984).

Results

Maternal Employment Patterns

Most of the employed women (85%) had worked continuously outside of the home for at least 1 year prior to our study; the nonemployed-mothers families had experienced similar continuity. Employed mothers sought work outside of the home both for personal fulfillment and financial incentive and reported that they would continue to work even if they did not need the money. Mothers' reasons for employment did not differ according to the sex of their child. Future plans of most mothers included employment, with 80% of the nonemployed women planning to seek employment after their children were in school. Child-related concerns were the primary reason why women who were currently nonemployed remained out of the work force. Husbands usually reported attitudes that supported their wives' employment status, whether or not she was employed. Furthermore, there was consonance in reasons for spouses' preferences regarding maternal employment; husbands of nonemployed women mentioned child-related concerns, and husbands of employed women cited their wives' personal fulfillment.

Perceptions of the Impact of Maternal Employment

With questionnaires we assessed all parents' perceptions of the effects of maternal employment (actual or hypothetical) on their own relationship with their child and their spouse's relationship with their child. Responses were coded as maternal employment exerting positive effects (e.g., "We appreciate each other more," "Work brings information and experience to the relationship," "There is more time for father and child to develop an intimate relationship"); negative effects (e.g., "She would be confused about who her mother is," "Someone else would be affecting her personality," "Time would be less quality, more utility"); or no effect.

Most employed women and their husbands reported that the impact of maternal employment on the mother-child relationship was entirely positive (67% of mothers, 74% of fathers). Some said it had no effect (6% of mothers, 22% of fathers), and a mixture of positive and negative or entirely negative effects was perceived by 26% of employed women and 4% of their husbands. In contrast, the majority of nonemployed women and their husbands anticipated negative effects of maternal employment on mother-child relationships: 63% of nonemployed women and 61% of their husbands expected negative effects, and only 20% of these mothers and 26% of their husbands expected positive effects; 17% of nonemployed mothers and 13% of their husbands anticipated no effect of maternal employment on mother-child relationships. Chi-square tests demonstrated significant associations between maternal employment status and perceived effects, with mothers and fathers in the nonemployed-mother group perceiving a more negative and less positive impact of maternal employment on mother-child relationships, $\chi^2(4,N = 73) = 21.16$, p < .001, for mothers, and $\chi^2(4,N = 72) = 12.37$, p < .05, for fathers.

The perceived impact on father-child relationships was similar. Employed mothers and their husbands most often felt maternal employment had a positive effect on father-child relationships: 58% mothers and 64% of fathers responded entirely positively, while negative or mixed responses were given by 23% of employed women and only 2% of their husbands; 18% of employed women and 34% of their husbands perceived no impact on the father-child relationship. In the nonemployed-mother group, 8% of mothers and 43% of fathers felt that maternal employment would have an entirely positive effect on the father-child relationship; entirely negative or mixed effects were reported by 50% of mothers and 24% of fathers; no effect was anticipated by 42% of nonemployed mothers and 33% of their husbands. Again, the differences in perceived effects of maternal employment between the employed and nonemployed groups were significant, $\chi^2(4,N = 73) = 16.60$, p < .01, for mothers, and $\chi^2(4, 72) = 19.66$, p < .001, for fathers. There were no differences related to sex of child or variations in part-time and full-time maternal employment status. In sum, there was consistency in families between their maternal employment status and positive or negative attitudes toward maternal employment.

Toddler-Parent Attachment

To examine the association between maternal employment status and security of toddler-parent attachment, chi-square tests were conducted. In our sample, there were no significant associations between maternal employment and quality of toddler-mother or toddler-father attachment. Across employment groups, there was a high proportion of secure (Group B) toddler-mother attachment (86%), with no difference according to maternal employment status (88% secure for nonemployed, 86% secure for employed [83% secure for part-time, 89% secure for full-time]). Less total security was evident in toddler attachments to father (65% secure), but this distribution was not related to maternal employment status (71% secure for nonemployed, 63% secure for employed [68% secure for part-time, 59% secure for full-time]). All chi-square tests examining associations between maternal employment and security of toddler-parent attachments were nonsignificant, $\chi^2(2,N = 73) = 0.40$ for mother, and $\chi^2(2,N = 72) = 1.07$ for father. Separate analyses conducted for girls and boys also failed to demonstrate relationships between maternal employment and either toddler-mother or toddler-father attachment (all χ^2s < 1.25). Table 1 lists the distribution of security of attachment to mother and father for the employment groups. Our analyses, then, did not support the claim that regular maternal employment would be related to insecure attachments to either mother or father for boys or for girls.

Table 1
Maternal Employment and Security of
Attachments to Mother and Father

Security of attachment	Mother			Father		
	NE	PT	FT	NE	PT	FT
Secure	21	19	23	17	15	15
Insecure	3	4	3	7	7	11

Note. NE = nonemployed mother; PT = part-time employed mother; FT = full-time employed mother.

Family Time, Child-Rearing Attitudes and Parent-Child Problem Solving

To further assess whether maternal employment status was related to family organization, a 3 × 2 × 2 (Maternal Employment Status × Sex of Parent × Sex of Child) multivariate analysis of variance (MANOVA; order of variable entry was maternal employment, sex of parent, sex of child) was conducted on the set of variables assessing family time allocation, parental child-rearing attitudes, and parental and child behavior in the problem-solving task. The following variables were subjected to the analysis: a set of time variables (six variables: daily time mother and father spend alone with the child, daily time spent in the family triad, and time spend playing with the child, each measured in hours per day, separately for weekdays and weekends); the set of child-rearing attitudes (four variables; warmth, strictness, encouragement of independence, and aggravation); and the behavioral indices of problem-solving behavior (three variables: child affect, child task orientation, and parental sensitivty).

Significant main effects were found for maternal employment, $F(2,135) = 3.96$, p < .001, and sex of parent, $F(2,135) = 7.88$, p < .001, but not sex of child. A two-way interaction between maternal employment and sex of parent, $F(2,135) = 3.03$, p < .001, also emerged from the analysis; there were no interactions between maternal employment and sex of child or between sex of child and sex of parent, and no significant three-way interaction.

Accompanying univariate analyses of variance revealed significant effects of maternal employment on hours per day that parents spent alone with their child during the weekdays, $F(2,135) = 11.34$, p < .001, the parental attitudes of warmth, $F(2,135) = 3.80$, p < .05, and strictness, $F(2,135) = 3.19$, p < .05, and behavioral sensitivity, $F(2,135) = 4.74$, p < .01. From examination of group means, we find that parents in employed-mother families spent less weekday time alone with the child, held less warm and less strict attitudes, and were less sensitive than the nonemployed group parents. The univariate analyses for sex of parent revealed significant differences on hours spent alone with the child during weekdays, $F(2,135) = 12.61$, $p < .001$, and weekends, $F(2,135) = 5.07$, $p < .05$, and for strictness $F(2,135) = 8.81$, $p < .01$. Mothers spent more time alone with their children and were less strict than were fathers. These results must be interpreted with caution owing to the significant interaction effect between maternal employment and sex of parent. Because of this interaction, we conducted separate main effect tests of maternal employment for mothers and fathers; both MANOVAs were significant, $F(2,135) = 4.53$, $p < .001$, for mothers, and $F(2,135) = 2.29$, $p < .01$, for fathers. Univariate analyses of variance demonstrated significant effects of maternal employment status for mothers only on the variables hours spent alone with the child on weekdays, $F(2,135) = 37.61$, $p < .001$, and hours spent playing with the child on weekdays, $F(2,135) = 12.43$, $p < .001$. Significant univariate tests emerged from the father analysis for aggravation, $F(2,135) = 7.43$, $p < .01$, and behavioral sensitivity, $F(2,135) = 5.58$, $p < .01$.

One of the aims of this study was to examine the contribution of the extent of maternal employment. Planned comparisons contrasting nonemployed with part-time, nonemployed with full-time, and part-time with full-time groups on all of the variables revealed that full-time versus part-time distinctions are important for the time that mothers have available to interact with their toddlers (see Table 2). Full-time employed mothers spent fewer hours per weekday alone with their child and playing with their child than did mothers employed either part-time or not at all. For time alone with child, both the nonemployed, $t(48) = 8.13$, $p < .001$, and part-time $t(45) = 6.59$, $p < .001$, groups were significantly different from the full-time group, but not from each other. A linear relation between weekday hours mothers played with their children and maternal employment emerged: Nonemployed mothers played with their child more than the part-time group, $t(45) = 2.08$, $p < .05$, and the full-time group, $t(48) = 4.97$, $p < .001$, and mothers employed part-time played more than those employed full-time, $t(47) = 2.73$, $p < .01$. Recall that there were no differences in weekend time or family triad time by maternal employment status.

Extent of employment was also related to maternal attitudes. Mothers not employed outside the home held warmer child-rearing attitudes than mothers employed full-time, $t(48) = 2.35$, $p < .05$, and were more strict than mothers employed part-time, $t(45) = 2.33$, $p < .05$. There were no differences between the part-time and full-time groups on these measures. Similar planned comparisons on paternal variables did not reveal time effects but demonstrated associations between extent of maternal employment and paternal attitudes and behavior. Husbands of nonemployed women were less aggravated than those whose wives were employed either part-time $t(45) = 2.72$, $p < .01$, or full-time, $t(47) = 3.72$, $p < .001$; the part-time and full-time groups did not differ from each other. Men whose wives were employed full-time were less behaviorally sensitive in the problem-solving task than

Table 2
Mean Values by Maternal Employment and Parent

Measures	Mothers				Fathers			
	NE	PT	FT	Significant comparisons	NE	PT	FT	Significant comparisons
Time allocation								
Alone with child								
Weekday	6.92	6.14	2.13	NE–FT***,	1.22	2.50	1.55	
Weekend	2.75	4.14	3.29	PT–FT***	2.32	2.70	2.65	
Play with child								
Weekday	3.23	2.57	1.71	NE–PT*,	1.64	1.65	1.91	
Weekend	3.06	3.12	3.48	NE–FT***	2.82	3.23	3.41	
Family triad								
Weekday	3.70	2.85	2.55		3.70	2.85	2.55	
Weekend	7.29	6.02	7.04		7.29	6.02	7.04	
Child-rearing attitudes								
Warmth	5.71	5.54	5.46	NE–FT*	5.52	5.30	5.29	
Strictness	2.62	2.16	2.42	NE–PT*	2.84	2.57	2.62	
Independence	5.16	5.07	4.93		5.01	4.98	4.81	
Aggravation	2.82	2.97	2.94		2.61	3.00	3.12	NE–PT**, NE–FT***
Problem-solving behavior								
Parental sensitivity	3.75	3.81	3.52		3.56	3.90	2.93	NE–FT*, PT–FT**
Child affect	3.48	3.33	3.39		3.57	3.60	3.57	
Child task orientation	3.19	3.02	2.64		3.40	3.19	3.28	

Note. NE = nonemployed mother; PT = part-time employed mother; FT = full-time employed mother. Time allocation is measured in hours per day.
* = $p < .05$. ** = $p < .01$. *** = $p < .001$.

were those whose wives were not employed, $t(47) = 2.18$, $p < .05$, or who were employed part-time, $t(46) = 3.26$, $p < .01$. The two latter groups were not significantly different.

Discussion

The present study had three aims: (a) to discuss the relation between maternal employment status and dimensions of adaptation in families with toddlers, (b) to examine whether these effects were both direct (on mother-child) and indirect (father-child) relationships, and (c) to investigate whether maternal employment effects varied according to the gender of the child.

Two dimensions of toddler adaptation were chosen for study: attachment and problem-solving behavior. Quality of toddler-parent attachment is considered an important index of socioemotional development in the first years of life; behavior in a difficult problem-solving task examines functioning in a social cognitive task. We found no associations between maternal employment and security of toddler-mother or toddler-father attachment. In fact, there was a strong propensity toward secure attachments in this middle-class sample, especially for toddler-mother relationships. Our data concerning toddler-mother attachment are consistent with other studies of maternal employment in middle-class families in the infancy period (Chase-Landsdale, 1981; Hock, 1980). The findings do not concur however, with Chase-Landsdale's report of more insecure attachments among 1-year-old sons and their fathers in full-time employed-mother families; we did not find more insecurity between toddler boys and their fathers in these families. Several factors may account for the discrepant results: (a) differences in child-father relationships related to the age or developmental period of the child (infant vs. toddler), (b) the fact that families in our sample had longer periods of time to develop adaptive family styles following resumption of maternal employment, and (c) differences in the type of maternal employment (we included both part-time and full-time employment groups).

Our second measure of toddler adaptation, behavior during a parent-child problem-solving task, also failed to reveal consistent differences among children that were related to their mother's employment status. The assessments of toddler affect and task orientation reflect the affective quality with which toddlers engaged with their parents in a task and how autonomous and persistent toddlers were in their efforts. We found no differences in affect or task orientation associated with maternal employment status and no interactions with sex of child or parents. These data are not in accord with possible expected outcomes of Zaslow et al.'s (1983) report that infants, particularly sons, of employed women experienced less parental cognitive stimulation and positive affect in the first year of life. They are consistent, though, with other research that failed to find cognitive differences among infants of employed and nonemployed mothers (Hock, 1980).

No differences were observed among the children, but there were some interesting differences among parents that were related to maternal employment status. Dimensions of parental functioning in this study included the allocation of time (alone with the child, playing with the child, and in the family triad, assessed separately for weekdays and weekends); child-rearing attitudes (warmth, strictness, encouragement of independence, and aggravation about the child); and behavior sensitivity in the parent-child problem-solving task. In our multivariate analysis, the overall main effect of maternal employment (indicating that parents in employed-mother families spend fewer weekday hours alone with their child, were less strict and warm, and less behaviorally sensitive than parents in nonemployed-mother families) was qualified by the finding that maternal employment influenced mothers and fathers differently.

It was not surprising to find that maternal employment was related to mothers' allocation of weekday but not weekend time. Nonemployed women spent an average of about 2 more hours alone with their children than did employed mothers. Mothers employed full-time spent fewer weekday hours alone with their children than did mothers employed part-time or not at all. There was a linear relation for mother-child play: The more hours mothers spent at work, the fewer hours they played with their toddler. These time data, though, do not address qualitative aspects of the interaction. Employed mothers may compensate for the lack of available time by intensifying their interaction (Pedersen et al., 1982) or by engaging in special activities with their children. Our toddler outcome data do not reflect differences among the daughters or sons of mothers differing in employment status. Furthermore, the number of hours spent together as a family did not vary with maternal employment status. Perhaps this complex triadic interaction offers the toddler opportunities for important developmental experiences.

Qualitative dimensions of mothers' child-rearing attitudes were related to maternal employment only when we specified the extent of employment hours. Nonemployed mothers held warmer attitudes than mothers employed full-time; in addition, they were more strict than the part-time group; but there were no group differences on encouragement of independence or aggravation attitudes or on behavioral sensitivity. Given that the magnitude of observed differences is quite small, these data do not present a consistent pattern of the effects of maternal employment on maternal attitudes and behavior.

While maternal employment status most regularly influences quantitative aspects of mother-child relationship, the indirect effects on fathers were demonstrated by qualitative differences among attitudes and behavior. Husbands of employed women were more aggravated about their toddlers, and those whose wives were employed full-time interacted less sensitively in the parent-child problem-solving task than did men whose wives were not employed or employed part-time. Although there were no differences in the amount of father-child time, it is possible that the content of father-child interaction in families of mothers employed full-time differs from other fathers. Other data from this sample indicate that these men assume more responsibility for child-care tasks (Easterbrooks, 1982); perhaps this renders the fathers more aggravated or limits opportunities for the types of interaction that would facilitate their behavioral sensitivity in our problem-solving task. Because husbands of employed women are somewhat more aggravated and less sensitive during a problem-solving task, one might expect their children to reflect these differences. There may be several reasons why we did not find these effects on children: The mean differences among groups of fathers were small in magnitude, differences among toddlers may be revealed by other measures or assessments in other domains, and differences among children may emerge at later points in development.

From this study, it is not possible to conclude whether the parenting differences related to maternal employment are a result of maternal employment itself or are a priori characteristics of parents who choose this family constellation. In many cases, maternal employment may be a positive characteristic, facilitating personal adjustment and adjustment to parenthood and, thus, optimal development of children. Correspondingly, women who desire to remain at home with their young children may be more sensitive mothers if they are able to do so. In these families, mother-child relationships are embedded in a larger system; the functioning of the mother-child relationship has indirect implications for father-child and spousal adaptation.

Family adaption may be more strongly related to congruence between attitudes and behavior about maternal employment status than to employment per se (Hock, 1980; Schubert et al., 1980). In our sample, mothers were generally satisfied with their employment status (whether employed or nonemployed) and their husbands were supportive of their roles. Husbands' positive attitudes toward maternal employment facilitate maternal satisfaction and lessen role strain for employed mothers (Coiner, 1978; Lidsky, 1979). Parents in our employed-mother families perceived employment as having a generally positive impact on parent-child relationships, whereas parents in nonemployed-mother families were concerned that maternal employment would have negative consequences for their relationships with their children. As Hoffman (1982) notes, the impact of maternal employment may be related to perceptions of how the child is faring. These parental perceptions, along with the extent of strain and satisfaction in integrating employment and family roles, may affect the ability of parents to be sensitive partners in family interaction. The high degree of role satisfaction in our sample may have minimized differences between families and increased positive family development. It should be noted that these mothers work outside of the home for personal as well as financial reasons. Family adjustment may differ when mothers are employed only for reasons of economic necessity.

Our data suggest that young children and their parents are able to adapt positively to a variety of life-styles, including maternal employment. In the present study, maternal employment status was well-established, with most mothers (85%) employed for more than 1 year. We might, then, expect that family interaction patterns would be relatively stable and that these children would continue to function optimally. On the other hand, much of early childhood is a process of transition, and families may enjoy or cope with different developmental phases differentially. Thus, we may witness sleeper effects of early maternal employment, with corresponding variations in characteristics of children and partners at various points in development. Further studies that provide a longitudinal perspective are vital to our understanding of young children's development in today's families.

REFERENCES

Ainsworth, M.D.S., Blehar, M.C., Waters, E., & Wall, S.N. (1978). *Patterns of attachment: A psychological study of the strange situation.* Hillsdale, NJ: Erlbaum.

Ainsworth, M.D.S. & Wittig, B.A. (1969). Attachment and exploratory behavior of one-year-olds in a strange situation. In B.M. Foss (Ed.), *Determinants of infant behavior,* (Vol. 4, pp. 111-136). London: Methuen.

Alvarez, W.F., Bronfenbrenner, U., & Henderson, C.H. (1983, April). *Working and watching: Maternal employment status and parents' perceptions of their three-year-old children.* Paper presented at the meeting of the Society for Research in Child Development, Detroit, Michigan.

Barnett, R.C., & Baruch, G.K. (1978). *The competent woman.* New York: Irvington.

Bowlby, J. (1951). *Maternal care and mental health.* Geneva, Switzerland: World Health Organization.

Chase-Lansdale, P.L. (1981). *Maternal employment and quality of infant-mother and infant-father attachmen*t (Doctoral dissertation, University of Michigan, 1981). Dissertation *Abstract International,* 42, 2562B.

Clarke-Stewart, K.A. (1977, March). *The father's impact on mother and child.* Paper presented at the meeting of the Society for Research in Child Development, New Orleans, Louisiana.

Coiner, M.C. (1978). *Employment and mothers' emotional states: A psychological study of women reentering the work force.* Unpublished doctoral dissertation, Yale University.

Easterbrooks, M.A. (1982). *Toddler development in a family context: Variations in maternal employment, father involvement and parenting characteristics* (Doctoral dissertation, University of Michigan, 1982). Dissertation Abstracts International, 43, 540B.

Easterbrooks, M.A., & Goldberg, W.A. (1984). Toddler development in the family: Impact of father involvement and parenting characteristics. *Child Development,* 55, 740-752.

Goldberg, W.A., & Easterbrooks, M.A. (1984). The role of marital quality in toddler development. *Developmental Psychology*, 20, 504-514.

Hock, E. (1980). Working and nonworking mothers and their infants: A comparative study of maternal caregiving characteristics and infant social behavior. *Merrill-Palmer Quarterly*, 26, 79-101.

Hoffman, L.W. (1982, October). *Maternal employment and the young child.* Paper presented at the Minnesota Symposium on Child Psychology, Minneapolis, Minnesota.

Hollingshead, A.B. (1978). *Four factor index of social status.* Unpublished manuscript, Yale University.

Lamb, M.E. (1977). The development of parent-infant attachments in the first two years of life. In F.A. Pedersen (Ed.), *The family system: Networks of interactions among mother, father and infant.* New York: Plenum.

Lidsky, A.M. (1979). *Dual-career families: A social psychological study from a systems theory perspective.* Unpublished doctoral disseration, Northwestern Unviersity.

Pedersen, F.A., Cain, R.L., Zaslow, M., & Anderson, B.J. (1982). Variation in infant experience associated with alternative family roles. In L. Laosa & I. Sigel (Eds.), *Families as learning environments for children.* New York: Plenum.

Schacter, F. (1981). Toddlers with employed mothers. *Child Development*, 52, 948-964.

Schubert, J.B., Bradley-Johnson, B., & Nuttal, J. (1980). Mother-infant communication and maternal employment. *Child Development*, 51, 246-249.

Schwartz, P. (1983). Length of day care attendance and attachment behavior in 18-month-old infants. *Child Development*, 54, 1073-1078.

Spitz, R.A. (1946). *Psychoanalytic Study of the Child*, 2, 313-342.

Vaughn, B.E., Gove, F.L., & Egeland, B. (1980). The relationship between out-of-home care and the quality of infant-mother attachment in an economically disadvantaged population. *Child Development*, 51, 1203-1214.

Waldman, E. (1983). Labor force statistics from a family perspective. *Monthly Labor Review*, 106, 16-20.

Zaslow, M., Pedersen, F., Suwalsky, J., & Rabinovich, B. (1983, April). *Maternal employment and parent-infant interaction.* Paper presented at the meetings of the Society for Research in Child Development, Detroit, Michigan.

Divorce: A Child's Perspective

E. Mavis Hetherington

The rate of divorce in the United States, particularly of divorce involving those who have children, has increased dramatically since 1965. It is estimated that 40% of the current marriages of young adults will end in divorce and that 40%-50% of children born in the 1970s will spend some time living in a single-parent family. The average length of time spent by children in a single-parent home as a result of marital disruption is about six years. The majority of these children reside with their mothers, with only 10% living with their fathers even though this proportion has tripled since 1960. Living with the father is most likely to occur with school-aged rather than pre-school children (Glick & Norton, 1978).

This article first presents an overview of the course of divorce and its potential impact on children and then uses research findings as a basis for describing the process of divorce as it is experienced by the child. Since the research on single-parent families headed by fathers is meager and since after divorce most children live in a single-parent family headed by the mother, the article focuses primarily on children in this family situation.

The Course of Divorce

In studying the impact of divorce on children, much confusion has resulted from

Originally published in the *American Psychologist*, 1979, 34, 851-858. Copyright ©1979 by the American Psychological Association. Reprinted by permission of the publisher and author.

viewing divorce as a single event rather than a sequence of experiences involving a transition in the lives of children. This transition involves a shift from the family situation before divorce to the disequilibrium and disorganization associated with separation and divorce, through a period when family members are experimenting with a variety of coping mechanisms, some successful and some unsuccessful, for dealing with their new situation. This is followed by the reorganization and eventual attainment of a new pattern of equilibrium in a single-parent household. For most children, within five years of the divorce there is also a later period of reentry into a two-parent family involving a stepparent, which necessitates further alterations in family functioning. The point at which we tap into the sequence of events and changing processes associated with divorce will modify our view of the adjustment of the child and the factors which influence that adjustment. Although divorce may be the best solution to a destructive family relationship and may offer the child an escape from one set of stresses and the opportunity for personal growth, almost all children experience the transition of divorce as painful. Even children who later are able to recognize that the divorce had constructive outcomes initially undergo considerable emotional distress with family dissolution. The children's most common early responses to divorce are anger, fear, depression, and guilt. It is usually not until after the first year following divorce that tension reduction and an increased sense of well-being begin to emerge.

A crisis model of divorce may be most appropriate in conceptualizing the short-term effects of divorce on children. In the period during and immediately following divorce the child may be responding to changes in his or her life situation—the loss of a parent, the marital discord and family disorganization that usually precede and accompany separation, the alternations in parent-child relations that may be associated with temporary distress and emotional neediness of family members, and other real or fantasized threats to the well-being of the child that are elicited by the uncertainty of the situation. In this period, therefore, stresses associated with conflict, loss, change, and uncertainty may be the critical factors.

The research evidence suggests that most children can cope with and adapt to the short-term crisis of divorce within a few years. However, if the crisis is compounded by multiple stresses and continued adversity, developmental disruptions may occur. The longer term adjustment of the child is related to more sustained or concurrent conditions associated with the quality of life in a household headed by a single parent-alterations in support systems, the increased salience of the custodial parent, the lack of availability of the noncustodial parent, the presence of one less significant adult in the household to participate in decision making, to serve as a model or disciplinarian, or to assume responsibility for household tasks and child care, and finally, changes in family functioning related to continued stresses associated with practical problems of living, such as altered economic resources.

Variability in Response to Divorce

In considering how the child experiences and responds to divorce and to life in a single-parent household, investigators are beginning to examine the interplay among situational factors, stresses, and support systems. However, even when these factors are comparable, wide variability in the quality and intensity of responses and the adaptation of children to divorce remains. Some children exhibit severe or sustained disruptions in development, others seem to sail through a turbulent divorce and stressful aftermath and emerge as competent, well-functioning individuals. Although there is increasing interest in the relative vulnerability or invulnerability of children to psychosocial stress (Garmezy, 1975; Rutter, in press-b), this issue has not been systematically explored in relation to divorce. It seems likely that temperamental variables, the past experience of the child, and the child's developmental status all contribute to individual differences in coping with divorce. There also have been some provocative findings suggesting that boys are more vulnerable to the adverse effects of divorce than are girls, although the reasons for this difference have yet to be clarified.

TEMPERAMENT AND THE RESPONSE TO DIVORCE

Temperamentally difficult children have been found to be less adaptable to change and more vulnerable to adversity (Chess, Thomas, & Birch, 1968; Graham, Rutter, & George, 1973; Rutter, in press-a) than are temperamentally easy children. The difficult child is more likely to be the elicitor and the target of aversive responses by the parent, whereas the temperamentally easy child is not only less likely to be the recipient of criticism, displaced anger, and anxiety but also is more able to cope with it when it hits. Children who have histories of maladjustment preceding the divorce are more likely to respond with long-lasting emotional disturbance following divorce (Kelly, Note 1). This, of course, could be attributable either to temperamental factors or to a history of pathogenic environmental factors.

CUMULATIVE STRESS AND THE RESPONSE TO DIVORCE

Rutter (in press-b) reported that when children experience only a single stress it carried no appreciable psychiatric risk. However, when children who have been exposed to chronic stress or several concurrent stresses must deal with family discord the adverse effects increased multiplicatively. The effects of stresses in the family also are compounded by those in the larger social milieu. Extrafamilial factors such as stresses and supports in other social institutions or networks, the quality of housing, neighborhoods, child care, the need for the mother to work, economic status, and geographic mobility will moderate or potentiate stresses associated with divorce (Colletta, 1978; Hodges, Wechsler, & Ballantine, Note 2). Finally, transactional effects may occur in cases where divorce may actually increase the probability of occurrence of another stressor. This is most apparent in the stresses associated with the downward economic movement that frequently follows divorce and makes raising children and maintaining a household more difficult (Bane, 1976; Brandwein, Brown, & Fox, 1974; Kriesberg, 1970; Winston & Forsher, 1971).

DEVELOPMENTAL STATUS AND THE RESPONSE TO DIVORCE

The adaptation of the child will also vary with his or her developmental status. The limited cognitive and social competencies of the young child, the young child's dependency on parents and more exclusive restriction to the home will be associated with different responses and coping strategies from those of the more mature and self-sufficient older child or adolescent who operates in a variety of social milieus. Note that I am saying the experience of divorce will differ qualitatively for children of varying ages rather than that the trauma will be more or less intense. The young child is less able accurately to appraise the divorce situation, the motives and feelings of his or her parents, his or her own role in the divorce, and the array of possible outcomes. Thus the young child is likely to be more self-blaming in interpreting the cause of divorce and to distort grossly perceptions of the parents' emotions, needs, and behavior, as well as the prospects of reconciliation or total abandonment (Tessman, 1978; Wallerstein & Kelly, 1974, 1975). Although most adolescents experience considerable initial pain and anger when their parents divorce, when the immediate trauma of divorce is over, they are more able accurately to assign responsibility for the divorce, to resolve loyalty conflicts, and to assess and cope with economic and other practical exigencies (Wallerstein & Kelly, 1974, 1975). It should be noted that this is often accompanied by premature, sometimes destructive disengagement from the family and an increased future orientation. However, if the home situation is particularly painful adolescents more than younger children do have the option to disengage and seek gratification elsewhere, such as in the neighborhood, peer group, or school.

SEX DIFFERENCES IN RESPONSES TO DIVORCE

The impact of marital discord and divorce is more pervasive and enduring for boys than for girls (Hetherington, Cox, & Cox, 1978, in press; Proter & O'Leary, in press; Rutter, in press-a; Tuckman & Regan, 1966; Hetherington et al., Note 3; Wallerstein, Note 4). Disturbances in social and emotional development in girls have largely disappeared two years after the divorce, although they may emerge at adolescence in the form of disruptions in heterosexual relations (Hetherington, 1972). Although boys improve markedly in coping and adjustment in the two years after divorce, many continue to show developmental deviations. Boys from divorced families and children from nuclear families, show a higher rate of behavior disorders and problems in interpersonal relations in the home and in the school with teachers and peers. Although especially in young children both boys and girls show an increase in dependent help-seeking and affection-seeking overtures following divorce, boys are more likely also to show more sustained noncompliant, aggressive behavior in the home (Hetherington et al., 1978, in press, Note 3).

Why should this be the case? It has been suggested that loss of a father is more stressful for boys than for girls. It also may be that the greater aggressiveness frequently observed in boys and the greater assertiveness in the culturally prescribed male role necessitates the use of firmer, more consistent discipline practices in the control of boys than of girls. Boys in both nuclear and divorced families are less compliant than girls, and children are less compliant to mothers than fathers (Hetherington et al., 1978). It also could be argued that it is more essential for boys to have a male model to imitate who exhibits mature self-controlled ethical behavior or that the image of greater power and authority vested in the father is more critical in controlling boys, who are culturally predisposed to be more aggressive. Although these factors may all be important, recent divorce studies suggest that these sex differences may involve a more complex set of mediators. Boys are more likely to be exposed to parental battles (Wallerstein, Note 4) and to confront inconsistency, negative sanctions, and opposition from parents, particularly from mothers, following divorce. In addition, boys receive less positive support and nurturance and are viewed more negatively by mothers, teachers, and peers in the period immediately following divorce than are girls (Hetherington et al., 1978, in press; Santrock, 1975; Santrock & Trace, 1978; Hetherington et al., Note 3). Divorced mothers of boys report feeling more stress and depression than do divorced mothers of girls (Colletta, 1978; Hetherington et al., 1978). Boys thus may be exposed to more stress, frustration, and aggression and have fewer available supports.

The Child's Changed Life Experiences Following Divorce

Keeping in mind the many factors that contribute to the wide variability in the responses of children to divorce, let us examine the changes in the child's experiences associated with divorce. Some of these changes are related to alterations in economic status and practical problems of living, others involve changes in family functioning, and still others are associated with social networks external to the family.

ECONOMIC CHANGES AND PRACTICAL PROBLEMS OF LIVING

Some of the most prevalent stresses confronting children of divorce are those associated with downward economic mobility. Poor parents and those with unstable incomes are more likely to divorce (Brandwein et al., 1974; Ross & Sawhill, 1975), and divorce is associated with a marked drop in income. This is in part attributable to the fact that less than one thrid of ex-husbands contribute to the support of their families (Kriesberg, 1970; Winston & Forsher, 1971). Moreover, many divorced women do not have the education, job skills, or experience to permit them to obtain a well-paying position or to pay for high-quality child care. Divorced mothers are more likely to have low-paying part-time jobs or positions of short duration. For the child this results in erratic, sometimes inadequate provisions for child care and, if the mother feels forced to work, in a dissatisfied, resentful mother.

If the divorced mother wishes to work and adequate provisions are made for child care and household management, maternal employment may have positive effects on the mother and no adverse effects on the children. However, if the mother begins to work at the time of divorce or shortly thereafter, the preschool child seems to experience the double loss of both parents, which is reflected in a higher rate of behavior disorders (Hetherington et al., 1978). In addition, maternal employment may add to the task overload experienced when a single parent is attempting to cope with the tasks ordinarily performed by two parents in a nuclear family. It has been suggested that as the divorced mother struggles to distribute her energies across the many demands placed on her, the child may be maternally deprived rather than paternally deprived (Brandwein et al., 1974). This is sometimes associated with what one mother termed a "chaotic lifestyle," where family roles and responsibilities are not well delineated and many routine chores do not get accomplished. Children of many divorced parents receive less adult attention and are more likely to have erratic meals and bedtimes and to be late for school (Hetherington et al., 1978).

The downward economic mobility of families headed by a divorced mother also involves a lower standard of living and relocation. Following divorce, families are likely to shift to more modest housing in poorer neighborhoods, and their greater social isolation may be exacerbated by moving (Marsden, 1969; Pearlin & Johnson, 1977). For the child, such moves not only involve losses of friends, neighbors, and a familiar educational system, but also may be associated with living in an area with high delinquency rates, risks to personal safety, few recreational facilities, and inadequate schools. For children involved in family dissolution, such moves represent further unraveling of the skein of their lives at a time when continuity of support systems and the environment can play an ameliorative role (Tessman, 1978).

CHANGES IN PARENT-CHILD RELATIONS

Many changes in family interaction are associated with divorce and living in a single-parent family. In early studies the role of the loss or relative unavailability of the father was emphasized. More recently, family conflict, the increased salience of the custodial mother, changes in mother-child interaction and in the life circumstances of the single-parent family have been the focus of attention.

Conflict. A high degree of discord characterizes family relations in the period surrounding divorce. The conflict between parents often enmeshes the child in controversy. Children are exposed to parental quarreling, mutual denigration and recrimination, and are placed in a situation of conflicting loyalties, with one parent frequently attempting to coerce or persuade children to form hostile alliances against the other parent. This results in demands for a decision to reject one parent which children are unprepared or unable to make. The vast majority of children wish to maintain relations with both parents. Conflict also gives children the opportunity to play one parent against the other and in some children develops exploitative manipulative skills (Tessman, 1978; Wallerstein, Note 4). The behavior of some children actively escalates conflict between divorced parents and between parents and stepparents following remarriage.

The frequent mutual demeaning and criticism of divorcing parents leads to dissonance, questioning, and often precipitous revision and de-idealization of children's perceptions of their parents (Hetherington, 1972; Tessman, 1978; Wallerstein, Note 4). When the mother is hostile and critical of the father, the child begins to view the father in a more ambivalent or negative manner and as a less acceptable role model. For young boys this is associated with disruption in sex typing (Hetherington et al., Note 3). For girls it may be associated with disruptions in heterosexual relations at adolescence (Hetherington, 1972). Elementary-school-aged children and adolescents in particular are concerned with their parent's morality and competence. Perhaps because of their own awakening sexuality, preadolescents and adolescents are particularly distressed by an increased awareness of their parents as sex objects, first when both parents are dating and then when parents remarry (Wallerstein & Kelly, 1974). Younger children are most anxious about the mother's ability to cope with family conflicts and stresses and her emotional condition following divorce, because of their precarious dependence on the single parent (Wallerstein, Note 4).

Research findings are consistent in showing that children in single-parent families function more adequately than children in conflict-ridden nuclear families (Rutter, in press-b; Hetherington et al., Note 3). The eventual escape from conflict may be one of the most positive outcomes of divorce for children. However, family conflict does not decline but escalates in the year following divorce (Hetherington et al., 1978; Kelly, Note 1; Hetherington et al., Note 3; Wallerstein, Note 4). During this period children in divorced families, particularly boys, show more problems than do children in discordant nuclear families.

Father absence. In the current eagerness to demonstrate that single-parent families headed by mothers can provide a salutary environment for raising children and that the presence of fathers is not essential for normal development in children, there has been a tendency to overlook the contribution of fathers to family functioning. In trying to escape from the earlier narrowly biased view emphasizing father absence as the cause of any obtained developmental differences between children from single-parent and nuclear families, the pendulum may have swung too far in the other direction. Fathers may have a relatively unique contribution to make to family functioning and the development of the child. In the single-parent home some of the father's functions may be taken over by the mother or by other people, social institutions, realtives, siblings, a stepfather, friends, neighbors, a housekeeper, day-care centers, and schools. However, the roles the alternative support systems play may be qualitatively different from those of an involved accessible father (Pederson, Rubenstein, & Yarrow, in press). Some of the roles fathers play in parenting are indirect and serve to support the mother in her parenting role; others impact more directly on the child. The father in a nuclear family indirectly supports the mother in her maternal role in a number of ways — with economic aid, with assistance and relief in household tasks and child rearing, and with emotional support and encouragement and appreciation of her performance as a mother. In addition, an intimate relation with the mother is valued and cherished contributes to her feelings of self-esteem, happiness, and competence which influence her relationship with her children (Hetherington et al., 1978).

The father also may play a more direct and active role in shaping the child's behavior as an agent of socialization, by discipline, direct tuition, or acting as a model. In a single-parent family there is only one parent to serve those functions. The single parent or even two adults of the same sex offer the child a more restricted array of positive characteristics to model than do two parents (Pederson et al., in press). A mother and father are likely to exhibit wider ranging interests, skills, and attributes than a single parent. In addition, the father with his image of greater power and authority may be more effective in controlling children's behavior and in serving as backup authority for the mother's discipline.

Finally, one parent can serve as a protective buffer between the other parent and the child in a nuclear family. In a nuclear family a loving, competent, or well-adjusted parent can help counteract the effects of a rejecting, incompetent, emotionally unstable parent. In a single-parent family headed by a mother, the father is not present to mitigate any deleterious behaviors of the custodial parent in day-to-day living experiences (Hetherington et al., Note 3). Thus, the constructive and pathogenic behaviors of the mother are funneled more directly onto the child, and the quality of the mother-child relationship will be more directly reflected in the adjustment of the child than it is in a nuclear family.

Divorced fathers and their children. A finding that should be of some concern to those making custody recommendations is that there is little continuity between the quality of pre- and post- separation parent-child interaction, particularly for fathers (Hetherington et al., 1976; Kelly, Note 1). This discontinuity is another factor contributing to the sense of unpredictability in the child's situation. Some intensely attached fathers find intermittent fathering painful and withdraw from their children. On the other hand, a substantial number of fathers report that their relationship with their children improves after divorce, and many fathers, previously relatively uninvolved, become competent and concerned parents.

The parents' response to divorce and the quality of the child's relationship with both parents immediately after divorce has a substantial effect on the child's coping and adjustment (Hetherington et al., 1976; Kelly, Note 1). In the first year after divorce, parents often are preoccupied with their own depression, anger, or emotional needs and are unable to respond sensitively to the wants of the child. During this period divorced parents tend to be inconsistent, less affectionate, and lacking in control over their children (Hetherington et al., 1978). However, they recover markedly in the second year after divorce.

Although in the early months following divorce fathers are having as much or even more contact with children as they did preceding the divorce, most divorced fathers rapidly become less available to their children. Fathers are more likely to maintain frequent contact with their sons than with their daughters (Hess & Camara, in press). Most children wish to maintain contact with the father, and in preschool children, mourning for the father and fantasies of reconciliation may continue for several years (Hetherington et al., 1978; Tessman, 1978; Wallerstein & Kelly, 1975). Unless the father is extremely poorly adjusted or immature, or the child is exposed to conflict between the parents, frequent availability of the father is associated with positive adjustment and social relations, especially in boys (Hess & Camara, in press; Hetherington et al., 1978, Note 3; Wallerstein, Note 4). A continued mutually supportive relationship and involvement of the father with the child is the most effective support system for divorced women in their parenting role and for their children. The recommendation that has been made that the custodial parent have the right to eliminate visitation by the noncustodial parent, if he or she views it as adverse to the child's well-being, seems likely to discourage parents from working out their differences and runs counter to the available research findings.

Divorced mothers and their children. With time, the custodial parent in single-parent families becomes increasingly salient in the development of the child (Hetheringtron et al., Note 3). Fathers who maintain frequent contact and involvement with their children have more impact on the child's development than do fathers whose contacts are relatively infrequent or who are relatively detached. However, even highly involved noncustodial fathers are less influential than the custodial mother in many facets of the child's personality and social and cognitive development. The well-being of the divorced mother and the quality of mother-child relations thus become central to the adjustment of the child. However, this is not a one-way street, since the mother's sense of competence, self-esteem, and happiness is modified by the behavior of her children, particularly her sons. The mother who must cope with too many young children or with acting-out, noncompliant behavior in sons becomes increasingly distressed and inept in her parenting. Divorced adults have more health and emotional problems, even after the initial crisis period of divorce, than do married adults (Bloom, Asher, & White, 1978). This suggests that the child may be coping with a mother who is not only confronting many stresses but who may be physically and psychologically less able to deal with adversity.

In most divorcing famil;ies there is a period in the first year after divorce when mothers become depressed, self-involved, erratic, less supportive, and more ineffectually authoritarian in dealing with their children. Divorced mothers and their sons are particularly likely to get involved in an escalating cycle of mutual coercion. As was noted above, parenting improves dramatically in the second year after divorce; however, problems in parent-child relations continue to be found more often between divorced mothers and children, especially sons, than between mothers and children in nuclear families.

Different aspects of the divorced mother's relationship with her children are important with children of different ages. With preschool children, organization of the home and authoritative control, accompanied by nurturance and maturity demands, seem to be particularly important in the adjustment of the child. Young children have more difficulty than older children in exerting self-control and ordering their changing lives and thus require more external control and structure in times of stress and transition (Hetherington et al., Note 3). On the other hand, divorced mothers of older children and adolescents are more likely to rely on their children for emotional support and for assistance with practical problems of daily life. The children are asked to fulfill some of the functions of the departed father. There is great pressure for elementary-school-aged children and adolescents to function in a mature, autonomous manner at an early age. Weiss (Note 5) described the phenomenon of great self-sufficiency and growing up faster in one-parent families. If the mother is not making excessive or inappropriate demands for emotional and sustenance, her greater openness about concerns and plans can lead to a companionate relationship between her and her children. However, being pushed toward early independence and the assumption of adult responsibilities leads to feelings of being overwhelmed by unsolvable problems, incompetence, and resentment about lack of support and unavailability of mothers, and to precocious sexual concerns in some school-aged children and adolescents (Kelly, Note 1; Wallerstein, Note 4).

EXTRAFAMILIAL SUPPORT SYSTEMS

Willard Hartup (in press) discussed how little we know about extrafamilial social and affectional systems and the relationships among familial and extrafamilial systems. This is nowhere more apparent than in the area of divorce, where the focus of study largely has been confined to parent-child relations and where the emphasis has been on supports for the divorced parents rather than for the children. Even the role of siblings and the extended family as support systems for children going through family disruption has received only cursory examination. The research thus far indicates that extended family and community services play a more active role as support systems for low-income than for moderate-income families (Colletta, 1978; Spicer & Hampe, 1975). With preschool children, family relations are prepotent in the adjustment of the child. Disruptions in family functioning are associated with maladaptive behaviors both in the home and in other social situations (Hess & Camara, in press; Wallerstein & Kelly, 1975; Hetherington et al., Note 3).

With older children, although the disruptive effects of divorce may flood over into other relations in the period immediately surrounding divorce, they are more rapidly able to circumscribe these effects. Older children are frequently able to confine their stress within the family arena and to use peers and schools as sources of information, satisfaction, and support (Hetherington et al., in press; Wallerstein, Note 4). The validation of self-worth, competence, and personal control are important functions served by peers, and positive school and neighborhood environments are to some extent able to attenuate the effects of stressful family relations (Hess & Camara, in press; Hetherington et al, in press; Rutter, in press-b; Wallerstein, Note 4; Hetherington et al., Note 3).

Summary

The best statistical prognostications suggest that an increasing number of children are going to experience their parents' divorce and life in a single-parent family. A conflict-ridden intact family is more deleterious to family members than is a stable home in which parents are divorced. An inaccessible, rejecting, or hostile parent in a nuclear family is more detrimental to the development of the child than is the absence of a parent. Divorce is often a positive solution to destructive family functioning; however, most children experience divorce as a difficult transition, and life in a single-parent family can be viewed as a high-risk situation for parents and children. This is not to say that single-parent familes cannot or do not serve as effective settings for the development of competent, stable, happy children, but the additional stresses and the lack of support systems confronted by divorced families impose additional burdens on their members.

Most research has viewed the single-parent family as a pathogenic family and has failed to focus on how positive family functioning and support systems can facilitate the development of social, emotional, and intellectual competence in children in single-parent families. Neither the gloom-and-doom approach nor the political stance of refusing to recognize that many single-parent families headed by mothers have problems other than financial difficulties is likely to be productive. We need more research and applied programs oriented toward the identification and facilitation of patterns of family functioning, as well as support systems that can help families to cope with changes and stress associated with divorce and that help to make single-parent families the basis of a satisfying and fulfilling life-style.

REFERENCE NOTES

1. Kelly, J.B. *Children and parents in the midst of divorce: Major factors contributing to differential response.* Paper presented at the National Institute of Mental Health Conference on Divorce, Washington, D.C., February 1978.

2. Hodges, F.H., Wechsler, R.C., & Ballantine, C. *Divorce and the preschool child: Cumulative stress.* Paper presented at the meeting of the American Psychological Association, Toronto, August 1978.

3. Hetherington, E.M., Cox, M., & Cox, R. *Family interactions and the social, emotional and cognitive development of children following divorce.* Paper presented at the Johnson and Johnson Symposium on the Family: Setting Priorities, Washington, D.C., 1978.

4. Wallerstein, J.S. *Children and parents 18 months after parental separation; Factors related to differential outcome.* Paper presented at the National Institute of Mental Health Conference on Divorce, Washington, D.C., February 1978.

5. Weiss, R. *Single-parent households as settings for growing up.* Paper presented at the National Institute of Mental Health Conference on Divorce, Washington, D.C., February 1978.

REFERENCES

Bane, M.J. Marital disruption and the lives of children. *Journal of Social Issues*, 1976, 32, 103-117.

Bloom, B.L., Asher, S.J., & White, S.W. Marital disruption as a stressor: A review and analysis. *Psychological Bulletin*, 1978, 85, 867-894.

Brandwein, R.A., Brown, C.A., & Fox, E.M. Women and children last. The social situation of divorced mothers and their families. *Journal of Marriage and the Family*, 1974, 36, 498-514.

Chess, S., Thomas, A., & Birch, H.O. Behavioral problems revisited. In S. Chess & H. Birch (Eds.), *Annual progress in child psychiatry and child development.* New York: Brunner/Mazel, 1968.

Colletta, N.D. *Divorced mothers at two income levels: Stress, support and child-rearing practices.* Unpublished thesis, Cornell University, 1978.

Garmezy, N. The experimental study of children vulnerable to psychopathology. In A. Davids (Ed.), *Child personality and psychopathology* (Vol. 2). New York: Wiley, 1975.

Glick, P.G., & Norton, A.J. Marrying, divorcing and living together in the U.S. today. *Population Bulletin*, 1978, 32, 3-38.

Graham, P., Rutter, M., & George, S. Temperamental characteristics as predictors of behavior disorders in children. *American Journal of Orthopsychiatry*, 1973, 43, 328-399.

Hartup, W. Two social worlds: Family relations and peer relations. In M. Rutter (Ed.), *Scientific foundations of developmental psychiatry*. London: Heinemann Medical, in press.

Hess, R.D., & Camara, K.A. Post-divorce family relations as mediating factors in the consequences of divorce for children. *Journal of Social Issues*, in press.

Hetherington, E.M. Effects of father absence on personality development in adolescent daughters. *Developmental Psychology,* 1972, 7, 313-326.

Hetherington, E.M., Cox, M., & Cox, R. Divorced fathers. *Family Coordinator,* 1976, 25, 417-428.

Hetherington, E.M., Cox, M., & Cox, R. The aftermath of divorce. In J.H. Stevens, Jr., & M. Matthews (Eds.), *Mother-child, father-child relations*. Washington, D.C.: National Association for the Education of Young Children, 1978.

Hetherington, E.M., Cox, M., & Cox, R. Play and social interaction in children following divorce. *Journal of Social Issues*, in press.

Kriesberg, L. *Mothers in poverty: A study of fatherless families*. Chicago: Aldine, 1970.

Marsden, D. *Mothers alone: Poverty and the fatherless family*. London: Allen Lane the Penguin Press, 1969.

Pearlin, L.I., & Johnson, J.S. Marital status, life strains, and depression. *American Sociological Review,* 1977, 42, 704-715.

Pedersen, F.A., Rubenstein, J., & Yarrow, L.J. Infant development in father-absent families. *Journal of Genetic Psychology,* in press.

Porter, G., & O'Leary, D.K. Marital discord and child behavior problems. *Journal of Abnormal Child Psychology*, in press.

Ross, H.L., & Sawhill, I.V. *Time of transition: The growth of families headed by women.* Washington, D.C.: Urban Institute, 1975.

Rutter, M. Mental deprivation 1972-1978: New findings, new concepts, new approaches. *Child Development,* in press. (a)

Rutter, M. Protective factors in children's responses to stress and disadvantage. In M.W. Kent & J.E. Rolf (Eds.), *Primary prevention of psychopathology: Vol. 3. Promoting social competence and coping in children.* Hanover, N.H.: University Press of New England, in press. (b)

Santrock, J.W. Father absence, perceived maternal behavior and moral development in boys. *Child Development*, 1975, 46, 753-757.

Santrock, J.W., & Trace, R.L. Effect of children's family structure status on the development of stereotypes by children. *Journal of Educational Psychology,* 1978, 70, 754-757.

Spicer, J., & Hampe, G. Kinship interaction after divorce. *Journal of Marriage and the Family*, 1975, 28, 113-119.

Tessman, L.H. *Children of parting parents.* New York: Aronson, 1978.

Tuckman, J., & Regan, P.A. Intactness of the home and behavioral problems in children. *Journal of Child Psychology and Psychiatry,* 1966, 7, 225-233.

Wallerstein, J.S., & Kelly, J.B. The effects of parental divorce: The adolescent experience. In A. Koupernik (Ed.), *The child in his family: children at a psychiatric risk* (Vol. 3). New York: Wiley, 1974.

Wallerstein, J.S., & Kelly, J.B. The effects of parental divorce: Experiences of the preschool child. *Journal of the American Academy of Child Psychiatry*, 1975, 14, 600-161.

Weiss, R. *Marital separation.* New York: Basic Books, 1975.

Winston, M.P., & Forsher, T. *Nonsupport of legitimate children of affluent fathers as a cause of poverty and welfare dependence.* New York: Rand Corporation, 1971.

The Developmental Effects of Day Care

Jay Belsky

Research on the effects of day care can be usefully organized around three topics—intellectual, emotional, and social development (Belsky and Steinberg, 1978; Belsky, Steinberg, and Walker, 1982). Before proceeding to present such a review, it is necessary to highlight once again the very real limits of research designs for studying the effects of day care. Up until the past five years, most inquiry into day care was restricted to university-connected centers providing high quality care (e.g., Ricciuti, 1974; Ramey and Campbell, 1979a and 1979b; Kagan, Kearsley, and Zelazo, 1978). More than ever, however, social scientists are moving beyond highly controlled settings to investigate the nature and effects of community sponsored day care (e.g., Blanchard and Main, 1979; Golden et al., 1978; Rubenstein and Howes, 1979; this volume). This new work tells us not simply what the effects of day care can be for children fortunate enough to be enrolled in special programs, but what they are likely to be for the overwhelming majority of children in day care who are not exposed to programs with special educational curriculums, well-trained staff, and good caregiver-child ratios.

An even more serious concern from the standpoint of design than sample limita-

Jay Belsky, "Two Waves of Day Care Research: Developmental Effects and Conditions of Quality," in *The Child and the Day Care Setting*, Ricardo C. Ainslie, Ed. (Praeger Publishers, a division of Greenwood Press, Inc., New York, NY, 1984), pp. 3-17.

tions are the potential pre-existing differences that characterize children reared in day care and at home. In most investigations of the effects of day care, two samples are compared, one using day care, the other being reared at home. Such comparative designs are founded upon the assumption that where developmental differences exist they can be attributed to variation in child care experience. But a major problem, perhaps the major problem, of such designs, and indeed the "Achilles' heel" of day care research, is that important differences are likely to characterize home reared and day care reared comparison groups *before* variation in child care is experienced (Roopnarine and Lamb, 1978). Under such circumstances the attribution of subsequent developmental differences to day care, and thus the very notion of day care effects, may be inappropriate.

This brief analysis of two of the major limits in day care research could easily and understandably lead the rigorous scientist to the conclusion that research on the effects of day care cannot be done well, or at least not well enough so that it is useful for drawing valid conclusions. There are two reasons why one should not draw this conclusion. The first is that if the principal question is whether day care is bad for children, then even nonperfectly controlled designs can answer this question. Unless we presume that families which place their children in day care do a better job of caring for their offspring before and during their placement, then comparisons which consistently reveal few differences between day care- and home-reared children should allay most fears that parents, scientists, and policymakers are likely to have. Thus, while research designs might not be the best possible to document the effects of day care per se, they appear to be good enough to chronicle deficits that may be associated with (as opposed to caused by) day care rearing.

The second cause for confidence in available day care research derives from the data themselves. Despite limits in design and especially measurement, findings across studies are surprisingly consistent, even if not perfectly uniform. And, as I hope to show, even where inconsistency is markedly apparent, this too appears both explainable and meaningful.

INTELLECTUAL DEVELOPMENT

Ever since the Soviet Union beat the United States into space with the launching of Sputnik in the 1950s, Americans have displayed great concern for the intellectual development of their children. In point of fact, this is one reason why the theories of Piaget and the cognitive perspective in general have come to dominate the American psychological scene over the past two decades. Concern for the effects of day care on intellectual functioning merely reflects this historical influence.

An overwhelming majority of studies of the effects of day care on subsequent intellectual development have indicated no differences between day care-reared children and matched home-reared controls (Belsky, Steinberg, and Walker, 1982). Although a number of these investigators had found initial gains in one or many test subscales, all significant differences between day care children and matched controls, disappeared during the program or soon after termination. In the only long-term follow-up study in this area, 102 of 120 Swedish children initially investigated by Cochran (1977) during infancy were found at 5-1/2 years of age to be equal in intelligence regardless of whether they had been continuously reared in a day care center, family day care home, or in their own homes by their parents (Gunnarson, 1978). For children from relatively advantaged families, then, exposure to day care, even to high quality, cognitively enriched programs, does not appear to result in any long-term gains in IQ test performance. Neither, though, does it seem that any losses in intellectual performance result from enrollment in day care.

In contrast to this conclusion regarding children from advantaged families, it is of significance that positive effects of the day care experience on performance on standardized tests of intellectual development have been reported by a handful of investigators for those children who have been categorized as higher risk than the average middle-class child. It should be noted, however, that most of the programs in which these economically-disadvantaged children were enrolled were specifically designed to provide cognitive enrichment, although they varied widely in the type and degree of special enrichment provided for the children and families involved (Belsky and Steinberg, 1978). Lally (1973), for example, found that while 29 percent of a low education, home-reared group obtained an IQ below 90 on the Stanford-Binet test, only 7 percent of a day care group did so. On the basis of these results, it would appear than an enriching day care experience may reduce some of the adverse effects typically associated with high-risk environments.

Further support for this conclusion comes from a longitudinal study of day care-rearing beginning in early infancy (Ramey, Dorval, and Baker-Ward, 1981). In this work, three groups of children were compared: (1) a high-risk experimental group enrolled in a specially designed cognitive enrichment day care program; (2) a high-risk, home-reared control group matched to the experimentals on a number of important variables (e.g., social class, age, sex, race); and (3) a general population contrast group reared at home in more economically advantaged households. During the period between six and 18 months, performance on the mental developmental subscale of the Bayley Infant Test declined for the high-risk controls (from 104 to 86), while it remained stable (near 104) for the high-risk experimentals (who were *randomly* assigned to the day care-rearing group). In addition, motor development subscale scores on this same test revealed significant differences between these two groups, favoring the day care-reared children.

Follow-up comparisons demonstrate that these patterns of decline in the level of functioning for the home-reared, economically disadvantaged children and of stability for their day care-reared counterparts continue into the child's third, fourth, and fifth years of life. In fact, while only 11 percent of the day care-reared children are scoring in the range of cognitive-educational handicap (i.e., IQ ≤ 85) at age five, a full 35 percent of the home-reared controls are scoring below this level of functioning. A possible reason for this difference is suggested by a recent analysis by O'Connell and Farran (1982) of these children's linguistic functioning when observed with their mother at 20 months during free play and a structured give-and-take-an-object session. The experimental children cared for in day care since their opening months of life engaged in more spontaneous showing of objects, and relied upon words more frequently when giving and requesting. In sum, they appeared more linguistically and communicatively competent, and it is just such competency upon which subsequent intellectual growth is likely to build.

The overall picture of evidence, duly qualified, suggests that the day care experience has neither beneficial nor adverse effects on the intellectual development (as measured by standardized tests) of most children. For economically disadvantaged children, however, day care may have an enduring positive effect, for it appears that such day care experience may *reduce the declines in test scores* typically associated with high-risk populations after 18 months of age (Belsky and Steinberg, 1978; Belsky, Steinberg, and Walker, 1982).

Emotional Development

Historically, the mother-child bond has been of prime concern to those interested in the influence of early experience upon emotional development. Psychoanalytic theory and early research on institutionalized children (e.g., Bowlby, 1951; Spitz, 1945) suggested that any arrangement which deprived the child of continuous access to its mother would impare the development of a strong maternal attachment and thereby adversely affect the child's emotional security. Since day care, by its very nature, entails the daily separation of mother from child, a good deal of attention has been devoted to discovering whether child care outside the home does indeed disrupt the child's emotional tie to his mother. The major strategy for making such an appraisal has been to observe young children's responses to separation from and reunion with their mothers (usually in an unfamiliar laboratory playroom), and to see whether children prefer to interact with their mothers, their caregivers, or a stranger in free play situations.

In a very early, and therefore noteworthy study, Blehar (1974) observed disturbances in the attachment relationships that children, 30 and 40 months of age, and enrolled in day care for five months, had developed with their mothers. Specifically, while the 30 month-old children were more likely to show "anxious-avoidant" attachments to their mothers (more resistance and avoidance behavior and less proximity seeking during reunion) than were their home-reared counterparts, the 40 month-old children manifested "anxious-ambivalent" attachments (less exploration prior to the separation, more crying and searching during separation, and more proximity seeking *and* resistance behavior to mother during reunion). In each age group, the home-reared comparison subjects were more likely to greet their mothers positively following the stressful separation experience, a behavioral style that is considered to index a secure emotional attachment (Sroufe, 1979). Much criticism has been levelled against this study (Belsky and Steinberg, 1978), and an attempt to replicate Blehar's 40-month results, using many more methodological controls, failed to find the home care/day care differences she discerned (Moskowitz, Schwarz, and Corsini, 1977).

Results from several other investigations are contradictory in showing that either day care (Cochran, 1977; Ricciuti, 1974) or home-reared children (Doyle and Somers, 1977) are more likely to get distressed upon separation from the caregiver. It seems ill advised, however, to interpret group differences on a single measure as indicative of a meaningful and functionally significant difference in psychological development (Belsky and Steinberg, 1978). This would seem especially true in the case of a measure of distress following separation from mother, since Kagan and his colleagues (1978) have observed that distress to separation shows virtually the same developmental course in children reared in markedly different contexts around the world, suggesting that it may be more maturationally programmed than experimentally influenced. This is probably the reason why Kagan et al. (1978) found, in the most comprehensive and controlled study to date, that at between 3 1/2 and 30 months of age, day care- and home-reared infants did not differ in their emotional responses to a separation from mother.

Further evidence of similar patterns of emotional development in day care- and home-reared children comes from a series of studies of 10-12 month olds (Brookhart and Hock, 1976), 5-30 month-olds (Doyle, 1975), 36 month-olds (Roopnarine and Lamb, 1978), and 41-45 month-olds (Portnoy and Simmons, 1978). In each investigation, response to a separation from a reunion with mother were generally equivalent between groups that varied in early rearing experience. Why then do Blehar's (1974) previous results differ so markedly? Two explanations come to mind—one historical, the other developmental.

It is important to note that Blehar's children were enrolled in day care in the early 1970s, at a time when day care, especially for very young children, was still looked upon negatively by many people. Possibly, then, the guilt that parents may have experienced in violating cultural standards, or even the quality of care that was offered when day care was such a relatively new phenomenon, could have adversely influenced the Blehar subjects. Thus, a cohort effect, emphasizing the historical timing of day care enrollment, might be responsible for her divergent results.

Additionally, it needs to be noted that Blehar's children were only in day care for five months when evaluated. Recent evidence indicates that a "transient distress reaction" may be associated with initial adaptation to daily separation from parents and thus may account for Blehar's data. Support for this possibility comes from several sources. First, Portnoy and Simmons (1978), who first proposed this explanation, were unable to replicate Blehar's results, but studied children who averaged 9 1/2 months of day care experience prior to assessment. And, in an entirely independent study, Blanchard and Main (1979) found that avoidance of mother, both during daily pick-up from day care and in a structured laboratory situation, decreased the longer the child had been in day care. These findings suggest, then, that young children may go through a period of *stressful adaptation* to supplementary child care. But once they come to understand that regular separation from parent need not imply loss of the attachment figure, adaptation is achieved and problematic behavior is reduced.

It is important to emphasize that beyond the just discussed transient-distress reaction, negative effects of day care may be absent primarily when supplementary child care arrangements are reasonably stable and care is of a reasonable quality. In fact, a recent study of infants enrolled prior to their first birthday in unstable (i.e., frequently changing) day care arrangements reveals that children in such poor quality care arrangements are at risk for developing anxious-avoidant attachment relations with their mothers (Vaughn, Gove, and Egeland, 1980). An unrelated investigation by Schwartz (1984) also indicates that infants starting full-time day care placement during the first year display more avoidance of their mothers when reunited with them following a brief separation at 18 months. Attachment relations characterized by high levels of such avoidance, and thus classified as insecure, have been found to predict problems in adjusting to peers during the preschool years (Arend, Gove, and Sroufe, 1979).

A follow-up study of the children in the Vaughn et al. (1980) investigation led its authors to conclude that even these apparently negative effects may not be long lasting: "at two years of age the effects of out of home care were no longer striking. . . For this sample, then, it appears that the cumulative adverse effects of out-of-home care were minimal" (Farber and Egeland, 1982, p. 120). Despite these conclusions, it should be noted that several trends were apparent in Farber and Egeland's data on children's behavior during a problem-solving episode which could lead a more cautious reader to a different conclusion. Specifically, toddlers whose mothers began working prior to their infants' first birthday displayed significantly less enthusiasm in confronting a challenging task than children who had had no day care experience. Furthermore, they tended to be less compliant in following their mothers' instructions and were less persistent in dealing with a difficult problem than children who had never been in day care or who began day care after their first birthday. Finally, they, like the late-entry day care children, tended to display more negative affect.

In a recent and provocative reanalysis of the Farber and Egeland (1982) data, Vaughn, Deane, and Waters (1984) demonstrate that the effects of early day care entry are indeed long lasting, "but can only be understood when the interaction of attachment history and nonmaternal care experiences are considered together" (p. 37, ms). For children classified as anxiously attached to their mothers at 18 months of age, no effect of day care emerged; such children, regardless of day care utilization or timing of entry into day care continued to display less competent and more maladaptive behavior in the problem solving situation at 24 months. For children evaluated as securely attached at 18 months, however, those who had entered day care before one year of age received "substantially less optimal scores on the 24-month measures than their home care counterparts" (p. 37, ms). Indeed, although children who were secure at 18 months and whose mothers never worked looked more competent at two years than the insecure children from the early work group, no differences in functioning in the problem-solving task were evident between children who were secure at 18 months and whose mothers started work before 12 months and insecure children whose mothers never worked.

Since the initial Vaughn et al. (1980) analysis indicated that early entry is associated with greater anxious-avoidant attachments, and since these new data indicate that limits in child functioning become evident by two years of age even when the attachment history was characterized by security, there seems to be cause for concern about early entry into the kind of routine day care that is available in most communities. This would seem to be especially true in view of two additional recent studies which also raise questions about early entry into day care. In one which was conducted in Bermuda, and will be discussed in more detail when we consider the second wave of day care research, McCartney and her colleagues (1982, p. 148) found that "children who began group care in infancy were rated as more maladjusted (when studied between three and five years of age) than those who were cared for by sitters or in family day care homes for the early years and who began to group care at later ages." These conclusions, it is important to note, were based upon analyses which controlled for a variety of important background variables, including child's age at time of assessment and mother's IQ, age, and ethnicity. In a retrospective investigation of eight to 10 year olds who had varied in their preschool experiences, Barton and Schwarz (1981) also found day care entry prior to 12 months of age to be associated with higher levels of misbehavior and greater social withdrawal, even after controlling for the education of both parents.

These new data lead one to modify conclusions that have been arrived at in past reviews in order to underscore the potentially problematic nature of early entry into community-based, as opposed to university-based, day care (Belsky and Steinberg, 1978; Belsky, Steinberg, and Walker, 1982). Supplementary child care exerts little influence on the child's emotional ties to his/her mother (other than *transient* distress) except under certain conditions, as when children are enrolled in unstable or poor quality day care arrangements prior to their first birthday. Under such conditions, infants may be more likely to develop a particular kind of disturbance in their relations with their primary attachment figure: they will be likely to avoid her. Further, they may be more likely to display emotional and social problems in subsequent years. Important to note, though, is the fact that such deleterious consequences may not be long-lasting or inevitable. Recall that Farber and Egeland themselves concluded that little effect of early entry was evident at two years. Further, studies of high quality care have failed to discern negative consequences of early entry (Picciuti, 1974; Kagan, Kearsley, and Zelazo, 1978; Ramey, Dorval, and Baker-Ward, 1981).

Social Development

Earlier it was noted that both economics and ideology play a major role in the utilization of day care in the United States, as increasing numbers of mothers with young children are working outside the home—either for reasons of financial necessity or personal fulfillment. To fully understand such early reliance on group rearing, one also needs to recognize the value that American culture places on independence. In marked contrast to the Japanese, for example, who view their newborns as independent and thus in great need of developing dependency relations with parents, family, and community, Americans view the newborn as exceedingly dependent, needing to be weaned from his excessive reliance on others if he is to succeed in a society as competitive and individualistic as United States (Caudill and Weinstein, 1969; Kagan et al., 1978). Thus, it should be of little surprise that one important reason American families place their children in group rearing situations is to give them the opportunity to be independent of their families and to learn how to get along with others, most especially their peers. When it comes to assessing the effects of day care on social development, then, primary attention has been directed toward children's behavior toward peers and nonparental adults.

With respect to peer relations, available evidence indicates that day care has both positive and negative effects. On the positive side, Ricciuti (1974) and Kagan et al. (1978) have shown that one- to two-year olds with group experience during infancy are more willing to approach a strange peer or continue their play in the presence of an unfamiliar agemate, and Clarke-Stewart (1979) has reported that two- and three-year olds cared for in day care centers, nursery schools, or family day care homes display more cooperation while playing with a strange peer and are better able to appraise the perspective of another than are agemates reared by their mother or a babysitter at home. More recently, Vliestra (1981) has reported, on the basis of observations of two and a half- to four and a half-year olds, that those experiencing full-day care, in contrast to those experiencing half-day care (for at least six months), engaged in significantly more positive interaction with peers and displayed more of what she regarded as prosocial aggression (tattling, defending property against counterattack, commanding, enforcing rules), but not more hostile aggression (physical or verbal attack on others). Studies such as these and others (Gunnarson, 1978) clearly suggest that day care rearing may enhance certain social competencies, probably by providing children with early and increased opportunities to relate to peers. That these effects may be enduring is suggested by Moore's (1975) study of adolescents: boys who had experienced group rearing prior to the age of five reported higher concern for social activities and were also observed to be more sociable with peers and found to be chosen more regularly by peers as likable than were boys who were home reared during their preschool years.

On the negative side, Moore (1964) observed that when these children were pre-schoolers those in supplementary child care arrangements (which were often unstable) were more prone to toilet lapses and were more self-assertive. Schwarz et al. (1974) found, in one of the first studies to raise concerns about the effect of day care, that preschoolers with day care experience in infancy were more aggressive (both physically and verbally) toward peers than a group of home-reared children who were enrolled in day care for the first time when three to four years old. Vliestra's (1981) earlier mentioned study raises some questions, however, about these results, which were based upon observer ratings. While her observational data comparing children with part-time and full-time exposure to day care failed to demonstrate that full-time care was associated with greater aggression, teacher ratings indicated that the full-time children were more aggressive. This contradiction, she suggests, may be a result of the greater activity levels of the full-time children which could have been interpreted as aggression by teachers. The relevance of this interpretation for the Schwarz et al. (1974) study is to be found in the fact that this early investigation discerned greater activity on the part of preschoolers with extensive day care experience. Could it be that aggression and activity were also confused in the Schwarz study?

While this possibility cannot be discounted, the situation is further confused by a recent retrospective study by Barton and Schwarz (1981), who compared the teacher and peer ratings of 191 eight- to ten-year olds from white middle-class families who varied in day care exposure during their preschool years. After controlling for mater-nal and paternal education, analyses revealed no differences on teacher ratings of children, but peer ratings indicated that full-time day care exposure was associated with more aggression and attention getting—what Barton and Schwarz referred to as misbehavior. Although the evidence is by no means totally consistent, it does repeatedly suggest that in some respects day care children engage in more negative in-teractions with peers. Another reading of these data is that with greater peer ex-posure comes greater peer interaction, which is more likely to be both positive and negative in quality.

When it comes to relations with adults, and the socialization of adult-like be-haviors, the available evidence also raises concerns. In the initial Schwarz et al. (1974) investigation, observations and teacher reports revealed that preschoolers with exten-sive day care experience were less cooperative with adults, more physically and verbal-ly aggressive toward them, and somewhat less tolerant of frustration. Results consistent with these data were reported a decade earlier by Raph et al. (1964) who found that negative interactions between middle- and upper-class first graders and their teachers varied directly with the amount of group-rearing the children experienced prior to first grade. Paralleling these results are recent findings from a retrospective analysis of five- and six-year olds who were reared at home or in day care during the preschool perod. Robertson (1982) observed that boys with day care histories were rated by their teachers as substantially and significantly more troublesome than peers cared for at home. Specifically, these day care-reared boys were more likely to be rated as having little respect for other children and as being quarrelsome, disobedient, and uncooperative. Consistent with these findings are those reported as part of a retrospective study of two-year olds from Bermuda who had been cared for in day care centers, by babysitters, or by mothers during their first years of life. Analyses which included statistical controls for variation in maternal and paternal IQ, education, and occupation indicated that, in testing situations with adults, center-reared children were more apathetic, less attentive, and less socially responsive (Schwarz et al. 1981).

Additional evidence also suggests that day care-reared children may orient to peers more than to adults. Schwarz et al. (1974) found, for example, that while preschoolers with prior day care experience interacted more with peers than teachers, the opposite was true of the home-reared children who were having their first group experience at age three to four (Lay and Meyer, 1973). Similar results have been reported by McCutcheon and Calhoun (1976) who observed that increased interaction with peers was accompanied by decreased interaction with adults in day care. The implications of this trend are suggested by several results from Moore's (1964) initial study that indicate that day care-reared preschoolers are less conforming and less impressed by punishment.

Given these potentially disturbing effects of day care on social development, several comments are in order. Lest these data be taken as a sweeping indictment of day care rearing, it must be noted that

> ...like all social and educational efforts, day care programs are likely to reflect, and in some measure achieve, the values held explititly or implicitly by their sponsors and, through the, by the community at large.

> From this perspective, the tendency we have observed for all-day group care to predispose children toward greater aggressiveness, impulsivity, and egocentricism may represent a phenomenon specific to American society, for these outcomes have been identified as characteristic of socialization in age-segregated peer groups in America generally. . . . That the phenomena may indeed be culturebound is in-

dicated by ... comparative studies of peer group socialization in the United States, the USSR, Israel, and other contemporary societies, which show that, depending on the goals and methods involved, group upbringing can lead to a variety of consequences, ranging from delinquency and violence at one extreme to unquestioning conformity at the other (Belsky and Steinberg, 1978, p. 942).

Ambron's (1980) recent suggestion that day care staff are more permissive, more tolerant of disobedience and aggression, and less inclined to set behavior standards than parents is consistent with these conclusions. So too is McCrae and Herbert-Jackson's (1975) claim that the effects of day care may be program specific. Empirical support for these speculations can be found in Gunnarson's (1978) Swedish day care study, the findings of which contradict much of the data reviewed above. Specifically, naturalistic observations of five-year olds reared since infancy in day care centers, family day care home, or in their own homes, revealed no rearing-group differences in children's compliance and cooperation with, and positive affect expressed towards, adults. Moreover, structured doll play assessments of these five-year olds revealed that day care children were no more likely than home-reared children to transgress against adult wishes in the face of peer pressures to do so. However, children reared in Swedish day care centers, in comparison to those reared in homes (by family day care providers or mothers), did engage more frequently in information sharing, compliance, and cooperation with peers. These data demonstrate not only that day care can promote positive peer skills, but that negative interactions with peers and adults which have been reported regularly enough so that they cannot be disregarded, need not be more frequent in any rearing environment. This leads us to reaffirm the conclusion quoted earlier: The effect of day care on social development will likely depend on the community and cultural context in which day care is employed as well as the particular practices of the day care program.

REFERENCES

Ambron, S. Causal models in early education research. In S. Kilmer (Ed.), *Advances in early education and day care,* Vol. II. Greenwich, CT: JAI Press, 1980.

Arend,R, Gove, F., and Sroufe, L.A. Continuity of individual adaptation from infancy to kindergarten: A predictive study of ego-resiliency and curiosity in preschoolers. *Child Development,* 1979, 50, 950-959.

Barton, M., and Schwarz, C. *Day care in the middle-class: Effects in elementary school.* Paper presented at the American Psychological Association Annual Convention, Los Angeles, August 1981.

Belsky, J., and Steinberg, L. The effects of day care: A critical review. *Child Development,* 1978, 49, 929-949.

Belsky, J., Steinberg, L., and Walker, A. The ecology of day care. In M.E. Lamb (Ed.), *Nontraditional families: Parenting and child development.* Hillsdale, NJ: Erlbaum, 1982.

Blanchard, M., and Main, M. Avoidance of the attachment figure and social-emotional adjustment in day care infants. *Developmental Psychology,* 1979, 15, 445-446.

Blehar, M. Anxious attachment and defensive reactions associated with day care. *Child Development,* 1974, 45, 683-692.

Bowlby, J. *Maternal care and mental health.* Geneva, Switzerland: World Health Organization, 1951.

Brookhart, J., and Hock, E. The effects of experimental context and experiential background on infants' behavior toward thier mothers and a stranger. *Child Development,* 1976, 47, 333-340.

Caudell, W., and Weinstein, H. Maternal care and infant behavior in Japan and America. *Psychiatry,* 1969, 12, 32-43.

Clarke-Stewart, A. *Assessing social development.* Paper presented at the Biennial Meeting of the Society for Research in Child Development, San Francisco, March 1979.

Cochran, M. A comparison of group day care and family child-rearing patterns in Sweden. *Child Development,* 1977, 48, 702-707.

Doyle, A. Infant Development in Daycare. *Developmental Psychology,* 1975, 11, 655-656.

Farber, E.A., and Egeland, B. Developmental consequences of out-of-home care for infants in a low-income population. In E. Zigler and E.W. Gordon (Eds.), *Day care: Scientific and social policy issues.* Boston, MA: Auburn House, 1982.

Golden, M. et al. *The New York City Infant Day Care Study: A comparative study of licensed group and family day care programs and the effects of these programs on children and their families.* New York, NY: Medical and Health Research Association of New York City, Inc., 1978.

Gunnarson, L. *Children in day care and family care in Sweden: A follow-up.* Bulletin No. 21, Department of Educational Research, University of Gothenburg, Sweden, 1978.

Kagan, J., Kearsley, R., and Zelazo, P. *Infancy: Its place in human development.* Cambridge, MA: Harvard University Press, 1978.

Lally, R. The family development research program: Progress report. Unpublished paper, Syracuse University, 1973.

Lay, M., and Meyer, W. *Teacher/child behaviors in an open environment day care program.* Syracuse University Children's Center, 1973.

Macrae, J.W., and Herbert-Jackson, E. Are behavioral effects of infant day care programs specific? *Developmental Psychology,* 1975, 12, 269-270.

McCartney, K., Scarr, S., Phillips, D., Grajek, S., and Schwartz, J.C. Environmental differences among day care centers and their effects on children's development. In E. Zigler and E.W. Gordon (Eds.), *Day care: Scientific and social policy issues.* Boston, MA: Auburn House, 1982.

McCutcheon, B., and Calhoun, K. Social and emotional adjustment of infants and toddlers in a day care setting. *American Journal of Orthopsychiatry,* 1976, 46, 104-108.

Moore, T. Children of full-time and part-time mothers. *International Journal of Social Psychiatry,* 1964, 2, 1-10.

Moore, T. Exclusive early mothering and it's alternatives: The outcome of adolescence. *Scandinavian Journal of Psychology,* 1975, 16, 255-272.

Moskowitz, D., Schwarz, J., and Corsini, D. Initiating day care at three years of age: Effects on attachment. *Child Development,* 1977, 48, 1271-1276.

O'Connell, J.C., and Farran, D.C. Effects of day-care experience on the use of intentional communicative behaviors in a sample of socioeconomically depressed infants. Developmental Psychology, 1982, 18, 22-29.

Portnoy, F., and Simmons, C. Day care and attachment. *Child Development,* 1978, 49, 239-242.

Ramey, C.T., and Campbell, F.A. Compensatory education for disadvantaged children. *School Review,* 1979, 87, 171-189. (a)

Ramey, C.T., and Campbell, F.A. Early childhood education for psychosocially disadvantaged children: The effects of psychological processes. *American Journal of Mental Deficiency*, 1979, 83, 645-648. (b)

Ramey, C., Dorval, B., and Baker-Ward, L. Group day care and socially disadvantaged families: Effects on the child and the family. In S. Kilmer (Ed.), *Advances in early education and day care*. Greenwich, CT: JAI Press, 1981.

Raph, J., Thomas, A., Chess, S., and Korn, S. The influence of nursery school on social interaction. *Journal of Orthopsychiatry*, 1964, 38, 144-152.

Ricciuti, H. Fear and development of social attachments in the first year of life. In M. Lewis and L.A. Rosenblum (Eds.), *The origins of human behavior: Fear.* New York, NY: Wiley, 1974.

Robertson, A. Day care and children's responsiveness to adults. In E. Zigler and E. Gordon (Eds.), *Day care: Scientific and social policy issues*. Boston, MA: Auburn House, 1982.

Roopnarine, J., and Lamb, M. The effects of day care on attachment and exploratory behavior in a strange situation. *Merrill-Palmer Quarterly*, 1978, 24, 85-95.

Rubenstein, J.L., Howes, C., and Boyle, P. *A two year follow up of infants in community based infant day care.* Paper presented at the biennial meeting of the Society for Research in Child Development, San Francisco, March 1979.

Schwarz, J.C., Scarr, S.W., Caparulo, B., Furrow, D., McCartney, K., Billington, R., Phillips, D., and Hindy, C. *Center, sitter, and home day care before age two: A report on the first Bermuda infant care study*. Paper presented at the American Psychological Association, Annual convention in Los Angeles, August 1981.

Schwarz, J., Strickland, R., and Krolick, G. Infant day care: Behavioral effects at preschool age. *Developmental Psychology*, 1974, 10, 502-506.

Schwarz, T. Length of Day Care Attendance and Attachment Behavior in 18 month olds. *Child Development*. In Press.

Spitz, R.A. Hospitalism: An inquiry into the genesis of psychiatric conditions in early childhood. *Psychoanalytic Study of the Child,* 1945, 1, 53-74.

Sroufe, L. The coherence of individual development. *American Psychologist*, 1979, 34, 834-841.

Vaughn, B., Deane, K., and Waters, E. *The impact of out-of-home care on child-mother attachment quality: Another look at some enduring questions.* Invited Presentation to the Department of Pediatric Psychology, Rush University Medical School, Chicago, Ill., March 1983.

Vaughn, B., Gove, F., and Egeland, B. The relationship between out-of-home care and the quality of infant-mother attachment in an economically disadvantaged population. *Child Development*, 1980, 51, 1203-1214.

Vliestra, A.G. Full versus half-day preschool attendance: Effects in young children as assessed by teacher ratings and behavioral observations. *Child Development*, 1981, 52, 603-610.

The Skills of Friendship

Zick Rubin

In this reading from his book on Children's Friendships, Rubin provides from his own work and that of others an interesting overview of the skills involved in making and keeping friends. In comparing children who are adept in establishing friendships with those who are not, Rubin makes two important points. The first concerns the complex nature of the social skills that are required to make friends. These skills include a series of tactics that are used to enter into play routines; and ways in which young children, when they recognize that another child is upset, take action to alleviate the problem. The second point Rubin makes is that given the complex nature of these skills, not all children readily use them to maintain friendships. Thus when children enter school, they reveal a range of social abilities. Some will settle securely, while others need help to establish friendships. To illustrate these differences between children, Rubin starts the chapter with reference to two children, Ricky and Danny, mentioned earlier in his book. Ricky makes friends easily, and on entry to school 'quickly proceeded to establish friendly relations with at least ten of the other children in the class'. Danny, on the other hand, has few friends, and '... made periodic attempts to join other children in their activities but with little success'.

I begin with reference to two boys in the same preschool class — Ricky, who made many friends, and Danny, who made none. Ricky's greater ability to make friends could not have been predicted from the two boys' physical or intellectual characteristics. But Ricky had mastered to an impressive degree the social skills needed to establish and maintain friendships. These skills include the abilities to gain entry into group activities, to be approving and supportive of one's peers, to manage conflicts appropriately, and to exercise sensitivity and tact. They are subtle skills, by no means easy to learn, and the fact that most children ultimately succeed in acquiring them is itself one of the most remarkable aspects of social development.

Consider, first, the immedaite problem confronting a child who enters a new group and wants to join other children in their play. During their first few days in a new preschool setting, children frequently avoid their peers and instead hover nervously on the sidelines. (McGrew, 1972; Putallaz and Gottman, 1981). As they become more familiar with their environment, the newcomers may try to approach other children. But these attempts — like Danny's — are not likely to succeed until the child has accumulated a repertoire of tactics for entering groups, complete with implicit rules about how and when a certain ploy can be used most effectively.

William Corsaro offers the following example of the 'access strategies' of four-year-olds in nursery school:

> Two girls, Jenny and Betty, are playing around a sandbox in the outside courtyard of the school. I am sitting on the ground near the sandbox watching. The girls are putting sand in pots, cupcake pans, bottles and teapots ... Another girl, Debbie, approaches and stands near me observing the other two girls. Neither Jenny nor Betty acknowledges her presence. Debbie does not speak to me or the other girls, and no one speaks to her. After watching for some time (five minutes or so) she circles the sandbox three times and stops again and stands near me. After a few more minutes of watching, Debbie moves to the sandbox and reaches for a teapot in the sand. Jenny takes the pot away from Debbie and mumbles, 'No.' Debbie backs away and again stands near me observing the activity of Jenny and Betty. Then she walks over next to Betty, who is filling the cupcake pan with sand. Debbie watches Betty for just a few seconds, then says:
> 'We're friends, right? We're friends, right Betty?'
> Betty, not looking up at Debbie and while continuing to place sand in the pan, says, 'Right.'

'I'm making coffee,' Debbies says to Betty.
'I'm making cupcakes,' Betty replies.
Betty turns to Jenny and says, 'We're mothers, right, Jenny?'
Jenny replies, 'Right.'
The three 'mothers' continue to play together for 20 more minutes,
until the teachers announce cleanup time. (Corsaro, 1979, pp. 320-
321).

Debbie's persistent efforts to join the group illustrates a variety of strategies. At first Debbie merely places herself in the area of the interaction, a strategy that Corsaro calls 'nonverbal entry'. When this tactic gets no response, Debbie proceeds to 'encircle' the area. When this strategy, too, is ignored, she enters the area directly and produces 'similar behaviour' (she picks up a teapot). And when this attempt is rebuffed, Debbie switches to a verbal strategy, making direct 'reference to affiliation' ('We're friends, right?'). After Betty responds positively to this move, Debbie once again produces behaviour similar to that of the others, this time explicitly describing it ('I'm making coffee'). At this point, Debbie's attempt to join the group finally succeeds. Betty responds in a way that includes Debbie in the activity ('We're mothers'), and the three now play together for some time.

Corsaro notes that nursery school children rarely use more direct verbal access strategies, such as saying 'Hi', 'What ya doing?' or 'Can I play?' One likely reason is that such direct approaches call for a direct response by the approached children, and this response is very likely to be negative. Once two or more children have structured and defined for themselves a particular activity, whether it is making cupcakes or blasting off in a spaceship, they often 'protect' their activity by excluding any outsiders who might dare to request entry. Sometimes this exclusive stance is established even before the activity begins. For example:

(David, Josh, and Jonah are in the sandbox together.)
David (to Josh): Will you help me make some soup?
Josh: Yeah- and Jonah can't play, right?

Unless the 'outsider' is already a highly accepted group member who has special rights of entry, young children will frequently refuse him admission. A 'Hi' may be ignored, a 'What ya doing?' responded with 'We're making cupcakes and you're not', and a direct 'Can I play?' answered with an equally direct 'No'. To enter the activity therefore, the child may have to be cautious and subtle, like Debbie. By first reconnoitring the situation unobtrusively, then quietly joining in the ongoing activity and finally making direct verbal statements—including the ingratiating 'We're friends, right?'—Debbie was able to include herself in Betty and Jenny's activity without mobilizing their resistance.

On the other hand, direct approaches may be more effective when the child wants to engage a single other child who is not already involved in a group activity. And as children grow older, specific verbal formulas for initiating interaction become more important. In a study of eight- and nine-year-olds, John Gottman and his co-workers asked children to pretend that the researcher was a new child in the class with whom they wanted to make friends. (Gottman, Gonso and Rasmussen, 1975). From the children's performance in this role-play situation, the researchers were able to assess their knowledge of friendship-making tactics. Offering greetings ('Hi, Mary'), offering appropriate information ('My favourite sport is basketball'), requesting information ('Where do you live?'), and extending invitations ('Wanna come over to my house some time?') were all scored as reflecting the child's knowledge of how to make friends. The researchers then compared these social-knowledge scores with popularity ratings derived from questions asked of all class members. They found, not surprisingly, that popular children knew more about how to make friends than unpopular children did.

'Knowing how' to make friends is no guarantee of social success, however. Some children may excel on a role-play test of social skills but at the same time may be unable or unwilling to put these skills to practical use. For example, an experience with rejection may lead some children to avoid approaching others for long periods of time; other children will bounce back from rejection much more easily. As Carol Dweck and Therese Goetz (1979) suggest, the difference in reactions may depend on the child's personal explanation of a rejection. Some children tend to blame any rejection on their own inadequacies ('I'm just a shy person') and, as a result, do not feel that the problem can be overcome. Other children will attribute the same rejection to temporary moods or misunderstandings ('Maybe her mother yelled at her that morning') and will persist in their efforts to gain acceptance. In the comparison, it is the resilient child who is more likely to establish friendships.

The skills of friendship include not only the ability to gain entry into group activities, but also the ability to *be* a friend—an attentive, approving, and helpful playmate and associate. Even in the first year of life, children have distinctive styles of interaction that can make them agreeable or disagreeable to their peers. Lee C. Lee (1973) observed a daycare group of five infants in Ithaca, New York, for a period of six months, beginning when the infants were all about nine months old. She found that one of the infants, Jenny, was by far the best-liked member of the group; throughout the six-month period, each of the other four babies approached her most often. Patrick was the least-liked group member; he was approached least often by three of the other four infants. On the basis of detailed observations of each baby, Lee was able to paint a picture of their contrasting styles of interaction. Jenny was a responsive, adaptive social partner. She displayed a range of emotion in her social encounters. And she seldom terminated social contracts that had been initiated by others. Patrick, on the other hand, was a belligerent and unfriendly baby. He frequently grabbed others and was reluctant to end encounters that he had initiated. But when others initiated contacts with him, he was passive and unresponsive. Patrick did not smile, laugh, or otherwise display positive feelings in a single one of the occasions in which he was contacted by another baby. To put it bluntly, Patrick was no fun. Not surprisingly, in light of their differing styles of response, Jenny continued to be approached by other babies while Patrick was shunned.

There is no strong reason to believe that such differences in the 'likeability' of infants are likely to persist past the second year in life. As children grow older, however, they become capable of producing a wider range of behaviour that may be either rewarding or unrewarding to their peers. In extensive observations of nursery school children, Willard Hartup and his colleagues at the University of Minnesota (Hartup, Glazer and Charles Worth, 1967) found that the most popular children—those whom their classmates enjoyed playing with most—were also the ones who most often paid attention to other children, praised them, showed affection, and willingly acceded to their requests. Children who frequently ignored others, refused to cooperate, ridiculed, blamed or threatened others were most likely to be disliked by their classmates. In short, for a child to be included and accepted, he must also include and accept.

Again, Ricky epitomizes such an inclusive and accepting child. He is an engaging, supportive boy who goes out of his way to involve others in his activities. When Caleb comes out to the big rotating swing, which already has four children on board, Ricky immediately shouts to him, 'You can get on it!' 'It's crowded,' Caleb shouts back. In Ricky's view of things, however, there is always room for one more. 'Someone else wants to get on,' he informs his fellow riders. Then he takes charge of slowing down the swing and shows Caleb where he can climb on. Ricky is a skilful social facilitator, and others like him for it.

It is important to stress, however, that 'friendly' behaviour does not always win friendship. Whether an affectionate act is in fact experienced as rewarding will depend on *how* the affection is expressed and, most important, how it is interpreted by the recipient. While some children must learn to be more outgoing, others must learn to stop 'coming on too strong'. At the beginning of the year, Fiona would regularly run up to other children and hug them effusively. She discovered, to her dismay, that this display of affection usually frightened off the others. She eventually learned that she could do better by approaching others more subtly—for example, by patting them on the arm and suggesting an activity.

What may be, for one child, a show of friendship is not necessarily viewed that way by another. Even gift giving can backfire, if the recipient attributes ignoble motives to the giver. Ann, who began to interact with other children only late in the school year, gave Craig a paper envelope she had made, as a gesture of friendship.

Later Craig tells me, 'I'm not going to take it home because it doesn't have a drawing.' 'Why do you think Ann gave it to you?' I ask. 'I don't know. Maybe she doesn't like it either.' Moreover, the same overt behaviour can be regarded as rewarding if it comes from a child one already likes and unrewarding if it comes from a child one already has doubts about. 'I'll tell you why I don't like David,' Rachel explains to me. 'Because he screams around all sorts of places. But I don't mind if Steven screams because he just screams a little bit.'

Studies of nursery school children have also indicated that the best-liked children are not highly dependent on teachers (Moore, 1967). Ricky often chatted amiably with teachers and generally followed their instructions, but only rarely went to a teacher for help in dealing with routine matters. Danny, in contrast, frequently called for help in a whiny tone of voice and would cry for the teacher whenever he received a minor injury or rebuff. Ricky's lesser dependence on teachers was almost certainly related to his greater ability to be supportive of his classmates. When a child must constantly turn to adults for support and assistance, he is unlikely to have the emotional resources necessary to be rewarding to his peers.

The skills of friendship also include the ability to manage conflicts successfully. Children learn that it is often valuable to talk out their hurt feelings in order to restore good will. While playing fireman, for example, John and Tony managed to offend each other. After a period of sullen silence, the following conversation ensued:

> *Josh:* I'm not going to be your friend, Tony. You're talking mean to me so I'm not going to be your friend.
> *Tony:* You're talking mean to me.
> *Josh:* You're calling me names—Bloody Boy, Fire Boy.
> *Tony:* Well, you're not letting me and David play by ourselves.

Once they put these feelings on the table, Josh and Tony quickly restored harmony. 'I can be a fireboy in the fireman game,' Josh declares. 'Let him spray out fires,' Tony orders his other fireman.

In order to maintain friendships in the face of the disagreements that inevitably arise, children must learn to express their own rights and feelings clearly while remaining sensitive to the rights and feelings of others. They must be able to suggest and to accept reasonable compromises, even as they stand up against unreasonable demands. As S. Holly Stocking and Diana Arezzo (1979) note, different children may start in different places in the quest for the ability to manage conflict appropriately:

> The overly aggressive child ... may need to learn how to listen to others without interrupting or putting them down, and how to accept reasonable disagreement gracefully, without anger or attack. The

overly submissive child, in turn, may have to learn to stand up for himself with a definite posture and a calm tone of voice that communicates conviction.

As children become more sensitive to the feelings of their peers, they also learn the subtle skills of tact that are needed to maintain friendships. Even four-year-olds may begin to display such tact, especially in the context of close friendships. When Tony took his pants off to go swimming, for example, his best friend David inadvertently burst into laughter. But a moment later, David turned to Tony and assured him, 'I'm not laughing at you, Tony. I'm laughing at Neil.' Although this explanation may have involved a white lie on David's part, it also illustrates his sensitivity to his friend's feelings and his ability to act in such a way as to protect them.

I observed a particularly striking example of tact among four-year-olds in the following conversation between David and Josh, who were walking together and pretending to be robots:

> *David:* I'm a missile robot who can shoot missiles out of my fingers.
> I can shoot them out of everywhere - even out of my legs. I'm a missile robot.
> *Josh* (tautingly): No, you're a fart robot.
> *David* (protestingly): No, I'm a missile robot.
> *Josh:* No, you're a fart robot.
> *David* (hurt, almost in tears): No, Josh!
> *Josh* (recognizing that David is upset): And I'm a poo-poo robot.
> *David* (in good spirits again): I'm a pee-pee robot.

As in the case of the interaction between David and Tony, Josh realized that he had said something ('you're a fart robot') that greatly distressed his friend. He handled the situation resourcefully by putting himself down as well ('I'm a poo-poo robot'), thus demonstrating that his insult was not to be taken seriously. David's response to Josh's move ('I'm a pee-pee robot') indicates that Josh had appraised the situation accurately and had successfully saved his friend's feelings.

Acquiring the skills of friendship can be a difficult struggle for the preschool child, especially if he has not had much previous experience in interacting with other children of his own age without direct adult supervision. Nursery schools often serve as valuable proving grounds for the development of such skills. Although the learning may sometimes be painful or frustrating, children gradually develop both more sophisticated concepts of friendship and more sophisticated techniques for establishing and maintaining such friendships for themselves. The development of communication skills through interaction with one's peers may itself be an important pre-requisite for the acquisition of skills specifically related to friendship. In this connection, Danny, who had doting parents but little experience with children of his own age before entering nursery school, probably suffered in his attempt at making friends because of his relatively undeveloped powers of communication. Ricky, in contrast, lived in the same household as several cousins of varying ages and had developed communications skills of an unusually high order. With additional experience, as it turned out, Danny, too, became more successful at making friends. When I revisited him a year after I had concluded my observations of the class, I found that he was interacting much more successfully and was sought out by several of his classmates.

Children, then, acquire social skills not so much from adults as from their interaction with one another. They are likely to discover through trial and error which strategies work and which do not, and later to reflect consciously on what they have learned. While playing with blocks one day, a four-year-old Alec remarked to his teacher 'Remember that day when I gave Colin a truck he needed? That was a very nice thing to do, don't you think, Miss Beyer?' (Beyer, 1956, p. 347). Children also learn social skills from the direct tutelage or examples provided by their peers. When David whines, 'Gary pushed me,' for example, Josh firmly advises him, 'Just say stop.' In other instances, children introduce their friends to one another, help others to launch joining activities, or show others how to resolve their conflicts. Rachel is one child who is successful, in her own soft-spoken way, in promoting good feeling among other children. For example, she serves as timekeeper while several other children take turns standing in a special hiding place. When Claudia occupies the space before it is her turn, Rachel calls her back to the table where the timekeeper's hourglass is kept and gently explains, 'Here, Claudia - when it goes all the way through there it's your turn, all right?' When all the sand has trickled through, Rachel happily informs Claudia that her turn has come, and lets Alison know that her time has run out. One suspects that such advice and assistance from respected peers may often be more effective than similar interventions by teachers or parents.

There are also cases, however, when children need help from adults in mastering particular skills of friendship. When children wish to make friends but lack the skills to do so, vicious circles can be set in motion. The friendless child must interact with his peers in order to develop the self-confidence and skills needed for social success. But the lack of social skills—for example, the inability to approach other children or the tendency to scare them off—may cut him off from just such opportunities. In such cases, intervention by paretns or teachers may be necessary. One approach is to steer a friendless child to a particular other child—sometimes one who also lacks friends - with whom the adult thinks the child might hit it off. In at least some cases, such matchmaking can help to give two withdrawn children an initial and valuable experience of social acceptance. Another tactic is to pair an older child who is too competitive or aggressive with a younger child to whom he can relate as a 'big brother' - and, in the process, learn that he can win the approval of others without being a bully (Furman, Rahe and Hartup, 1979).

Psychologists have also developed a variety of training programmes for both pre-school and school-age children. In such programmes, children who have been identified as isolates or outcasts are given a series of sessions which may include demonstrations of specific social skills, opportunities to practise them, and feedback on their performance. In at least some cases, these programmes have been notably successful in increasing the social acceptance of initially isolated children. (For a review of such programmes see Combs and Slaby, 1977, and Oden and Asher, 1977.

Because training programmes tend to be focused on increasing 'social acceptance' or 'popularity', they bring up some troublesome questions of values. Do the programmes really help children develop the capacity for friendship, or are they geared to some 'American' ideal of glib sociability and congeniality that has little to do with real friendship at all? The answer to this question depends both on the details of the programme and on the values of the adults who administer it. In the view of at least some leading practitioners, however, 'The objective of social skills instruction is not to create "popular" or "outgoing" children, but to help youngsters, whatever their personality styles, to develop positive relationships ... with at least one or two other children.' (Stocking and Arezzo, 1979). One can also ask whether it is ethically acceptable to impose social skills training on children who have little choice in the matter and who in some instances may not really want to be changed into 'friendlier' people. In the last analysis, though, the most compelling defence for such programmes is that they may be able to increase the child's degree of control over her own life. As Melinda Combs and Diana Arezzo Slaby note, 'A child who has the skills to initiate play and communicate with peers may still choose to spend a good deal of time alone. But that child will be able to interact effectively when she (he) wants to or when the situation requires it. On the other hand, a socially unskilled child may be alone or 'isolated' out of necessity rather than by choice (Combs and Slaby, 1977, p. 165).

Even without instituting formal training, parents and teachers can make use of similar demonstrations, explanations, and feedback, in order to teach the skills of freindship in school or home settings. In making use of such procedures, however, adults must be sensitive to the fine line that exists between help and interference. Although adults have a role to play in teaching social skills to children, it is often best that they play it unobtrusively. In particular, adults must guard against embarrassing unskilled children by correcting them too publicly and against labelling children as shy in ways that may lead to children to see themselves in just that way (Zimbardo, 1977).

Rather than 'pushing' social skills indiscriminately, adults should respect the real differences between children that motivate some to establish friendly relations with many others, some to concentrate on one or two close friendships, and some to spend a good deal of time by themselves. Children's friendships take many forms and involve different styles of interaction. In our efforts to help children make friends, we should be more concerned with the quality of these friendships than with their quantity.

Adults must also recognize that there are many personal attributes, some of them relatively immutable, which are likely to affect the way a child is viewed by his peers in a particular setting, including physical appearance, athletic prowess, intellectual abilities, and family background (see for example Dion and Berscheid, 1974; McCraw and Tolbert, 1953; and Asher, Oden and Gottman, 1977). As a result, different children may be best equipped with somewhat different skills of friendship. Finally, adults must be sensitive to events in children's lives that may underlie problems with making and keeping friends. Moving to a new school or neighbourhood may create special difficulties, and so may stressful family events such as divorce (Hetherington, Cox and Cox, 1979). For the most part, as we have seen, children learn the skills of friendship not from adults but from each other. But parents and teachers who are sensitive to individual children's distinctive needs and circumstances can play a crucial role in facilitating this learning.

Section 5

Social Development: Aggression, Altruism, Moral Development, and Sex Differences

The previous section on social development contained papers that addressed the questions and issues of how family and peer relationships can shape and influence children's social behavior: it was a chapter about the *agents* of socialization. This section is devoted to research on the *outcomes* or *results* of socialization. When we are children, the other people in our lives explicitly and implicitly teach us the lessons of our culture and our society. Although democratic societies such as ours allow flexibility in lifestyle and freedom of expression, and permit individual differences in the goals and values that families set for their children, there are also common goals and concerns that many members of society seem to share. Some of these are the subject of the readings selected for this section.

One of the most prominent outcomes of socialization is the acquisition of sex role behavior. These are the attributes and behaviors that are perceived to be characteristic of us because we are male or female. Although researchers have found that there are in fact more similarities than differences between the sexes, there are certain behaviors that seem to consistently differentiate between males and females. For example, males are generally more aggressive than females, and females are generally more nurturant toward small children than males are. However, researchers have also found that there is overlap in the expression of these traits. There are aggressive women and nurturant men. Sex differences in behavior have received much attention, as scientists have tried not only to establish whether there are genuine sex differences in behavior, but also if any such differences are due to the biological differences between males and females or to patterns of socialization.

Two of the papers in this section address the question of sex differences. Doreen Kimura looks at a well documented sex-difference, the tendency of males to perform relatively better on spatial skill tasks than verbal tasks, and of females to show the opposite pattern. She discusses the evidence that these and other differences may exist at least in part because of fundamental differences in the way male and female brains are structured, perhaps from before birth. A different perspective is suggested by Beverly Fagot, who examines the role that reinforcement and observational learning play in the establishment of sex role behaviors in preschool children.

Aggression is a pervasive characteristic of human interaction and a phenomenon that has intrigued historians, scientists and writers for generations. To explain the origin and development of "man's inhumanity to man" has been an enduring challenge. The first paper in this section is a classic work by Albert Bandura. He demonstrated how readily children acquire aggressive responses that they see preformed by a filmed model. He also showed that while all of the children learned the model's aggressive behavior, imitation of the behavior depended on whether they saw the model rewarded or punished for the aggression. Bandura's work stimulated further research on observational learning and imitation, and has had important implications for the debate over whether or not viewing violence on television contributes significantly to children's aggressive behavior in the real world. Leonard Eron's paper is a report of his work on some of the factors that he and his colleagues have found enable us to predict aggressive behavior in children. Consistent with Bandura's results, he has found a significant positive correlation between the amount of violence that children watch on television and their overt aggression. However, he has also found that other variables, such as having had punitive and rejecting parents, also contribute to overt aggression. Kenneth Dodge presents a social cognitive analysis of aggressive behavior which focuses on the way that boys interpret ambiguously motivated interpersonal conflicts with peers. He found that highly aggressive boys are more likely to interpret and react to these ambiguous situations aggressively than are non-aggressive boys. Dodge discusses these differences in terms of cue distortion deficiencies in cue-utilization.

All human societies share a belief that certain behaviors are "good" and morally correct and that other behaviors are "bad" and morally reprehensible. While the specific acts that fall into these categories are defined differently in different cultures and social groups, rewarding what is good and punishing what is bad are generally believed to be necessary for the maintenance of social order. We try to teach our moral values to our children, who comply initially to gain approval or to avoid disapproval. However, as they mature, they adopt and try to live by moral values because they are seen to be the "right thing to do". The process by which children develop this internalization of moral thought, feeling and behavior is the subject of the paper by Martin Hoffman. He reviews important literature on these questions. Sharon Nelson reports on the way in which young children learn to evaluate the relative importance of the consequences of an act and the intention of the actor in judging good and bad. She found that 3-year-olds have some ability to evaluate these variables correctly in simple, familiar situations.

Prosocial behavior and altruism are important goals of the socialization of children, and are an integral part of the moral and ethical values that parents teach their young. The paper by Terry Orlick describes his work on the facilitative effects of a cooperative games program on subsequent sharing and happiness in 5-year-old children. Finally, the paper by Philippe Rushton is a review of some of the literature on the potential of television to affect the development of characteristics such as altruism, friendliness, and self-control. While most of the studies on the impact of television as a socializer have focused on the effects of aggressive programming on children's behavior, this review looks at the potential of the medium for the development of positive and adaptive behavior

Influence of Models' Reinforcement Contingencies
on the Acquisition of Imitative Responses

Albert Bandura

In order to test the hypothesis that reinforcements administered to a model influence the performance but not the acquisition of matching responses, groups of children observed an aggressive film-mediated model either rewarded, punished, or left without consequences. A postexposure test revealed that response consequences to the model had produced differential amounts of imitative behavior. Children in the model-punished condition performed significantly fewer matching responses than children in both the model-rewarded and the no-consequences groups. Children in all 3 treatment conditions were then offered attractive reinforcers contingent on their reproducing the model's aggressive responses. The introduction of positive incentives completely wiped out the previously observed performance differences, revealing an equivalent amount of learning among children

Originally published in the *Journal of Personality and Social Psychology*, 1965, 1, 589-595. Copyright ©1965 by the American Psychological Association. Reprinted by permission of the publisher and author.

in the model-rewarded, model-punished, and the no-consequences conditions.

It is widely assumed that the occurrence of imitative or observational learning is contingent on the administration of reinforcing stimuli either to the model or to the observer. According to the theory propounded by Miller and Dollard (1941), for example, the necessary conditions for learning through imitation include a motivated subject who is positively reinforced for matching the rewarded behavior of a model during a series of initially random, trial-and-error responses. Since this conceptualization of observational learning requires the subject to perform the imitative response before he can learn it, this theory evidently accounts more adequately for the emission of previously learned matching responses, than for their acquisition.

Mowrer's (1960) proprioceptive feedback theory similarly highlights the role of reinforcement but, unlike Miller and Dollard who reduce imitation to a special case of instrumental learning, Mowrer focuses on the classical conditioning of positive and negative emotions to matching response-correlated stimuli. Mowrer distinguishes two forms of imitative learning in terms of whether the observer is reinforced directly or vicariously. In the former case the model performs a response and simultaneously rewards the observer. If the modeled responses are thus paired repeatedly with positive reinforcement they gradually acquire secondary reward value. The observer can then administer positively conditioned reinforcers to himself simply by reproducing as closely as possible the model's positively valenced behavior. In the second, or empathetic form of imitative learning, the model not only exhibits the responses but also experiences the reinforcing consequences. It is assumed that the observer, in turn, experiences empathetically both the response-correlated stimuli and the response consequences of the model's behavior. As a result of this higher-order vicarious conditioning, the observer will be inclined to reproduce the matching responses.

There is some recent evidence that imitative behavior can be enhanced by noncontingent social reinforcement from a model (Bandura & Huston, 1961), by response-contingent reinforcers administered to the model (Bandura, Ross & Ross, 1963b; Walters, Leat, & Mezei, 1963), and by increasing the reinforcing value of matching responses *per se* through direct reinforcement of the participant observer (Baer & Sherman, 1964). Nevertheless, reinforcement theories of imitation fail to explain the learning of matching responses when the observer does not perform the model's responses during the process of acquisition, and for which reinforcers are not delivered either to the model or to the observers (Bandura et al., 1961, 1963a).

The acquisition of imitative responses under the latter conditions appears to be accounted for more adequately by a contiguity theory of observational learning. According to the latter conceptualization (Bandura, in press; Sheffield, 1961), when an observer witnesses a model exhibit a sequence of responses the observer acquires, through contiguous association of sensory events, perceptual and symbolic responses possessing cue properties that are capable of eliciting, at some time after a demonstration, overt responses corresponding to those that had been modeled.

Some suggestive evidence that the *acquisition* of matching responses may take place through contiguity, whereas reinforcements administered to a model exert their major influence on the *performance* of imitatively learned responses, is provided in a study in which models were rewarded or punished for exhibiting aggressive behavior (Bandura et al., 1963b). Although children who had observed aggressive responses rewarded subsequently reproduced the model's behavior while children in the model-punished condition failed to do so, a number of the subjects in the latter group described in postexperimental interviews the model's repertoire of aggressive responses with considerable accuracy. Evidently they had learned the cognitive equivalents of the model's responses but they were not translated into their motoric forms. These findings highlighted both the importance of distinguishing between learning and performance and the need for a systematic study of whether reinforcement is primarily a learning-related or a performance-related variable.

In the present experiment children observed a film-mediated model who exhibited novel physical and verbal aggressive responses. In one treatment condition the model was severely punished; in a second, the model was generously rewarded; while the third condition presented no response consequences to the model. Following a post-exposure test of imitative behavior, children in all three groups were offered attractive incentives contingent on their reproducing the models' responses so as to provide a more accurate index of learning. It was predicted that reinforcing consequences to the model would result in significant differences in the performance of imitative behavior with the model-rewarded group displaying the highest number of different classes of matching responses, followed by the no-consequences and the model-punished groups, respectively. In accordance with previous findings (Bandura et al., 1961, 1963a) it was also expected that boys would perform significantly more imitative aggression than girls. It was predicted, however, that the introduction of positive incentives would wipe out both reinforcement-produced and sex-linked performance differences, revealing an equivalent amount of learning among children in the three treatment conditions.

METHOD

Subjects

The subjects were 33 boys and 33 girls enrolled in the Stanford University Nursery School. They ranged in age from 42 to 71 months, with a mean age of 51 months. The children were assigned randomly to one of three treatment conditions of 11 boys and 11 girls each.

Two adult males served in the role of models, and one female experimenter conducted the study for all 66 children.

Exposure Procedure

The children were brought individually to a semi-darkened room. The experimenter informed the child that she had some business to attend to before they could proceed to the "surprise playroom," but that during the waiting period the child might watch a televised program. After the child was seated, the experimenter walked over to the television console, ostensibly tuned in a program and then departed. A film of approximately 5 minutes duration depicting the modeled responses was shown on a glass lenscreen in the television console by means of a rear projection arrangement, screened from the child's view by large panels. The televised form of presentation was utilized primarily because attending responses to televised stimuli are strongly conditioned in children and this procedure would therefore serve to enhance observation which is a necessary condition for the occurrence of imitative learning.

The film began with a scene in which the model walked up to an adult-size plastic Bobo doll and ordered him to clear the way. After glaring for a moment at the non-compliant antagonist the model exhibited four novel aggressive responses each accompanied by a distinctive verbalization.

First, the model laid the Bobo doll on its side, sat on it, and punched it in the nose while remarking, "Pow, right in the nose, boom, boom." The model then raised the doll and pommeled it on the head with a mallet. Each response was accompanied by the verbalization, "Sockeroo ... stay down." Following the mallet aggression, the model kicked the doll about the room, and these responses were interspersed with the comment, "Fly away." Finally, the model threw rubber balls at the Bobo doll, each strike punctuated with "Bang." This sequence of physically and verbally aggressive behavior was repeated twice.

The component responses that enter into the development of more complex novel patterns of behavior are usually present in children's behavioral repertoires as products either of maturation or of prior social learning. Thus, while most of the elements in the modeled acts had undoubtedly been previously learned, the particular pattern of components in each response, and their evocation by specific stimulus objects, were relatively unique. For example, children can manipulate objects, sit on them, punch them, and they can make vocal responses but the likelihood that a given child would spontaneously place a Bobo doll on its side, sit on it, punch it in the nose and remark, "Pow ... boom, boom," is exceedingly remote. Indeed, a previous study utilizing the same stimulus objects has shown that the imitative responses selected for the present experiment have virtually a zero probability of occurring spontaneously among preschool children (Bandura et al., 1961) and, therefore, meet the criterion of novel responses.

The rewarding and punishing contingencies associated with the model's aggressive responses were introduced in the closing scene of the film.

For children in the model-rewarded condition, a second adult appeared with an abundant supply of candies and soft drinks. He informed the model that he was a "strong champion" and that his superb aggressive performance clearly deserved a generous treat. He then poured him a large glass of 7-Up, and readily supplied additional energy-building nourishment including chocolate bars, Cracker Jack popcorn, and an assortment of candies. While the model was rapidly consuming the delectable treats, his admirer symbolically reinstated the modeled aggressive responses and engaged in considerable positive social reinforcement.

For children in the model-punished condition, the reinforcing agent appeared on the scene shaking his finger menacingly and commenting reprovingly, "Hey there, you big bully. You quit picking on that clown. I won't tolerate it." As the model drew back he tripped and fell, the other adult sat on the model and spanked him with a rolled-up magazine while reminding him of his aggressive behavior. As the model ran off cowering, the agent forewarned him, "If I catch you doing that again, you big bully, I'll give you a hard spanking. You quit acting that way."

Children in the no-consequences condition viewed the same film as shown to the other two groups except that no reinforcement ending was included.

Performance Measure

Immediately following the exposure session the children were escorted to an experimental room that contained a Bobo doll, three balls, a mallet and pegboard, dart guns, plastic farm animals, and a doll house equipped with furniture and a doll family. By providing a variety of stimulus objects the children were at liberty to exhibit imitative responses or to engage in nonimitative forms of behavior.

After the experimenter instructed the child that he was free to play with the toys in the room, she excused herself supposedly to fetch additional play materials. Since many preschool children are reluctant to remain alone and tend to leave after a short period of time, the experimenter reentered the room midway through the session and reassured the child that she would return shortly with the goods.

Each child spent 10 minutes in the test room during which time his behavior was recorded every 5 seconds in terms of predetermined imitative response categories by judges who observed the session through a one-way mirror in an adjoining observation room.

Two observers shared the task of recording the occurrence of matching responses for all 66 children. Neither the raters had knowledge of the treatment conditions to which the children were assigned. In order to provide an estimate of interscorer reliability, the responses of 10 children were scored independently by both observers. Since the imitative responses were highly distinctive and required no subjective interpretation, the raters were virtually in perfect agreement (99%) in scoring the matching responses.

The number of different physical and verbal imitative responses emitted spontaneously by the children constituted the performance measure.

Acquisition Index

At the end of the performance session the experimenter entered the room with an assortment of fruit juices in a colorful juice-dispensing fountain, and booklets of sticker-pictures that were employed as the positive incentives to activate into performance what the children had learned through observation.

After a brief juice treat the children were informed that for each physical or verbal imitative response that they reproduced, they would receive a pretty sticker-picture and additional juice treats. An achievement incentive was also introduced in order to produce further disinhibition and to increase the children's motivation to exhibit matching responses. The experimenter attached a pastoral scene to the wall and expressed an interest in seeing how many sticker-pictures the child would be able to obtain to adorn his picture.

The experimenter then asked the child, "Show me what Rocky did in the TV program," "Tell me what he said," and rewarded him immediately following each matching response. If a child simply described an imitative response he was asked to give a performance demonstration.

Although learning must be inferred from performance, it was assumed that the number of different physical and verbal imitative responses reproduced by the children under the positive-incentive conditions would serve as a relatively accurate index of learning.

RESULTS

Figure 1 shows the mean number of different matching responses reproduced by children in each of the three treatment conditions during the no-incentive and the positive-incentive phases of the experiment. A square-root transformation ($y = \sqrt{f + 1/2}$) was applied to these data to make them amenable to parametric statistical analyses.

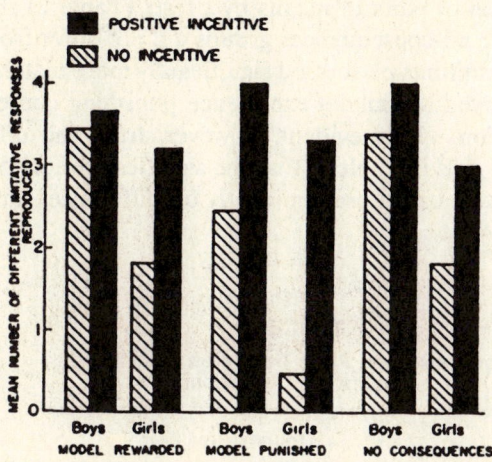

Fig. 1. Mean number of different matching responses reproduced by children as a function of positive incentives and the model's reinforcement contingencies.

TABLE 1
ANALYSIS OF VARIANCE OF IMITATIVE PERFORMANCE SCORES

Source	df	MS	F
Treatments (T)	2	1.21	3.27*
Sex (S)	1	4.87	13.16**
T × S	2	.12	<1
Within groups	60	.37	

* $p < .05$.
** $p < .001$.

Performance Differences

A summary of the analysis of variance based on the performance scores is presented in Table 1. The findings reveal that reinforcing consequences to the model had a significant effect on the number of matching responses that the children spontaneously reproduced. The main effect of sex is also highly significant, confirming the prediction that boys would perform more imitative responses than girls.

Further comparisons of pairs of means by t tests (Table 2) show that while the model-rewarded and the no-consequences groups did not differ from each other, subjects in both of these conditions performed significantly more matching responses than children who had observed the model experience punishing consequences following the display of aggression. It is evident, however, from the differences reported separately for boys and girls in Table 2, that the significant effect of the model's reinforcement contingencies is based predominantly on differences among the girls' subgroups.

TABLE 2

COMPARISON OF PAIRS OF MEANS BETWEEN
TREATMENT CONDITIONS

Performance measure	Treatment conditions		
	Reward versus punishment *t*	Reward versus no consequences *t*	Punishment versus no consequences *t*
Total sample	2.20**	0.55	2.25**
Boys	1.05	0.19	1.24
Girls	2.13**	0.12	2.02*

* $p < .05$.
** $p < .025$.

Differences in Acquisition

An analysis of variance of the imitative learning scores is summarized in Table 3. The introduction of positive incentives completely wiped out the previously observed performance differences, revealing an equivalent amount of imitative learning among the children in the model-rewarded, model-punished, and the no-consequences treatment groups. Although the initially large sex difference was substantially reduced in the positive-incentive condition, the girls nevertheless still displayed fewer matching responses than the boys.

Acquisition-Performance Differences

In order to elucidate further the influence of direct and vicariously experienced reinforcement on imitation, the differences in matching responses displayed under nonreward and positive-incentive conditions for each of the three experimental treatments were evaluated by the t-test procedure for correlated means. Table 4 shows that boys who witnessed the model either rewarded or left without consequences per-

TABLE 3

ANALYSIS OF VARIANCE OF IMITATIVE LEARNING SCORES

Source	df	MS	F
Treatments (T)	2	0.02	<1
Sex (S)	1	0.56	6.22*
T × S	2	0.02	<1
Within groups	60	0.09	

* $p < .05$.

formed all of the imitative responses that they had learned through observation and no new matching responses emerged when positive reinforcers were made available. On the other hand, boys who had observed the model punished and girls in all three treatment conditions showed significant increments in imitative behavior when response-contingent reinforcement was later introduced.

TABLE 4

SIGNIFICANCE OF THE ACQUISITION-PERFORMANCE DIFFERENCES IN IMITATIVE RESPONSES

Group	Treatment conditions		
	Reward *t*	Punishment *t*	No consequences *t*
Total sample	2.38*	5.00***	2.67**
Boys	0.74	2.26*	1.54
Girls	3.33**	5.65***	2.18*

* $p < .025$.
** $p < .01$.
*** $p < .001$.

DISCUSSION

The results of the present experiment lend support to a contiguity theory of imitative learning; reinforcements administered to the model influenced the observers' performance but not the acquisition of matching responses.

It is evident from the findings, however, that mere exposure to modeling stimuli does not provide the sufficient conditions for imitative or observational learning. The fact that most of the children in the experiment failed to reproduce the entire repertoire of behavior exhibited by the model, even under positive-incentive conditions designed to disinhibit and to elicit matching responses, indicates that factors other than mere contiguity of sensory stimulation undoubtedly influence imitative response acquisition.

Exposing a person to a complex sequence of stimulation is no guarantee that he will attend to the entire range of cues, that he will necessarily select from a total stimulus complex only the most relevant sitmuli, or that he will even perceive accurately the cues to which his attention is directed. Motivational variables, prior training in discriminative observation, and the anticipation of positive or negative reinforcements contingent on the emission of matching responses may be highly influential in channeling, augmenting, or reducing observing responses, which is a necessary precondition for imitative learning (Bandura, 1962; Bandura & Walters, 1963). Procedures that increase the distinctiveness of the relevant modeling stimuli also greatly facilitate observational learning (Sheffield & Maccoby, 1961).

In addition to attention-directing variables, the rate, amount, and complexity of stimuli presented to the observer may partly determine the degree of imitative learning. The acquisition of matching responses through observation of a lengthy uninterrupted sequence of behavior is also likely to be governed by principles of associate learning such as frequency and recency, serial order effects, and other multiple sources of associative interference (McGuire, 1961).

Social responses are generally composed of a large number of different behavioral units combined in a particular manner. Responses of high-order complexity are produced by combinations of previously learned components which may, in themselves, represent relatively complicated behavioral patterns. Consequently, the rate of acquisition of intricate matching responses through observation will be largely determined by the extent to which the necessary components are contained in the observer's repertoire. A person who possesses a very narrow repertoire of behavior, for example, will, in all probability, display only fragmentary imitation of a model's behavior; on the other hand, a person who has acquired most of the relevant components is likely to perform precisely matching responses following several demonstrations. In the case of young preschool children their motor repertoires are more highly developed than their repertoires of verbal responses. It is, perhaps, for this reason that even in the positive-incentive condition, children reproduced a substantially higher percentage (67%) of imitative motor responses than matching verbalizations (20%). A similar pattern of differential imitation was obtained in a previous experiment (Bandura & Huston, 1961) in which preschool children served as subjects.

It is apparent from the foregoing discussion that considerably more research is needed in identifying variables that combine with contiguous stimulation in governing the process of imitative response acquisition.

It is possible, of course, to interpret the present acquisition data as reflecting the operation of generalization from a prior history of reinforcement of imitative behavior. Within any social group, models typically exhibit the accumulated cultural repertoires that have proved most successful for given stimulus situations; consequently, matching the behavior of other persons, particularly the superiors in an age-grade or prestige hierarchy, will maximize positive reinforcement and minimize the frequency of aversive response consequences. Since both the occurrence and the positive reinforcement of matching responses, whether by accident or by intent, are inevitable during the course of social development, no definitive resolution of the reinforcement issue is possible, except through an experiment utilizing organisms that have experienced complete social isolation from birth. It is evident, however, that contemporaneous reinforcements are unnecessary for the acquisition of new matching responses.

The finding that boys perform more imitative aggression than girls as a result of exposure to an aggressive male model, is in accord with results from related experiments (Bandura et al., 1961, 1963a). The additional finding, however, that the introduction of positive incentives practically wiped out the prior performance disparity strongly suggests that the frequently observed sex differences in aggression (Goodenough, 1931; Johnson, 1951; Sears, 1951) may reflect primarily differences in willingness to exhibit aggressive responses, rather than deficits in learning or "masculine-role identification."

The subgroups of children who displayed significant increments in imitative behavior as a function of positive reinforcement were boys who had observed the aggressive model punished, and girls for whom physically aggressive behavior is typically labeled sex inappropriate and nonrewarded or even negatively reinforced. The inhibitory effects of differing reinforcement histories for aggression were clearly reflected in the observation that boys were more easily disinhibited than girls in the reward phase of the experiment. This factor may account for the small sex difference that was obtained even in the positive-incentive condition.

The present study provides further evidence that response inhibition and response disinhibition can be vicariously transmitted through observation of reinforcing consequences to a model's behavior. It is interesting to note, however, that the performance by a model of socially disapproved or prohibited responses (for example, kicking, striking with objects) without the occurrence of any aversive consequences may produce disinhibitory effects analogous to a positive reinforcement operation. These findings are similar to results from studies of direct reinforcement (Crandall, Good, & Crandall, 1964) in which nonreward functioned as a positive reinforcer to increase the probability of the occurrence of formerly punished responses.

Punishment administered to the model apparently further reinforced the girls' existing inhibitions over aggression and produced remarkably little imitative behavior;

the boys displayed a similar, though not significant, decrease in imitation. This difference may be partly a function of the relative dominance of aggressive responses in the repertoires of boys and girls. It is also possible that vicarious reinforcement for boys, deriving from the model's successful execution of aggressive behavior (that is, overpowering the noncompliant adversary), may have reduced the effects of externally administered terminal punishment. These factors, as well as the model's self-rewarding and self-punishing reactions following the display of aggression, will be investigated in a subsequent experiment.

REFERENCES

Baer, D.M., & Sherman, J.A. Reinforcement control of generalized imitation in young children. *Journal of Experimental Child Psychology*, 1964, 1, 37-40.

Bandura, A. Social learning through imitation. In M.R. Jones (Ed.), *Nebraska symposium on motivation: 1962.* Lincoln: University Nebraska Press, 1962. Pp. 211-269.

Bandura, A. Vicarious processes: A case of no-trial learning. In L. Berkowitz (Ed.), *Advances in experimental social psychology*. Vol. 2. New York: Academic Press, 1965, in press.

Bandura, A., & Huston, Aletha C. Identification as a process of incidental learning. *Journal of Abnormal and Social Psychology*, 1961, 63, 311-318.

Bandura, A., Ross, Dorothea, & Ross, Sheila A. Transmission of aggression through imitation of aggressive models. *Journal of Abnormal and Social Psychology,* 1961, 63, 575-582.

Bandura, A., Ross, Dorothea, & Ross, Sheila A. Imitation of film-mediated aggressive models. *Journal of Abnormal and Social Psychology*, 1963, 66, 3-11. (a)

Bandura, A., Ross, Dorothea, & Ross, Sheila A. Vicarious reinforcement and imitative learning. *Journal of Abnormal and Social Psychology*, 1963, 67, 601-607. (b)

Bandura, A., & Walters, R.H. *Social learning and personality development*. New York: Holt, Rinehart, & Winston, 1963.

Crandall, Virginia C., Good, Suzanne, & Crandall, V.J. The reinforcement effects of adult reactions and non-reactions on children's achievement expectations: A replication study. *Child Development*, 1964, 35, 385-397.

Goodenough, Florence L. *Anger in young children*. Minneapolis: University Minnesota Press, 1931.

Johnson, Elizabeth Z. Attitudes of children toward authority as projected in their doll play at two levels. Unpublished doctoral dissertation, Harvard University, 1951.

McGuire, W.J. Interpolated motivational statements within a programmed series of instructions as a distribution of practice factor. In A. A. Lumsdaine (Ed.), *Student response in programmed instruction: A symposium*. Washington, D.C.: National Academy of Sciences, National Research Council, 1961. Pp. 411-415.

Miller, N.E., & Dollard, J. *Social learning and imitation*. New Haven: Yale University Press, 1941.

Mowrer, O.H. *Learning theory and the symbolic processes*. New York: Wiley, 1960.

Sears, Pauline S. Doll play aggression in normal young children: Influence of sex, age, sibling status, father's absence. *Psychological Monographs,* 1951, 65(6, Whole No. 323).

Sheffield, F.D. Theoretical considerations in the learning of complex sequential tasks from demonstration and practice. In A.A. Lumsdaine (Ed.), *Student response in programmed instructions: A symposium*. Washington, D.C.: National Academcy of Sciences, National Research Council, 1961. Pp. 13-32.

Sheffield, F.D., & Maccoby, N. Summary and interpretation on research on organizational principles in constructing filmed demonstrations. In A.A. Lumsdaine (Ed.), *Student response in programmed instruction: A symposium*. Washington, D.C.: National Academy of Sciences, National Research Council, 1961. Pp. 117-131.

Walters, R.H., Leat, Marion, & Mezei, L. Inhibition and disinhibition of responses through empathetic learning. *Canadian Journal of Psychology,* 1963, 17, 235-243.

Social Cognition and Children's Aggressive Behavior

Kenneth A. Dodge

The application of concepts from the literature on the development of social cognition to the problem of inappropriate and persistent aggression among certain children provides the basis for two connected studies constituting this investigation. These studies deal specifically with children's defensive aggression, that is, aggression which is a hostile and assertive response to perceived threat or intentional frustration. Defensive aggression is differentiated from instrumental aggression, which is injurious behavior intended to gain an independent reward and which may be altered by the appropriate manipulation of reward and punishment (Hartup 1974; Rule 1974).

The moral-judgment literature is abundant with studies demonstrating the importance of social cognitions in inhibiting defensive aggression. When a person perceives that a peer is *intentionally* causing a negative outcome, that person's modal response is aggressive against the peer. When a person perceives that a peer causes a negative outcome accidentally, his modal response is inhibition of aggression. This finding holds for adults (Burnstein & Worchel 1962; Pastore 1952) and for children (Mallick & McCandless 1966; Rule, Nesdale, & McAra 1974; Shantz & Voydanoff 1973).

Since a child's ability to differentiate the intentions of others and his ability to integrate that intention information into his own behavior are milestones which are thought to be developmentally acquired (Flavell 1977; Heider 1958; Piaget 1965), it has been hypothesized that variations in defensive aggressive behavior in children may be related to variations in cognitive development (Feshbach 1970; Hartup 1974). That is, the 10-year-old child who persistently responds with aggression to a nonintentional negative outcome may be doing so because of a *cue-utilization deficiency* related to a lag in his ability to integrate intention information into his behavior.

An alternative explanation of persistent aggressive responding to nonintentional negative outcomes by a certain child is that this child is not deficient in *cue utilization*, but rather engages in *cue distortion*. This hypothesis is that the child makes a distortion in the perception of intention which is related to his expectation about the intentions of others. If a child strongly expects that a peer will behave with hostile intent, then he may be likely to perceive the peer's behavior as hostile, particularly when the behavior produces a negative outcome. This perception may justify the child's retaliatory aggressive behavior from his own point of view.

This process of making an inaccurate attribution in the direction of one's expectations has been identified as a "complementary apperceptive projection" by Murray (1933). He suggested that the likelihood of one making a misperception of this kind increases with the ambiguity of the stimulus. Translated to the inappropriately aggressive child, it may be hypothesized that, given a negative outcome, this child will be most likely to mistakenly attribute a hostile intention to a peer (and consequently, to retaliate aggressively) when the peer's behavior seems ambiguously intended.

As a test of these hypotheses, in the first study of the present investigation, known aggressive and nonaggressive children in three grades were presented with a negative outcome which was the consequence of the behavior of a peer who had acted with hostile intent, benign intent (accidental behavior), or ambiguous intent. The child's behavioral responses were recorded by a video camera and constituted the dependent measure.

Study 1

Method

Selection of subjects. — Samples of 15 aggressive and 15 nonaggressive boys in each of grades 2, 4, and 6 (90 boys in all) of a semi-rural lower-middle-class school were selected on the joint bases of peer nominations and teacher assessments. Subjects selected by this method have been found to differ in their actual aggressive behavior, both in the classroom and on the playground (Dodge and Coie, Note 1). Informed consent for all phases of participation, including consent to videotape children, was obtained from parents of all participating children. Through a sociometric interview and with the aid of grade-level rosters, the 326 children in these grades were asked to nominate three peers who fit a particular behavioral description. Two of the descriptions were about consistent aggressive behavior ("This child starts fights," and "This child upsets everything when he gets in a group"). Also, children were asked to nominate three peers whom they liked most and three peers whom they liked least. Scores for each nomination category were computed for each child by summing the numbers of nominations received from all peers. Teachers were asked to privately assess each of their students by rating, on a scale of 1 to 9, each child's behavior in the areas of social relations, initiation of fights, and total involvement in fights.

In order to be selected as "aggressive," a boy had to be placed above the median of his teacher's ratings on each of the aggression questions and below the median on the favorability of social relations questions. From this pool, the boys in each grade whose peer nomination scores for aggression were highest, *and* whose cooperation and liking scores were low, were selected as the aggressive sample. Only males were selected since the total pool of aggressive children was predominantly male. The "nonaggressive sample of boys was matched to the aggressive sample by race. One-third of the same was black, paralleling the overall racial composition of the school. The nonaggressive sample was similarly selected on the basis of teacher ratings and peer nominations, but for the prosocial and nonaggressive behavior.

Overview of experimental design. — Subjects were exposed to a frustrating negative outcome during the course of a puzzle-assembling task in which a prize could be won. A negative outcome (destruction of the subject's puzzle) was instigated by an unseen peer who through simulated "live" audio information, was heard to be acting with a hostile intent, with a benign intent, or ambiguously. Assignment to condition was random. The boy was then given an opportunity to retaliate by destroying the unseen peer's puzzle. His verbal and behavioral responses were recorded by a video camera and constituted the dependent measure in a 3 × 2 × 3 (grade level of subject × status of subject × experimental condition) factorial experiment.

Procedure. — Each boy was escorted into a research trailer which was divided into two rooms and was told by the white female experimenter that he could win a prize by performing well in a puzzle-assembling task. He was told that another boy, in the adjoining room, would also be working at this task, even though they were not competing against each other. By means of a contrived demonstration the boy was led to believe that a microphone and speaker system had been connected between the two rooms, which allowed the two boys to communicate openly with each other. The "other boy" was actually a tape-recording of scripts read by a 9-year-old boy. The tape player was operated by a technician in the other room. The experimenter then went on to explain the task to the child. He could win one of three prizes of differing value, or no prize depending on how many pieces of his puzzle were assembled at the end of the task.

The boy would have a limited amount of time and was to work as rapidly as possible on the 50-piece jigsaw puzzle, which was large and simple enough that all children could assemble at least some pieces. Boys unfamiliar with the task were given time to practice.

The experimenter then began timing the boy's efforts. When the boy had assembled 13 puzzle pieces, she announced that they would stop for a break. She told the subject she wanted the boys to look at each other's puzzles, so she left the room with this partially completed puzzle, which was in a wooden tray. A few seconds later the tape player was turned on, and the subject was led to believe he heard the experimenter talk to the other boy. She told the other boy to look at the puzzle while she left the room. The subject then heard one of three recordings by the fictitious other boy.

In the hostile condition, the other boy made the following statement, in a hostile voice: "Gee, it looks like he's got a lot done. Well, I don't like it. I don't want him to win that dumb prize, so there I'll mess i up. [Crashing sounds are heard.] There ... that'll do it." In the benign condition, the other boy stated, in a friendly voice: "Gee it looks like he's got a lot done. I think I'll help him put some more pieces together. Hey, there's one. I'll put it here. [Crashing sounds are heard.] Oh, no, hey, I didn't mean to drop it. I didn't mean it." In the ambiguous condition, the other boy made only the following statement, in a nondescriptive voice: "Gee it looks like he's got a lot done." [After a long pause, crashing sounds are heard.]

Following this sequence, the experimenter was heard to return to the room and collect the two puzzles. Moments later, she returned to the subject's room with both puzzles. The subject's puzzle had been disassembled, the other boy's puzzle was partially competed. She told the subject to look over the two puzzles while she was gone, and then she left the room. At all stages of the experiment, the experimenter remained blind to the status of the child and to the experimental condition.

Following the experimenter's departure, a video recorder filmed the subject's behavior through a one-way mirror and recorded his voice for the next 3 min. Subjects were not made aware of the filming. The subject's behavior during this period constituted the dependent measure. Following this period, the experimenter returned to the room and told the child that the task was over. The experimenter awarded him the best prize for his positive performance on the task, thereby reinforcing the child for his *performance* and not the *outcome*, and escorted him back to the classroom. He was asked to not tell other children about the task.

While cognizant of ethical considerations, the experimenter did not inform the child that his behavior had been videotaped, or that the task had been "rigged." This information was withheld so that children would not be tempted to "divulge the trick" to peers and because it was felt that the information would only confuse the children. Both parents and school personnel had given fully informed consent for this procedure.

As an informal check on the credibility of the manipulation, the experimenter questioned the child about the procedure as she escorted him back to the classroom. No children appeared to disbelieve the reality of the procedure. Teachers acted as a check on the experimenter's request that each child not tell other children about the procedure. By anecdotal accounts of teachers, all children appeared to honor this request.

Observer coding and reliability.—Two observers independently coded the occurrences of each child's behavior in seven categories, which were derived after observation of the range in behaviors displayed: (A) disassembled one or more pieces of the other's puzzle, (B) expressed verbal hostility, (C) showed indirect hostility (such as hitting the wall, pounding the table, or making a fist), (D) assembled one's own puzzle, (E) attempted a neutral communication with the other child, (F) made a positive verbal statement, and (G) helped assemble the other's puzzle. The percentage of times in which both coders agreed whether or not a particular category of behavior occurred was calculated as the measure of observer reliability. The median agreement for the seven categories was 97%, with a range of 94%-100%.

In addition, an a priori single measure which assessed the affective valence of the child's behavior was derived from the seven observer categories. If the observer had recorded an occurrence of any of the aggressive categories (A, B, or C), the child received a score of 3. A child received a score of 2 if no valenced behavior was recorded, and a score of 1 if he had demonstrated positive behavior (categories F or

TABLE 1

PERCENTAGES OF SUBJECTS IN EACH CONDITION DISPLAYING VARIOUS BEHAVIORS, STUDY 1

	BEHAVIOR CATEGORY						
SUBJECTS	A	B	C	D	E	F	G
Aggressive:							
Hostile peer........	47	60	33	33	27	13	0
Ambiguous peer.....	20	13	33	20	20	53	7
Benign peer.........	0	7	13	20	27	13	53
Nonaggressive:							
Hostile peer........	40	27	13	7	0	7	0
Ambiguous peer.....	7	7	0	27	0	47	7
Benign peer.........	0	0	0	20	0	7	20

NOTE.—A = disassemble puzzle, B = verbal hostility, C = indirect hostility, D = assemble own puzzle, E = neutral communication with peer, F = positive verbal behavior, G = help assemble peer's puzzle.

G), in absence of aggressive behavior. Cases in which the two observers disagreed on this coding were resolved by a joint review, so that 100% agreement was reached for this measure.

Results and Discussion

The occurrence rates for the seven categories of behavior were analyzed by a multi-variate analysis of variance and are displayed in table 1. A significant multi-variate effect for experimental condition was found, $F_{(14,132)} = 4.55$, $p < .0001$. Univariate analyses revealed that the hostile condition elicited more disassembling of the other's puzzle, $F_{(2,72)} = 10.64$, $p < .0001$, and more verbal hostility, $F_{(2,72)} = 10.78$, $p < .0001$, than either of the other conditions. The benign condition elicited the greatest occurrence of helping behavior, $F_{(2,72)} = 11.44$, $p < .0001$, and the ambiguous condition elicited the greatest occurrence of positive verbal behavior, $F_{(2,72)} = 10.29$, $p < .0002$.

A significant multivariate main effect for subject status was also found, $F_{(7,66)} = 3.68$, $p < .0002$. Univariate analyses revealed that aggressive boys, relative to nonaggressive boys, were more likely to display verbal hostility, $F_{(1,72)} = 4.26$, $p < .05$, indirect hostility, $F_{(1,72)} = 8.70$, $p < .01$, neutral communications with the peer, $F_{(1,72)} = 15.13$, $p < .001$, and helping behavior, $F_{(1,72)} = 2.78$, $p < .07$. An interaction of subject status with experimental condition for helping behavior, $F_{(1,72)} = 2.78$, $p < .07$, showed that the aggressive boys helped the peer more than did the nonaggressive boys only in the benign condition.

These data show that all groups of children reacted to the hostile condition with aggression and to the benign condition with relative restraint from aggression. The aggressive group of boys were more likely than their nonaggressive peers to display aggression, as one might predict. Interestingly, they were also more likely to help the peer, but only when the situation called for it, as in the benign condition. The latter finding suggests that the boys in the aggressive group were not blindly aggressive, but were highly discriminating and were reacting to the interpersonal stimuli to a greater extent than were nonaggressive boys. The "increased reactivity" of aggressive boys is a finding which is distinct from a hypothesis of "increased activity" in these children and which could be explored further in other studies.

Analysis of the variance in the derived aggression score revealed a main effect for experimental condition, $F_{(2,72)} = 14.64$, $p. < .00001$. Post hoc examination of the mean scores by Newman-Keuls tests revealed that the hostile condition ($M = 2.6$) elicited significantly ($p < .05$) higher aggression scores than did the benign condition ($M = 1.75$). The mean score in the ambiguous condition ($M = 1.9$) fell in between the two extreme scores.

Neither a main effect of grade level nor an interaction of grade level with experimental condition was found for the aggression score, indicating that in all three grades children displayed aggression when the peer was hostile and refrained from aggression when the peer was benign. This finding differs from the data of Shantz and Voydanoff (1973) but is consistent with the findings of other researchers (Berndt 1977; Darley, Klossen, & Xanna 1978) who have studied children's verbal responses in various hypothetical situations. The present data extend those findings to boys' behavioral responses in actual interpersonal situations, and suggest that, when the intentions of another are defined clearly, young boys (7 years of age) incorporate intention cues into their ongoing behavior in the same fashion as do older boys. However, it remains plausible to speculate that age effects might have been found had even younger boys served as subjects.

Aggressive boys received a higher mean aggression score than did nonaggressive boys, $F(1,72) = 6.56$, $p < .02$. However, a marginally significant interaction of subject status with experimental condition was also found, $F(2,72) = 2.64$, $p < .08$. Newman-Keuls analysis of mean scores revealed that, in the hostile condition, aggressive boys ($M = 2.7$) and nonaggressive boys ($M = 2.5$) received similar high scores. In the benign condition, aggressive boys ($M = 1.8$) and nonaggressive boys ($M = 1.7$) received similar low scores, which were significantly lower than their scores in the hostile condition ($p < .05$). In the ambiguous condition, however, aggressive boys ($M = 2.3$) received a significantly higher mean aggression score than did nonaggressive boys ($M-1.5$) ($p < .05$). In fact, the aggressive boys' mean score in the ambiguous condition was significantly higher than their score in the benign condition ($p < .05$) and was not significantly different from that in the hostile condition. The nonaggressive boys' mean score in the ambiguous condition was significantly lower than their score in the hostile condition ($p < .05$) and was not significantly different from their score in the benign condition.

The present data show that, when a peer's intention is stated clearly, aggressive boys alter their retaliatory behavior according to that intention as appropriately as do nonaggressive boys. These data do not support the cue-utilization-deficiency hypothesis. When the intention of the peer remains ambiguous, aggressive and nonaggressive boys diverge in their behavioral reactions. Aggressive boys react as if the peer had acted with hostile intent, that is, with aggression, while nonaggressive boys behave as if the peer had acted benignly, that is, by refraining from aggression. These data support the cue-distortion hypothesis that aggressive and nonaggressive boys differ in their perceptions of the intentions of peers in ambiguous circumstances. However, in this study, only behavioral reactions of the subjects were measured. The attributions made by the boys must be inferred. In order to more directly assess specifically the attributions of these children in negative outcome ambiguous circumstances, a second study was run. This study employed an interview methodology in which children were asked to attribute reasons for a negative outcome which was hypothetically inflected upon them by a peer. Also, they were asked to state their probable behavioral response. According to the cue-distortion hypothesis, aggressive boys would be more likely than nonaggressive boys to attribute a hostile intention to the peer and would therefore be more likely to state that they would responde aggressively to the peer.

It may be suggested that characteristics of the specific peer who caused the negative outcome in this second study could additionally affect the attributions of these children. A study by Zadney and Gerard (1974) has shown that predetermined attributes of a person could affect other's interpretations of his behavior. It may be hypothesized that if a peer is known to be aggressive, then children will be more likely to attribute hostile intentions to him in an ambiguous situation than if the peer is known to be nonaggressive. To test this hypothesis, the status of the actors in the second study was manipulated by using the names of actual known aggressive and nonaggressive boys as actors.

Study 2

Method

Subjects. — The same children who served in study 1 also served in study 2. The two studies were administered at separate times, in random order, by independent experimenters, so that the children did not associate the two studies.

Procedure. — This study was conducted as an interview in which each child was brought to a private room and assured of the confidentiality of his responses, which were tape recorded. The child was asked a series of four questions about each of four peers. In each series, the interviewer told subjects one of two hypothetical stories in which a peer was involved in a negative outcome for the child. In one study, the child was to imagine that he was sitting at a lunch table. As the peer (identified by name) approached the table, a carton of milk on the peer's tray spilled all over the child's back. In the other story, the child was to imagine that he was on the playground playing catch with a ball. When the peer got the ball, he threw it, and it hit the child in the back, hurting him. Each of the two stories was worded so that the intention of the peer was left ambiguous. The child's task was to describe how the incident might have happened. His responses were probed in a nonleading direction until the child responded about the intentionality of the peer. Subsequently, he was asked how he would respond behaviorally and two additional question about the peer.

Selection of peer targets. — The four peers who were targets of each series of questions were selected because they had been identified by the subject as aggressive or nonaggressive during the course of the above-mentioned peer nomination interviews which were conducted 6 weeks prior to the experimental interview by independent administrators. Two aggressive peer targets were chosen from the subject's nominations for the "starts fights" and "disrupts group" categories. Two nonaggressive peer targets were chosen from the subject's nominations to the "cooperates in a group" category. When subjects had made more than two nominations for a category the nominated peers who also happened to be subjects in the study were selected as targets for the stories. No peer name was used as a target figure in a category opposite to the category in which he was a subject. In other words, no aggressive subject served as a nonaggressive target, and vice versa.

Experimental design and dependent measures. — The study followed a $2 \times 3 \times (2 \times 2)$ factorial design in which subject status (aggressive vs. nonaggressive) and grade level (2, 4, or 6) were between-subject factors and target status (aggressive vs. nonaggressive) and story content (lunch vs. playground) were within-subject factors. Subjects were interviewed in random order. Target status and story content were factorially combined into four conditions and were presented to subjects in an order which was counterbalanced across all subjects. The first dependent measure was the subject's attribution about the intention of the peer target and was scored as 1 if inten-

TABLE 2

MEAN SCORES OF AGGRESSIVE AND NONAGGRESSIVE SUBJECTS' RESPONSES TO INTERVIEW QUESTIONS ABOUT AGGRESSIVE AND NONAGGRESSIVE PEERS, STUDY 2

	QUESTION			
	1:	2:	3:	4:
			Prediction	Lack of
	Attributions	Aggressive	of	Trust in
SUBJECTS	of Hostility	Retaliation	Aggression	Peer
Aggressive:				
Aggressive target............	1.40	1.48	1.86	1.46
Nonaggressive target.........	1.10	1.31	1.38	1.14
Nonaggressive:				
Aggressive target............	1.31	1.39	1.70	1.30
Nonaggressive target.........	1.03	1.20	1.17	1.08

tional and 2 if accidental. The second dependent measure was the subject's stated behavioral response, which was scored as 1 if aggressive retaliation and as 2 if no aggressive retaliation. In the third question, the subject was asked what he thought the peer target would do next after the negative outcome, and his response was scored as 1 if he said the peer would continue to aggress, 2 if he said the peer would do nothing, and 3 if he said the peer would act benevolently. In the fourth question, the subject was asked if he would trust the peer by allowing himself to be placed in a position to let the act be repeated. His response was scored as 1 if he said yes he would trust the peer, and 2 if he said no he would not trust the peer. Since all interviews were tape recorded, an independent coder was able to check the reliability of the interviewer's coding of responses. This coder listened to 20 tapes and agreed with the interviewer in over 85% of the cases. Thus, the interviewer's coding was used for all subjects.

Results and Discussion

Since parametric analyses have been empirically justified with dichotomous data (Lunney 1970), the children's responses to each question were analyzed by a repeated-measures analysis of variance. Mean scores of subjects' responses to the four questions are displayed in table 2. As the results of the first study would have one predict, aggressive subjects attributed a hostile intention to the peer 50% more often than did nonaggressive subjects $F(1,84) = 3.00, p < .09$. Aggressive subjects also predicted that the target would continue to behave aggressively more often than did nonaggressive subjects, $F(1,84) = 4.28, p < .05$, and they said that they would not trust the target in the future more often than did nonaggressive subjects, $F(1,84) = 5.08, p < .03$.

These findings support the major hypothesis. In a hypothetical, negative-outcome, ambiguous circumstance, aggressive boys are more likely than nonaggressive boys to attribute a hostile intention to the peer instigator of the behavior. They also expect continued hostility from the peer and will not trust him. It is worth noting that when subjects attributed a hostile intention to the peer, they also said they would retaliate aggressively in 60% of the cases. When they attributed a benign intention to the peer, they retaliated in only 26% of the cases. This difference is significant by χ^2 analysis, $\chi^2(1) = 40.18, p < .0001$. Apparently, even in this ambiguous circumstance the subject's attributions about the intention of the peer is highly predictive of his stated response.

The status of the peer target who instigated the behavior had an even more sizable effect on subjects' attributions and stated behavior than did the status of the subject. As table 2 shows, aggressive targets were attributed a hostile intention five times more often than were nonaggressive targets, $F(1,84) = 46.51, p < .0001$. This effect held true at all grade levels (all t tests were significant at the .05 level), although the disparity between attributions for aggressive and nonaggressive targets was greater among sixth graders and fourth graders than among second graders, as revealed by a significant interaction of grade with target status, $F(2,84) = 4.15, p < .02$. In other words, being labeled as aggressive has an increasingly negative effect on children's attributions about a peer as he gets older.

The status of the peer target also had a significant effect on subject's hypothetical reactions to the negative outcome in the story. Subjects proposed aggressive retaliation more often against aggressive targets than against nonaggressive targets, $F(1,84) = 19.37, p < .0001$. Subjects predicted that aggressive targets would be more likely to continue behaving in aggressive ways than would nonaggressive targets, $F(1,84) = 36.60, p < .0001$. Subjects also refused to trust aggressive targets more often than nonaggressive targets, $F(1,84) = 37.95, p < .0001$. These data amply demonstrate the importance of a peer's reputation in the determination of a child's attributions about the peer's behavior and in that child's behavior toward the peer. Specifically, children who are known to be aggressive are more likely than others to be attributed hostile intentions, to be the objects of aggressive retaliation, and to be expected to continue to aggress. Also, they are less likely to be trusted by their peers than are their nonaggressive counterparts.

General Discussion

The two studies reported provide complementary data concerning the attributions and behavior of aggressive and nonaggressive boys. In the first study, it was found that both aggressive and nonaggressive boys in each of three grades could differentiate their retaliatory behavior in a negative-outcome situation according to the clearly stated intention of the peer instigator of the outcome. This finding does not support the hypothesis that aggressive boys lack the ability to integrate intention cues into their behavior. Only when the peer's intentions were ambiguous in producing a negative outcome did aggressive and nonaggressive boys' responses differ. The aggressive boys reacted with aggression, as if the peer had acted with a hostile intent, while the nonaggressive boys reacted with restraint from aggression, as if the peer had acted benignly.

This difference in the behavior of aggressive and nonaggressive boys in the ambiguous circumstance may have broad implications about the naturally occurring interpersonal behavior of these children. First, aggression in the ambiguous circumstance may bring negative reactions from peers who believe that aggression is not warranted in that situation. Lesser (1959) reported that warranted aggression (such as that elicited by the present hostile condition) was actually positively correlated to popularity among children of this age range while unwarranted aggression was linked to social rejection. Aggressive responding in the ambiguous circumstance, if considered unwarranted by peers, may bring about social rejection. Second, it is reasonable to assume that since many naturally occurring peer interactions are filled with ambiguous, or multi-intentioned circumstances the present ambiguous experimental condition approximates many of the actual situations in which boys find themselves. It is these situations that aggressive boys are more likely than others to aggress against peers.

Data from the second study show that aggressive and nonaggressive boys differ in their attributions about a peer who ambiguously instigates a negative outcome. Aggressive boys are relatively more likely to attribute a hostile intention to the peer, to expect continued aggression from the peer, and to mistrust the peer. In addition, the second study demonstrates the overwhelming importance of a child's reputation in determining attributions made about his behavior and in determining how others will behave toward him. Children known to be aggressive were more often than others attributed hostile intentions in ambiguous circumstances. They were more often the objects of aggression. Peers expected continued aggression from them and refused to trust them. Unfortunately for these children, the data suggest that the negative consequences associated with this label may actually increase over time, even when differences in the attributions and behavior of aggressive and nonaggressive children have *not* changed.

Based on the present data, a cyclical relationship between attributions and aggressive behavior may be proposed. Given a negative outcome in the context of unclear intentions, an aggressive child may be likely to attribute a hostile intention to a peer who is responsible for this negative event. This attribution may confirm his general image of peers as hostile and may increase the likelihood of his interpreting future behavior by the peer as hostile. Consequently, he may retaliate against the peer with what he feels is justified aggression. Subsequently, the peer, who has become the recipient of a negative outcome, may attribute a hostile intention to the aggressive child. This attribution confirms the peer's view of the child as being inappropriately aggressive in general and increases the peer's likelihood of interpreting future behavior by the aggressive child as being hostile. Consequently, the peer may aggress against the aggressive child, which could start the cycle over again.

Given a series of negative outcomes, which is inevitable, the cycle could turn into a self-perpetuating spiral of increased hostile attributions, aggressive behavior, and social rejection. Indeed, data from the second study showed that the effects of being labeled as aggressive increased with age. Older children suffered more negative consequences of their label than did younger children. Certainly, this label becomes known to the child himself and may serve to incite and justify his continued aggressive behavior as he grows up.

Supportive evidence for the proposed cyclical process has been found in studies in related behavioral areas. Snyder, Tanke, and Berscheid (1977) showed that, in a dyadic interaction, when person A was led to expect (by the experimenter) that person B would be friendly, then A unwittingly behaved toward the naive B in such a way as to cause B to actually become friendly. An implication of this study is that B's behavior will actually confirm A's expectation and cause him to respond accordingly, thus perpetuating the cycle. The durability of the expectations that could be built by such a process was demonstrated in a longitudinal study by Campbell and Yarrow (1961) in which it was inferred that changes in a child's behavior did not always change his social label.

The present investigation has shown that attributions and behavior may interact in a way that could perpetuate their relationship. For children who are developing aggressive styles of social interaction, this relationship could make behavioral change for them very difficult. The present data do not explain how children initially become aggressive, but do suggest a way in which defensive aggressive behavior is maintained and strengthened.

REFERENCE NOTE

1. Dodge, K.A., and Coie, J.D. *Behavioral patterns among socially rejected, average, and popular fifth graders.* Paper presented at the Biennial Southeastern Conference on Human Development, Atlanta, April 1978.

REFERENCES

Berndt, T.J. The effect of reciprocity in norms on moral judgments and causal attribution. *Child Development*, 1977, 48, 1322-1330.

Burnstein, E., & Worchel, P. Arbitrariness of frustration and its consequences for aggression in a social situation. *Journal of Personality*, 1962, 30, 528-540.

Campbell, J.D., & Yarrow, M.R. Perceptual and behavioral correlates of social effectiveness. *Sociometry*, 1961, 24, 1-20.

Darley, J.M.; Klossen, E.C.; & Zanna, M.P. Intentions and their contexts in the moral judgments of children and adults. *Child Development*, 1978, 49, 66-74.

Feshbach, S. Aggression. in P. Mussen (Ed.), *Carmichael's manual of child psychology*. New York: Wiley, 1970.

Flavell, J.H. *Cognitive Development*. Englewood Cliffs, N.J.: Prentice-Hall, 1977.

Hartup, W.W. Aggression in childhood: development perspectives. *American Psychologist*, 1974, 29, 336-341.

Heider, F. Perceiving the other person. In R. Tagiuri and L. Petrullo (Eds.), *Person perception and interpersonal behavior*. Stanford, Calif.: Stanford University Press, 1958.

Lesser, G.s. The relationship between various forms of aggression and popularity among lower class children. *Journal of Educational Psychology*, 1959, 50, 20-25.

Lunney, G.H. Using analysis of variance with a dichotomous dependent variable: an empirical study. *Journal of Educational Measurement*, 1970, 7, 263.

Mallick, S.K., & McCandless, B.R. A study of catharsis of aggression. *Journal of Personality and Social Psychology*, 1966, 4, 591-596.

Murray, H.A. The effect of fear upon estimates of maliciousness of other personalities. *Journal of Social Psychology*, 1933, 4, 310-329.

Pastore, N. The role of arbitrariness in the frustration-aggression hypothesis. *Journal of Abnormal and Social Psychology*, 1952, 47, 728-731.

Piaget, J. *The moral judgment of the child.* New York: Free Press, 1965.

Rule, B.G. The hostile and instrumental functions of human aggression. In W.W. Hartup and J. deWit (Eds.), *Determinants and origins of aggressive behaviors*. The Hague: Mouton, 1974.

Rule, B.G.; Nesdale, A.R.; & McAra, M.J. Children's reactions to information about the intentions underlying an aggressive act. *Child Development*, 1974, 45, 794-798.

Shantz, D.W., & Voydanoff, D.A. Situational effects of retaliatory aggression at three age levels. *Child Development*, 1973, 44, 149-153.

Snyder, M.; Tanke, E.d.; & Berscheid, E. Social perception and interpersonal behavior: on the self-fulfilling nature of social stereotypes. *Journal of Personality and Social Psychology*, 1977, 35, 656-666.

Zadney, J., & Gerard, H.B. Attributed intentions and informational selectivity. *Journal of Experimental Social Psychology*, 1974, 10, 34-52.

Parent-Child Interaction, Television Violence, and Aggression of Children

Leonard D. Eron

In the early 1960s I reported an incidental finding uncovered in a large-scale study in which we were attempting to determine the relation between child-rearing practices of parents and the aggressive behavior of their children in school (Eron, 1963). This finding, that there was a relation between the violence of the television programs children preferred and how aggressive they were in school, received a lot of attention, overshadowing other results of the study that I believe were equally important and theoretically just as interesting. As has been amply demonstrated by Bandura (1973), Berkowitz (1962), Buss (1961), Feshbach (1970), and my collaborators and me (Eron, Walder, & Lefkowitz, 1971; Lefkowitz, Eron, Walder, & Huesmann, 1977), aggression is to a great extent a learned behavior, and the findings in regard to television represent just one example of how aggression can be learned from the interaction of the individual with the environment. There are other ways in which aggression can be learned, however, than from viewing the behaviors of television characters. I will discuss these other processes and present some relevant recent data later in this article. However, now I would like to bring you up to date on the work that my colleagues and

I have been doing, which is concerned with the television-aggression relation. Because the original finding was incidental and largely serendipitous does not mean that it is unimportant in adding to our understanding of how children learn to be aggressive and, also, how this behavior can be unlearned.

The original finding of a relation between television violence viewing and subsequent aggressive behavior in natural situations outside the laboratory has now been replicated by a number of investigators (Greenberg, 1975; Hartnagel, Teevan, & McIntyre, 1975; McCarthy, Langner, Gersten, Eisenberg, & Orzeck, 1975; Parke, Berkowitz, Leyens, West, & Sebastian, 1977). Further, my collaborators and I have demonstrated that the continued viewing of television violence is a very likely cause of aggressive behavior and that there is a long-lasting effect on children (Eron, Huesmann, Lefkowitz, & Walder, 1972; Huesmann, in press; Huesmann & Eron, in press). The causative direction of the relation has also been confirmed by other investigators (Belons, 1978; Singer & Singer, 1981).

The subjects of our original study, 875 eight-year-old children, included the entire third-grade population of a semi-rural county in upstate New York. This is referred to as the *Rip Van Winkle Study*. Ten years later we interviewed 475 of these subjects in a follow-up study. A surprising finding was that the correlation between television violence viewing and aggressive behavior was higher for boys over the 10-year period than it was contemporaneously. This led us to conclude that the effect of viewing violence was probably cumulative. Since there was no relation between the amount of violence viewed in the later period and aggression at that time, however, we further concluded that there must be a sensitive period, around age 8, when a youngster is especially susceptible to the effect of continued violence viewing. It was assumed this period began sometime before age 8 and was probably over by age 12.

Because our original sample included only eight-year-old children, it was impossible to determine when this sensitive period began and when it ended. Therefore, Rowell Huesmann and I undertook a new study, some 17 years later, in a different area of the country. In this new study we followed approximately 750 children for three years. By using two overlapping samples, we encompassed an age range of 6-10 years during this period. We were interested in determining the boundary conditions of the relation between television violence viewing and aggression that we and others had demonstrated. In addition, however, we were interested in learning more about the intervening variables. What were the essential child and parent factors that could mediate the relation between television violence viewing and aggressive behavior? And since the correlation between the two was far from perfect, were there certain kinds of parent and child variables that made some children more vulnerable than others to the effect of violence on television? Thus we interviewed as many of the parents of our child subjects as possible and obtained additional information from the children themselves. The variables we chose to investigate were primarily ones that had been suggested as likely precursors or mediators in our previous 10-year study. Another way in which we looked for important intervening variables was with a manipulative field experiment with subsamples of the subjects from our longitudinal study. The manipulation was an intervention designed to attenuate the relation between exposure to TV violence and aggressive behavior among high violence viewers.

In this article, I will try to integrate the results of this manipulative field experiment with the findings in regard to precursor variables from the three-year longitudinal study. This longitudinal study, not including the manipulation, has been and is being replicated in Finland, Poland, Holland, Australia, and Israel, and I will comment on the preliminary findings of this cross-national research that are now available. Finally, we are currently in the last stage of data collection in a 21 year follow-up of our original third-grade subjects. Of course since these data are not yet all collected, there are no analyses that I can report.

We turn now to the three-year longitudinal survey completed in the United States, which we will refer to as the *Chicago Circle Study*. Our original group included 672 children in the public schools of Oak Park, Illinois, an economically and socially heterogeneous suburb of Chicago, and 86 children from an inner city school in the Chicago Archdiocese. Half of these children were in the first grade and half in the third grade during the first year of the study, 1977. All of the children were tested in their classrooms in two hourly sessions a week apart in that year and then again in 1978 and 1979. In 1978 607 children remained in the sample, and in 1979 there were 505. In addition 591 of their parents were also seen for individual interviews. Almost all of the subject attrition was attributable to children leaving the school system, and the attrition rate did not differ by grade or sex. Measures taken at the three points in time included peer-nominated aggression and popularity; self-ratings of aggression, fantasy, and preference for sex-typed behaviors; and various measures of television habits including frequency of viewing, violence of favorite programs, and identification with aggressive male and female television characters. The parent variables included rejection, nurturance, physical punishment for aggression, self-ratings of aggression, social mobility, and the violence of the television programs the parents themselves watched. A brief description of the measures follows.

Child Measures

PEER-NOMINATED AGGRESSION AND POPULARITY

Aggression and popularity of children were measured by a version of the Peer Rating Index of Aggression (Walder, Abelson, Eron, Banta, & Laulicht, 1961), in which every child in the classroom rates every other child on a series of 10 aggression and two popularity items embedded in a total list of 15 items. The reliability of this instrument as well as its concurrent predictive and construct validity have been amply demonstrated (Eron et al., 1971; Lefkowitz et al., 1977). In the current study coefficient alpha was .95 and test-retest reliability over one month was .91.

SELF-RATINGS OF AGGRESSION

This included four items in which the subject rates his or her similarity to fictional children described as engaging in specific aggressive behaviors; for example, "Steven often gets angry and punches other kids. Are you just like Steven, a little bit like Steven or not at all like Steven?" Test-retest reliability over one month was .54.

SEX-TYPED BEHAVIOR

A measure of preference for sex-typed toys and games was used to determine appropriate sex role behavior. This measure of preference for sex-typed activities comprised a booklet of four pages, each of which contained six pictures of children's activities. Two pictures of each set had been previously rated as masculine, two as feminine, and two as neutral by 67 college students who had been asked to designate the activities as popular for boys or girls or both. The task for the children was to select the two activities they liked best on each page, and they received a score for the number of masculine, feminine, and neutral pictures they chose. The reason for including a neutral category is that even though less masculine boys may not like traditionally feminine activities, they might prefer neutral over traditionally masculine ones. Similarly, for girls we anticipated that those who did not prefer traditionally feminine activities might also eschew masculine activities but subscribe to neutral ones. Coefficient alpha is not an appropriate measure of reliability for this scale. However, one-month test-retest reliabilities ranged between .55 and .60. Only the masculine and neutral sex-typed preferences are included in the analyses, since preference for feminine activities did not relate to aggression either positively or negatively.

FANTASY

Two of the fantasy scales devised by Rosenfeld, Huesmann, Eron, and Torney-Purta (in press) were used to measure extent of aggressive fantasy and active heroic fantasy (each with six items; e.g., "Do you sometimes have daydreams about hitting or hurting somebody you don't like?" or "When you are daydreaming, do you think about being the winner in a game you like to play?"). Coefficient alphas for these scales were .64 and .61, respectively; one-month test-retest reliability, .44 and .62.

FREQUENCY OF VIEWING

This measure was obtained from the subjects themselves, who rated the frequency with which they watched specifically named programs. These were the 80 television shows chosen from the Nielson data as the most popular for children of ages 6-11. The shows were divided into eight lists of 10 programs each. The lists were equivalent in terms of the violence and popularity of the shows in each list, the sex of the central character, the the time and day of the week in which the programs were shown in the Chicago area. The children were given booklets with each of the eight lists on a different colored sheet of paper and were asked to draw a line through the one program they watched the most on that list. They were then asked to indicate, by checking an appropriate box, whether they "watched every single time the program was on," or "watched a lot, but not every single time," or "just once in a while." A TV frequency score was then obtained by summing the scores for all eight shows selected. Test-retest reliability over one month was .76.

VIOLENCE OF FAVORITE TELEVISION PROGRAMS

Two psychology graduate students who had small children, but were not associated with this research project, rated all 80 programs for the amount of visually portrayed physical aggression in the show on a five-point scale from "not violent" to "very violent." Interrater reliability was .75. A child's TV violence score was the sum of the violence ratings of the eight shows that the child had indicated he or she watched, weighted by the frequency with which the child reported watching the program. Test-retest reliability over one month was also .75.

REALISM OF TELEVISION PROGRAMS

The children were asked to rate how realistic they judged television to be. They were given a list of 10 violent shows, including cartoons as well as police shows and "bionic" shows. They were then asked, "How true do you think these programs are in telling what life is really like: just like it is in real life, a little like it is in real life, or not all all like it is in real life?" The subject's total realism score was then the sum of the ratings on all 10 items. One-month test-retest reliability was .74. Coefficient alpha was .72.

IDENTIFICATION WITH TV CHARACTERS

Ratings were made by the children to indicate how much they were like certain television characters. These characters included two aggressive males, two aggressive females, two unaggressive males, and two unaggressive females. From their responses a reliable identification with aggressive character score was derived. Coefficient alpha for this measure was .71, and test-retest reliability over one month was .60.

Parent Measures

REJECTION

This was a 10-item scale dealing with change-worthy behaviors, other than aggression, in the child. The greater the number of items on which the parent indicated disapproval of the child's current behavior, the higher the rejection score; for example, "Are you satisfied with Johnnie's manners?" "Does he read as well as could be expected for a child of his age?" "Is he too forgetful?" This measure has been demonstrated to be reliable and reasonably independent of rejectability of the child (Eron et al., 1971).

NURTURANCE

This scale included eight items having to do with the amount of attention the parent devotes to the child and the parent's awareness of the child's needs and activities. For example, "Do you usually have time so that Johnnie can talk to you about things that interest him?" "What does Johnnie dream about?" (scored + if parent can name at least one topic). The reliability and validity of this and the other parent measures have been reported by Eron et al. (1971) and Lefkowitz et al. (1977).

PUNISHMENT

This was a five-item scale tapping the parents' use of physical punishment; for example, "How many times in the past year have you spanked Johnnie until he cried?" Our previous research (Lefkowitz, Walder, & Eron, 1963) indicated that use of non-physical punishment by parents did not relate to aggression in children. It was only physical punishment by the parents that bore this relation to their child's aggression.

SELF-RATINGS OF AGGRESSION

There were two measures of the parents' own aggression. The first included the sum of Scales 4 and 9 (psychopathic Deviate and Hypomania) of the Minnesota Multiphasic Personality Inventory (MMPI). These combined scales have been shown to be reliable and valid as a measure of antisocial behavior (Huesmann, Lefkowitz, & Eron, 1978). The other measure was a self-rating of how often the parent engaged in seven specific aggressive behaviors; for example, "Have you ever slapped or kicked another person?"

SOCIAL MOBILITY

This included five items designed to tap how strongly motivated the parent was toward occupational and social achievement; for example, "Would you give up your friends and move to a new location in order to get ahead?"

TV VIOLENCE

Sum of violence scores for parents' favorite program, weighted by the frequency with which the program was watched. This was identical to the child television measure (see above).

AGGRESSIVE FANTASY

This measure for parents included one of the six items used in the aggressive fantasy measure for child subjects (see above).

Television Violence and Aggression

The Chicago Circle Study and its replication in other countries were undertaken to determine the generality of the original findings obtained with eight-year-old children in a semi-rural area of New York state. As indicated in table 1, the positive relation was found to hold up in a different geographical and more urban area of the United States and in three other countries with a range of political and economic systems as well as different organizations of control and distribution of television than in the United States. The correlations in all four countries are positive and, except for the first grades in Australia and Finland, are of roughly the same order and for the most part highly significant. Further, at least in the United States, the increasing size of the correlation with each succeeding year is consistent with our original assumption of a cumulative effect. Part of this trend may be the result of a methodological factor-- The measures used are not as reliable with first graders as they are with older children. But probably even more important is a developmental factor. As demonstrated in an article by Eron, Huesmann, Brice, Fischer, and Mermelstein (in press), aggression, as measured by the peer rating index, increases significantly for both boys and girls from the first to the fifth grade, whereas the viewing of television violence increases up to the third grade and then starts to decline. Over the same period the child's perception of television violence as realistic is decreasing. Thus the third grade may be a period during which a number of factors converge and make the child unusually susceptible to the effects of television. It is interesting that the strongest relations between television violence and both simultaneous and later ag-

TABLE 1

Correlations Between Television Violence and Aggression

	U.S.	Finland	Poland	Australia
1				
1st grade	.21**	.14	.23*	.02
2nd grade	.23**	.26**	.19*	
3rd grade	.25**	.20*		
2				
3rd grade	.22**	.16	.29**	.22**
4th grade	.23**	.23*	.23**	
5th grade	.26**	.22*		

gression have been reported for children of this age (Chaffee, 1972; Lefkowitz et al., 1977).

At any rate there is no denying that the relation between television viewing and aggressive behavior is ubiquitous. Indeed, although 20 years ago we found a significant relation only for boys, we now find the same effect for girls. In general, this is true in all four countries, Finalnd, Poland, Australia, and the United States (Lagerspetz, Note 1; Fraczek, Note 2; Sheehan, Note 3). The recent extension of the findings to include girls has been reported and commented on elsewhere (Eron, 1980; Huesmann, in press; Huesmann & Eron, in press). Though the existence of the positive relation between violence viewing and aggression is clear, the reasons for it are debatable. A number of processes have been hypothesized (Huesmann, in press), suggesting various causes. The evidence seems compelling that excessive violence viewing is a cause of increased aggression in many children, but this does not necessarily eliminate other causal hypotheses as well. For example, on the basis of our most recent data, it appears that not only does continued exposure to violence on television influence a young person to be more aggressive, but aggressive youngsters continue to watch an increased amount of violence. It is quite possible that a number of processes in addition to observational learning account for the bidirectional nature of the relation between television violence and aggression. I will comment further on the likely circularity of the relation after discussing the evidence for the presence and effect of other intervening variables and processes.

Intelligence, Aggression, and Television Violence

In research in personality and child development, there is one variable that is invariably related to just about everything else, and that is intellectual ability. It is the prime example of a third variable that can often be invoked to explain away the correlation between two other variables. Thus it is usually necessary to control for intellectual ability, either in the experimental design by using randomized blocks or statistically by using partial correlation in the data analysis. Most observational and field studies have used the latter procedure. For example, Belson (1978) in England and Singer and Singer (1981) in New Haven partialed out the effect of intelligence and still detected a significant relation between television violence viewing and aggression. In our 10-year research in New York, we also found that low academic achievement was related both to television viewing and to aggression, but achievement could not account completely for the relation between the latter two. Again, in the Chicago Circle Study, as noted in Table 2, reading achievement is one of the highest correlates of aggression and, at least for boys, is also related to observation of violence. Further, for both boys and girls, the lower the intellectual ability, as indicated by scores on a reading achievement test, the more the youngster believes television violence is real. When achievement is partialed out, there is a substantial diminution in the relation between television viewing and aggression for boys, from .245 to .134, which, however, is still significant in this large group. Of course the partialed variable here is reading achievement, which may be influenced by television viewing as well as influencing both television viewing and aggression. As we see in Table 2, less-achieving children watch television more often, identify more strongly with aggressive television characters, and are more apt to believe aggressive television content is real. Thus they are more likely to be influenced by the behaviors they observe on the screen. In addition, they are likely to be frustrated more often. Thus intelligence, as reflected in reading achievement, accounts for some of the variance in the relation between television violence and aggressive behavior, but its role seems to be that of an exacerbating variable.

TABLE 2
*Correlations Between Reading Achievement
and Other Variables*

Variable	Boys	Girls
Peer-nominated aggression	−.44***	−.24**
TV violence	−.30***	−.14
TV frequency	−.26**	−.05
TV realism	−.32***	−.30***
Identification with aggressive		
TV characters	−.20*	−.10
Parents' education	.35***	.21**
Fathers' occupation	−.19*	−.19*

*p < .05. **p < .01 ***p < .001*

Other Variables and Aggression

Although television violence by itself may be an important precursor of aggressive behavior, it would be foolish to maintain that it is the only one of importance. Ordinary common sense would tell us that other socializing agents, especially parents, should have at least equally as great an effect on children's behavior. Our previous research (the Rip Van Winkle Study) did indicate that parental punishment of aggression, the model of behavior parents provide, and the instigations to aggression implied in their rejecting and non-nurturant child-rearing practices all contribute to aggressive behavior in children. The Chicago Circle Study and the cross-national replications have furnished an opportunity to check further on the child-rearing antecedents of aggressive behavior as well as other child behaviors that might have some bearing on the relation between television violence and aggression, in addition to any independent influence they might have on aggressive behavior.

Table 3 presents those variables that, based on our previous findings in semi-rural New York, we posited would be most closely related to aggressive behavior of the children. The correlations of these variables with aggression are shown separately for boys and girls in Table 3. Most are significantly related to aggression, although not markedly so. Since most of the variables are not normally distributed, the correlation coefficient probably underestimates the true relation. A better understanding of the meaning of these relations can be obtained by dividing the male and female samples into high, medium, and low groups, according to each of the variables, and computing the mean peer-nominated aggression score for each level of the variable. It then becomes clearer how aggression increases with each of the hypothesized precursors or concomitant variables.

TABLE 3

Correlations of Predictor Variables With Peer-Nominated Aggression Scores

Variable	Total	Girls	Boys
Child			
Self-rating of aggression	.322	.281	.300
Masculine sex role	.242	.163	.188
Neutral sex role	−.204	−.148	−.189
Aggressive fantasy	.164	.113	.195
Active heroic fantasy	.195	.171	.153
TV violence	.221	.171	.206
TV realism	.135	.115	.151
Identification with aggressive			
TV characters	.103	.122	.126
Popularity	−.372	−.355	−.409
Parent			
Mother's MMPI 4 + 9	.155	.062	.245
Father's MMPI 4 + 9	.191	.222	.187
Self-rating of aggression	.023	.001	.027
Rejection	.233	.132	.274
Nurturance	.053	−.023	.132
Mobility orientation	.034	−.01	.086
Punishment	.207	.175	.236
Television violence (parent)	−.060	−.058	−.063
Aggressive fantasy (parent)	.071	.053	.084
Father's occupation	.169	.085	.237

Let us look first at the measures obtained directly from the children. As noted in Figure 1, self-ratings of aggression were significantly related to aggression. Children who were rated as more aggressive by their peers also said they had more aggressive daydreams. It seems that the more youngersters rehearse aggression in fantasy, the more aggressive they are in overt behavior. Generally the same results were found with both sexes and in the other two countries for which data have thus far been analyzed, Finland and Poland (Fraczek, Note 2; Lagerspetz, Note 1). Similarly, peer popularity, as also seen in Figure 1, was negatively related to aggression for both boys and girls. This was true in the other countries as well. The more aggressive youngsters are, the more unpopular they are. In Figure 2 it can be seen that preference for masculine activities is generally related to aggression for both boys and girls. This is true for all groups in all countries, and preference for neutral activities almost always goes along with lessened aggression. Preference for feminine activities is not at all related to aggression, either positively or negatively, in any of the samples. These data have also been discussed elsewhere (Eron, 1980; Huesmann, in press; Huesmann & Eron, in press).

Television violence observed by children, as we mentioned previously (seen in

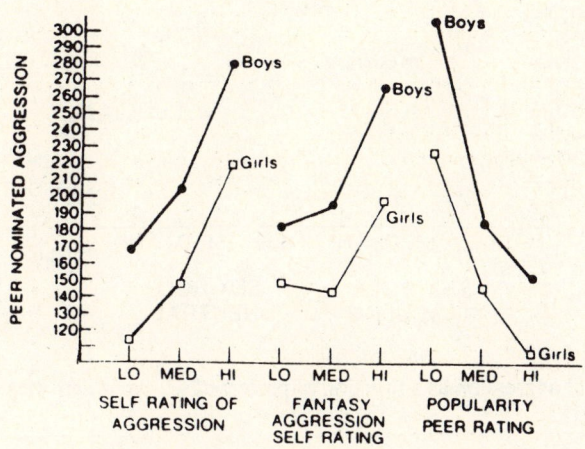

Fig. 1. Child aggression as a function of self-evaluation and peer popularity.

Figure 3 for the United States only), is actually related to aggression in all four countries (as indicated previously in Table 1). As for the other television variables, the relation of aggression to TV realism or how realistic the youngster believes television to be does not reach significance in the United States. Nor does it in Finland, although it does in Poland. The results are the same for identification with TV characters.

Insofar as the parent-child interaction variables are concerned, in the United States, Finland, and Poland physical punishment by parents relates significantly to aggression for both boys and girls, as seen in Figure 4 for the United States. Rejection by parents is another important concomitant of aggression in school. The less satisfied the parents are about their child's accomplishments, manners, and behaviors, the more aggressive is that child in school. In Poland and Finland results were essentially the same, but the relation seemed stronger for boys than girls. Nurturance by parents has no consistent relation to aggression in school. This was true in all three countries.

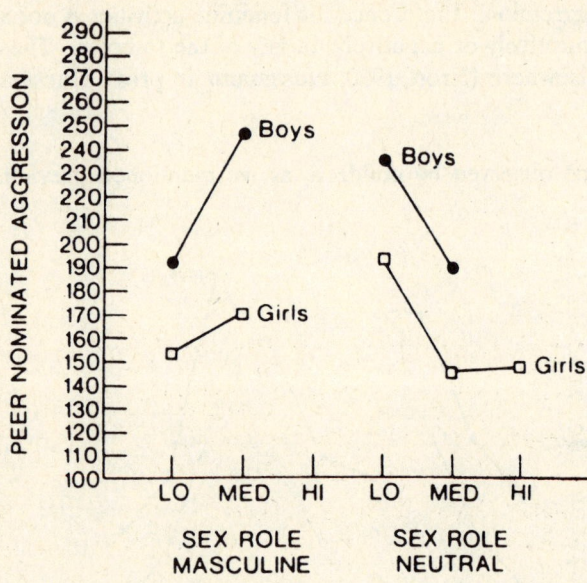

Fig. 2. Child aggression as a function of preferred sex-types activities.

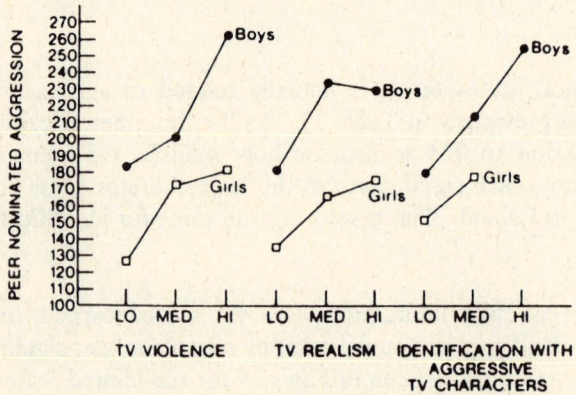

Fig. 3. Child aggression as a function of television habits and attitudes.

By and large, then, in terms of interaction between parent and child, those parents who punish their children physically and express dissatisfaction with their children's

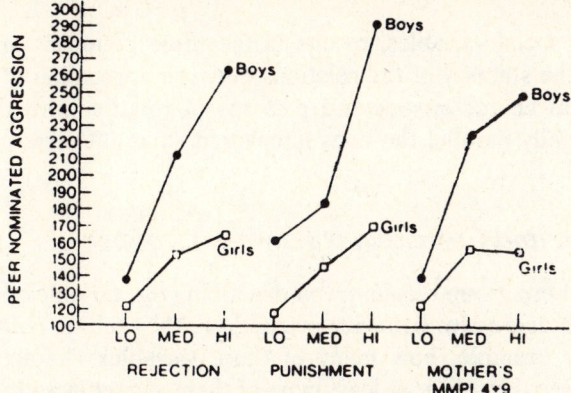

Fig. 4. Child aggression as a function of parent behaviors

accomplishments and characteristics have the most aggressive children. This finding holds largely for both boys and girls and in Finland and Poland as well as the U.S.

How about the characteristics of the parents themselves and how they relate to child aggression? One might guess from what we have said thus far that aggressive parents who watch violent television would have the most aggressive children. Well, not quite. We found no relation between either parent's television habits and the child's aggression in any of the three countries and no relation between parent and child aggression in Finland and Poland. In the United States, however, a mother's aggressiveness, as measured by Scales 4 + 9 of the MMPI (and as seen in Figure 4), was very highly related to her son's aggression. Fathers' agression, as measured by these scales, also varied positively with sons' aggression. There was no relation between either parent's aggression and daughter's aggressiveness in the United States.

Similarly, for sociological variables such as age, education, occupation, and mobility strivings of parents, there were no significant correlations with children's aggression in Poland and Finalnd. In the United States, however, fathers' age and education were related to boys' aggression. The younger and less educated the father, the higher the boy's aggression. For girls in the United States, fathers' occupation was related to aggression. The lower the occupation, according to census standards, the higher the aggression of girls. The relation was in the same direction for boys but did not reach statistical significance. The reason for the lack of relations in the other two countries may be their greater homogeneity on these characteristics. Social class distinctions are not widely prevalent, or at least so our foreign collaborators claim. One finding of considerable interest is that the children of working mothers obtain significantly higher aggression scores than children of nonworking mothers. This is probably not due to a confounding with social class in general, since 129 of the 352 working mothers were in Class 1 and 2 occupations (Huesmann & Eron, Note 4).

Except for these social variables, results in the three countries are remarkably similar and attest to the stability of the relations between aggression of children and their parents' personal characteristics and patterns of relation with their children. These findings essentially parallel the ones uncovered some 20 years earlier in New York state (Eron et al., 1971).

Individual Children and Correlations Between Groups

As suggestive as these group results are in describing the variables that are important in influencing the aggressive behavior of children, they tell us nothing about individual children; for example, how many of these variables characterize a given aggressive child, and are they all or at least most of them absent in a given nonaggressive child? To accomplish this analysis we sampled the 10 most and the 10 least aggressive boys in each cohort, as well as the 10 most and 10 least aggressive girls in each cohort — a total of 80 children in all, 40 high aggressive and 40 low aggressive, equally divided according to grade and sex. We compared these eight groups by inspection, first, in mean score on the nine child variables and eight parent interview variables previously described. Table 4 presents a sign analysis of the difference between the extreme subgroups on these variables. A plus indicates that the difference in means between the high and low aggression groups is greater than one SE of the means and in the direction hypothesized; a minus sign indicates the opposite direction from that hypothesized; a zero signifies there was less than one SE difference in mean score between the two groups. For third-grade boys 16 of the 17 comparisons are in the right direction; for first-grade boys 11 of the 17 are correct, three are in the wrong direction, and three show no difference between high and low aggression groups. For third-grade girls 15 of the 17 are in the correct direction, 1 is in the wrong direction, and on 1 variable there is no appreciable difference between high and low aggressive girls; for first-grade girls there are 14 in the predicted direction and 3 show no appreciable difference.

In general it can be said that these 17 variables do discriminate between the most and the least aggressive boys and girls in each cohort. Parental nurturance and parental preference for TV violence, however, are least likely to discriminate between the groups and, thus, will not be used here to characterize the background variables of extremely aggressive and nonaggressive children, leaving a total of 15 variables for this analysis.

Let us then look at these samples of the extremely aggressive and nonaggressive girls and boys and see how many in each group can be described as possessing many or most of the 15 discriminating group characteristics we have isolated. To do this we

TABLE 4

Agreement With Stated Hypothesis of Direction of Difference Between Most and Least Aggressive Boys and Girls

Variable	Third-grade boys	First-grade boys	Third-grade girls	First-grade girls
Child				
Aggression self-rating	+	+	+	+
Neutral sex role	+	0	+	+
Masculine sex role	+	−	+	0
Aggressive fantasy	+	+	+	+
Active fantasy	+	0	+	+
Popularity	+	+	+	+
TV violence	+	+	+	+
Identification with aggressive TV character	+	+	+	+
TV realism	+	+	+	+
Parent				
MMPI 4 + 9	+	+	+	+
Parent's self-rating of aggression	+	+	+	+
Rejection	+	+	+	+
Nurturance	−	−	+	0
Mobility orientation	+	+	0	+
Punishment	+	+	+	+
TV violence (parent)	+	−	−	+
Aggressive fantasy (parent)	+	0	+	0

assigned each child a score of 0-4 on each of the 15 variables, corresponding to how far from the mean for his or her grade and gender group the specific score lay. A designation of 1 indicated that the subject's score was over .5 standard deviation from the mean; a designation of 2, that the score was greater than one standard deviation from the mean; 3, that it was more than two standard deviations removed; and 4, that it was three or more standard deviations removed from the mean. A plus sign was used to designate a deviation from the mean in line with the hypothesis; a minus sign, that it was in the opposite direction from the hypothesis.

Table 5 represents the deviation scores of each of the 10 most aggressive boys in the third grade on the 15 characteristics that we have indicated as important. The reason for less than 15 in some cases is that three of the mothers of these high aggressive children were unavailable for interview and one of the children was absent from school on one of the days we were collecting data. None of the children in this group had fewer than one half of the designated characteristics. Seven of the 10 have at least two thirds of them. The behaviors we have been discussing, then, are not merely group abstractions. Together they characterize specific children who have been designated by their peers as the most aggressive in the group.

TABLE 5
Scores of the 10 Most Aggressive Third-Grade Boys in Terms of Their Distance From the Mean for All Third-Grade Boys

	Subject									
Variable	1	2	3	4	5	6	7	8	9	10
Child										
Self-rating	+1	+4	−1	+4	−2	+1	+4	+3	+2	−2
Neutral sex role	+3	−1	+3	+1	+3	+1	+1	+1	+3	+3
Masculine sex role	+3	−1	+3	−1	+3	+2	+2	−1	+2	+3
Aggressive fantasy	+4	+3	+3	+3	−3	+3	+4	x	+3	−3
Active fantasy	+4	+3	+3	+3	−3	−1	+4	x	+3	−3
Popularity	+3	+3	−1	+2	+3	+3	+2	+3	+2	+3
TV violence	−1	+3	+3	−3	+3	+3	+3	x	+3	+3
Identification with aggressive										
TV character	+2	+3	−1	+1	−2	−2	+3	x	+3	+4
TV realism	+3	+2	−2	+4	+1	−1	−1	x	+3	+3
Parent										
MMPI 4 + 9	+3	−1	+3	x	x	+2	+1	−1	−1	x
Self-rating of aggression	−1	+1	+3	+2	−3	−2	−1	−1	+3	x
Rejection	−1	+2	+1	+3	−1	+3	−3	+1	+2	x
Punishment	+2	+3	+3	+4	+4	+3	+1	−1	+4	x
Mobility orientation	+1	+1	+2	−2	+1	−2	+3	−2	+3	x
Aggressive fantasy	+4	−1	+4	+4	−1	−1	−1	+4	+1	x

Note. A + indicates deviation in direction appropriate for hypothesis regarding high aggressive boys. A − indicates that it was in the opposite direction from the hypothesis. An x indicates data not available for that child or parent. 1 means subject's score was over 5 SD from the mean; 2, greater than one SD; 3, more than two SDs; 4, three or more SDs.

We look now at Table 6, which contains similar data for the 10 least aggressive third-grade boys. All of the mothers of these children agreed to be interviewed, and none of the children was absent on the data collection day. None has as many as half of these characteristics and half of the subjects have three or fewer. And so it is with the other groups, first-grade boys and first- and third-grade girls. Significantly more of the behaviors and attitudes we have been discussing are jointly present in the subjects and parents of the high aggressive than in those of the low aggressive group.

To illustrate the salience and concomitance of these characteristics in a specific individual, I would like to tell you about a subject in our 10-year longitudinal study, which is now a 21-year old study. One of the bonuses of doing longitudinal research in a small community is that you get to know some of your subjects and the milieu in which they live quite well and from a number of perspectives. It is perhaps out of place in a scientific paper to give a case report, but I am after all a clinical psychologist

TABLE 6

Scores of the 10 Least Aggressive Third-Grade Boys in Terms of Their Distance From the Mean for All Third-Grade Boys

Variable	Subject									
	1	2	3	4	5	6	7	8	9	10
Child										
Self-rating of aggression	−2	−3	−2	−3	−3	−3	+2	−3	−2	−2
Neutral sex role	−1	+1	−3	+3	+1	−3	+1	+2	−3	−1
Masculine sex role	−1	−1	−4	+1	+1	−3	+1	+3	−3	−1
Aggressive fantasy	−2	+1	+1	−1	−3	−3	−2	−3	−3	−1
Active heroic fantasy	−1	+2	−2	+1	−4	−3	−1	−4	−2	−1
Popularity	−3	+1	−1	+1	+1	−4	−3	−4	−3	−4
TV violence	−2	0	−2	−1	−2	−3	−2	+3	−3	−2
Identification with aggressive TV character	−2	−2	−2	−2	−2	−2	+1	−2	−2	+2
TV realism	−3	−3	−3	−2	−3	−3	+1	−1	−2	−3
Parent										
MMPI 4 + 9	−3	−2	+2	+3	x	+2	−2	x	−2	−3
Self-rating of aggression	−1	−3	+1	−3	−2	+2	−3	−3	−3	−1
Rejection	+3	+3	+4	−3	−2	−3	−3	−2	−3	−3
Punishment	−1	−1	−2	−1	−2	−1	−2	−1	+2	−2
Mobility orientation	−1	+2	+2	+1	0	+1	+3	−1	−1	+2
Aggressive fantasy	+3	−1	+3	−1	−1	−1	+1	+1	−1	−1

Note. A + indicates deviation in direction appropriate for hypothesis regarding high aggressive boys. A − indicates that it was in the opposite direction from the hypothesis. An x indicates data not available for that parent. 1 means subject's score was over .5 SD from the mean; 2, greater than one SD; 3, more than two SDs; 4, three or more SDs.

and for a clinician the proof of a valid piece of research is whether it can be applied to a specific case in which the clinician has some interest.

Case Example of a Highly Aggressive Child

Ronald was first seen by me when he was eight years old and in the second grade. His teacher, who described him as "a likable and happy-go-lucky child," had referred him because of immature behavior and poor work habits. He had repeated first grade, but the teacher felt he was brighter than group tests indicated. Ronald was the youngest of three children. His brother, age 11, was out of the home at a special school for emotionally disturbed youngsters and his sister, age 12, was progressing normally in school. Ronald had been sickly from infancy, having suffered from severe attacks of asthma until the previous year. The parents reported that because the attacks were so frightening, they had overindulged him. However, the father, who had to hold two jobs to support the family, did not spend much time with the children. The mother's primary complaint about Ronald was that he was always hungry and "would eat from morning to night."

An intelligence test indicated that Ronald was of average ability. He was, however, one year retarded in reading, due perhaps to a disturbance in spatial orientation that was apparent in the way he handled test materials. It was noted that he was impulsive and did not go about problem solving in any ordered, planned way, relying solely on trial and error. He was uncritical of his own performance.

Ronald was next seen by another psychologist when he was 12 years old and in the sixth grade. At this time he was failing in school, reading at a second-grade level, and a management problem in his class. He talked back to the teacher, provoked fights, and was constantly making noise. He was not allowed to go to the lavatory with his classmates because he would get into fights with them. Ronald was also having difficulty on the school bus and in the neighborhood, continually getting into fights with other boys by taunting them and egging them on. The parents did not seem to be concerned about the boy's behavior. The father never appeared for a parent interview and the mother said it was the school's problem, not hers. She usually took the boy's part and accused the school officials of picking on her son.

By coincidence Ronald was a subject in the longitudinal study of aggression. It was possible to retrieve the parent interviews conducted when Ronald was nine years old and his own interview, when he was 19. In the third grade Ronald was already seen by his peers as one of the most aggressive boys in class, doing things that bothered others, starting a fight over nothing, saying mean things, not obeying the teacher, and pushing other children. At the same time the father and mother indicated that Ronald was disobedient at home, that he annoyed and pestered them, had a bad temper, and used foul language. They did not approve of a number of things that he did, giving many indications of a rejecting attitude toward Ronald and little indication that they understood him or were concerned about him. They related having had many arguments between themselves that did not settle anything; they moved around a lot, so Ronald continually had to find new friends. These behaviors and occurrences must have created a very frustrating situation at home that probably instigated Ronald to be aggressive both there and at school. The father related using many physical punishments when Ronald was aggressive, including spanking him severely and washing out his mouth with soap, thus adding to the youngster's frustration and providing the model of an aggressive adult. Other aggressive models were furnished on Ronald's favorite TV programs, "Maverick," "Have Gun Will Travel," and "The Three Stooges." The parents indicated that Ronald showed few signs of internalized standards of behavior, such as feeling sorry after he disobeyed, worrying about telling a fib or a lie, or confessing when he had done something naughty. Thus according to information furnished by his parents at that time, Ronald at age nine was experiencing many instigations to aggression at home, had a physically punitive father as well as other aggressive models, and showed little indication of having developed a conscience.

When Ronald was interviewed at the age of 19, he was on probation for three years for petty larceny. A few weeks after the interview, he was picked up by the police and charged with "criminal mischief in the third degree" and one week later with "criminal possession of drugs, fourth degree." During the interview it was revealed that he had dropped out of high school in the 10th grade, but he insisted that he expected to go to graduate school so that he could eventually do research in "brain biology." He admitted that he engaged in many aggressive behaviors. On the MMPI he had high scores on a pattern of scales characteristic of recalcitrant delinquents (Scales 4, 8, and 9--psychopathic deviate, schizophrenia, and mania, respectively). He continued to prefer violent television programs and thought that "Mod Squad," "Mannix," and "Dragnet" were very realistic in showing what police work is really like.

Unfortunately Ronald is no longer a subject in our 21-year longitudinal study. He was killed in a violent accident within a year of the second interview. In his brief life, however, we can discern the joint occurrence of most of the factors, detailed in Table 4, that we have been discussing. And it is the joint occurrence of these factors, as demonstrated in Tables 5 and 6, that is important in determining the extent of aggressive and violent behavior in young people. Aggressive behavior, like most other behaviors, is overdetermined. But we have some knowledge about what many of those determinants are.

We know that observation of television violence is a cause of aggressive behavior in children, and we know that the effect is not confined to boys or to a certain geographical or socioeconomic area in the United States. We know that because of a convergence of developmental trends occurring around age eight, children of that age may be unusually susceptible to the effect of violent television. Also, it seems likely that how closely a youngster identifies with aggressive TV characters and how realistic he or she believes aggressive television content to be are related to both aggression and television viewing. We know further that academic achievement is negatively related to aggression and that aggressive youngsters tend not to be popular with their peers. We know that rejection and physical punishment by parents are concomitants of aggression in children and that the attitudes and behaviors of parents, especially mothers, which are known predictors of antisocial behavior, are highly related to the aggressive behaviors of their sons. Is that sufficient knowledge to enable us to intervene sensibly with a program to counteract the influence of violent television and, in general, reduce aggressive behavior in individual children?

The Chicago Circle Study

Huesmann and I (Huesmann, Eron, Klein, Brice, & Fischer, Note 5) were simpleminded enough to think it might be. Therefore, we introduced an intervention into our Chicago Circle Study aimed at reducing the aggressive behavior of 169 high violence viewers. In the second year of the study, these high violence viewers were randomly assigned to one of two groups. The experimental group was exposed to three training sessions designed to help the children discriminate television fantasy from real life events. They were shown excerpts from violent programs and were informed about how the sound and visual effects were used to simulate reality. The control group spent a similar amount of time watching folk dancing programs and learning more about such activities. As I reported in 1980 (Eron, 1980), this effort did not appear to be successful, since on a posttest the experimental subjects did no better than the control subjects in discriminating between television fantasy and real life behavior. At that time we half-facetiously said that we were hoping for a "sleeper" effect that would show up later (Gruder et al., 1978). As a matter of fact, the next year a strong effect did show up that may be a confound of the effect of our new procedures with the sleeper from the old procedure, since at the beginning of the third year we instituted a new training procedure with the same subjects. This new procedure consisted of techniques traditionally associated with attitude change experiments and has been described in detail elsewhere (Huesman et al., Note 5). I will mention them briefly here.

Each of the experimental subjects was asked to write a paragraph on "why TV violence is unrealistic and why viewing too much of it is bad." Over the course of two sessions, the child in the experimental group wrote the paragraph, received suggestions, and rewrote it; were taped reading the paragraph; and watched a TV tape of themselves and their classmates reading the paragraphs. The subjects were told that the tapes were going to be shown to the school children in Chicago. The placebo group also made a tape, but it was about "what you did last summer." Four months after this intervention, the final wave of data on all of the children in the study was collected. Remarkably it was found that the mean peer-nominated aggression score for the experimental group was now significantly lower than the score for the placebo group, although a year previously the two groups were approximately equal in score. The difference was highly significant, as evaluated by analysis of covariance with sex, grade, and pretreatment aggression score as covariates (Huesmann et al., Note 5).

Even more striking was the lack of relation between television violence and aggression in the experimental group and the continued positive relation in the placebo group, almost the same degree of relation as in the general population. The best predictor in the experimental group, however, was identification with aggressive TV characters. Another good predictor was judgment of TV realism. Those subjects who had higher self-rated identification with TV characters had higher peer-nominated aggression scores. The more realistic the experimental subjects thought TV was, the more aggressive they were. In the placebo group there was no significant independent relation between realism or identification and aggression. For all boys in the Chicago Circle Study (N = 375), however, there was an interaction between identification and TV violence, so those who watched violent television and also identified with the aggressive characters were the most aggressive of all subjects.

Why were those subjects who identified with TV characters less susceptible to the treatment? The treatment attempted to change attitudes about television and about aggression as well. As a manipulation check six attitudinal questions were asked before and after treatment; for example, "How much of what kids see on television shows would make a kid meaner?" The subjects responded to these questions on a five-point scale. The score was the sum of the weighted responses. A change score was calculated for each child by subtracting the pretreatment score from the posttreatment score. The larger the score, the more the child changed toward the desired attitude. We found that the most important predictor of change was identification with TV characters. The more the subjects identified with TV characters, the less likely they were to change their attitudes toward television as a result of the intervention. It will be remembered that the more the youngsters identified with TV characters, the more aggressive they were. Extent of identification with TV characters is thus demonstrated to be an important mediating variable in the relation between television violence and aggression. The only other significant predictor was a self-report on the extent to which the subjects read fairy tales or had fairy tales read to them. The more extensive the reading of fairy tales, the more likely was the attitude toward television to change. This latter finding is in keeping with the Singers' (Singer & Singer, 1981) contention that training in fantasy can affect the relation between television violence

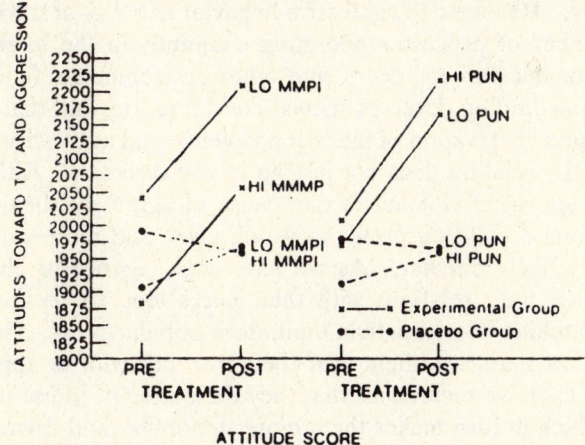

Fig. 5. Change in attitude toward TV as a function of parent variables and experimental treatment.

and behavior.

So with a very simple, brief technique, we were able to intervene in the real life relation between television violence viewing and aggressive behavior. It is almost too simple—almost unbelievalbe—that we who were strangers to the children could do this in three hours. What about the effect of parents—their personalities and behaviors? Is it possible that these brief procedures could overpower those effects?

Figure 5 shows that indeed it is possible. The strongest parent predictors of aggressive behavior in their children were the sum of Scales 4 and 9 on the MMPI and the extent of parental punishment for aggression. This figure shows that whether a parent was a high or low punisher or was high or low in the behaviors and attitudes measured by Scales 4 and 9 had no effect on how much attitudes changed from the pretreatment to posttreatment sessions. This, of course, is just one study, which demands replication. But it certainly suggests that we are not helpless in the face of that insidious teacher in our living rooms. There are simple instructional procedures that can be used by parents and teachers to counteract the negative effects television is having on our children.

Conclusion

I have tried to summarize and integrate the findings to date of two ongoing, large-scale, longitudinal studies of the development of aggression. One, the Rip Van Winkle Study, located in semirural New York, is now in its 21st year, and we are in the midst of the third wave of data collection. The second, the Chicago Circle Study, has drawn its subjects from suburban and inner-city Chicago, has completed three consecutive years of data collection, and is now being replicated in five other countries. The overriding conclusion, which should come as no surprise, is that aggression can be learned in many ways. Recourse to aggressive behavior as a way of solving problems is the result of a number of processes operating conjointly in the interactions of the youngster with his or her parents, peers, and other environmental figures. One persistent and ubiquitous finding deserves special consideration, and that is the relation between the continued observation of television violence and aggressive behavior. It is now apparent that the relation does not just go in one direction. Although we have demonstrated that television violence is one cause of aggressive behavior, it is also probable that aggressive children prefer to watch more and more violent television. The process is very likely circular. As we have seen, aggressive children are unpopular, and because their relations with their peers tend to be unsatisfying, they spend more time watching television than their more popular peers. The violence that they see on television reassures them that their own behavior is appropriate while teaching them new coercive techniques that they then attempt to use in their interaction with others, which in turn makes them more unpopular and drives them back to television, and the circle continues. Similarly, aggression is associated with low acheivement--for reasons we may not yet know. But we do know that children who do not succeed in school spend more time watching television than scholastically successful children and therefore have more opportunity to observe aggressive models. They tend to identify with these models more than their achieving peers and are therefore more influenced by the violent acts that they observe their favorite characters performing. Since their resources for problem solving are more limited than those of scholastically successful youngsters, the easy solutions they observe on television are more readily employed in their interactions with others. This type of behavior isolates them from their peers, leads them to more television, with less time for study, and so on and so on.

We have demonstrated, however, that it is possible to break into this cycle with simple interventions and short-circuit the connection between television violence and aggression. Unfortunately, with the procedures we have used, there is less chance for successful intervention when children identify strongly with TV characters and believe that the violence they observe on television is an accurate description of real life. The simple instructional procedures we have used may have to be modified for children already severely entrenched, by reason of constitution or environment, in these attitudes and beliefs.

REFERENCE NOTES

1. Lagerspetz, K. Personal communication, April 12, 1981.

2. Fraczek, A. *Cross cultural study of media violence and aggression among children. Comments on assumptions and methodology.* Paper read at the Twenty-Second International Congress of Psychology, Leipzig, Germany, July 6-12, 1980.

3. Sheehan, P. Personal communication, March 7, 1981.

4. Huesmann, L.R. & Eron, L.D. *The influence of mother's personality on children aggression* (Tech. Rep. No. 5). Chicago: University of Illinois at Chicago Circle, 1981.

5. Huesmann, L.R., Eron, L.D., Klein, R., Brice, P., & Fischer, P. *Mitigating the imitation of aggressive behaviors by changing children's attitudes about media violence* (Tech. Rep. No. 3). Chicago: University of Illinois at Chicago Circle, 1981.

REFERENCES

Bandura, A. *Aggression: Social learning analysis.* Englewood Cliffs, N.J.: Prentice-Hall, 1973.

Belson, W. *Television violence and the adolescent boy.* Hampshire, England: Saxon House, 1978.

Berkowitz, L. *Aggression: A social psychological analysis.* New York: McGraw-Hill, 1962.

Buss, A.H. *The psychology of aggression.* New York: Wiley, 1961.

Chaffee, S.H. Television and adolescent aggressiveness (overview). In G.A. Comstock & E.A. Rubinstein (Eds.), *Television and social behavior. Vol. 3: Television and adolescent aggressiveness.* Washington, D.C.: U.S. Government Printing Office, 1972.

Eron, L.D. Relationship of TV viewing habits and aggressive behavior in children. *Journal of Abnormal and Social Psychology,* 1963, 67, 193-196.

Eron, L.D. Prescription for reduction of aggression. *American Psychologist,* 1980, 35, 244-252.

Eron, L.D., Huesmann, L.R., Brice, P., Fischer, P., & Mermelstein, R. Age trends in the development of aggression, sex typing, and related television habits. *Developmental Psychology,* in press.

Eron, L.D., Huesmann, L.R., Lefkowitz, M.M., & Walder, L.O. Does television violence cause aggression? *American Psychologist,* 1972, 27, 253-263.

Eron, L.D., Walder, L.O., & Lefkowitz, M.M. *The learning of aggression in children.* Boston: Little, Brown, 1971.

Greenberg, B.S. British children and televised violence. *Public Opinion Quarterly,* 1975, 38, 531-547.

Gruder, C.L., Cook, T.D., Hennigan, K.M., Flay, B.R., Allessis, C., & Halamaj, J. Empirical tests of the absolute sleeper effect predicted from the discounting cue hypothesis. *Journal of Personality and Social Psychology,* 1978, 36, 1061-1074.

Hartnagel, T.F., Teevan, J.J., Jr., & McIntyre, J.J. Television violence and violent behavior. *Social Forces,* 1975, 54, 341-351.

Huesmann, L.R. Television violence and aggressive behavior. In D. Pearl & L. Bouthilet (Eds.), *Television and behavior: Ten years of scientific progress and implications for the 80's.* Washington, D.C.: U.S. Government Printing Office, in press.

Huesmann, L.R., & Eron, L.D. Factors influencing the effect of television violence on children. In M.J.A. Howe (Ed.), *Learning from television: Psychological and educational research.* London: Academic Press, in press.

Huesmann, L.R., Lefkowitz, M.M., & Eron, L.D. Sum of MMPI Scales F, 4, and 9 as a measure of aggression. *Journal of Consulting and Clincial Psychology*, 1978, 46, 1071-1078.

Lefkowitz, M.M., Eron, L.D., Walder, L.O., & Huesmann, L.R. *Growing up to be violent.* New York: Pergamon, 1977.

Lefkowitz, M.M., Walder, L.O., & Eron, L.D. Punishment, identification and aggression. *Merrill Palmer Quarterly of Behavior and Development,* 1963, 9, 159-174.

McCarthy, E.D.., Langer, T.S., Gersten, J.C., Eisenberg, J.G., & Orzeck, L. Violence and behavior disorders. *Journal of Communication*, 1975, 25, 71-85.

Parke, R.D., Berkowitz, L., Leyens, P., West, S., & Sebastian, R.J. Some effects of violent and nonviolent movies on the behavior of juvenile delinquents. In L. Berkowitz (Ed.), *Advances in experimental social psychology* (Vol. 10). New York: Academic Press, 1977.

Rosenfeld, E., Huesmann, L.R., Eron, L.D., & Torney-Purta, J.V. Measuring patterns of fantasy behavior in children. *Journal of Personality and Social Psychology*, in press.

Singer, J.L., & Singer, D.G. *Television, imagination and aggression: A study of preschoolers' play.* Hillsdale, N.J.: Erlbaum, 1981.

Walder, L.O., Abelson, R., Eron, L.D., Banta, T.J., & Laulicht, J.H. Development of a peer rating measure of aggression. *Psychological Reports,* 1961, 9, 497-556.

Television as a Socializer

J. Philippe Rushton

The results of many surveys have now shown that, in North America (1) almost every family has at least one television set, (2) the television is turned on for almost 6 hours per day in the average household, (3) both children and adults watch, on the average, over 3 hours of television daily, (4) about 40% of all leisure time is spent with television, and (5) television ranks third (behind sleep and work) as a consumer of time (e.g., *Ontario*, 1977). The figures relating to children are particularly interesting. Children begin watching television on a regular basis 3 or 4 years before entering Grade One and most children watch television every day. It has been estimated that by the time the child is 16 years of age he or she will have spent more time with television than will ever be spent in any kind of classroom. Another comparison also demonstrates perspective: by the time a child is 5 and reaches kindergarten, he or she has spent more time watching televison than a liberal arts student spends in the classroom throughout his or her 4 years at a university!

An important question that arises from such considerations is: Can the content of what is watched influence viewers' behavior? It is certainly true that people learn by watching others. Indeed, this is one of the most fundamental ways by which people learn new behavior. By watching others, people who enter new occupations learn skills and attitudes necessary to their new job. Also by watching others, people can

Originally published in *Altruism and Helping Behavior*, edited by Lawrence Erlbaum and Associates. Reprinted with permission of the author.

learn the complex skills involved in new sports and leisure-time activities. Such learning often involves a great deal of effort and concentration. Other such learning, however, takes place quite automatically. Think of speech as an example. The majority of words we use are learned without conscious effort. Simply by observing others, people acquire the vocabulary and many of the rules of grammar that they use. People also acquire their accents and styles of delivery by observing others. Thus whether people use a wide or a more limited range of expressive gestures when they talk will depend to a large extent on the particular models they watched when they were learning the language. Much of this learning took place without their even being aware of it.

Children are particularly likely to learn by watching others. They are at a most formative period in their lives where they are striving to gain some understanding and mastery of the social world that they inhabit. By watching others and then imitating what they have seen they can learn the "rules" of social behavior. Although adults have very often learned to distinguish between who is appropriate and who is inappropriate to watch and learn from, young children very often have not made this distinction.

Of particular importance for the current purpose is the research that confirms that watching others leads to learning the norms and emotional responses that people have for each other (Rushton, 1980). One of the most important implications of this pertains to television. If one of the main ways in which people learn is by observing others, then it follows that people can learn a great deal from viewing others on television. This has been a question of concern for more than two decades now (Himmelweit, Oppenheim & Vince, 1958).

In recent years, concern has focused primarily on whether violence on television contributes to the amount of violence in society. Many governmental inquiries as well as scholarly researchers have investigated this question and a vast literature has come into being. Although there were still dissenters (e.g., Halloran, 1978; Kaplan & Singer, 1976), the weight of the evidence appears to demonstrate that television portrayals of violence do increase the amount of antisocial behavior in society. For example, a recent Canadian Royal Commission of inquiry into the problem concluded:

> If the amount of depicted violence that exists in the North American intellectual environment could be expressed in terms of a potentially dangerous food or drink additive ... there is little doubt that society long since would have demanded a stop to it...[*Ontario*, Vol. 1, 1977, p. 51].

Other recent reviews have also concluded that the portrayal of violence on television increases antisocial behaviors (Comstock, Chaffee, Katzman, McCombs, & Robers, 1978; Liebert & Schwartzberg, 1977; Murray & Kippax, 1979; Parke,

Berkowitz, Leyens, West & Sebastin, 1977; Rushton, 1980).

It is not the intention in this chapter to consider this evidence yet again; rather it is to focus on television as a force for good. Although there has long been a research interest in the possible harmful effects of media violence, the other side of the coin, the potential for good, has only recently been investigated. Notwithstanding its recency, this research literature is now burgeoning. It demonstrates that television can have quite diverse effects, including the power to influence prosocial behavior. (The term "prosocial" is used to specify that which is socially desirable and which in some ways benefits another person or society at large.) This definition will involve a value judgment based on the wider social context. The present chapter views some of the key studies in this more recent line of inquiry into television effects. It borrows heavily from the outline and content I have followed in previous discussions of this same literature (Rushton, 1977, 1979, 1980).

This chapter investigates the consequences of showing five types of television content to viewers. The first type of programming is altruistic in nature, and includes such behaviors as generosity, helping, and cooperation. The second concerns showing friendly behavior. The third involves showing self-control behaviors such as resisting temptation and delaying gratification. The fourth involves showing both adults and children coping with their fears. Finally the portrayal of occupational, ethnic group, and sex roles is examined. Some of the studies examined the television effects in laboratory situations and others used more naturalistic environments. As we shall see, the results from both settings come to similar conclusions. Nonetheless, throughout the review a clear demarcation is made between the two types of testing environments. The term *television* is used here in the widest sense; i.e., it will include specially constructed videotapes used purely for experimental or therapeutic purposes in addition to commercial television programs. The nature of the programming is clearly specified throughout the review.

THE EFFECTS OF SHOWING ALTRUISTIC BEHAVIORS ON TELEVISION

Laboratory Studies

In a series of experiments, reviewed by Bryan (1975) several hundred 6- to 9-year-old children, of both sexes, were shown specially constructed 5-minute videotape film of a model who played on a bowling game, won gift certificates, and donated or did not donate some of these gift certificates to a charity. Subsequently, the child was watched through a one-way mirror to see how much of his or her winnings he or she donated to a similar charity. The results showed that children were strongly influenced by what they had seen the models doing on TV. Children who had watched generosity on the videotape gave more of their certificates to the charity than did those

children who had watched selfishness portrayed. Other studies, using similar procedures, have replicated Bryan's findings. Elliot and Vasta (1970) showed that 5- to 7-
year-old children were influenced by television models to share both candy and
money. Rushton and Owen (1975) found that 8- to 10-year-old British children were
influenced to donate tokens to a charity by watching TV models do so.

The film material used in these studies was not like that produced for commercial
purposes however. It lasted for only 5 minutes and showed one person acting a number of times in just one way (e.g., being generous) in one highly specific situation. In
addition the child who watched was then tested in exactly the same situation in which
he or she had seen the model act. Sprafkin, Liebert, and Poulos (1975) went further
than the aforementioned studies and conceptually replicated the previous findings
with a highly successful commercial television program, *Lassie*. They divided 30 5-
year-old white middle-class children into three groups and showed each group one of
three half-hour television films, complete with commericals. A prosocial *Lassie*
program involved Jeff, Lassie's master, risking his life by hanging over the edge of a
mine shaft to rescue Lassie's pup. A neutral *Lassie* film and a neutral non*Lassie* film
made up two control groups. After watching the programs the children were taken to
another room where they could earn points toward a prize by playing on a game.
During the course of playing the game they had an opportunity to aid puppies in distress by calling for help by pressing a Help button. Pressing the Help button, however,
would interfere with earning points toward the prize. The average time spent pressing
the Help button for children who had watched the prosocial Lassie was 93 seconds,
whereas in the two neutral conditions it was 52 and 38 seconds respectively. Thus this
study supported the previous laboratory studies using a program from a highly successful commercial series.

Collins and Getz (1976) also carried out a laboratory investigation using a regular
program complete with commercials. They edited a television action-adventure
drama made for adults such that in one version a model responded constructively to
an interpersonal conflict while in another he responded aggressively. Fourth, seventh,
and tenth graders saw one of these versions or a wildlife documentary control. They
were then given an opportunity to either help or hurt a fictitious peer who was apparently completing a task by either pressing a "help" button which shut off a distract-
ing noise or a "hurt" button which increased it. Children of all ages who had seen
models of constructive coping showed greater prosocial responding than subjects in
the other two conditions, i.e., they gave more help responses than children who viewed
either the aggression or the control programs.

Naturalistic Studies

Friedrich and Stein (1973) carried out a study with 97 nursery school children.
First, the children's naturally occurring free play behavior was coded into categories

such as "aggressive," "prosocial," and "self-control." The children were then randomly assigned to one of three groups and exposed to 4 weeks of selected television. The first group watched aggressive television films such as *Batman* and *Superman* cartoons. A second group watched "neutral" films such as children working on a farm, and a third group watched *Mister Rogers' Neighborhood,* a prosocial education television program that stresses cooperation, sharing, sympathy, affection and friendship. During the 4-week exposure to one of the three television diets, the children's free play behavior was recorded by observers who were "blind" as to experimental condition.

The results of this experiment demonstrated that the programs did have some effect on the children's subsequent aggressive or prosocial behavior. The aggressive television content led to increased interpersonal aggression for those children who were above average in such aggression at baseline. However the effects did not generalize to a 2-week retest. Although exposure to the prosocial television content led to increased prosocial behavior, it did so only in the children from the lower half of the socioeconomic status distribution. Here too, however, the results failed to extend to the 2-week retest. Both the aggressive and prosocial films had stronger effects on the measures of self-control as we shall see when we come to that section.

In a subsequent study with *Mister Rogers' Neighborhood,* Friedrich and Stein (1975) randomly assigned 73 preschoolers to one of five conditions. One group of children watched four "neutral" programs about nature and other topics unrelated to interpersonal behavior. The other four groups saw four programs from *Mister Rogers' Neighborhood* chosen to form a dramatic sequence. In this sequence, a crisis arose in which one of the characters feared that she would be replaced by a fancy new visitor. Action centered on the attempts of friends to understand her feelings, reassure her of her uniqueness, and help her. Children watched the television programs in groups of three or four over 4 days. Results indicated that when children were asked questions such as "How do friends show they like you?" those who had watched the prosocial television films reported more ways of showing how friends demonstrated affection than children who had watched neutral films. This was true both in situations that were similar to those in the *Mister Rogers' Neighborhood* program and also to those that involved new situations. On another test a behavioral measure of helping another child in a quite different context; while there were no overall differences between those children who had watched prosocial television programs and those who had watched the neutral television programs, it was found that if watching the prosocial television had been paired with direct training to be helpful through "role-playing" techniques, then children in this condition were more helpful than those who had been given the training but no diet of prosocial television. This suggests the possibility that prosocial television might be used as an adjunct to other training procedures when attempting to teach or enhance prosocial tendencies in children—as nursery school teachers and parents might well wish to do.

This latter conclusion gains additional credence from a study by Friendrich-Cofer, Huston-Stein, Kipnis, Susman, and Clewett (1979). They found that even 8 weeks of prosocial television, by itself, did not influence the behavior of urban poor children. However, if the prosocial television was augmented with themes from *Mister Rogers' Neighborhood* acted out in class, then significant behavioral gains in prosocial behavior were found compared to control groups.

A particularly ambitious and realistic study was carried out by Moriarty and McCabe (1977) with 259 children and youth engaged in organized team sports. Participants in Little League baseball, lacrosse and ice-hockey were included. Both the antisocial and prosocial behavior of the players on the field, before, during, and after experimental treatment were measured. The experimental treatment consisted of providing antisocial, prosocial, and control video presentations of the relevant sport to the randomly assigned teams. The prosocial material consisted of (1) altruism — helping, encouraging, and team work; (2) sympathy — compassion, pity, and caring for another's plight; (3) courtesy — displays of respect; (4) reparation — correcting a wrong, or apologizing; and (5) affection — any overt expression of positive feelings towards another. The results indicated that exposure to the prosocial content clearly increased the level of prosocial behavior for the hockey and lacrosse players, although not for baseball players. The showing of the antisocial programs had no effect in this particular study.

Finally a study might be reported that assessed the relative influence of role-playing and prosocial television content in facilitating altruism. Ahammer and Murray (1979) showed Australian kindergarten children television programs such as *Lassie, I Love Lucy, The Brady Bunch* and *Father Knows Best*. On the basis of a content analysis some of these programs were designated as high in prosocial television while others were designated as neutral. The prosocial programs had a high frequency of expressing concern for others' feelings, sympathy, task persistence, and explaining feelings of self or others. The children were either assigned as a class to a "prosocial" viewing condition or to a "neutral" viewing condition. The viewing took place 1/2 hour per day, 5 days per week, for 4 weeks. The children were pretested on a variety of measures one week prior to the onset of television viewing and were posttested on these same measures one week after the conclusion of training. The results indicated that the prosocial television condition was associated with increases in a situational test of helping (for boys only) and increases in a test of cooperation (for both boys and girls). Helping had been measured by the child's willingness to forego playing with some attractive toys in order to help another absent child complete a task which consisted of placing marbles in a box one at a time. Cooperation was indexed by the number of candies that the child won in contrast to his or her partner, while playing on a Madsen cooperation/competition table. Thus observation of standard television programs in which the main characters displayed concern for others, could be effective in facilitating altruism in specific situational tests quite dissimilar from the situations seen on the programs. Of interest in this study was the finding that role-playing techniques were even more effective in facilitating altruism than was the prosocial television. This latter finding, of course, does not detract from the fact that prosocial television had independent effects.

THE EFFECTS OF SHOWING FRIENDLY BEHAVIORS ON TELEVISION

Laboratory Studies

Fryrear and Thelen (1969) assigned boys and girls of nursery school age to one of two main television viewing groups: one which observed an adult demonstrating "affectionate" behavior toward a small stuffed clown, and a control group. Children were subsequently given an opportunity to play with a group of toys which included the small clown. An observer sat in the back of the room and watched to see whether the child imitated the affectionate behavior toward the toy. Children who watched television films of affectionate behavior were subsequently more likely to express similar affection than children who had not seen such behavior on television.

Gorn, Goldberg and Kanungo (1976) carried out a study in Canada to investigate whether prosocial television content could increase nursery school children's friendliness toward ethnic minorities. After being exposed to special "Sesame Street" inserts containing nonwhite children, a sample of 3- to 5-year old white children showed a strong preference for playing with nonwhites as opposed to whites. This sharply contrasted with the preferences of a control group not exposed to these inserts.

Naturalistic Studies

O'Connor (1969) conducted a dramatic and potentially important study to see if television programs could be used to enhance social interaction among those nursery school children who tended to isolate themselves from their peers. Thirteen severely solitary children were chosen for the study. These children were interacting on fewer than five of 32 possible interactions reliably observed over an 8-day period. One group of these isolated children was then shown a specially prepared sound-color film shown over a television console. This film portrayed a graduated sequence of 11 scenes in which children interacted in a nursery school setting with reinforcing consequences ensuing. All the scenes were accompanied by a female narrator describing the actions of the model and the responses of the other children. For comparison purposes, a second group of children were shown a film of dolphins engaging in acrobatic feats.

The results were quite dramatic. Children who had watched the specially made film about others engaging in social interaction increased from their baseline score of an average of nearly 2 interactions out of the 32 possible to an average of nearly 12 interactions out of the possible 32. The control group showed no increase over their baseline scores. Furthermore, a follow-up at the end of the school year showed that the changes were durable over time.

In a subsequent study, O'Connor (1972) selected 33 social isolates from four nursery school populations according to both teacher ratings and behavioral samples obtained by trained observers. In a 2 ×2 factorial design, half of the children viewed a specially constructed 23-min modeling film depicting appropriate social behavior, while the other half viewed a control film. Half of the subjects in each film condition then received social reinforcement contingent upon the performance of peer interaction behaviors. Modeling was shown to be a more rapid modification procedure than was shaping-through-reinforcement, and resulted in more stable social interaction patterns over time, with or without the attendant social reinforcement. In the follow-up assessments, modeling subjects remained at the original baseline level of nonisolates, while social reinforcement and control subjects returned to isolate baseline level.

In a study of similar nature, Keller and Carlson (1974) showed 19 socially isolated preschoolers either four 5-minute videotapes in which social skills (e.g., how to socially reinforce peers) were modeled (treatment) or 4 sequences of a nature film (control). The frequency with which subjects dispensed and recieved social reinforcement and the frequency of social interaction were rated by observers pre- and post-treatment and at follow-up. Results indicated that treatment produced increases in all 3 dependent measures for the treatment group.

Coates, Pusser, and Goodman (1976) assessed the effects of both *Sesame Street* and *Mister Rogers' Neighborhood* on 32 preschool children. The frequency of these children's behaviors were recorded into one of three categories:

(1) Positive reinforcement: giving positive attention such as praise and approval, sympathy, reassurance, and smiling and laughing; giving affectionate physical contact such as hugging, kissing, and holding hands; giving tangible reinforcement such as tokens, prizes and other objects; (2) Punishment: giving verbal criticism and rejection such as criticism, negative greetings, obvious ignorings, and scarcasm; giving negative physical contact such as hitting, biting, and kicking; withdrawing or refusing tangible reinforcement such as taking away a toy; and (3) Social contact: any physical or verbal contact between a child and another child or adult.

Following these baseline measures children watched either 15 minutes of *Sesame Street* or 15 minutes of *Mister Rogers' Neighborhood* for each of four days. These programs had previously been content analyzed for the frequency of occurrence of positive reinforcement and punishment. After watching the programs, the children were observed and the frequency with which they behaved in any of the categories mentioned above was recorded. In addition, a four day follow-up was undertaken. The results showed that the television programs affected the children's social behavior in a significant manner, particularly on the immediate post-viewing tests. For all children *Mister Rogers' Neighborhood* significantly increased the giving of positive reinforcement to, and social contacts with, both other children and adults. For *Sesame Street* the effects were only found for children who had low baseline scores.

THE EFFECTS OF SHOWING SELF-CONTROL BEHAVIORS ON TELEVISION

Laboratory Studies

Stein and Bryan (1972) explained to 80 8- and 9-year-old girls the rules by which they could win money by playing an electronic bowling game. Before playing the game the children watched a television program in which they saw a same sex peer playing the same game. This peer model behaved either in violation of these rules or in accordance with them. Children who observed the transgressing model cheated more than twice as much as those who observed a model adhering to the rules.

Wolf and Cheyne (1972) carried out an experiment with 7- to 8-year-old boys. First the children were taken to a games room and allowed to play with some toys. They were forbidden, however, to touch or play with one particularly attractive toy. It was found that an average of 4 minutes and 40 seconds would go by before an average boy in this situation would touch the toy. However, if the toys and this TV child had *not* touched the toy, then the average boy would wait nearly 8 minutes before transgressing. If, on the other hand, the TV program had shown another boy violating the rule and touching the forbidden toy, then the subject would be likely to touch the toy in less than 3 minutes. Very similar results were found when the measure of the child's resistance to temptation was based on the *length* of time he played with the toy. The average boy would play with the forbidden toy for about 1 minute out of the 10 that was observed. If he watched a TV program depicting violation of the rules then he would play with the forbidden toy for nearly 4 out of 10 minutes. If however, he watched a TV program showing adherence to the rules then he would touch the forbidden toy for only about 7 seconds. Wolf and Cheyne (1972) brought the boys back one month later and put them into the same situation. The results still showed an effect for the television program. Whereas children who had seen no television film one month earlier managed to resist the temptation for nearly 6 minutes, boys who had seen a model giving in to the temptation, only resisted for 4 minutes. In this 4-week retest no effect was found for the "self-controlled" model however. These results were replicated by Wolf (1973).

Another form of self-control is the ability to delay gratification to a later point in time. Yates (1974) carried out a study with 72 8-year-old New Zealand children. Baselines were established by asking children if they would prefer a small reward such as money immediately, or a larger one by waiting for 7 days. Some time later, some of the children watched television programs of an adult female model exemplify high-delay behavior and/or verbalize reasons for delaying gratification. Other children did not watch such programs. Compared to controls, children who had watched the television programs showing delay of gratification were subsequently more likely themselves to choose to delay their gratification for a larger reward later. Furthermore, when the children were retested 4 weeks later their behavior still showed the effects of the exposure to the television films.

Naturalistic Studies

In a study described previously in the section on altruistic behavior (Friedrich & Stein, 1973), either the prosocial television program *Mister Rogers' Neighborhood*, the aggressive television programs of *Superman* and *Batman*, or neutral fare was shown to 93 4-year-old nursery school children for a 4-week period. During this time their naturally occurring free-play-behavior was observed. Three categories of self-control behavior had been recorded. These were: obedience to rules, tolerance of delay, and persisting at task. In regard to the obedience to rules category, aggressive films decreased this behavior in relation to neutral films, whereas the prosocial films increased it, producing an overall difference. In regard to tolerating delay, the aggressive films significantly decreased such behaviors over both the neutral and prosocial conditions that did not differ from one another. Furthermore, these particular effects were maintained across the 2-week retest. Finally the prosocial television content increased persistence at tasks over the neutral and aggressive films on both immediate and later observations.

THE EFFECTS OF SHOWING PEOPLE COPING WITH THEIR FEARS ON TELEVISION

Laboratory Studies

The first study to be reported concerns young children who were inappropriately afraid of dogs. Bandura and Menlove (1968) first measured 3- to 5-year-old children's willingness to approach and play with a cocker spaniel on a number of occasions, to determine which children were afraid of dogs. Some children were then shown eight specially prepared 3-minute film programs over an 8-day period in which they saw other children playing with dogs. Another group of fearful children were shown movies of Disneyland instead. After watching these films, the children who had watched other children showing courage were now much more likely to approach and play with the dogs than the children in the control group were. Furthermore, this reduction in fear generalized to dogs quite different from those seen in the film, and was maintained over a 4-week retest period.

A study by Bandura, Blanchard, and Ritter (1971) investigated whether film programming could help adolescents and adults reduce their fear of snakes. Only those who reported having a severe fear of snakes took part. For example, their dread of snakes had actually to be so severe as to interfere with their ability to do gardening or go camping. These people were then shown films of young children, adolescents, and adults engaging in progressively threatening interactions with a large king snake for 35 minutes. Behavioral measures were then taken in the presence of live snakes. The findings were clear. People who had watched the film significantly reduced their fears. It might be mentioned that the behavioral measures were quite stringent and included actually holding the snake in the hands. The ultimate test (which 33% of the subjects performed) included allowing the snake to lie in their laps while they held their hands passively at their sides.

Weissbrod and Bryan (1973) attempted to see whether similar techniques would succeed with 8- to 9-year-old children who had indicated an extreme fear of snakes on a fear inventory, and also refused to pet a snake during a pretest. These children watched a 2 min. videotaped sequence involving a model either approaching a live 4-ft. boa constrictor (the experimental group) or a stuffed 5-ft. toy snake (the comparison condition). All children watched their respective films twice through and then, 2 days later, watched them twice through again. Following this second showing of the film the children were taken to an aquarium that housed a 4-ft. boa constrictor and asked to touch, then pet, and then hold the snake. The experimental group were able to go further into the sequence than the control comparison group, and furthermore, maintained their superiority on another test taken 2 weeks later. For example, although none of the ten children in the control were able to actually handle the snake 2 weeks after watching the "neutral" film, 11 out of the 40 children in the experimental condition could.

Naturalistic Studies

Melamed and Siegel (1975) showed 60 children aged 4 to 12 who were about to undergo elective surgery for hernias, tonsillectomies, or urinary-genital tract difficulties, either a relevant peer modeling film of a child being hospitalized and receiving surgery or an unrelated control film. The experimental film was 16 minutes in length and consisted of 15 scenes showing various events that most children hospitalized for elective surgery encounter. Both groups received extensive preparation by the hospital staff. State measures of anxiety, including self-report, behavioral observation, and Palmar Sweat Index, revealed a significant reduction of preoperative (night before) and postoperative (3-4 week postsurgery examination) fear arousal in the experimental as compared to the control film group. In addition parents reported more problem behavior in the children who had not seen the modeling film.

Effects for the therapeutic value of the film modeling have been demonstrated in a number of other studies. O'Connor (1969, 1972) used film models to decrease children's fear of social interaction. Jaffe and Carlson (1972) and Mann (1972) treated test-anxious university and high school students with videotaped modeling procedures and found significant improvement on performance measures. Shaw and Thoresen (1974) demonstrated that specially constructed films can effectively reduce adults fears of dental treatment. These authors used actual visits to the dentist for treatment as their measure of success. Video desensitization has also been successfully applied to the treatment of sexual dysfunction among women (Wincze & Caird, 1976).

Only a very few of the many studies that have used modeling films to systematically diminish anxiety in therapeutic contexts have been reviewed here. Major reviews of this particular literature have been carried out by Rosenthal and Bandura (1978) and Thelen, Fry, Fehrenbach and Frantschi (1979). Both reviews conclude that such films have vast therapeutic potential.

THE EFFECTS OF SHOWING OCCUPATIONAL, ETHNIC GROUP, AND SEX ROLE BEHAVIOR ON TELEVISION

To what extent are our conceptions about occupations, ethnic groups, and sex roles influenced by how we see them portrayed on television? Given the power of television to alter both viewer's aggressive and prosocial behavior, it might well be expected that such expectations *would* be readily influenced. Strangely enough, far less research has been aimed at this particular question. Although researchers have carried out several content analyses of the social roles portrayed on television they have not, in the main, carried out research to see whether these particular portrayals are subsequently mirrored in viewers' perceptions. Let us examine the content analyses.

In regard to occupational roles, Smythe (1954) in an early study, found that teachers were portrayed as the kindest and fairest, journalists the most honest, and scientists the least kind, the most unfair, and the least honest of all the occupations he looked at. DeFleur (1964) found that television portrayed the police as generally hardened and often brutal; private investigators as resourceful and more capable than the police; salesmen as glib; journalists as callous; and truck drivers as aggressive. In a more recent study, Williams, Zabrack and Joy (1977) found that the police were portrayed as powerful, interesting, satisfied with their lives, and overwhelmingly emotionally stable. This was similar to a finding by Dominick (1978) who also found that television police were far more efficient than are police in real life. Dominick (1978) also noted that the portrayal of law enforcement on prime time television had increased dramatically over the years from 7% in 1953 to 27% in 1977.

Psychiatrists and their mentally ill patients have also been represented in different ways from earlier times to more recent ones. Winick (1978) found, for example, in an analysis of 151 movies made from 1919 to 1978 that there was a increasing trend that as mental illness and its treatment became more accepted, there was a tendency to make the pateint and his therapist less exotic, magical, frightening, and more human.

In regard to ethnic groups, the characters portrayed on North American television are overwhelmingly young, white, middle class, and American (Williams et al., 1977). Most ethnic minorities and citizens of foreign countries are ignored. When they are presented they are often made to look either ridiculous or villanious and this has been a source of hurt and irritation to groups as far flung as Chinese, Italians, Mexicans, and perhaps particularly, Native Peoples. Even Canadians have sometimes been concerned at the way in which they have been portrayed, particularly in Hollywood movies (Berton, 1975). In response to black American protest, portrayals of black Americans seem to have shifted somewhat in recent years, so that they are now presented both more frequently and in higher-status positions. In a recent content analysis, Donagher, Poulos, Liebert, and Davidson (1975) found that black males, for example, were usually portrayed as nonaggressive, persistent, altruistic, and more likely to make reparation for injury than any other group. Black women expressed a high ability to explain feelings in order to increase understanding, resolve strife, and reassure others. Unfortunately, as mentioned, very few studies have actually been carried out to see whether television portrayals are ever mirrored in viewers' perceptions.

One interesting study that did look at viewers' perceptions was carried out by Vidmar and Rokeach (1974). These authors investigated racially prejudiced and nonprejudiced viewers perceptions of Archie Bunker, the chief protagonist in the comedy satire *All in the Family*. Archie Bunker is a conservative, superpatriotic working-class American who engages in a great deal of racial and ethnic prejudice but who is at the same time very endearing in many ways, especially when everything goes wrong for him (as it often does). One of the stated aims of the program is to bring racial bigotry into the open and make fun of it, thus serving to reduce it. Vidmar and Rokeach (1974) found however that how the viewers perceived the program depended on their preexisting attitudes. High prejudiced viewers, as measured by a questionnaire, were more likely to perceive Archie as admirable and to make better sense and win arguments than low prejudiced viewers. Thus, the authors concluded, the program may inadvertently be reinforcing prejudice and racism in those already prejudiced. The selectivity of perception was further documented by Vidmar and Rokeach (1974) by some data these authors had collected about another program *Sanford and Son*. This is a situation comedy modeled after *All in the Family* about a black junk dealer who is prejudiced against whites. Sanford, the junk dealer, is lazy, lives in a junkyard, and throws his beer cans out the front door. On the other hand, his son Lamont is ambitious and hard working. The authors found that high prejudiced persons were sig-nificntly more likely to perceive Sanford as typical of blacks than were low prejudiced viewers.

Although studies such as that by Vidmar and Rokeach (1974) clearly demonstrate that television content is perceived differently by different types of people, they do not speak directly to the question of whether television programs can modify prejudiced attitudes. At least two such studies have been carried out directly on this question. One very early British study did find that television could increase children's knowledge about foreigners (Himmelweit, Oppenheim & Vince, 1958). A recent Canadian study found that children's play preferences could be made more favorable to minority groups after viewing special inserts on *Sesame Street* (Gorn, Goldberg, & Kanungo, 1976).

In regard to the portrayal of sex roles, some concern has been expressed in regard to the way females have been portrayed. A study by Sternglanz and Serbin (1974) provided support for this concern. These authors content analyzed a number of children's programs that had high Nielsen ratings. They found, first of all, that males were portrayed nearly twice as often as females. There were also major differences between the sexes in the types of behavior protrayed. Males, for instance, were more often portrayed as aggressive and constructive (e.g., building, planning) than females, while females were more likely to be shown as deferent and passive. In addition, the consequences that males and females received for emitting behavior were different, with males more often being rewarded and females more often receiving no conse-quence. An exception to this was that females were more often punished for high levels of activity than were males. On the other hand, at least when women were portrayed they were presented as "interesting" and "emotionally stable" (Williams et al., 1977).

Finally, Silverman, Sprafkin & Rubinstein (1979) in an analysis of sexual behavior on prime time TV, found that sexual innuendos have dramatically increased in fre-quency in recent years; while the TV viewer in 1975 could hear an average of about one innuendo per hour, in 1977 he or she could hear about seven. Interestingly enough, it was white females who were disproprotionately responsible for the physical-ly suggestive behaviors. (Black females affectionately touched children; males engaged in aggression!)

It appears that commercially produced television programs are carrying quite dif-ferent messages about the appropriate behavior for males and females. Given the general evidence on the powerful effectiveness of modeling on television as a means of teaching behavior, television may well be an important source in the learning of stereotyped sex roles.

SUMMARY AND CONCLUSION:
UNDERSTANDING TELEVISION EFFECTS

People learn norms, the "rules" of social behavior, from watching others. This is the key to understanding the effects of television. Television is much more than mere entertainment; it is also a major source of observational learning experiences, a setter of norms. It determines what people will judge to be appropriate behavior in a variety of situations.

In this chapter, over two dozen experimental investigations were reviweed from an even larger body of data. These studies, from both laboratory and naturalistic settings, demonstrated that television programming can modify viewers' social behavior in a prosocial direction. Generosity, helping, cooperation, friendliness, adhering to rules, delaying gratification, and a lack of fear can all be increased by television material. This suggests that television is an effective agent of socialization; that television entertainment is modifying the viewers perception of the world and how to live in it.

From the present vantage point, therefore, it would appear that television does act as a socializer. The evidence suggest that it influences the social behavior of viewers in the direction of the content of the programs dictate. If, on the one hand, prosocial helping and kindness make up the content of television programming, then this is what may be learned by viewers as appropriate, normative behavior. If, on the other hand, antisocial behaviors and uncontrolled aggression are shown, then these are what viewers may learn to be the norm. This view will fit well with the fact that billions of dollars are spent annually by advertisers on North American television. Advertisers believe correctly, that brief, 30 second exposures to their product, repeated over and over, will significantly modify the viewing public's behavior in regard to those products. The message therefore seems clear: people learn from watching television and what they learn will depend on what they watch. As discussed in detail elsewhere (Rushton, 1980), it might very well be that television has become one of the major agencies of socialization that our society currently possesses.

REFERENCES

Ahammer, I.M., & Murray, J.P. Kindness in the Kindergarten: The relative influence of role playing and prosocial television in facilitating altruism. *International Journal of Behavioral Development*, 1979, 2, 133-157.

Bandura, A., Blanchard, E.B., & Ritter, B. The relative efficacy of desensitization and modeling approaches for inducing behavioral, affective and attitudinal changes. *Journal of Personality and Social Psychology*, 1971, 13, 113-199.

Bandura, A., & Menlove, F.L. Factors determining vicarious extinction of avoidance behavior through symbolic modeling. *Journal of Personality and Social Psychology,* 1968, 8, 99-108.

Berton, P. *Hollywood's Canada.* Toronto: McClelland and Stewart, 1975.

Bryan, J.H. Children's cooperation and helping behaviors. In E.M. Hetherington (Ed.), *Review of child development research* (Vol. 5). Chicago: Unviersity of Chicago Press, 1975.

Coates, B., Pusser, H.E., & Goodman, I. The influence of "Sesame Street" and "Mister Rogers' Neighborhood" on children's social behavior in the preschool. *Child Development,* 1976, 47, 138-144.

Collins, W.A., & Getz, S.K. Children's social responses following modeled reactions to provocation: Prosocial effects of a television drama. *Journal of Personality,* 1976, 44, 488-500.

Comstock, G., Chaffee, S., Katzman, N., McCombs, M., & Roberts, D. *Television and human behavior.* New York: Columbia University Press, 1978.

DeFleur, M.L. Occupational roles as portrayed on television. *Public Opinion Quarterly,* 1964, 28, 57-74.

Dominick, J.R. Crime and law enforcement in the mass media. In C. Winick (Ed.), *Sage Annual Reviewers of Studies in Deviance, Vol. 2. Deviance and Mass Media.* Beverly Hills, Ca.: Sage Publications, Inc., 1978.

Donagher, P.C., Poulos, R.W., Liebert, R.M., & Davidson, E.S. Race, sex and social example: An analysis of character portrayals on interracial television entertainment. *Psychological Reports*, 1975, 37, 1023-1034.

Elliot, R., & Vasta, R. The modeling of sharing: Effects associated with vicarious reinforcement, symbolization, age, and generalization. *Journal of Experimental Child Psychology*, 1970, 10, 8-15.

Friedrich, L.K., & Stein, A.H. Aggressive and prosocial television programs and the natural behavior of preschool children. *Monographs of the Society for Research in Child Development,* 1973, 38 (4, Serial No. 151).

Friedrich, K.L., & Stein, A.H. Prosocial television and young children: The effects of verbal labeling and role playing on learning and behavior. *Child Development,* 1975, 46, 27-38.

Friedrich-Cofer, L.K., Huston-Stein, A., Kipnis, D.M., Susman, E.J., & Clewett, A.S. Environmental enhancement of prosocial television content: Effects of interpersonal behavior, imaginative play, and self-regulation in a natural setting. *Developmental Psychology,* 1979, 15, 637-646.

Fryrear, J.L., & Thelen, M.H. Effect of sex of model and sex of observer on the imitation of affectionate behavior. *Developmental Psychology,* 1969, 1, 298.

Gorn, G.J., Goldberg, M.E., & Kanungo, R.N. The role of educational television in changing the intergroup attitudes of children. *Child Development,* 1976, 47, 277-280.

Halloran, J.D. Studying violence and the media: A sociological approach. In C. Winick (Ed.), *Sage Annual Reviews of Studies in Deviance. Vol. 2. Deviance and Mass Media.* Beverly Hills, Ca.: Sage Publications, Inc., 1978.

Himmelweit, H., Oppenheim, A.N., & Vince, P. *Television and the child: An empircial study of the effects of television on the young.* London: Oxford Unviersity Press, 1958.

Jaffe, P.G., & Carlson, P.M. Modeling therapy for test anxiety: The role of model affect and consequences. *Behavior Research and Therapy,* 1972, 10, 329-339.

Kaplan, R.M., & Singer, R.D. Television violence and viewer aggression: A re-examination of the evidence. *Journal of Social Issues*, 1976, 32(4), 35-70.

Keller, M.F., & Carlson, P.M. Social skills in preschool children with low levels of social responsiveness. *Child Development*, 1974, 45, 912-919.

Liebert, R.M., & Schwartzberg, N.S. Effects of mass media. *Annual Review of Psychology*, 1977, 28, 141-173.

Mann, J. Vicarious desensitization of test anxiety through observation of videotaped treatment. *Journal of Counseling Psychology*, 1972, 19, 1-7.

Melamed, B.G., & Siegel, L.J. Reduction of anxiety in children facing hosptialization and surgery by use of filmed modeling. *Journal of Consulting and Clinical Psychology*, 1975, 43, 511-521.

Moriarty, D., & McCabe, A.E. Studies of television and youth sport. In *Ontario. Royal Commission on Violence in the Communications Industry Report (Vol. 5). Learning from the Media (research Reports)* Toronto: Queen's Printer for Ontario, 1977.

Murray, J.P., & Kippax, S. From the early window to the late night show: A cross-national review of television's impact on children and adults. In L. Berkowitz (Ed.), *Advances in Experimental Social Psychology* (Vol. 12). New York: Academic Press, 1979.

O'Connor, R.D. Modification of social withdrawal through symbolic modeling. *Journal of Applied Behavior Analysis*, 1969, 2, 15-22.

O'Connor, R.D. Relative efficacy of modeling, shaping, and the combined procedures for modification of social withdrawal. *Journal of Abnormal Psychology*, 1972, 79, 327-334.

Ontario, Royal Commission on Violence in the Communciations Industry. Report. Vol. 1. *Approaches, concusions and recommendations* Vol. 2. *Violence and the media: A bibliography* Vol. 3. *Violence in television, films and news* Vol. 4. *Violence in print and music* Vol. 5. *Learning from the media* Vol. 6. *Vulnerability to media effects* Vol. 7. *The media industries: From here to where?* Toronto, Ontario: Queen's Printer for Ontario, 1977.

Parke, R.D., Berkowitz, L., Leyens, J.P., West, S., & Sebastian, R.J. Some effects of violent and nonviolent movies on the behavior of juvenile delinquents. In L. Berkowitz (Ed.), *Advances in experimental social psychology* (Vol. 10). New York: Academic Press, 1977.

Rosenthal, T.L., & Bandura, A. Psychological modeling: Theory and practice. In S.L. Garfield & A.E. Bergin (Eds.), *Handbook of Psychotherapy and Behavior Change.* New York: Wiley, 1978.

Rushton, J.P. Television and prosocial behavior. In *Ontario: Royal Commission on Violence in the Communications Industry.* Report. (Vol. 5). Toronto: Queen's Printer for Ontario, 1977.

Rushton, J.P. The effects of prosocial television and film material on the behavior of viewers. In L. Berkowtiz (Ed.), *Advances in Experimental Social Psychology* (Vol. 12). New York: Academic Press, 1979.

Rushton, J.P. *Altruism, socialization, and society.* Englewood Cliffs, N.J.: Prentice-Hall, 1980.

Rushton, J.P., & Owen, D. Immediate and delayed effects of TV modeling and preaching on children's generosity. *British Journal of Social and Clincial Psychology*, 1975, 14, 309-310.

Shaw, D.W., & Thoresen, C.E. Effects of modeling and desensitization in reducing dental phobia. *Journal of Counseling Psychology*, 1974, 21, 415-420.

Silverman, L.T., Sprafkin, J.N., & Rubinstein, E.A. Physical contact and sexual behavior on prime-time TV. *Journal of Communication*, 1979, 29, 33-43.

Smythe, D.W. Reality as presented by television. *Public Opinion Quarterly*, 1954, 18, 143-156.

Sprafkin, J.M., Liebert, R.M., & Poulos, R.W. Effects of a prosocial example on children's helping. *Journal of Experimental Child Psychology*, 1975, 20, 119-126.

Stein, G.M., & Bryan, J.H. The effect of a televised model upon rule adoption behavior of children. *Child Development*, 1972, 43, 268-273.

Sternglanz, S.H., & Serbin, L.A. Sex role stereotyping in children's television programs. Developmental Psychology, 1974, 10, 710-715.

Thelen, M.H., Fry, R.A., Fehrenbach, P.A., & Frantschi, N.M. Therapeutic videotape and film modeling: A Review. *Psychological Bulletin,* 1979, 86, 701-720.

Vidmar, N., & Rokeach, M. Archie Bunker's bigotry: A study in selective perception and exposure. *Journal of Communication,* 1974, 24, 36-47.

Weissbrod, C.S., & Bryan, J.H. Filmed treatment as an effective fear-reduction technique. *Journal of Abnormal Child Psychology*, 1973, 1, 196-201.

Williams, T.B., Zabrack, M.L., & Joy, L.A. A content analysis of entertainment television programming. In *Ontario: Royal Commission on Violence in the Communications Industry Report* (Vol. 3). *Violence in Television Films and News*. Toronto: Queens Printer for Ontario, 1977.

Wincze, J.P., & Caird, W.K. The effects of systematic desensitization and video desensitization in the treatment of essential sexual dysfunction in women. *Behavior Therapy,* 1976, 7, 335-342.

Winick, C. Mental illness and psychiatrists in movies. In C. Winick (Ed.), *Sage Annual Reviews of Studies in Deviance*. Vol. 2. *Deviance and Mass Media*. Beverly Hills, Ca.: Sage Publications, Inc., 1978.

Wolf, T.M. Effects of televised modeled verbalizations and behavior on resistance to deviation. *Developmental Psychology,* 1973, 8, 51-56.

Wolf, T.M., & Cheyne, J.A. Persistence of effects of live behavioral, televised behavioral, and live verbal models on resistance to deviation. *Child Development,* 1972, 43, 1429-1436.

Yates, G.C.R. Influence of televised modeling and verbalization on children's delay of gratification. *Journal of Experimental Child Psychology*, 1974, 18, 333-339.

Development of Moral Thought, Feeling, and Behavior

Martin L. Hoffman

Research on moral development has proceeded without letup for over half a century. One reason for the sustained interest is the topic's obvious social significance in an urban industrialized society characterized by increasing crime, declining religious involvement, and events like Watergate, Jonestown, and the Kitty Genovese murder, which are brought home by the mass media. More fundamentally, morality is the part of personality that pinpoints the individual's very link to society, and moral development epitomizes the existential problem of how humans come to manage the inevitable conflict between personal needs and social obligations.

The legacy of Freud and Durkheim is the agreement among social scientists that most people do not go through life viewing society's moral norms (e.g., honesty, justice, fair play) as external, coercively imposed pressures. Though initially external and often in conflict with one's desires, the norms eventually become part of one's motive system and affect behavior even in the absence of external authority. The challenge is to discover what types of experience foster this internalization. The research, which initially focused on the role of parents, has now expanded to include peers and the

Originally published in *American Psychologist*, 1979, 34, 958-966. Copyright ©1979 by the American Psychological Association. Reprinted by permission of the publisher and author.

mass media as well as cognitive development and arousal of affects such as empathy and guilt. The aim here is to pull together relevant findings and theories, drawing heavily from previous critical reviews (Hoffman, 1977, 1978, 1980).

CHILD-REARING PRACTICES AND MORAL INTERNALIZATION

Since the parent is the most significant figure in the child's life, every facet of the parent's role- disciplinarian, affection giver, model- has been studied.

Discipline and Affection

Moral internalization implies that a person is motivated to weigh his or her desires against the moral requirements of a situation. Since one's earliest experience in handling this type of conflict occurs in discipline encounters with parents, and since discipline encounters occur often in the early years- about 5-6 times per hour (see, e.g., Wright, 1967) – it seems reasonable that the types of discipline used by parents will affect the child's moral development. Affection is important because it may make the child more receptive to discipline, more likely to emulate the parent, and emotionally secure enough to be open to the needs of others. A large body of research done mainly in the 1950s and 1960s dealt with correlations between types of discipline and moral indices such as resisting temptation and feeling guilty over violating a moral norm. The findings (reviewed by Hoffman, 1977) suggest that moral internalization is fostered by (a) the parent's frequent use of inductive discipline techniques, which point up the harmful consequences of the child's behavior for others, and (b) the parent's frequent expression of affection outside the discipline encounter. A morality based on fear of external punishment, on the other hand, is associated with excessive power-assertive discipline, for example, physical punishment, deprivation of privileges, or the threat of these. There is also evidence that under certain conditions- when the child is openly and unreasonably defiant – the occasional use of power assertion by parents who typically use induction may contribute positively to moral internalization (Hoffman, 1970a).

The mid-1960s saw a shift from correlational to experimental research. In the most frequently used paradigm the child is first trained, or "socialized," by being presented with several toys. When the child handles the most attractive one, he or she is punished (e.g., by an unpleasant noise, the intensity and timing of which varies). The child is then left alone and observed surreptitiously. Resistance-to-temptation scores are based on whether or not, how soon after the experimenter left, and for how long the child plays with the forbidden toy. Recently, a verbal component has been added – a simple prohibition or a complex, inductionlike reason. The general findings are that (a) with no verbal component, intensity and timing of punishment operate as they do in animals- the child deviates less when training consists of intense punishment applied at the onset of the act; (b) with a verbal component, these effects are reduced;

and (c) the verbal component is more effective with mild than severe punishment and with older than younger children.

Both types of research are limited. Thus it may seem as plausible to infer from the correlations that the child's moral internalization contributes to the parent's use of inductions as it is to infer the reverse. I have argued, however, that although causality cannot automatically be inferred from correlations, in this case the evidence warrants doing so (Hoffman, 1975a), at least until the critical research employing appropriate (e.g., cross-lagged longitudinal) designs has been done. The experimental research, on the other hand, lacks ecological validity, since the socialization process is telescoped. In addition, the distinction between moral action and compliance with an arbitrary request is blurred, since compliance is used as the moral index. Compliance is also a questionable index in light of Milgram's finding that it may at times lead to immoral action. Despite these flaws, the experiments are useful because they may tell something about the child's immediate response to discipline, and as such, the findings are compatible with the correlational research (Hoffman, 1977).

I recently proposed a theoretical explanation of the findings (Hoffman, Note 1). Briefly, it consists of the following points: (a) Most discipline techniques have power-assertive and love-withdrawing properties, which comprise the motive-arousal component needed to get the child to stop and pay attention to the inductive component that may also be present. (b) The child may be influenced cognitively and affectively, through arousal of empathy and guilt, by the information in the inductive component and may thus experience a reduced sense of opposition between desires and external demands. (c) Too little arousal and the child may ignore the parent; too much, and the resulting fear or resentment may prevent effective processing of the inductive content. Techniques having a salient inductive component ordinarily achieve the best balance. (d) The ideas in inductions (and the associated empathy and guilt) are encoded in "semantic" memory and are retained for a long time, whereas the details of the setting in which they originated are encoded in "episodic" memory and are soon forgotten. (e) Eventually, lacking a clear external referent to which to attribute the ideas, they may be experienced by the child as originating in the self.

Parent as a Model

It has been assumed since Freud that children identify and thus adopt the parents' ways of evaluating one's own behavior. The intriguing question is, Why does the child do this? Psychoanalytic writers stress anxiety over physical attack or loss of the parent's love. To reduce anxiety, the child tries to be like the parent—to adopt the parent's behavioral mannerisms, thoughts, feelings, and even the capacity to punish oneself and experience guilt over violating a moral standard. For other writers, the child identifies to acquire desirable parent characteristics (e.g., privileges, control of resources, power over the child).

The research, which is sparse, suggests that identification may contribute to aspects of morality reflected in the parent's words and deeds (e.g., type of moral reasoning, helping others). It may not contribute to feeling guilty after violating moral standards (Hoffman, 1971), however; perhaps because parents rarely communicate their own guilt feelings to the child, children lack the cognitive skills needed to infer guilt feelings from overt behavior, and children's motives to identify are not strong enough to overcome the pain of self-criticism.

In the early 1960s Bandura suggested that identification is too complex a concept; imitation is simpler, more amenable to research, yet equally powerful as an explanatory concept. Numerous experiments followed. Those studying the effects of adult models on moral judgment and resistance to temptation in children (reviewed by Hoffman, 1970b) are especially pertinent. The results are that (a) children will readily imitate an adult model who yields to temptation (e.g., leaves an assigned task to watch a movie), as though the model serves to legitimize the deviant behavior, but they are less likely to imitate a model who resists temptation. (b) When a child who makes moral judgments of others on the basis of consequences of their acts is exposed to an adult model who judges acts on the basis of intentions, the child shows an increased understanding of the principle of intentions, and the effect may last up to a year.

It thus appears that identification may contribute to the adoption of visible moral attributes requiring little self-denial, which may become internalized in the sense that the child uses them as criteria of right and wrong in judging others, but it may not contribute to the use of moral standards as an evaluative perspective for examining his or her own behavior.

PEER INFLUENCE

Despite interest, there is little theorizing and still less research on the effects of peers. The theories boil down to three somewhat contradictory views about the effects of unsupervised peer interaction: (1) Since gross power differentials do not exist, it allows everyone the kind of experiences (role taking, rule making, rule enforcing) needed to develop a morality based on mutual consent and cooperation among equals (Piaget, 1932). (2) It may release inhibitions and undermine the effects of prior socialization—a view reflected in Golding's novel *Lord of the Flies* and Le Bon's (1895/1960) notions about collective behavior. (3) Both 1 and 2 are possible, and which one prevails depends, among other things, on the hidden role of adults (Hoffman, 1980). For example, 1 may operate when the children come from homes characterized by frequent affection and inductive discipline. Parents may also play a more direct, "coaching" role, as when they do not just take their child's side in an argument with a peer but sometimes provide perspective on the other child's point of view.

The research indicates that parental influence wanes and peer groups become more influential as children get older (Devereux, 1970). The direction of the influence is less clear. Some studies report broad areas of agreement between peer and adult values (e.g., Langworthy, 1950). Others show disagreement—radical disagreement, as in the finding by Sherif et al. (1961) that newly formed unsupervised groups of preadolescent boys may undermine the preexisting morality of some members, or modest differences in emphasis, as in high school subcultures stressing athletics and popularity rather than academic achievement (see, e.g., Coleman, 1961). There is no evidence that children are more apt to endorse peer-sponsored misbehavior as they get older, and that this may reflect a growing disillusionment with the good will of adults rather than an increasing loyalty to peers, whose credibility may actually decline (Bixenstine, DeCorte, & Bixtenstine, 1976). Finally, the peer-model research (reviewed by Hoffman, 1970b) suggests that exposure to a peer who behaves aggressively or yields to temptation and is not punished increases the likelihood that a child will do the same; if the model is punished, the subject behaves as though there were no model. These findings suggest that if children deviate from adult moral norms without punishment, as often happens outside the home, this may stimulate a child to deviate; if they are punished, however, this may not serve as a deterrent. The immediate impact of peer behavior may thus be more likely to weaken than to strengthen one's inhibitions, at least in our society.

SEX-ROLE SOCIALIZATION AND MORAL INTERNALIZATION

Contrary to Freud and others, females appear to be more morally internalized than males, and their moral values are also more humanistic (Hoffman, 1975b). The difference may be due partly to the fact hat parents of girls more often use inductive discipline and express affection (Zussman, 1978). More broadly, since females have traditionally been socialized into the "expressive" role (Johnson, 1963)—to give and receive and receive affection and to be responsive to other people's needs—they are well equipped to acquire humanistic moral concerns. Boys are also socialized in this way, but as they get older they are increasingly instructed in the "instrumental" character traits and skills needed for occupational success, which may often conflict with humanistic moral concerns (e.g., Burton, Note 2, found that under high achievement pressure, parents may communicate that it is more important to succeed than to be honest). Since females may now be receiving more instrumental socialization than formerly, the sex difference in morality may soon diminish.

TELEVISION

The burgeoning work on effects of television on aggression and helping is tangential to mainstream research on moral development, but any assessment of social influences would be incomplete without reference to it. It may also be useful to provide an alternative to the frequent assumption that important effects have been demonstrated (see, e.g., Murray, 1973; Stein & Friedrich, 1975). To begin, the correlations between watching violent television programs and behaving aggressively are inconclusive because the causality is unclear. The one study that used a cross-lagged design and found that a childhood preference for violent programs relates to aggressive behavior in adolescence (Eron, Huesmann, Lefkowitz, & Walder, 1972) may have serious flaws (see, e.g., Kaplan, 1972).

Numerous experiments done mainly in the 1960s showed that children exposed to a live or filmed model behaving aggressively—or helping or sharing—are apt to behave like the mdoel shortly afterward. It thus appeared that the content of television programs might affect children's moral development. To demonstrate this convincingly, however, may require controlling the television viewing of children and observing their social behavior over an extended time in a natural setting. This has been done in four studies. I will summarize one (Friedrich & Stein, 1973). For four weeks, children in a summer nursery school watched three 20-minute episodes per week of an aggressive (*Batman* or *Superman*), neutral, or prosocial (*Mister Rogers' Neighborhood*) program. Measures of interpersonal aggression (physical and verbal) and prosocial behavior (cooperation and nurturance) were based on observations made during free play for two weeks before, during, and following the exposures. The only expected effect found in the postexposure period was a decline in prosocial behavior by middle-class children who saw the aggressive film. It was also found, however, contrary to expectations, that lower-class girls who saw the aggressive film showed an increase in prosocial behavior, and the total sample showed an increase in aggression when exposed to either the aggressive or prosocial film. It is difficult to make sense of these findings, as well as those obtained in the other three studies (see review by Hoffman, Note 3). Further research is needed, perhaps using more subtle measures of aggression and prosocial behavior. It is possible, however, that even the most sophisticated designs may not reveal long-term effects because the effects may be overridden by one's overall television experience (including newscast violence), not to mention one's actual socialization experiences as well as other pressures and frustrations to which one is exposed, which may be impossible to control. The measurable effects of television on behavior may thus be largely momentary.

COGNITIVE DEVELOPMENT AND MORAL THOUGHT

Piaget's view that cognitive development contributes to moral development continues to stimulate research. Children's moral judgment, for example, has been found to relate positively to their cognitive level, as shown in solving mathematics and physics problems, and to their ability to take the role of others (Kurdek, 1978).

Piaget thought that children under 7 or 8 years of age are egocentric and thus often miss crucial aspects of moral actions (e.g., intentions). Recent research minimizes the cognitive and linguistic demands on subjects, however, shows that even 4-

year-olds consider intentions when the amount of damage is controlled (Keasey, 1978). They can also allocate rewards in a way that coordinates other children's needs and contributions in simple group tasks (Anderson & Butzin, 1978). And they recognize that norms about the human consequences of actions are more important than social conventions; for example, they resist attempts to convince them that it would be all right to hit someone if the rules said so, but they are more flexible about dress codes (Turiel, 1978).

Kohlberg (1969) saw morality as developing in a series of six stages, beginning with a premoral one in which the child obeys to avoid punishment and ending with a universal sense of justice or concern for reciprocity among individuals. Each stage is a homogenous, value-free, moral cognitive structure or reasoning strategy; moral reasoning within a stage is consistent across different problems, situations, and values. Each stage builds on, reorganizes, and encompasses the preceding one and provides new perspectives and criteria for making moral evaluations. People in all cultures move through the stages in the same order, varying only in how quickly and how far they progress. The impetus for movement comes from exposure to moral structures slightly more advanced than one's own. The resulting cognitive conflict is resolved by integrating one's previous structure with the new one.

Kohlberg's theory has been criticized as follows (Hoffman, 1970b, 1980; Kurtines & Greif, 1974): The stages do not appear to be homogeneous or to form an invariant sequence. There is no evidence that exposure to appropriate levels of moral reasoning inevitably leads to forward movement through the states or that it leads to "structural" rather than value conflict. Though low positive correlations exist between moral reasoning and moral behavior, the stages are not associated with distinctive patterns of behavior. These problems may be due to the manner of scoring moral reasoning, and future research with the new scoring system (Kohlberg, Colby, Speicher-Dubin, & Lieberman, Note 4) may produce different results. The theory has also been criticized for neglecting motivation which may be needed to translate abstract moral concepts into action (Peters, 1971), and for having a western, a male, and a "romantic individualistic" bias (Hogan, 1975; Samson, 1978; Simpson, 1974).

Cognitive conflict may underlie the previously noted finding that adult models affect children's moral judgments (see "Parent as Model" section above). Since the subjects' understanding of intentions was increased and the effect lasted long, they were not mindlessly imitating the model. Rather, they probably knew the difference between accidental and intended action initially (as noted, even 4-year-olds know this) but were influenced by the more severe consequences in the accident stories. Exposure to adults who repeatedly assign more weight to intentions despite the disparity in consequences must therefore have produced cognitive conflict, which may have led the subjects to change their minds. This interpretation does not assume that cognitive conflict always leads to progressive change, since models who espouse consequences, the less mature response, might have similar effects.

Whether or not cognitive-conflict theory is confirmed, it has called attention to people's active efforts to draw meaning from experience. It has also led to a new approach to moral education (Kohlberg, 1973): Different moral stages are assumed to be represented in the classroom; in discussing moral dilemmas lower-stage children are thus exposed to higher-stage reasoning, and in the course of handling the resulting conflict their moral levels advance. This approach appeals to educators partly because they are not expected to make moral judgments or state their values. They need only present moral dilemmas, foster discussion, and occasionally clarify a child's statement. In actual practice, the children are also encouraged to participate in decisions about making rules and assigning punishments for violating them. Should the program be effective, it will therefore still remain for research to determine whether cognitive conflict is necessary.

EMPATHY AND PROSOCIAL BEHAVIOR

Empathy, the vicarious emotional response to another person, has long interested social thinkers. Philosophers like David Hume and Adam Smith and early personality theorists like Stern, Sheler, and McDougall all saw its significance for social life. Despite the interest, there has been little theory or research. The topic is discussed below in some detail, nevertheless, because it bears on the affective side of morality, which has long been neglected. The focus thus far has been on the response to someone in distress, since this seems central to morality. A brief summary of a developmental theory of empathic distress (Hoffman, 1975c, 1978) follows.

When empathically aroused, older children and adults know that they are responding to something happening to someone else, and they have a sense of what the other is feeling. At the other extreme, infants may be empathically aroused without these cognitions. Thus, the experience of empathy depends on the level at which one cognizes others. The research suggests at least four stages in the development of a cognitive sense of others: for most of the first year, a fusion of self and other; by 11-12 months, "person permanence," or awareness of others as distinct physical entities; by 2-3 years, a rudimentary awareness that others have independent inner states — the first step in role talking; by 8-12 years, awareness that others have personal identities and life experiences beyond the immediate situation.

Empathy thus has a vicarious affective component that is given increasingly complex meaning as the child progresses through these four stages. I now describe four levels of empathic distress that may result from this coalescence of empathic affect and the cognitive sense of the other: (1) The infant's empathic response lacks an awareness of who is actually in distress (e.g., an 11-month-old girl, on seeing a child fall and cry, looked like she was about to cry herself and then put her thumb in her mouth and buried her head in her mother's lap, which is what she does when she is hurt). (2) With person permanence, one is aware that another person and not the self is in distress, but the other's inner states are unknown and may be assumed to be the same as one's own (e.g., an 18-month-old boy fetched his own mother to comfort a crying friend, although the friend's mother was also present). (3) With the beginning of role taking, empathy becomes an increasingly veridical response to the other's feelings in the situation. (4) By late childhood, owing to the emerging conception of self and other as continuous persons with separate histories and identities, one becomes aware that others feel pleasure and pain not only in the situation but also in their larger life experience. Consequently, though one may still respond empathically to another's immediate distress, one's empathic response is intensified when the distress is not transitory but chronic. This stage thus combines empathically aroused affect with a mental representation of another's general level of distress or deprivation. If this representation falls short of the observer's standard of well-being, an empathic distress response may result even if contradicted by the other's apparent momentary state, that is, the representation may override contradictory situational cues.

With further cognitive development, one can comprehend the plight of an entire class of people (e.g., poor, oppressed, retarded). Though one's distress experience differs from theirs, all distress had a common affective core that allows for a generalized empathic distress capability. Empathic affect combined with the perceived plight of an unfortunate group may be the most advanced form of empathic distress.

These levels of empathic response are assumed to form the basis of a motive to help others; hence their relevance to moral development. A summary of the research follows: (a) Very young children (2-4 years) typically react empathically to a hurt child, although they sometimes do nothing or act inappropriately (Murphy, 1937; Zahn-Waxler, Radke-Yarrow, & King, 1979). (b) Older children and adults react empathically too, but this is usually followed by appropriate helping behavior (see, e.g., Leiman, Note 5; Sawin, Note 6). (c) The level of empathic arousal and the speed of a helping act increase with the number and intensity of distress cues from the victim (see, e.g., Geer & Jarmecky, 1973). (d) The level of arousal drops following a helping act but continues if there is no attempt to help (see, e.g., Darley & Latané, 1968).

These findings fit the hypothesis that empathic distress is a prosocial motive. Some may call it an egoistic motive because one feels better after helping. The evidence suggests, however, that feeling better is usually not the *aim* of helping (see, e.g., Darley & Latané, 1968). Regardless, any motive for which the arousal condition, aim of ensuing action, and basis for gratification in the actor area all contingent on someone else's welfare must be distinguished from obvious self-serving motives like approval, success and material gain. It thus seems legitimate to call empathic distress a prosocial motive, with perhaps a quasi-egoistic dimension.

Qualifications are in order. First, though helping increases with intensity of empathic distress, beyond a certain point empathic distress may become so aversive that one's attention is directed to the self, not the victim. Second, empathic distress and helping are positively related to perceived similarity between observer and victim: Children respond more empathically to others of the same race or sex and, with cognitive development, to others perceived as similar in abstract terms (e.g., similar "personality traits"). These findings suggest that empathic morality may be particularistic, applied mainly to one's group, but they also suggest that moral education programs which point up the similarities among people, at the appropriate level of abstraction, may help foster a universalistic morality.

Despite the qualifications, a human attribute like empathy that can transform another's misfortune into distress in the self demands the attention of social scientists and educators for its relevance both to moral development and to bridging the gap between the individual and society.

GUILT

The reemergence of interest in affective and motivational aspects of morality includes a revived interest in guilt. I have suggested a relation between guilt and empathy (Hoffman, 1976), summarized as follows: The attribution research suggests a human tendency to make causal inferences about events. One can thus be expected to make inferences about the cause of a victim's distress, which serve as additional inputs in shaping one's affective empathic response. If one is the cause of the distress, one's awareness of this may combine with the empathic affect aroused to produce a feeling of guilt (not the Freudian guilt which results when repressed impulses enter consciousness).

I have been constructing a developmental theory of guilt that highlights the importance of empathic distress and causal attribution (Hoffman, in press-b). Space permits mentioning only that the guilt stages correspond roughly to the empathy stages described above and that some gaps in the theory reflect a lack of research on certain aspects of cognitive development such as the awareness that one has choice over one's action and that one's actions have an impact on others, as well as the ability to contemplate or imagine an action and its effects (necessary for anticipatory guilt and guilt over omission).

A summary of the findings follows: (a) A full guilt response appears in children as young as 6 years (Thompson & Hoffman, in press), and a rudimentary one appears in some 2-year-olds (Zahn-Waxler et al., 1979). (b) As noted earlier, discipline that points up the effects of the child's behavior on others contributes to guilt feelings. (c) Arousal of empathic distress appears to intensify guilt feelings (Thompson & Hoffman, in press). (d) Guilt arousal is usually followed by a reparative act toward the victim or toward others (see, e.g., Regan, 1971) or, when neither is possible, a prolongation of the guilt. (e) Guilt arousal sometimes triggers a process of self-examination and reordering of values, as well as a resolution to act less selfishly in the future (Hoffman, 1975b). It is interesting that this response, which should contribute to moral development, might be missing in children who are too "good" to transgress and thus may not have the experience of guilt. The findings suggest, somewhat paradoxically, that guilt, which results from immoral action, may operate as a moral motive.

CONCLUDING REMARKS

To pull together the findings and most promising concepts, I suggest three somewhat independent moral internalization processes, each with its own experiential base:

1. People often assume that their acts are under surveillance. This fear of ubiquitous authority may lead them to behave morally even when alone. The socialization experiences leading to this orientation may include frequent power-assertive and perhaps love-withdrawing discipline, which results in painful anxiety states becoming associated with deviant behavior. Subsequently, kinesthetic and other cues produced by the deviant act may arouse anxiety, which is avoided by inhibiting the act. When the anxiety becomes diffuse and detached from conscious fears of detection, this inhibition of deviant action may be viewed as reflecting a primitive form of internalization (perhaps analogous to the Freudian superego).

2. The human capacity for empathy may combine with the cognitive awareness of others and how others are affected by one's behavior, resulting in an internal motive to consider others. As contributing socialization experiences, the research suggests exposure to inductive discipline by parents who also provide adequate affection and serve as models of prosocial moral action (e.g., they help and show empathic concern for others rather than blame them for their plight). Reciprocal role taking, especially with peers, may also heighten the individual's sensitivity to the inner states aroused in others by one's behavior; having been in the other's place helps one know how the other feels in response to one's behavior.

3. People may cognitively process information at variance with their preexisting moral conceptions and construct new views, that resolve the contradiction. When they do this, they will very likely feel a special commitment to—and in this sense internalize—the moral concepts they have actively constructed.

These processes are not stages. The first, in one form or another (e.g., anxiety over retribution by God), may be pervasive in all ages and most cultural groups. The second may also occur in all ages, though primarily in humanistically oriented groups. The third may be true mainly among adolescents in groups for whom intellectually attained values are important.

The three processes may develop independently, since their presumed socialization antecedents differ. They may sometimes complement one another, as when the rudimentary moral sense originating in the child's early capacity for empathy and in discipline encounters contributes direction for resolving moral conflicts in adolescence. They may sometimes be noncomplementary, as when an early, anxiety-based inhibition prevents a nonmoral behavior from occurring later, when its control might be acquired through moral conflict resolution. Perhaps the processes are best viewed as three components of a moral orientation, with people varying as to which one predominates, and individual differences being due to cognitive abilities and socialization. A mature orientation in our society would then be based predominantly on empathic and cognitive processes, and minimally on anxiety. The challenge is to find ways to foster this morality. Whether this is possible in the context of the prevailing competitive-individualistic ethic is problematic. The finding by Burton (Note 2) noted earlier highlights the dilemma confronting parents who want to socialize children for both morality and achievement.

To test hypotheses implicit in the processes suggested above and to gain new knowledge as well may require complex designs including close observations of children's behavioral, cognitive, and affective responses to a socialization agent. A longitudinal dimension will also be needed to permit cross-lagged or other analyses for assessing causality and finding out which of the agent's actions are responsible for the child's moral growth. To do all this in a single study is a tall order, but it should be feasible with the aid of new procedures such as Zahn-Waxler et al.'s (1979) method of observing children's behavior in and out of discipline encounters, over long periods of time, Cheyne and Walter's (1969) use of telemetered heart-rate data to assess children's emotional responses to simulated discipline techniques, and Leiman's (Note 5) use of videotaped facial expression to tap empathic arousal. If techniques like these were appropriately combined and modified for use in naturalistic or laboratory settings as needed, I would anticipate new levels of knowledge about how affect and cognition interact in moral development.

REFERENCE NOTES

1. Hoffman, M.L. *Parental discipline and moral internalization: A theoretical analysis* (developmental Report 85). Ann Arbor: University of Michigan, 1976.

2. Burton, R.V. *Cheating related to maternal pressures for achievement.* Unpublished manuscript, State University of New York at Buffalo, Department of Psychology, 1972.

3. Hoffman, M.L. *Imitation and identification in children.* Unpublished manuscript, University of Michigan, Department of Psychology, 1978.

4. Kohlberg, L., Colby, A., Speicher-Dubin, B., & Lieberman, M. *Standard form scoring manual.* Unpublished manuscript, Harvard University, Moral Education Research Foundation, 1975.

5. Leiman, B. *Affective empathy and subsequent altruism in kindergartners and first graders.* Paper presented at the meeting of the American Psychological Association, Toronto, September 1978.

6. Sawin, D.B. *Assessing empathy in children: A search for an elusive construct.* Paper presented at the meeting of the Society for Research in Child Development, San Francisco, March 1979.

REFERENCES

Anderson, N.H., & Butzin, C.a. Integration theory applied to children's judgments of equity. *Developmental Psychology*, 1978, 14, 593-606.

Bixenstine, E.V., DeCorte, M.S., & Bixenstine, B. Conformity to peer-sponsored misconduct at four grade levels. *Developmental Psychology*, 1976, 12, 226-236.

Cheyne, J.A., & Walters, R.H. Intensity of punishment, timing of punishment, and cognitive structure as determinants of response inhibition. *Journal of Experimental Child Psychology*, 1969, 7, 231-244.

Coleman, J.S. *The adolescent society.* New York: Free Press of Glencoe, 1961.

Darley, J.M., & Latané, B. Bystander intervention in emergencies: Diffusion of responsibility. *Journal of Personality and Social Psychology*, 1968, 8, 377-383.

Devereux, E.C. The role of peer-group experience in moral development. In J.P. Hill (Ed.), *Minnesota symposia on child psychology* (Vol. 4). Minneapolis: University of Minnesota Press, 1970.

Eron, L.D., Huesmann, L.R., Lefkowitz, M.M., & Walder, L.O. Does television violence cause aggression? *American Psychologist*, 1972, 27, 253-263.

Friedrich, L.K., & Stein, A.H. Aggressive and prosocial television programs and the natural behavior of preschool children. *Monographs of the Society for Research in Child Development*, 1973, 38 (4 Serial No. 151).

Geer, J.H., & Jarmecky, L. The effect of being responsible for reducing another's pain on subject's response and arousal. *Journal of Personality and Social Psychology*, 1973, 26, 232-237.

Hoffman, M.L. Conscience, personality, and socialization techniques. *Human Development,* 1970, 13, 90-126. (a)

Hoffman, M.L. Moral development. In P.H. Mussen (Ed.), *Carmichael's handbook of child psychology* Vol. 2 . New York: Wiley, 1970. (b)

Hoffman, M.L. Identification and conscience development. *Child Development,* 1971, 42, 1071-1082.

Hoffman, M.L. Developmental synthesis of affect and cognition and its implications for altruistic motivation. *Developmental Psychology*, 1975, 11, 607-22. (a)

Hoffman, M.L. Moral internalization, parental power, and the nature of parent-child interaction. *Developmental Psychology*, 1975, 11, 228-239. (b)

Hoffman, M.L. Sex differences in moral internalization. *Journal of Personality and Social Psychology,* 1975, 32, 720-729. (c)

Hoffman, M.L. Empathy, role-talking, guilt, and development of altruistic motives. In T. Kilona (Ed.), *Moral development: Current theory and research*. New York: Holt, Rinehart & Winston, 1976.

Hoffman, M.L. Moral internalization: Current theory and research. In L. Berkowitz (Ed.), *Advances in experimental social psychology* (Vol. 10). New York: Academic Press, 1977.

Hoffman, M.L. Empathy, its development and prosocial implications. In C.B. Keasey (Ed.), *Nebraska symposium on motivation* (Vol. 25). Lincoln: University of Nebraska Press, 1978.

Hoffman, M.L. Adolescent morality in developmental perspective. In J. Adelson (Ed.), *Handbook of adolescent psychology*. New York: Wiley-Interscience, 1980.

Hoffman, M.L. Empathy, guilt, and social cognition. In W. Overton (Ed.), *Relation between social and cognitive development*. Hillsdale, N.J.: Erlbaum, in press. (b)

Hogan, R. Theoretical egocentrism and the problem of compliance. *American Psychologist,* 1975, 30, 533-540.

Johnson, M.J. Sex role learning in the nuclear family. *Child Development,* 1963, 34, 319-333.

Kaplan, R.M. On television as a cause of aggression. *American Psychologist*, 1972, 27, 968-969. (Comment)

Keasey, C.B. Children's developing awareness and usage of intentionality and motives. In C.B. Keasey (Ed.), *Nebraska symposium on motivation* (Vol. 25). Lincoln: University of Nebraska Press, 1978.

Kohlberg, L. The cognitive-developmental approach. In D.A. Goslin (Ed.), *Handbook of socialization theory and research*. Chicago: Rand McNally, 1969.

Kohlberg, L. The contribution of developmental psychology to education—Examples from moral education. *Educational Psychologist*, 1973, 10(1), 2-14.

Kurdek, L.A. Perspective-taking as the cognitive basis of children's moral development: A review of the literature. *Merrill-Palmer Quarterly,* 1978, 24, 3-28.

Kurtines, W., & Greif, E.B. The development of moral thought: Review and evaluation of Kohlberg's approach. *Psychological Bulletin*, 1974, 31, 453-470.

Langworthy, R.L. Community status and influence in a high school. *American Sociological Review*, 1959, 24, 537-539.

Le Bon, G. *The crowd: A study of the popular mind.* New York: Viking Press, 1960. (Originally published, 1895).

Murphy, L.B. *Social behavior and child personality.* New York: Columbia University Press, 1937.

Murray, J.P. Television and violence: Implications of the Surgeon General's research program. *American Psychologist,* 1973, 28, 472-478.

Peters, R.S. Moral development: A plea for pluralism. In T. Mischel (Ed.), *Cognitive development and epistemology*. New York: Academic Press, 1971.

Piaget, J. *The moral judgment of the child.* New York: Harcourt, 1932.

Regan, J.W. Guilt, perceived injustice, and altruistic behavior. *Journal of Personality and Social Psychology,* 1971, 18, 124-132.

Samson, E.E. Scientific paradigms and social values: Wanted--A scientific revolution. *Journal of Personality and Social Psychology,* 1978, 326, 1332-1343.

Sherif, M., Harvey, O.J., White, B.J., Hood, W.R., & Sherif, C. *Intergroup conflict and cooperation: The Robber's Cave Experiment.* Norman, Okla.: University Book Exchange, 1961.

Simpson, E.L. Moral development research: A case study of scientific cultural bias. *Human Development,* 1974, 17, 81-106.

Stein, A.H., & Friedrich, L.K. The impact of television on children and youth. In E.M. Hetherington, J.W. Hagen, R. Kron, & A.H. Stein (Eds.), *Review of child development research* (Vol. 5). Chicago: University of Chicago Press, 1975.

Thompson, R., & Hoffman, M.L. Empathic arousal and guilt feelings in children. *Developmental Psychology,* in press.

Turiel, E. Distinct conceptual and developmental domains: Social convention and morality. In C.B. Keasey (Ed.), *Nebraska symposium on motivation* (Vol. 25). Lincoln: University of Nebraska Press, 1978.

Wright, H.F. *Recording and analyzing child behavior.* New York: Harper & Row, 1967.

Zahn-Waxler, C., Radke-Yarrow, M., & King, R.M. Childrearing and children's prosocial initiations toward victims of distress. *Child Development,* 1979, 50, 319-330.

Zussman, J.U. Relationship of demographic factors to parental discipline techniques. *Developmental Psychology,* 1978, 14, 685-686.

Factors Influencing Young Children's Use of Motives and Outcomes as Moral Criteria

Sharon A. Nelson

Piaget (1932) found a developmental trend in the preferred basis of moral judgments made by 6-10-year-old children in response to hypothetical situations. In children under 9-10 years he found no clear preference for motives as the basis for judgments. After the age of 10 years, judgments were consistently based on motive. However, in the same work, he pointed out that young children's tendency to base their judgments more on consequence information need not imply that they are unaware of intentions. In fact, Piaget (1926, 1932) has observed that the concepts of intention and motive emerge at about the same time as the first "whys," that is, around the age of 3-4 years. The present research was undertaken to determine the conditions under which the moral judgments of 3-4-year-old children would reflect their consideration and use of motives as well as outcomes.

Recent investigators have been successful in demonstrating the use of motives in addition to outcomes in children as young as 6 years of age. This has been achieved by departing from Piaget's method. Whereas Piaget used forced-choice situations, recent

Originally published in *Child Development*, 1980, 50, 823-829. Copyright ©1980 by the Society for Research in Child Development Inc.; reprinted with permission of the publisher and author.

investigations have presented single stories in which motives and outcomes are systematically varied and have used quantitative response measures (e.g., Constanzo, Coie, Grumet, & Farnhill 1973). Some researchers have also stated the actor's motive explicitly (e.g., Bearison & Isaacs 1975). Some have increased the salience of the actor's motive by using videotaped situations (e.g., Chandler, Greenspan, & Barenboim 1973) or by reversing the order in which the motive and outcome information is presented (e.g., Feldman, Klosson, Parsons, Rholes, & Ruble 1976; Nummedal & Bass 1976).

Studies that have examined 3- and 4-year-olds' use of motives report conflicting findings. Lyons-Ruth (Note 1) found no evidence that these children differentiate between actors with good versus bad motives, but Keasey (1978) reports opposite findings. However, no outcome information was presented to children in the Lyons-Ruth study, and the study reported by Keasey did not vary the outcome. Thus, it is not known whether the type of outcome affects young children's understanding and use of motives as moral criteria.

The assumption underlying this research is that young children do regard both motive and outcome as relevant criteria for moral judgments. However, procedures employed thus far have not allowed young children to demonstrate their understanding and use of these criteria. Young children may believe that motives provide information important for making moral judgments, yet fail to interpret or remember accurately cues about the actor's motive. They may also believe that the relationship between motive and outcome is logical (i.e., one implies the other). Children may, therefore, consider the motive as they have understood it and not as it was presented. It was hypothesized that a mode of presentation which makes both motives and outcomes explicit and salient and which keeps them available at the time of judgment, would allow children as young as 3 years old to demonstrate their sensitivity to both these moral criteria.

In order to test the assumption, a series of pictures depicting the actor's motive, behavior, and outcome were developed to accompany verbally presented stories. To compensate for the greater pictorial explicitness of outcomes relative to motives, additional cartoon-like drawings were made to portray the actor's motive.

Study 1

Method

SUBJECTS

Subjects were 60 preschool children between the ages of 3 and 4 years (mean = 3-4) and 30 second-grade children between the ages of 6 and 8 years (mean = 7-4). Approximately half of the children in each grade level were females and half were males. These children, mostly white, were from a middle-class, urban area and participated with parental consent.

MATERIALS

Stories

Two levels of motive and two levels of outcome were combined factorially to make four versions of a story. In each story version a boy acting from a good or bad motive purposely threw a ball toward a friend, resulting in a good or bad outcome. This situation was chosen because "throwing a ball" was consistently regarded by children in pilot studies as a neutral act (see Lyons-Ruth, Note 1). Motive descriptions always preceded outcome descriptions, and the actor's overt behavior was the same in all versions. The motive and outcome levels were as follows.

Motive statements. — (1) Good motive: This boy was playing with a ball; his friend did not have anything to play with. He wanted to throw the ball to his friend so they could play catch together with the ball. (2) Bad motive: This boy was playing with a ball; he was very mad at his friend that day. He wanted to throw the ball at his friend so he could hit him on purpose.

Outcome statements — -(1) Good outcome: The boy threw the ball. His friend caught the ball and was happy to play with it. (2) Bad outcome: The boy threw the ball. His friend did not catch the ball; the ball hit his friend on the head and made him cry.

Story example — This boy was playing with a ball; his friend did not have anything to play with. He wanted to throw the ball so he and his friend could play catch together with the ball. He threw the ball. His friend did not catch the ball; the ball hit his friend on the head and made him cry.

Pictures

In order to alleviate memory constraints and to examine the effects of motive salience, two sets of black-and-white line drawings were constructed to accompany the information presented in each of the four stories described above. Each set contained a series of 25-cm × 23-cm drawings illustrating the motive, the behavior, and the outcome in each story. The two sets of drawings differ in the manner in which they convey the motive of the actor. In the first set, positive and negative motives are merely implied by the actor's facial expressions. In the second set, positive and negative motives are conveyed explicitly by connecting to the actor's head cartoon-like representations of the goal which he intends to achieve (see Fig. 1).

RESPONSE SCALE

Children who judged the actor to be good were required to make judgments of goodness by pointing to one of three smiling faces whose diameter increased in size from 5.5 to 7.5 cm so that judgments could be represented from "a little bit good" to "very good." A similar series of frowning faces was used to represent the judgments

Fig. 1. Example of drawings used to convey motive, action, and outcome in picture-motive explicit presentations of stories.

from "a little bit bad" to "very bad." At the small end of each series there was a 4.5-cm-diameter neutral face representing the judgment "just okay," (a term used by the majority of children in the pilot work to convey the neutral judgment). By using this as a neutral endpoint common to both positive and negative ratings, the two scales were combined to form a seven-point scale for all judgments ranging from "very bad" (1) to "very good" (7) with the "just okay" judgment as a mid-point

PROCEDURE

Children of each age were randomly assigned to one of the three story-presentation conditions. There were 20 children per group at the 3-year-old level and 10 children per group at the 7-year-old level. Children in each group heard all four stories. Order of presentation to each child was randomly determined.

Children were interviewed individually by the experimenter. At the beginning of the test session, the children were familiarized with each point on the rating scale and then given two practice stories to define the "very good" and "very bad" endpoints of the scale. The very good story was about a little boy with a good motive and outcome; the very bad story was about a little boy with a bad motive and outcome. The children in the picture-motive explicit group were also given practice to familiarize them with the cartoon conventions used to illustrate the actor's motive.

In the experimental session the children were told to listen very carefully to the stories because later they would have to tell them aloud. After each story, children were asked whether the little boy in the story was a good boy or a bad boy, or "just okay." Then they were asked to indicate how good or how bad the little boy was by pointing to one of the faces. In both picture presentation conditions, the drawings were introduced one by one at the appropriate points of the story as the experimenter read. They were placed side by side in front of the child where they remained available for reference while the child made his judgment.

After the judgment was made, the drawings were removed and children were asked to tell the story aloud exactly as they had heard it. If motive or outcome information was omitted in recounting the story, specific questions were asked to elicit the information: for example, "Why did the boy throw his ball?"; "What was the boy trying to do?"; "What happened after the boy threw his ball?"

Results

MORAL JUDGMENT

A 2 (age: 3- and 7-year-olds) $\times 3$ (mode of presentation: verbal only, picture-motive implicit, and picture-motive explicit) $\times 2$ (motive: good or bad) $\times 2$ (outcome: good or bad) repeated measures analysis of variance was performed on the judgment data. Age and story presentation were between subject variables, and motive and outcome were within subject variables. If children perceived the stories as they were designed to be perceived, their judgments for positive motives and outcomes should have been more positive than their judgments for negative motives and outcomes. Indeed, the mean ratings for the motive and outcome conditions were in the expected direction. The overall mean rating of the main character in the good-motive conditions was 5.35, and 2.27 in the bad-motive conditions. The main effect for motive was highly significant, $F(1,84) = 217.13$, $p < .0001$, accounting for over one-third of the total variance in the data (estimated $\omega^2 = .362$). The overall mean ratings for good and bad outcomes were 4.70 and 2.92, respectively, $F(1,84) = 116.98$, $p < .001$. The

TABLE 1

MEAN RATING OF ACTOR'S GOODNESS/BADNESS IN STUDY 1 AS A FUNCTION OF SUBJECTS' AGE, LEVEL OF MOTIVE, AND LEVEL OF OUTCOME

	3-Year-Olds ($N = 60$)		7-Year-Olds ($N = 30$)	
	Good Motive	Bad Motive	Good Motive	Bad Motive
Good outcome............	6.55	2.27	6.20	3.46
Bad outcome.............	4.17	1.60	4.47	1.56

main effect for outcome accounted for considerably less variance (estimated ω^2 = .120).

A significant motive × outcome interaction was found, F(1,84) = 4.83, p < .03. Whenever there was a negative cue in the motive outcome pair, especially a negative motive, the other cue had a diminished influence on the judgment. An age x motive x outcome interaction, F(1,84) = 3.54, p < .051, was analyzed for age trends because the older children were expected to show greater use of both motive and outcome than the younger children. Indeed, the motive x outcome interaction was significant for the 3-year-olds, F(1,59) = 5.52, p < .03, but not for the 7-year-olds, F < 1 (see table 1).

Of interest for present purposes was the question whether the mode of presentation affected children's use of motive and outcome information in making moral judgments of the main character. Contrary to expectations, only the influence of outcome

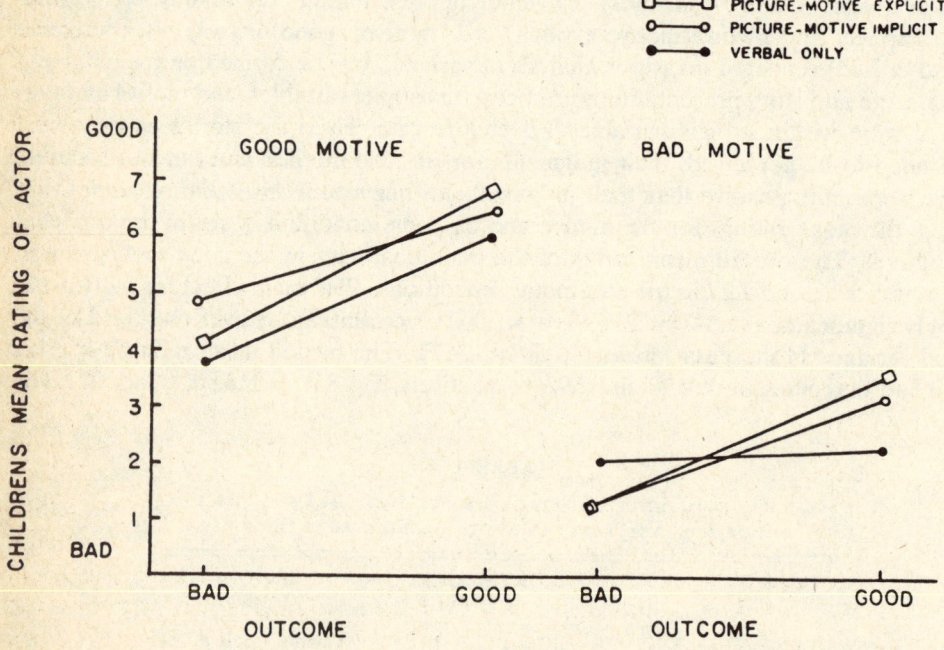

Fig. 2. Mean rating of actor's goodness/badness in study 1 according to level of motive and outcome in each story presentation.

varied significantly with the mode of presentation of story information (presentation $\times$ outcome interaction, $F[2,84] = 4.60$, $p < .01$). A more detailed analysis was conducted using Scheffé's procedure for post hoc comparisons among means. When the motive information was explicitly pictured, good and bad outcomes had a greater effect on judgments than when it was implicitly pictured or not pictured at all, $p < .01$.

The increased effectiveness of outcome information across story presentation modes is due to the increased use of this information when the motive is bad (mode of presentation x motive x outcome interaction, $F[2,84] = 3.06$, $p < .05$). That is, whereas children show substantial use of outcome information in the good-motive stories under all modes of presentation, only in the picture presentations do they show use of information about outcomes when the motive is bad, $F(2,84) = 9.67$, $p < .01$. The form of this interaction can be seen in figure 2.

RECALL

To obtain an estimate of reliability in coding the accuracy of children's recall of motive and outcome information, a second observer independently coded responses for approximately one third of the sample. Rater agreement was 97%. Recall frequencies were compared with chance levels: only the motive recall frequencies for 3-year-olds in the verbal-only conditions did not depart significantly from binomial chance.

Errors made in recalling the valence of motive and outcome information were analyzed in a 2 (age) $\times 3$ (story presentation) $\times 2$ (motive) $\times 2$ (outcome) repeated measures analysis of variance. As expected, age emerged as a significant main effect. Three-year-old children made more errors in recalling motives and outcomes than seven-year-old children. Analyses of variance performed separately on motive errors and outcome errors indicated that, while there was no effect of story presentation on outcome recall errors, recall of motives was significantly affected, $F(2,84) = 5.38$, $p < .006$. As expected, fewer errors occurred in recalling motive valences in the picture presentations than in the verbal-only presentation.

It was hypothesized that the younger children might assume a necessary correspondence to exist between motive and outcome and that, when presented with stories in which this information was incongruent, they would tend to distort motives and outcomes so as to make them congruent. Because of discrepancies between the variances in some of the cells, assumptions appropriate to parametric analyses could not be made; therefore, nonparametric analyses were undertaken. Separate series of Wilcoxin matched pairs signed-ranks tests (Siegel 1956) were performed on the recall data from each age group. Comparison of motive and outcome errors indicated, as expected, that the 3-year-olds made relatively more errors recalling motive valences than outcome valences when this information was conflicting ($Z = 1.72$, $p = .05$) than when it was congruent ($Z = -60$). The congruency or incongruency of valence information had no effect on the pattern of recall errors made by 7-year-olds.

Discussion

The unexpected fining that, for 3-year-olds in the verbal-only presentation group, motive rather than outcome had the more potent effect on their judgment prompted a closer examination of judgment data from individual subjects. Inspection of these data suggests distinct patterns of judgment responses. The predominant pattern, shown by 40% of this sample, was to rate the actor negatively whenever there was at least one negative cue, regardless of its source. The second pattern, shown by 28.33% of the sample, was to ignore the outcome and to rate the actor according to the valence of the presented motives. The remaining children showed the following patterns: ratings that depended equally on the valence of motive and outcome (1.67%); ratings that varied only with the valence of the outcome (6.67%); positive ratings whenever at least one positive cue was presented (10%); and random responses (13.33%).

A very large percentage of the preschoolers seem to give more emphasis to the valence, especially negative valence, of the cue rather than to its source (motive or outcome). It has been reported that children develop the concept of bad before the concept of good (Hill & Hill 1977); McKechnie 1971; Piaget 1932; Rhine, Hill, Wandruff 1967). In formulating a moral judgment, children may be more alert to cues regarding badness of any kind. Since children commonly define good as the absence of bad (Hill & Hill 1977), positive judgments may tend to be made only when no negative cue is encountered. Thus it may be that the first negative cue- motive or outcome- encountered by the preschooler in the story situation will be sufficient to establish a negative judgment.

Study 2

In Study 1, when the 3-year-olds in the verbal-only condition rated the actors in the bad-motive stories, their judgments reflected the bad motive but not the outcome which followed. Is it possible that motive may have been utilized as a basis for judgment simply because it was always the first cue encountered? If preschoolers are really more concerned with negative valence than with the source of the cue, then reversing the order of presentation of motive and outcome within the stories should lead to judgments which disregard motives whenever bad outcomes are encountered. This is expected to be so, especially for the verbal presentations of the stories. Therefore, a second study was undertaken to investigate the possibility that the emphasis given to motive by the 3-year-olds in study 1 reflects a confounding of information about the valence of the cues with the order of presentation of the source of the cues within the stories.

SUBJECTS AND PROCEDURE

Twenty-seven preschool boys and girls (mean age = 3-8) participated as subjects in the second study. Children were randomly assigned to one of the three presenta-

TABLE 2

MEAN RATING OF ACTOR'S GOODNESS/BADNESS IN STUDY 2 ACCORDING TO PRESENTATION MODE, OUTCOME, AND MOTIVE

PRESENTATION	GOOD OUTCOME		BAD OUTCOME	
	Good Motive	Bad Motive	Good Motive	Bad Motive
Verbal only	6.11	3.56	2.67	1.78
Picture–motive implicit	7.00	2.11	2.33	1.11
Picture–motive explicit	7.00	3.56	4.22	1.11

tion groups. The materials and procedure were identical with those of study 1. In all stories and presentation modes, description of the outcome preceded description of the motive.

RESULTS AND DISCUSSION

Judgments

Moral judgment ratings were analyzed in a 1 (presentation mode) $\times 2$ (outcome) $\times 2$ (motive) repeated measures analysis of variance. Table 2 presents the mean judgments made by children in study 2. As in study 1, good outcomes were rated more positively (mean = 4.89) than bad outcomes (mean = 2.20); $F(1,24) = 102.06$, p < .001 (estimated ω^2 = .250). Likewise, good motives were rated more positively (mean = 4.89) than bad motives (mean = 2.20); $F(1,24) = 144.50$, p < .001 (estimated ω^2 = .251). Again, a significant motive x outcome interaction was found, $F(1,24) = 6.88$, p < .02, indicating that, whenever either motive or outcome is negative, the other cue in the pair has diminished influence on the judgment. The presentation x outcome interaction found in study 1 did not occur in these data. Rather, as predicted, a significant presentation x motive interaction was found, $F(2,24) = 4.73$, p < .02. As hypothesized, judgments made in the verbal-presentations condition were less influenced by motive than those made in the picture conditions (see table 2).

Recall

Errors made in recalling the valence of presented motives and outcomes were analyzed in a 3 (mode of presentation) $\times 2$ (outcome) $\times 2$ (motive) repeated measures analysis of variance. The analysis revealed only one significant effect: an outcome x motive interaction, $F(2,24) = 6.68$, p < .03. Children made more errors recalling story information in good-motive stories when outcomes were bad (mean = 0.167) than when outcomes were good (mean = 0.074); in bad-motive stories, there were more errors made for good outcomes (mean = 0.130) than for bad outcomes (mean = 0.055).

The results of Wilcoxin tests performed on the recall data clarify the above finding. Recall errors were compared for stories with congruent versus incongruent motive outcome pairings. More errors were made for incongruent pairings than for congruent pairings (32 errors vs. 14 errors), $Z = -2.57$, p = .005. Errors made in the incongruent stories consisted primarily of distorting the positive cue presented so as to make it congruent in valence to the accompanying negative cue.

General Discussion

The results from the present studies show that the modality in which story information is presented significantly affects young children's use of motives and outcomes in making evaluative judgments. When stories are presented verbally, information following negative cues has diminished impact on preschoolers' moral judgments. In contrast, when stories are presented accompanied by pictures, judgments are more likely to be influenced by both good and bad motives and by good and bad outcomes.

The 3-year-old children in these studies made judgments that consistently relied on one cue. In the verbal presentations, this cue was most likely to be the first negative cue encountered in the stories. In picture presentations, children's judgments can be described as reflecting any one of three cues: negative valence, motive, or outcome. This finding is consistent with Piaget's (1932) observation that younger children made judgments relying either on motive or on outcome and that the same child might judge sometimes by outcome and sometimes by motive. Rather than viewing such a child's behavior as inconsistent, the present research suggest that it may reflect consistent application of a judgmental strategy influenced by the child's concepts of "good" and "bad."

It is noteworthy that in the second study, where outcome preceded motive in the stories, the effect of motive on moral judgments was not less than that of outcomes. This suggests that while cue valence does influence the preschooler's moral judgment motive is influential in its own right as a source of relevant information. The finding that many children's judgments reflected the use of motive alone supports this notion.

The finding that the 3-year-olds tended to recall stories containing conflicting motive and outcome information so as to make these cues congruent is in line with the observations of previous researchers (e.g., Berndt & Berndt 1975; Piaget 1932) that young children assume some logical and necessary connection between motives and outcomes. They may assume, for example, that a bad outcome necessarily implies a bad motive and, therefore, encode the actor's motive as bad. Even when the story information is made explicit, children may infer that the actor's motive must have changed. It was not uncommon for children, when questioned about their judgments, to remark that the actor whose presented motive was incongruent with the effected outcome had "changed his mind" (i.e., changed the goal he sought to achieve). The fact that these children sought to justify their evaluations by the actor's motive as well as by the outcome indicates an awareness that the motivation for behavior should be considered.

In conclusion, the results of the present research suggest that making a moral judgment requires understanding of the evaluative concepts (i.e., "good," "bad") to be applied. Also required is comprehension of the motives or goals involved (e.g., "sharing," "helping," "hurting"). A child must also be able to recognize and interpret the interrelationship between action, motives, goals, and outcomes in order to make evaluative judgments. The development of these competencies deserves further investigation if we are to advance out present understanding of the beliefs children have about purposeful actions and social relationships.

REFERENCE NOTE

1. Lyons-Ruth, K. *Factors affecting the value judgments of preschool children.* Paper presented at the biennial meeting of the Society for Research in Child Development, New Orleans, March 1977.

REFERENCES

Bearison, D., & Isaacs, L. Production deficiency in children's moral judgments. *Developmental Psychology*, 1975, 11, 732-737.

Berndt, T., & Berndt, E. Children's use of motives and intentionality in person perception and moral judgment. *Child Development*, 1975, 46, 904-912.

Chandler, M.; Greenspan, L.; & Barenboim, C. Judgments of intentionality in response to videotaped and verbally presented dilemmas: the medium is the message. *Child Development*, 1973, 44, 315-320.

Constanzo, P.; Coie, J.; Grumet, J.; & Farnhill, D. A reexamination of the effects of intent and consequences on children's moral judgments. *Child Development*, 1973, 44, 154-161.

Feldman, N.; Klosson, E.; Parsons, J.; Rholes, W.; & Rubble, D. Order of information presentation and children's moral judgments. *Child Development,* 1976, 47, 556-559.

Hill, K., & Hill, C. Children's concepts of good and bad behavior. *Psychological Reports*, 1977, 41, 955-958.

Keasey, C.B. Children's developing awareness and usage of intentionality and motives. In C.B. Keasey (Ed.), *Nebraska Symposium on Motivation.* Vol. 25. Lincoln: University of Nebraska Press, 1978.

McKechnie, R. Between Piaget's stages: a study in moral development. *British Journal of Educational Psychology,* 1971, 41, 213-217.

Nummedal, S., & Bass, S. Effects of salience of intention and consequence on children's moral judgments. *Developmental Psychology*, 1976, 12, 475-476.

Piaget, J. *The language and thought of the child*. New York: Harcourt, Brace, 1926.

Piaget, J. *The moral judgment of the child.* London: Kegan Paul, 1932.

Rhine, R.; Hill, S.; & Wandruff, S. Evaluative responses of preschool children. *Child Development*, 1967, 38, 1035-1042.

Siegel, S. *Nonparametric statistics for the behavioral sciences*. New York: McGraw-Hill, 1956.

Positive Socialization via Cooperative Games

Terry D. Orlick

The purpose of this study was to assess the effects of a cooperatively structured games program on sharing and on happiness when playing games among 5-year-old children. Subjects consisted of four intact, half-day kindergarten classes from two different schools. Each school had one experimental group and one control group, both of which were taught by the same classroom teacher. Experimental groups were exposed to an 18-week cooperative games program, and control groups were exposed to a traditional games program of equal duration. Premeasures and postmeasures on a candy-sharing task revealed that children in the cooperative games program increased their sharing significantly more than did those in the traditional games program. Overall happiness when playing games outside of school increased for all groups.

Positive socialization (i.e., teaching children to cooperate, to get along well, and to share with one another) is one of the stated aims of many educational, therapeutic, sport, and recreation programs. Yet little has been done to structure environments to accomplish this objective.

Originally published in *Developmental Psychology*, 1981, 17, 426-429. Copyright ©1981 by the American Psychological Association. Reprinted by permission of the publisher and author.

Deutsch (1949) was among the first researchers to demonstrate experimentally that cooperative learning structures result in greater harmony among people than do competitive learning structures. Stendler, Damrin, and Haines (1951) confirmed this finding in a study with 7-year-old children. What made young children cooperative or competitive was primarily a function of the social situation to which they were exposed.

Sherif's (1956) Robber's Cave Experiment showed that when 12-year-old boys were placed in situations in which one group could achieve its aims only at the expense of another group, group members became hostile toward members of the opposing group, even though the groups were composed of "normal," well-adjusted individuals. Sherif maintained that the probability of achieving harmony is greatly enhanced when individuals or groups are brought together to work toward common ends.

Aronson (1975) took this principle to the classroom. After a series of studies, he concluded that cooperative interdependent learning led to improvements in self-esteem, to feelings of increased importance in school, and to a fostering of group affection and friendship and did so without interfering with academic learning and performance.

Orlick (1976, 1978a, 1978b, 1979) experimented with the physical medium of play and games as a means of influencing positive cooperative socialization among children. A series of games was designed so that it was necessary for children to interact in a cooperative way to meet a challenge or to achieve the goal of the game. Behavior observations within the game environment verified that cooperatively structured games were effective in eliciting cooperative social interaction among elementary school children.

Subsequent observational studies demonstrated that through a well-designed cooperative games program, it was possible to increase spontaneous cooperative behavior among kindergarten children during unstructured free time in the classroom (Orlick, McNally, & O'Hara, 1978), among kindergarten children during free play in a playroom (Jensen, 1979), and among preschool children during free play in a gym (Orlick & Foley, 1979). The purpose of this study was to assess the effects of a cooperative games program on the willingness of a 5-year-old children to share with other children and on the perceived happiness of these children when playing games outside of school.

Method

Subjects

Four intact kindergarten classes in two different schools in Ottawa served as subjects for this study. Each school had one experimental group and one control group.

In each school, the children in both the experimental and the control groups lived in the same community, were taught by the same classroom teacher in the same room, and followed the same daily kindergarten schedule with the exception of the experimental games program. In School 1, the morning class (N = 17, 10 boys and 7 girls) was exposed to a cooperative games program, and the afternoon class (N = 21, 15 boys and 6 girls) was exposed to a traditional games program. In School 2, this procedure was reversed, with the morning class (N = 19, 10 boys and 9 girls) being exposed to a traditional games program and the afternoon class (N = 14, 10 boys and 4 girls) being exposed to a cooperative games program.

Procedure

The experimental cooperative games program was drawn directly from the activities presented for this age group in *The Cooperative Sports and Games Book* (Orlick, 1978a). All activities in the cooperative games program were designed to be done with partners or in groups, varying in size up to involvement of the whole group. Activities for the traditional games program were similar with respect to physical demands and utilization of equipment but stressed individual pursuits in which children could work independent of the group. For example, in a game called "bridges," children in the cooperative group teamed together in twos or threes to make a bridge with their bodies. They then connected their bridges until the whole group formed one long bridge. In the traditional games group, the objective was for each individual to make his or her own independent bridge. The major difference between the activities for the different groups was the component structure of the activity and the behavior it was designed to elicit (i.e., cooperative vs. individual). Competition was introduced in some traditional activities such as relay races, but direct competition against others was de-emphasized in the program because of negative responses to such competition by similarly aged children during pilot work.

The kindergarten games programs consisted of four 30-minute sessions per week for a period of 18 weeks. For each group, two of the four sessions were conducted in a large gymnasium and the other two sessions took place in a smaller room. All of the games were taught by a qualified, female physical education teacher who was hired from outside to teach in this program. She was experienced in teaching both traditional and cooperative games to this age group and was familiar with the games there were to be taught in both programs. The teacher was instructed by the experimenter to try to (a) ensure that most feedback is positive in both groups, (b) give relatively equal amounts of feedback in both groups, and (c) reinforce game objectives in each group. In an attempt to assess whether these basic guidelines were followed, unobtrusive behavioral observations of the teacher were conducted intermittently during various cooperative and traditional games sessions. The frequency of positive and negative feedback, along with the behavior preceding reinforcement, was recorded on 6 different days. It was found that the teacher engaged in positive feedback on an average of 26 times per games sessions with the traditional games group and an average of 19 times per session with the cooperative games group. Negative feedback occurred an average of .8 times per session with the traditional games group and an average of 2.1 times per sessions with the cooperative games group. In the traditional games group, positive feedback was generally contingent on individually oriented behavior, and in the cooperative games group it was contingent on cooperative behavior.

Sharing. In an attempt to assess children's willingness to share with other children, a candy-sharing task was devised. The children were told that each of them was going to receive five candies, which they could keep for themselves or share with children in another kindergarten class who had no candies (i.e., the other kindergarten class who used the same room). While sitting in a class circle (facing outward), each child was then given a small brown bag that had five candies inside, along with another small bag with a red dot on it, which was empty. The children were simply asked to keep those candies they wanted for themselves and to put the ones they wanted to share in their empty bag with the red dot on it. They were then asked to put their "red dot" bag in a big brown bag in the center of the room even if they had decided to keep all five candies for themselves. This procedure was an attempt to ensure that neither their peers nor their teacher would know whether the children had actually given away any candies. Each bag was marked to that individual subjects could be identified by the researcher for pre-post comparisons. To ensure that all children would like the "treats" provided and would not be adversely affected by eating them, the kindergarten teachers consulted with the children in an informal way before the study began.

Happiness. Happiness when playing games outside was assessed by having the children respond to a Happy Faces Scale (Orlick et al., 1978), both before and after the respective programs. Each child was asked to mark one of five faces ranging from very happy (weighted 5) to very sad (weighted 1) in response to the question, "Which one is you when you're playing games outside of school?"

Pretests and posttests. Pretests for both "sharing" and "happiness" were administered at a quiet time during the day approximately 1 week before the games program commenced. Posttests were administered at the same time of day approximately 1 week after the termination of the study.

Results

The investigator was primarily interested in whether the program resulted in any change in an individual's willingness to share. Consequently the focus for data analysis was on determining how many children made a change in either a positive or a negative direction. The nonparametric sign test was chosen for data analysis, as it is designed for measuring the significance of the direction of change and is particularly appropriate in small sample cases in which each subject can act as her or his own control. The only assumption underlying this test is that the variable under consideration has a continuous distribution (Siegel, 1956). The data from each school were analyzed separately to maintain control for as many external effects as possible, particularly the classroom teacher effect.

Sharing

In School 1, the cooperative games group remained relatively stable in their willingness to share their candies over the course of the study, whereas the traditional games group underwent a significant decline (p = .03). In School 2, the cooperative games group underwent a significant increase in their willingness to share their candies from pretest to posttest (p = .03), whereas the traditional games group registered a nonsignificant trend in the opposite direction.

Of the children in the combined cooperative games groups, 35% increased their candy-sharing behavior over the course of the study compared with 12% of the combined traditional games groups. Of the children in the combined traditional games groups, 43% decreased their candy-sharing behavior over the course of the study compared with 16% of the combined cooperative games groups.

Happiness

In School 1, both groups registered increases in game-playing happiness "outside of school" over the course of the study. Only the cooperative games group, however, gained significantly (p = .02). In School 2, both groups also underwent an increase in game-playing happiness outside of school. In this case, however, only the traditional games group registered a significant increase (p = .05).

Discussion

The results of this study stress the important socialization function of children's games and provide additional evidence for the potential value of cooperatively structured play and game experiences in the socialization of sharing. For many children, the cooperative play experiences appeared to set the stage for sharing, or at least served to balance the conditioning toward unsharing orientations, in a way that was not apparent in traditional play experiences. The increase in scores on the Happy Faces Scale for many children in both cooperative and more traditionally oriented games groups may have been a result of exposure to a variety of enjoyable physical activities that were presented in a positive and nonthreatening way.

Many research questions are raised as a result of this study. For example, what is the difference between children who respond to cooperative games and who consequently increase their sharing responses and those who do not? Can sharing behavior be more dramatically influenced by a more extensive exposure to cooperative games or by multi-dimensional approaches to cooperation (including television)? What is the long-term effect of cooperative socialization on children's willingness to share and on the quality of their lives? The potential impact of positive socialization research in the realm of play and games appears promising for helping us to orient children's behavior in a positive direction.

REFERENCES

Aronson, E. The jigsaw route to learning and liking. *Psychology Today*, February 1975, pp. 43-50.

Deutsch, M. An experimental study of the effects of cooperation and competition on group processes. *Human Relations*, 1949, 2, 199-231.

Jensen, P. *Effects of cooperative games programme on subsequent free play of kindergarten children.* Unpublished doctoral dissertation, University of Alberta, Edmonton, Alberta, Canada, 1979.

Orlick, T.D. Games of acceptance and psycho-social adjustment. In T. Craig (Ed.), *The humanistic and mental health aspects of sports, exercise and recreation.* Chicago: American Medical Association, 1976.

Orlick, T. *The cooperative sports and games book.* New York: Pantheon Books, 1978. (a)

Orlick, T. *Winning through cooperation: Competitive insanity--Cooperative alternatives.* Washington, D.C.: Acropolis, 1978. (b)

Orlic, T. Children's games: Following the path that has heart. *The Elementary School Guidance and Counseling Journal,* 1979, 14(2), 156-161.

Orlick, T., & Foley, C. Pre-school cooperative games: A preliminary perspective. In M.J. Melnick (Ed.), *Sport sociology: contemporary themes* (2nd ed.). Dubuque, Iowa: Kendall/Hunt, 1979.

Orlick, T.D., McNally, J., & O'Hara, T. Cooperative games: Systematic analysis and cooperative impact. In F. Smoll & R. Smith (Eds.), *Psychological perspectives in youth sports.* Washington, D.C.: Hemisphere, 1978.

Sherif, M. Experiments in group conflict. *Scientific American*, 1956, 195(32), 54-58.

Siegel, S. *Nonparametric statistics for the behavioral sciences.* New York: McGraw-Hill, 1956.

Stendler, C., Damrin, D., & Haines, A. Studies in cooperation and competition: The effects of working for group and individual rewards on the social climate of children's groups. *Journal of Genetic Psychology*, 1951, 79, 173-179.

Male Brain, Female Brain: The Hidden Difference

Doreen Kimura

The idea that male and female brains are organized differently has been around for a long time. After all, since men and women are dissimilar in size, appearance and sexual role, why shouldn't their brain organization differ too? Research has documented in the past 25 years that there are intellectual differences in the way the two sexes solve problems: On average, women do better in certain verbal skills and men in spatial and mathematical skills.

The notion that men's and women's brains are differently organized began to take hold in earnest as a result of experiments spanning the 1960s and 1970s. It began with the work of psychologist Herbert Lansdell, who studied neurosurgical patients. Others before him had found that, in general, removing the brain's left temporal lobe interfered with verbal skill, while removing the right impaired nonverbal skills. Lansdell found that although such injuries caused a similar overall pattern of impairment in women and men, women were less severely affected than men.

These preliminary findings were confirmed and given support by people working

Originally published in *Psychology Today*, November 1985; reprinted with permission. From Psychology Today magazine, copyright ©1985 by the American Psychological Association.

MAJOR AREAS OF THE LEFT HEMISPHERE

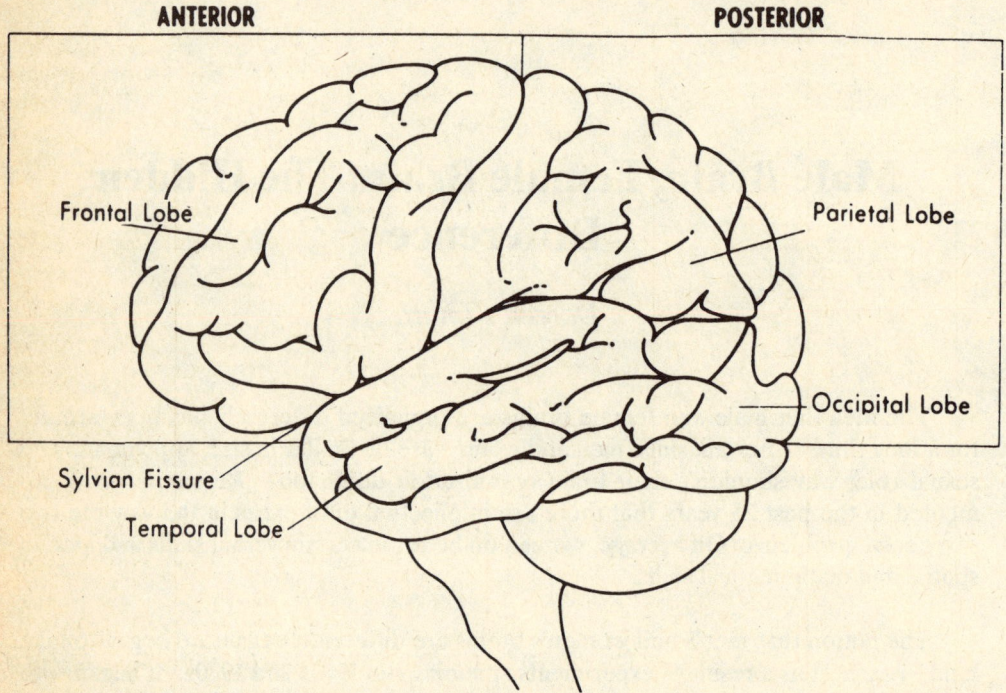

ANTERIOR   **POSTERIOR**

Frontal Lobe

Parietal Lobe

Occipital Lobe

Sylvian Fissure

Temporal Lobe

in my laboratory and in other laboratories. Studies of both brain-damaged and normal people revealed that while men and women tend to use one hemisphere more than the other for certain verbal tasks, such as recognizing spoken or seen words, women seem to rely less strongly on a single hemisphere than men do. Particularly striking was a finding by psychologist Jeanette McGlone, then a graduate student in my laboratory, that damage to the left hemisphere (the one usually dominant for language) caused less aphasia (language disorder) in women than in men.

These findings led to what seemed to be an obvious conclusion: certain thinking skills are more lateralized—more dependent on one hemisphere—in the male brain than in the female. Or, putting the comparison the other way, the women's brains are more diffusely organized than men's.

A number of explanations were offered for this apparent sex difference: women were more verbal, meaning that both their hemispheres were given up to speech; women developed more quickly and lateralization required slower development; women were just as lateralized as men but used verbal strategies more often; connections between the hemispheres were stronger in women and, therefore, the asymmetrical organization of their brain was less detectable. And so on.

Anatomical studies began to suggest that there were structural differences between men's and women's brains, but results were inconsistent regarding the question of men's greater lateralization. After neurologist Norman Geschwind and coworker Walter Levitsky at Harvard Medical School had found that a verbal part of the brain was generally larger on the left than the right side (see "Of Hemispheres, Handedness and more," this issue), neuroscientist Juhn Wada reported that these anatomical differences were smaller in women. In addition, biologist Christine de Lacoste-Utamsing, working with anthropologist Ralph Holloway at Columbia University, claimed that part of the corpus callosum, the major connection between the hemispheres, was slightly larger in women.

The problem with viewing men's brains as more lateralized than women's was that it left a lot of questions unanswered. Why, for example, are women more often right-handed than men? Even among right-handers, more women are purely right-handed, suggesting that, if anything, women rely more on one hemisphere than do men. And why was there no evidence that speech disorders occur more often in women following right-hemisphere brain damage, as one would expect if they, unlike men, depended on both hemispheres for speech?

In the course of looking at how damage to specific regions of one hemispehre affects speech and related functions, I came across some unexpected findings that, I believe, help to clarify some of these issues. One of the difficulties in doing research on neurological patients is finding enough people with various kinds of brain damage to study—enough women, for example, with damage limited to particular regions of one hemisphere. It took me 10 years to gather enough data on brain-damaged patients to make meaningful comparisons. But an important and surprising sex difference emerged.

I was looking at people whose brain damage was restricted to either the front (anterior) or back (posterior) sections of the brain. I found that left-hemishpere damage could cause aphasia in both men and women, but different sites within that hemisphere were involved in the two sexes. Men were equally likely to have a severe speech disorder with anterior or posterior damage, in keeping with the classical picture of "speech areas" in the left hemisphere. Women, however, were much less likely than men to become aphasic after restricted posterior damage, and so far, in all women with damage to the posterior area, the left temporal lobe was affected. No woman has lost her capacity for speech because of damage to the left parietal lobe, but several men have.

This seemed to suggest that the brain area involved in women's speech is, if anything, more localized than in men, at least in the left hemisphere. This idea was so radical that it took me some time to accept it. After all, according to the prevailing wisdom, speech was supposed to be more broadly represented in the female brain than in the male. But there was support for this idea from another type of research evidence: a study of how speech is affected when the cortex is electrically stimulated in awake patients during brain surgery.

Since the brain itself cannot feel pain, patients do not need a general anesthetic during brain surgery; local anesthesia to the scalp and skull will suffice. Catherine Mateer, a neuropsychologist who worked with neurosurgeon George Ojemann at the University of Seattle, found that electrical stimulation in the brain area near the Sylvian fissure interfered with a picture-naming task, but the particular brain areas responsible for such interference differed in men and women. In men, stimulation almost anywhere in the vicinity of the Sylvian fissure resulted in naming difficulties, while in women the pattern was more restricted. In particular, posterior parietal stimulation in women did not result in any naming problems, while it did in men. Thus, both my own data on brain damage and Mateer's on stimulation suggested that speech was not, as believed, more diffusely organized in women's left hemisphere than in men's.

What's more, the right hemisphere does not seem to contribute to speech any more in women than in men. Reviewing our own series of right-handed cases with damage restricted to the right hemisphere, we found that aphasic disorders after such damage are very rare (1 to 2 percent of cases), and there is absolutely no difference between men and women in this respect. So we are left with the very strong probability that speech is organized differently within women's left hemisphere compared with men's. It looks as though in women's brains—but not men's—speech favors anterior systems and avoids the parietal region.

When, then, is aphasia less common after left-hemisphere damage in women? Presumably, it's just a matter of odds: If speech is localized in a more restricted area of the women's left hemisphere, and we look at a random series of patients with left-hemisphere damage, the speech systems are simply less likely to be hurt in women and aphasia is less likely to occur.

The different representations of speech functions within the left hemisphere might also partially explain why normal women are slightly less dependent on a single hemisphere than men in dichotic listening tests (see "Listening in to the Hemispheres" box). (In the 1970s psychologists Richard Harshman and Philip Bryden found inde-

Kimura's Model of Dichotic Listening

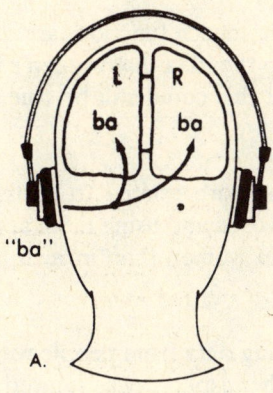
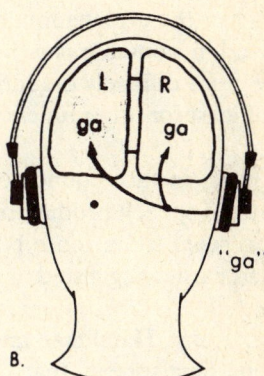
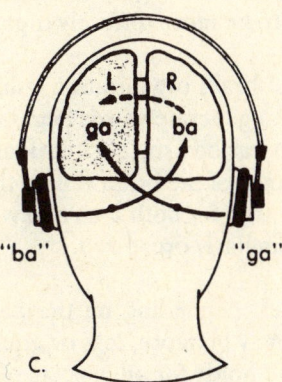

Fig 2. A. Syllable ("ba") sent to the left ear goes to right and left hemispheres by different pathways. Subjects report syllable accurately. B. Syllable ("ga") sent to right ear also goes to both hemispheres by different pathways and is reported accurately. C. "Ba" sent to left ear and "ga" sent to right ear simultaneously. "Ga" goes only to the left (speech) hemisphere and "ba" to the right. So "ga" is usually reported more often and more accurately than "ba".

pendently that women have a less pronounced advantage in the right ear, that is, in the left hemisphere, on these tests.) In women, the left auditory cortex may be less directly connected to the speech centers than it is in men because the speech areas are differently located. It's also possible that by having a greater number of fibers in the corpus callosum, women have more effective transmission from the less-favored left ear to the left hemisphere.

Whatever the explanation, our findings that basic speech functions are quite focally organized in women mean that we have to give up the idea that women's brains are generally more diffusely organized than men's. But this could still be true, if not for speech, at least for other functions.

We have, in fact, found some verbal functions more related to abstract verbal ability than to speech production, such as defining words and using them appropriately, that do seem to be more bilaterally organized in women than in men, as several people had earlier suggested.

In particular, Harshman and I found, on analyzing data from people with damage to only one hemisphere, that regardless of which hemisphere was injured, women's vocabulary — the ability to define words — was impaired. I then found this was true whether I looked at anterior or posterior damage in either hemisphere, suggesting that defining words is a function of the whole brain in women. Men had problems in defining words only after left-hemisphere damage. So for this kind of thinking at least, women's brains do indeed seem to be more diffusely organized.

I found different patterns of brain organization using other verbal tests, ones in which people were asked either to generate words beginning with a certain letter or to describe what they should do in various social situations. Other people have found that damage to the left anterior part of the brain causes the most difficulty in performing such tasks. I found this to be true for both men and women. So for this task, men's and women's brains were quite similarly organized.

In short, we are finding that, depending on the particular intellectual function we're studying, women's brains may be more, less or equally diffusely organized compared with men's. No single rule holds for all aspects of thinking. When it comes to speaking and making hand movements that contribute to motor skill, the brain seems to be very focally organized in women compared with men. This may relate to the fact that girls generally speak earlier, articulate better and also have better fine motor control of the hands. Also, a larger proportion of women than men are right-handed, and unequivocally so. But when it comes to certain, more abstract tasks, such as defining words, women's brains are more diffusely organized than men's, although men and women don't differ in overall vocabulary ability.

I have been describing the average state of affairs. But there is reason to believe that there is a lot of variation in brain organization from person to person. We know, for example, that the brains of left-handers and right-handers are organized somewhat differently, yet on average they function quite similarly.

In addition to individual variations, there are some interesting combined effects. Harshman and his colleagues at the Unviersity of Western Ontario found, for example, when they looked separately at people with above-average reasoning ability that sex and hand preference interacted. Left-handed men with above-average reasoning ability showed poorer scores on certain spatial tests, as well as other tests, than did right-handed men; but left-handed women were better at these tests than were right-handed women. When Harshman and coworkers looked at people with below-average reasoning ability, just the opposite happened: Now the left-handed men performed better than right-handed men on spatial tasks, but left-handed women did worse than the right-handed women.

What does this confusion suggest? It must mean that brain organization for such problem-solving abilities is related not only to sex and hand preference but also to overall intelligence level. And more to the point, it indicates that we have probably not one or two types of brain organization but several.

How are these different patterns of brain orgnaization determined? There have been several suggestions in recent years that they may be related to the organism's rate of development both before and after birth. Biopsychologist Jerre Levy of the University of Chicago suggested some time ago that the two halves of the body, including the brain hemispheres, might grow at different rates in boys and girls, even before birth. The left hemisphere may develop more quickly in girls, and the right hemisphere in boys, thus favoring verbal skills in girls and spatial skills in boys. This idea has persisted in modified form in much of the literature on sex differences.

A recent report by biologist Ernest Nordeen and psycobiologist Pauline Yahr of the University of California at Irvine on the effect of injecting hormones into the brain of newborn rats suggested that even the hypothalamus, a very basic regulating system, is asymmetrically organized for sexual behavior; injections on the left or right side affected sex-typical behavior differently. So although it may seem a bit farfetched at first, there do appear to be basic asymmetries in the developing organism and these asymmetries may well have far-reaching repercussions for later differences between the sexes.

Functions such as speech and spatial ability traditionally have been thought to depend primarily on the cerebral cortex. Although we should not dismiss the idea that deeper brain structures contribute something to these abilities as well, it would be particularly interesting if there were sex-related differences in the structure of the cortex.

BRAIN ORGANIZATION: MEN AND WOMEN COMPARED

FUNCTION	BRAIN LOCATION		SUMMARY	
	Men	**Women**	**Men and women same**	**Men and women different**
Producing speech	Left hemisphere, front and back	Left hemisphere, mostly front		X Women more focal
Hand movements for motor skill	Left hemisphere, front and back	Left hemisphere, mostly front		X Women more focal
Vocabulary-defining words	Left hemisphere, front and back	Both hemispheres, front and back		X Women more diffuse
Other verbal tests (Naming words beginning with certain letters; describing appropriate social behavior)	Left hemisphere, front	Left hemisphere, front	X	

Neuropsychologist Marian Diamon of the University of California at Berkeley, comparing cortical thickness in male and female rats, did find that the right cortex is thicker in males at most ages, while the left cortex is thicker in females but only at some ages (see "A Love Affair with the Brain," *Psychology Today*, November 1984). Also very suggestive is her finding that, when ovaries are removed at birth, the female rat develops a pattern of hemispheric dominance more like that of the male.

These studies on anatomical asymmetries in the brain are in a very early stage, of course, but they indicate quite strongly that the biological sex differences in brain organization are probably dynamic, rather than a crystallized pattern that is laid down entirely by the genes. At various periods in life, different brain structures may be undergoing more- or less-rapid growth, and patterns of brain organization will vary from time to time as a result. This may very well go on throughout a person's life, in fact, since hormonal environments are in lifelong flux.

The role of sex hormones in prenatal development is quite dramatic and profound (see "What Are Little Boys and Girls Made of?" box). It may also be appreciable in adult life, even affecting cognitive abilities in men and in women. While hormonal changes occur in both sexes over a variety of short and long cycles, the changes in women during stages of the menstrual cycle have been most thoroughly studied. For example, there is some evidence that spatial ability in women may vary monthly as natural levels of sex hormones in the bloodstream change; it may be best during the phase when the level of the female sex hormone estrogen is lowest.

WHAT ARE LITTLE BOYS AND GIRLS MADE OF?

One of the most fascinating facts of biology to emerge in the past few years is that sex is not determined by the genetic makeup of a person in any simple, direct way. An individual can be born with an XY genetic make-up (the male chromosomal pattern), yet grow up to have female genitals and look and behave like a woman. Another individual may have XX chromosomes (the female pattern) and become a man.

What determines whether a group of cells carrying XY or XX chromosomes will turn into a male or female human being is the presence of critical sex hormones early in fetal life. The Y chromosome appears to be necessary for converting the gonads into testes. The testes, in turn, are responsible for secreting androgens, male hormones, which result in the development of a penis rather than a vagina. If no Y chromosome is present, the gonads become ovaries.

But curiously, no hormones are needed to develop the female reproductive tract. If there are no hormones, or if female hormones are present, a vagina rather than a penis develops. This means that we have a biological bias toward being female. It also means that through variations in fetal and perhaps even pubertal hormones, it is possible to have somewhat wider biological variations in "maleness" and "femaleness" than we previously suspected.

Psychologist June Reinisch of the Kinsey Institute in Indiana has shown that girls who have had a higher-than-usual exposure to androgens before birth tend to be tomboyish. And researcher Günther Dorner's work in East Germany suggests that even some instances of homosexuality may reflect variation in fetal hormones. These examples may mean that, although the two sexes differ sharply in genital appearance, each has a range of potential behavior broad enough to defy characterizing behavioral patterns as exclusively limited to one sex or the other.

In contrast to these findings, Elizabeth Hampson, one of my graduate students, has found that women perform best on tests of motor skill when their female sex hormones are at their highest level. So, as in brain organization, the pattern we see may very well depend on the particular function that we study.

What do all these findings tell us about the inherent capabilities of the two sexes? And what can we, as a result, deduce about the abilities of an individual man or woman? The fact seems inescapable that men and women do differ genetically, physiologicaly and in many important ways psychologically. This should not be surprising to us, since as a species we have a long biological history of having two sexual forms and have had a sexual division of labor dating back perhaps several million years. Men and women probably have been evolving different advantages for a wide range of activities for at least hundreds of thousands of years. In short, given two genetically different sexes, we can expect differing behavioral capabilities extending even beyond directly sexual roles.

LISTENING IN TO THE HEMISPHERES

Before the early 1960s, people interested in the differing roles of the left and right hemispheres depended almost entirely on evidence drawn from animal research, from studies of neurological patients with one-sided brain damage or from patients who had had their corpus callosum, the conduit connecting the two hemispheres, surgically severed. But I found that it was possible to detect which brain hemisphere was most involved in speech and other functions in normal people by having them listen to two different words coming to the two ears at the same time. This became known as the "dichotic listening" procedure. When several word pairs are given in a row, people are unable to report them all, and most right-handers prefer to report—and report more accurately—words given to their right ear. This seems to be related to the fact that signals from the right ear, although sent to both hemispehres, are preferentially sent to the left hemisphere, which controls speech. People who have speech represented in the right hemisphere, a very unusual occurrence even in left-handed people, more accurately report what their left ears hear.

In contrast to the right-ear (left-hemisphere) advantage for speech, there is generally a left-ear (right-hemisphere) advantage for another type of auditory signal: music. When right-handed people listen to melodic patterns, which neuropsychologist Brenda Milner at the Montreal Neurological Institute has shown depend more on the right hemisphere, they report them beter from the left ear.

But having said all that, I also have a number of important caveats. First, biological sex itself has turned out to be much more variable and dynamic than we ever imagined. And brain-organization patterns are even more variable from person to person, and probably even within the same person at different times. Further, on most tests of cognitive ability there is enormous overlap of men and women. We strain to look for differences and, of course, tend to emphasize the few we find.

Given these facts, it follows that while genital sex is related to our mental capabilities, it is going to be a very poor screening device for intellectual assessment. Numerous environmental events interact with our genetic heritage from prenatal development onward, and the human brain is extraordinarily malleable and variable. Thus, we can predict very little about an individual's mental capabilities based on his or her sex. A number of men and women can and do excel in activities that, on average, favor the other sex. There may be no inherent characteristics unique to the brains of either sex that necessarily limit the intellectual achievements of individual men or women.

Beyond the Reinforcement Principle: Another Step Toward Understanding Sex Role Development

Beverly I. Fagot

Forty children, ages 21 to 25 months, participated in ongoing play groups. Observers then studied these groups, noting the reactions of both peers and teachers to behaviors that could be identified and coded as male, female, or neutral. Teachers, both female and male, were found to respond primarily to the category of behavior. Regardless of the sex of the child, they gave positive reactions to behaviors that were female-preferred or neutral but seldom to those that were male-preferred. Responses among the peer group were more complicated. Girls responded more positively to other girls than to boys, regardless of the catgeory (male, female, or neutral) of the behavior. Boys responded to the category of the behavior and to the sex of their peer. They gave more positive responses to other boys when the boys were engaged in male-preferred activities. Both girls and teachers were effective in changing the behavior of other girls, but neither could influence boys to change; boys were effective

Originally published in *Developmental Psychology*, 1985, 21, 1097-1104.

in influencing other boys but not in influencing girls. Although reinforcements do appear to affect the likelihood of a behavior continuing, other factors must be at work, for behaviors are maintained even under conditions of no responses, and, most important, the reinforcements themselves are most effective when they have been processed in terms of gender.

Existing studies imply that peers', parents', and teachers' differential reinforcement of sex-typed behavior of young children does exist in the natural environment, but the process by which the children use such information is not at all clear (Fagot 1977, 1981; Lamb, Easterbrook, & Holden, 1980; Lamb & Roopnarine, 1979; Serbin, Connor, Burchardt, & Citron, 1979). So far, most of these studies can be used to argue that peer reinforcement and teacher reinforcement may help maintain sex-typical behaviors, but they tell us very little about the role played by such reinforcement in the learning of sex-typical behaviors. Only a very few researchers (Fagot, 1978; Lewis & Brooks-Gunn, 1979) have observed children younger than 3 years in the natural settings where this learning must take place.

McCall (1977) suggested that many factors can produce change under controlled conditions, but perhaps do not in the naturalistic setting. As differential reinforcement for sex-typical behaviors exists in the natural environment and children show behavioral differences, it was reasonable to hypothesize that sex role behaviors were learned through a shaping process. However, if we examine what we know about the shaping of behaviors in the laboratory and compare that process to those occurring in the natural environment, problems arise. We know that to shape a child's behavior, the most effective procedure is to give repeated trials with immediate reinforcement. This is not the situation in the natural environment; and, although differential reinforcement undoubtedly has a part in the child's learning of sex-typical behaviors, it becomes difficult to argue that the traditional shaping process could account for the rapid acquisition and tenacious quality of typical sex role behaviors. In fact, Serbin, Tonick, and Sternglanz (1977) showed that cross-sex play could be shaped with specific teacher instructions to always reward such episodes, but when natural contingencies were reasserted, cross-sex play also dropped.

Perry and Busses (1979) presented a modified social learning theory view of how imitation contributes to sex-role development. The proposed that the child observes the different frequencies at which each sex performs certain behaviors in different situations. The child then employs the different frequencies as abstractions of what constitutes male-appropriate and female-appropriate behavior as models for imitative performance. It would seem reasonable to hypothesize that children also abstract information from the differential frequencies of reinforcement they receive for performance of different types of behavior. The major focus of the study was on the observation of play behaviors in a natural setting and on the influence of peers' and teachers' reactions on the child's choice of these behaviors.

We were interested in getting answers to four quite specific questions: (a) Are the reactions of teachers and peers influenced by the sex of the child, the type of behavior the child is engaging in, or both? (b) Does the effectiveness of teacher and peer response depend on whether the child's behavior is classified as typically male, typically female, or neutral, as defined by exisiting preferences for the play? (c) Is there any effect on the child's behavior that can be attributed to the perceived sex of the person responding to it—male peer, female peer, or teacher? (d) Does the kind of feedback received by boys and girls, particularly negative feedback, contain the same or similar types of information?

Method

Subjects

Forty children, 20 boys and 20 girls, were subjects in this study. The children were 20 to 25 months of age when they entered a play group consisting of children from 20 to 48 months of age. Eight different play groups were observed for this study. The major criteria for selection of the subsample consisted of continued participation in the project over at least two university terms and an appropriate age range upon entry to the group. As part of their participation in the longitudinal study, the children were routinely tested on entry with the gender identity interview designed by Slaby and Frey (1975), which has questions concerning gender identity, stability, and constancy. The Slaby-Frey interview was given, but only the gender identity questions were used to determine the sample. The child was asked to identify a series of hand-cut figures as a boy or a girl or a man or woman in appropriate combinations. The child was also asked to identify whether he or she was a boy or girl. The standard administration, which was followed, of the Slaby-Frey calls for reversal of the question each time children answer to insure they are not simply guessing or repeating the last response.

Because the intent was to study children who were initially still defining their own gender, three children, out of total of 43 tested, were excluded, even though they were members of this age group, because they already were giving consistent answers to the gender identity questions. All the children were from two-parent families in which the mother was the primary caretaker, and one had extensive daycare experience. The families included both working-class and middle-class parents, and all were Caucasian.

Behavior Checklist

A list of 34 child behaviors and 15 teacher and peer reactions was used for this study (Behavior Checklist, available from author). The child behavior categories consisted of activities such as rough-and-tumble play, build with small blocks, and dance, whereas the reactions included categories of behaviors such as hug and give physical affection, parallel play, and continue alone. For each observation, the child behavior was always recorded first, then the reactor (if there was one), and then the reaction.

Procedure

The children were observed in play groups of 12 to 15 children, with a fairly equal division among boys and girls in each group. Approximately one third of the children in each group were in the 21- to 25-month age range at the beginning of each year. At least two undergraduate students served as teachers throughout the term. Both males and females served as teachers, about three females for every male.

The play groups were held in a large playroom (approximately 6 m $\times$ 7.6 m), equipped with standard preschool toys such as blocks, dolls, books, and transportation toys. The playroom was not as sex typed as those of many preschools are. There was a large slide that was very popular with all of the children. There were no domestic play areas such as a kitchen, and toys were not segregated along traditional sex-typed lines, for example, blocks and trucks were separated, whereas dolls were kept in a large red wagon.

Observers were in an observation room with a separate entrance and observed the children through a one-way mirror. Teachers were instructed to let the children choose their own activities and to interfere only when a child was obviously disturbed. The teachers did provide varied activities each day by placing toys on the tables or the floor for the children to choose, but no attempt was made to have each child sample all activities.

Two hours of observation were completed during each play session. The children were observed in two different ways with the same behavior checklist. First, all children were observed each session using a scan sampling technique. Each child was observed in a predetermined order for 2 to 5 s, and the child's behavior, the reactors, and the reactions were coded. Using this technique, each child in the play group was observed 12 times per hour. Each child was observed from 480 to 720 times per term.

This technique gives a picture of the types of activities favored by the children in the group and gives a pattern of peer and teacher reaction within the group. However, scan sampling doesn't allow for any sequential analysis or for any estimate of length of episode. For these, each child was observed at least five times each term using a continuous sampling technique. The same behavior checklist was used, but the target child was observed continuously for a period of 10 min, and the child's behavior, the reactors, and the reactions to the behaviors were recorded. The observers recorded all behaviors as they occurred and were alerted each 10 s so that a new recording line could be started.

Observers were first trained using videotapes of children enrolled in the play groups in previous terms. The tapes were precoded so that, over the two years of the study, all observers were checked against criterion tapes. None of the videotaped interactions are included as data in this study. Throughout each term of data collection, reliability spot checks were run at least once a week and sometimes three times a week. There was an average of 12 reliability checks in a term of data collection, with a range of 10 to 15.

The observers had to give exactly the same code number on each observation to be considered in agreement. Each spot check last approximately 15 min, which gave the observers time to code all children in the room three different times, so that each set of coders working at the same time shared 120 or more observations. The pairs of observers all exceeded 90% agreement for the child behaviors (range = 91% to 98%) and 77% agreement for the reactions (range = 78% to 92%).

Definition of Male, Female, and Neutral Behaviors

Behaviors were categorized as male, female, or neutral in a previous study (Fagot, 1984) in which tests for sex differences in behavior were made for a separate sample of 180 children. At least 12 and as many as 80 hours of observation per child were coded using the behavior checklist described above. Eight play activities showed significant sex differences (i.e., were more likely to be engaged in by one sex or the other as determined by t tests significant at the .01 level). Male-typical activities included rough-and-tumble play, transportation toys, large blocks, and carpentry play. Female-typical activities were doll play, dress up, art activities, and dance. The 10 following behaviors showed no significant sex differences and were designated as neutral behaviors; play in wagon, climb and slide, play with clay, play with design boards and puzzles, play with small blocks, play with puppets, play ball or frisbee, fantasy play, sing or listen to records, and look at books. This system was used to classify the behavior observed in this study, so that scores for the play behavior categories were combined to yield male-typical, female-typical, and neutral behavior scores for each child. The three clusters were not signficantly different in the present playgroups. Scores for each behavior in the three clusters were standardized within each class. Standard scores were computed for each target child. We found that only doll play and play with transportation toys showed significant sex differences during the child's first term of attendance, but that by the second term of attendance all the sex differences found in the original sample were replicated.

Results

The first question of importance in this study is: Are the responses of teachers and peers influenced by the sex of the child, the type of behavior the child is engaging in, or both? This question is answered primarily for positive responses, because negative responses to children of this age are very rare (at least in this context). However, it is worth noting that boys were much more likely to receive negative responses than girls: 16 of 20 boys and only 6 of 20 girls received two or more negative responses. This difference was statistically significant, $\chi^2(1, N = 40) = 10.10, p < .01$.

To test for differences in positive responses, a separate ANOVA design was used for each of the three reactor categories (teachers, female peers, male peers). The design was a two-way factorial--sex of child (boys, girls) by category of play activity (male-typical, female-typical, neutral). All tests were run first with class as an additional factor; however, there were no significant differences among the classes, so the design was collapsed to a two-way factorial. There were 20 boys and 20 girls as "targets" to whom the reactors were responding. There were therefore repeated measures over category of activity. The dependent variable was proportion of positive responses by a reactor given that the child was engaged in a specific activity (e.g., male-typical); i.e., the dependent variable was a "conditional" proportion (or probability estimate). The analyses for each of the reactors follows.

Positive responses: Teachers. Table 1, Section A shows the mean proportion of positive responses for teachers. Male and female teachers did not differ in their responses, so their scores were combined. The main effect of play activity was significant, $F(2,76) = 6.01, p < .01$, but sex of child was not. The interaction was also not significant. Tukey comparisons revealed that teachers responded less to male-typical behavior regardless of the sex of the child.

Positive responses: Female peers. Table 1, Section B shows the mean proportion of positive responses for female peers. The only significant effect was sex of child, $F(1,38) = 5.75, p < .05$.

Postive responses: Male peers. Table 1, Section C shows the mean proportion of positive responses for male peers. All effects were significant: Sex of child, $F(1,38) = 8.92, p < .01$, play activity, $F(2,76) = 9.21, p < .01$, and interaction of sex by play, $F(2,76) = 16.21, p < .01$. Comparing all 6 individual cell means using Tukey comparisons, the mean of male peer response to male role category differed from all other means (.01), and male peers to neutral role category differed from all other means (.05).

To summarize, teachers, female peers, and male peers provided three distinct patterns of positive responses. (a) Teachers are not influenced by the sex of the child, but the frequency of positive response is much higher for female typical and neutral activity compared to male typical activity. (b) Female peers, on the other hand, completely reverse this pattern, not being influenced by category of play activity in dispensing positive responses but being strongly influenced by the sex of the child. Little girls give positive responses to other little girls regardless of the play activity

Table 1
Mean Proportion of Positive Responses by Teachers and Peers

Sex	Play activity			
	Male typical	Female typical	Neutral	*M*
A. Teachers				
Boys	.12	.25	.20	.190
Girls	.10	.22	.22	.180
M	.110	.235	.210	.185
B. Female peers				
Boys	.09	.11	.09	.097
Girls	.19	.22	.22	.210
M	.140	.165	.155	.153
C. Male peers				
Boys	.32	.06	.19	.190
Girls	.10	.07	.08	.083
M	.210	.065	.135	.137

Note. Table gives the mean proportions of positive responses made by each reactor (teachers, female peers, and male peers) given that the child (boy or girl) was engaged in a specific play activity (male typical, female typical, neutral).

about twice as often as to little boys. (c) The pattern for male peers is more complex (as can be seen in Table 1, Section C) and shares similarities and differences with both teachers and female peers. Like teachers, male peers are influenced by type of activity, and, like female peers, they are influenced by sex of child, but these influences are interactive. Boys dispense positive responses to girls at a low level relatively independent of the girls' behavior. They are markedly influenced by the behavior of other boys, however, responding much more frequently with positive responses to male-typical behavior and least frequently to female-typical behavior for boys.

Effectiveness of Teacher and Peer Responses

In the preceding section the data revealed how positive responses of teachers and peers were related to the sex of the child and the type of behavior engaged in by the child. The next logical step was to determine if the responses of the reactors were followed by changes in the behavior of the target child. Does the effectiveness of responses depend on the type of behavior the child is engaged in, that is, typically male, female, or neutral? Is there any effect on the child's behavior that can be attributed to the class of person responding to it, that is, male peer, female peer, or teacher?

For this analysis, sequence data were collected while the child was observed continuously for a 10-min interval. The raw data for each child consisted of the relative frequency with which the child continued a specific behavior (male typical, female typical, or neutral) given no response or a specific response (positive or negative) by

Table 2
Proportion of Continuation of Activity

	Reactor and response								
	Male peers			Female peers			Teachers		
Behavior	+	0	−	+	0	−	+	0	−
	Boys								
Male typical	.160	.45	.34x	.55	.45	.51	.67	.45	.57
Female typical	.39	.38	.21x	.39	.38	.34	.41	.38	.36
Neutral	.57	.39	.31x	.42	.39	.35	.45	.39	.38
	Girls								
Male typical	.59	.51	.48	.63	.51	.46x	.60	.51	.43x
Female typical	.72	.56	.53	.77	.56	.51x	.76	.56	.50x
Neutral	.67	.54	.52	.72	.54	.43x	.73	.54	.45x

Note. Positive and negative responses were compared for each behavior type (male typical, female typical, and neutral), with each type of reactor (male peers, female peers, and teachers). Neutral responses (0), included so that readers can see continuation proportion, are affected both by behavior type and by class of person doing the reinforcing. x = $p < .01$ t tests.

one of the reactors. These related frequencies, called continuation proportions, are the dependent variables, based on one proportion (score) for each of the 20 target children under each of the conditions. Mean continuation proportions were obtained for no response, positive response, and negative reponse by reactors, for each of the conditions.

It was not possible to do an ANOVA for these data because not all children are represented in all categories of behavior and types of responses. Instead, the mean proportions were examined first to answer the two questions: Is reinforcement effective, and does the category of behavior make any difference? The data are presented in Table 2 separately for boys and girls by respondents and category of play activity.

Two patterns of continuation were predicted each with a probability of occurring by chance of 1/6.
(a) Behavior should be more likely to continue under conditions of positive reaction than nonresponse, and least under negative. This was true in 16 of 18 cases. The probability of this occurring by chance is 1×10^{-10}. These data are represented in the rows of Table 2. Note that negative reinforcement doesn't effect male-typical behavior

for boys when given by female peers and teachers.

(b)Next we predicted that boys would continue longer in male-typical behaviors, then neutral and then female-typical, whereas girls would continue longer in female-typical, then neutral, and then male. This was true in all 18 cases. The probability of only the predicted pattern occurring by chance is 1×10^{-14}. These data are represented in the columns of Table 2.

Next, to test the effectiveness of the different types of reactions for individual children, t tests were computed on the difference between proportions for continuation of the behaviors given positive or negative reactions for each category of behavior for boys and girls. When male peers are the reinforcers for boys' behaviors, the prob-

Table 3
Type and Percentage of Negative Peer Reactions

Sex of child and category of activity	Percentage of negative peer reactions		
	Physical	Verbal	Sex typed
Girls			
Neutral	32	68	
Female typical	34	66	
Male typical	42	54	4
Boys			
Neutral	42	57	
Male typical	38	63	
Female typical	40	24	24

Note. Examples of types of negative peer reactions are as follows: Physical—Toy snatching, bumping, hitting, pushing; Verbal—"that's my crayon (chair, doll, book)"; Sextyped—"you're silly, that's for girls"; "now you're a girl"; "that's dumb, boys don't play with dolls"; "you can't play, you're a girl."

ability of continuation is significantly different, given positive or negative responses for male-typical, female-typical, and neutral behaviors. Teacher and female peer reactions do not significantly affect the continuation of boys' behavior. For girls, both female peers and teachers—but not male peers—affect the continuation of behavior, with the positively rewarded behaviors being more likely to be continued. Because of the large number of tests on the data, p levels were set at .01. Also each set of data has a different sample size so the absolute value of the p (.01) level differs for each test.

To summarize these analyses, we see that reinforcement is effective, but the effect is moderated by the individual giving the reinforcement and the category of behavior which is being reinforced. In effect, both reinforcement pattern and category of behavior can be used to predict continuation, but different reinforcers are effective for boys and girls.

Types of Negative Feedback

The last question was, "Does the kind of feedback received by boys and girls, particularly negative feedback, contain the same or similar types of information?" We found that negative feedback is a rare event for these toddler children; so rare that using group statistics and computing conditional probabilities for negative behaviors is not possible. But when duration data are examined, negative feedback is seen as effective in terminating some behaviors. In a sample of 20 hours of videotapes of the 40 children taken from these same play groups, all negative reactions that occurred were coded as verbal, physical, or sex-typed. Table 2 is a summary of the kinds of negative responses that children received for different kinds of behaviors. As can be seen, most negative interactions are disputes over ownership of a particular toy or place, but part of the negative feedback that boys received for participating in female-typical activities is of a type given only to boys. This kind of negative feedback appears to carry an information value that other types do not.

Discussion

In the present study, children (21 to 25 months old) who were entering their first play group were chosen as subjects. Because we wished to study children who were in the process of gender role development, we chose to look at children who could not yet answer gender identity questions consistently at the beginning of the study. In retrospect, it would have been more informative if children had been tested on their knowledge of sex stereotypes as well as their understanding of gender throughout the course of observations. Weinraub et al. (1984) found that sex stereotype knowledge and gender knowledge developed as different systems, so that data on both systems would have been informative. Emmerich and Shepard (1984), with slightly older children, also found evidence of two systems, with sex stereotypes being more highly developed in young children than gender understanding.

Both boys and girls received more positive feedback when they played with members of their own sex. Boys also received a different kind of negative feedback when they engaged in female-typical behaviors, which very directly told them that such behavior is inapporprite. Boys' peer groups gave two kinds of feedback: stay away from certain behaviors and play with others like you. Girls' peer groups have the message, play with those like you; but they do not limit play behaviors by category in the same way that boys do. We see that the male peer group starts defining what is *not male* very early, and that the behaviors that are defined as not male drop out of the boy's repertoire. Fagot (1981) found that participation by boys in this not-male category received more negative feedback and dropped over a period of one year. We even see in these young children what might be called the tyranny of the male group, if one is not enthralled with the consequences, or the beginnings of the male bonding process, if one is.

From the data in this study, we also start to see some of the differences in responses to adults that last through childhood. Boys did not respond to teachers as readily as did girls, even though there were both male and female teachers in this study. However, not all classes had male teachers, and a more effective analysis with carefully matched teachers is needed. From Table 1, one can see that teachers give feedback to boys at the same rate as to girls; but from Table 2 we see that this teacher feedback has less effect on the duration of behavior for boys than for girls. This is true even when behaviors are not sex-typed, such as the neutral categories.

This sex difference in the response to teachers' overtures has also been shown in a different kind of study. Feldbaum, Christenson, and O'Neal (1980) showed that teachers made consoling overtures about equally as often to new boys and new girls entering established preschool groups. Girls accepted the teachers' overtures, whereas boys rejected them. The question of why boys and girls respond so differently to adults from such a young age needs continued study. Serbin, Connor, and Citron (1981) found that teacher presence overcame girls' resistance to play with opposite-sex-typed toys, but boys were not influenced in this way.

As might be expected, the answer to the question of how effective peers and teachers are in shaping sex role behaviors is complex and different for boys and girls. It seems to this author that social learning theorists have shown over the past 10 years that differential reinforcement of boys and girls does take place in the natural environment and that it is effective at least in maintaining the status quo. That still leaves us a long way from understanding the process underlying sex role development and why the learning that takes place is so tenacious. However, children in this study also reacted to the category of respondent, so it is necessary to assume that the child had some concept of gender that would lend greater value to some individuals than to others. While the children in this study were not consistent in answering gender identity questions at the beginning of the study, it is likely that in the course of the study with appropriate tasks we could have measured their knowledge. In order to understand the total process of sex role development, it is now time to make the transition to a complete theory of development by examining how the child makes use of the information provided by the environment, and that means understanding how the child interprets that information. As Kuhn (1978) pointed out, developmental psychologists have studied cognitive processes with cognitive approaches and social processes using social learning theory. Within each world view, methods have been developed that have given us insight, but each world view is incomplete and fails to use whole realms of data. Kohlberg's (1966) theory was a first step, but it has not been very helpful in explaining the early (1 to 3 years) processes of sex role development. Yet is it just that time period that seems crucial in the establishment of gender identity, which then most influences the child's sex role adoption. We can now start searching for more subtle indicators of differential socialization, particularly in the informational and affective qualities of the reactions to the behaviors preferred by boys and girls. At the same time, it is increasingly necessary to try to show how the child's cognitive categories are used to interpret this environmental information. Lewis and Brooks-Gunn (1979) and Thompson (1975) have started to examine the child's use of gender during the first two years of life, but so far only a few studies have attempted to understand how the child's developing gender identity guides development of sex role behaviors (Fagot, 1985; Weinraub et al., 1984). The young child's responses to others are influenced by the gender of that other, even though we were not able to measure the extent of the child's understanding of gender. To understand the complete process of sex role development, we are going to need to use the methodologies of both the laboratory and the field.

By asking these questions of toddlers who are just acquiring a sense of gender in others and in themselves, we think we have begun to study the origins of sex role behaviors, not just their maintenance, and to delineate the processes by which they are acquired.

REFERENCES

Emmerich, W.C., & Shepard, K. (1984). Cognitive factors in the development of sex-typed preferences. *Sex roles*, 11, 907-1007.

Fagot, B.I. (1977). Consequences of moderate cross-gender behavior in preschool children. *Child Development*, 48, 902-907.

Fagot, B.I. (1978). The influence of sex of child on parental reactions to toddler children. *Child Development*, 49, 459-465.

Fagot, B.I. (1981). Continuity and changes in play styles as a function of sex of the child. *International Journal of Behavioral Development*, 4, 37-43.

Fagot, B.I. (1984). Teacher and peer reactions to boys' and girls' play styles. *Sex Roles*, 11, 691-702.

Fagot, B.I. (1985). Changes in thinking about early sex-role development. *Developmental Review*, 5, 83-98.

Feldbaum, C.L., Christenson, T.E., & O'Neal, E.C. (1980). An observational study of the assimilation of the new-comer to the preschool. *Child Development*, 51, 497-507.

Kohlberg, L. (1966). A cognitive-developmental analysis of children's sex-role concepts and attitudes. In E. Maccoby (Ed.), *The development of sex differences* (pp. 82-173). Stanford: Stanford University Press.

Kuhn, D. (1978). Mechanisms of cognitive and social development: One psychology or two? *Human Development*, 21, 92-118.

Lamb, M.E., Easterbrooks, M.A., & Holden, C.W. (1980). Reinforcement and punishment among preschoolers: Characteristics, effects, and correlates. *Child Development*, 51, 1230-1236.

Lamb, M.E., & Roopnarine, J. (1979). Peer influences on sex role development in preschoolers. *Child Development*, 50, 1219-1222.

Lewis, M., & Brooks-Gunn, J. (1979). *Social cognition and the acquisition of self*. New York: Plenum Press.

McCall, R.B. (1977). Challenges to a science of developmental psychology. *Child Development*, 48, 333-344.

Perry, D.G., & Bussey, K. (1979). The social learning theory of sex differences: Imitation is alive and well. *Journal of Personality and Social Psychology*, 37, 1699-1712.

Serbin, L.A., Connor, J.H., Burchardt, C.J., & Citron, C.C. (1979). Effects of peer presence on sex typing of children's play behavior. *Journal of Experimental Child Psychology*, 27, 303-309.

Serbin, L.A., Connor, J.M., & Citron, C.C. (1981). Sex differentiated free play behavior: Effect of teacher modeling, location, and gender. *Developmental Psychology*, 17, 640-646.

Serbin, L.A., Tonik, I.J., & Sternglanz, S. (1977). Shaping cross sex play. *Child Development*, 48, 924-929.

Slaby, R.G., & Frey, K.S. (1975). Development of gender constancy and selective attention to same-sex models. *Child Development*, 46, 849-856.

Thompson, S.E. (1975). Gender labels and early sex role development. *Child Development*, 46, 339-347.

Weinraub, M., Brown, L.M., Sockloff, A., Ethardyl, T., Gracely, E., & Myers, B. (1984). The development of sex-role stereotypes in the third year: Relationships to gender labeling, gender identity, and sex-typed toy preference, and family characteristics. *Child Development*, 55, 1493-1503.